Thomas Procter Wadley

Notes or Abstracts of the Wills

contained in the volume entitled the Great orphan book and Book of wills, in the

council house at Bristol

Thomas Procter Wadley

Notes or Abstracts of the Wills
contained in the volume entitled the Great orphan book and Book of wills, in the council house at Bristol

ISBN/EAN: 9783337301248

Printed in Europe, USA, Canada, Australia, Japan

Cover: Foto ©Lupo / pixelio.de

More available books at **www.hansebooks.com**

NOTES OR ABSTRACTS OF THE WILLS

CONTAINED IN THE VOLUME ENTITLED

THE

GREAT ORPHAN BOOK

AND

BOOK OF WILLS,

In the Council House at Bristol.

By the Rev. *T. P. WADLEY*, *M.A.*,

RECTOR OF NAUNTON BEAUCHAMP;

Honorary Member of the Bristol and Gloucestershire Archæological Society,

and of the Worcester Diocesan Architectural and Archæological Society.

BRISTOL:
Printed for the Bristol and Gloucestershire Society by C. T. JEFFERIES AND SONS,
Printers, Redcliff Street, 1886.

INTRODUCTION.

THE following notes or abstracts were made towards the end of the year 1879, and in the early part of 1880, under the auspices of the Bristol and Gloucestershire Archæological Society, which had previously obtained the requisite permission from the Bristol Town Council.

In making these abstracts, care was taken to give the names of all the persons mentioned in each will, adhering to the original spelling of their surnames, and setting down full particulars of the bequests in every case of real property. And for the satisfaction of other antiquaries, besides the genealogist, it was deemed advisable to note all the places, streets, lanes, and ships of which the testators make mention.

The Orphan Book has been rightly described as the "great" book, being of much larger size than either of its companion volumes, which are entitled—Register Book of Wills, No. 2, and Register Book of Wills, No. 3. It will be seen that, viewed chronologically, these two books have been wrongly numbered.

The great book contains 448 wills. There appears to have been no will preceding that of John Woderoue as far back as the year 1479. It may be remarked that in Additional MS., 29866, at the British Museum, there are some copies of wills, which one might have expected to find in this collection : viz., those of Margery Spert, A.D., 1389, who owned property in the town and suburb of Bristol, and was mother of Thomas Spert, whose will is here ; Thomas Berkeley, burgess, 1436, nephew of John Clyve, whose will is also here ; Hugh Withyford, merchant of Bristol, 1441 ; and William Withyford, son and heir of the said Hugh, 1449.

There are 113 wills in the second book, the dates ranging from 1630 to 1674. The third book contains nearly 300 wills, upwards of sixty of them bearing date towards the end of the reign of Elizabeth, and the last one dated May 13th, 1633.

There are also two volumes of Recognizances at the Council House. The first of these recites the charter granted by King Edward III. to the burgesses of Bristol, in reference to the protection of the lands, tenements, and goods bequeathed to orphans and children who were minors in the town and its suburb. The seventh year of the reign of that king seems to be the earliest date, mentioned in this volume, of the appearance of persons before the Mayor as guardians of orphans and their property : in which year, on Monday in the vigil of the Purification of the B.V.M., William de Cropenhull came and made a declaration (recognovit) at the Guildhall, before Roger Turtle, then Mayor, relative to the will of John de Aschton, deceased, and as guardian of Walter and Isabel, children of the said John, Alan de Wrington being a bondsman for Cropenhull. It is further shown that when an orphan had arrived at his full age, and been put in possession of his legacy, it was his duty to acknowledge the receipt thereof personally before the Mayor. One of the most interesting entries in this book of Recognizances relates to the family of the celebrated William Canynges. It states that his father John being dead, and his mother Joan having become the wife of Thomas Yonge, burgess, the said Thomas appeared before the Mayor, on Monday next after the feast of St. Thomas Martyr, 9 Henry IV., and acknowledged that he had undertaken the guardianship of Thomas, son of the said John Canynges, being of the age of ten years and a half, and of William, son of the same John, aged five years and a half. This book does not seem to have been much used between the reigns of Edward IV. and Elizabeth. In the second book of Recognizances, 18 Charles I. appears to be the latest date.

Repeated mention of the exercise of this jurisdiction occurs in the Orphan Book. Reference is made to it in the earliest dated will, that of John Dodyng, No. 18. The following note is inserted after the record of proof, at the Guildhall, of the will of Walter Frompton, burgess, who made his will in 1423, having then an only son :—
" Et co'misim' admi'straco'em lib'or' ten'tor' infra dict' test'm content' qua'tu' ad officin' n'rm p'tinet executrici infrascripte in forma iuris iurate salua & res'uata nob' & Succ' n'ris potestate quacu'qz

t'ras & ten'ta Orphani infrascripti p'inf'scriptu' nup' p'rem suu' du' vixit eid'm Orphano p' p'sens test'm legata sufficient' p'sonis quibz nobis fore videbit' co'mittend' & eid'm Orphano inde modo debito se'd'm tenore' & eff'em eiusd'm testame'ti respondend' *iux' tenorem Carte d'ni Regs' in auxiliu' & fauore' Orphanor' ville p'dce burgensibz eiusd'm ville concesse* Jn cui' rei testi'o'm sigillu' Officij Maiorat' ville Bristoll' p'sentibz est appensum." The will of John Suche, merchant of Bristol, made March 21st, 1565, after mentioning his children, who were minors, and the property therein bequeathed to them, contains the clause—"J do hartely pray mr. Mayor and his brethren the aldremen that the same legases may be assured to the said children Accordinge to the Laudable and godlye ordere of the Charter of orfants graunted to this cytie."

Towards the end of the sixteenth century, however, there is evidence that the system was often regarded with the disfavor expressed by Robert Taylor, whose will is numbered 447.

The earlier contents of the Orphan Book show the practice of proving the wills of Bristol testators before the Mayor, at the Guildhall, as well as before the Ecclesiastical Authorities. There is no record of probate before the Mayor appended to any will in the book after that of John Prewett, No. 364.

In addition to the Wills and notes of proof, the Orphan Book contains a number of indentures and some other manuscripts. Among the latter are "Ordinances" made by the Mayor and Burgesses of Bristol, assembled in the Common Council House, July, 1545, for the due ordering and disposing of the money bequeathed, in 1532, by Robert Thorne, of the city of London, merchant tailor, for the furtherance of the manufacture of broadcloth in Bristol, and for providing corn and wood to the advantage of purchasers among the poor of the same place. The last indenture is dated May 15th, 1633. But this is followed by two more writings belonging respectively to the reigns of Henry VII. and Edward VI.; so little was chronological order attended to in the arrangement of these documents when the book was bound.

There are two lists of testators at the end of the Orphan Book; the one complete, and apparently written, though not by the same hand, in the reign of James I., or Charles I.; the other ending with "Test'm Will'i Rowley Jun'"—date 1478. This list is preceded by the words—" Kalendar' testamentor' in isto paupiro content' de test'o in aliu' fact' p' Thomam Oseney Co'em Cl'icum ville Bristoll'."

The wills have been registered in Latin down to that of Elizabeth Ferre, which is in English, and was made in February, 1487. There are only a few in the former language between that date and 1503, the year in which the will of Thomas Edwarde was made and proved; English being employed for all wills thereafter recorded.

  NAUNTON BEAUCHAMP,
    JULY. 1886.

1.—JOHN WODEROUE.

This is only part of a will, the first leaf of the Orphan Book having been lost. Testator mentions his wife Cristina, and children John, Avice, and Agnes; his property called Berewyke, and adjacent lands in the Redclond, in which Joan, widow of John Stoke, had a life interest, a tenement in Redeclyvestret inhabited by William Filberd, another in Wynchestret inhabited by John Muryweder, and property "in vico Templi;" while a note of the "reclamacio" of testator's widow subjoined to the will speaks of four tenements in the street of St. Mary de port, between the tenement of Henry Wyveliscombe and that of John Borne, a tenement in Wynchestret occupied by Thomas Redeberd, baker, and John Dyar, a tenement "in alto vico" inhabited by Tibot formerly wife of John Fagan, a garden and shops in the suburb of Bristol as one goes towards Elebrugg, and a garden between the said shops and the King's way, as one goes from Elebrugg to the Market. Testator left legacies to his sister Beatrix Whityng, his servant Maud, servant Sibil de Erlyngham, John Willyams, Thomas Colston, Walter Derby and his wife Joan. A chaplain was to celebrate in the church of All Saints, and another in the Guildhall chapel of St. George. If neither of testator's children left issue, Berewyke and adjoining lands to go to William Canynges and his heirs male; in default of such issue, remainder to Isabel wife of John Barstaple and her heirs male; in def., rem. to Alice wife of William Wermynstre and her heirs male; in def., rem. to Thomas Colston and his heirs male; in def., rem. to Agnes dau. of Thomas Denehawde and her heirs; in def., rem. to Philip Execstre and his heirs male; in def., rem. to John Thorp and his heirs male; and in def. of such issue, rem. to the Mayor and Commonalty of the town of Bristol, who were to make due provision for the two chaplains above referred to. Executors to be Walter Derby, Cristina, wife of testator, Thomas Knap, Henry Wyveliscombe, Nicholas Warreyn, Henry Darleston, Thomas Colston, and Philip Execstre. Given at Bristol.

Proved (approbatum) at the Guildhall, Bristol, on Monday next after the feast of St. Laurence, 6 Richard ii. Previously proved (probatum) in the church of St. Nicholas of Bristol.

2.—JOHN BOWNES.

Will made 1382, May 8th. To be buried in the cemetery of St. James of Bristol. His wife Margaret to possess all his lands, tenements, rents, &c., in the town of "Droughda," in Ireland; the said property to be sold after her death, and the money expended in masses for the souls of testator and wife, of their parents, and all the faithful. Legacies to the fabric of St. John's church, Bristol, to that of the church of St. Peter of Droughda, to Sir Thomas Tankard of that place, and to each order of mendicant friars there. Wife Margaret, Henry Colmere, and the said Sir Thomas Tankard to be executors.

Proved at the Guildhall on Thursday next before the feast of St. Matthew Apostle, 6 Richard ii. Previously exhibited in the church of St. Michael of Bristol.

3.—JOHN STOKE, burgess of Bristol.

1381. Oct. 5th. To be buried in the chapel of the blessed Mary in the parish church of St. Thomas of Bristol, diocese of Bath and Wells. To wife

Joan, a tenement with 15 shops in the street of St. Thomas in the suburb of Bristol, near to the entrance of the house called Berewykesyn; the reversion of the said property to be sold and the money applied to the payment of his debts, and to the rebuilding of the said chapel of St. Mary. To the same Joan, his dwelling house, &c., in Redcliff-street, between what was formerly the tenement of Stephen Pollesworth and what was formerly the tenement of John Hornecastell; also his property called Berewykescroft and all other lands in the Redelond; which property is to go, after her death, to John Woderoue the elder, of Bristol, and to his heirs. To Robert Cheddre, William Canynges, Walter Derby, and John Woderoue, the messuage called Berewykesyn in Redcliff-street, between what was formerly the tenement of Thomas Colston and the messuage (formerly) of Stephen le Spicer; also other possessions in the same street: which parties are to provide two chaplains to celebrate in the chapel of B.V.M. in the church of St. Thomas of Bristol, for the healthful estate of K. Richard ii., for that of the Mayor and Commonalty of the town of Bristol, also of Sir Maurice Whych knt., Robert Cheddre, Joan wife of testator, Walter Derby, William Canynges, John Woderoue, and for their souls "cum ab hac luce mig'uerint"; for the souls of my lord K. Edward iii., Philippa his consort, Edward his eldest son, and their progenitors; and for the souls of Roger and Agnes Stoke, testator's father and mother, Andrew Bremcote, late a monk at Glastonbury, Walter Monyngton, late abbot, and Thomas White, late a monk there, Alice and Isold former wives of testator, Hugh Pecche, Geoffrey Beanflour, and of all the faithful dead; attending also to other works of charity specified in certain indentures. If the aforenamed feoffees should not duly carry out testator's directions, the aforesaid property was to be held by the Mayor and Commonalty of Bristol and their successors for the same purpose; and if these should refuse to act, it was to be sold, and the money distributed and divided for the benefit of the souls above named, and for the construction of the aforesaid chapel, for the conveying of water "in conducco'e plumbi" to the church of St. Thomas, and for poor widows and maidens of the town of Bristol. The rents and services paid by Simon Halewey for a tenement held of testator in Redcliff-street, and 10 shillings of yearly rent issuing from the tenement held by John Fleccher, at the end of the bridge of Avon, to be sold for the completing of the abovesaid chantry, and for all other things contained in the said indentures; also the tenement in the suburb of Bristol, "in Skatepulstret alias dict' Merschestret," and other property in Tuckersstreet and Redcliff-street, to be sold, and the money thereby raised to be divided between testator's wife and the children of Sir Thomas Arthur knt. and his wife Isabel. To testator's wife a messuage in the High-street called Ropefeld, together with the residue of his goods. Legacies to the church of St. Thomas of Bristol, to the poor, to each chaplain of the four orders of mendicant friars in Bristol, to the abbot and prior of Glastonbury and every monk there, to the prior and convent of Wytham, to Nicholas Geyl lately vicar of Redcliff church, to the present vicar, to Roger Hayward of "Oblee," to John Taber, William Coke, Robert Haddon, William Wallop of Berewykesyn, Joan Burton, to her marriage, the daughter of Robert Stoke of the county of Oxford, to her marriage, Agnes Hame, Richard Barbour, to servants William, Alice, and Isabel; to Sir Thomas Arthur knt. a black horse; to William Canynges "vnu' lectu' blodij coloris enbraud' en' J Egle & Cs."; to

Walter Derby "vnu' lectum album enbraud' & C$.$"; to John Woderoue " vnu' lectum Rubij color' enbraud'eu'vna aucill' (a shield ?) & C$.$" Executors to be William Canynges, Walter Derby, Joan wife of testator, and John Woderoue.

Proved before William de Wolleye, rector of "Porteshened," in the chapel of St. Thomas of Bristol, June 6th, 1382; also at the Guildhall on Monday next after the feast of St. Bartholomew Apostle, 6 Richard ii.

4.—JOHN ERNEAWEY, burgess.

1382. Thursday in the feast of St. Edmund King. To be buried in the cemetery of the parish church of St. James of Bristol. Legacies to the fabric of that church, to the prior of St. James, to William the brother, Edith the daughter, and John the son of testator, to the parish chaplain and parish clerk of St. James, and to the cathedral church of Worcester. To John Floyt and Geoffrey Hilde "vill' Bristoll comburg'" all testator's interest in the tenement in Brodemede, Bristol, purchased by him of Elias Whitawyer and Milcensia his wife, according to certain indentures. Residue of goods to wife Agnes and children. The said Agnes and his brother William to be executors.

Proved before John de Dunclent, clerk, commissary and sequestrator general for Henry bishop of Worcester, in the parish church of St. Augustine the Less of Bristol, Dec. 5th, 1382.

5.—ROGER TAUNTON, burgess.

1383. August 3rd. To be buried in the church of "Charthous de Henton," to which convent the sum of £10 sterling is to be given for his burial. Legacies to the fabric of Worcester cathedral, to the fabric of the parish church of St. James in Bristol, to the prior of St. James there, to friar John Welyngton of the order of Friars Preachers in Bristol, and to their convent, to the Friars Minors, the Carmelite Friars, and the Augustinian Friars of the same town. Bread to the value of 40 shillings to be distributed on the day of testator's burial. To the offspring about to be brought forth by his wife Joan £20 sterling. If the child should die under age, £5 to the fabric of the parish church of St. James aforesaid, and £5 to the priory church of St. James: of the remaining sum, £5 for a chaplain to celebrate in the aforesaid church of St. James for the benefit of testator's soul, and the souls of his parents and former wife Alice; and £5 for other pious uses. To wife Joan, all his tenements within the liberty of Bristol for her life, and residue of goods. She and John Thluyt to be executors, and the prior of St. James overseer.

Proved in the parish church of St. Nicholas of Bristol, Oct. 31st, 1383, and at the Guildhall, before the Mayor and Sheriff, on Monday next after the feast of St. Hilary, 7 Richard ii.

6.—ROBERT TILLY.

1382. Saturday next after the feast of St. James Apostle. To be buried in the church of the Friars Minors of Bridgwater. To the said friars for his obsequies, and the keeping of his anniversary among them for ever, 100 shillings. To each of the three other orders of friars 20 shillings. To friar

William Aumiger 10 shillings. Legacies to the poor on the day of burial, to the fraternity and chaplain of the blessed Mary of Kingston, to the vicar of Kingston, for tithes and offerings forgotten, and to celebrate for his soul, to John Ruspyn parson of Bradford, to Robert Amyet parson of Beanford, to Reginald Meddon ; to Joan, wife of testator, eight shops, with garden, dovehouse, and arable land adjoining, in the suburb of Bristol, outside Temple gate ; also two messuages, with the void place adjoining, in the town of Bristol in the street of St. Mary in Foro, which messuages, purchased of Hugh Cansi (or Causi), are held of testator by John Woderoue and Cristina his wife ; also a yearly rent issuing from a messuage in the town of Bristol in All Saints lane, by the cemetery of All Saints, held by the Master of the hospital of St. Laurence by Bristol ; also a void place in the town of Bristol in Marsh-street, called Kepesishey (?) ; all which property to remain, after the death of the said Joan, to testator's son John and his lawful heirs ; if he should die, s.p., it was to be equally divided, according to the custom of England, between Alice, Elianor, and Margaret, daughters of testator, and be held by them and their lawful heirs for ever ; but in case of their death s.p., the said possessions were to be sold, and the money distributed for the benefit of the souls of testator, his wife, and their parents, in masses and other divine services. To each of the three daughters 20 marks for their marriage. Executors to be Joan wife of testator, Thomas Ralegh, and Hugh Causy, to each of whom 20 shillings.

Proved in the church of Taunton, Oct. 1st, 1382, and in the Guildhall at Bristol on Friday next after the feast of St. Gregory Pope, 6 Richard ii.

7.—NICHOLAS CHEPMAN, burgess.

1382. May 15th. To be buried in the chapel of the blessed Thomas of Bristol. Legacies to the fabric of that chapel, to every priest attending his funeral, to each order of mendicant friars in Bristol, to the fabric of the chapel of the Assumption on the bridge of Bristol, to the anchoress of Stapleton, to William Hauker and John Oweyn chaplains, and to his servants. To his son John £20 and his silver cup having a shield in the bottom thereof. A chaplain was to celebrate for five years for the health of the soul of testator and for all the faithful dead. His wife Alice during her life to find a lamp "ardentem coram Cruce" in the chapel of the Assumption of B.V.M. His son Bernard to be assisted by his mother if need shall be, and to have £20 in the name of the third part of testator's goods, his mother keeping the money until he shall be 30 years of age. To Alice, wife of testator, a croft "cu' le Rekk in ead'm situat' apud lez Rekkes" between the land of the blessed Mary of Redcliff on the one part, and the land of the abbot and convent of Keynsham on the other, for her life, that she may yearly keep his obit, and that of Richard and Maud his parents, and of Sir William White chaplain, and of Joan testator's former wife ; and so dispose of the said croft that her own obit as well as the aforesaid be kept up every year in the chapel of St. Thomas of Bristol. She, John Palmere, and John Canntelbury, to be executors ; to the last two 20 shillings apiece. Written at Bristol.

Proved in the chapel of St. Thomas of Bristol, March 7th, 1382 ; at the Guildhall on Monday next after the feast of SS. Philip and James, 7 Richard ii.

8.—WALTER GLOVERE, of Bristol.

1383. Kalends of December. To be buried in the crypt of St. Nicholas in the town aforesaid. Legacies to the vicar of that church, to the parish chaplain, to the suffragan clerk, to the work of the church of St. Nicholas, to the fraternity of the Cross of the crypt, to the mother church of Worcester, and the four orders of friars, who are to celebrate for his soul. Residue of goods to Julian his wife and Thomas and Agnes their children. The said Julian to be executrix.

Proved before John de Dunclent, clerk, &c., Jan. 22nd, 1383; before the Mayor and Sheriff on Monday next after the feast of St. James Apostle, 8 Richard ii.

9.—JOHN HERVY, burgess.

1384. Monday next before the feast of St. Michael Archangel. To be buried in the cemetery of the church of St. James in Bristol. Legacies to the fabric of that church and of St. Nicholas of Bristol, and to the vicar of the latter, to each chaplain celebrating therein, and taking part in the funeral, to the clerk and suffragan of the same, to the fabric of the cathedral church of Worcester, to each order of mendicant friars in Bristol, to Elena his servant, and to Thomas Vyne. To Sir Robert, chaplain, "vnu' Nouu' Haldyng," to Sir Nicholas, chaplain, a like bequest. To John, son of testator, £10, to be kept by the mother until he shall be of full age. Executors to be Alice, testator's wife, and William Stiel; the latter to have 40 shillings, if willing to act.

Proved before John de Dunclent in the parish church of St. Augustine the Less of Bristol, Oct. 6th, 1384; at the Guildhall, before the Mayor and Sheriff, on Monday next after the feast of St. Andrew Apostle, 8 Richard ii.

10.—WILLIAM CHEDDRE, the elder, of Bristol.

1382. Nov. 21st. To be buried in the chapel of the blessed Mary in the parish church of Cheddar. For funeral expenses £20. Legacies to the prior and convent "domus Cartus' in Selwode," the prior and convent of "Worspryng," the religious women of the mendicant house of St. Mary Magdalene in Bristol, the vicar of the Temple church, Bristol, poor people holding houses and land in Cheddar and Axbridge, and the needy poor near to those parishes, the fabrics of the churches of Cheddar and holy Cross Temple at Bristol, to John and Thomas Selsy and Margaret their sister, to Philip Brown, chaplain. To the three sons of my brother Roger Seward 20 pounds of silver, that is to say, 10 marks to each. Testator remits to Isabel wife of Robert Aleyn her debt of 100 shillings of silver, also other money. Residue of goods to Agnes testator's wife. She, his brothers Robert Cheddre and Roger Seward, William Draper, clerk, and John Stanys of Bristol, to be executors.

Proved in the parish church of Temple, Feb. 27th, 1383; at the Guildhall on Monday next after the feast of Gregory Pope, 8 Richard ii.

11.—ROBERT CHEDDRE, of Bristol.

1382. March 21st. To be buried in the chapel of St. Mary in the parish church of Cheddar, "de nouo fundata." Legacies to the vicar of the church of holy Cross Temple at Bristol, to every chaplain of the four orders of mendicant friars of Bristol, and to other brethren in the said town and suburb, to the poor on the day of burial, to each chaplain, deacon, and sub-deacon in the church of the Temple at Bristol, and every chaplain of the town and suburb attending his funeral and mass, to the fabric of the chapel upon the bridge of Avon at Bristol, to the sisters of St. Mary Magdalene, and those of the House of St. Bartholomew there, to the sisters of "Mochenbarugh." To Richard, son of testator, "vj Ciphos vocat' Bolles de argento," and other plate; to the fabric of the hospital of St. John Baptist of Bristol 40 shillings; to Margaret daughter of Lucy Selsy 100 marks for her marriage; to William Draper, clerk, a third best silver cup which was then at Cheddar. Also legacies to William Bierden testator's clerk, Joan his servant, Thomas Crede, John Perent, John Primlok, and William David. Residue of goods to Joan, testator's wife. She, William Draper clerk and the aforesaid William Bierden to be executors.

Proved in the parish church of holy Cross Temple of Bristol, June 30th, 1384; at the Guildhall on Monday next after the feast of St. Bartholomew Apostle, 9 Richard ii.

12.—JOHN CLIFFORDE, of Bristol.

1383. Thursday next after the feast of the Nativity of B.V.M. To be buried in the crypt under the church of St. Nicholas in Bristol. Legacies to the fabric of that church, to the vicar, and every chaplain celebrating divine offices there, and attending his obsequies, to each clerk of the same, to the fabric of Worcester cathedral, and each order of mendicant friars at Bristol. To Agnes, wife of testator, and her heirs and assigns, his dwelling-house in the suburb of Bristol, on the Back of Avon, between a shop of William Somerwell and a tenement of John Viel; also the residue of his goods. She and Thomas Parlebien to be executors.

Proved before John de Dunclent, clerk, &c., in the parish church of St. Nicholas of Bristol, Oct. 31st, 1383; before the Mayor and Sheriff at the Guildhall on Monday next after the feast of St. James, 9 Richard ii.

13.—ROBERT GRADELEY. In the margin *Grateley*.

1385. Sept. 26th. To be buried in the church of the Friars Minors of Bristol, where the bodies of his wives were interred. Legacies to the fabric of the mother church of Worcester, and to that of the parish church of St. John of Bristol, and to the rector of the same church. To the said friars a whole cloth of blanket "p' courcell inde faciend'." To each order of mendicant friars in Bristol 5 shillings. Testator's wife Cristina to choose a fit chaplain, who is to have £20, and celebrate *pro anima* for four years. To his said wife, a tenement in the street called Knyzt-masstret in Bristol, situate between his own dwelling-house and the tenement of Walter Goos, while his interest therein lasted, for the term of her life; also two halls and two shops in the street called Horstret in the suburb of Bristol, between the tenement of Nicholas Mason and that of Thomas Malverne: also 14 shops in the street called Gropelane, Bristol, between the tenement of Elias Whitawyer and the garden of John Viel; also a yearly rent of 14 shillings issuing from two shops on the bridge of Avon, Bristol, formerly held by

John Axston ; the said property to be sold after her death, and the money bestowed for the benefit of the souls of both of them and their friends. Legacies to his kinsman Geoffrey, his three servants Alice Mablie, Thomas, and Elen, and to Richard Harderley, whose name is written *Athurleye* in note of probate. Cristina, wife of testator, to be executrix, and Richard Hardeley (*sic*) overseer.

Proved in the parish church of St. Augustine the Less, Oct. 30th, 1385 ; at the Guildhall on Monday next before the feast of Simon and Jude Apostles, 9 Richard ii.

14.—ADAM POUNTFREYT, of Bristol.

1385. Tuesday in the feast of the Assumption of the blessed Mary. To be buried in the crypt under the church of St. Nicholas, " in noua tumba quam ib'm construxi." Legacies to the fabric of that church, to each chaplain celebrating there who shall take part " in obsequijs meis," to the clerk and the suffragan of the said church, to each order of mendicant friars of Bristol, to the fabric of the cathedral church of Worcester, and to William Pountfreit his servant. To Eve, testator's wife, property consisting of 5 shops, &c., in the suburb of Bristol, " apud le Barres," between the King's way eastward leading to the priory of St. James on the one part, and Wynchelane westward on the other part ; also 4 shops in the aforesaid suburb " in la Brodemede," situate between the shop of the aforesaid William Pountfreyt and the shops which Maud le Frensch held ; the said property to go, after the death of testator's wife, to his daughter Alice and her lawful heirs. If Alice should die s.p., all the said property to be sold, and the money applied to charitable purposes for the benefit of testator's soul and all the souls " quibz teneor." Sir David Newton, chaplain, and Thomas Gylemyn to be executors, and each to have £5.

Proved in the parish church of All Saints of Bristol, Aug. 30th, 1385 ; at the Guildhall on Monday next after the feast of St. Martin Bishop, 9 Richard ii.

15.—RICHARD PEAUTRER, burgess.

1384. Thursday next before the feast of St. Martin Bishop and Confessor. To be buried in the crypt of the church of St. Nicholas of Bristol, by the tomb of Thomas Gloucestre. Legacies to the vicar and the fabric of that church, also to the deacon and suffragan ; to the fabric of Worcester cathedral ; to the poor on the day of burial 10 shillings in bread ; to each of the four orders of mendicant friars of Bristol. To Richard Portbury, late servant and apprentice, my sword. To my sister Edith Sowey " vnu' fletherbed & mea' armilausam meliorem." To Isabel, wife of testator, for the term of her life, his half share in the two tenements inhabited by Adam atte Corner and John Carsewell carpenter, in the suburb of Bristol in Baldewynstret, as one goes towards the Back of Avon, between the tenement in which Robert Camel, skinner, dwells, and the shop inhabited by Agnes Golde, which Richard Spicer gave in his life and left by will to David Newton, now chaplain of the chantry, to pray for his soul and the souls of all the faithful dead. The property to be sold after the death of the said Isabel, and masses to be celebrated in the church of St. Nicholas aforesaid. The other half to be disposed of in alms, &c. The said Isabel and John Carsewell to be executors. Given at Bristol.

Proved in the church of St. Nicholas there, before Walter Chiltenham and Martin Lydeforde, commissaries of the Archbishop of Canterbury, March 5th, 1384 ; before the Mayor and Sheriff on Monday next after the feast of the Conception of B.V.M., 9 Richard ii.

16.—JOHN PEDEWELL, burgess.

1385. Thursday next after the feast of All Saints. To be buried in the cemetery of the parish church of St. James of Bristol, to the fabric of which church half a mark. All his effects to be divided into two equal parts, one to be disposed of by the executors for the benefit of his soul and for his burial, the other to Julian his wife. Legacies to Sir Richard, prior of St. James, Robert Cole and Sir Thomas monks there, Sir Richard parish chaplain, and Sir Richard chaplain of the blessed Mary there, Sir John Pygas monk of Tewkesbury, the four orders of friars of Bristol, the fabric of the chapel of the blessed Mary on the bridge of Avon, and the cathedral church of Worcester. If money enough be left, 20 shillings-worth of white bread to be bought and bestowed for the benefit of his soul, &c. To his wife Julian all his interest in the tenement by the Castle mill, with an acre of land lying in Cadden : if she should die "infra temp' status mei," the said tenement and acre to go to the Master and the house of St. Laurence. The tenement inhabited by testator to be repaired in the roof, &c., and secured against wind, rain, and ruin ; his son Walter, monk at Glastonbury, to have therein "p' se armig'o suo & Garc'one," a chamber, and stable for his horses, and free ingress and egress whenever he shall come without any condition during the life of the said Julian. His tenement at the "barres" together with the garden, to be sold by the executors, and one half of the money to be expended *pro anima*, &c., the other for his wife. She, William Worcestre, Roger Chaundeler, and John Chapeleyn to be executors, and Richard the prior of St. James overseer. "Jt'm lego Joh'i filio Will'i Hathewey cui compat' existo si continuet scolas xl^d. ad soluend' p' labore Mag'ri sui."

Proved in the parish church of St. Augustine the Less of Bristol, Nov. 30th, 1385.

17.—JOHN CHICHELEW, burgess.

1384. Sunday next after the feast of the Conversion of St. Paul Apostle. To be buried in the cemetery of the parish church of holy Cross Temple at Bristol "coram ymagine sc'i Joh'is bap'te." Legacies to the vicar, the parish chaplain, and the fabric of that church. To Edith, wife of testator, for her life, three shops in the suburb of Bristol, in Temple-street, between the tenement inhabited by William de Ele and the shop inhabited by William Wodelond ; which three shops with their appurtenances extend from the aforesaid street in front to Lawdiche of the friars *(sic)* of the order of St. Augustine behind. The said property to go, after the death of Edith, to testator's daughter Alice for her life, and afterwards to the procurators and brethren of the fraternity of St. John Baptist in Bristol for ever, that they may tend the welfare of testator's soul, the souls of his parents, &c. The said Edith to be executrix, and William de Ele overseer.

Proved in the church of holy Cross Temple at Bristol, Feb. 3rd, 1384.

18.—JOHN DODYNG, mariner and burgess.

1379. March 22nd. To be buried in the church of St. Laurence of Bristol. Legacies to the work of that church, to Sir Thomas the rector, to each priest celebrating there, and to the clerk. To Elizabeth, wife of testator, a shop in the suburb, in Horstret, which he had purchased of the Commonalty of the town of Bristol; also a new tenement, with shops adjoining, in the suburb, by the gate called "ffromebrug;" and the tenement in Merschstret bought of Henry Carpenter, shipman, and Cristina his wife; to go, after her death, to testator's son John and his lawful heirs. If at length there should be no heir, the said property was to be sold, and the money laid out in masses, and bread, cloth, and shoes for the poor. To Joan, daughter of testator, certain goods and a yearly rent issuing from the tenement lately inhabited by him in Horstret aforesaid, also a yearly rent from the tenement in which John Rawlyn, shipcarpenter, now dwells in the same street; if she should die s.p., the said rent to go to the procurators of the aforesaid church of St. Laurence, for the sustentation and reparation thereof for ever. The said Joan and her effects to be in the keeping of Walter Goos, burgess of the town aforesaid, until she be of full age, he providing good security for the said effects before the Mayor for the time being. Residue to wife Elizabeth. No mention of any executor.

Proved in the parish church of St. Nicholas of Bristol before Robert Cros, clerk, sequestrator general for the Bishop of Worcester, March 6th, 1380; administration of all the effects committed to the dean of Bristol.

Proved at the Guildhall on Monday next before the feast of St. George Martyr, 9 Richard ii.

19.—WALTER TEDISTILLE, burgess.

1385. March 12th. To be buried in the parish church of St. Stephen of Bristol. To daughters Margaret and Joan all his tenements in the town and suburb of Bristol, except one shop inhabited by Maud Coucle which was to belong to the said Maud for her life, and to revert afterwards to the said Margaret and Joan and their lawful heirs; if they should die s.p., the property was to be sold by the executors, if still living, if not, by the Mayor and Bailiffs of Bristol, and the money divided in equal portions, one half to his wife Agnes, if still living, the other to be distributed for the good of his soul. To the said Agnes all his term in a certain tenement in Baldewynstret, also in one in Bradstret extending from the said street in front to Smalstret behind. The said Agnes to have the keeping of his daughters: William Frome to receive the rent of the tenements bequeathed to them, and deliver it to the said Agnes. To the church of St. Stephen of Bristol £20 to buy a pair of vestments "cum toto apparatu." Legacies to his needy kinsmen, to the rector, chaplain, and clerk of the church of St. Stephen aforesaid, to William Fawkener, Thomas Coke, Joan Yrys, Emmot Perle, and John Bourne; to Joan the kinswoman, and Richard the son of John Sloo; to Margaret the servant, and John and William the apprentices of testator; to Maud servant of Robert Gardyner. To Richard son of Walter Frompton, the silver bowl (ciphum) with cover, which the same Walter had given to testator. To Maud Coucle a note (or *nut*, a species of cup) chased with silver. All effects to be divided into three parts, one part to remain in the possession of testator's wife, the second in that of his two daughters, the third to be divided, *pro anima*, by the executors, viz., William Frome, burgess of Bristol, Sir John Knyghton, and Sir Richard Hegg, chaplains.

Proved before John de Dunclent, clerk, &c., March 23rd, 1385; before William Canynges, Mayor, and John Somerwell, Sheriff of Bristol, on Monday next after the feast of St. George Martyr, 9 Richard ii.

20.—JOHN STANES, of Bristol. In the margin *Stanys*.

1385. Friday next after the feast of St. Petronilla Virgin. To be buried in the new chapel of the church of "Redeclyue," by the tomb of Joan, formerly wife of testator. To the fabric of that church 40 shillings; but if his burial there should not be permitted, then only 20 shillings. Legacies to the vicar of that church for tithes forgotten, if there be any, to the parish chaplain and the clerks of the same, and every chaplain celebrating there, and attending the funeral; to the fraternity of All Souls of Bristol; to the fabric of the cathedral of Wells; to that of the chapel of the blessed Thomas of Bristol, and the parish chaplain, the deacon, sub-deacon, and suffragan; also to each chaplain celebrating therein, and at the funeral; to the fabric of the chapel of the blessed Mary on the bridge of Avon; to the fraternity of the holy Cross in the crypt under the church of St. Nicholas; to the poor in bread on the day of burial; to each order of mendicant friars in Bristol; to Clement atte Merk of Stanes, and John Okerforde. To testator's daughter Margaret, the younger, £40 for her marriage, if she survived him, and arrived at her full age; also certain goods; John Bount to have charge of the said Margaret and all her effects; if she should die under age, her legacies were to be disposed of in masses and other charitable works. To testator's daughter Margaret, the elder, 20 shillings; to her husband Thomas Pedewell my cloak of blue. To Joan, daughter of testator, £20, and the tenement in Bradestret, Bristol, inhabited by John Swelle, after the decease of Elen her mother; also a tenement in the High-street, in which John Millyng, "Botemaker," dwelt; and a garden, with dove-house, which garden, called Tophey, lay in the suburb of Bristol, by the orchard of the priory of St. James. If the said Joan should die s.p., the aforesaid property was to be sold, and the money distributed by the executors in works of piety, &c. Of the residue of goods, one part to testator's wife, and the other for masses for his soul, and that of former wife Joan, and others, in the chapels of St. Mary on the bridge and St. Thomas. Elen, his wife, Sir William Hanker, chaplain, and Thomas Gylemyn, to be executors, and each to have £3.

Proved in the chapel of St. Thomas of Bristol, July 14th, 1385; at the Guildhall on Monday next after the feast of St. Laurence Martyr, 10 Richard ii.

21.—JOHN BORD. In the margin *Borde*.

1382. Monday next after the feast of St. Lambert Bishop. To be buried in the church of St. Stephen of Bristol, where a chaplain was to celebrate *pro anima* for three or four years. Legacies to his mother Lucy, wife Agnes, and son John; to the fabric of Worcester cathedral; the fraternity of the Nativity of the blessed Mary in the said church of St. Stephen, and to the rector there; to each order of friars in Bristol. Wife Agnes, John Swell, and William Nywbury, to be executors. By a codicil under the date 13th kal. May, 1385, "temp'e quo languebat in Mari inf' dioc' Exon'," testator bequeathed a pipe of wine, or 100 shillings, to the fabric of St. Stephen's church in Bristol, and the same to the fraternity at Coventry.

Proved before Walter Cheltenham and Walter Gybbes, commissaries of the Archbishop of Canterbury, in the church of St. Augustine the Less of Bristol, 3rd kal. May, 1385; at the Guildhall on Monday next before the feast of St. Bartholomew Apostle, 10 Richard ii.

The will of Walter Cheltenham, rector of "Wythyndon" in the diocese of Worcester, and commissary general of the Archbishop, was proved Sept. 15th, 1385, and will be found in the archiepiscopal library at Lambeth, *Courteney* 211.

22.—WILLIAM MILTON, tucker and burgess.

1386. Monday next before the feast of St. Laurence. To be buried in the cemetery of St. Werburgh of Bristol. Legacies to the fabric of that church, to the rector, and every chaplain, clerk, and suffragan thereof, Robert Milton, sherman, to John Crompe and Magot, servants of testator, the prior and brethren of the house of the Kalendaries, and each order of friars at Bristol. Poor and needy people to have bread on the day of burial. To son Walter, shops in Gropelane, late the property of Master Nicholas Ryner, also the tenement inhabited by testator in Cornestret. Son Walter and the said Robert Milton to be executors; the rector of St. Werburgh overseer.

Proved before John de Dunclent, Sept. 16th, 1386; at the Guildhall on Monday next before the feast of St. Michael Archangel, 10 Richard ii.

23.—WALTER DERBY, burgess.

1385. Thursday next before the feast of Simon and Jude Apostles. To be buried in the church of St. Werburgh of Bristol in the chapel of St. Anne "de nouo edificand'." Legacies to the fabric of the said chapel, to the rector of the said church, the clerk, suffragan, and every chaplain there, to the vicar and the fabric of St. Leonard's, and to the clerk and each chaplain, to the four orders of friars in Bristol and every friar belonging thereto, to the prioress and nuns of Barugh, and Isabel Poleyne a nun there, to the prior and convent of Bradstoke, to the vicar, and each chaplain, and the clerk, and the fabric of the church of Erlyngham, to the prioress and sisters of St. Mary Magdalene, and the poor of the same town. Two chaplains to celebrate in the church there during one year for testator's soul, his father's and mother's, &c. To the prioress and sisters of the house of St. Bartholomew of Bristol, and Joan Maryon sister there, to the chapel of the Assumption on the bridge of Avon, to the fabric of the chapel of the blessed Mary of Redcliff, to the master and brethren of the hospital of St. John by Redcliff, to Henry prior of the Kalendaries of Bristol and each of his brethren being chaplains there, to the fabric of All Saints' church in Bristol, and Sir William Lench vicar thereof, to the fabric of the churches of St. Peter and St. James of Bristol, to the fabric of the church of Worcester, to each order of medicant friars in Gloucester and Oxford, to the Carmelite friars of Marlborough, to every poor person in the hospital of St. John at Bristol, in the house of Langrewe and in the almshouse by Temple gate, to every blind or lame poor person in Bristol. Twenty-four poor men clothed in white or in black to sit about testator's corpse on the day of burial, twelve of whom to carry torches; twelve wax tapers also to be provided " circa corpus meu' ardent' die sepultur'." No feastings for the rich on the occasion, but for the poor. Legacies to each master of wine-drawers in Bristol, and every other wine-drawer, to every carrier of salt in the town, and every laborer upon the Key; to Master Thomas Spert a gilt girdle given to testator by John Barstaple, &c.; to Master John Dene, and his sister Elizabeth and her children; to John Stephenys the fourth part of the ship called the "Marie;" to testator's servant William Godewyn £20, and one half of the said ship, of which Walter Cogan is master; to servant Nicholas and John Castell half the ship called the "Nicholas;" to the said John Stephenys and Nicholas "dimidia' p'tem del Balynger vocat' Trinite cum toto app'at' medictat' p'tinent';" to Julian testator's nurse, and John Berkeley his servant, to Joan Reynold, to the children of John Ailly for their marriage, to Richard Portyngale, Maud Frensch, Robert Cordy, and John Benham, to servants Walter Beauflour, William Sampson, and Joan Asshton, to William and John Spaynell, to Sir William Bryghtlamton, Philip Excestre, Letice Chaunger, Alice Williams, and Richard Morewey. To wife Joan £200, in the name of the third part of goods, and certain vessels; the rent of a tenement inhabited by John Candevere in Cornestret, with reversion after the death of the said John, also a tenement in the aforesaid street, and one in the High-street, both of which belonged formerly to John Blanket, and rent of the tenement in Wynchestret, bought of the executors of Joan Sampson, opposite the church of the Holy Trinity of Bristol, with reversion of the same, and five shops in the corner of Langrewe, formerly purchased of John Warwyk, and six shops, with garden adjoining, in the suburb of Bristol in Bastestret, bought of William Peyto, and the corner tenement in High-street, by the high Cross, and the corner tenement opposite the house of the Kalendaries in Bristol; all which property to be held by her during her life, if she shall keep herself single and chaste, if not, all the said property to be forthwith sold, and the money applied to pious uses. To John Stephenys a tenement in Cornestret, in which William Wermynstre............A leaf missing.

24.—RICHARD MULEWARD, merchant.

1386. Aug. 8th. " Ego Ric'us Muleward m'cator sup' Pontem Bristoll manens." To be buried in the chapel of St. Thomas the Martyr, before the altar of the fraternity of the same. Legacies to the work (op'i) of the chapel of Redcliff, to the vicar there for tithes, to the work of the chapel of St. Thomas, to each friar of the four mendicant orders, and to the poor in the almshouses in Bristol, to other poor on the day of burial, for funeral expenses and celebrations *pro anima*, to William Hewyssche, to the needy prisoners of Monkbridge in Bristol, to servants Joan Abraham and Cristina Priour, to John Newton my apprentice, to sons John and Bernard; residue to wife Edith; she, and son John, and Walter Martyn, executors. Witnessed by William Wiche, John Corby chaplain, and William Hewyssche.

Proved in the chapel of St. Thomas of Bristol, June 25th, 1387; at the Guildhall on Monday next after the feast of St. Bartholomew Apostle, 11 Richard ii.

25.—THOMAS SAMPSON, burgess.

1387. June 9th. To be buried in the cemetery of the church of the blessed Mary of Redcliff " int' pueros meos ib'm sepultos." Legacies to the fabric and vicar of that church, to the fabric of the church of St. Thomas of Bristol, to the parish chaplain of the said church, and to each chaplain, and the deacon, sub-deacon, and suffragan there, to the poor on day of burial, to Philip my brother, and his son Richard, and daughter Benet, to kinswoman Agatha, to Sir William, chaplain at the Kalendaries, my wife's kinsman, to chaplains of honest conversation, to pray for my soul, and the souls of all the faithful, to William More, and his daughter Joan, and wife Cristina, testator's daughter, and to her daughter Joan, to Thomas Borgeys, to servants John Hulle, Thomas Pen'ell, Margery, and George, to John Deye and John Hore, late servants, to Peres my kinsman and late servant, to Thomas Person, to the sick poor, and for the marriage of poor maidens; to wife Joan and her heirs and assigns, a ship "vocat' la Cog-Johan;" to Janyn of Norton, a helmet, with its garniture (auentall'), habergeon, lance, and small breastplate; to wife Joan the tenement in which I dwell, situate between that of William Combe and the one inhabited by Philip Dyar, to go, after her decease, to son William and his lawful heirs; if he should die s.p., the property to be sold by my executors, or their executors "p' visum Maioris ville Bristoll," who is to have twenty shillings for his pains, and the money to be disposed of among the poor, feeble, and lame, and in the marriage of poor maidens; to wife Joan the reversion of the tenement in Redcliff-street, between the tenement of John Yong and that of Robert Cheddre, when it shall fall after the death of Thomas Inhyne; to go, on the death of the said Joan, to my son William and his lawful heirs; if the said William should die s.p., to go to testator's daughter Cristina, wife of William More, and her lawful heirs. To wife Joan £300 in money, or in merchandise wares, as they are set down "in p'cio in Jnuentar' meo," in the name of the third part of all my goods, also vessels of silver, brass, wood, and lead. To son William £300 in money, or in merchandise wares, as set down in the said inventory, some of the wares being beyond the sea. To wife Joan, the keeping of son William and the effects bequeathed to him, she finding sufficient security before the Mayor, "p'ut mos est." The said Joan, Thomas Colston, William Wermynstre, and William More, executors. Witnessed by Sir William Kene chaplain, Thomas Person, and others.

Proved in the chapel of the blessed Mary of Redcliff, July 15th, 1387; at the Guildhall on Monday next after the feast of the Exaltation of the holy Cross, 11 Richard ii.

26.—THOMAS CLERK, burgess.

1387. Tuesday before the feast of the Decollation of St. John Baptist. To be buried in the church of St. Werburgh. Legacies to the fabric of that church and of St. Leonard's, to each priest in the latter and the clerk, in which also two priests are to celebrate *pro anima*; to the mother church of Worcester; to son John £20 sterling, also vessels, including "vnu' Ciphum de Degun;" the said John and his legacies to be in the keeping of John Stephens: to John Florys 40 shillings and all testator's armour; to servant Isabel. Sir Philip Sherrer and John Stephens executors.

Proved before John Barell clerk, commissary and sequestrator general for the Bishop of Worcester, in the church of All Saints of Bristol, Sept 7th, 1387; at the Guildhall on Monday next after the feast of St. Matthew Apostle and Evangelist, 11 Richard ii.

We have here an ancient Gloucestershire and Bristol surname. The will of John Barell the younger, son of Robert, of the parish of Holy Trinity, Bristol, was proved in P.C.C., Dec. 4th, 1406.

27.—JOHN WARMYNSTRE.

1388. Aug. 21st. To be buried in the church of St. Thomas of Bristol, before the altar of St. Nicholas. Legacies to the fabric, the parish chaplain, and the three clerks of that church, to the mother church of Wells, to the vicar of the church of Redcliff, Bristol; for burial and obit 100 shillings; to servant Thomas Wolf articles of clothing; to each order of mendicant friars at Bristol. All lands, tenements, &c., in the town and suburb of Bristol, late the property of Walter Muleward burgess, and purchased by testator of John Milward, the said Walter's brother, to be sold, and the residue of the money, after payment of all debts, to remain with wife Cristina; to servant John 20 shillings if he shall stay with the said Cristina for the term agreed on between us, otherwise "nichil." To Thomas atte Hay and John Sharp 20 shillings apiece, if they will act as executors with the said Cristina.

Proved in the parish church of Redcliff, Sept. 4th, 1388; at the Guildhall on Monday next after the feast of St. Vincent, 12 Richard ii.

28.—JOHN MULEWARD.

1388. April 2nd. "Quond'm filius Ric'i Muleward burgens' ville Bristoll." To be buried in the church of St. Thomas the Martyr of Bristol. Legacies to the work of the said church, and of Redcliff, to the vicar of the latter for tithes, to the work of St. Peter's of Bristol, and that of the chapel of the blessed Mary on the bridge of Avon, to the four orders of mendicant friars, and the needy in the various almshouses of Bristol, to the poor on the day of burial, to John Thomme and his wife, to Joan Abraham, John Newton, Cristina Priour, John son of Thomas Norton, John son of John Momfort, and William Hewyhs. To my brother Bernard a shop in the suburb of Bristol, on the bridge of Avon, between the tenement of John Bunt and the shop which Edith our mother holds for her life, with reversion of the same, after her death, for the term of five years after the feast of the Annunciation of B.V.M., 11 Richard ii., according to a writing. Four Trentals of St. Gregory to be celebrated *pro anima*. Residue to the said Edith. The aforesaid Bernard and Thomas Norton, executors.

Proved in the chapel of St. Thomas of Bristol, May 11th, 1388; at the Guildhall on Monday next after the feast of St. Vincent, 12 Richard ii.

29.—EDITH MULEWARD.

1388. Sunday next after the feast of Easter. Testatrix was relict of Richard Muleward, of the parish of St. Thomas of Bristol, in the diocese of Bath and Wells. To be buried in the tomb of the aforesaid Richard, in the chapel of the said St. Thomas. Legacies to the fabric of that chapel, and the parish chaplain there, to the fabric and vicar of St. Mary of Redcliff, to the four orders of mendicant friars of Bristol. Forty pounds of wax to make tapers for use at the time of burial. "Jt'm lego vlt' hoc tres libras monete Anglicane ad tenend' exequias meas." To the needy prisoners in Monkbridge, to the aged, needy, &c., in the various almshouses of Bristol, to my servant Joan Abraham, and apprentices John Newton and Cristina Priour, to Janyn David, to Cecily Hewyhs and her husband William, to John Thommys of Middlezoy and his wife, to former servants Joan Barbour and Cristina Shippester, to my spiritual daughter Edith, daughter of Roger Taillour, to William White, and Master Simon Uphull. Residue to son Bernard; he and William White executors. Witnessed by Sir Henry Netherhaven perpetual vicar of Redcliff, Walter Martyn, the aforesaid William White, John Newton, Master Simon Uphull notary public, and others.

A codicil was added June 28th, 1388, witnessed by John Mounford, and some of the parties already named: half the residue of the goods of testatrix and her husband to be disposed of for the benefit of the soul of Richard, her husband, of John her deceased son, and of herself, at the discretion of Thomas Norton, burgess of Bristol.

Proved in the chapel of St. Thomas the Martyr, Sept. 10th, 1388; at the Guildhall on Friday next after the feast of the Conversion of St. Paul, 12 Richard ii.

30.—NICHOLAS TYMTENHULL.

1388. Sept. 28th. Testator, who belonged to the parish of Temple in Bristol, made his (nuncupative) will at sea, during a violent storm: "lego ai'am meam d'o & corpus meu' sacre sepultur' iuxta disposic'oem clemencie diuine." All debts to be paid, and Margery his wife to have the residue, and his tenement in Temple-street, and be executrix.

Proved at Chew, before Ralph Canon, commissary general of the Bishop of Bath and Wells, Jan. 18th, 1388; at the Guildhall on Monday next before the feast of the Purification of B.V.M., 12 Richard ii.

31.—WALTER FROMPTON, burgess.

1388. Dec. 6th. To be buried in the parish church of St. John of Bristol. To wife Isabel, for her life, the shop inhabited by Geoffrey Padirstowe in the High-street, also the rent of a tenement, with reversion thereof, opposite the church of St. Peter, next the tenement of John Laucastre, also a shop in Fisscherstret, held by Thomas Pyke, and the rent, with reversion, of a shop held by Andrew Anketill, and of one inhabited by Robert Hoper, in the same street, and a shop on the Key inhabited by Simon Spert, and the rent of a tenement on the Key inhabited by Ralph Blanket, next a tenement of the prior and brethren of the Kalendaries, and six shops in Gropelane next the tenement of John Slo, also the rent, with reversion, of the shop inhabited by Joyce Webbe, and a yearly rent from a tenement in Langrewe inhabited by John Bissy, and the rent of a tenement inhabited by Elizabeth Dodyng, opposite the church of St. Laurence, next the tenement of John Hanam; on condition that the said Isabel carefully preserves the said possessions; but if she should marry again, or live unchastely, they are to be sold after three proclamations at the high Cross "cum tuba & plus offerenti;" the money thereby raised to be divided into four equal parts, one for the blind, lame, &c.; the second for the marriage of poor young women within the province of Canterbury; the third for the mending of the roads and bridges about Bristol, &c.; the fourth for the four mendicant religious orders in Bristol and other places. To son Walter and his heirs a tenement in the corner in St. Ewen's parish, and one at Newgate, between a tenement of Robert Chedder on either part; and the rent of a tenement in Bradstret, by the cemetery of holy Cross on the one part, and a tenement of the prior and brethren of the Kalendaries on the other; also two shops annexed to the aforesaid tenement, and a yearly rent from the tenement inhabited by Nigel Fisscher in Worschupstret, and a shop on the Key held by Walter Michell next a tenement of Robert Chedder, and the rent, with reversion, of a tenement inhabited by John Wyke on the Key, next a tenement of John Vyel, and the rent, with reversion, of three shops in Merschstret occupied by John Pakker, and six shops in Merschstret and Lovelane next a tenement of the prior and brethren of the Kalendaries, and the rent, with reversion, of four shops "situat ext' p'tam Aillewardi," next a tenement of John Pedewell, and a tenement on the bridge of Avon, inhabited by Richard Chippenham, and a garden "situat' en la Market." If the said Walter should die s.p., the property to be sold in the manner expressed above, and the money similarly distributed. To Walter Frompton clerk, son of Roger, testator's brother, the shop inhabited by Roger Chaundeler in the High-street, in the corner opposite the church of the Holy Trinity, next the tenement of Richard Cobyndon, and the rent, with reversion, of the shop held by John Hynebest, next a tenement of the Augustinian convent at Bristol, and the rent, with reversion, of a tenement in Merschstret, inhabited by Edmund Beauflour, next the tenement of Thomas Graunt, and a yearly rent from a tenement on the Key, inhabited by John Roper; to have and to hold the said possessions until he has been promoted to an ecclesiastical benefice, when they are to remain to testator's son Walter and his lawful heirs. To servant Joan Asscheworthy, for her life, the shop held by John Hunteley in Cokynrewe, also two marks of yearly rent from the tenement of Thomas Sutton in Cornestret, and the rent of a tenement in Wynchestret, next the tenement of Roger Dyar; the said property to go afterwards to son Walter and his heirs. To servant John Ranlyn, for his life, a shop in Lewynesmede in which Thomas Screven dwelt. The tenement inhabited by Hugh Plommer, and the one inhabited by Henx Goldsmyth, and the reversion of the tenement given to Joan Asscheworthy for her life in Bradstret, next the tenement of the prior of Henton, also the reversion of twelve shops in Gropelane "inf' portam Alwardi," granted to William Conley for his life, to be sold, and the money distributed "in forma p'missa;" also reversion of tenement in Knyfmestret and of yearly rent from the tenement of Yvo Fluyt in Brodemede, given to the aforesaid Joan Asscheworthy, to be sold in like manner. To my son Richard, for his life only, three shillings of yearly rent issuing from the shops built by David Seys. To son Walter 100 marks, also a gold ring "quo solebam sigillare," a horn, &c. To John Knygton (sic) my chaplain £20, a silver charger, &c. Legacies to the blind and lame, to William Conley and Simon Olyver. Certain household goods to be divided into three parts, one share together with 100 marks, to wife Isabel. If the said Walter shall marry without the executors' consent, he is to have none of the moveable goods bequeathed to him. Two chaplains to celebrate for ten years in the church of Frompton for testator's soul and his benefactors. Celebrations also for the soul of John Wyseman of Coscombe. To John Champeney £3 on condition that he asks for nothing more from the executors. Richard Adekyn is to serve Sir John Knyghton, William Couley, John Raulyn, and Nawdyn. To Robert Dudbroke is left the remainder of the term of the apprenticeship of John Thomas. Residue of goods to be divided into four parts, one for the blind, lame, &c., the second for the marriage of poor young women and the support of widows, the third for mending roads and bridges, and other works of piety in the province of Canterbury, the fourth for the four mendicant religious orders of Bristol and other places within the said province. To Sir John Cook chaplain and Nawdyn 40 shillings apiece. Sir John Knyghton chaplain, Walter son of Roger Frompton, William Couley, and Robert Dudbroke, executors. Witnessed by Sir John Walter, William Couley, John Raulyn, Richard Cook, John Nawdyn, and others.

Proved in the parish church of St. Dunstan in London, Jan. 21st, 1388; before the Mayor and Bailiffs of Bristol on Friday next before the feast of the Purification of B.V.M., 12 Richard ii.

This will is also in the archiepiscopal library at Lambeth, *Courteney*, 227, 8.

32.—NIGEL CHEPSTOWE, burgess.

1383. April 23rd. To be buried in the church of the blessed Nicholas of Bristol, under the campanile, near the place where the body of late wife Joan rests. Legacies to the fabric, the vicar, Richard the clerk, and the fraternity of the holy Cross in the crypt of the said church, to every chaplain there, or serving in the chapel on the bridge of Bristol, to the fraternity of the blessed Katharine in the church of the blessed Mary "ad portum Bristoll," to that of the blessed Mary on the bridge, for repairing the bridges of Chepstow, Usk, and Caerleon, to the four orders of friars in Bristol, to the fabric of the church of Worcester, to Sir David Newnton, to Maud Stevens for her marriage, to Elen my maid, to every prisoner in Monkbridge, to the poor, to every decayed beggar in Bristol too feeble to leave his bed. To son Robert £10; and half the price of my dwelling house in Bristol to be divided between him and Edith my daughter, the other half for masses and alms for the soul of my wife Joan and my own. To son John the debt he owes for a cloth, also the debt of Henry Rirran formerly my servant. The garden in the suburb of Bristol called Brodemede, to be sold for pious uses; and as daughter Edith wishes to give ten marks for it, she is to be preferred to all other persons in the purchase. Sir David Newnton and son Robert executors.

Proved before John Barell, clerk, Nov. 30th, 1387; at the Guildhall on Friday next after the feast of the Purification of B.V.M., 12 Richard ii.

33.—THOMAS CHAPELEYN.

1388. Monday next before the feast of Agapitus. To be buried within the western entrance of St. Stephen's church in Bristol. Towards glazing one of the windows vjs. viijd., on condition that the procurators of that church are willing that testator should be buried in that place: the same sum to the rector, on condition that the four torches used on the day of burial shall serve at the four altars of the same church in honor of the elevation of the Body of Christ. Legacies to son William and daughter Isabel, to each chaplain attending the funeral rites, to the fabric of the mother church of Worcester, to Sir Philip Hoke, to Sir Richard Egger chaplain, to Richard Chapeleyne my brother, and John Chapeleyne my godson, to Agnes Brewer; residue to wife Maud. If son William and daughter Isabel should both die under age, the money bequeathed to them to be divided between the poor and a chaplain who is to celebrate *pro anima*. Wife Maud, John Chapeleyn, and Peter atte Wode to be executors. Richard Egger overseer. The aforesaid John and Peter to have for their pains those sums of money which they owe.

Proved in the parish church of St. Ewen of Bristol, Oct. 1st, 1388; at the Guildhall on Monday next after the feast "Cathedr' sc'i Petri," 12 Richard ii.

34.—RICHARD DERNEFORD.

1388. Jan. 26th. To be buried in the cemetery of holy Cross Temple of Bristol. Legacies to the vicar and each chaplain celebrating in that church, and the two clerks. To wife Alice and her unborn infant, a white cloth not yet completely finished. To servant Edward an article of clothing—*un' sloppa'*—of Irish cloth. Legacies to servant Philip, to Robert Makeatese, to sons John and Stephen, and daughter Joan, who is left to the keeping of Stephen Plastrer. One "chayne" of cloth, and one "doseyn" of russet to be sold for funeral expenses and payment of debts. Residue to wife Alice; she, and Stephen Plastrer, and Robert Makeatese, executors.

Proved in the parish church of Redcliff, Feb. 23rd, 1388; at the Guildhall on Wednesday in the second week of Lent, 12 Richard ii.

35.—WALTER MICHELL, burgess.

1388. On the day of St. Valentine Martyr. To be buried in the church of St. Stephen of Bristol. Legacies to each chaplain celebrating there, to Richard the clerk, and Richard the suffragan of that church, in which a chaplain is to celebrate for a year after testator's decease; to the mother church of Worcester, to John Glise "co'morant' in fforest," to sons Robert, John, and Richard Michell. Son Thomas Michell and wife Isabel to be executors. Memorandum—the said Walter Michell bequeathed xxj^{li}. xiij^s. iiij^d. to each of his sons Robert, John, and Richard, as was declared before John Viell, Mayor of Bristol, " in plena Cur'."

Proved in the parish church of St. Augustine the Less of Bristol, April 24th, 1389; at the Guildhall on Monday next after the feast of the Lord's Ascension, 12 Richard ii.

36.—KATHARINE CALF.

1389. May 21st.—"licenciata p' Henricu' Calf maritum meu'." To be buried in the church of St. Werburgh of Bristol, in the chapel of the blessed Mary. Legacies to the poor and for masses, to servants Joan Jacob, Joan Sparewe, and Joan Saundres, to former servants Alice Cartere and Katharine Perell, to kinswoman Edith, wife of Adam Taillour. To my executors the reversion of messuages and lands in the town and suburb of Bristol; viz., reversion of dwelling-house in Smalstret, tenement, &c., in

Baldewynstret, one in Bastestret, another on the bridge of Avon ; reversion of a curtilage in Mersshstret, and of a grange and croft "in la Redeloud ;" which property husband Henry Calf holds for his life ; also reversion of all property in the town and suburb, purchased by John Spicer, father of testatrix, of Walter Broun and Thomas Mynty, chaplains, and left to her by will, the same to be sold, and the money expended in masses, &c., *pro anima*. To the said Henry Calf, for his life, a half share in all messuages, lands, tenements, rents, &c., with reversions, in the town and suburb, on the death of my brother Robert Newmaystre, for which half Thomas Lyonns and his wife Margaret received of my husband and me £50 for seisin —"antoq'm possemus h're s'si'am." The aforesaid half share to go, after the death of the said Henry, to sister Margaret and her heirs for ever. The said Henry Calf, and John Warwyke, rector of St. Werburgh's in Bristol, to be executors.

Proved in the parish church of St. Ewen, June 21st, 1389 ; at the Guildhall on Monday next after the feast of the Translation of St. Thomas Martyr, 13 Richard ii.

37.—SIMON HALEWEY, burgess.

1389. June 12th. To be buried in the church of the Friars Preachers of Bristol, before the image of the blessed Mary. Legacies to the fabric of that church, and every friar of the house, to each other order of mendicant friars in Bristol, to the fabric of All Saints' church, and to the vicar and clerk thereof, to the prior of the Kalendaries, and every chaplain "ad exequias meas venient'," to the fabric of the church of St. Peter. On the day of burial, four torches to burn about testator's body, and 40 shillings for the needy poor. To wife Margery £40 of silver, and her chamber, &c. To son John house property in Worschupstret, for his life, to be afterwards sold, and two chaplains to celebrate as long as the money lasts, one in All Saints' church, and the other in St. Peter's aforesaid. To Thomas Halewey with Joan my daughter £30, six silver spoons, a silver girdle, &c. To brother Thomas Halewey, to Richard Halewey, to servant Elen, to John Hachet, Joan Strete, and Richard atte Feiradon. To daughter Joan Brayne "vnn' Ciphum meu' voc' Note." All the debts of William Brid forgiven. Philip Excestre and Thomas Halewey executors. Son John may, if he should desire, purchase the aforesaid property, and pay £10 less than any one else might wish to give.

Proved in the parish church of St. Ewen of Bristol, June 18th, 1389 ; at the Guildhall on Monday next after the feast of St. Margaret Virgin, 13 Richard ii.

38.—HUGH LE HUNT, burgess.

1389. Monday next after the feast of the Annunciation of B.V.M. To be buried in the chapel of the blessed Mary in the church of St. Werburgh of Bristol, by former wife Cristina, and under the same stone. Legacies to the fabric, and Sir John Warwyke rector of that church, to each order of mendicant friars of the town, to the fabric, and Sir Thomas rector of St. Ewen's, the water-bearing clerk (aquebaiulo), and the fraternity of St. John Baptist in the same church, to Richard Portingale, to Richard son of testator's wife Katharine, to Simon Olyver. To wife Katharine all lands, tenements, rents, &c., in the town and suburb of Bristol, for her life, to go afterwards to son John; if he should die s.p., the said property to be sold, one half of the money for the church work of St. Werburgh, the other for masses, &c., *pro anima*. To the said John £20, also swords, poleaxes, bows and arrows, four gold rings, &c.; wife Katharine to be his guardian, and to have the residue of goods. She and Simon Olyver executors.

Proved in the church of St. Ewen of Bristol, July 18th, 1389; at the Guildhall on Friday next before the feast of St. Michael Archangel, 13 Richard ii.

39.—JOHN RIPER.

1389. Sept. 14th. To be buried in the church of the Friars Preachers of Bristol. Legacies to the prior and each friar of that house, and to my three sons. Executors to have the keeping of sons Robert and Adam and their effects during their minority (name of third son not given). To kinsman Richard articles of clothing, including a pair of scarlet hosen; to kinswoman Mariot 40 shillings; to wife Maud 60 ounces of silver vessels, and all interest in the messuage held of the prior of St. James of Bristol, in Wynchestret, between testator's property and that of William Somerwell. Dwelling house and six adjoining shops in that street, to be sold for the payment of debts, and provision for wife Maud. Nicholas Wareyn, John Bailly, otherwise called Tibbys, of Bedmynstre, and John Richardys, executors; Simon Olyver, overseer.

Proved in the church of St. Ewen of Bristol, Oct. 1st, 1389; at the Guildhall on Monday next after the feast of All Saints, 13 Richard ii.

40.—JOHN SWELL.

1389. May 5th. To be buried in the church of the Holy Trinity of Bristol, before the altar of St. Katharine. Legacies to the rector of that church, the parish clerk, and each chaplain celebrating there "die obitus mei," and to friars who shall say *Dirige* and mass, which they are to do in their own houses,—"in suis pp'is domibz & non veniant ad mansionem meam nec ad eccl'iam vbi sepult' fue'." To the said altar of St. Katharine, after the death of wife Margaret, a chalice "cum toto apparatu," also "vnam picta' tabulam;" and a breviary to that church. Cloth of russet to be laid over my body, and given, after burial, to the poor and needy *pro anima*. Eight poor people to have russet cloaks and carry four torches and four round tapers, "& non portet' plus de lumine c'ea corpus meu'." To the fabric of St. Ewen's of Bristol 20 shillings; for mending the roads near Bristol £5. Legacies to poor people holding houses, and other needy people, having wives and children, in and near the town, and certain men who have lost their goods "p' auenturam;" to the marriage of poor maidens, to Robert and Joan Dedbroke, to Coneley, to former servant Alice, to Joan Waleys, Thomas Blount, John Spyne, William Wilteschire, to my chaplain Sir Richard, to servants Walter and Philip, to Bydowe, and Hykedon. "Jt'm lego omibz Wynhalyers de Bristoll xs." To John son of Joan wife of Stephen Ferrour of Glastonbury, also to John son of Stephen Ferrour and Joan his wife. To the Commonalty of the town of Bristol £5. To Richard Inhyne and John Chiltenham barber, £5 apiece, if they will administer. To Maud Coneley, Nawdyn, John Rawdyn, Thomas Passemer, Sir William, chaplain, celebrating at St. Ewen's, John Hamme, John Cameleigh, and the mother church of Worcester. To unmarried daughter Alice and her heirs, a tenement in Smalstret held by John Toftrang; if she should die s.p., wife Margaret to have it for her life, to be afterwards sold, and the money given to the poor. To the said Margaret, for her life, the rent and services paid by William Solers and Agnes his wife for a tenement in the suburb of Bristol, in Knyfsmythstret, in the corner, as one goes towards Gropelane; also two shops annexed to that tenement: to be dealt with, after her death, in the above-written manner; also to the said Margaret, a garden in the suburb, in Puthay, to go, after her death, to daughter Alice. A chaplain to celebrate for ten years on the altar of St. Katharine in the church of the Holy Trinity of Bristol. Wife Margaret, Richard Inhyne, Thomas Blount, and John Chiltenham, executors.

Proved before John Barell, clerk, &c., Sept. 30th 1389; before the Mayor and Bailiffs on Monday next after the feast of Philip and James Apostles, 13 Richard ii.

41.—WALTER STODELEY, burgess.

1387. Monday, Sept. 2nd. To be buried in the church of St. Laurence of Bristol, before the altar of the blessed Mary. Legacies to the rector of that church, and Sir William, the rector's kinsman, to the clerk, and each chaplain celebrating there, to the four orders of friars of Bristol, to the hospitals of St. Mary Magdalene and St. Bartholomew, to every poor man and woman in the hospital of St. John Baptist, of Bristol, to the almshouse "in la langrewe," to the fabric of the churches of St. Ewen, St. Augustine, St. Michael, All Saints, and St. James, of Bristol, to the sustentation of the bridges of Chepstow and Newport in Wales, to the sustentation and repair of the bridge of Tewkesbury, for mending the common way between Pontley and the park of Harefeld, as one goes towards Gloucester. To wife Elen, for her life, a tenement in Knyfsmythstrete, and three shops in Gropelane; which tenement and shops were lately bought of John Canynges and Joan his wife. If she should marry again, son John and his heirs to come into possession. If the said John should die s.p., the property to be sold for the benefit of the poor and other works of charity. To the same John, my interest in the shop which John Bury, chaplain, and I bought of Joan formerley wife of Hugh Leyg'ne, in the suburb of Bristol, in Temple-street, also a tenement in the suburb "in vico vocat' Redeelynestret," lately purchased of John Coton, also a cellar, &c., in the cemetery of St. Stephen of Bristol, lately purchased of John Champenes of Pennesford and Alice his wife. To the same John £100, two brass pots, &c., and a girdle which John Seymour bequeathed to me. John Stephenys to be guardian of the said John and his effects during minority. Legacies to sister Alice, Thomas my son and his mother Maud, to Walter Davy, John Wolf "webbe," Anketill Moygne, Edith Colet, to each of my god-children, to Simon Pert, and his three sons, to the work of the Commonalty of Bristol, to infirm men and women "infra Com' Bristoli," to the prisoners in Monkbridge bread and drink, to every porter "p' Kayam" who formerly served testator, to the mother church of Worcester, to each chaplain at the funeral and mass in the aforesaid church of St. Laurence, to Walter son of Richard Carpenter, to friar John Derneford of the order of Preachers, to the fabric of the chapel of the blessed Mary on the bridge of Avon, to William Norton, William Waleys, John Cobyndon, Richard Portingale, John Anstyn, Peryn, Alice Williams, Joan Cornyssh,

Richard son of wife Elen, servant Agnes, Robert Greynyle, Walter Seymour, John Stephenys, and John Goos. Two honest and well reported chaplains to have 80 marks, and celebrate divine offices for four years in the church of St. Laurence of Bristol for the souls of testator, his former wife Joan, his father and mother, John Seymour, &c. Wife Elen, who is to have the third part of all effects, Walter Seymour, and John Stephenys, to be executors.

Proved in the parish church of St. Ewen of Bristol, April 6th, 1390; at the Guildhall on Monday next after the feast of Corpus Christi, 13 Richard ii.

42.—BERNARD OBELEYE.

1389. Ides of March.—"p'ochus eccl'ie sc'e Crucis de Temple Bristol." To be buried in the cemetery of that church. Legacies to Sir William the vicar, Sir Henry parish chaplain, and the fabric of the bell of the same church, to each chaplain and the two clerks there, to maid Beatrix, Walter Taverner, William Stede, William Asch, William Knyzt, sister Joan, daughter Alice, John and Felix de Well'. To wife Agnes a tenement in the parish of holy Cross, to be disposed of, after her death, for the benefit of our souls. A tenement in the market, in the parish of St. Philip of Bristol, to be sold for the payment of debts. Residue to wife Agnes. She and Peter atte Barugh to be executors.

Proved in the church of holy Cross Temple of Bristol, April 9th, 1390; at the Guildhall on Thursday next after the feast of the Lord's Epiphany, 14 Richard ii.

43.—JOHN INHYNE, of St. Leonard's parish in Bristol.

1390. Day of St. Bartholomew Apostle. To be buried in the church of St. Nicholas in the same town. Legacies to the mother church of Worcester, to the fabric and vicar of the church of St. Leonard of Bristol, to the fraternity of the holy Cross in the church of St. Nicholas "in le Crowde," to two chaplains to celebrate *pro anima*, one in the church of St. Leonard, the other in that of St. Nicholas. To wife Margery, for her life, tenements in the town and suburb of Bristol, and lands in the fee of Bedemynstre and Knoll. All tenements situate "sup' la Were & in Berlane" to be sold for payment of debts, and the remainder for the chaplains celebrating for our souls. Adam Inhyne, if he should desire, may have all the said property for £5 less than others offer. After the death of the said Margery, the tenements at Redcliff, with all lands in the aforesaid fee, to go to son John and his heirs. If he should die s.p., the said property to be sold by the procurators of the churches of St. Leonard, St. Nicholas, and St. Thomas the Martyr, and the money given to pious uses. Wife Margery and Adam Inhyne, executors.

Proved in the church of St. Ewen of Bristol, Dec. 8th, 1390; at the Guildhall on Friday next after the feast of St. Wolstan Bishop, 14 Richard ii.

44.—ELIAS SPELLY, burgess.

1390. Jan. 13th. To be buried in the church of the blessed Mary of Kingswood. Legacies to the vicar and fabric of St. Leonard's in Bristol, to each chaplain coming "ad exequias meas," to the cathedral church of Worcester, to the abbot and convent and every monk at Kingswood, the four orders of friars of Bristol, the poor in the hospital of St. Bartholomew of Bristol, the fabric of the house of St. Mary Magdalene there, the fabric of the houses of Friars Preachers and Friars Minors in the city of Worcester, the fabric of the house of St. Mary Magdalene there, and Elen Spelly—"d'ne Elene Spelly sorori eiusd'm domus," to poor and very needy churches, to John Ombersey (Ombersley) monk of Evesham, to my most needy kinsfolk, to every godchild in the street "vocat' Baldewynstr'," to all sick people lying in their beds, and unable to help themselves, in the town and suburb of Bristol, to the fabric of a certain bridge between Calne and "Chiriell," for the making and mending of causeways about Bristol and elsewhere, and mending the "Cawsey de Bedmynstre," to ten maidens, and the daughter of Henry Spelly, for their marriage. Two chaplains to celebrate in the said church of St. Leonard for twenty years for my soul, and the souls of my father and mother, &c., and have £200. To Thomas Norton, burgess of Bristol, a tenement called "le Niewynne" in the town of Bristol, in the High-street, also the corner tenement in Smalstrete inhabited by John Sely, and the corner tenement at the end of the bridge of Avon, as one goes towards Toukerstret, purchased of William Combe, and lately held by John Luk, also a shop next the said tenement lately purchased of the said William Combe, and now held by John Gyna, turner, also four shops in the suburb of Bristol in Temple-street, between property of John Yong and Sir Thomas Broke, knt., also two tenements in Temple-street held by Henry Stokmer and John Archor, between property of the procurators of the Temple church, also shops in Berlane in the same parish of Temple, also a messuage in Baldewynstret between the tenement of Henry Spelly and that which John Poculchurche holds of testator, which messuage was lately held by William Salesbury, also three shops in the same street, between the said tenement held by John Poculchurch and the shops of Joan Brompton, also a messuage in the same street, between the tenement of Richard Braillys and testator's dwelling house, also tenements in the street of St. Nicholas in Bristol, and a hall and shop in Gropelane, held by Richard Frere, and a shop there held by John Mamfras, also a tenement in Lewynesmede inhabited by Richard Stephenys, and the rent received from a tenement of Roger Spert in the street of the blessed Mary "de fforo;" the said Thomas Norton, his heirs and assigns, to pay yearly to Agnes, testator's wife, 20 pounds of silver. Legacies to the said Agnes, to John Poculchurch, Philip Excestre, and his dau. Agnes, Philip Kyngton, William Hogekyn, to all testator's servants and maids, to each master of "Wynchaliers" in Bristol, to each porter "vocat' sakberer" in the town, and each other porter about the Key and the Back. To Elias son of Philip Excestre two shops in in the suburb of Bristol, opposite the Cross, in Baldwynstreet; if the said Elias should die s.p., the property is to remain to Alice, daughter of the said Philip; if the said Elias and Alice should die under age, the said Philip and his wife Margaret to have it for their life, and Thomas Norton, his heirs and assigns, to possess afterwards. The aforesaid Philip Excestre to have the keeping of the aforesaid Elias, Alice, and Agnes, with the property bequeathed to them, according to the custom of the town. To John Poculchurch and his wife Amy, and their heirs, the tenement in Baldewynstrete now inhabited by them, with a shop "post'ius in vico sc'i Nich'i." If the said John and Amy should die s.p., Thomas Norton, his heirs and assigns, to have the said property. To Henry son of Roger Specheley, and his heirs, the rents and services paid to testator by Juliana Southwode for a tenement on the Back of Avon, with reversion of the same; which property was lately purchased of Isabel Arthur. To the same Thomas Norton all the other lands, &c., in the town and suburb of Bristol, also all my ship "vocat' la George." To Thomas Norton, son of the said Thomas, all my lands, tenements, rents, &c., in the city and suburb of Worcester, the same Thomas to provide a chaplain to celebrate *pro anima* in the chapel of St. Oswald at Worcester. Residue of goods to be disposed of by executors, Thomas Norton, Philip Excestre, and John Poculchurch.

Proved before John Chewe, clerk, sequestrator general and commissary for the Bishop of Worcester, Feb. 2nd, 1390; before the Mayor and Bailiffs on Thursday next after the feast of the Purification of B.V.M., 14 Richard ii.

The registers of the Bishops of Worcester state that a William Spelly was ordained a secular deacon in the parish church of Chipping Campden, Dec. 18th, 1406, on a title from the hospital of St. Oswald, by the city of Worcester. Elias Spelly's will is also registered at Somerset House, in *Rous*, 8, where May 22nd, 1391, is given as the date of probate. It is followed, in the Orphan Book, by a deed in which Alan son and heir of Robert de Wrington formerly burgess of Bristol, grants and confirms to Sir Robert Broforde and others, chaplains, all his lands, tenements, &c., in the said town and suburb, the deed being dated at Bristol Oct. 20th, 14 Richard ii., and witnessed by Elias Spelly, then Mayor, Thomas atte Hay, Sheriff, Robert Dudbroke and John Selwode, Bailiffs, Thomas Baupyne *(sic)*, Thomas Knap, William Frome, and many others. Which deed is followed by what purports to be a will made by Walter Derby, burgess of Bristol, on Monday in the feast of St. Silvester Pope, 1386. All his lands, tenements, rents, &c., are bequeathed to John Stephenes, Thomas Colston, and Nicholas le Clerk. No witnesses are named, and there is no record of probate. A fuller copy of the document occurs in the Library at Lambeth, in *Courteney*, 230; and the names of William Canynges, John Sloo, Simon and John Olyver, John Candaver, John Somerville, and Walter Cogan are there given as witnesses. In the note of proof, dated 1389, Colston's name is spelt *Golston*. In the margin is written—"Probacio dci' testamenti ac reprobacio probac'ois habit' circa illud et falsor' codicill' eid' testamento annex'."

45.—WILLIAM FILBERD, burgess.

1391. April 15th. To be buried in the chapel of St. Thomas of Bristol "ante altam Crucem." Legacies to Sir Richard Leonis parish chaplain of that chapel, and all the clerks and chaplains there; to the fabric thereof 30 shillings, and a mazer bowl called *Godezere*; to the fabric of the church of Redcliff, and Sir Henry Netherhaven perpetual vicar thereof, to the almshouses of Langrewe and Templestrete, to the abbot and convent of St. Augustine, to Roger the brother, Alice the servant, and John at Glastonbury, son of testator, to Robert Cleyvile and Walter Martyn, co-executors with wife Alice, who is to have residue of goods and the term of 30 years granted to testator by John Staunford, burgess of Bristol, in the house inhabited by John Frere in St. Thomas's street; the remainder of the term to revert, after the death of Alice, to the said John Staunford, who makes oath that, provided seven of the 30 years then remain, he or his representatives will pay a chaplain of good and honest conversation 100 shillings to celebrate for one year in the aforesaid chapel, and on that agreement he is enrolled in the great missal of the high altar of that chapel, the procurators thereof, namely, Thomas Hay and William White, as also testator and his wife and executors, and Sir Richard Leonus, priest (p'b'ro) of the diocese of London, with others, being witnesses. In addition to this, a chaplain is to celebrate in the said chapel for two years, or two chaplains for one year, and to have £10.

Proved in St. Mary's chapel by the close of Wells cathedral, May 8th, 1391, and before the Mayor and Bailiffs of Bristol on Monday next after the feast of the Lord's Ascension, 15 Richard ii.

46.—ALAN WRYNGTON.

1392. Sunday next before the feast of Philip and James Apostles. To be buried in the chapel of the blessed Mary next the church of holy Cross Temple of Bristol. Legacies to the work of that chapel and of the church of St John in Bristol, to the rector of the latter, to the fabric of Worcester cathedral; to servant John Basset a life interest in lands and tenements "iuxta les Barres voc' la Redelond." All the charitable works ordered by testator in a certain schedule—*Cedula*—written "de manu Thome Hendy" to be fulfilled and performed. Sir Richard Peautrer, Sir John Blake, and all the other feoffees of the gift of lands, rents, tenements, &c., in the town and suburb of Bristol, to sell the same according to the arrangement and promise of Thomas Knap of Bristol and Simon Olyver; the money to be expended on solemn masses and other pious uses. Executors to be Henry Wyvelescombe, Sir William Broun "de Bromezerd iuxta Herford," Philip Excestre, John Sutton son of Thomas Sutton, and John Chiltenham barber.

Proved, with codicil annexed, before John Chewe, clerk, &c., May 6th, 1392; before the Mayor and Bailiffs on Monday next after the feast of St. Laurence, 16 Richard ii.

47.—RALPH COLNE, of Bristol. In the margin *Collys*.

1391. Feb. 20th. To be buried in the parish church of the Holy Trinity of Bristol before the altar of the blessed Mary. Bequeaths a silver bowl to be made into a thurible for that church, and vi^s viii^d yearly for 20 years out of the rent of the house held of testator by William atte Lane, that two tapers may be burned on Sundays and feast-days before the image of the blessed Mary in the church aforesaid. Legacies to each chaplain and the clerk of that church. To wife Elen for her life that part of the messuage in Wynchestret inhabited by testator, and the house held by William atte Lane; the said messuage to be sold, and the money, after payment of debts, to be divided into 3 equal parts, one for the making of a bell "tenorem h'entem ad alias Campanas," another for the maintenance of a chaplain, and the third for the work of the said church; part of the messuage being reserved for wife Elen as bequeathed above. Testator's lawful heirs are to possess his burgage in "seint Mariestret" in Bridgwater which John Leye used to hold, and the other held by Nicholas Marler in Lenestrete (?) in the same town. If the said heirs should die, that property is to be sold and the money expended on the work of the church of St. Andrew at Stokecursy. Half of the burgage outside the western gate of Bridgwater, which Nicholas Croute used to hold, to be sold for the maintenance of a chaplain at the altar of the blessed Mary of Bridgwater *pro anima*. The other half of the burgage in that town, which Nicholas Marler holds of testator, and testator holds of the house of St. John of Eston, to revert to the said house for ever for the support of the needy poor there. Residue of goods to wife and children. She, Richard Sadeler, and John Tanner executors.

Proved before John Chewe, sequestrator general, &c., July 19th, 1392; before the Mayor and Bailiffs on Monday next after the feast of St. James Apostle, 16 Richard ii.

48.—ROBERT SAUNDRES, burgess.

1391. June 15th. To be buried in the cemetery of the church of holy Cross Temple of Bristol opposite the southern cross there. Legacies to the vicar, the chaplains, and the two clerks of that church, to kinswoman Isabel, and wife's dau. Cristina. To wife Alice, for her life, his dwelling-house with curtilage and drying-room adjoining in Temple-street, on condition that she remains sole and chaste; if she does not, and in the event of her death during the lifetime of William testator's son, the said William to possess for his life; the property to be afterwards sold *pro anima*; also to him, for his life, the tenement now held by John Norton tucker adjoining this property in the same street; to be sold for the like purpose. The yearly rent issuing from the tenement possessed and inhabited by William Norton in the suburb of Bristol, to be similarly dealt with immediately after testator's death. To son William and his heirs and assigns, a tenement in the same street, held by John Caunterbury and his wife Joan for their life, between one of Sir Thomas Brook knt. and that of William Norton. Residue of goods to be equally divided between wife Alice and son William. The aforesaid William Norton to be guardian of the latter and of his legacies until he arrive "ad plenam etatem suam," finding security before the Mayor of Bristol according to the custom of the town, and acting as co-executor with the said William.

Proved before Ralph Canon, clerk, &c., July 5th, 1391; before the Mayor and Bailiffs on Monday next after the feast of the Assumption of B.V.M., 16 Richard ii.

49.—WILLIAM SPAYNELL, burgess.

1391. Oct. 4th—"corpus men' t're." Legacies to the rector of the parish church of St. Stephen of Bristol, and to each order of mendicant friars in that town, to kinsmen Nicholas Rawe and Nicholas Wigan, to the two daughters of Dayowe Brathelyn, and to Dayowe himself, if alive, to the poor, to my two maids, to old John Wynne of the balinger; to wife Soneta 100 marks and a fourth part of my bark (bargea), to son Mark a similar bequest, to son Richard a fourth part of the same bark, one half of my balinger, and 100 marks "de auro." My "place" beyond the Avon at Bristol, of the yearly value of 6 marks, to be sold *pro anima*. Residue of goods for pious uses, my debts being first wholly paid. Wife and two sons to be executors, and to have 100 marks in salt. Given under my seal at Lyepe in Spain.

Proved in the church of St. Stephen of Bristol before John Chewe, commissary of the Bishop of Worcester, Dec. 2nd, 1391, and also before John Wyke rector of the said church, and Simon Uphulle bachelor of laws, representing the Archbishop of Canterbury, March 10th in the year aforesaid.

50.—AMY WESTON.

1392. Monday next before the feast of the Nativity of the blessed Mary. "Ego Amicia vxor Joh'is Weston Baker." To be buried in the cemetery of the blessed Mary of Redcliff. Legacies to the vicar there, to each priest celebrating in the church of St. Thomas the Martyr and present at the funeral rites, and each of the three clerks. Articles of clothing to Joan Burgeys, to the wife of Nicholas Tiperton, and Joan Bole. To John my husband, for his life, a tenement in the suburb of Bristol "sup' la Were," to be afterwards sold, and the money distributed in masses and alms for the benefit of the souls of Thomas Bristelton and Julian his wife, their dau. Amy, and John my husband after his departure "ab hac luce," our progenitors, all our benefactors, and all the faithful dead. Residue of goods to the said John. He and John Yong clerk to be executors.

Proved before Thomas Polton, clerk, commissary general of the Bishop of Bath and Wells, in the church of St. Cuthbert of Wells, Sept. 21st, 1392; before the Mayor and Bailiffs of Bristol on Monday next after the feast of St. Matthew Apostle and Evangelist, 16 Richard ii.

51.—WILLIAM WALEYS, draper and burgess.

1392. Thursday in the feast of the Decollation of St. John Baptist. To be buried in the church of holy Cross Temple of Bristol. Legacies to the work of that church, the vicar, each chaplain, and the two clerks serving therein, to Sir William Burton chaplain, to sons Walter and Richard, and daughters Agnes and Joan. If all the said children should die under age, the money bequeathed to them was to be distributed "in pijs elemosinis" for their souls and testator's. Legacies to servants William Stoke, Richard Woderoue, Nicholas Bougham, Edith, Margaret, Alice, Isabel, and Petronilla; to Thomas Blount, John Heth, John Delyn the elder, and John Delyn my apprentice. For funeral expenses £40. Residue to wife Alice. She, Richard Inhyne, and Thomas Blount, executors.

Proved in the parish church of Redcliff, Oct. 1st, 1392; before the Mayor and Bailiffs on Monday next before the feast of the Conception of B.V.M., 16 Richard i.

52.—JOHN ROPER.

1390. May 5th.—"filius Will'i Rop' quond'm burgens vill' Bristoll, moram t'hens ante pypam in suburbio Bristoll sup' Kayam." To be buried in the church of the Friars Minors of Bristol, if happening to die in the said town or suburb. Legacies to the four orders of mendicant friars there, to the rector of St. Stephen's, Bristol, for tithes forgotten and not forgotten, to the mother church of Worcester. To wife Julian, for her life, a yearly rent with reversion of the tenement inhabited by John Donster "smyth" in the suburb of Bristol in Cristemastret, also six shops, with garden behind, on St. Michael's hill, bought by testator of Master Roger White, formerly rector of St. Stephen's, Bristol, and the garden, bought of Sir Henry Fayreford chaplain, "iacens ex alia p'te dict' shopar' sup' dict' montem," and the void place on the same hill, bought of the said Henry, opposite the mill "voc' Gauntysmyll," to go, after her death, to Richard Panys and his wife Alice, testator's dau., and their lawful heirs. The six shops with garden aforesaid to go to Margaret dau. of the said Richard and Alice, and her lawful heirs:

if she should die s.p., remainder to her brother William Panys; to the said Margaret a girdle which had been testator's mother's—" zonam M'ris dict' Joh'is Rop' meliorem." The aforesaid garden and void place, bought of the said Sir Henry, to go to John Panys son of the said Richard and Alice. Residue to wife Julian. She and the said Richard to be executors. "Jt'm lego ffirmam q'm h'eo de d'no Rege de ten' (tenementis) en' p'tin' que fuer' Will'i Roper p'ris dict' Joh'is Rop' deo' Ric'o Panys soluend' debit' mea."

Proved before John Chewe, clerk, &c., Nov. 14th, 1392; before the Mayor and Bailiffs on Monday next after the feast of the Lord's Epiphany, 16 Richard ii.

53.—THOMAS ATTE HAY, burgess.

1393. March 27th. To be buried in the chapel of St. Thomas the Martyr of Bristol, where my daughters are buried. Legacies to the fabric, the vicar, and the three clerks of that chapel. Sir David Walsch, chaplain, to celebrate there *pro anima* for four years, and to have £21 6s. 8d., and my best gown "de Baudekyn;" and a chaplain to celebrate in the church of Stoke-Giffard for two years, and have £10. The funeral rites to be attended by twenty-two chaplains. Legacies to the mother church of Wells, to my sister Alice, Thomas Goode, John Palmer in the market, William Hurdeman, Henry Branktre, John Pay, tucker, to whom a gown "de Motley," John Scot in the market, servants Robert Russell, John Person, Thomas Clerk, and Thomas Cooke, who is also testator's apprentice, and whose legacy is bequeathed on condition of faithfully keeping his agreement. Forty shillings to be distributed among poor weavers and fullers holding houses and having wives and families. For mending roads between the towns of Bristol and Gloucester, and between Bristol and Almondesbury, £20. For the poor and feeble in the country and in town £10. To wife Julian, my horse, a silver girdle, all the utensils of my house, and one half of all effects; the other half to be disposed of by the executors *pro anima*. To the same Julian a tenement in Brodemede inhabited by William Tanner, also four shops in the suburb of Bristol, opposite the cemetery of St. James, two shops in the town "iuxta le Newyate," my dwelling-house in the suburb in Touker-strete, and my state in those three shops, &c., in Bradstrete, by the Guildhall, except the last ten years of my term " quibz (*sic*) lego Maiori & Co'itati vill' Bristoll." All the said possessions to be eventually sold for the benefit of my soul, my wife Julian's, &c. To Elen Oseborne, for her life, a shop in Brodemede "iuxt' reddit' Capellor' Eborard le ffrensch." To John my brother, for his life, a shop in the suburb "iuxta Templeyate." Wife Julian, John Palmer in the market, and William Hurdeman to be executors.

Proved before John Lynton, commissary general of the Archbishop of Canterbury, in the chapel of St. Thomas of Bristol, diocese of Bath and Wells, April 3rd, 1393; before the Mayor and Bailiffs on Monday next after the feast of Corpus Christi, 16 Richard ii.

This will is also registered in *Rous*, 9.

54.—JOHN FREWEYN, burgess.

1393. May 12th. To be buried in the parish church of St. Ewen of Bristol, before the altar of St. Katharine, " iuxt' vx'em meam." To the fabric of that church xiijs. iiijd., and a chest worth that sum to put vestments in. Legacies to the rector and clerk thereof, to the fabric of Worcester cathedral, to Sir Robert Gloucestre chaplain, to each order of mendicant friars at Bristol, to dau. Margaret, sister Amy, and Alice, kinswoman and servant. Twenty shillings sterling to be distributed in bread on the day of burial. A chaplain to celebrate in the above-named church for testator's soul and the souls of his parents and all the faithful dead. Half of his unbequeathed goods to wife Joan, also four yards of cloth "blod' color'," a bowl of "Mazer" bound with silver, with a foot, one cow, &c. She, Sir Thomas the aforesaid rector, and William atte Lane, executors.

Proved before Richard Winchecombe, clerk, sequestrator general for the Bishop of Worcester, May 26th, 1393; before the Mayor and Bailiffs on Wednesday next before the feast of St. Petronilla Virgin, 16 Richard ii.

55.—ROBERT GARDENER.

1392. Jan. 8th. My soul to God and body to the earth. Legacies to the cathedral church of Worcester, to John rector of St. Stephen's in Bristol, and the fabric of that church, on condition that there be no objection to testator's burial therein; to son John, who, together with his goods, until he have discretion, is to be in the keeping of John Bannebury of Bristol; to brother William and uncle William, to dau. Cecily, to servants William Brent, William Brook, and Agnes Huchons, *Joh'i* Chepstowe famul' *mee*, to Agnes wife, Elizabeth daughter, and Hugh son of John Dere, to William Cook, John Englissh, and Maud his wife, Thomas Baillebien, Cristina Grove, Thomas Wyneley tailor, Alice Williams, Sir William Kerdyf chaplain, John Spray, John Hadecome, David Ewyas chaplain; to John Martell for his support at school; to the four orders of mendicant friars of Bristol. To son Robert and his lawful heirs two tenements with three adjoining shops in Fisschernelane, occupied by John Lytell tailor and Reginald Hoper: if he should die s.p., son John and his heirs to possess. To James Myagh, my apprentice, five marks, when he shall come to the end of his term; son Robert to have the said James in the mean time. David Codde, my chaplain, to celebrate *pro anima* for four years, and have a yearly salary of ten marks. Residue of goods to be distributed for the benefit of testator's soul and the souls of his parents and friends. Executors to be John Stanschawe, John Bannebury, John Bryt, and William Gardyner; the first three to have £30 divided between them.

Proved before Richard Wynchecombe, clerk, &c., Jan. 27th, 1392; before the Mayor and Bailiffs on Monday next before the feast of St. Barnabas Apostle, 16 Richard ii.

56.—HENRY LONDON.

1391. Sept. 24th. To be buried "vbi deus disposu'it." All debts to be wholly paid. A censer to be made for the church of Holy Trinity of Bristol, for which 100 shillings are bequeathed. The fourth part of a ship "voc' Cristofer de Bristoll" to be sold, and 40 shillings of the price to go towards making the said censer, if the said 100 will not suffice; executors James Cokkys and John Chiltenham barber to dispose of what remains, and find a fit chaplain to celebrate in the aforesaid church of Holy Trinity at the altar of St. Mary. Legacies to each chaplain and the clerk of that church, and each chaplain celebrating in St. Ewen's of Bristol, to Peret Taverner, to servant John, to unmarried daughters Alice and Maud, to John Chiltenham barber, to Simon Olyver, if he will see that the will be fulfilled, and to the Mayor of Bristol on the same condition. If either Alice or Maud should die before marriage, executors to dispose of the bequest *pro anima*. Twenty shillings to be equally divided among the four orders of mendicant friars of Bristol, for the celebration of four trentals—*trintal' miss.*' All my term in the lands, built and not built on, in the town of Bristol in Tourstrete, to be sold " plus offerenti," preference being given to the aforesaid James Cokkys ; wife Agnes to have the third part of the money and certain household goods. Residue to his daughters.

Proved before Richard Wynchecombe, clerk, &c., June 21st, 1393 ; before the Mayor and Bailiffs on Monday next after the feast of St. Alban, 17 Richard ii.

57.—WILLIAM BEKESWELL, burgess.

1392. Saturday next after the feast of St. Martin Bishop. To be buried in the crypt of St. Nicholas of Bristol. Legacies to the fabrics of that church and crypt, and to the vicar, the chaplains, and the two clerks there ; to Walter Bekeswell my brother, to the mending of the common way in Chippenameslane and of that near Calne, to each order of mendicant friars of Bristol, to Agnes Loue. Three dozen pairs of new shoes for poor needy people on the day of burial. To servant Alice a mazer called *lewte*, and a small silver cup serving for my shop. To wife Alice, for her life, a tenement in the surburb of Bristol on the Back of Avon, between a tenement of Richard Spicer's chantry and Thomas Gilmyn's tenement ; to be afterwards sold for providing celebrations *pro anima* in the crypt of St. Nicholas aforesaid, for mending roads where most needful, and other works of charity. Wife Alice, Adam Pykenham, and Thomas Hendy, executors ; to the last two 20 shillings apiece.

Proved before Richard Wynchecomb, clerk, &c., Jan. 27th, 1392 ; before the Mayor and Bailiffs on Monday next after the feast of the Nativity of St. John Baptist, 17 Richard ii.

58.—WILLIAM SOMERWELL, burgess.

1392. Dec. 6th. To be buried in the church of St. Thomas the Martyr of Bristol. Legacies to the work or profit of that church, to the vicar, the deacon, sub-deacon, suffragan, and each chaplain celebrating therein : to the house of the Friars Preachers, to celebrate *pro anima*, and friar John Sherborne of that order, to the Augustinian Friars, and William Lyndraper friar of that house, to the Minors and Carmelites, to friar Walter Loryng, to Margaret and the other servants. To son John £20 ; Gilbert Joos to have the keeping and governing of him and the money during his minority. To Richard Fynch and John Clage 100 shillings apiece, on condition that they serve my wife well and faithfully during their term. For burial, the poor, &c., £40 sterling. To Gilbert Joos a jasper bedecked with silver— *cun' Jesp' jallerat' argent'*—and 40 shillings sterling. To wife Cassandra, for her life, tenements and mansion houses ; to be afterwards sold for the benefit of our souls and of all the faithful dead ; also all my "vtensil' lib'e & quiete." She, Thomas Prestbury (to whom 100 shillings), and Gilbert Joos, executors. Thomas Colston to help them, and have 40 shillings. Sir William Sydbury chaplain to be their overseer, and have £4 sterling. Witnessed by William White, Thomas Goode, John Frere, Sir John Olyver, and others.

Proved in London March 16th, 1392 ; before the Mayor and Bailiffs at Bristol on Thursday next before the feast of St. Margaret Virgin, 17 Richard ii.

This will is also registered in *Rous*, 9.

59.—RICHARD BYDDESTON.

1393. April 26th. To be buried in the cemetery of the church of holy Cross Temple of Bristol. Legacies to that church, to William Burton chaplain, and each of the other chaplains celebrating there, to servants John Coke and John Taillour ; to servant John Ruddoc a short gown of divers colors " vz de rub' colore & sendry." To Maud Barstaple 3 ells of red woollen cloth to make her a gown. Residue of goods to son John. William Berford vicar of the church aforesaid and William Burton chaplain to be executors ; the former to have the keeping of the said John ; but in case of his death before the goods have been expended on the said John, " quod absit," the guardianship is to be undertaken by William Burton chaplain aforesaid. If John should die before coming to man's estate, the goods are to remain for the benefit of our souls.

Proved before Thomas Polton, clerk, &c., in the chapel of B.V.M., by the close at Wells, July 1st, 1393 ; before the Mayor and Bailiffs at Bristol on Thursday next before the feast of St. Margaret Virgin, 17 Richard ii.

60.—HENRY WYVELESCOMBE.

1393. April 18th. To be buried in the church of holy Cross Temple of Bristol, before the altar of St. James, or wheresoever it shall please God. To the use of that church two pairs of vestments, with a chalice, a missal, and other appurtenances, already in the church, in a chest before the altar of St. James, to serve at that altar. Masses to be celebrated "infra diem exit' mei & diem sepulture mee," if it may be, or within eight days after. The poor to have bread on the day of burial. The vicar of that church or his parish chaplain to pray for my soul and the souls of Clarice my wife and Walter Kebbe on Sundays "in Pulpito." Legacies to the vicar, the chaplains, the deacon, and sub-deacon, to the four orders of friars of Bristol, to the prior and convent of Witham, to William Champion, formerly my servant, dwelling at Hereford, to Master Simon Sydenham and his sister Joan Sydenham, to my (female) servant who is called Ismay (?), to servants Juliana Riche, Juliana Broke, William Palmer, and Matthew Dorset, to William Norton, Nicholas Knyght, the sisters of St. Mary Magdalene of Bristol, each of my godchildren, and the Commonalty of the town of Bristol. To my apprentice William Knyght 10 shillings and the term of his apprenticeship. To a chaplain to celebrate for one year before the aforesaid altar of St. James, for my soul, and the souls of John and Gunnilda (?) my parents, and Clarice my wife, &c., 100 shillings. To Sir Thomas Frenssh chaplain 20 shillings and my psalter in the chest aforesaid. To Henry Sydenham my silver seal with a chain. Executors to sell two large furnaces, and distribute the money for the good of the souls of Walter and Thomas Kebbe, and the souls "quibz ip'i tenebantur" and all the faithful dead. Executors also to sell for pious purposes, the soul of John Wycombe being mentioned, those shops "in vico Templi" between the shops of John Badecok and what was formerly the shop of William Hendy, extending from the said street in front to the Temple cemetery behind. To Henry son of Richard Sydenham and his lawful heirs the tenement inhabited by testator in the same street, bought of John Woderoue, John Pryschton and Alexander Moys, situate between what were formerly the tenements of John Framceys and Henry Babbecary, and extending from the said street in front to the Avon behind. If the said Henry should die s.p., remainder to his brother Simon Sydenham, and in default of issue, rem. to their sister Joan and her heirs. If she should die s.p., the property to be sold ; £20 of the price to the Commonalty of Bristol, and the rest for pious purposes. John Slape to have the said tenement "ad firmam" at a reasonable rent. To Sir Henry Inct, chaplain, my book called *Orologium sapiencie* and 20 shillings of silver. To Richard Inhyne twelve new silver spoons and my new saddle and bridle. To John Slape a furnace standing in my kitchen, with all wooden vessels for brewing, and lxxviij^s. of his debt of x^{li}. iiij^s. To Geoffrey Hole four pieces of lead "vocat' p'sse" for dyeing cloth. William Norton, Richard Inhyne, and Henry Sydenham, executors.

Proved before Master Thomas Polton, commissary general of the Bishop of Bath and Wells, Aug. 19th, 1393 ; before the Mayor and Bailiffs on Monday next after the feast of the Nativity of B.V.M., 17 Richard ii.

61.—WILLIAM HERVY.

1393. Jan. 10th. To be buried in the cemetery of the church of holy Cross Temple "si in Bristoll decessero." Legacies to the fabric of that church, to the abbots and convents of Sherborne, Milton, Cerne, and Abbotesbury, to the prior of St. John of Wells and his brethren, to the prioress and convent of Mynchenberugh, to the prior and convent of Staverdene (?), to the four orders of friars of Bristol, to William Gate "de Langebridie in Cors'," John Shirborn of Cerne, William Winterborne of Bristol, and William Mason of Wells. To John Middelton and his heirs, after the decease of testator and wife, a tenement with garden in Tempulstrete, between the tenement of William Winterborne and that of John Tanner. Residue of goods to wife Joan. She and John de Middelton to be executors.

Proved before Thomas Polton, clerk, &c., August 28th, 1394 ; before the Mayor and Bailiffs on Monday next after the feast of the Nativity of B.V.M., 18 Richard ii.

62.—JOHN BEKET, of co. Somerset.

1392. Saturday in the feast of the Conversion of Paul Apostle. To be buried in the monastic abbey of the blessed Mary of Keynsham. Legacies to the abbot and convent of that monastery, the vicars of Keynsham and Comptoundando, Sir Richard chaplain of St. Anne, Richard Champeneys, John

Wyke late my servant, the fabrics of the churches of Farnburgh and Markesbury, the parish chaplain and the clerk at the latter place, the poor of St. Bartholomew's hospital beyond Frome gate at Bristol, my servant John Galon, and Sir Richard Okeley, canon of Keynsham. To wife Maud 100 marks, which are in the keeping of Sir Thomas Broke knt. To son John Beket 100 marks, also in the keeping of the said Thomas, to provide a chaplain to celebrate *pro anima* for seven years. To the said John and his heirs and assigns, all my lands, tenements, rents, reversions, &c., in the town and suburb of Bristol. To Maud wife of the aforesaid John Beket and to her children 40 marks. To Sir John Babestoke the bed in which I have lain in my sickness, &c. Executors to be John rector of "Northyate Bathon," Richard Sutton, and Richard Clerk of Pensford: to the first two 40 shillings apiece.

Proved before Master Thomas Polton, clerk, &c., at Wells, Dec. 23rd, 1393; before the Mayor and Bailiffs at Bristol on Monday next before the feast of St. Hilary, 17 Richard ii.

63.—JOHN WYNCHESTRE, tanner and burgess.

1394. Wednesday in the feast of the Annunciation of the blessed Mary. To be buried in the parish church of St. James of Bristol, before the altar of St. Thomas the Martyr "quod de nouo fieri feci." Legacies to the prior of that place, to each monk accustomed to celebrate there, to the parish chaplain and parish clerk, to the mother church of Worcester, to the poor, and each order of mendicant friars at Bristol. Twelve pounds of wax to burn about my body on the day of burial. To wife Isabel, for her life, the tenement inhabited by testator in Lewynesmede; remainder to kinswoman Maud Yerdesleigh and her heirs and assigns; also to Isabel my state of three shops which I built "in la Brodemede" on land purchased by me of the abbot and convent of Tewkesbury, and a tenement with shop, &c., in Lewynesmede, held of me by John Stephenys webbe; to be sold, after her decease, for pious purposes. To Thomas Piers, late servant, property in Brodemede, to be held by him, his wife, and one son for their lives. John Arthur, late servant and apprentice, his wife, and son, and John Heryng, wife, and son, to hold other property in like manner; the money raised by the sale of which possessions to be employed *pro anima*. Residue of goods, after payment of debts, to wife Isabel. Executors to be John Stone and Stephen Reve, to each of whom 40 shillings.

Proved in the parish church of St. James of Bristol, April 3rd, 1394.

Testator added a codicil March 27th, 1394, bequeathing to John Stone, burgess of Bristol, property in the street called "le Brodemede," between land held by testator of the prior of St. James of the said town, and the void land held by John Brewer, and extending from the aforesaid street in front to the land of John Devenysch behind. Which codicil was exhibited before Richard Wynchecombe, clerk, &c., in the church of All Saints of Bristol, May 8th, 1394.

Proved before the Mayor and Bailiffs on Monday next after the feast of Peter and Paul Apostles, 18 Richard ii.

64.—WILLIAM TEMPLE, of Bristol.

1393. Nov. 25th. To be buried in the cemetery of holy Cross Temple. Legacies to all the priests celebrating in that church and the one officiating at the burial, to the orders of friars, to friar "W. Wroxale," to servant John, to William, son of Th. Carpenter, to the four children of Richard White of Keynesham, to godson William of Kyngeswode, to daughters Alice and Agnes. To my apprentice a broad axe, otherwise chipaxe, and a "pollax" which "Daud smyth" made, also two augers, &c. Executors to receive the rents of the two tenements inhabited by Walter Turke and Richard Chaloner for twelve years after my decease, during which term a payment to be made to Sir Walter Brynyng chaplain; the said tenements to be afterwards possessed by the Master of the hospital of St. John Baptist in Redeclynepytt, and his successors for ever. Nicholas Taillor and Richard White to be executors, and dispose of goods "p' sal' aie' mee."

Proved before T. Polton, clerk, &c., Dec. 4th, 1393; before the Mayor and Bailiffs on Monday next after the feast of St. James Apostle, 18 Richard ii.

65.—MARGERY WALES. In one part of the will *Walees*.

1390. Thursday in the feast of the Translation of St. Thomas Martyr. Testatrix describes herself as wife of Master Nicholas Wales, Mason, and dau. and heir formerly of Master Thomas Cook. To be buried in the monastic church of St. Augustine by Bristol. Legacies to St. Mary of "Wircestre," to the Friars Preachers, the Minors, and Carmelites of Bristol, to Walter Cogan, to servant Thomas Barri, and to the poor. Two shillings for bell-tolling in the aforesaid monastery. Ten shillings to be laid out in bread, ale, &c., on the day of burial. To husband Nicholas and his heirs and assigns, a tenement with two shops in Horstret on the south, and five shops on the north side of the same street, also residue of goods. He and Walter Cogan executors.

Proved before John Barell, clerk, &c., Oct. 14th, 1390; before the Mayor, Sheriff, Bailiffs and Chamberlains, on Monday next before the feast of the Assumption of B.V.M., 19 Richard ii.

66.—JOHN HUNTE.

1388. Wednesday in the feast of St. Kalixtus Pope. To be buried in the church of All Saints of Bristol, before the altar of the holy Cross. Legacies to the fabric of that church, Sir William parish chaplain, and every other chaplain, and Richard the clerk there, to the fabric of the church of St. Peter of Bristol, to Walter Wotton, to the mother church of Worcester. To son John four entire beds &c., and to him and dau. Katharine "vasa mea stangnea" in equal portions; to the said dau. six entire beds, and ten marks of silver; she and the said marks to be in the keeping of James Bokebynder until she come to full age. If she should die, her bequests to be distributed for the benefit of my soul, and that of wife Cristina, &c. To John Savage a bed wherein I have lain for the last two weeks. To the aforesaid church of All Saints, my third best coverlet to lie before the high altar. Residue of goods to be sold for pious purposes. James Bokebynder and John Saverey executors, to each of whom vj^s viij^d.

Proved before John Barell, clerk, &c., Nov. 28th, 1388; before the Mayor, &c., on Monday next after the feast of the Assumpton of B.V.M., 19 Richard ii.

67.—HENRY CALF, burgess.

1394. May 26th. My soul to Divine mercy, and body to be buried in St. Werburgh's of Bristol, or in the church of St. Michael of Chipping Torrington, if I shall happen to die there. Legacies to the rector of St. Werburgh's as well for my own forgotten tithes as for those of John Godereste, spicer, to the six priests and two clerks serving therein ; for making an altar "ad claudend' vestiariam" in the chapel of St. Mary there ; to the four orders of friars of Bristol for the celebration of forty trentals in their churches for my soul, and that of the said John and his wife Alice and dau. Katharine, to the poor lying and abiding in the church of St. Bartholomew in Bristol, and those in the hospitals of Langrewe and St. John Baptist in the suburb, and St. Laurence by Bristol, and at Bryztbowe, and the poor and decrepit in the town and suburb ; to the sisters of St. Mary Magdalene serving God in the suburb, to the abbot and convent of St. Augustine of Bristol for the work of the campanile, to the prior and monks of St. James of Bristol for the glazing of a window in their church, to the master and brethren of St. Mark of Bristol, to the work of the church of the blessed Mary of Redcliff, to the procurators of St. Ewen's of Bristol, for the renovation of the roof of that church, to Alice dau. of William Rede, late my servant, for her marriage, to John son of the said William, to help him at school, to kinsman John Torrynton, and godson Henry, son of Richard Bris, for the same purpose ; to Elen wife of Adam Taillour, kinswoman of the aforesaid John Gotereste *(sic)*, to Thomas Wyngtley, tailor, and Roger Bore ; to servants Richard Bloundel, and Richard Austyn, son of Robert Niwemaistre, kin to my late wife Katharine ; to servant Edith, to her marriage ; to late servants Robert Wyot, Roger Russell, John Wilkyns, William Westley, and Alice Carter, wife of Richard Brys ; to Richard son of Henry Cobyndon, and John son of Hugh Hounte. All my lands, tenements, &c., once the property of the aforesaid John Goterest and his dau. Katharine, late my wife, are made over to John Candever for a certain sum, remaining in his hands, that he may pay and distribute all the legacies aforesaid ; to him 100 shillings. Of the residue four pence to each chaplain taking part in the obsequies, namely, *placebo*, *dirige*, and *mass*, two pence to each clerk, and a penny to every poor person attending ; 100 men to be clothed in cloth of russet or white ; 20 marks to be expended on the day of burial in bread, ale, wine, cheese, and flesh. To wife Katharine all silver cups, spoons, &c., and all the store in my dwelling-house in Bristol, so that she claim no part of my real and personal property in Chipping Torrington, co. Devon. She, Roger Russell, and Sir Richard Boilon, chaplain, to be executors, and dispose of the residue for the benefit of my soul, and the souls of the said John and Katharine, and all the faithful dead. John Candever to enfeoff the executors in all lands, tenements, &c., according to an indenture between him and testator. Brother Richard Wocestre, prior of St. James of Bristol, to be overseer.

Proved before Master John Wyke, bachelor of decrees, rector of St. Stephen's, Bristol, in that church, being deputed by John Lynton, commissary general of the Archbishop of Canterbury, Jan. 13th, 1394 ; before the Mayor, and others, on Monday next before the feast of St. Bartholomew, 19 Richard ii.

68.—JOHN WATTIS. In the margin *Wattys*.

1393. Saturday next before the feast of the Nativity of St. John Baptist. To be buried in the chapel of the blessed Mary within the church of the Carmelites of Bristol, on the south side. Legacies to the said order, to my dau. Joan, and her dau. Alice, to Alice servant of John Canynges, and Amy dau. of the same. To wife Joan the rent of two messuages and five adjoining shops in the suburb of Bristol in Knyfsmythstret, between Frome gate and the tenement inhabited by Nicholas Warreyn, extending from the aforesaid street in front "vsq' ad le Portwalle" behind; with reversion of half the aforesaid messuages, shops, &c., to be held by her and her heirs and assigns. A fit chaplain to celebrate *pro anima* for four years. Residue of goods, after payment of debts, to wife Joan. She, John Prisshton, and William Bierden, executors.

Proved before Richard Wynchecombe, clerk, &c., in the parish church of All Saints of Bristol, Oct. 11th, 1393; before the Mayor, and others, on Monday next before the feast of St. Giles Abbot, 19 Richard ii.

69.—WILLIAM BRACI, burgess.

1395 (1394?). Wednesday before the feast of St. Matthias Apostle. My soul to Almighty God, the blessed Mary, and the company of all the saints, and body to be buried in the church of St. Stephen of Bristol. Legacies to the fabric of that church for making bells, to every priest who has no benefice therein, to the suffragan, to the mother church of Worcester. To 100 poor people a penny apiece. To dau. Agnes ten marks sterling, half a dozen silver spoons, a bed, a chest "de sprnyce," a posnet, &c. To my sister and her son, to Nicholas Hokere, John Saundre, John Wellys, Thomas Scherman, and servant Robert Bury. Wife Maud to have the residue and be executrix.

Proved in the church of St. Ewen of Bristol, July 6th, 1395, before John Chewe, clerk, sequestrator general for the Prior of Worcester cathedral, the see being vacant; before the Mayor, and others, on Monday next after the feast of St. Giles Abbot, 19 Richard ii.

70.—JOHN REDE, burgess.

1394. Tuesday next after the feast of St. Benedict Abbot. To be buried in the cemetery of St. Augustine of Bristol. Legacies to Worcester cathedral, to divers chaplains to celebrate *pro anima* on the day of burial, to poor people of the town of Bristol lying in their beds, to each priest celebrating in the church of St. Leonard of Bristol. To John son of Thomas Sutton of Bristol, and his heirs, a tenement with shops, &c., in Oldecorne street in the said town held by John Sherp, also a garden opposite the Friars Preachers, in the suburb, held by the said John Sutton, and two tenements in the said suburb in Baldewynstret, and two in Lewynesmede, and one in Redeclynestret, and a garden in that street, extending from the land of the abbot and convent of St. Augustine of Bristol in front to the bank of Avon behind, and all my other lands, tenements, rents, services, and reversions in the said town and suburb. The said John to be executor, and have the residue of goods.

Proved before the sequestrator general for the diocese of Worcester, April 3rd, 1394 (1395?); before the Mayor, and others, on Monday next before the feast of the Nativity of the blessed Mary, 19 Richard ii.

71.—WALTER FROMPTON.

1395. April 2nd.—"fili' Walt'i ffrompton nup' b' vill' Br.'" To be buried in the church of St. John of Bristol. Legacies to the rector thereof, and each order of mendicant friars at Bristol. To servant John Bernelee a cup "numcup' a Note." All goods to be divided for the benefit of my soul, my wife Joan's, &c. All lands, tenements, rents, and services in Bristol to be divided for the said Joan and my children. Nicholas Wareyn and John Sloo, executors. John Knyghton, clerk, overseer.

Proved before Walter Rooke, sequestrator general for the Archbishop of Canterbury, April 6th, 1395; before the Mayor, and others, on Monday next after the feast of the Nativity of the blessed Mary, 19 Richard ii.

72.—JOAN STOKE.

1393. May 20th. "Ego Johanna Relicta Joh'is Stoke quondam burgens' ville Bristoll." To be buried in the church of St. Thomas the Martyr, by John Stoke, my late husband. Twenty pounds of wax to be made into eight tapers, four of which are to be about my body "in exequijs meis & in Missa in Crastino," namely, one at the head—*ad caput*,—another at the feet, and two on either side, and four to stand above the breast; also six torches, to be disposed of and divided *pro anima*. Four pounds of silver for clothing the bearers of the said torches, and other people near of kin to me. Legacies to the vicar of the church aforesaid, to 100 of the poor who keep their beds, to servant Robert Hyne, to Thomas Backe. To Richard Barbor the 20 shillings bequeathed in the will of John Stoke late my husband. Executors to sell those two acres of meadow lying next Bedmynstre. To John son of Henry Spicer, son of Stephen Spicer, formerly burgess of Bristol, the tenement called Ropfelde in High-street, Bristol. If the said John should die s.p., remainder to Alice his sister; in case of her death s.p., rem. to my nearer kin. To the said John and Alice a tenement in Cornstret, Bristol; their father Henry to have the keeping of them for 24 years. Executors to collect the money due from Sir Thomas Arthur knt. for rent of the manor of "Nyce," unpaid for eleven years past, he being bound to pay me five marks yearly. The messuage inhabited by John Barth in Catepulstret, Bristol, in the parish of St. Stephen, to be sold *pro anima*. To dau. Isabel, wife of Sir Thomas Arthur, knt., the best cup with cover, "qui ciphus vocat' Chalice coppe." To dau. Alice, wife of John called lord of Kenne, the second best. To son Henry the third best silver cup, six silver spoons, a bed "cum Capeto & vno quelto," &c. To Agnes, wife of William Canynges, a silver cup wherein the image of St. John is engraved, with the cover of the same. Son Henry Spicer to be executor.

Then follows a note, dated Sept. 17th, 1395, to the effect that Henry Spicer, burgess of the city of London, son of testatrix, refused to act; and Sir Thomas Arthur knt. was appointed to administer.

Proved before William Frome, Mayor, John Stephenys, Sheriff, and John Prischton and John Castell, Bailiffs and Chamberlains, on Monday next after the feast of the Exaltation of the holy Cross, 19 Richard ii.

73.—WILLIAM FROST, boucher and burgess.

1391. Wednesday in the vigil of the Exaltation of the holy Cross. To be buried in the church of the Apostles Peter and Paul of Bristol, "coram se'a Cruce." A thousand masses to be celebrated *pro anima*. To wife Margaret, for her life, my dwelling-house in Bristol in Worschipstret, by St. Edith's well, also a cottage with lands and meadows within the hundred of Barton "extra portam Laffardi;" all which porperty to go, after her decease, to dau. Margaret and her lawful issue; if she should die s.p., it is to be sold for pious uses, for the benefit of my soul, the souls of my wives, our children, &c. Residue to wife Margaret. She, Richard Crokker, and John Baath, mason, to be executors.

Proved before John Chewe, clerk, sequestrator general for the Bishop of Worcester, September 23rd, 1391; before the Mayor and Bailiffs on Monday next before the feast of St. Kalixtus Pope, 19 Richard ii.

74.—ROBERT MAY. In the margin *John* May, "Coke."

1395. Aug. 29th. To be buried in the church of All Saints of Bristol. Legacies to the fabric, vicar, and clerk of that church. To each order of mendicant friars in Bristol, 30 pence for a trental to be sung for my soul; to my mother Alice, and sons Richard and Walter. Residue to wife Agnes. She and Nicholas Churchey to be executors.

Proved before Thomas Wybbe, clerk, sequestrator general for the Bishop of Worcester, Oct. 4th, 1395; before the Mayor, Sheriff, and Bailiffs on Monday next before the feast of All Saints, 19 Richard ii.

75.—JOAN SEYS, daughter of John Seys, glazier.

1395. Oct. 3rd. To be buried in the chapel of St. Mary in the parish church of St. Augustine of Bristol. Legacies to the vicar and fabric of that church, in which a chaplain or chaplains are to celebrate *pro anima*; lands, tenements, &c., in the town and suburb of Bristol to be sold for that purpose. For funeral expenses on the days (*sic*) of my burial 40 shillings. All my lands, tenements, rents, &c., in the town of Taunton, co. Somerset, to be sold *pro anima*. To Alice Bawdon a bed, that is to say, a coverlet with tester of green and yellow, also "J lilod' Toga" and a furred hood. Executors to be Richard Ledbury and Thomas atte Mede, to each of whom iij^s. iiij^d.

Proved in the church of St. Augustine the Less, Nov. 14th, 1395; before the Mayor, and others, on Monday next after the feast of St. Martin Bishop, 19 Richard ii.

76.—JOHN WYKE, merchant.

1393. July 15th. To be buried in the chapel of the blessed Mary in the church of St. Stephen, Bristol, "iux' sepuler' Ed'i Beauflo'," to whose son, John, xl^s. Legacies to the rector, the fabric, and Sir John Modeford parish chaplain of that church, to the clerk there for bell-tolling, and the suffragan for the cross, to Richard Egger and John Steph', chaplains, to David Cod and John Poul, priests, to the mother church of Worcester, to each chaplain coming to the obsequies on the day of my burial, namely to *placebo*, *dirige*, and *mass*, to every chaplain in Bristol celebrating immediately after my decease. To the poor on the day of burial £3 in bread. For cloth and shoes for the poor and needy 120 shillings. To each order of mendicant friars, and to friar John Derneford of the order of Friars Preachers of Bristol, to John Ley, tailor, John Wyke, Anketill Moyne, Andrew Anketill, Richard de le Beche of Berwyke, to my spiritual son John Tipet, to Marion Brynt servant, and Robert Brynt her brother ; to the poor lying in the house of St. Bartholomew 10 shillings, according to the disposing of John Thomas chaplain there ; to each leper house in Bristol, to the house called Langrewe, to the poor house opposite the church of the Augustinian Friars, to the poor lying in the church of St. John beyond the Avon at Bristol, to the needy in the prison called Monkebrig, to Thomas Pedmore of Worcester, to Richard Reve, Margaret Stoke, Ismaeta Devenysch, Margaret Grenell, Mariota, John Faunt, Perot, Godeyer skinner, and his wife, to Wygan, Sara Skynner, Virly dwelling beyond Avon, Stapulton beyond Avon, and Alice Piers, widow, of Bristol. For mending the roads 40 shillings. Residue to be disposed of *pro anima*. Richard Panes, Sir David Cod, and Sir John Don, executors, to each of whom 100 shillings.

Proved before Walter Roke, sequestrator general for the Archbishop of Canterbury, Aug. 20th, 1395 ; before the Mayor on Monday next after the feast of St. Clement Pope, 19 Richard ii.

77.—RICHARD ASCH, merchant.

1395. Monday in the vigil of the Exaltation of the holy Cross. To be buried in the church of St. Laurence of Bristol before the altar of the Holy Trinity. To the fabric of that church for my said place xiij^s. iiij^d. A fit chaplain to celebrate there for one year after my decease. To each order of mendicant friars of Bristol ij^s. vj^d. To wife Rose, for her life, my state in all those cellars, shops, and solars opposite the church of St. John of Bristol, beginning in the corner which Wiliam Shephurd holds of me, and reaching to the tenement of John Knyzton chaplain ; to go, after her death, to John Hervy and his wife Cecily. Also to wife Rose a garden, with the pool, at Irischmede, formerly the property of Alan de Wryngton ; to go, after her death, to William Poulet and his heirs and assigns. All other lands, tenements, &c., bought by me in the town and suburb of Bristol, to remain to the said Rose for her life, and afterwards to be sold for pious uses for the benefit of our souls. To Richard Panys and Geoffrey Barbour £3 apiece : they, wife Rose, and John Hervy to be executors.

Proved before the ecclesiastical authorities Nov. 8th, 1395 ; afterwards before the Mayor.

78.—THOMAS HALLE.

1395. Wednesday next after the feast of St. Matthew Apostle. To be buried in the crypt of St. John Baptist of Bristol. Legacies to that church and the rector. A chaplain to celebrate therein *pro anima* for two years, and have £10. To each order of mendicant friars of Bristol ij^s. vj^d. Legacies also to my brother Robert and servant Margaret. Executors to be Cristina my wife and Thomas Drynkewater. To the latter 20 shillings, if he will undertake administration : if not, Richard Halle is to be an executor, and have that sum.

Exhibited in the church of Redcliff Nov. 8th, 1395, and proved before the Mayor on Monday next after the feast of St. Andrew Apostle, 19 Richard ii.

79.—JOHN ROWBERWE, burgess. In the margin *Rowborwe.*

1395. Sept. 16th. To be buried in the cemetery of the blessed Mary of Redcliff. To wife Margaret and her heirs and assigns a tenement in Redcliff-street, between a tenement of John Castell, inhabited by John Lenam, and the lane leading to the Avon, also all my goods within the said tenement. To dau. Alice and her heirs two shops on Redcliff hill, between the tenement of Walter Newcomb and that of John Hame; also a tenement in Temple-street, between the rent of the abbot of Keynsham and the tenement of Thomas Broke. To Robert Lemenstour, and his lawful heirs, two shops "sup' le Were," between the tenement of William Stiel "crokker" and the rent of St. Bartholomew. If Robert should die s.p., the said two shops are to revert to me and my heirs for ever. William Foxhull and Robert Cadbury executors.

Proved before Ralph Canon, clerk, &c., in the chapel of B.V.M. by the close at Wells, Dec. 13th, 1395; before the Mayor of Bristol on Monday next after the feast of the Lord's Epiphany, 19 Richard ii.

80.—JOHN BROKE, burgess.

1395. Feb. 15th. To be buried in the cemetery of St. James of Bristol. All the grain found in my tenement at Sutton and in the barn thereof to be divided into three parts; one to be expended on my burial, another for the sowing of the land there, and the residue to be equally divided between wife Maud and son William. A chaplain to celebrate *pro anima* for a whole year, and to have 100 shillings. Legacies to the rector and fabric of the church of St. John of Bristol, and the prior of St. James there. To wife Maud, for her life, the tenement in Gropelane, Bristol, in which she lives; the said tenement, with all the leaden vessels therein, to remain, after her death, to son William for his life; to be sold afterwards, and the money divided into five parts, four of which to the orders of friars at Bristol equally, and the fifth for pious uses. To son William a silver cup, also a mazer bound with silver, with a silver cover, and another mazer bound with silver, of which the binding is somewhat broken. To dau. Isabel a silver cup. Another silver cup, with a foot and cover of silver, to be sold for the benefit of my soul and son Walter's. The mark which William Grene hooper owes me to be expended *pro anima.* Residue to wife Maud. She, the rector of St. John's aforesaid, Richard Hoper, and Thomas atte Hulle, executors.

Proved before Thomas Wybbe, clerk, &c., Feb. 22nd, 1395; before the Mayor on Monday next before the feast of St. Gregory Pope, 19 Richard ii.

81. WILLIAM SAMPSON, son of Thomas Sampson, of Bristol.

1395. Aug. 19th. To be buried in the cemetery of the blessed Mary of Redcliff, by the tomb of my father. Legacies to the fabric of that church and of the church of St. Thomas, to Sir William Kene chaplain, Cristina More, Thomas Burgeys, John Burton the younger, Margery Lokyer, and

Isabel Douster. To the children and servant of William Wermynstre 8 marks. To my mother Joan 300 marks and residue of goods. She, John Burton her husband, and the aforesaid Sir William Kene, executors.

Proved before Walter Roke, clerk, &c., in the church of St. Thomas of Bristol, diocese of Bath, Sept. 30th, 1395; before the Mayor on Monday next after the feast of St. Gregory Pope, 19 Richard ii.

82.—JOHN TOSTRONG.

1396. Monday next after the feast of St. John Baptist. To be buried in the choir of the church of the Friars Preachers. Legacies to the said friars and the fabric of their church, to the Augustinians, Carmelites, and Minors, to the vicar of St. Leonard's, to Thomas son of William Wermystre, and Sir John Don. To wife Agnes the half of all my moveable goods. To Alice Wermystre £20, and all my land and rent in the city and county of Waterford. Henry Lane, who is enfeoffed in the said property conditionally for the performance of my will, is to cause the aforesaid Alice to be enfeoffed in fee simple for herself and her heirs and assigns for ever, holding the same of the chief lords of that fee, &c. Residue of goods to Alice Wermystre. She, and John Don, priest, executors.

Proved before Thomas Wybbe, clerk, &c., July 7th, 1396; before the Mayor on Wednesday next after the feast of the Translation of St. Thomas Martyr, 20 Richard ii.

The name John *Toftrang* occurs in will 40.

83.—ROBERT CAMMELL, otherwise Arnald, burgess.

1395. Wednesday next after the feast of St. Gregory. To be buried in the crypt of the church of St. Nicholas, Bristol. Legacies to the fabric, the vicar, and every chaplain there, to the church at Worcester, to each order of mendicant friars at Bristol, to the church of St. Barnabas of Quenecammell, to William Hobbes of Westcammell, John Baggewell of Estecammell, Isabel Carter, William Fort, John Shephurd, Alice wife of Hugh Screven, and Edith Donhede. For mending the road of Bisschupworthfeld £5. For celebrations in the aforesaid church of St. Nicholas for four years £20. To the poor 100 yards of woollen cloth "de Bergony." To Henry Fodyngdon, for his life, a shop and garden at Elebrigge, near the land of St. John, held by Philip Excestre, out of which the sum of eight pence to be paid yearly to the chief lord of that fee; the property to remain to my heirs after the said Henry's decease. To dau. Joan £60 sterling and the third part of the utensils in my house. A silver girdle to the blessed Mary of Redeclyve. To wife Alice, for her life, lands and tenements in the town and suburb of Bristol; remainder to dau. Joan and her lawful issue. If the said Joan should die s.p., all the property to be sold : the fourth part of the money to the fabric of the aforesaid church of St. Nicholas; the rest to be distributed for the good of my soul, wife Alice's, our parents, benefactors, &c. Residue to wife Alice. She, John Mey, and John Donhede, executors. To the last two, for their pains, xxvj^s. viij^d. apiece.

Proved before Henry de Netheravene, vicar of the chapel of the blessed Mary of Redeclyve, May 2nd, 1396; before the Mayor on Friday next before the feast of St. Margaret Virgin, 20 Richard ii.

84.—WILLIAM CARY, burgess.

1395. May 4th. To be buried in the cemetery of St. Werburgh of Bristol. Legacies to Sir John Warwyk the rector, to each chaplain accustomed to celebrate there, and the clerk, to the mother church of Worcester, to each order of mendicant friars of Bristol, to the sick poor in the hospital of St. Bartholomew, to servant Alice. Clothing of Welsh russet for 13 very needy poor people. To 13 other poor a pair of shoes apiece. Bread to be distributed on the day of burial. To son John Cary £40, also one piece of silver, &c.; executors and Sir John Warwyke his godfather to have the keeping and governance of him and his goods, and buy him a corrody in the abbey of Keynsham, made secure to him under the seal both of the convent and abbot, so that he shall have no lack of proper victuals. To the offspring about to be brought forth £10, if it live to lawful age, if not, wife Agnes to have the money. To the same Agnes my dwelling-house in Bristol, in Cornestr,' and one parcel of meadow in the suburb "iuxta les fllodegates." Remainder to her offspring, if it shall survive. A chaplain to have eight marks, and celebrate for a year in the church of St. Werburgh for my soul and the souls of Gervase Cari and his wife Julian. Executors to be wife Agnes and Henry Roper, to whom xiij^s iiij^d. if willing to undertake.

Proved before Thomas Wybb May 8th, 1396: before the Mayor on Monday next after the feast of St. James, 20 Richard ii.

85.—ALEXANDER MOYS, burgess.

1394. Friday next after the feast of St. Michael Archangel. To be buried in the church of holy Cross Temple of Bristol. Legacies to the fraternity of the chapel of St. Katharine therein, to the vicar, the two clerks, and the work of that church, to each priest celebrating there and taking part in my funeral rites; to Sir Henry, chaplain, to celebrate for my soul; to each order of mendicant friars in Bristol. To wife Sibil, for her life, my dwelling-house in the suburb in Temple-street, between the tenement now inhabited by John Wodeley and the tenement of Richard Inhyne, and extending from the aforesaid street in front to the Avon behind; remainder to Henry Bokerell and Alice my dau., and their lawful issue. If they should die s.p., the property to be sold, and the money expended on masses and other charitable works. To the said Henry and Alice my messuage in Temple-street between the shops of William Dyme and those of Master de Templecombe, and extending from the aforesaid street in front to Lawdyche behind; which messuage I had by gift from Joan Elcok, dau. and heir of Adam Dyme. Also to the said Henry and Alice, three shops, with drying-room, a "place" of land, and curtilage adjoining, in the suburb of Bristol "in vico se'i Thome iuxta les Rekkes." To wife Sibil, for her life, a shop in the suburb in Redcliff-street, between what were formerly the shops of John Bathe and the shop now held by John Coton; remainder to my brother Peter Touker for his life, to be sold afterwards, and the money applied as above written. To the said Peter 20 shillings. Residue to wife Sibil. She, and Richard Inhyne, executors. To the latter xxvj^s. viij^d. if he will act.

Proved before Ralph Canon, clerk &c., Feb. 21st, 1395: before the Mayor on Monday next after the feast of St. James, 20 Richard ii.

86.—ELENA BARRY.

1396. June 5th. To be buried in the cemetery of St. Augustine the Less of Bristol. Legacies to the vicar of that church for a trental of masses, and to the fabric thereof, and the parish clerk ; to the mother church of Worcester, and to Joan Brewer. To William Clerk, mercer and burgess of Bristol, a tenement in the suburb in Horstret, situate between the tenement inhabited by John Brompton and the one inhabited by Thomas Cocus, monk of St. Augustine, and extending from the aforesaid street in front to Frome ferry behind; which tenement I had by gift from Master Stephen Barry, my uncle. The said William Clerk to have residue of goods, and be executor.

Proved before the dean of Bristol, in the absence of Master Thomas Wybbe, clerk, in the church of St. Leonard, Sept. 3rd, 1396; before the Mayor on Monday next before the feast of the Exaltation of the holy Cross, 20 Richard ii.

87.—PETER ATTE BARUGH, burgess.

1396. Sept. 15th. To be buried in the chapel of St. Katharine the Virgin in the church of holy Cross Temple of Bristol. Legacies to the fabric, the vicar, the two clerks, the parish chaplain, and other chaplains of that church. A chaplain to celebrate for my soul and wife Margaret's for 20 years at the altar of St. Katharine in the said church, and to have 100 shillings yearly. For the better keeping up of the light on the beam before the altar in the said chapel 20 shillings. Another chaplain to celebrate at the altar of St. Nicholas in the aforesaid church for 20 years next after the sale of the reversion of the tenement bequeathed to wife Margaret, and to have £100. For two pairs of vestments and two chalices, with other things needful for the two chaplains at the altars aforesaid, vj^{li} xiij^s iiij^d. For funeral expenses £60. For keeping testator's anniversary in the aforesaid church for twenty years £10. To the work of every parish church in the town and suburb of Bristol vj.^{s} viij^d, and to each clerk thereof xx^d, if there be solemn bell-tolling for the good of my soul in the said churches on the eve before my burial, otherwise let them have nothing. Three common whole cloths of black, price of each xxxiij^s iiij^d, for clothing poor people on the day of burial, and covering my body. Two good whole cloths of black, price of each liij^s iiij^d, to clothe my executors and friends on the same day. Legacies to the four orders of friars, and the poor of the hospitals of St. John and St. Bartholomew in Bristol, to the poor of the renovated hospital at Laffardisyate, and the poor and leprous in the hospital of St. Laurence, Bristol, to the nuns of the blessed Mary Magdalene there, to the poor, feeble, lame, blind, leprous, and those lying in bed in the said town and suburb; to the poor of Charleton, Whitechurch, Saltford, Niewton Seyneloo, Metford, Henton Prior's, Keynesham, Phelippesnorton, Bekynton, Norygge, Chapmanslade, Tholnyston, and Corslee by Wermynstre. To son John £100, also my bastard, a silver cup, &c. In case of his death under age, masses were to be celebrated at Tholnyston (Thurloxton ?) with the said money and goods. To the use of the church there 40 shillings; sums of money also to the parson for himself, and to lay out in food and drink for the poor on the day of burial. To the work of the church of

Corslee xiij^s. iiij^d. For the mending of a bridge in the wood "voc' la holt in alto vico" 40 shillings. To dau. Alice, wife of William Pays, £20; to the two sons of Alice, and to the said William. To Joan Tryne, dau. of wife Margaret, £10, and a quarter of woad, for her marriage. To uncle John Spryngot of Chapmanslade; my brother Thomas Persons, of the same town; my brother Michael; my sister Cristina Venour; servants Joan Bowyer, Richard Coke, and Julian his wife, William Dorchestre, and Edith for her marriage; to the prisoners of Monkebrigg; to the third son of William Pays; which William is made overseer, and is to attend to the bestowing of the money bequeathed to the poor in Somerset and Wilts. To wife Margaret 20 sacks of wool, price of each 10 marks; also 10 quarters of woad, price of each liij^s. iiij^d., and a girdle of silk guarded with silver. To the same Margaret, for her life, a tenement in the suburb of Bristol, in Tuckers-street, held, for her life, by Edith late the wife of John Berkeley; and another tenement in the same street, held by John Comer, webb, and his wife Is', for their life; and another at the end of the bridge of Avon, held by William Halteby, goldsmith, and his wife Margaret, for their life; also a tenement in the town of Bristol, in High-street, held by Thomas London, cook, for his life; and a tenement in the suburb, in Temple-street, next to what was lately the shop of Richard Eweyn; which tenement I purchased of John Thorp. The said property to be sold after her death, and the money expended in masses *pro anima*. To Stephen Milman of Keynesham vj^s. viij^d; to his wife Agnes three yards of cloth, price of each ij^s. vj^d. To Edmund Bierden my best green gown. To Walter Ferthyng my gown "de Motley." To Isabel, dau. of the said Walter, 20 shillings for her marriage. To the fullers, for their common feast in the first year after my death, 20 shillings. To the weavers, for their same feast in the same year, 20 shillings. To my lady Joan, wife of Sir Thomas Broke knt., one dozen of cloth of blue (blod') good and well made. To John Harreys 100 shillings. Wife Margaret, William Bierden, and Thomas Blount, executors. To the said William vj^{li}. xiij^s. iiij^d. To the said Thomas 100 shillings.

Proved in the chapel of the blessed Mary of Redcliff Nov. 11th, 1396; before the Mayor, and others, on Monday next before the feast of St. Thomas Apostle, 20 Richard ii.

88.—WILLIAM CANYNGES, burgess and merchant.

1396. Oct. 2nd. To be buried in the chapel of the blessed Mary in the church of St. Thomas the Martyr of Bristol, by the tomb of John Stokes. Legacies to the chaplains, the fabric, &c., of that church, the vicar of Redcliff, the friars, the poor in the hospitals of St. Bartholomew, St. Laurence, and St. John Baptist, the lame and bedridden within a mile round Bristol, Cristina Codyngton and children, Joan widow of Thomas Bocher of Cirecstre, and Richard Hanham; for mending ways between Laffardesyate and Ruggewey. To Simon Canynges all my share of the ship "voc' Rodecog de Bristoll." A chaplain to celebrate in Hausdon (Alveston?) church for my soul, and that of John Codynton, Margery Smythes, Geoffrey and Agnes Beauflour. Residue to wife Agnes, except a plate of iron in my hall, which is to go, after her death, to John Canynges. She, Simon Canynges, and William Warre, executors.

Proved before Henry de Netherhaven Nov. 10th, 1396; before the Mayor on Monday next after the feast of the Lord's Epiphany, 20 Richard ii.

89.—NICHOLAS DERBY.

1396. Last day of March. To be buried according to the wish and ordering of his executors. Legacies to servant William Aschcote, the mother church of Worcester, the rector of St. Werburgh's for tithes, and Sir John Forster rector of St. Laurence's, Bristol. Residue to wife Margaret. She, Thomas Griffyn, and the rector of St. Werburgh's aforesaid to be executors.

Proved before Thomas Wybbe, clerk, &c., May 8th, 1396; afterwards before the Mayor.

90.—JOHN DRAYCOT, merchant and burgess.

1396. Thursday in the feast of St. Thomas Apostle. To be buried in the church of St. Werburgh of Bristol. Legacies to the rector and every chaplain celebrating therein, to each order of mendicant friars of Bristol, to servants Geoffrey, Margaret, Walter, and Richard. To wife Lucy, for her life, a tenement on the bridge of Avon; remainder to daughter Joan and her lawful issue. Also to the said Lucy, lands, tenements, rents, &c., in the town of Wells and in Wokyhole: if testator's children should all die s.p., rem. to the procurators of St. Cuthbert's church in Wells, and their successors, on condition that they maintain yearly for ever a suitable priest to celebrate for his soul, his wife Lucy's, &c., in the chapel of the Holy Trinity, within the said church, at the altar of St. James; the priest aforesaid to celebrate every day "ad septem de Campana id est la Clok." The said procurators to attend to the keeping of his anniversary every year, and have xx^d, and distribute to the poor xiij^s iiij^d in bread. To the said Lucy all lands and tenements in Redclond, formerly the property of John le Spicer; rem. to dau. Alice and her heirs; in def., rem. to her sister Joan and her heirs; in def., rem. to son Thomas; after him to son John; afterwards to son William and his heirs. To the said Lucy, household goods, and a third part of all effects after payment of debts; £20 to remain for increasing the portions of our children. She, son William, and John Cable of Frome, executors. Richard Panys of Bristol overseer.

Proved before Henry de Netherhaven and Simon Uphull, Jan. 17th, 1396; also before the Mayor.

91.—ADAM FRENSCH, fletcher and burgess.

1396. Oct. 12th. To be buried in the church of the Friars Minors of Bristol, beside late wife Maud. Legacies to the said friars, to the rector and every chaplain accustomed to celebrate in the church of St. John, to the mother church of Worcester, to the fraternity of St. John of Jerusalem, to the poor in the hospital of St. Bartholomew of Bristol, to my poor neighbours. My clothes to be distributed for the good of my soul, &c. To wife Alice lands, tenements, &c., in the town and suburb of Bristol, for her life, while she keeps herself single; in case of her marriage, the said property to be sold; half the money to be given to the said Alice, and the other half to be disposed of for the benefit of the soul of wife Maud, our parents, &c. Residue of goods to wife Alice. She, Richard Screven, and Robert Bowyer, executors, to each of whom vj^s viij^d.

Proved before Thomas Wybbe, clerk, &c., Jan. 22nd, 1396; also before the Mayor.

E

92.—WILLIAM STEYL, "crokker" and burgess.

1396. Nov. 15th. To be buried in the cemetery of St. Philip of Bristol. Legacies to the fabric, chaplain, and parish clerk of that church, to the mother church of Worcester, to each order of mendicant friars of Bristol. Poor people to be clothed in white cloth of our making, and to have xxx^s in bread on the day of burial. Cloth to kinsman John Steyl, his sisters Cecily and Sarah, and to Maud Bekeford. To son John and his heirs a hall in the suburb of Bristol, in the market, between testator's shop and that of John Palmer. To son William and his heirs a shop next to the aforesaid hall. To son Thomas and his heirs two shops between the one bequeathed to William and that next to the entrance by my tenement. After the death of the last of them and their lawful heirs, the aforesaid shops and hall to be sold, and the money applied to pious uses. To wife Alice two tenements, with shop, &c., inhabited by testator in the market, also two shops there, built by him, next the lane as one goes to Elebrig on the one part, and what was formerly the shop of Hugh Hunte on the other, to be held for her life of the chief lords of that fee; to be sold afterwards, and the money expended in masses and other works of charity. The three shops "apud le Wer iuxta Will'm Borne," to be sold immediately after testator's decease, and the money employed to find a chaplain to celebrate in the church of St. Philip, for his soul, the souls of Sarah and Alice his wives, &c. To son Thomas certain goods; also goods to John and William, brothers of Thomas, including two "helyngs." To servant Philip Cave (or Cane) a bed suited to his stature—"statui sue (sic) competens"—and xl^d. Residue to wife Alice. She, and Richard Bovy (or Bony), to whom xiij^s iiij^d, to be executors. Richard Bole, tucker, overseer, to whom x^s.

Proved before Thomas Wybbe, clerk, &c., Dec. 1st, 1396; also before the Mayor.

93.—HENRY ROPERE, burgess.

1394. Feb. 4th. To be buried in the church of St. Werburgh beside former wife Cristina. All goods and chattels to be divided into two parts; of one half, son Thomas to have twenty marks sterling, and the residue of the said half to wife Joan. Of the other half, ij^s to the mother church of Worcester. Legacies also to the four orders of mendicant friars of Bristol, the fabric of St. Werburgh's aforesaid, and Sir John Warwyke rector of that church, in which a chaplain is to celebrate *pro anima* for three years, and have yearly eight marks sterling; to every chaplain celebrating therein, and the clerk and suffragan; to Gilbert Joce, Clarice my sister, John Ropere, William Perlour, John Swalwe, servant John Gibbys, former servant Cristina, Richard, Peter, John, and *John*, sons of Thomas Ropere, the fabric of the church of St. Augustine of Bristol, and that of St. Michael's church at Milton in Dorset. To John Dunsterr, smith, xx^s, and a girdle of green silk worked with silver. To the aforesaid Thomas Ropere divers necessaries pertaining to testator's craft, as perches, "coppys," iron, &c., in his house on St. Augustine's place. Twenty poor people to be clothed, on the day of burial, in French cloth, and each to have one penny, a pair of shoes, and meat and drink enough. John Dounster and Thomas Ropere executors. The aforesaid Sir John Warwyk overseer.

Proved before Henry de Netherhaven and Simon Uphull, Jan. 17th, 1396; also before the Mayor.

94.—JOHN FOLYOT, burgess.

1396. Given at Bristol in the feast of the Conversion of St. Paul. To be buried in the cemetery of the church of the blessed Mary atte port in Bristol. Legacies to John Wythsyd and wife. To Thomas Northton, burgess of Bristol, and his heirs and assigns, testator's dwelling house; the said Thomas to pay to him, his heirs, or executors, forty pounds of silver of English money, of which sum testator has received from him xl^s. Residue of goods to dau. Agnes Neel, who is made executrix.

Proved before Thomas Wybbe, clerk, &c., March 3rd, 1396; also before the Mayor.

95.—JOHN RUSSELL, burgess.

1396. Oct. 20th. To be buried in the church of the Carmelite Friars of Bristol "coram Cruce." To the said friars xiij^s iiij^d, and a silver cup called *Roundeboll*, to pray for his soul, also the residue of the wax used at his burial, the cloth of russet after lying over his body, &c. Bread to the value of xl^s. to be distributed on the day of burial. Legacies to the rector of St. John's of Bristol, Sir Richard parish chaplain, and the clerk there, the rector of St. Leonard's of Bristol, dau. Alice, servants John Barbour, Thomas, and Henry. To servant Roger all testator's barrels and pipes in Ireland, his sword, &c. To wife Agnes a garden in the suburb of Bristol by the "Barres," purchased by testator of the executors of Alan Wryngton late burgess, to be held to the end of a term of twelve years, she paying to the said executors xl^s; the said garden, after that term, to go to son Edmund and his heirs and assigns. If he should die under age, dau. Alice and her heirs to have it. If she should so die, it shall remain to wife Agnes for her life, and afterwards be sold *pro anima*. Son Edmund to have C^s, and be under the control of Walter Seymour. Residue to wife Agnes. She and John Chiltenham, barber, to be executors.

Proved before Thomas Wybbe Dec. 2nd, 1396; also before the Mayor.

96.—WILLIAM DOWNE.

1392. Aug. 20th. To be buried in the cemetery of holy Cross Temple of Bristol. For burial expenses xl^s; the whole residue of goods to son Thomas and dau. Agnes, who are to be under the guardianship of the executors, John Comber and John Ferthyng "burg' Bristoll." If both children should die, the whole residue to be distributed for the welfare of testator's soul, his wife's, and children's, according to the disposal of the said executors.

Proved before Thomas Palton, clerk, &c., in the chapel of St. Mary by the cathedral close at Wells, Sept. 16th, 1393; before the Mayor of Bristol (Thomas Knap) on Monday next before the feast of St. Dunstan Bishop, 20 Richard ii.

97.—WILLIAM SAUNDRES.

1396. Thursday in the feast of St. Clement Pope. —"filius quond'm Rob'ti Saundres burgens' vill' Bristoll." To be buried in the cemetery of the church of holy Cross Temple of Bristol, beside his parents. Legacies to that church, the vicar, parish chaplain, deacon, and subdeacon, the chaplain of the blessed Mary there, and every other chaplain celebrating therein. The tenement in Temple-street, between one of Sir Thomas Brook knt., inhabited by William Wermynstre, and that of William Norton, and extending from the aforesaid street in front to the Lawdych behind, to be sold for pious uses for the benefit of testator's soul, his parents', and all " quibz tenor." William Norton and William de Ele executors, to each of whom xx^s.

Proved before Ralph Canon, clerk, &c., Jan. 8th, 1396; also before the Mayor.

98.—JOHN BRYT, burgess.

1397. Sept. 2nd. To be buried in a certain place of the cemetery near the parish church of St. Stephen of Bristol, next the body of late wife Margaret. Legacies to the rector, and every priest of that church attending the funeral, to each order of friars in Bristol, John Bannebury burgess of Bristol, the vicar of Redcliff, the parish priest of St. Thomas the Martyr of Bristol, in which parish testator was living, and the suffragan and subdeacon of that church. Residue to wife Agnes. She and the aforesaid John Bannebury to be executors.

Proved before Henry de Netheravene, vicar of the chapel of the blessed Mary of Redcliff, Oct. 5th, 1397 ; also before the Mayor.

99.—THOMAS SPERT, chancellor and canon of the church of Wells.

1395. Tuesday in the feast of the Invention of St. Stephen Martyr. To be buried in the cathedral church of Wells, before the image of St. Thomas the Martyr of Canterbury, at the altar of the blessed Stephen, next the tomb of Margery my mother. Legacies to the cathedral church of Sarum, to Master Thomas Benet, Walter son of William and Elizabeth Escote, Thomas Moigne, Thomas Lye, Sir John Strode, Sir Stephen Lucas, John Wycombe and his wife Agnes, and each valet and page in testator's service at the time of his death. To Joan Lye a silver cup with cover, bequeathed to testator by John Hope. To William Escote a horse. To Elizabeth, wife of the said William, a silver cup with cover, given to testator by Richard Cornewale, dean of Westbury. Executors are to sell a tenement, once the property of Nicholas Portbury, in the street of the blessed Mary in Foro, Bristol, lately held by Simon Olyver, and another tenement, annexed to the aforesaid on the east side, purchased by Roger Spert, testator's father, of John Blanket and David Brounenesyng, executors of John Famer, now held by Ralph Baker, and dispose of the money for the welfare of the souls of testator's father and mother, of Nicholas Portbury and his wife Julian, of John Reynald, &c. To William Escote and his wife Elizabeth, for their lives, a shop on the Key of Bristol "iuxta la p'pe," with the chamber over it, inhabited by Simon Oysell, otherwise Spert ; also, for their lives, another tenement in the street aforesaid, and the rents and reversion of the same, held by John Bruer, between the abovenamed tenement inhabited by Ralph Baker and a tenement of the abbot and convent of St. Augustine of Bristol; the said property to remain, after their death, to their son Walter and his lawful issue : in default of such issue, remainder to the said Walter's brother Stephen and his heirs: in def., rem. to Stephen's brother John ; in def., rem. to John's sister Alice : in def., rem. to Alice's sister Elizabeth ; if Elizabeth should die s.p., the said property to be sold for pious uses. Testator bequeaths 1000 silver pence for the celebration of

1000 masses in the churches of Wells and Sarum, and in those dioceses. Executors to be Master Thomas Benet, John Strode, Stephen Lucas, chaplains, William Escote, John Wycombe, and Thomas Lye, rector of "Obeley."

Proved in the chapel of the blessed Mary by the close at Wells, Feb. 18th, 1397 ; also before the Mayor of Bristol.

Master Thomas Spert was named as an executor and legatee in the will of John de Harewell, bishop of Bath and Wells ; proved Aug. 20th, 1386, and registered at the Lambeth Library, *Courteney*, 218.

100.—JOHN MULEWARD, burgess.

1398. June 7th. To be buried in the church or cemetery of St. Peter of Bristol. Legacies to the fabric and high altar of that church, and the parish clerk, to the mother church of Worcester, the fabric of the church of "Axmystre," the Friars Minors and Carmelites, dau. Joan, and servant Agnes. To son John thirteen marks sterling, a bed, three silver spoons, &c., to be kept during his minority by John Bagpath. If he should die under age, the aforesaid goods to be disposed of for the benefit of testator's soul, his son John's, &c. To wife Joan, so long as she shall live in pure widowhood, half a bushel of flour a week ; the said flour to go, after her marriage, to John Bagpath for the sustentation of son John, and to be received weekly from Leonard's mill. Residue of goods to wife Joan. John Bagpath and John Plommer executors, to each of whom vj^s viij^d.

Proved before Thomas Wybbe, clerk, &c., July 9th, 1398 ; before the Mayor on Monday next before the feast of St. Margaret Virgin, 22 Richard ii.

101.—WILLIAM KEDWELLY, of the parish of Holy Trinity, of Bristol.

1397. Tuesday in the vigil of the Assumption of B.V.M. To be buried in the cemetery of the church of Holy Trinity aforesaid, by his deceased wife. Legacies to the fabric, the rector, and each chaplain of that church, to the cathedral church of Worcester, to his mother, kinsman Henry, servants Thomas and Petronilla, and former servant Maud Kempe. Five tapers to be arranged about his body on the day of burial. To his wife and daughter six marks of good money, and all cups, beds, spoons, wool, yarn, &c. Residue to be disposed of for the welfare of his soul. Richard Willy, John Devenysch, and John Reynald executors, to each of whom vj^s viij^d.

Proved before Henry de Netherhaven, Oct. 1st, 1397 ; also before the Mayor.

102.—NICHOLAS HASTYNG, burgess.

1397. Dec. 3rd. To be buried in the church of St. James of Bristol "ext' int'clausum." Legacies to the prior, and every monk in the said priory, accustomed to celebrate, also to the fabric, the parish chaplain, and clerk of the church. Testator's second best piece of silver, and one small piece, to be made into a chalice to serve in the said church, and to be in the keeping of the chaplain who shall celebrate therein for his soul, and the soul, or estate of his wife Margery. His tenement in Lewynesmede, lately purchased of Rose Assch, to be sold for the purpose of keeping up celebrations in the said church of St. James. The reversion also of his dwelling house in Lewynesmede, and the half of all his unbequeathed goods, to be sold, and the money applied to the finding of a chaplain to celebrate in the said church before the altar of the holy Cross, for his soul, the souls of his wives, their and his parents, benefactors, &c., while the money shall hold out. To wife Margery the said dwelling house, for her life, on condition of her paying yearly to the Friars Minors and Carmelites of Bristol ij^s vj^d each for their prayers, and also maintaining the same taper "cora' su'mo Crucifixo" in the said church of St. James, which he was wont to maintain; also to her the half of all his goods. His anniversary to be kept, and vj^s viij^d expended thereon while she lives. To his brother William his horse "de Bay colo'," with saddle and bridle, and xx^s. To the poor in bread or in silver on the day of burial xl^s. Legacies also to Agnes and Joan daughters of Henry Portbury, to their marriage, the mendicant friars of Bristol, Walter Portlond, goddaughter Joan Holewey, and every other godchild, Thomas Halewey, and the mother church of Worcester. Wife Margery and Walter Portlond executors. John Halewey to be executor, in testator's place, with William Rogers executor of the will of Walter Horugge.

Proved before the ecclesiastical authorities May 15th, 1398; before the Mayor on Wednesday next after the feast of St. Laurence Martyr, 22 Richard ii.

103.—JOHN FREMAN, burgess.

1397. Nov. 14th. To be buried in the cemetery of holy Cross Temple of Bristol. Legacies to Sir William parish chaplain, and the other chaplains celebrating in that church, and Thomas Fyl clerk there; to the mendicant friars of Bristol; to friar Thomas my son, and each of the three sons of myself and wife Alice; to John Romesay. For funeral expenses £5 of lawful money. Residue to wife Alice. She and John Romesay executors.

Proved before Thomas Benet, canon of Wells, and commissary general for the Bishop of B. and W., in the chapel of the blessed Mary of Redcliff, Bristol, Feb. 9th, 1397; before John Canynges, Mayor, and others, on Monday next after the feast of All Saints, 22 Richard ii.

104.—REGINALD TAILLOUR, tucker and burgess.

1397. Sept. 11th. To be buried in the church of holy Cross Temple of Bristol, before the altar of the Holy Trinity. To the work of the tower there, if it shall be renovated, C^s. Legacies to the vicar, the two clerks, and all the chaplains celebrating in that church, if they come daily from testator's death to the day of burial, and say, with due devotion, after vespers, "Placebo & Dirige cu' noue' l'ec'onibz" for his soul and the souls of all the faithful dead; to the poor on the day of burial, and to xxiij poor widows; to the work of the churches of St. Peter of Bristol, St. Ewen, St. Mary Magdalene, and St. Mary of Redcliff; to the poor in the hospital of St. Bartholomew; infirm and leprous men and women in that of St. Laurence outside "Laffardesyate;" the abbot and convent of Kingswood; my brother William Heynes of Bristol; my sister Julian and her sons; the lame, blind, &c., lying in places and lanes in the town and suburb of Bristol; the prisoners at Monkbridge; Thomas Frenssh chaplain; William Norton executor; each godchild; late servant John Doddesley. To my brethren of St. John's, at St. Ewen's church, for the use of the fraternity xx^s. For mending the roads about Bristol iiij^{li}. To each of the four orders of friars at Bristol xx^s., and a whole cloth of white, price fifty shillings, for their prayers. A whole cloth of burnet color to be laid over testator's body before burial, and given to the poor immediately after his month's mind. A whole cloth of the same color for clothing his wife, executors, and other friends. The four men who shall carry his body to burial, and also his servants, to be clad in a whole cloth of black, price forty shillings. A priest to celebrate *pro anima* at the altar of the Holy Trinity, in the Temple church aforesaid, for four years, and have C^s. yearly. To buy a missal for the same altar Cvj^s viij^d. To wife Joan a tenement in Wynchestret, Bristol, bought by testator of John Marchall; also his dwelling house in the suburb, in Tuckersstreet, and a tenement in Temple-street, bought of Richard Grove and Margery his wife, and another in the same street, bought of Thomas Sutton, and other property in the same, bought of Henry Wyvelescombe, and Thomas atte Hay, executor of the will of John Wermynstre, and the tenement there in which Robert Wether dwells, also that messuage and twelve shops in the suburb, in the lane called "Wryngtoneslane," next a tenement of Sir Thomas Brook knt. lately inhabited by Stephen Dyar, on the one part, and the aforesaid lane on the other, and extending from the street called "Toukerstrete" to the Avon ; which messuage and shops were lately bought of Richard Armys clerk and Thomas Danyell ; the said Joan to hold them, for her life, of the chief lords of those fees. After her death, the one of the three shops (in Temple-street) now held by Elias Tyler, to remain to testator's brother William Heynes and his lawful issue. If the said William should die s.p., it is to be sold for pious purposes. The tenement purchased of Richard and Margery Grove to remain, after the said Joan's death, to late servant John Doddesley and his lawful issue, but to be dealt with as the other property in case of his death s.p. The reversion of all the other tenements to be sold within a year after testator's death, and the money disposed of in celebrations, alms, &c. Residue to wife Joan. She, brother William Heynes, and William Norton of Bristol, executors.

Proved before William Bryghtlampton, in the chapel of the blessed Mary outside the entrance of the parish church of Temple, Jan. 7th, 1398 ; before John Canynges, Mayor, on Monday next before the feast of St. Vincent Martyr, 22 Richard ii.

It has been supposed that Bernard Obeleye (will 42), as well as this testator, bequeathed money towards the "building" of the Temple tower ; the supposition originating in Obeleye's words—"Jt'm lego ffabrice *Campane* eiusd' eccl'ie vj^s viij^d."

105.—WILLIAM POYNEZ. Indexed *Poynis* and *Poines*.

1395. Friday next after the feast of Simon and Jude. To be buried in the church of St. Peter of Bristol, in the chapel of the blessed Mary, before the image of St. George. Legacies to the fabric and rector of that church, and the clerk for tolling the bells and his other pains. To wife Elizabeth, for her life, a tenement next the "Blyndezate" in Bristol ; to go afterwards to Robert Wylde for his life, and at length to be disposed of *pro anima* ; also to her, for her life, the messuage called the "Mille place" at Bristol, situate "ex' portam Laffordie" in Barton hundred ; to go afterwards to the aforesaid Robert for his life. Residue of goods to wife Elizabeth. She and Robert Wylde executors.

Proved before Thomas Wybbe, clerk, &c., Feb. 22nd, 1395; also before the Mayor.

106.—RICHARD BROKEWORTH, burgess.

1397. Oct. 12th. To be buried in the church of the blessed Mary of Redcliff, next the burial-place of wife Edith. To the fabric of that church "vnu' Garnement' de Bawdekyn" and twenty shillings sterling. Legacies to "my vicar" for tithes, to every priest celebrating in that church, and each of the four orders of friars at Bristol. Testator's cups to be halved between his wife Agnes and son John, who are also to have twelve silver spoons between them. If the said John should die under age, his legacy is to be disposed of *pro anima*. Residue of goods to be divided into three parts; one to wife Agnes, another to son John, the third to be religiously disposed of by the executors, William Whyte and John Whytyng, to each of whom xl^s sterling.

Proved before Henry de Netherhavene kal. Dec., 1397; also before the Mayor.

107.—JOHN FYTELTON, the elder.

1398. Sunday, Feb. 16th. To be buried in the church of Gothurst, or in that of Hengestrygge (Henstridge). Executors are to grant to William son of John Yonge, if he should live to be 28 years of age, the tenements in Bristol in which testator purchased a state of Henry Boteler, to be held during the life of the said Henry. But if William should die before attaining to that age, provision is to be made, by means of the aforesaid tenements, for the marriage of testator's daughter Elizabeth. K...? my Master and friend Sir John Wadham knt., John Russell, and William son of Stephen Doddesham, to be executors.

Proved before the Bishop of Bath and Wells, in his manor of Wiveliscombe, Apr. 6th, 1399; also before John Canynges, Mayor of Bristol.

108.—THOMAS GRAUNT, burgess.

1398. March 4th. To be buried in the church of the Carmelite Friars of Bristol. Funeral to be arranged by his wife Elena and son friar John Graunt. To the rector of St. Stephen's for tithes or offerings xiij^s iiij^d. To wife Elena and son John his dwelling house in Mersshstrete, and all his state in the shops &c. built by him in the suburb of Bristol in Gropelane. His said wife and son to be executors.

Proved before Thomas Wybbe, clerk, Apr. 30th, 1399; also before the Mayor.

109.—JOHN FRENSSH, burgess.

1398. Feb. 22nd. To be buried in the church of the blessed Mary of Redcliff, by the holy font and the tomb of late wife Julian. Legacies to the vicar of that church, to the lame, blind, or leprous lying in the hospital of St. John Baptist of Bristol, and such people in the suburb; to Richard Pedewell, Agnes Plomere, Joan Freman, and Juliana Hastyne. To wife Joan, for her life, a tenement in the suburb in "Redclynestret," between the rent of Sir Thomas Broke knt. and the tenement of William Selcok; also, for her life, three shops on Redcliff hill, between the rent of the blessed Mary of Redcliff and that of the hospital of St. John Baptist; the said property to be afterwards sold under the inspection of the procurators of Redcliff church, and the money given to a fit priest to celebrate therein for testator's soul, and the souls of his wives Julian and Joan. Wife Joan, John Wodle, and Thomas Erle, burgess of Bristol, executors. "Dat' & act' in hospicio meo."

Proved before Thomas Benet, canon of Wells, June 2nd, 1399; also before the Mayor.

110.—JOHN VIELL, burgess.

1398. May 25th. To be buried at the Friars Preachers of Bristol. Legacies to the mother church of Worcester, to every chaplain celebrating divine offices in the church of St. Stephen of Bristol, and the parish clerk and suffragan there, to Joan Marion of "Bertolomew," Richard Hamond of Lamborne, every mendicant friar of Bristol being a priest, each almshouse "in le Langerew & Templestrete," Bristol, Sir John Warwyke, rector of St. Werburgh's, the poor in the hospital of St. Bartholomew of Bristol, according to the disposal of Sir John Tommas chaplain, the bedridden poor, the Commonalty of Bristol, Andrew Anketyll, Thomas Botener the elder, John Leveden, servants Agnes and Juliana. For the liberation of people detained in the prison of "Monkebrugge" for small debts xx^{li}. To the fraternity of Linne in which I am a brother xl^s. To the fraternity of Conyntre (Coventry) xl^s. To the procurators of the church of St. Stephen of Bristol, a ring carrying with it (ferent') a stone from the pillar to which our Lord Jesus Christ was bound, to be laid up with the reliques in that church for ever. Executors to provide two tapers, and no more, about testator's body on the day of burial, one at the head, and the other at the feet. To wife Elizabeth fifty shillings of yearly rent, purchased for a term of twenty years, and issuing from a tenement in the town of Bristol, in Bradestrete, now inhabited by Thomas Botener; to remain, after her death, to son John, who is also to have the best cup with a cover. To son Henry a hundred marks sterling "ad p'quirend' xx marcat' terre" for himself and his wife Alice. Immediately after testator's decease 1000 masses were to be celebrated for his soul and the souls of all the faithful dead. If any one would swear upon the Book that testator was in his debt, he was to be paid. Residue to wife Elizabeth. She, son Henry, and John Leveden, executors.

Proved in the house of John Vyell, upon the Key of Bristol, before Simon Uphull, 14th kal. May, 1399; before William Frome, Mayor, Robert Dudbroke, Sheriff, Mark William, and John Sely, Bailiffs and Chamberlains, on Friday in the vigil of St. Leonard, 2 Henry iv.

This will contains no mention of any "Canynges Guild," as alleged by several Bristol historians, who evidently did not give themselves time enough to decipher the word "Conyntre." The ancient MS. roll of the fraternity or guild entitled that of the Holy Trinity, St. Mary, St. John Baptist, and St. Katharine, of Coventry, is fortunately extant; and therein occurs the entry—"Joh'es Vyel de Brystoll & Elizabeth ux' eius." Many other members are also described as of Bristol; as Elias Spylly, and his wife; Gilbert

Joos, and wife Agnes, and his parents Anthony and Alice Joos; John Candouer; John Burgeys, chapman, and wife Margery; Roger Russell, and wife Emma; Richard Fynche, and wife Katharine, and late wife Joan; Thomas Sutton, and wife Joan; Walter Seynmore, and wife Margaret; William Kannyngges, and wife Agnes; William Mareschall, &c.

111.—ROBERT WYOOTE, otherwise Grawnte, burgess.

1398. Oct. 15th. To be buried in the parish church of St. Stephen of Bristol. Legacies to the fabric, to Master John Wyk the rector, and Sir Nicholas Mathew, parish chaplain of that church, to each order of friars in Bristol, and the fabric of Worcester cathedral. To wife Elizabeth all household vessels. To mother Denis ten marks of lawful money. Provision to be made for a priest to celebrate for testator's soul in the next year after his decease. Residue of goods to be divided: one half to his six sons and dau. Margaret, the other to wife Elizabeth. She to be executrix. Roger Calff overseer, to whom £5.

Proved before Thomas Wybbe, clerk, &c., Dec. 3rd, 1398; also before the Mayor.

112.—WILLIAM PEDEWELL, burgess.

1392. Wednesday in the feast of St. Denis. To be buried in the crypt of the church of St. Nicholas of Bristol. Legacies to the fabric and vicar of that church, and every chaplain celebrating divine offices therein, and taking part in the funeral rites, each order of mendicant friars in Bristol, the fabric of the chapel of the Assumption of the blessed Mary on the bridge of Avon, and the cathedral church of Worcester. Forty shillings in loaves to needy people on the day of burial. Testator's dwelling house on the bridge aforesaid to be sold by his executors, and with the money, after the death of wife Emmot, and the payment of debts, fit chaplains to be provided to celebrate for his soul in the aforenamed chapel of the Assumption. Residue to wife Emmot. She and son John executors, and Sir Nicholas Adams overseer, by these presents.

Proved before John de Derlton, commissary general for the Prior of Worcester cathedral, the see there being vacant, May 4th, 1395; also before the Mayor.

113.—THOMAS CARPYNTER.

1397. March 12th. To be buried in the cemetery of the blessed Mary of Redcliff. Legacies to "my vicar," the hospital newly made at "Laffardisyate," the house of St. Bartholomew, the poor lying in "le langerewe," and in the hospital of St. John Baptist of Bristol, each of the orders of mendicant friars, Henry Lekas, Henry Cory, John Cadbury, and Thomas Benet. To wife Margaret ten marks; to dau. Alice the same, to be kept, until she is of full age, by Thomas Benet. To Richard Wallyce a gown "de blew Ray cum Capicio." To the chapel of Hanham, a brass pot. Residue to wife Margaret. She and Thomas Bene (sic) executors.

Proved before Thomas Benet, canon of Wells, May 5th, 1399; also before the Mayor.

114.—HUGH PLOMER, burgess.

1400. July 26th. To be buried in the crypt of the parish church of St. John of Bristol, in which crypt a fit chaplain is to celebrate for a whole year for testator's soul, and the souls of all the faithful departed. To the fabric of that church xx^s. To son Richard a share of a ship called " le Nicholas de Bristoll," of which Walter Fysshprest is master. To son William xx^{li}. To dau. Isabel xx^{li}. To servant Thomas certain goods pertaining to one of testator's houses called " le Werkhous." To son Laurence x^{li}. To William Castell iij^{li}, if he will undertake the administration of this will. To wife Edith, a tenement in Bradestret, between the tenement inhabited by Thomas Clerk, mariner, and testator's shop inhabited by Frederick Golsmyth, and extending from the aforesaid street to the garden of John Spyne ; to go, after her death, to son John, and after John's death, to be disposed of *pro anima*. The said shop and the house within it inhabited by Richard Mertok, and all testator's other tenements, rents, reversions, &c., in the town and suburb of Bristol, to be sold for the full payment of all his debts and funeral expenses. Residue to wife Edith. She, son John, and William Castell, executors.

Proved before John Chewe, clerk, &c., Aug. 5th, 1400 ; also before the Mayor.

115.—HENRY SEYDON, of Bristol.

1400. Sept. 23rd. To be buried in the crypt of St. Nicholas. Legacies to the vicar, each chaplain, and the fabric of that church. Five pounds of wax to be made into four tapers, " vt ardeant circa corpus men' duo quol't die ad Missam in dict' Crippa durante quatuor septiman' post obitum meum." Bread to the value of ten shillings to be distributed to the poor. To each order of mendicant friars of Bristol, for a trental of masses, ij^s vj^d. Residue to wife Beatrix and children, who are to pay his debts. She and Sir Richard Peautrer chaplain to be executors.

Proved before John Barstaple, Mayor, Thomas Norton, Sheriff, Richard Panys and Simon Algode, Bailiffs, on Monday next after the feast of All Saints, 3 Henry iv. Previously proved before the ecclesiastical authorities.

116.—JOHN SOMERWELL, burgess.

1401. April 18th. To be buried in the church of St. Werburgh of Bristol, by late wife Alice. Two chaplains to celebrate therein for four years, for the good of his own soul and that of his said wife. His anniversary to be kept for twenty years, and forty shillings to be yearly expended thereon. Legacies to John Warewyke rector of that church, to the mother church of Worcester, the four orders of friars at Bristol, the prioress and convent of St. Mary Magdalene, the poor in the house of St. Bartholomew of Bristol, in the hospital of St. John " de Redeclyneputte," in the almshouse next " Templefrerys," and at " Langrewys ende ;" to Alice dau. of my sister and her sons ; to servants Henry, Margaret, and Agnes ; to John Bery, John and Thomas Naillesey, John Willy, little Roger and John Rye, Robert Wotton, former servants John Davy and Marion ; John Berclay and his wife Isabel ; Robert, Joan, and Alice, children of Gilbert Joce, and his two nurses ; John son of William Somerwell, John Wynkeley and wife, William

Blakeney, Agnes relict of Roger Frompton, Thomas Swyft, one called Payn, John Prisshton, and William Markes. To kinswoman Margaret 20 shillings, and a barrel of oil in the keeping of Roger Calff. For mending the ways 20 shillings. For funeral expenses £20; and the same sum to be divided among the poor and needy who keep their beds. "Jt'm lego Aunori consanguin' mee lx^s." To Agnes Joce "aulam meam esteyne cu' Costur' & alijs p'tin' suis." To Agnes my now wife twenty cloths, worth 100 marks, with all utensils had with her in marriage; also, after the death of Agnes Bluet, the reversion of lands, tenements, rents, and services within the town and suburb of Bristol, for her life; remainder to Gilbert Joce. To Robert, son of the said Gilbert, and his heirs and assigns, a tenement in Bath. Residue of effects to be disposed of for the welfare of testator's soul, his late wife Alice's, &c. Gilbert Joce and William Markes executors. John Pryssheton overseer.

Proved before the Mayor on Monday next after the feast of St. Bartholomew Apostle, 2 Henry iv. Previously exhibited in the church of Redcliff.

117.—JOHN CASTELL, burgess.

1401. Sept. 1st. To be buried "vbicumqz deo placu'it." To the rector of St. Werburgh's of Bristol, for tithes, xl^s. Sir Adam who had been testator's chaplain was to celebrate *pro anima* for two years in that church, and have eight marks yearly. "Jtem lego eccl'ie p'och'i sc'i Clementis in qua natus fui in Northfolk x^{li}." Legacies to the friars of Bristol, to John son of John Stephenes, and the poor and infirm. To John Stephenes the elder xx^{li}, if willing "supportare onus testamenti mei." To wife Alice £100, and the value of half his goods, &c.; also all his tenements in the town of Bristol, for her life; remainder to John Stephenes. These two to be executors, and to order and dispose with the other half of the goods "p' salute anime mee."

Proved before the Mayor, Sheriff, and Bailiffs, on Friday next before the feast of the Conversion of St. Paul, 3 Henry iv. Previously proved before the ecclesiastical authorities.

118.—JOHN HALLE, rector of Buscot.

1400. Given at "Burwardiscote" Feb. 4th. To be buried in the chancel of my church. Legacies to that church, to Worcester cathedral, the churches of the blessed Mary of Cardiff, and St. Stephen of Bristol, and servant William. "Jtem lego Will'mo Smyth Cl'ico meo xx^s & vnam Togam furrat' de lib'at' Sacrist' Wygorn'." To the vicar of Lechlade a gown furred with fitchew, and a cup called *Cobhard*. To the master of the hospital of St. John of Lechlade 20 shillings. To Master John Chewe two messuages with eight adjoining shops in the suburb of Bristol, outside the new gate as one goes towards the Were, between that gate and the mill of our lord the King called "Castelmyll;" the said trustee to sell the property "cariori p'cio quo pot'it," and distribute the money in the celebration of masses and other works of piety, for the benefit of the soul of Walter Tedistill, testator's soul, and all the faithful dead. John Sutton of Bristol may purchase the said property, and give ten marks less than any one else might offer. To the said Master John Chewe a bed "de Worsted panel' cum Curteyns & toto app'atu sid'm p'tinent'," also six silver spoons, &c. He, and Sir Richard master of the house or hospital of Lechlade, and Sir Richard the vicar of that place, to be executors, and have xiij^s iiij^d apiece, and dispose of the residue of goods as they would answer before God.

Proved before Thomas by divine permission abbot of Pershore, in the parish church of Leigh (de Lega), diocese of Worcester, Oct. 12th, 1401; afterwards in the Guildhall of Bristol "in pleno hundr' ib'm tent'."

The episcopal registers at Worcester mention that Richard Porter vicar of Lechlade, having died, was succeeded by Sir Richard Bedhampton, Dec. 7th, 1404.

119.—ROBERT LYGH, burgess.

1401. Thursday next after the feast of St. James Apostle. To be buried in the cemetery of the blessed Mary of Redcliff, to the fabric of which church xx^s and my best silver girdle. Legacies also to the vicar, the deacon, suffragan, and every chaplain celebrating there, the mendicant friars of Bristol, friar John Derneford, John Dyhuce, William Wroxhale, Nicholas Harper, the poor of Congesbury, John Blekker, my brother John and sister Alice, John Selke, Nicholas Lygh, my father John Lygh, my sons John and Thomas, and daughters Margaret, Joan, and Agnes; in case of their death under age, one half of their goods to be distributed *pro anima*, the other to revert to testator's surviving brothers and sisters. To five poor maid-servants, for their marriage, ten shillings apiece. A white cloth, price xl^s, to cover his body before burial, and afterwards, on the same day, to be distributed to the poor there present, each to have two yards. A black cloth of russet to be bought for the same sum, and distributed to his servants and poor domestics. Twenty shillings "ad corrigend' vias debiles." Bread to the value of £3 for the poor on the day of burial, and £6 sterling to make a feast—*couiuiam*—among his neighbours, rich and poor, on that day. The sum of vj^s viij^d yearly to the procurators of the blessed Mary of Redcliff for his anniversary for six years; but if they or their successors will not attend to it, the forty shillings are to revert to his next of kin. To the poorest church "istius patrie" a silver bowl to make a chalice, to celebrate for testator's soul and that of Maud Lygh. To wife Margaret residue of goods, and £40 in gold and merchandise. John Blekker and son Thomas Lygh to be executors.

Exhibited before Henry de Nethirhaven Oct. 15th, 1401; proved also before the Mayor, Sheriff, and Bailiffs.

"Test'm Henrici de Netherhauen" is written in the margin opposite the note of "exhibition;" and the same mistake occurs in the later index at the end of the volume.

120.—WILLIAM POUNDE..

1400. Jan. 8th.—"p'ponens me p'tes t'nsmarinas m'candisando visitare." To be buried wherever God shall appoint. To the mother church of Worcester ij^s. Legacies to the fabric and rector of St. Stephen's of Bristol, the clerk, suffragan, and every chaplain celebrating therein, each order of mendicant friars, daughters Alice, Margaret, and Alexandra, and servant Elen. To the Carmelite Friars in Bristol xl^s to make a chalice to continue always in memory of me. To daughter Alice all lands, tenements, &c.,

which I have, or which may fall to me in fee simple within the island "de Portclond," to be held of the chief lords of those fees by due and accustomed services for ever. All lands, tenements, rents, &c., that shall fall to me and my heirs in fee tail, to remain and revert to my heirs according to the same tenure for ever. Sir John Burford, chaplain, to sell, for the payment of debts, testator's interest in the tenement purchased of the procurators of the church of the blessed Mary of Redcliff, situate on St. Augustine's Back at Bristol. To wife Agnes, for her life, a tenement in Mersshstrete in the suburb, purchased of the executors of Thomas Graunt ; the said property to be afterwards sold by the aforesaid Sir John ; one half of the money to be employed *pro anima*, the other to be divided equally among the above named three daughters, who are "infra etatem," and are to be in the keeping of Sir John Burford. Residue of goods to wife Agnes. She, and the said Sir John, executors ; to the latter xx^s.

Proved before the ecclesiastical authorities Jan. 2nd, 1401 ; also before the Mayor.

121.—JOHN FLUYT, burgess.

1398. Tuesday next before the feast of St. Margaret Virgin. To be buried in the parish church of St. James of Bristol, in the chapel of the blessed Mary there, next the tomb of late wife Thomasine. Legacies to the fabric and rector of that church, the parish chaplain, and clerk, and two monks there ; the mother church of Worcester, the Augustinian convent, and the other mendicant friars in Bristol, the fabric of the chapel of Betisley, and that of the chapel of " Northewyke in Salso Marisco ;" servants Henry Hemyng and David, and late servant Gerard ; Jenn' Gough, John Poleyn, and Joan Cobbe. Ten marks sterling for burial expenses and the poor. To the chapel of the blessed Mary of St. James of Bristol, three large pieces of timber—*merem'*—two of which support the scaffold in the church of St. James aforesaid, and the other lies on St. James's Back. To wife Agnes, for her life, a hall with two shops in the town of Bristol, in Worschipstret, lately acquired by the gift and grant of Walter Vynour ; remainder to my heirs, on condition that when the said Walter or his executors shall pay £16 sterling to my heirs executors or assigns, the property shall remain to the said Walter, his heirs and assigns, for ever. Thomas Maistre and Philip Rigelyn of Betisley are to levy the money due to testator from Roger Ripe, John Long of Betisley, and the wife of Philip Boteman of that place, lately wife of John Yewen ; after which a chaplain is to celebrate *pro anima* in the chapel of Betisley as long as the money will hold out. To children John, Nicholas, William, and Agnes, five marks of silver apiece. If all should die under age, executors are to find with the money a chaplain to celebrate for four years in the aforesaid church of St. James. To dau. Joan forty shillings of silver, and one entire bed now at Lanneyre (Llanyre ?) in Wales ; also, during my state, half of the messuage and shop held by lease of the prior of St. James. Stephen Reve to have the keeping of the said Joan and her legacies. To dau. Agnes, all interest in the two shops in Worschipstret had by the grant of John Keynesham. To dau. Isabel xx^s. To wife Agnes, a red cow, 20 marks sterling, &c., also the half of a tenement in Worschipstret lately bought of Stephen Reve, and half of two tenements in the suburb of Bristol in Brodemede, which tenements are held of testator by John Randolf and William Tought ; the said halves to remain, after her decease, to children John, Nicholas, William, and Agnes ; to each of whom an entire bed, price xiij^s. iiij^d. Silver girdles, &c., to sons John and William ; a dagger to son Nicholas. To John son of John Poleyn, a horse " videl't le Grey ameler," and one piece of timber, price viij^s., to which testator has proved his right in the court of Hembury ; also to the said John all interest in the croft called Hychepyll, with a meadow by the same, called Ha'me, until the end of the life of John Hamme, or of testator ; paying yearly to the chief lords of that fee lviij^s. Residue of goods to be halved ; one part to wife Agnes, and children John, Nicholas, William, and Agnes ; the other to be employed for the benefit of testator's soul, his late wife's, their parents', &c. William Brewer and John Peyntour, baker, to be executors, and have xiij^s. iiij^d. apiece. Sir Richard Wircestre, prior of St. James of Bristol, and John Sherp, overseers.

Proved in the chapel of the blessed Mary of Redcliff, Aug. 3rd, 1398 ; afterwards before the Mayor.

122.—THOMAS TANNER, of Wells, co. Somerset.

1401. Wednesday in the feast of St. Clement Pope and Martyr. To be buried in the church of St. Cuthbert of Wells, in the chapel of the blessed Mary, under the southern window, in a tomb about to be newly made for his body and that of Isabel his wife. For the reconstruction of the aforesaid window £20. To the fabric of that church 60 shillings, and the 40 shillings now in the hands of John Blith. Legacies to Sir Walter Hamme, vicar of St. Cuthbert's, for tithes, each canon, vicar, chorister, &c., of the church of the blessed Andrew, in which, as well as in St. Cuthbert's, mass and other offices were to be celebrated ; eight poor people to hold tapers about his body in the one church, and eight more in the other. For bell-tolling ij^s. Legacies to the prior and poor inmates of the hospital of St. John of Wells, and each brother there being a chaplain, to the priors and convents of Wytham and Henton, the prioress and nuns of Minchinbarugh, co. Wilts, the prior and convent of the Carmelites in Bristol, and the other friars there ; servants Robert Asby, Edward Curteys, John Waryn, William Heryng, and John Croter ; kinsmen Philip Smyth and John Bradford ; Julian Huth and her daughter Alice ; Sir William atte Water, chaplain ; Nicholas More ; Elias Jones, and Walter Menyber, both of Axbridge. To the annuelleres of the new hall, dwelling in New-street, Wells, for their common table, lx^s. To the abbot and convent of Glastonbury a pipe of red wine. "Jt'm lego Co'ne Aule nou' Clausi vicar' Well' ad oraud' p' anima mea xl^s." To wife Isabel and her heirs and assigns, a tenement, with two cellars and three shops adjoining, in the town of Bristol, situate in the south part of a certain street called Smalstret, between the cemetery of St. Werburgh's church and a tenement of the lord of Burnell. Residue of goods to the said Isabel. She, Thomas Hore, John Broun, John Wykyng, and John Panes, executors ; to the last two 100 shillings apiece.

Proved before Richard Bruton, canon of Wells cathedral, Dec. 12th, 1401 ; also before John Barstaple, Mayor of Bristol, &c.

123.—JOHN CHEPPYSTOWE, burgess.

1402. June 9th.—"p'ochianus sc'i Jacobi Bristoll' Wygorn' dioc'." To be buried in the parish church of the said St. James, by former wife Edith.

Legacies to the fabric of that church, the prior of St. James of Bristol, and the three monks there, each secular priest now serving there in the parish church, the fabric of the church of the blessed Mary of Redcliff, the mother church of Worcester, and each house of mendicant friars in Bristol. Twenty shillings-worth of bread for the poor on the day of burial. Ten pounds of wax for a light to burn about my body at mass, &c., on the same day. To wife Isabel my dwelling-house in Lewenysmede, and a tenement in the same street inhabited by Roger Libbe; the said property to be sold after her death, and the money expended for the good of our souls, and those of my parents, ancestors, and benefactors. The said Isabel and Adam Arthur to be executors; to the latter 20 shillings, if willing to administer.

Proved before John Whyte, perpetual vicar of the church of SS. Philip and Jacob of Bristol, diocese of Worcester, in the parish church of St. James, June 30th, 1402; also before the Mayor, Sheriff, and Bailiffs.

124.—RICHARD FEROUR, burgess of Wells.

1402. Thursday in the morrow of the feast of St. Andrew Apostle. To be buried in the cemetery of St. Cuthbert of Wells, by wife Mabil and children. Legacies to the vicar of that church, and the chaplains serving in the same and taking part in the funeral rites, and on the days of the anniversary; 100 masses to be celebrated before burial, and 40 shillings to be distributed in bread to the poor on that day. A fit chaplain to celebrate for one year for testator's soul, and that of his former wife, and for the healthful estate of his now wife. To brother Henry all clothing, as well woollen as linen, except two cloaks. To kinsman John Houghlot a dagger, silver chain, &c., if he will cause, during his life, that four masses be celebrated on the day of the anniversary, for the souls of John Possebury, John Greynton, and others. To Ralph Ferant of Exeter a baselard, &c. To wife Felicia 4 marks of yearly rent from the two shops held by John Devenyssh for his life, with reversion of the same; which shops testator had by the gift and enfeoffment of John atte Celer, burgess of Bristol, and are situate in the south part of Wynchstr't in that town, between a messuage of the abbot of St. Augustine's of Bristol on the east, and one of John Clyve on the west; also two marks of yearly rent from a tenement in Wells inhabited by Nicholas Cristisham and his wife Maud; the said six marks and reversion to remain to daughter Isabel and her lawful issue. One mark of the rent in Wells to be expended yearly on testator's obit on the day of the anniversary. To dau. Katharine a cup which belonged to her mother Mabil, and a coffer "cum Wykett'," also a messuage in Wells, situate in "la Niewstr't apud lez barres." If testator's daughters should die s.p., the said property to revert and remain to his rightful and next heirs. His wife to be executrix, and John Wycombe and kinsman John Houghlot overseers. Witnessed by Sir Walter Hamme, vicar of St. Cuthbert's of Wells, Nicholas More, and others.

Proved before the Mayor, Sheriff, and Bailiffs of Bristol on Thursday in the feast "Cathedre sc'i Petri" 4 Henry iv.

This will is followed by a writing setting forth that Edith, relict of Hugh Plommer, lately burgess of Bristol, and John Plommer his son, and William Castell, executors of the will of the said Hugh, have sold o Ralph

Persevale, John Deye, parson of Baggeworth, and John Briggewatir, a tenement in Baldewynstret, in the suburb of Bristol, situate between a tenement lately possessed by Richard Bromdon and one formerly possessed by Richard Horlok, and extending from the aforesaid street to a tenement which was formerly Roger Turtle's, and is now held by Juliana Sonthwode; which property was to be sold for the payment of the said testator's debts and the good of his soul: Will 114. The said Edith and the other executors conclude with the statement that because their seals were unknown "pl'ribz," they caused that the seal of the office of the Bristol mayoralty be affixed to the document. Witnessed by John Barstaple, Mayor, and many others. Given at Bristol, Aug. 17th, 3 Henry iv.

125.—WILLIAM SOLLERS, burgess.

1402. Sept. 18th.—" p'ochianus eccl'ie sc'i Joh'is Bristoll." To be buried in the crypt—*Crouda*—of the said church, to the fabric of which £3. To wife Agnes all interest in a property, including a garden, in the suburb of Bristol in the market; remainder to son Thomas for his life; then to son William; after him to dau. Margaret; then to dau. Elen for her life, "si tunc aretro fu'it." Also to wife Agnes, a house and garden in Gropelane, lately purchased of Robert Bakkester; to remain, after her death, like the other property, and at length be sold for the benefit of the poor and needy. The tenement in Gosham to be disposed of for the good of testator's soul, and the souls of all the faithful dead. Residue to the said Agnes, who is appointed guardian of all the children. She, Sir John Knyghton, clerk, and Sir John Tovy (or Tony), rector of St. John's aforesaid, to be executors.

Proved before John White, perpetual vicar of the church of SS. Philip and Jacob Apostles, in the parish church of St. John of Bristol, Oct. 6th, 1402; afterwards before the Mayor.

126.—NICHOLAS WALEYS, mason.

1402. March 22nd. To be buried in the monastic church of St. Augustine of Bristol, by the side of wife Margery. To the abbot and convent of that monastery xl^s, for their prayers. Five tapers to burn about my body. For burial expenses xx^s. " Jt'm lego Belryngers Mon' p'dict' ad pulsand' campan' p' a'i'a mea ij^s." Legacies to the vicar of St. Augustine the Less, the fabric of the church of St. Michael of Bristol, and each order of friars. Four shops in the suburb in Horstrete, between the garden of the Kalendaries of Bristol on the one part, and a shop of testator's inhabited by John Bridport on the other, to be sold *pro anima*. To dau. Isabel and her lawful posterity, a hall with two shops in front, in the aforesaid street, situate between a tenement of the abbot and convent of St. Augustine and the tenement of William Berdon, and extending from the street to Frome ferry. The said Isabel, or her executors, to give away on Friday in every week for ever a penny-worth of bread for the good of testator's soul. To servant Margery ten shillings; also a shop with two gardens behind, in the same street, situate between the said four shops and the tenement of Adam Abraham, and extending from the street in front to the land of John Stoke, merchant, behind. But if Margery should die in the lifetime of dau. Isabel, this property is to belong to the latter and her lawful issue. The said

F

Margery, Peter Webbe, and John Bridport, executors; to the last two vj^s viij^d apiece.

Proved before William Forster, clerk, bachelor in laws, commissary general of the Bishop of Worcester, June 9th, 1403; before the Mayor on Monday next before the feast of St. Alban, 4 Henry iv.

127.—JOHN BORTON, burgess.

1401. Feb. 9th. To be buried in the church of St. Thomas the Martyr of Bristol. Legacies to that church, to my vicar, to each chaplain now serving there, and the parish chaplain; to the church of the blessed Mary of Redcliff; the four orders of friars in Bristol; for the poor and funeral expenses; to Sir William Kene, John Hull, Nicholas Hulle, John Falaunce, servant Agnes, John Penard, Peter Gasquyn, and William Caball. A fit chaplain to celebrate in the aforesaid church of St. Thomas for a whole year, for the soul of testator and of Elen his former wife; the said chaplain not to absent himself from the church at any of the canonical hours, without leave of the executors, or other reasonable cause; also a trental of St. Gregory Pope to be celebrated by him, according as it may be lawfully sung at certain festivals in the year, namely, through the octave of the Lord's Epiphany, and during other feasts. Another chaplain to celebrate in the same church for two years. Testator's body to be covered with half a cloth "de Bernet" at the mass and other mortuary offices; to be given, immediately after his burial, to four poor people, that they might pray for his soul. All his cups and silver spoons to be halved between his wife Joan and son John Borton. Residue of goods, except household vessels, to be also divided; one part for his wife, the other to the executors for payment of legacies. To son John £100 sterling, &c., and testator's dwelling-house in the suburb of Bristol in Redcliff-street, situate between the tenement of Elias Combe and that of John Bathe inhabited by Thomas Dier, and extending from the said street to Lawdiche; which tenement is held by wife Joan for her life. John Newton, Richard Dyer, and Richard Borton, tucker, executors, to each of whom £3, if willing to act; son John overseer.

Proved before the Mayor on Monday next before the feast of St. Alban, 4 Henry iv. Previously proved before the ecclesiastical authorities.

128.—WILLIAM BOUGHAN.

1403. July 11th. To be buried in the chapel of St. Katharine "eccl'ie p'ochial' se'e Crucis Templi Bristoll." Legacies to each priest celebrating in that church, and the two clerks; to John Combur, John Hillard, servant Maud, and apprentices Robert and William. To wife Joan, for her life, a tenement in the suburb of Bristol in Toukerstrete, between the tenement of John Selwode on the north, and a certain way called Contasslipe which leads to the Avon on the south; remainder to "Joh' & Joh'" our children, and their lawful issue; in default, to be disposed of for the good of all our souls. The said two children to have 100 shillings sterling, and be under the guardianship of wife Joan during their minority. If they should die under age, one half of that sum to remain to their mother, the other to be employed for the benefit of the soul of former wife Margaret, &c. To son John the second best gown and best cloak. To my brother William a furred gown "existentem coloris virid' & de storion'." Wife Joan, John Combar, and William Boughan, son of William Boughan the younger, executors. To the said William, a silver bowl called *le Taster*.

Proved before Thomas Barton, clerk, commissary general of the Bishop of B. and W., in the chapel of the blessed Mary next the close of Wells cathedral, Aug. 14th, 1403; before the Mayor, Sheriff, and Bailiffs of Bristol on Monday next before the feast of St. Valentine, 5 Henry iv.

129.—JOHN PALMER, tucker and burgess.

1403. Jan. 29th. To be buried in the parish church of St. Philip of Bristol, to the fabric of which a brass pot and platter. Legacies to the vicar, and each chaplain celebrating there ; to the mother church of Worcester, each order of friars in Bristol, and servants Agnes Edward, and Margaret Seysdon. Six marks for the poor and expenses on the day of burial. Testator wills that Edward Palmer and Robert his brother be made burgesses of the town of Bristol "sup' costag' & expens' meis," and have all his implements pertaining to a fuller's craft, his wonted clothing, &c. His tenement and garden in the suburb of Bristol in the market, situate between the land of John Droys and the tenement of Richard Brewer, and extending from the street in front to the land of Richard Ledbury behind, to be sold for the benefit of the destitute. To wife Edith, napkins, cushions, &c.; also four shops with garden and drying-room in the said market, situate between the tenement of John Stiel and that of John Stephenys, and extending from that street to Baftestrete. But when dau. Agnes arrives at full age, or is married, she is to hold this property, paying out of it two shillings yearly for the keeping of testator's anniversary and that of John Stiel and his wife Maud. Also to the said Edith, a state in other property in the market situate between a tenement of the abbot and convent of Stanley and a shop of the Kalendaries of Bristol, and extending from the street to what was formerly the garden of John Vyell. If she and dau. Agnes should both die "durante statu meo," the said state to be sold, and the money distributed among the destitute. To the said Edith and Agnes, a barn in the market, between the tenement of John Stephenys and the garden of the aforesaid abbot and convent ; to be sold after their decease for the benefit of the destitute. Residue of goods to be divided into three parts ; the first to be distributed *pro anima*, the second for wife Edith, the third for dau. Agnes. William Hurdeman, to whom xx^s, to have the keeping of the third part for the use of the said Agnes. Edmund Broun, to whom xiij^s iiij^d, and the said Edith, executors.

Proved in the parish church of All Saints of Bristol, Feb. 9th, 1403 ; also before the Mayor.

130.—THOMAS GILEMYN, burgess.

1404. Monday in the feast of the Translation of St. Thomas Martyr. To be buried in the crypt under the church of St. Nicholas of Bristol, in the tomb where his children lie interred. A silver girdle to the fabric of that church. To Sir Nicholas Adames the vicar, six silver spoons, bequeathed to testator by Sir John Croume, also a maser bound with silver engraven with a bishop's (?) head—*cu' ruo capite cp'ali inp'sso*. Legacies to the clerk, the suffragan, and each chaplain celebrating there, and taking part in the funeral rites; and to all other chaplains attending. Loaves of bread to the value of £10 to be given to the poor and needy on the day of burial, and 10 shillings for the needy inmates of the almshouses in Bristol. To the fabric of the cathedral church of Worcester xij^d. The second best silver girdle to the church of the Holy Trinity of Bradeford. His breviary to be delivered to a chaplain of good conversation, who is to have it for his life, and find security for its proper and safe keeping, that it may be afterwards handed over to another fit chaplain. A brass pot to the hospital of St. Bartholomew of Bristol. The sum of 100 shillings for a year's celebrations in the church of St. Nicholas. Lands, tenements, &c., in the town and suburb, to be sold immediately after testator's death, and the money divided into three parts; one for the fabric of the church aforesaid; the second for chaplains to celebrate for his soul, and the souls of wife Agnes, and Richard, and all the faithful dead; the third for the needy poor. Thomas Hendy, John Penrice, Roger Peny, and Robert Clement, executors, to each of whom a silver cup with a silver cover.

Proved before the ecclesiastical authorities July 16th, 1404; before the Mayor, Sheriff, and Bailiffs, on Monday next after the feast of the Assumption of B.V.M., 5 Henry iv.

This will is also recorded in the probate registry at Somerset House, where a considerable number of the ensuing wills are registered.

131.—WALTER NEWCOMBE, burgess.

1401. Jan. 11th. To be buried "apud Redeclyue" in the chapel of St. Nicholas. Legacies to the fabric and vicar of the church of Redcliff, every chaplain serving there on the day of burial, and the two clerks now serving therein; to Thomas Eston. To Walter son of Adam Lyme, and his heirs, a bed; also, after the death of testator's wife, the reversion of a shop by the common sink of the town of Bristol. To wife Alice, this property, if the said Walter should die s.p.; also lands and tenements in the town and suburb, or in any other place, and all goods and chattels. She and John Blecker to be executors.

Proved in the cathedral church of Wells, March 28th, 1402; before John Barstaple, Mayor of Bristol, &c., on Monday next after the feast of the Exaltation of the holy Cross, 5 Henry iv.

132.—THOMAS KNAPPE, burgess.

1404. Sunday next after the feast of St. Barnabas Apostle. To be buried in the chancel of the chapel of St. John the Evangelist, on the Back of Bristol, diocese of Worcester. To the fabric of the parish church of St. Nicholas £20. To the vicar thereof for tithes and offerings 100 shillings. Legacies to each chaplain of that church, the four orders of friars, and William Penseforde. To servant Avice Knappe, for her marriage, and my brother William Knappe, 50 pounds of silver apiece. To the Commonalty of Bristol 200 marks of silver. To John Dreyse all effects, lands, and tenements in Bristol or elsewhere; the said John and his wife Margery being made testator's heirs. A yearly rent of £20 for providing two chaplains to celebrate in all future time in the chapel of St. John the Evangelist, where testator's body shall rest, for his soul, and that of Avice his deceased wife, and the souls of his progenitors, and all the faithful dead. John Dreyse and William Penseford executors. Witnessed by Sir Henry Hassefeld, chaplain, Thomas Bartelote, William Nele, and others.

Proved before Robert Dudbroke, Mayor, &c., on Friday next after the feast of the Purification of B.V.M., 6 Henry iv. Previously proved before the ecclesiastical authorities.

133.—ROBERT SPISOUR, burgess.

1404. Thursday next before the feast of St. Michael. To be buried in the crypt—*Crippa*—of St. Nicholas of Bristol. Legacies to the fabric of that church, Thomas Smyth, chaplain, and each chaplain celebrating therein, the four orders of friars of Bristol, servants Reginald, John, Thomas, and Maud; to twelve poor people, and nurse Alice. To William "de Capella" on the bridge iij^s iiij^d. "Jt'm lego fabrice eccl'ie Pedrici in Cornubia videl't edificat' in Badman vj^s viij^d." Thirteen poor people to have a shirt and pair of shoes apiece. Twenty shillings to be distributed in bread for the good of testator's soul. A chaplain to celebrate, and have eight marks. To wife Alice the dwelling-house, third part of effects, &c. The said house to go, after her decease, to son Roger; if he should die s.p., remainder to John, Roger's brother; in default of issue, rem. to his brother Thomas; in def., rem. to their sister Avice. If at length there should be no heir, the said property to be disposed of *pro anima*. Wife Alice, Richard Pewtrer, chaplain, and Roger Mynde, executors, to each of whom xx^s.

Proved before the Mayor, &c., on Thursday next after the feast of the Purification of B.V.M., 6 Henry iv. Previously proved before the ecclesiastical authorities.

134.—JOHN SLOO, burgess.

1404. April 21st. To be buried in the church of St. Stephen of Bristol, by the image of the Holy Trinity on the north side. Legacies to the fabric and rector of that church, and every chaplain attending on the day of burial, the fabric of the church of St. Augustine the Less, and each order of friars in Bristol; Joan Phelpys, Isabel seynt Mariechurche, and Nicholas "s'nient' mee." To servant William Dyme xx^s, and a gown with hood of red and murrey color, in the name of a debt. To son Richard, a bassenet, with ventail, a pair of iron gloves, and a halberd. To wife Margaret the rents and services due from Walter Power, baker, and his wife Alice, for testator's share of a tenement in the suburb of Bristol in Knyfsmythstrete, inhabited by the same Walter and Alice; also a rent bought of Thomas atte Celer, clerk, the rents and services paid by Thomas Lumbard, shoemaker, the half of a shop in the street aforesaid inhabited by Alice Crane, and the rents due from Thomas Drynkwater, with the reversion after the death of the said Thomas. John Porter, chaplain, to whom a piece of silver worth x^s, and the said Margaret to be executors, and to order and dispose " p' ai'a mea."

Proved before William Forster, clerk, &c., in the church of St. Stephen of Bristol, August 5th, 1404; afterwards before the Mayor.

135.—EDWARD TANNER, burgess.

1404. Nov. 29th. Of the parish of the holy Apostles Philip and Jacob. To be buried within the church of St. Peter of Bristol, to the fabric of which xx^s. To the mother church of Worcester vj^d. A chaplain to celebrate for a year, and have 100 shillings. For funeral expenses 50 shillings. Legacies to the fabric of St. Philip's church, the vicar, curate, and clerk; male servant Denis; servants Joan and Alice. "Jt'm lego Edwardo filioll' meo sussept' de sacro fonte vnam Murram in cui' fundo infra scribit' hoc nomen Jhc in asura p'cij x^s & xl^s cum p'uen'it id'm Edwardus ad etatem xx annor'." Residue to wife Joan. She, and John Bagpath, to whom vj^s viij^d, to be executors. Witnessed by Sir John Wyte, vicar of St. Philip's, Robert Chepe on the bridge of Bristol, and Nicholas Alwey, burgess of the town.

Proved before the Mayor on Monday next after the feast of the Purification of B.V.M., 6 Henry iv. Previously proved before the ecclesiastical authorities.

136.—RICHARD KENFEKE, burgess.

1404. Saturday in the feast of St. Cecily Virgin and Martyr. To be buried in the church of St. Werburgh of Bristol. To the fabric thereof vj^s viij^d. To sons William, John, and Henry £5 apiece. To dau. Joan £11, a piece of silver with a foot, a maser of less value—*prior*'—with a silver foot, and a bed. To my brother William Carse vj^s viij^d. Two marks and a half to be laid out in bread for the poor and needy *pro anima*. Legacies to John Thomas, chaplain at St. Bartholomew's, and Thomas and Hugh Carse. Residue to wife Katharine. She and servant Thomas Carse to be executors.

Proved before the Mayor on Friday next after the feast of St. Valentine, 6 Henry iv. Previously proved before William Forster, clerk, &c.

137.—JOHN BANNEBURY, burgess.

1404. Dec. 30th. To be buried before the altar of the blessed Mary in the church of St. Werburgh of Bristol, to the fabric of which xxx^s. All effects to be halved; one part to wife Joan, the other for payment of legacies. To the mother church of Worcester xx^d. Twenty-four poor people to carry torches at his burial and the previous offices, and have a gown with hood, and ij^d apiece. Legacies to the five priests celebrating in the church aforesaid, on condition of their diligently occupying themselves in divine rites on the occasion, and to nineteen other priests, that they may attend; to servants Thomas Whete, John Carue (or Carne), Margaret, and Katharine; kinswoman Elianor, William Brent, Robert Asshton, and his wife Denis, Sir William Howell, chaplain, William Broke, clerk, the friars of Bristol, and the procurators of the fraternity of All Souls at Redcliff. Ten marks for one or two chaplains to celebrate at St. Werburgh's or elsewhere. John son of Robert Gardyner to have the £200 bequeathed by his father's will, and release from all further claim testator's executors, and those who were bound for him at the Guildhall: Will 55. To the same John Gardyner a silver cup with cover, and a cup of ivory bound with silver. To the fabric of the church and house of the Friars Minors at Limerick in Ireland, eight marks of silver, on condition that the prior and brethren of that house and place provide due security for the proper expending of that sum on the reparation of the said church and house, the overseers of the work to be chosen by the executors. To the fabric of the church of the blessed Mary of Limerick aforesaid xxxiij^s iiij^d. To wife Joan two water-mills situate in Limerick, and all testator's tenements and rents in and outside that city ; to be sold after her decease, and the money applied to pious purposes for the good of her soul and his. She, Robert Assheton, and William Broke, executors.

Proved in the parish church of All Saints of Bristol, before Thomas Lye, rector of St. Peter's, and Thomas Marchall, perpetual vicar of the former church, Feb. 7th, 1404 ; afterwards before the Mayor.

138.—THOMAS WHITE, of the town of Bristol, fisherman.

1404. Thursday in the feast of St. Leonard. To be buried in the crypt of the church of St. Nicholas, to the fabric of which iij^s iiij^d. Legacies to daughter Alice, and Thomas Smyth, chaplain. Residue of goods to the executors, viz., John Clerke and wife Alice.

Proved in the church of All Saints of Bristol Feb. 11th, 1404 ; afterwards before the Mayor.

139.—ADAM FORSTER, burgess.

1402. Jan. 18th. To be buried in the crypt of St. Nicholas of Bristol. Legacies to the vicar and fabric of that church, each chaplain celebrating therein, and the suffragan. "Jt'm lego mat'ce *(sic)* eccl'ie xij^d." To Thomas son of John Donne xx^s ; if he should die under age, testator's son John to have that sum. To son John ten marks ; if he should die, one half to wife Alice, and the other *pro anima*. Residue to the said Alice. She, John Bathe, and William Hurdeman, executors.

Proved before Nicholas Adam, vicar of St. Nicholas's church, June 30th, 1403 ; afterwards before the Mayor.

140.—JOHN HALEWEY.

1404. Nov. 20th. To be buried in the church of St. James of Bristol, "coram ymagine sc'e Crucis ib'm iuxta sepultura' Nich'i Hastyng in dext'a p'te ciusd'm sepult'e." Legacies to the fabric of that church, the parish chaplain, the clerk, each monk of the house of St. James, and the prior ; each order of friars, the fabric of St. Peter's of Bristol, and the mother church of the blessed Mary of Worcester. To Margery Hastyng, testator's mother, the rents and services due from Robert Brayn, "Bouchour," and his wife Joan, for a hall and two adjoining shops in Worshepstret, Bristol, with reversion of the same ; also a shop there inhabited by Joan Possh, and a stable held of testator by Robert Prat "Boucho'." The said property to remain, after her death, to daughter Margery and her lawful issue ; in default of such issue, to be sold ; preference being given, at the sale thereof, to Thomas Halewey and his wife Joan, testator's sister ; and with the money a fit chaplain to be paid for celebrating in the church of St. Peter of Bristol. If testator and wife Alice should leave no lawful heir, his mother Margery to possess, for her life, a tenement in Lewlynnesmede *(sic)*, situate between the tenement of the abbot and convent of Tewkesbury, and that of Philip Faunt ; also the rents and services paid by Richard Venour and his wife Cristina for a messuage in Worshepstret, with reversion of the same ; and the rents and services paid by Thomas Engelond and his wife Julian for a tenement in the same street, with reversion ; and also the rents and services paid for a tenement, shop, and cellar, in the street aforesaid, by Thomas Powke and his wife Agnes, and by Henry Honsome (?) and his wife Maud, with reversion of the same: which property, with the exception of the tenement in Lewlynnesmede, to remain to dau. Margery, and to be sold, in case of her death s.p., for providing celebrations *pro anima*. With the money obtained by the sale of the excepted tenement after the death of testator's mother, a chaplain was to celebrate in the church of St. James of Bristol, for the souls of testator's father and mother, Nicholas Hastyng, Walter Horngge, &c. To the aforesaid Thomas Halewey and his wife Joan, and the heirs of the latter, a garden in the suburb of Bristol in the market, lately bought of Isabel Predy, dau. and heir of William Predy ; also the reversion of a messuage in Lewlynnesmede, after the death of testator's mother, who was then occupying it. To wife Alice a bed, &c. To John Sutton a coat of mail, a saddle with bridle, " vnu' p'kyngpalet," &c. Residue to mother Margery. She and Thomas Halewey to be executors. John Sutton overseer.

Proved before William Forster, clerk, &c., March 13th, 1404 ; afterwards before the Mayor.

141.—WILLIAM FOLKYSHULL, burgess.

1405. April 2nd. To be buried in St. Mary's chapel in the church of St. Augustine by Bristol, to the fabric of which church £10. To each house of the four orders of mendicant friars of Bristol 40 shillings, that they might celebrate for testator's soul. £20 for poor people on the day of burial, one penny to each ; and the same sum for funeral expenses, and mourning apparel for the poor—*restita paup'u' sera*. To William Kendall £3, for his praiseworthy service, and wages for a year, as agreed upon. Legacies to the fabric of the blessed Mary of " Redeclefl," to the reparation of St. Werburgh's, and the rector of that church for tithes, each person in testator's service, his sister Agnes, and Alice " Auc mee." To daughter Joan £200. To wife Joan all his lands and tenements in the town and suburb of Bristol ; remainder to dau. Joan and her lawful issue. If the said Joan should die s.p., the property to remain to the Mayor and Commonalty of Bristol, on condition that they find two fit chaplains to celebrate for his soul ; the said Mayor and the Sheriff to take for their pains 40 pence out of the lands and tenements. To the clerk £100 to distribute at various times in clothing for the poor, visiting the decrepit sick, mending the roads, &c. Wife Joan and Walter Seymour executors ; to the latter £10.

Proved before the ecclesiastical authorities, Aug. 8th, 1405 ; afterwards before the Mayor.

142.—AGNES LEMMAN, relict of John Lemman.

1405. May 18th. To be buried in the church of St. Mary of Redclifl, diocese of Bath and Wells. To elder son Thomas, the tenement built on the Back of Bristol, and inhabited by testatrix. If he should die within the term, "q'd absum," remainder to brother John. Residue to sons Thomas and John. In case of their death, the said tenement and the whole residue to be disposed of for the good of the soul of testatrix, and the souls of Richard Brockworth, John Lemman, &c. William Whyte and his wife Edith to be executors. John Stephyn overseer. Witnessed by Sir Thomas Smyth, chaplain, Sir William Hervey, chaplain, Thomas Lemman, and many others.

Proved before William Forster, clerk, &c., July 10th, 1405; afterwards before the Mayor.

143.—RICHARD BRAYLE, burgess.

1405 (1404?). Thursday next before the feast of St. Thomas Archbishop. To be buried in the cemetery of St. Nicholas "cu' filijs meis." Legacies to the vicar of that church for tithes, and Richard Brokworth. To wife Edith a tenement in the suburb of Bristol, for her life; remainder to son Richard and his lawful posterity. If he should die s.p., the property to be disposed of *pro anima*. Residue of goods to wife Edith and son Richard, who are to pay what is due to Richard Clement "Cofferare." If Edith should die during the minority of son Richard, he is to be in the keeping of Robert Rowe and his wife Joan; if these should die, Richard Brokworth is to take charge of him. Robert Rowe and Richard Brokworth executors.

Proved before Richard Wynchecombe, clerk, &c., in the parish church of St. Nicholas of Bristol, Jan. 25th, 1404; afterwards before the Mayor.

144.—JOHN BOUNT.

1404. Aug. 24th. Testator describes himself as son and heir of John Bount, late a burgess of the town of Bristol, and commends his soul to Almighty God, the B.V.M., His Mother, St. John Apostle and Evangelist, and all the saints: his body, if he died in Bristol, to be buried in the cemetery of the blessed Mary of Redcliff, by the bodies of his brother Thomas and sister Margaret. Legacies to the fabric and vicar of that church, the parish priest of St. Thomas's, each order of mendicant friars of Bristol, friar John Dirneford, Sir Adam Cantwell of the order of Carthusians, Sir Adam of the Temple in London, Maud Canyng, Walter Wotton, weaver, William Taillour, John Bath, and apprentice William Han'sam (or Han'sam). To John Caunterbury 40 shillings, for his good and true affection, &c., also testator's book of the Gospels in English, which was then in the keeping of William Stourton. To uncle Roger articles of clothing, &c., and a yearly rent of 40 shillings for his life. To John Pochyn, burgess of Bristol, 33 shillings of rent from a tenement in Cornstret inhabited by John Austyn and his wife Joan; also, for his life, land and meadow ground in Tykenam and Hele, co. Somerset; remainder to Alice Wermystre, after whose death, to the right heirs of Thomas Morell, testator's kinsman. The said John to dispose of the residue of goods *pro anima*. To apprentice John Beoff, "Cur' & Socio meo dilecto," xl^s, and testator's new "Statuta," and sword garnished with silver, also his large harp, and guitar "cu' facie Damisell'." He wills that Richard Appulby, whom he releases from his apprenticeship, be liberated from the prison of Newgate, on condition that he agrees with the aforesaid John Beoff. To Robert "Mancipio medij Templi" two marks "p' inmensa (sic) bonitate sua michi impensa." Testator wills that when Thomas Bokelond, brother on the side of his mother, "cui' anime p'picietur deus," shall come to his full age, viz. 21, Richard Pensford and Roger Bount, feoffees in all his lands and tenements in the town and suburb of Bristol, shall enfeoff the said Thomas of and in the tenement inhabited by Richard Fembrigg. To the same Thomas and his lawful issue, the tenement inhabited by Thomas Williams, tailor. If he should die s.p., the tenement inhabited by Richard Fembrigg to remain to William Warmystre and his wife Alice for their life, and that inhabited by Thomas Williams to remain to John Thorp for his life; both tenements to be afterwards sold, with preference to testator's next of kin on his mother's side, and the money given for celebrations in the church of St. Thomas the Martyr of Bristol, for the good of his soul, the souls of his parents, Juliana Frox, John Wale and Margaret his wife, as long as the money would hold out. To the Mayor of Bristol vj^s viij^d, and each of the Bailiffs of the said town xl^d, to see that the will in this respect be faithfully carried out. Alice Wermystre to have the keeping of the said brother Thomas and his legacies during his minority. The other lands and tenements in the town and suburb to be sold, immediately after testator's decease, to John Bath, if he should wish to purchase, if not, to John Barstaple, and the money employed "ad maiore' cultu' dininn'," also for payment of debts, and celebrations for his soul, the souls of his father and mother, and my lord William Wykeham, bishop of Winchester "fundatoris mei," and for the good estate of his colleges at Winchester and Oxford. To Walter Wale of Wroxall and his heirs, all testator's land at Cokelesford in Wroxall. John Pochyn, otherwise Bath, John Beoff, William Pensford, to whom 100 shillings, and William Robrok, to whom 40 shillings, to be executors.

Proved before John Barstaple, Mayor, Mark William, Sheriff, John Clyve and John Niewton, Bailiffs, on Monday next after the feast of the Conception of B.V.M., 7 Henry iv. Previously proved before the ecclesiastical authorities.

145.—THOMAS BENET, tanner.

1405. Sept. 11th. To be buried in the cemetery of the blessed Mary of Redcliff. Legacies to the fabric of that church, the fabric and rector of the church of St. John of Bristol, William Benet the elder, Alice Filter, the poor, and every child raised by testator from the holy font. To dau. Joan 20 marks, for her marriage; Thomas Filter to have the keeping of her and her effects until she be of full age. To wife Julian £20, also a tenement in the suburb in Gropelane, between the tenement of Richard Frere and that of William Glaccare; remainder to the said Joan and her lawful issue. If she should die s.p., the property to be disposed of *pro anima*. Wife Julian, William Benet the younger, and Thomas Fylter, executors. To the said William xiij^s iiij^d, if willing to act. To the said Thomas x^s, on the same condition.

Proved before William Forster, Oct. 31st, 1405; afterwards before the Mayor.

146.—ROBERT CROSMAN.

1405. Wednesday next after the feast of St. Matthew Apostle and Evangelist. Testator describes himself as of the parish of the Holy Trinity of Bristol, in the diocese of Worcester, and invokes the name of Christ. To be buried in the church of All Saints of Bristol "cora' alta cruce," where the bodies of his father Thomas and mother Agnes were interred. His wife Agnes every year during her life, on the feast of the Apostles Simon and Jude, to have four masses celebrated in that church, and give alms to the poor, for the good of the souls of Thomas, Agnes, Robert, Isabel, and all the faithful dead. The vicar of All Saints to have xl^d, and put the above-said names "in Tabula memoriar'," and rehearse them on Sundays. The rector of Holy Trinity to do the same at his church, to the fabric of which xx^d, and to him xl^d for tithes and offerings forgotten. Legacies to the procurators of All Saints', and to priests for the celebration of masses on the day of burial, for the soul of testator's father and mother, his former wife Isabel, &c., and at his month's mind. To wife Agnes a tenement in Temple-strete, with two adjoining shops, and a garden ; to be sold, after her death, for pious uses ; also two shops in "le Market" between the tenement of William Fader and that of John Neel, fisher; also arable lands and meadows at Compton Dando and Marksbury, co. Somerset ; to be sold at length for procuring masses for the souls of testator's father and mother, and uncle William Wydebornwe, &c. Residue to wife Agnes. She, and John Tyler, brewer, of the parish of Holy Trinity aforesaid, executors.

Proved before the Mayor, &c., on Monday next before the feast of St. David Bishop, 7 Henry iv. Previously proved before the ecclesiastical authorities.

147.—JOHN DUNSTER, burgess.

1406. May 17th. To be buried in the chancel of St. Laurence of Bristol. Legacies to the rector of that church, the mother church of Worcester, William Dene, chaplain, and Thomas Michell. To wife Isabel, and sons William, Elias, and John, all and singular the utensils pertaining to the chamber, hall, and kitchen, &c. To the said sons ten marks. All money remaining after payment of funeral expenses to be divided into three parts ; one to be distributed *pro anima*, the second for the said Isabel, the third for the sons in equal portions. To the said sons for their life, all interest in the shop, with solar built over it, in Knyfsmythstrete, lately purchased of the Mayor and Commonalty of Bristol for a term of years. If they should all die within the term, the property to be for the poor in the hospital of the Holy Trinity at Lafford's gate. Wife Isabel, Sir William aforesaid, and Thomas Michell, executors.

Proved before John Pavy, clerk, bachelor in laws, commissary general of the Bishop of Worcester, in the parish church of St. Augustine of Bristol, June 9th, 1406. No note of proof at the Guildhall.

148.—WILLIAM LE ELE, burgess.

1405. Wednesday in the feast of Julian Bishop, viz. the 27th day of January. To be buried in the cemetery of the parish church " sc'e Crucis de Temple Bristoll," diocese of Bath and Wells. Legacies to the vicar of that church, to William Howys, chaplain, and every other priest celebrating therein, to each of the four orders of friars in Bristol, and Alice daughter of Robert Scherbay. To the chapel of St. Katharine, in the church aforesaid, a cup of mazer garnished with silver and gilt, not to be sold at any time; also vj^s viij^d for the adornment of the high altar, namely, for a frontal. To wife Agnes testator's dwelling-house; the reversion thereof to be sold for procuring celebrations *pro anima*. The said Agnes and Thomas Clerk to be executors.

Proved before Thomas Barton, clerk, commissary general of the Bishop of Bath and Wells, in the parish church of Keynsham, March 15th, 1405; afterwards before the Mayor.

149.—SIMON ALGODE, burgess.

1405 Dec. 28th. To be buried in the chapel of the blessed Mary within the church of St. Thomas the Martyr of Bristol. All effects to be divided into three parts; one for wife Agnes; the second for testator's lawful children, his son Thomas by his former wife Joan, to have an equal share with the rest; the third to be dealt with by the executors in carrying out the will. Of that third part, five marks of silver for vestments for the church aforesaid. Legacies to my vicar for tithes, Sir Henry Inet, chaplain, Agnes at Berkyng, kinsman John Hasplond, and servant Simon Fissher. Ten marks to the fabric of the church of Bassyngborugh, co. Cambridge, at the disposing of Warine White and John Pynke. To John Knotynglay a ring of gold, with a pouch, worth two marks. William More to have the keeping of the aforesaid Thomas. If all the children should die under age, the effects were to be divided into two parts; one for wife Agnes, the other to be disposed of *pro anima*. The said Agnes, Richard Halle, and Robert Colvyle, executors; to the last two 5 marks apiece. Robert Russell and John Sodbury overseers, to each of whom 40 shillings.

Proved before the Mayor on Monday next before the feast of St. Giles Abbot, 7 Henry iv. Previously proved before the ecclesiastical authorities.

150.—JOHN WODELEY, burgess.

1404. Jan. 27th. To be buried within the chapel of St. Thomas the Martyr of Bristol. Legacies to the fabric of that chapel, every chaplain who shall be celebrating therein on the day of testator's death, the three clerks serving there, the vicar of Redcliff for tithes, the church of holy Cross Temple, Sir Henry Inet, chaplain, each order of mendicant friars in Bristol, and Thomas Clerk, tucker. To wife Alice tenements, lands, rents, meadows, gardens, &c., in the town and suburb of Bristol, or elsewhere: remainder to sons Thomas and Walter, and their lawful issue, in equal portions; the property not to be given away or sold. If both the sons should die s.p., it is to be disposed of *pro anima*. The said Alice, Thomas, and Walter, executors.

Proved before the Mayor on Monday next before the feast of the Nativity of B.V.M., 7 Henry iv. Previously proved before the ecclesiastical authorities.

151.—JOHN CANYNGES, burgess and merchant.

1405. March 30th. To be buried in the chapel of St. Thomas the Martyr of Bristol, "in Tomba mea" within the chapel of the blessed Mary, on the east side. All goods and chattels, except clothing, and all other ornaments and armor pertaining to testator's body, to be divided into three parts; one for wife Joan, the second for his lawful children in equal shares, the third to be distributed for the benefit of his soul. If all the children should die under age, their legacies are to be disposed of *pro anima*. To wife Joan four shops in Toukerstret in the suburb, situate between the land of Thomas Barough and that of testator, and abutting on William Baker's; also two halls in the same street, between the land of John Harrys and that of John Broun; and eight shops in the suburb "iuxta lez Rekkys;" and three shops in the same, in the street of St. Thomas, between the land of Sir Thomas Broke knt. and that of William Pays; also a garden lying in the suburb, next "le Hondynlane," and another in Redclynestrete, between the land of Hugh Hoper and that of Alice Clyvedon; and rent issuing from two tenements held by the said William Pays in the street of St. Thomas, situate between testator's three shops and the tenement inhabited by Hugh Stoventon (or Stonenton). All the said tenements to remain, after Joan's death, to son John and his lawful posterity. To the said Joan, a hall with shop adjoining in Toukerstrete, situate between what was lately the land of Thomas Beaupyne and testator's land, and extending from the street aforesaid to Lawdych; also property in the same street between testator's land on either side; and other property there abutting on land of the prior and convent of Wytham and the tenement of James Cokkis, and extending in like manner; also a garden in Pylestrete in the said suburb: remainder to son Thomas. If he should die s.p., the property to remain to the lawful heirs of testator and wife Joan; to her heirs in case of their death s.p. The said property not to be alienated. Also to Joan, a tenement in Smalstrete, situate between a tenement of Walter Seymour, and one of John Pochen, and extending from the street to the Guildhall of Bristol; and six shops in the same suburb, next "le Castelledyche;" and property in Castellstrete, between the land of John Brwton and that of the prior and convent of Monkynfferlygh; and in Wynchestrete, between the land of David Vaughan and that of the said prior and convent; also a garden lying on St. Michael's hill, between the land of Sir Thomas Broke knt. and that of John Hurell; and another on Brendenhull, held by Joan wife of Richard Knyzt, "crokker," within the liberty of Bristol; and property in Leweynesmede, between the shop of Martin Bouch' and that of Hugh Carleton; also a void place in Wynchestrete, held by John Tanner; and another in Baldewynstrete, between what was formerly the tenement of William Wodefford and the land of Thomas Gloucestre; and one acre and a half of land between what was lately the land of Alan de Wryngton and that of John Folyet: remainder to son William and his lawful issue. If he should die s.p., rem. to son Thomas. If Thomas should die s.p., rem. to female heirs; in default of such, to be sold by the Mayor and Bailiffs, and four honest men of the parish of St. Thomas the Martyr, of Bristol; the Mayor to take for his pains 20 shillings sterling, and each Bailiff 10 shillings; the money raised by the sale of the property to be employed *pro animæ.* To wife Joan, a tenement in Templestrete, between the tenement of Sir Thomas Broke knt. and that of Richard Innyng, extending from the street to Lawdych; and another in Redcclyuestrete, between the tenement of John Hau'yng and that of Henry Brent, extending from the street to the Avon behind; and the reversion of the tenement in "Netherwer," co. Somerset, held of testator by John Lane, of that place, and Alice his wife, for their life; and 10 shillings of yearly rent, for the term aforesaid; to remain, after the death of the said Joan, to the offspring about to be brought forth by her. If her offspring should die s.p., these tenements, reversion, and rent, to remain to her rightful heirs, and be held of the chief lords of those fees. To the said Joan, the keeping of son William and dau. Agnes, and their effects, until they shall be of full age, finding security before the Mayor and Bailiffs of the town of Bristol, as the manner and custom is. Margaret Beaupyne to have the keeping of son Thomas, and daughters Joan and Margaret, together with their legacies during their minority. To John Sodbury, the keeping of son John. Wife Joan, Sir Henry Darleston, and John Frere, executors.

Proved in the church of St. Thomas the Martyr of Bristol, before Thomas Lye, rector of St. Peter's, and Thomas Marchall, perpetual vicar of All Saints', Aug. 12th, 1405; before John Barstaple, Mayor, &c., on Monday next before the feast of St. Matthew Apostle, 7 Henry iv.

The will of Thomas Beaupyne, who is referred to above, is registered in the Library at Lambeth, *Arundel*, i. 205. It was made at "Horslegh" on Saturday next after the feast of Corpus Christi, 1403, and "letters" were granted to the executors June 30th, 1404. Testator described himself as a burgess of Bristol, and desired to be buried in the abbey of the blessed Mary of Cirencester, in the chapel constructed there by Sir Henry Mourton. He bequeathed £60 sterling for the making of roads and causeways, and a yearly rent of ten marks of silver to his servant Arnald de Spynaw, out of lands and tenements in the town and suburb of Bristol lately purchased of the executors of Richard de Brompton; the reversion of the rent, after the death of the said Arnald, to be sold "p' salute animæ meæ." Residue to Margaret Beaupyne, his wife. She, John Bluet, John Harrewell, Thomas Colston, and Robert Orchard, executors. Sir Thomas Broke, overseer.

152.—NICHOLAS COMPAIGNONN.

1406, Sept. 24th.—" in bona existens p'speritate & sana memoria." To be buried by his late wife Elen in the cemetery of St. Werburgh "p' erucem." Legacies to the fabric and rector of that church, each chaplain constantly celebrating therein and taking part in the funeral rites, and the suffragan. "Jt'm lego aquibainlo p' classico campanar' pulsand' xij^d." To each order of mendicant friars of Bristol, the poor, the mother church of Worcester, daughter Margaret, Isabel dau. of wife Katharine, and servant Margaret. To the said Katharine, all testator's interest in a shop in Wynchestrete, situate between the shop of John Southfolke, web, on the one part, and the rents of the prioress of Barugh on the other; which property he had by the grant of the aforesaid John Southfolke for a term of twenty-three years from the day of a certain indenture made between him and testator,—Monday next after the feast of the Purification of B.V.M., 4 Henry iv. If she should die within that term, the said state or possession of that shop to be put up for sale, and the money employed for the good of his soul, the souls of his wives, &c. She, John Lavynton, chaplain, and William Markes, executors. Adam Sopemaker, overseer, to whom, for his pains, vj^s. viij^d.

Proved before John Droys, Mayor, John Fyssher, Sheriff, James Cokkys and David Dudbroke, Bailiffs, on Monday next after the feast of the Purification of B.V.M., 8 Henry iv. Previously proved before the ecclesiastical authorities.

153.—RICHARD PAANS, merchant.

1406. Dec. 17th. To be buried, if it shall please God, in the chapel of B.V.M. within the church of St. Stephen of Bristol, " vbi sum p'ochianus." Legacies to Master John Wyke, rector of that church, and each chaplain celebrating therein, and attending the funeral rites, and each clerk of the parish who shall attend ; to the Friars Minors and Carmelites, and the poor in the hospitals of St. Bartholomew and St. John of Bristol. Sixty shillings-worth of wax to be made into torches and tapers to burn about testator's body " in honore dei" on the day of burial. Linen and woollen clothing, to the value of £40, for a hundred of the more feeble and hospital poor ; thirteen of whom to be clad in one suit, and be present on that day. Forty marks for the maintenance of honest chaplains, to celebrate within the aforesaid chapel, with all possible speed after the death of testator, for his soul, the souls of his parents, and friends, &c. To son William £20, for his advancement, together with armor and weapons. To daughters Joan, Alice, and Elizabeth, 28 marks in equal portions. If they should all die s.p., the third part of that sum to remain to wife Alice, and with the two other parts, sacred books, vestments, &c., to be bought for the use of the church aforesaid, and alms to be given. To servants Adam, Joan, and Agnes, 60 shillings in equal portions. To William Popylton " heremite de Rounh'm " 40 shillings, to pray for testator's soul. To son William and his lawful posterity, a capital hall, with chambers and kitchen pertaining thereto, and five cellars adjoining, situate on the Key of Bristol, " que h'ni & adquesiui de hered' Joh'is de Lyme," with free ingress and egress. If he should die s.p., the property to remain to the aforesaid three daughters, and their lawful issue, equally divided. If they should die s.p., wife Alice to possess it for her life ; and, afterwards, sacred books, vestments, and other ornaments, to be bought for the use of the aforesaid church of St. Stephen, with one part of the price thereof, and the celebration of masses, &c., to be had with the other. To the said dau. Joan and her lawful issue, a tenement with shop adjoining on the Key ; of which tenement John Tommes is tenant, William Stephenes being tenant of the shop. To dau. Alice, and her lawful issue, other property on the Key, inhabited by William Hoper, on the south side by the common lane. To dau. Elizabeth, and her lawful issue, that tenement on the aforesaid Key lately inhabited by Walter Broun, and adjoining the tenement of Bourne " Sadeler " on the north. If the daughters should die s.p., rem. to son William and his lawful issue. If he should die s.p., rem. to wife Alice. In case of the death of all s.p., the property to be sold ; one half of the price to the aforesaid church of St. Stephen, the other to be distributed for the health of testator's soul, his wife's, &c. To wife Alice 200 marks, and all vessels and needful stuff pertaining to his house ; also a yearly rent of 40 pence in M'sshstrete, Bristol, paid by the tenant Robert Shepeward; rem. to son William and his heirs. Also to Alice, and our issue, tenements and garden on the land formerly belonging to John Roper at St. Augustine's green by Bristol; which property was lately bought of the executors of John Brampton. To the fraternity of St. John Baptist of Bristol, for a perpetual alms in memory of my name, and for the souls of my progenitors, &c., a tenement upon the Key, in the south part of the entrance "port' eiusd'm Keye." To Sir John Broke, rector of Stretton, five marks, "cu' quad'm casula & vestimento p' celebrand' miss'." Nicholas Devenyssh, to whom ten marks, the said Sir John, and wife Alice, executors. William Stephenes overseer, to whom ten marks.

Proved before the Mayor, &c., on Monday next before the feast of St. Gregory Pope, 8 Henry iv. Previously proved before the ecclesiastical authorities.

154.—WILLIAM SELCOK.

1406. Monday next before the feast of the Nativity of the blessed Mary. To be buried in the church of Hunspull (Huntspill). Forty pence to the roodloft, and the same sum "ad batelliamentum" of that church. Legacies to John Bonde, parish chaplain, John Cake the clerk, William Toker chaplain of the blessed Mary there, and William Chepe. "Jt'm lego Dionis' Godesone vj^d." Testator bequeathed to his wife Joan all his burgages, lands, and tenements at Bristol in "Radeclestrete," together with all other property in the suburb; to be held, for her life, of the chief lords of that fee; remainder to his and her lawful issue; in default of such, to be sold, and the money distributed for the good of his soul and the souls of his parents. The said Joan and her brother John Forster executors.

Proved in the chapel of B.V.M., by the close at Wells, April 20th, 1407; also at Bristol, before John Droys, Mayor, &c., on Friday next after the feast of Peter and Paul Apostles, 8 Henry iv.

155.—CRISTINA CHESEWELL.

1407. Aug. 20th. Testatrix mentions that she was wife of John Chesewell, burgess of the town of Bristol, and bequeaths to him all her effects, to be disposed of for the good of her soul. To be buried in the crypt of St. Nicholas. To Robert Nemot (?) and his wife Margaret, their heirs and assigns, the reversion of six shops, a curtilage, and croft in the suburb on Redeclynehill, between the shop (or shops) of Sir John Lavynton, chaplain, and the land of the prioress of Barugh; which property is held by John Chesewell, husband of testatrix, for his life, and reverts afterwards to her and her heirs. The said John to be executor.

Proved before John Pavy, clerk, in the parish church of All Saints of Bristol, Sept. 26th, 1407; before Thomas Blount, Mayor, Thomas Yonge, Sheriff, John Spyne and Robert Barstaple, Bailiffs, on Monday next after the feast of the Conversion of St. Paul, 9 Henry iv.

There can be but little doubt that the surname to which it has appeared advisable to append a query, is really "Nemot;" and, if so, it may have been originally *Emmot*, as the name Nash was otherwise *Ash*.

156.—THOMAS GLOUCESTRE, burgess.

1407. June 5th. To be buried in the church of the Carmelite Friars of Bristol, to the fabric of which xl^s. Legacies to the vicar, fabric, and crypt of the church of St. Nicholas, every chaplain present at the funeral rites, the chapel of the Assumption of the blessed Mary on the bridge of Avon, the mother church of Worcester, the mendicant friars of Bristol, Sir William Tamworth chaplain, Isabel wife of John Pembroke, apprentices John Smert, John Shiryngton, and John More, nurse Alice, and servant Joan Thlau' (or Thlau'). To wife Isabel, for her life, a garden in the market, lately bought of Richard North, dyer and burgess of Bristol, now held by Angellinus John; remainder to dau. Agnes and her lawful issue. In default, rem. to testator's right heirs. Also to Isabel, his dwelling house in the suburb, on the bridge of Avon; the reversion of a tenement on the bridge, inhabited by John Burbache, after the death of the said John; a tenement, with lands, meadows, &c., in Bristilton, co. Somerset, lately bought of the executors of Thomas Bakke; a garden in the suburb in Mersshstrete, between the garden of the rector of St. Stephen's and that of John Stephenes; and a tenement in the town of Gloucester, in a lane called Oxbodelane; remainder to dau. Margaret and her lawful issue. In default, rem. to the procurators of St. Nicholas's of Bristol, who are to provide a fit chaplain to celebrate there for his soul, his wife Isabel's, late wife Agnes's, Thomas Bakke's, &c. To wife Isabel, a tenement in Oldecornestrete, Bristol, inhabited by Gilbert Gaveler (or Ganeler), between the tenement inhabited by John Rokell and one belonging to the Commonalty inhabited by Robert Barstaple; also a tenement in Baldewynstrete inhabited by Thomas Reyneshury, situate between property of James Cokkys on either side; six shops in Mersshstrete, between the tenement of John Stephenes and that of the rector of St. Stephen's of Bristol; the reversion, after the death of John Burbache, of two shops with garden adjoining in the market, between property of John Parys and Elizabeth Vyell; the reversion of a curtilage in the Redelond, between property of William Hoke and Elen Thornebury; and the reversion of a curtilage with three acres and a half of land lying "apud lez Barres," between property of Robert Michell and John Veell; remainder to the fraternity of the chapel of the Assumption of the blessed Mary, in which a chaplain is to celebrate for his soul, the souls of Adam Inhyne, Thomas Hendy, &c. To Alice wife of William Benley, a bequest including a pair of beads, one gold ring, with a sapphire, "& duobz filarijs vocat' flylettys cum perlis." Wife Isabel and Adam Inhyne executors; to the latter xl^s if willing to act. Sir William Tamworth overseer.

Proved before Thomas Blount, Mayor, &c., on Monday next before the feast of St. Valentine, 9 Henry iv. Previously proved before the ecclesiastical authorities.

157.—JOHN SOMERVYLE, of Trowbridge.

1407. Saturday next before the feast of St. Laurence Martyr. To be buried in the church of St. James the Apostle at Troubrigge. Legacies to every light in the said church, and to the cathedral church of Sarum. To daughter Margaret the third part of all moveable goods, after the funeral and payment of debts; residue to wife Elizabeth, that she may order and dispose for the health of my soul. To the said Elizabeth, forty shillings of yearly rent from the tenement inhabited by John Rokell in Oldecornestrete in Bristol, also two solars pertaining to that tenement, and a house called "le Scolehous" in the street of St. Nicholas in the same town; the said property to remain, after her decease, to dau. Margaret. If Margaret should die s.p., the Mayor and Sheriff of Bristol were to sell the property, and apply the money to the celebration of masses for the soul of his late wife Agnes, his own, wife Elizabeth's, &c. The said Elizabeth and Margaret to be executrices, and William Kaynell overseer. Given at Tronbrigge. Witnessed by Richard Kaynell, of that place, Hugh Dauntesey, William Wolff, John Frank, and John Draper.

Proved before Thomas Blount, &c., on Wednesday next after the feast of the Translation of St. Thomas Martyr, 9 Henry iv. Previously proved before the ecclesiastical authorities.

158.—PHILIP WYNTER, burgess.

1407. Oct. 8th. To be buried in the church of the Carmelite Friars of Bristol. Legacies to that house, and each of the three other orders: the fabric of the parish church of St. Thomas of Bristol; John, chaplain of the chapel of St. Mary of Kemmesford, and the poor and needy. To son Thomas £20. If he should die under age, the said sum to be divided into two parts, one for wife Constance, the other *pro anima*. To son John ten marks sterling, and a piece of silver. Testator's brother, Sir John Wynter, to have the keeping of the said John and his legacies during minority. To daughter Katharine ten marks. To daughter Margaret 100 shillings; of which sum those who now have the boy in their keeping are to have the value of 20 shillings in cloth; "si domi (?) non euen'it vel infra tempus obierit q'd absit," the residue of the said sum to wife Constance, that she may have the boy's soul in remembrance. To brother Sir John one piece of black "Worstede," price xx^s, and a fur of fitchew. To apprentice John a coat of mail, a basenet, a barrel of soap, &c., on condition of his rendering to testator's wife a faithful account of all the goods. Executors to be wife Constance, John Cokkyng, merchant of Bristol, and Sir Thomas Lye, clerk, rector of Obeley. To the last two vj^s viij^d apiece.

Proved before the Mayor on Monday next after the feast of the Assumption of B.V.M., 9 Henry iv. Previously proved before the ecclesiastical authorities.

159.—WILLIAM NORTON, tucker and burgess.

1407. Wednesday in the vigil of the Purification of B.V.M. To be buried in the cemetery of the church of holy Cross Temple of Bristol "exoppo'ito Cruc' austral' ibidem." Legacies to the vicar, each chaplain, and the two clerks of that church; to each order of mendicant friars of Bristol, servant Robert Benet, John Hyndebest, Alice Blount, William Fylle, John Bleys, and friar Thomas Camell. To Thomas Blount and his wife Alice, testator's dwelling house in Temple-street, Bristol, situate between a tenement of Sir Thomas Broke, knt., and that of John Caunterbury; to be sold after their decease, and the money to be expended on the work of the aforesaid church. To son Robert the best silver cup with a cover, also 60 shillings of silver, and two leaden vessels. Residue to the poor and needy. Alice Blount and John Bleys to be executors.

Proved before John Fissher, Mayor, John Clyve, Sheriff, John Sherp and John Leycestre, Bailiffs, on Monday next before the feast of Simon and Jude, 10 Henry iv. Previously proved before the ecclesiastical authorities.

160.—KATHARINE CALFE, of Bristol.

1408. May 10th. To be buried in the church of St. Werburgh of Bristol, before the altar of the blessed Mary, beside late husband Henry Calfe. Legacies to the rector, and each chaplain there who shall be at mass on the day of burial and at the previous rites, to the water-bearer, and the suffragan. To the fabric of the church vj^s viij^d, on condition that her body be allowed interment in the above named place without any further demand on the executors, otherwise nothing. Twenty masses to be celebrated for her soul immediately after her decease, and her body to be delivered for burial without any delay. Thirteen poor women sitting at table in her house, on that day, to have meat and drink enough, and one penny apiece for their prayers. Three yards of russet cloth to be laid over the hearse at the mortuary offices and mass, and bestowed, after the burial, upon the poorest woman the executors could find lying in her bed on account of infirmity, together with a linen cloth to make her a shift (camisiam). Two tapers to stand, one at the head of the hearse, and the other at the foot, each of the weight of three pounds, and no other lights. To the procurators of St. Werburgh's, a coverlet of a bed " glauci & rubij op'at' cum fllowres de luys," to make vestments therewith. To each of the orders of mendicant friars in Bristol ij^s. Legacies also to Lucy Stephenes, Dionysia Asshton, servant Clarice, William Brooke, Edmund Scosy, Elen Shepisby, and Joan wife of son John. To the said John, the third part of certain household stuff, half a dozen "quissons de arras," &c.; also all that share inherited by testatrix in a tenement on the Back of Avon, inhabited by John Lemman while he lived, and by one John Coton afterwards; also a yearly rent from a tenement on the Back of Avon aforesaid, inhabited by Thomas Bertlot and his wife Maud. The said son John and his executors to keep the anniversary of testatrix once in every year, for six years next after her decease, in the aforesaid church of St. Werburgh. Her tenement in the suburb of Bristol, in Mersshstrete, situate between the tenement of James Cokkes and one inhabited by Richard Abell, to be sold, and a chaplain provided to celebrate yearly in St. Werburgh's, at the altar of the blessed Mary, for the souls of Henry Cobyndon, Hugh Hunte, late husband Henry Calfe, &c., as long as the money would hold out. Son John and William Brooke executors. Lucy Stephenes overseer.

Proved before John Fyssher, Mayor, &c., on Friday next before the feast of the Annunciation of B.V.M., 10 Henry iv. Previously proved before the ecclesiastical authorities.

161.—ALICE WODEFORD.

1407. Friday next after the feast of St. Matthew. Testatrix describes herself as belonging to the parish of St. Nicholas of Bristol, in the diocese of Worcester, and desires to be buried in the chapel of St. Thomas the Martyr, before the Cross, by the tomb of her husband. Legacies to each priest celebrating in the said chapel, and the three clerks there; to each order of friars in Bristol, the poor women of the hospital of St. John Baptist outside Redcliff gate, the nuns of the blessed Mary Magdalene, the sisters of St. Bartholomew, bedridden sick people, my brother John Botiller, Maud his wife, to whom a gown "ffurrat' cum wyldeware," &c., Isabel and Joan his daughters, and Isabel Aungell. For wax to burn about the body of testatrix on the day of burial xl^s, and the same sum for other expenses on that day. Two marks to be spent at her month's mind. James Cokkes of Bristol to find a fit chaplain to celebrate in the aforesaid chapel for two whole years, and another chaplain to be provided by her executors to celebrate for one year therein for her soul, the souls of her husbands William Wodeford and Nicholas Chepman, and for all the faithful dead. To servant Maud, for her life, a yearly rent of 20 shillings issuing from three shops on St. Augustine's Back; remainder to my son Bernard. Also to him and his heirs, tenements, rents, reversions, and services in the town and suburb of Bristol. If he should die s.p., the said possessions to be sold for pious uses. To apprentice Joan, two coverlets of the least value, five ells and a half "de westvale," &c. John Caunterbury and John Palmer, merchant, to be executors. Witnessed by Robert Shepeward, Bernard Mulleward, William White, Peter Pedewell, and Sir William Seriaunt, parish chaplain of the said chapel of St. Thomas, and others.

Proved before John Fissher, Mayor, &c., on Friday next before the feast of the Invention of the holy Cross, 10 Henry iv. Previously proved before the ecclesiastical authorities.

This will is registered twice in the Orphan Book.

162.—AGNES CLIFFORD.

1408. March 14th. Testatrix was relict of John Clifford, late a burgess of the town of Bristol; "in pura viduitate mea & legitima potestate." To be buried in the crypt under the parish church of St. Nicholas of Bristol. To the fabric of the cathedral church of Worcester xij^d. To John Yeuelton, "ffuyster" and burgess of Bristol, and his wife Beatrix, dau. of testatrix, a tenement in the suburb on the Back of Avon, between the tenement of John Vyell and that held by Walter Sawyer; to be held by them and the lawful posterity of the said Beatrix. If she should die s.p., rem. to Margery dau. of testatrix, for her life; to be afterwards sold "plus dare volenti," and the money distributed *pro anima*. Roger Mynde and the said Beatrix to be executors, and have the residue of goods. Witnessed by Mark Williams, David Duddebroke, Roger Mynde, and others.

Proved before John Droys, Mayor, James Cokkes, Sheriff, John Sutton and William Beneley, Bailiffs, on Monday next after the feast of St. Matthias Apostle, 11 Henry iv. Previously proved before William Hayles, clerk, commissary general of the Bishop of Worcester, in the parish church of St. Augustine of Bristol.

163.—WALTER SEYMOUR, burgess.

1409. Feb. 26th. To be buried in the church of St. Werburgh of Bristol, in the chapel of the blessed Mary there, under the graven stone where the bodies of John Seymour, late my master, and Margaret my wife are buried. Twenty four chaplains to take part in the mortuary offices, and have vj^d apiece. The poor and needy to have bread, ale, and money on the day of burial. The bedridden to have the like, and also beds, coverlets, &c. To the rector of St. Werburgh's xl^s for tithes, and a gown of scarlet furred with grey. A pair of vestments, with a chalice, to that church, for the chaplains celebrating there for testator's soul. Legacies also to every chaplain celebrating therein, to the fabric of the church, and the clerk for bell-tolling at the mass and previous rites ; to the four orders of friars at Bristol, the mother church of Worcester, the house of the blessed Mary Magdalene on St. Michael's hill at Bristol (bequest including a pair of vestments and two cruets), apprentices Richard and Juliana, apprentice John Littilton, servant Agnes sister of the said John, servant Richard, late servant Edmund, friar John Camvyle of the order of Carmelites in Bristol, John Austyn, and John Bailly. Testator's lands, tenements, rents, reversions, and services in the town and suburb of Bristol ; namely, a tenement in Baldewynestrete inhabited by John Body ; two new shops with the adjoining garden in Templestret, situate between the tenement of the procurators of holy Cross Temple church, and what was lately the tenement of Hugh Carleton ; a tenement opposite St. Peter's church, inhabited by John Wever, situate between testator's land and the tenement of John Bruton, carpenter ; the shop annexed thereto ; a corner tenement inhabited by John Parmyter, weaver, in St. Peter's street, as one goes through the lane towards Wynchestret, opposite the house where Simon Olyver dwells ; two tenements with garden in Wynchestret, by the gate called Blyndegate, between the tenement of John Bruton and the lane as one goes towards St. Peter's church ; thirteen shops in Tourestret, between the tenement of Walter Touker and the common gate of the town ; testator's dwelling house, with cellar adjoining, in Smalstrete ; this property to be sold, and with the money, after payment of debts, fit chaplains to be provided to celebrate in the church of St. Werburgh, and other churches where it shall please the executors, for the furtherance of Divine worship, for the soul of testator and his wife Margaret, and the souls of John Seymour, Walter Goos, friar Matthew Tyderley, and all the faithful dead. Twelve new torches and four round wax tapers to burn about testator's body on the day of burial. Twelve poor men to carry the said torches, and each to have a gown with hood. The dwelling house in Smalstrete to be sold to John Fyssher, before all others, if he should wish to buy it, at a less price by £40 than any one else might be willing to give "r'onabilit' iuxta valorem eiusdem." John Rokell and Nicholas Devenyssh executors, to whom ten marks apiece.

Proved before the registrar of the Court of Canterbury, March 15th, 1409. No record of proof at the Guildhall.

164.—JOHN BASSET, of Bristol.

1410. Oct. 25th. To be buried in the cemetery of the parish church of St. James of Bristol, by the burial place of late wife Alice. To the fabric of the mother church of Worcester iiij^d. Legacies to the fabric of the church of St. James aforesaid, the parish chaplain, and parish clerk there, godson John, son of John Gusshe, Katharine Buttiller, and Margaret Prynce. To wife Alice her dowry of lands, tenements, rents, &c., in the parish of Slimbridge, co. Gloucester. To son Thomas ten marks, of which 100 shillings are to be received from Sir Thomas lord of Berkeley, at son

Thomas's own costs, for a messuage with curtilage and appurtenances in Wotton, or that property itself, to be held by the said son Thomas and his heirs in the name of the aforesaid 100 shillings. All the lands, tenements, gardens, crofts, rents, reversions, and services in the town and suburb of Bristol, lately purchased of the executors of Alan de Wryngton, formerly burgess of the said town, to be sold, and provision to be made, with five marks of the money, for the child which testator's wife Alice is about to bring forth. The said Alice to have the residue, and dispose of it *pro anima*; and have also the five marks, if the said child should die under age. She and Roger Libbe to be executors, and John Stephenes, merchant, overseer.

Proved before William Hayles, clerk, canon of Lincoln, and commissary general of the Bishop of Worcester, in the parish church of All Saints of Bristol, Dec. 10th, 1410; afterwards before John Sely, Mayor, and Nicholas Excestre, Sheriff.

165.—JOHN HUNTE, otherwise Calf.

1410. Monday next after the feast of the Conversion of St. Paul Apostle. Testator was of the parish of the Holy Trinity of Bristol, and desired to be buried in the church of St. Werburgh, beside his mother. Legacies to the fabric of that church, the rector and the fabric of the church of the Holy Trinity, the cathedral church of Worcester, each order of friars in Bristol, John Rede, smith, and every godchild of testator. To son William a saddle and bridle, bow and arrows, sword, buckler, &c.; his brother to have the said things, if he should die. To wife Joan, for her life, testator's dwelling house, and other tenements in the town and suburb; rem. to his right heirs. The whole debt of the above mentioned John Rede is remitted, and he may have the tenement inhabited by him without paying any rent for one whole year after the death of testator. Wife Joan and Peter atte Wode to be executors. Robert Burlas overseer. Given in testator's dwelling house in Wynchestrete. The same John owes to divers persons xxx^s; to William Spicer xviij^d ob.; to John Richard ij^s vj^d; to Robert Sadlere x^d.

Proved before John Sely, Mayor, &c., on Monday next before the feast of St. Gregory Pope, 12 Henry iv. Previously proved before William Hayles, clerk, &c.

166.—ISABEL BARSTAPLE.

1411. March 2nd. Testatrix describes herself as formerly wife of John Barstaple, late a burgess of the town of Bristol, and desires to be buried in the chapel of the Holy Trinity " iux' portam Laffard," before the image of the Holy Trinity. To the poor there £10. Sir William Rijs, chaplain, to have ten marks sterling, and celebrate in that chapel, in the next year after the decease of testatrix, for her soul, her late husband's, &c.; and have a further sum of 40 shillings for the celebration of a trental of St. Gregory. Her son Sir Nicholas, chaplain, the said Sir William, Robert Shepward, William Scot, and Roger Batte, to be provided with clothing of one sort " contra dirige meu'." To Sir Thomas Thorpp, celebrating in the chapel of the Holy Trinity, 20 shillings. To Sir William Hawvyle, rector of St. Werburgh's, £3 sterling, on condition that neither he, nor any other in his name, shall hinder the direct conveyance of the body of testatrix to the aforesaid chapel. Also, forty pence to the said rector; the same sum to the clerk of that church for bell-tolling, and twelve pence to every priest celebrating therein. Four tapers, each of the weight of six pounds, to be about the body "ad exequias meas," and five tapers, weighing eight pounds apiece, to stand upon the hearse. Poor people to have white cloth to the value of £8, and follow the body to burial. To daughter Alice £10 sterling; also the best girdle garnished with silver and gilt, a pair of beads, a cross of silver and gilt, and a broche of gold, worth £3; to remain, after her decease, to dau. Joan. To the said Joan, wife of Robert Shepward, and her heirs, the best silver cup, and £10 sterling. To son Sir Nicholas the best silver bowl with a cover, the best bed, "videli't de Tapserywork," two blankets, &c., and the sum of £10, which is to be distributed *pro anima*, if he should die before testatrix. To son Thomas 100 shillings, a bed "de Tapserywork," tester, coverlet, &c., and a silver cup worth 30 shillings. To Sir Henry, prior of the Kalendaries of Bristol, 20 shillings. To Alice Castell "vna' Nigr' Seynt" garnished with silver and gilt. Legacies also to bedridden people, maids Joan Clerk and Agnes Peawtrer, John Power, Richard Brond, John Harreys, and John Torre. Residue to be distributed for the good of the above mentioned souls by the executors, namely, Robert Shepward, to whom 10 marks, William Scot, to whom 100 shillings, and Roger Batte, to whom £4.

Proved before Thomas Yonge, Mayor, and John Spyne, Sheriff, on Monday next before the feast of St. Margaret Virgin, 13 Henry iv. Previously proved before the ecclesiastical authorities.

The name of Henry Darleston, or Derlaston, prior of the house of the Kalendaries, who is mentioned here, and in several wills of earlier dates, does not occur again. The episcopal registers at Worcester record the admission of his successor, Sir Thomas Colman, on the presentation of Thomas Norton, Mayor of Bristol, Aug. 30th, 1414; in which year the said Henry's will was proved. It was made May 9th, 1410. He desired to be buried according to the appointment of Sir Thomas Marchal, vicar of All Saints' in Bristol, in which church the chantries of that fraternity had been founded; and left legacies to the vicar and the fabric of that church, Sir Richard Brownwyn and Sir John Dyere, brethren of the house, Sir John Blake, St. Thomas's church in Bristol, and the church of "Todyngtown." The said Sir Thomas Marchal, Sir Thomas Lye, rector of St. Peter's, and Sir John Dyere, executors. Registered in the Library at Lambeth, *Arundel*, ii. 204.

167.—MARTIN BOUCHER, burgess.

1411. Sept. 12th.—"sanus mente eger tamen in corp'e sciens me viam vniu'si carnis ingredi ignorans penitus diem neq' horam." To be buried in the church of St. Mary "de foro," in the chapel of St. Katharine the Virgin, on the north side of the altar. A chaplain to celebrate in that church, and have 100 shillings. Legacies to the procurators, the rector, and the clerk there, the mother church of Worcester, each order of friars, wife's dau. Alice Squihere, and kinsman (whose name is not given either here or in the copy at Somerset House). To wife Margaret, and her heirs and assigns, tenements in the town and suburb of Bristol, except royal services customary by law. She and Matthew Squyer to be executors, and Reginald Peytevyn overseer.

Proved before the Mayor and Sheriff on Monday next before the feast of the Nativity of B.V.M., 13 Henry iv. Previously proved before the ecclesiastical authorities.

168.—JOHN RICHARD, burgess.

1411. Sept. 8th. To be buried in the parish church of the Holy Trinity of Bristol, before the altar of the holy Cross under the window on the south side. Legacies to the rector, the parish clerk, the reredosse of that church, and each chaplain celebrating therein ; the mother church of Worcester, each order of mendicant friars in Bristol, the poor in the hospital of St. Bartholomew, the sick in the almshouse "en le langcrewe Bristollie," John Stratton, John Combe, William Voghan, servant Walter, William Holebrond, and the bridge of Cardiff. For funeral expenses 100 shillings. To the fabric of St. Ewen's of Bristol xx^s. To the fraternity of St. John in that church vj^s viij^d. Twenty four poor people to have shoes, and twenty shillings to be distributed in bread on the day of burial. Thirteen poor people to be clad in Welsh russet on that day. Testator forgives the debts due from all such men and women as are not in a position to pay him. A fit chaplain to have £25, and celebrate for his soul, and the souls of all the faithful dead, in the aforesaid church of the Holy Trinity, on the altar of the holy Cross, for five years. To wife Julian £60, and all household goods; also the tenement inhabited by testator, with four shops and a cellar underneath, and two gardens behind, situate in Bradstrete, Bristol. To John Mavyle all testator's accoutrements (harnisia), as well in armor as in girdles, &c., and all the cloth in his shop and in a certain house called "le Clothhous" under his dwelling house, also debts, and a rent from a tenement in the High-street, at the corner as one goes towards "Seynt mariestrete in foro;" also the said cloth-house, and a hall with a cellar and chambers adjoining, which hall the. said John inhabits ; and the reversion of the said tenements, shops, and gardens, when it shall fall after the death of wife Julian. The said John Mavyle and William Eglesale, goldsmith, executors, to each of whom 40 shillings.

Proved before the Mayor and Sheriff on Monday next after the feast of the Purification of B.V.M., 13 Henry iv. Previously proved before the ecclesiastical authorities.

169.—WILLIAM MORE, burgess.

1411. Oct. 9th.—"diem obitus mei ignorans." To be buried in the chapel of St. Thomas the Martyr. Legacies to the works (op'ibz) of that chapel, the perpetual vicar, Sir Henry Inet, chaplain of the blessed Mary, celebrating there, and each of the other priests of the said chapel, if present at the mass and previous offices ; to kinswoman Alice, wife of Walter Baker of Bristol; servant James Mershe, when the agreement between him and testator has been faithfully fulfilled ; servants Joan and Alice ; William Webbe of Badmyngton, and late servant Thomas Crull. To Cristina Halle, wife of Richard Halle, merchant and burgess of Bristol, a whole woollen cloth. To Cristina, testator's wife, all the silver and brass utensils, and half.of the goods ; also a yearly rent of five marks from a tenement on the Key, paid by William Stevenys, burgess of Bristol, in the name of the heirs of John Draycote, formerly burgess of the said town, deceased. Wife

Cristina, Sir Walter Blakeford, chaplain, and the aforesaid Richard Halle to be executors, and distribute the residue of effects to the feeble and lame among the poor, and in other pious works and alms, for the health of testator's soul and the souls of all the faithful dead.

Proved before John Clyve, Mayor, and John Sherp, Sheriff, on Friday next after the feast of All Saints, 14 Henry iv. Previously proved before the ecclesiastical authorities.

170.—JOHN CAUNTERBURY, burgess.

1411. May 15th. To be buried in the church of St. Thomas the Martyr of Bristol. Legacies to the fabric, and Sir William, vicar of the said church, Dionisia Gunnet, servant Robert, late servant John Attewelle, John Wexmaker, John Golde, and William Barbour, servant to Nicholas Caunterbury. The sum of 100 shillings to be divided among testator's nearest kinsfolk, and his son Nicholas to have 40 shillings, if he will faithfully distribute it. To the said Nicholas, and his lawful issue, the tenement called "le Redehall," which is to revert to the right heirs of testator in default of issue. To John, elder son of the said Nicholas, the tenement in Temple-strete inhabited by Simon "zong." If John should die s.p., remainder to son Nicholas. If at length there should be no heir, the said two tenements are to remain to William Canon. If William should die s.p., they are to be sold *pro anima*. To son Nicholas "om'ia vtensilia mea." He and the aforesaid John Chepman "wexmaker" to be executors. Testator's will to be fulfilled in the first year after his decease.

Proved before the Mayor, &c., on Friday next after the feast of All Saints, 14 Henry iv. Previously proved before the ecclesiastical authorities.

171.—RICHARD SPYSER, burgess.

1412. Wednesday, Feb. 8th. To be buried in the parish church of St. James of Bristol. To the work of the church of the blessed Mary of Worcester xij^d. Legacies to the prior of St. James aforesaid, each monk of the priory, William, parish chaplain, and every chaplain of the aforesaid parish church celebrating there. To wife Cecily cups, spoons, &c.; also a tenement with five adjoining shops, situate in the suburb of Bristol "in le Broodemede," which tenement John Daubmne inhabited; also a garden "apud le Barres." If the said Cecily should marry again, son John Spyser, his heirs and assigns, to have the property. To the said John a girdle and dagger, each bedecked with silver. Residue to be disposed of *pro anima*. Son John and William Selcok executors, to each of whom 20 shillings of silver.

Proved before John Weston, clerk, inceptor of decrees, commissary general of the Bishop of Worcester, March 17th, 1412; afterwards before the Mayor.

172.—RICHARD SPALDYNG, esquire, burgess.

1412. March 20th. To be buried before the altar of St. George the Martyr in the church of the Carmelites of Bristol. To the said friars, to have "puteu' menm ib'm," vj^s viij^d. Legacies to the vicar of the church of the blessed Mary of Redcliff, each order of mendicant friars in Bristol, and the mother church of Bath. To the poor on the day of burial xiij^s iiij^d in bread. Six wax tapers to be about testator's body on that day. To his wife Margaret, the whole state which he had in the corrody lately bought of John Hastyng of Reading, issuing from the monastery of St. Augustine of Bristol, and purchased by the said John for the term of his life; the said Margaret and her assigns to pay yearly to the said John four marks sterling, and during her life, " si contingat ip'am viuere statu' p'd'em," to give and distribute on Friday in every week, through the whole term of four score and ten years, a penny loaf of white bread, for the good of testator's soul, and the souls of all the faithful dead; xij^d also in white loaves to be distributed to the poor every year in the feast of All Saints during the term aforesaid. The said Margaret or her assigns to keep his obit, and expend yearly during that term vj^s viij^d at his anniversary. Residue of unbequeathed effects to be disposed of by her for the good of his soul. She and John Burbach executors. William Benley overseer. Witnessed by John Droys, Roger Smyth, Thomas Spicer, John Wyke, Robert Wilteschire, John Uphulle, and many others.

Proved before Thomas Norton, Mayor, and John Nuton, Sheriff, Nov. 8th, 1 Henry v. Previously proved before the ecclesiastical authorities.

173.—SIMON CANYNGES, burgess.

1413. Nov. 10th. To be buried in the chapel of St. Katharine, in the parish church of St. Stephen of Bristol, before the image of the blessed Mary. Legacies to the rector, parish chaplain, parish clerk, suffragan, and fabric of that church. To the fabric of the mother church of Worcester xij^d. The sum of xiij^s iiij^d to be distributed in bread to the poor, for the good of his soul, and all the souls " quibz tencor." Residue of effects to be divided into three parts; the first for pious uses, the second for wife Margaret, the third for son Thomas. If the said Thomas should die under age, his legacy to remain to wife Margaret, who is made executrix.

Proved before Thomas Norton, Mayor, &c., on Monday next after the feast of St. Scolastica Virgin, 1 Henry v. Previously proved before John Weston, clerk, &c.

The above mentioned Margaret Canynges was daughter of William Botener, or Botoner, " of the diocese of Coventry and Lichfield," and sister of John Botoner, whose will was proved in P.C.C. July 20th, 1391.

174.—RICHARD VENER.

1413. The morrow of St. Lucy Virgin and Martyr. Testator describes himself as " de p'ochia b'te Marie in foro Bristollie." To be buried in the church of the blessed Peter, to the work of which vj^s viij^d, and the same sum to that of St. Mary aforesaid. To the rectors of those churches forty pence apiece. Twelve entire woollen cloths to be sold and expended for the health of testator's soul, and the souls of his deceased wives, &c., on the day of burial, and the day of his trigintal, and in other pious works at different times. His executors to pay to Sir Thomas Holme what is agreed on for celebrations on behalf of his wives for the present year, and to find a chaplain to celebrate in the aforesaid church of the blessed Peter of Bristol during another whole year, for the souls of his wives, and his own soul, from the proceeds of the said twelve cloths. Legacies to the mother church of Worcester, daughter Margaret, and John and Joan, her son and dau. To Robert Ledbury and his wife Agnes, dau. of testator, his dwelling house in the street of the blessed Mary "in foro;" they and their heirs to pay twelve pence yearly for the perpetual and future sustentation of a lamp burning in the church of the blessed Mary aforesaid, before the Lord's Body in the chancel. If Robert and Agnes should die s.p., the said mansion house to remain to John Teffent and his wife Margaret, dau. of testator. In default of issue, rem. to Nicholas Derlyng, testator's sister's son, and his heirs. Laurence Brokke, to whom xiij^s iiij^d, and Robert Ledbury to be executors. Master Thomas Lye, rector of St. Peter's aforesaid, overseer.

Proved before John Weston, clerk, &c., Jan. 20th, 1413; afterwards before the Mayor.

175.—ROBERT DIDBROK, merchant.

1409. March 28th. To be buried in the church of St. Stephen of Bristol, before the high altar, in a place already fixed upon. Legacies to the rector, parish chaplain, priests, clerks, and fabric of that church, each order of friars in Bristol, Robert Hywes, and John Halperton. A vestment to the altar of the blessed Mary in the said church of St. Stephen. "Jt'm lego matrice eccl'ie vj^s viij^d." To wife Alice 200 marks, which testator had with her in marriage; also the third part of all his effects, some of which were "vltra mare." The second part to be distributed for the health of his soul. The third to be divided into two portions; one for Richard Haukeslow and his wife Joan, testator's dau.; the other to be distributed by the executors, according to the ordering of the overseer of the will, that is, to John Vynour, testator's brother, £10, "in relaxando s' q' tantu' michi dz," and to John, son of the said John, £5; the residue of this second portion to his servants, &c. To Margaret wife of John Stephn' of Bristol, ten marks and rents in the town and suburb. To Richard Haukeslow, and Joan his wife, and their daughter Alice, certain tenements in the suburb at the "Were," &c.; to be disposed of *pro anima* after the death of these three, who are also to have testator's interest for a term of years in all the shops and tenements bought by him in the town and suburb, except one shop and garden in Merstrete held by William Yong, carpenter, which he is to hold for his life without payment of rent, and the reversion of which is to revert to them in case of his death before the expiration of the term agreed on in the writings. But if they should die before the said term, the reversion is to be sold and religious distribution made. Also, in this case, the two shops which were built by testator in Merstrete, on the land or fee (su' fudu') of St. Stephen's of Bristol, and which were to be held by the said Richard, Joan, and Alice, to remain to the said church. To wife Alice his interest in the messuage standing on the land of the town, which messuage "est p'tine's ad iiij soppas" in Merstrete. She and Richard Haukeslow to be executors. John Droys overseer.

Proved before John Droys, Mayor, &c., on Monday next after the feast of the Purification of B.V.M., 11 Henry iv. Previously proved before the ecclesiastical authorities.

176.—JOHN SELY, burgess.

1413. Dec. 22nd. To be buried before the altar of the Holy Trinity in the church of holy Cross Temple of Bristol. To the vicar of that church for tithes and offerings xx^s. To the work of the chapel of St. Katharine there xl^s. "Jt' lego op'i Campanil' einsdem eccl'ie si de nouo fu'it constructu' C^s." To every chaplain of that church celebrating there xij^d., and the same sum to each of the two clerks. A chaplain to celebrate therein *pro anima* for twenty years, and have £100. Every priest attending the funeral rites to have four pence. To the poor on the day of burial 100 shillings. Forty poor men and women to have a pair of shoes apiece, &c. To each of the four orders of friars of Bristol 20 shillings. A whole cloth of black to be laid over the body before burial, and bestowed on the poor immediately after the month's mind. A cloth of the same color for wife, executors, and friends. For funeral expenses £12. For the month's mind 60 shillings. For mending the roads about Bristol £4. To wife Isabel lxvj^li xiij^s iiij^d., and all household vessels; also all lands and tenements in the town and suburb, for her life, if she shall keep herself sole and chaste. The reversion of that property to be sold within one year after testator's death, and the money distributed to the poor, and for the marriage of poor women, and other pious purposes, for the good of his soul, and the souls of all the faithful departed. To the work of the chapel of St. George at the Guildhall of Bristol vj^li xiij^s iiij^d. To the work of the chapel of the fraternity of St. John Baptist in the church of St. Ewen of Bristol xl^s. To the work of the chapel of the Assumption of B.V.M. on the bridge of Avon xl^s. To the common work of the pipes of Bristol xl^s. To the work of the cathedral church of St. Andrew of Wells xx^s. To late servant Matthew Sqnyer xl^s, and a silver flat cup. Legacies also to servants Robert Sendel, William Broun, and Richard Wayn, tucker. Wife Isabel, Thomas Blount of Bristol, to whom C^s, and a silver cup and silver cover to the same with a dragon upon it, and Thomas Michel of Bristol, to whom lx^s, to be executors.

Proved before Thomas Norton, Mayor, &c., on Monday next before the feast of the Translation of St. Thomas Martyr, 2 Henry v. Previously proved before the ecclesiastical authorities.

This will is also registered in the Library at Lambeth, *Arundel*, ii. 201.

177.—JULIANA RICHARDES.

1413. Aug. 26th. Testatrix was widow of John Richardes, draper, late a burgess of the town of Bristol. To be buried in the church of the Holy Trinity, beside the said John. A cup called "stondyng Maser," with a cover bound with silver and gold, also another cup with a silver cover, and a piece of silver called "fllatpece," with a new dozen of silver spoons, to be sold by the executors, and with the money celebrations to be procured for the soul of testatrix and the souls of all the faithful dead, and the window next the cross of the aforesaid church to be glazed. John Mavyle to have these goods, if willing to buy them. For the forming and repair of the cross in that church xx^s. A fit chaplain to celebrate *pro anima* for three whole years at the altar of the holy Cross there. Legacies to the rector of that church, every chaplain coming to the funeral rites, the mother church of Worcester, each order of mendicant friars in Bristol, the needy poor, John Mavyle, and John his son, and Alice his daughter, former servant Joan Bryd, and present servant Margaret, who is to be in the keeping of Margaret Hansford. John Chiltenham, barber, and John Bertram, executors, to whom xiij^s iiij^d apiece. John Mavyle overseer.

Proved before John Weston, clerk, &c., Oct. 1st, 1413.

Then follows a codicil, in which testatrix bequeaths clothing, &c., to the wife of John Mavyle, William Solas, and his wife Alice, Margaret wife of John Batter, Cristina Kynge, Magot wife of Hugh Coryour, Joan Backwell wife of William Fourbour, the wife of John Sherman, the wife of William Goldsmyth, the wife of John Stephanys, barber, and the wife of Nicholas Taillour.

Will and codicil proved before Thomas Norton, Mayor, &c., on Wednesday next before the feast "Carniprenij," 1 Henry v.

178.—RALPH YEUELE, of Bedminster.

1414. Wednesday in the feast of St. Peter, which is called "aduincla." To be buried in the south entrance of the church of "Bedmystre," beside wife Cristina. To the vicar of that church vj^s viij^d, that he may come to the furneral rites and mass. To every chaplain of the chapel of Redcliff, coming with him, iiij^d. Legacies also to each clerk there, the parish chaplain of Bedmystre, the clerk for bell-tolling, "& cl'ico ib'm aquebaiulo," each order of friars at Bristol, the cathedral church of Wells, St. John of Jerusalem, St. Anthony, the prisoners of Monkbridge, the almshouses in Langerew, Templestreet, St. Bartholomew, St. John in "Redeclyneput," St. Katharine by Bristol, and at Laffard's gate. A sufficient taper to burn at testator's head, and another at his feet, immediately after death, and while the "exequie" are being said, and two other tapers about his body on the day of burial at the church of Bedmystre during mass, &c. The vicar, priests, friars, and others attending, to have bread and ale to the full. The chaplain celebrating at the mass to have four pence besides bread, cheese, and ale enough. An honest secular chaplain to celebrate for a whole year in the said church, for the soul of testator and of his wife Cristina, and have eight marks sterling. A silver cup (cupa) with a cover of silver to be made into a chalice and bestowed on some needy church where their souls may be especially prayed for. A bequest of goods to wife Amy (Amisia) and son Ralph. To John son of daughter Edith xl^s to find him at school. To Margaret dau. of the said Edith, and her lawful issue, a yearly rent from a hall and shop in Tuckers' street, Bristol, inhabited by Richard Bourton. If Margaret should die s.p., the said rent to be disposed of for the benefit of testator's soul "& ffelicie vx'is mee." To wife Amy, for her life, a furnace for the craft of a brewer, &c.; remainder to son Ralph. If he should die before the said Amy, rem. to the aforesaid Margaret, who is also to have one half of testator's hall on Redcliff hill, situate between a hall of the blessed Mary of Redcliff on the south and John Staunford's shop on the north. Residue of goods to be halved by son Ralph and wife Amy. The latter to keep, every year during her life, testator's anniversary and that of his wife Cristina. The said Amy, son Ralph, and Philip Hassok of Bristol to be executors, and have xx^s apiece. Witnessed by Richard Chynham, Thomas Mayes, William Paltysmore, Robert Pedewell, John Ardern, Walter Waterman, and Thomas Waky.

Proved before John Storthwait, clerk, commissary general of the Bishop of Bath and Wells, Sept. 20th, 1414; afterwards before the Mayor, &c.

179.—WILLIAM WARMYNSTRE, burgess.

1414. May 23rd. To be buried in St. Werburgh's of Bristol. Legacies to the fabric of that church, the rector, each chaplain celebrating therein, the parish clerk for bell-tolling, and the suffragan thereof; each order of mendicant friars at Bristol, every chaplain attending the funeral, John Daton, tailor, Henry Hemyng, William Frere, Gilbert Badecok dwelling at "Jrynacton," the wife of Robert Riggewey in the market, and servants Joan and Katharine. Cloth to the value of £20 to be distributed among the poor on the day of burial. Half a hundred of wax (dimid' Centu' Cere) for making torches to burn about testator's body. To wife Alice and her heirs a garden in the suburb of Bristol, situate in the market, and held by John Lymnour; also a messuage in Redclyvestret, between the tenement of William Berdene and what was formerly that of Simon Uphull; a messuage and shop in "le Brodemede" formerly acquired by the gift of John Michell; two messuages in Horsestret once the property of Edward Pounsot of Bristol, goldsmith, and his wife Amy; and a messuage and adjoining garden in Redclyvestrete, held of testator and inhabited by Matthew Garewey. Also to the said Alice, for her life, the rents and services paid by Roger Wanstre and his wife Alice for a messuage and garden in the suburb, in Bastestret, with reversion when it shall fall; remainder to son John and his lawful issue. If John should die s.p., the said rents, &c., to be disposed of *pro anima*. Also to the said Alice, the rents and services paid by John Tristy and his wife Agnes for two shops in Wynchestrete; remainder, with reversion, to son John; in default of issue, to be disposed of in like manner. Also to the said Alice, a tenement and garden in Mersshstret occupied by John Yalton, situate between the tenement of Nicholas Excestre and that of David Dudbroke; rem. as before; also that tenement in the same street which testator had by the gift and enfeoffment of Edith Hoker, late the wife of Nicholas Hoker, situate between a tenement of John Droys on the one part, and that of John Roddeney, inhabited by John Viell, on the other; rem. as before; also a tenement with two shops "in vico de Redeclyuestret" in the suburb, between the lane called Southrenlane on the one part, and what was lately the messuage of Isabel Torynton, formerly held by Walter Dybon, on the other; rem. as before: also testator's dwelling house in Cornstret, with the three adjoining shops; rem. as before; also twenty shillings of yearly rent of assize, formerly bought of William Combe, and issuing from the tenement inhabited by Richard Shirwyn, shoemaker, in Redclyvestrete; and the rent issuing from a messuage of Sir Thomas Brooke knt. in Cornstrete inhabited by Elen Auncell; rem. as before. Also to the said Alice a tenement with shops, &c., in Baldewynstrete and Bastestrete, between the tenement inhabited by Thomas Strech and that of Gilbert Joce; and property in Horstrete, between what was formerly the tenement of Thomas Sutton, on the one part, and a garden of the Commonalty of Bristol which Reginald Knap lately held, on the other; to be held for her life only, and afterwards sold for providing celebrations in the aforesaid church of St. Werburgh for twenty years next after her death, for the good of her soul and testator's, &c. She and John Lymnour executors. To the latter xxˢ.

Proved before John Droys, Mayor, and Robert Russell, Sheriff, on Monday next after the feast of St. Agnes, 2 Henry v. Previously proved before the ecclesiastical authorities.

180.—JOHN STONE, burgess.

1414. March 8th. To be buried in the parish church of St. James of Bristol "cora' hostio sc'i Thome Martiris in ead'm." To the fabric of that church xx^s. To every chaplain celebrating there xij^d. To the prior of St. James for tithes and offerings, xx^s. To each monk of the said prior xx^d To the fabric of the mother church of Worcester xl^d. To the fraternity of St. John Baptist in the church of St. Ewen of Bristol xl^d. Legacies also to the Friars Preachers, Carmelites, and Minors of Bristol. To wife Edith, who is to dispose *pro anima*, all testator's interest in his three shops in "Brodemed," and the residue of his effects. She and John Umfray executors.

Proved before John Weston, clerk, &c., in the parish church of St. Augustine of Bristol, April 21st, 1415; afterwards before the Mayor.

181.—JOHN SUTTON, burgess.

1415. Tuesday next after the feast of St. Matthew Apostle and Evangelist. To be buried in the church of the Carmelite Friars at Bristol. To the mother church of Worcester xij^d. To the prior of St. James of Bristol and the rector of St. Stephen's, for tithes, vj^s viij^d apiece. Legacies also to John Tilly of Clopton, and servant John White. To wife Joan the rent due from William Harper for a tenement, held by him for his life, in Templestret, with reversion of the same; also the rent paid by William Temple for a tenement held by him in like manner in the same street, with reversion after the death of the said William Temple. If she should die s.p., remainder to Thomas son of John Harper of "Chilmeley," and his heirs male; in def., remainder to Thomas Janyns; in def., remainder to John Shoppe; in def., rem. to the prior and convent of the Carmelite Friars of Bristol, who are to sell the property, and expend the money upon their house for the benefit of testator's soul and the souls of all the faithful dead. To the same Joan the rent due from Henry Lokier for a tenement, held by him for his life, in the suburb of Bristol in Lewenysmede, with reversion after the death of the said Henry; the rent paid by Thomas Peseley for a tenement in the same street, with reversion after the death of the said Thomas; the rent paid by Richard Priour for two shops opposite the cemetery of St. James of Bristol, with reversion after the said Richard's death; three shops by the aforesaid cemetery, held of testator by the same Richard; the rent paid by Roger Sylly and William Brewer for a garden by the "Barres," with reversion thereof; the rent paid by William Worcestre, the younger, for a tenement on St. James's Back, with reversion of the same. If the said Joan should die s.p., these rents, reversions, and shops to remain to Thomas Janyns and his heirs male; in default of such issue, rem. as before. To the same Joan the rents and services paid by John Sherp and his wife Joan, and by William Baret and his wife Margery, for a tenement, cellar, and adjoining shops in the town of Bristol, in Oldecornestret, with reversion thereof; in default of issue, rem. to Thomas son of John Harper of Chilmeley; in def., rem. to Thomas Janyns and his heirs and assigns. To Sir John Burford, chaplain, all testator's interest in "le Hawkehows," with solar, &c., situate at the gate of St. Giles at Bristol; to be disposed of *pro anima* if the said John should die before the expiration of the term. To dame Mabilla Sutton, sister of testator, for her life, all his interest in a house at the Barres, and in two acres of arable land "iux' lez barrez" adjoining the same house; also three acres of land lying at Apesherd by the "Redelond," held by Henry Brayn; remainder to the prioress and convent of "Mynchen Barugh." To the prioress of Kington all testator's interest in two shops in Baststret in the parish of St. Nicholas, and 50 shillings. Wife Joan to be executrix.

Proved before Thomas Blount, Mayor, and David Duddebroke, Sheriff, on Wednesday next after the feast of St. Gregory Pope, 4 Henry v. Previously proved before the ecclesiastical authorities.

182.—BELINUS NANSMOEN.

1416. March 20th. To be buried in the church or cemetery of the blessed Mary of Redcliff. Legacies to the perpetual vicar of that church, every priest of Redcliff coming to the funeral rites, each clerk, and each scholar (puero scolari) serving in the choir there. His exequies were to be held "sine pompa." He also willed that his two books, of which one was called the Sixth, "continens textum & glosam ordinariam" together with the doctors John Andreas, archdeacon of Bologna, " & d'ne digne," and the other book containing the doctors upon the Clementines, namely, Paul Jacelyn and others, be shut up in the church of the blessed Mary of Redcliff, so that the vicar and chaplains there might study them when they pleased; the same vicar, priests, and clerks to keep his anniversary every year, and also that of Alexander Bagenham, in a fitting manner in the choir, at their own costs. If they should neglect or refuse to do so, the said books were to remain in the parish church of St. Thomas the Martyr "sub forma p'de'a." If his anniversary should be neglected in that church, they were to remain in the church " se'e Crucis de Temple." And in case of omission there, they were to remain to the hospital of St. Katharine on the aforesaid condition for ever. Residue of goods to wife Isabel and daughter (?) Avice. The said Isabel and John Dawborn, to whom 20 shillings, executors. Robert Colvyll, to whom 20 shillings, overseer. Witnessed by Isabel, wife of the said Belinus, and William Clyve, clerk.

Proved before John Estcourt, bachelor in laws, examiner general of the Court of Canterbury, April 2nd, 1417; before Thomas Blount, Mayor, &c., on Wednesday next before the feast of St. Germanus Bishop and Confessor, 5 Henry v.

There is a copy of this will at Somerset House, *Marche*, 37, but it throws no light on the description of the books as given above. "d'ne digne" is obviously a mistake for the name of some doctor. The word translated "Clementines" is *Clementinos*, which should evidently be *Constitutiones Clementinas*—the Constitutions of Pope Clement v. The will of Alexander Bagenham, who is mentioned here, is registered in the Library at Lambeth, *Arundel*, ii. 202. It was made Feb. 9th, and proved on the last day of the same month, 1413. He styles himself clerk, and desires to be buried in the collegiate church of the Holy Trinity of Westbury. Legacies to dame Joan Stowell, Alexander and Joan Clyvedon, Agnes

Sylney, Sir John Long, priest, Thomas Russell and his wife Joan, Thomas Harethorn, Thomas Bydow, John Brydd, my sister Joan, the Friars Minors at Oxford and Bristol, and Master Peter Russell, who is to celebrate for testator's soul, and the souls of all the faithful dead. To Sir Hugh Loterell knt. the breviary 'which lately belonged to William Courtenay. Belinus Nansmoen and Thomas Russell executors. To the former, 20 shillings, a share in the residue of the effects, and the *Sixth book of the Decretals*. Sir Thomas Stowell knt. and Alexander Clyvedon overseers. Given at Bristol. The episcopal registers at Worcester mention Alexander Bagenham as rector of "Staple," in that diocese, in 1412, and state that the Bishop collated John Arondell, clerk of the King, to the deanery of Westbury, vacant by the death of the said Alexander, Feb. 17th, 1413.

The name "Nansmoen" is written *Nasmeon* in *Marche*, 37, which mentions wife Isabel and *daughter Amicia*. The Bristol copy has wife Isabel and *wife Auicia!*

183.—MARGARET STEPHENUS.

1417 (1416?). March 20th. Testatrix was wife of John Stephenus the elder, and made her will in the presence of the vicar of St. Leonard's of Bristol, and others, desiring to be buried in the cemetery of the said St. Leonard's. Legacies to the vicar, and clerk of that church, the mother church of Worcester, Sir John Bole, chaplain, the daughter of John Draper, servant Cecily, and Isabel Person. To John Herford, clerk, the rents and services paid for a tenement in the suburb of Bristol "sup' Keyam," with reversion thereof; the said tenement being situate between what was formerly the tenement of Walter Frompton, inhabited by Andrew Parle, on the one part, and a tenement of the prior and brethren of the Kalendaries, inhabited by Martin Wysebeche, on the other, and extending "a vico regio" to the said tenement inhabited by Andrew Parle. To John Stephenus, husband of testatrix, all her right or state in a shop situate in Cropelane, inhabited by William Pascowe. The said John to be executor.

Proved before the Bishop of Worcester, in the parish church of Hembury in Salt Marsh, in his diocese, July 9th, 1417; afterwards before the Mayor.

184.—JOHN BENLEY, burgess.

1416. Jan. 7th. To be buried in the cemetery of the chapel of St. Nicholas of Bristol. To the fabric of the cathedral church of Worcester xij^d. A priest to celebrate for one year, for the soul of testator and the souls of all the faithful dead, in the said church of St. Nicholas, and have ten marks, on condition of his celebrating a trental of St. Gregory. Legacies to Sir John vicar of that church, each priest celebrating therein on the day of testator's death, John Tustayn suffragan thereof, the fraternity of the holy Cross in the crypt of the same church, the fraternity of the blessed Mary upon the bridge, and servant Agnes for her marriage. The sum of 40 shillings to be divided among poor and needy people on the day of the funeral, that they may pray for the health of his soul. Torches and tapers to be provided. To wife Joan £40, the third part of the jewels, and certain goods. To son Thomas £20, a pair of beads "de lamber," a silver horn, a dagger, &c. If he should die under the age of 21, half of the money to be distributed among the poor, and the other half together with the rest of the legacies to remain to wife Joan. To son Robert Benley certain pieces of armor, as a "Jack defense," helmet, breastplate, a pair of rerebraces, two pairs of gauntlets, &c. To daughter Isabel £20, a pair of beads "de curell," &c. If she should die under age or before marriage, her legacies were to be divided, as those of Thomas in case of his death. Wife Joan to be executrix.

Proved before John Estcourt, bachelor in laws, &c., April 10th, 1417. No record of proof before the Mayor.

185.—JOHN HAVERYNG, burgess.

1416. March 6th. To be buried in the cemetery of the blessed Mary of Redcliff. Legacies to the vicar of that church for tithes, the procurators for the fabric thereof, and for bell-tolling at the accustomed times for three days between the death and burial, during which time the celebration of his exequies was to be continued; to each priest assisting thereat; the poor on the day of burial; servants John Lang and Sibilla for their good service. To the chapel of St. Thomas of Bristol a pair of red vestments of cloth of gold. To John Clerk, deacon thereof, sixpence. To each boy ministering therein one penny. To son John 40 shillings. To wife Joan, for her life, a tenement in Redeclyvestrete, situate between the tenement inhabited by William Westerley upon the south, on the one part, and that inhabited by William Laurence upon the north, on the other part, and extending from the said street to the Avon; also sixteen shops, with gardens adjoining, in the suburb of Bristol in Boketeslane, between the street of St. Thomas on the west and the garden held by William Tiler, weaver, on the east, and extending from the said lane to the garden of John Droys, late that of John Sutton; remainder to testator's children Philip, Thomas, and Joan, and their lawful issue; in default, remainder to son John and his lawful issue; in default, remainder to the right heirs of wife Joan. To the said Joan, for her life, all interest in those shops built by testator, with the gardens, meadows, &c., in the suburb in the street of St. Thomas, in a certain place lately named "Seynt mary Reckehey," which property he bought for a term of years of the procurators of the church of the blessed Mary of Redcliff; remainder to the aforesaid Philip, Thomas, and Joan. Wife Joan, Philip Hassok, and John Talbot, executors, to whom xx^s apiece.

Proved before John Storthwayt, commissary general of the Bishop of Bath and Wells, in the parish church of St. Thomas of Bristol, Oct. 7th, 1417; before Robert Russell, Mayor, and John Leicestre, Sheriff, on Monday next before the feast of the Conversion of St. Paul, 5 Henry v.

186.—WILLIAM CROPENEL.

1417. Oct. 1st. My soul to its Redeemer, and body to be buried in the crypt of the church of the blessed Nicholas at Bristol, in which two secular honest priests are to serve daily for a year at the canonical hours, and celebrate *pro anima*, not omitting a trental of the blessed Gregory (b'ti gg'); the said priests to have two marks apiece. Legacies to my vicar, the fabric of the said church, Sir Thomas Merston parish chaplain thereof, Stephen the parish clerk for bell-tolling at the mortuary offices, his fellow the suffragan, every priest celebrating in the said church and present at the offices, the fabric of the cathedral church of Worcester, each order of mendicant friars, every poor-house "vocat' Almyshouse" within the county of Bristol, Margaret wife of William Colston, William son of Richard Coferer, and his sister Cristina, Joan the maid servant of the said Richard, Alice Weremystre servant of William Normore, each of the maids of Richard Goodechild, Thomas his servant, William his son, and Isabel the sister of the said William. To the said Richard Godechilde, all testator's right and the residue of his term in a messuage in "Balwynstrete," held of the fraternity of the blessed Mary on the bridge of Bristol. Ten marks to be distributed to the poor and needy on the day of burial, or as soon after as convenient. Woollen and linen cloth, to the value of xlvj^s viij^d, for bedridden poor people "& alijs mis'abilibz p'sonis." Residue of goods for pious uses. The aforesaid Richard Coferer to be executor, and Sir Richard Peutrer overseer; to whom xl^s apiece.

Proved before Robert Russell, Mayor, &c., on Wednesday in the morrow of St. Edmund Archbishop, 5 Henry v. Previously proved before the ecclesiastical authorities.

187.—THOMAS MALVERNE, burgess.

1416. July 6th. My body to the earth. To the cathedral church of Worcester vj^d. To daughter Joan and her heirs a tenement with garden and shop adjoining in Stepstret. The tenement situate between the hospital of St. Bartholomew of Bristol on the one part, and Stepstret on the other, with all "cotagijs siue Shopis" in Horsestrete, to be sold for payment of debts, and the residue of the money to be distributed for the health of testator's soul. To William Pownam, brewer, a term in shops held of the prioress and sisters of the house or hospital of the blessed Mary Magdalene on St. Michael's hill, situate between a tenement of David Dudbroke and the shop of Agnes Morys. Sir William Tye, chaplain, and Thomas Walsche, weaver, to be executors, and Sir John Boure, rector of St. Michael's, overseer. Furthermore, I will that my lord the Bishop of Worcester have the proving of my will, "Quia no' habeo bona in aliqua alia dioc' q'm in dioc' Wygorn'."

Proved before the Mayor and Sheriff of Bristol on Wednesday next before the feast of St. Martin in the winter, 4 Henry v. No record of proof before the ecclesiastical authorities.

188.—JOHN DROYS, burgess.

1417. Jan. 24th. To be buried in the chapel of St. John the Evangelist on the Back of Avon. For funeral expenses £20. Legacies to the vicar and fabric of the church of St. Nicholas of Bristol, each chaplain thereof taking part in the mortuary offices, and the four orders of friars. To wife Isabel the messuage inhabited by John Draper, with two shops and cellars, in the suburb of Bristol at the end of the bridge, between the shop inhabited by Thomas Turnour and the gate called "Seint Nicholasyate;" also four shops in Worshipstrete between the said gate and the shop held by Walter Clerk "Boucher;" six messuages in Redeclyvestrete, inhabited by Henry Brent, David Hopkyns, Robert Benet, Peter Chaloner, John Gonette (?), and Ralph Lombard; two messuages in Tonkerstret, inhabited by Richard Borton and John Lese; a rent issuing from a tenement inhabited by John Malyns, cardmaker, in that street; two messuages in Templestrete, inhabited by Robert Harrys and John Merston; a rent issuing from what was lately the tenement of Henry Glasier in Worshipstrete; a shop with cellar at the end of the bridge, inhabited by the aforesaid Thomas Turnour; a large garden, with houses and dovehouse therein, lying within the suburb of the town, in the market, and held by testator; also two gardens in the market, one of them held by him, and the other held of him by Robert Russell: this property to be held by the said Isabel for her life, on condition of keeping herself sole and chaste. If she did not, the executors were to expel her, and immediately sell it. The reversion of the said messuages, shops, gardens, and rents to be sold within two years after testator's death, and the money applied to pious uses. To William Nele, burgess of Bristol, and his wife Alice, the messuage inhabited by them in Cristenmastrete in the suburb. Wife Isabel, David Duddebroke, and John Draper, executors. Thomas Blount overseer. Witnessed by Sir John Vaghan, vicar of St. Nicholas's, William Nele, John Bolton, and others.

Proved before the Mayor and Sheriff on Monday next after the feast of St. Gregory Pope, 5 Henry v. Previously proved before the ecclesiastical authorities.

189.—WILLIAM HURDEMAN, burgess.

1417. March 28th. To be buried in the church of St. Thomas the Martyr at Bristol "coram magna cruce." Legacies to the fabric and vicar of that church, the fabric of the chapel of the blessed Mary on the bridge of Bristol, Joan elder daughter of William Boghan the elder, and Joan "sorori sue," Isabel Thoms', Elen Broun, William son of Edmund Broun, and his sisters. The whole of testator's moveable effects, on this side the sea and beyond the sea, to be divided into three parts; one for wife Joan, the second for son William and daughters Agnes and Elizabeth, the third, after payment of legacies, to be divided into three portions, two of which to remain to the said three children, and the other *pro anima*. If son William should die under age, his portion to remain to the said Agnes and Elizabeth. To wife Joan all household vessels, except cups, masers, and spoons, of which she is to have the third part, and the children the rest. To the said Joan four shops, with garden, &c., in Templestrete, situate between property of Sir Thomas Broke knt. and the lane called Hundelane in the corner, and extending from the aforesaid street to "lawdiche;" to be held by her until son William shall arrive "ad etatem suam competentem," when the property is to pass to him and his lawful issue. In default of issue, rem. to dau. Agnes; in def., rem. to dau. Elizabeth; in def., rem. to wife Joan, if still living, and after her decease, to Edmund Broun and his lawful issue; in def., the said property to be disposed of *pro anima* by William Kylderton and the executors of the said Edmund. If dau. Elizabeth should die under age, or before marriage, William and Agnes to have her effects. Wife Joan, Edmund Broun, to whom xl^s, and William Kilderton, to whom xx^s, executors.

Proved before John Nuton, Mayor, and John Leicestre, Sheriff, Oct. 31st, 6 Henry v. Previously proved before the ecclesiastical authorities.

190.—ROBERT LODELOW, shoemaker and burgess.

1418. July 16th. To be buried in the cemetery of holy Cross Temple of Bristol. To the work of my mother church of Wells xxd. To the sustentation of the chapel of the blessed Mary "ex' ostium eccl'ie se'e Crucis

Templi p'dict' vjs viijd," Legacies also to the vicar of that church, Thomas Fylle the clerk, each chaplain celebrating therein, and for funeral expenses. To son William 100 shillings sterling, and a cup bound with silver "vocatu' Note," to be had after the death of wife Agnes. To son Roger the same sum, also a girdle, and a dagger bound with silver. If either son should die within age, his goods to remain to the other. If both should die, the goods were to be expended on celebrations in the aforesaid chapel of the blessed Mary, and for other pious purposes. Wife Agnes and John Brues to be executors. Sir William Cragge, chaplain, overseer.

Proved before John Storthwayt, bachelor of laws, canon of the church of Wells, and commissary general of the Bishop of B. and W., Sept. 19th, 1418; afterwards before the Mayor and Sheriff of Bristol.

191.—ALICE NEWCOMBE.

1418. Sept. 20th. Testatrix was relict of Walter Newcombe of Bristol, and desired to be buried in the chapel of St. Nicholas within the church of the blessed Mary of Redcliff. Legacies to the fabric and vicar of that church, every priest celebrating there, both the clerks, and each clerk singing and reading therein, the cathedral church of St. Andrew of Wells "matr' eccl'ie mee," each order of mendicant friars, and Richard Pedewell. To Thomas Eston, a loom, three sleys, &c.; also a tenement in Redeclyvestrete, held of testatrix by Richard Blakemore for a term of sixty years, the tenement inhabited by testatrix, "inxta Templeyate," a garden in Templestrete, three shops with gardens upon Redcliff hill, a croft called "le Mullewey" by the road where one goes to Trynelmulle, and a garden held of testatrix by John Cabell in Pilestrete; this property to be held by the said Thomas Eston for his life, and the reversion to be afterwards disposed of *pro anima*. The said Thomas to distribute vjs viijd in bread to the poor and needy every year during his life. To kinsman John Wetham, for his life, the two shops occupied by him, together with a certain parcel of garden; the said property to be sold "vt in ren'sione," and the money expended as directed above. The procurators of the parish church of Poulet to have yearly iijs iiijd sterling, for twenty years, and keep the anniversary of testatrix and that of her husband Walter. Thomas Eston and John Bloys executors; to the latter xxs.

Proved before John Nuton, Mayor, &c., March 27th, 7 Henry v. Previously proved before John Estcourt, bachelor in laws, &c.

192.—RICHARD BOKELOND, brewer and burgess.

1418. Dec. 15th. To be buried in the parish church of holy Cross Temple of Bristol, diocese of Bath and Wells, by my pew (inx' sedem meam). Legacies to the work of that church, Sir Richard the vicar, and each priest celebrating therein; to servant Thomas Smyth, apprentice Richard Young, and John Suelle. Certain household goods, as brazen vessels, &c., to testator's three daughters, Alice, Margery, and Joan; rem. to wife Joan, in case of their death under age. To Richard Dollyng and his wife Cristina, for their life, the tenement held of testator and inhabited by them, paying yearly to his wife Joan, and to his heirs after her decease, 20 shillings sterling for four years after his death, and 40 shillings after the lapse of the said four years ; the said Richard and Cristina within those four years to repair the front of the said tenement, commonly called *Jares*, at their own cost, except that they were to have the oak timber which was in that tenement and in testator's dwelling house. To daughter Alice Bokelond, for her life, after the decease of wife Joan, a tenement in the suburb in Temple-street, situate between tenements inhabited by John Broun and John Hellewyse ; rem. to daughter Joan Bokelond for her life ; rem. to daughter Margery Bokelond for her life ; rem. to son Richard Bokelond and his heirs. To John Grynder, a green gown with a fur, and a hood of the livery of St. Katharine. Wife Joan and Richard Dollyng executors.

Proved before the Mayor and Sheriff, March 27th, 7 Henry v. Previously proved before John Storthwayt.

193.—ADAM INHYN, burgess.

1418. Jan. 27th. To be buried in the church of the blessed Mary "de fforo," before the altar of St. Katharine the Virgin, beside the body of late wife Maud. To the said church, for making windows of glass, 100 shillings sterling. A fit chaplain to celebrate *pro anima* for four years at the altar of St. Katharine in that church, and have £20. To every chaplain present at the mass, &c., four pence. Forty shillings' worth of wax to be burned about testator's body at the mortuary offices ; and twelve poor men to carry torches at the same, and have a new gown of frize apiece. Thirty shillings to be distributed to the poor in bread on the day of the funeral in the aforesaid church. Legacies to the mother church of Worcester, each order of mendicant friars at Bristol, John Sutton, son of wife Katharine, Alice sister of the said John, servant Humphrey, late servant Henry, and Sir Stephen Blancombe, rector of my parish church aforesaid. To son William ten pounds " in pecunia munerata," and cups of the weight of twelve ounces of silver ; also to him and his heirs two messuages with four shops in front, situate in the suburb on "le Were," and held by Joan Tanner. To son Thomas ten pounds, &c., and two messuages situate in the same part, and inhabited by Alice Waterfall and John Cokkes. To son John, the elder, ten pounds, &c., and two messuages situate in the same part, and inhabited by John Glover and Henry Bagpath. To son John, the younger, ten pounds, &c., and a messuage in the suburb on St. James's Back, inhabited by Alia Peyntom ; also a messuage in the parish of St. Stephen, opposite " le churchestile," between the tenement of James Cokkes on the west, and the common gutter on the east ; and eight shillings of rent from the tenement inhabited by William Pownham in Lewynsmede. To daughter Margaret ten pounds, &c., and five shops with gardens in the suburb on "le Were," situate between a tenement of testator and one of the prior and convent of "Chartehouse ;" also two cellars in the town of Bristol, situate in the street of St. Nicholas, and for a long time occupied by testator. To wife Katharine, for her life, fifteen shops in the suburb in Berelane, three drying-rooms in Templecombe, and a tenement lately held by William atte Welle opposite the said shops ; remainder to testator's rightful heirs. Wife Katharine and the aforesaid Stephen Bancombe (*sic*) to be executors.

Proved before John Nuton, Mayor, &c., April 5th, 7 Henry v. Previously proved before the ecclesiastical authorities.

194.—FELICIA HOLEWEY.

1417. Sept. 23rd. Testatrix describes herself as of the parish "b'te Marie de fforo Bristoll' Wygornien' dioc'," and desires to be buried in the chancel of the church there, beside her late husband Edward Forster. To the fabric of that church xx^s; to Sir Stephen the rector, for tithes and offerings, x^s; to the water-bearer xij^d. A fit chaplain to celebrate therein for four years for the soul of late husband Edward Forster, &c., and have £20. The same sum for funeral expenses and the poor. Legacies to the mother church of Worcester, each order of friars at Bristol, the fabric of the church of the Carmelites, and friar John Camylle of that order. To late servant John Gele and his heirs, a shop in the town of Bristol in "la Cokenerewe" inhabited by Thomas Dagyn, cook. To late servant Roger Androw "Boucher" and his heirs, the rent due from Cristina Hede, late wife of John Hede, tucker, formerly, burgess of Bristol, for a tenement, held of testatrix, opposite the parish church of St. Peter of Bristol, with reversion of the same after the said Cristina's death. To servant Thomas Seysell and his heirs, a garden in the suburb "sup' le Casteldyche" between the garden held by William Beneley and a certain lane leading "de le Casteldyche versus le Watryngplace ib'm." Residue of goods to the said Thomas. He and Edward Googh "parchemynmaker" to be executors. To the latter 20 shillings.

Proved before William Burdon, clerk, commissary and sequestrator general of the Bishop of Worcester, Jan. 4th, 1418; afterwards before the Mayor.

195.—JOHN FRERE, burgess.

1419. Aug. 20th. To be buried in the chapel of St. Thomas the Martyr of Bristol, beside wife Margery. Legacies to the perpetual vicar of Redcliff, the said chapel, each order of mendicant friars, the fraternity of the blessed Katharine at the Temple, and the fraternity of the blessed Mary outside the entrance of the Temple. To the fraternity of St. John Baptist in Bristol ten shillings. Testator's moveable goods to be distributed in three parts; one for wife Joan, the second for the children in equal portions, the residue of the third for sons John, Roger, Thomas, and Richard, and daughters Agnes, Isabel, and Joan, in equal portions. If these should die under age, the said residue of the third part to be equally divided between my sons Robert and Henry. If all the children should die under age, the said moveable goods to be disposed of *pro anima*. To son Robert and his lawful issue, a tenement in the suburb in St. Thomas's street, situate between a tenement of Sir Thomas Broke knt. and Mark Spaynell's tenement, and extending from the street to Lawdych. In default of issue, rem. to son Thomas and his lawful issue; in def., rem. to son John and his lawful issue; in def., rem. to son Roger and his lawful issue; in def., rem. to son Richard and his lawful issue; in def., rem. to son Henry and his lawful issue; in def., rem. to daughters Agnes, Isabel, and Joan, and their lawful issue; in def., rem. to son Walter for his life; afterwards to Thomas, son of the said Walter, and the lawful heirs of the said Thomas. To son Henry and his heirs, a tenement in Templestrete, situate between a tenement of the chief lord of the Temple fee, on the one part, and a tenement of the procurators of the Temple church, on the other, and extending from the said street to Lawediche. In def. of issue, rem. to son

Roger and his heirs ; in def., rem. to son John and his heirs ; in def., rem. to son Thomas and his heirs ; in def., rem. to son Robert and his heirs ; in def., rem. to son Richard and his heirs ; in def., rem. to daughters Agnes, Isabel, and Joan, and their lawful issue; in def., rem. to son Walter for his life ; afterwards to Thomas, son of the said Walter. If Thomas should die s.p., the said two tenements were to be sold by the Mayor and Bailiffs of Bristol, and the money distributed by them *pro anima* ; " et capiet dns' Maior p' labore suo sup' vendic'oe p'dict' viginti solid' st'ling," and each Bailiff ten shillings. Robert Collevyle, and Thomas Colyns, " burgens' ville," executors.

Proved before James Cokkes, Mayor, and David Ruddok, Sheriff, on Monday next before the feast of the Purification of B.V.M., 7 Henry v. Previously proved before the ecclesiastical authorities.

196.—SIMON OLYVER, burgess.

1419. May 2nd. Testator describes himself as of the parish of St. Peter, and desires to be buried in the church there, under the stone prepared by him for his monument, and under which his former wife Agnes lies. To his brother John Olyver, his dwelling house, and four shops built by him in St. Peter's street, heretofore, " ante edificac'oem p'me fact'," called " le plase sc'i Petri ;" also his tenements in Lewynsmede. To Joan Boxwell, who was relict of Robert Boxwell, and guardian of testator's person after his wife Agnes departed, the sum of twelve marks six shillings and eight pence, for her good guardianship, the money to be levied by the same Joan, or by her assigns, " temp'ibz obligac'onum a Joh'e Sherp " formerly Mayor of the town of Bristol, as it is more plainly contained in the letters of the bonds. Sir Thomas Lye, rector of St. Peter's, James Cokkes, and John Boxwell, executors. Witnessed by Thomas Perys, Thomas Wylmott of Bristol, and others.

Proved before the commissary of the Prior of Worcester, " sede vacante," May 10th, 1419 ; before the Mayor, on Wednesday next before the feast of the Nativity of St. John Baptist, 7 Henry v.

197.—JOHN GOODSON, burgess.

1419. Sept. 5th. To be buried in the cemetery of St. Nicholas of Bristol. Legacies to the fabric of that church, the vicar, and each chaplain celebrating therein ; to John Cole, apprentice Agnes Pegge, John son of testator's sister, the nuns of Barowe, John Lucas, chaplain, John Piers, John Talbot servant of the said John Piers, Isabel daughter of John Covyntre, and each of the four convents of friars, who were to celebrate *pro anima*. Thirteen poor men to be clothed in russet gowns and hoods, and have a shirt and pair of shoes apiece. All testator's effects to be divided into three equal parts ; one for wife Margaret, the second for son John. "Tercia vero p's sit michi hoc modo "--the half of my part to my brother John, for the allowance (exhibic'oem) and support of my mother, and of John my sister's son. To brother John two gowns, &c. The legacies of son John to be in the keeping of John Peris during his minority. If he should die under age, one part of them to be disposed of for the good of testator's soul, and the souls of all the faithful dead ; the other for wife Margaret. Brother John Godeson and John Peris executors.

Proved before the Mayor, &c., on Monday next before the feast of St. Luke Evangelist, 7 Henry v. Previously proved before the ecclesiastical authorities.

198.—ROBERT BONCE, weaver and burgess.

1408 (1418?). March 17th. To be buried in the church of the blessed Mary of Redcliff, before the altar of St. Blaise, by the grave of son John. To the work of that church xxxiij[s] iiij[d]. To the vicar, for tithes, vj[s] viij[d]. A fit chaplain to celebrate *pro anima* at the said altar for two years, and have yearly eight marks. Twenty marks for funeral expenses. To wife Agnes, for her life, two tenements with gardens adjoining in Redclyvestrete, situate between the tenement inhabited by Robert Browne and Houndenlane, and extending from the street to "le Lawdiche ;" rem. to son John and his lawful issue; in def., rem. to daughter Agnes and her lawful issue. To the said Agnes, two shops in Wynchestrete, situate between a tenement of the prior of St. James in Bristol and one of the prioress of "Bargh," and extending from the street to the land of the said prior. To wife Agnes all household vessels. To son John 20 marks, twelve whole cloths, &c. To the mother church of St. Andrew of Wells vj[s] viij[d]. To the work of the church of Compton Dando, co. Somerset, "ad orand' p' a'ia mea," vj[s] viij[d]. Legacies also to David Hopkyn, tucker, Sir Thomas Godefelawe, chaplain, and William Lygh, testator's apprentice. Wife Agnes, son John, and Thomas Filour, mercer, to be executors.

Proved before James Cokkes, Mayor, &c., on Monday next before the feast of Simon and Jude Apostles, 7 Henry v. Previously proved before the ecclesiastical authorities.

199.—RICHARD WYKYNG, burgess.

1419. Aug. 20th. To be buried in the church of holy Cross Temple. All testator's lands and tenements in the town and suburb of Bristol to be sold, and the money bestowed "in pios vsus & in alijs elemosinis" for the good of his soul, his wife Julian's, &c. To John Broun and his wife Beatrix three pounds of silver, half a dozen silver spoons, &c. To the same Beatrix a chest "vocat' Sprnys tye." The said John Broun and John Chepman "Wexmaker" to be executors, and have xiij[s] iiij[d]. apiece.

Proved before John Storthwayt, in the parish church of St. Thomas of Bristol, Sept. 13th, 1419; afterwards before the Mayor.

200.—MARGARET GLOUCESTRE.

1420. Monday, May 20th. Testatrix describes herself as daughter and heir of Thomas Gloucestre, late a burgess of the town of Bristol, and desires to be buried among the Carmelite Friars, beside the tomb of her said father. To Alice wife of Walter atte Rode a pair of beads "de Coraille." To Margaret Grove a gown of green and kirtle of red. The residue of clothing to be distributed *pro anima*. To brother John Coton, and Agnes his wife, sister of testatrix, and their heirs, lands, tenements, rents, and services in the town and suburb of Bristol, together with all the property held by John Burbage for his life, also a tenement in the town of Gloucester in Oxbodelane, and a tenement, with lands, meadows, &c., in Brislington, co. Somerset. The said John Coton and his wife Agnes to be executors. To the latter a chaplet and fillet of pearls.

Proved before the Mayor, &c., on Monday next after the feast of St. Laurence Martyr, 8 Henry v. Previously proved before the ecclesiastical authorities.

201.—JOHN POWLYSHAM, merchant and burgess.

1420. Oct. 8th. To be buried in the church of holy Cross Temple of Bristol, to the fabric of which a table-cloth, to pay for his interment. Legacies also to the vicar, every other chaplain celebrating in that church on the day of testator's death, Richard Cabull, clerk thereof, Thomas Fyll, clerk, the fabric of the mother church of Wells, each order of friars at Bristol, William Bowde, servant of John Hawley, and my daughter Joan Bowde. For funeral expenses xl^s. Testator's dwelling house and garden " in vico Templi," situate between a messuage of the abbot and convent of the blessed Mary of Keynsham and his own shop, and extending from the King's way to Lawdiche, to be sold by the executors for the benefit of divers lame and needy poor people. To Maud Wyppay, for her life, on account of the good service rendered by her to testator, his said shop, with two selions of land annexed to the garden of his house, situate between the said house and the shops of Joan late wife of Sir Thomas Brook knt. The reversion of testator's property to be disposed of by the executors, namely, John Jaye, tucker and burgess of Bristol, and Maud Whyppay (*sic*).

Proved before John Storthwayt, bachelor of laws, canon and succentor of the cathedral church of Wells, in the said cathedral church, Dec. 7th, 1420; before Thomas Yonge, Mayor of Bristol, and Roger Lyveden, Sheriff, on Wednesday next after the feast of the Conception of B.V.M., 8 Henry v.

202.—WILLIAM PAYS, burgess.

1420. May 17th. To be buried in church of St. Thomas the Martyr of Bristol. To dau. Agnes, a girdle of silver and gilt, formerly the property of Agnes testator's mother, " de qua due zone modo sunt fact' p'cij xxxiij^s iij^d." Also to the aforesaid Agnes, at present unmarried, and to her lawful issue, three shops in the suburb of Bristol, in St. Thomas's street, situate between the tenement of John Wodevile, inhabited by John Garnet, on the one part, and that of Henry Bokerell, inhabited by Hugh Avynee, on the other; in def. of issue, rem. to son John and his lawful issue ; in def., rem. to son Thomas and his lawful issue ; the said property to be disposed of *pro anima*, if Thomas died s.p. To son John and his heirs, two tenements in St. Thomas's street, situate between a tenement of the procurators of Redcliff church and one of Thomas Yong, inhabited by Philip Hassok and John Pycheford ; in def., rem. to daughter Agnes and her lawful issue ; in def., rem. to son Thomas ; to be sold, if Thomas died s.p. To the said Thomas testator's whole state and term in three shops in Templestrete, situate between the tenement of John Bokerell and " le langrewe ; and in two shops in "le langrewe," between a tenement of the procurators of holy Cross Temple and the aforesaid shops. If all the children died within the state and term, the executors were to sell, and distribute the money in alms. To son John and his lawful issue, a shop with garden in Templestrete, situate between the tenement of John Arthur esquire, held by Roger Wellischotte, on the one part, and the tenement inhabited by William Baker, on the other ; rem. to Richard Mason, weaver, and his heirs and assigns, if all testator's children should die s.p. To daughter Agnes, the whole state in a hall and two shops in Redeclyvestrete, between the tenement of John Langley, on the one part, and one of testator's tenements, on the other, lately inhabited by Richard Blakemore; to be disposed of by the executors *pro anima*, if all testator's children should die "infra statum." To son John, a baselard, &c., also a weaver's loom, worth xxxiij^s iiij^d, in the occupation of Parice. To son Thomas, a silver cup weighing xxvij oz., two brass pots, worth ix^s, &c. The said John and Thomas were under age. Residue of goods to wife Alice. Roger Lyveden and Thomas Colyns executors. Witnessed by Sir William Duddellesbury, vicar of Redcliff, Sir William Skragge, John Gosham, and others.

Proved in the church of All Saints, Bristol, diocese of Worcester, before Sir Thomas Marchall, perpetual vicar of the said church, Nov. 28th, 1420; before Thomas Yonge, Mayor, &c., on Friday next before the feast of Pentecost, 9 Henry v.

203.—SIMON WALSH, burgess.

1420. May 4th. To be buried in the cemetery of the church of holy Cross Temple at Bristol. To the work of the cathedral church of Wells iiij^d. To son John, ten marks sterling, six silver spoons, &c.; to remain, in case of his death, to wife Katharine, who is to dispose therewith *pro anima*. To testator's apprentice Dionisius, some cloth according to the discretion of the said Katharine, who is to have the residue of goods, and be co-executor with John Baskervile. To the latter vj^s viij^d sterling.

Proved before John Storthwait, but no date is given; and there is no record of proof before the Mayor.

204.—JOHN ROBYNS, burgess.

1420. May 1st. To be buried in the cemetery of St. Stephen of Bristol. Legacies to the rector of the church there, the mother church of Worcester, the poor, and each order of friars at Bristol. To Joan, wife of testator, his dwelling house, and the third part of all his goods; the second part to be for his children " Ric'o Joh'e Joh'e Joh'e & Alicie," in equal portions; but, in case of their death, to be divided equally, one portion "p' salute a'ie mee," the other for wife Joan. She, and Richard Fynche, and his wife Katharine, executors.

Proved before the ecclesiastical authorities, June 8th, 1420. No record of proof before the Mayor.

205.—WILLIAM WORCESTRE, the elder, burgess.

1420. Oct. 20th. To be buried in the east corner of St. James's cemetery at Bristol, beside Sir Richard, formerly parish chaplain of that church. Legacies to the prior of St. James, for tithes, each monk there, the parish chaplain of the aforesaid church, and every chaplain celebrating therein, the fabric of the chapel of the blessed Mary on the bridge of Avon, each order of mendicant friars at Bristol, and the cathedral church of Worcester. Ten pounds of wax to burn about testator's body on the day of his burial. Twenty shillings sterling for the poor and decrepit, and bedridden sick people, having two or three children. To wife Joan, for her life, a tenement in the suburb of Bristol "in le Brodemede," situate between a curtilage of the prior and brethren of the Kalendaries, on the one part, and what was formerly the tenement of Henry Stanley, now inhabited by John Bole, on the other, and extending from the King's way in front to the course of the Frome behind; to be disposed of *pro anima* after her decease. Also to her, for her life, a tenement in the same part, situate between what was lately the tenement of Walter Taunton, inhabited by John Harry "whyttewyer," on the one part, and what was lately the curtilage of John atte Celer, inhabited by John Tiler, glover, on the other; rem. to Joan Griffethe, wife of Thomas Griffethe, mariner, and to Geoffrey their son; to be religiously disposed of after the death of the said Geoffrey Griffethe. Wife Joan and John Prowte "whittewyer" executors. To the latter vj^s viij^d.

Proved before John Spyne, Mayor, and Edmund Browne and Richard Arvas, Bailiffs, on Monday next after the feast of St. Matthias Apostle, 9 Henry v. Previously proved before John Byrymore, clerk, sequestrator and commissary general of the Bishop of Worcester.

206.—JOHN HEYTESBURY, weaver and burgess.

1422. Dec. 3rd. To be buried in the cemetery of the blessed Thomas the Martyr. Legacies to the vicar of Redcliff, and Sir Richard parish chaplain there, elder daughter Agnes, and John Bayon. To younger daughter Agnes £10 sterling, and a bowl of silver, price xx^s. If the said Agnes should die "an'q'm alicui viro fu'it disponsata in facie eccl'ie," her said legacies to be equally divided between wife Joan and daughter Agnes, wife of Robert Bayon. To the said Joan ten marks sterling, and all household utensils. For funeral expenses xx^s. Residue *pro anima*. Robert Bayon and John Yevyll executors. To the former a whole cloth "de plonket."

Proved before William Brett, clerk, commissary general of the Bishop of Bath and Wells, March 8th, 1422. No record of proof before the Mayor.

207.—THOMAS SHIRWYN, burgess.

1422. March 6th. To be buried "in terra sac' sc'i Thome" at Bristol. Four pence to each priest celebrating there, and taking part in the funeral rites. Legacies also to the vicar of Redcliff, the fabric of St. Andrew's church, son John, and daughter Joan. To wife Isabel, and her heirs, all testator's interest in a shop (schopa) opposite the church of Holy Trinity, situate between property of the prioress and sisters of the house of the blessed Mary Magdalene, on the east, and what was formerly a tenement of Walter Derbi, on the west, and extending from the street to a tenement of the abbot of St. Augustine of Bristol; also for her life, six shops in St. Thomas's lane, on condition of her granting to son Matthew one house called "Tanhowse" situate in the messuage inhabited by testator, with two chambers and cellar, one pertaining to the work of a baker, the other called "banyschambre;" the six shops to revert, after the death of wife Isabel, to the said Matthew and his heirs. She and son Matthew to be executors.

Proved before Mark William, Mayor, and Thomas Erle and John Piers, Bailiffs, on Wednesday in the morrow of St. Matthew Apostle and Evangelist, 2 Henry vi. Previously proved before William Britt, clerk.

208.—JOHN GY, burgess.

1424. March 28th. To be buried in the parish church of St. Stephen of Bristol, to which, for his burial, xxxiij^s iiij^d. To the rector of that church vj^s viij^d, on condition of his permitting the executors freely to arrange the tapers and torches burning about testator's body. One mass, with *placebo* and *dirige*, to be daily celebrated therein for thirty days after his burial. To the parish chaplain there xx^d. To the fabric of the mother church of Worcester vj^s viij^d. Legacies to the prior of St. James, and the parish chaplain of that church, each order of mendicant friars at Bristol, the fabric of the chapel of the blessed Mary of Redcliff, that of the chapel of the blessed Mary of Kingswood, and that of the parish church of St. Peter of Saltwyche; to the hungry and naked poor, and the inmates of the almshouses of Langrewe and within Temple-gate. Testator's effects, after payment of debts, to be divided into three parts; the first to be disposed of *pro anima*, the second for his wife Alice, the third for his sons and daughters in equal portions. Two chaplains to celebrate for a whole year in the parish church of St. James of Bristol, and have sixteen marks. Ten marks for the celebration "optima forma" of two trentals of St. Gregory. Six marks for the liberation of prisoners. "Jt'm q'd delib'ac'o vnins cuinsq' non p'cedat xl^d." Residue of goods to be bestowed for the welfare of testator's soul in the seven works of mercy. Wife Alice and Philip Faunt executors. To the latter xl^s. Thomas Halewey overseer. Witnessed by John Chapeleyn, John Hosschekyns, Thomas Whelyngton, and others.

Proved before John Byrymore, clerk, &c., in the parish church of St. James of Bristol, May 23rd, 1424. No record of proof before the Mayor.

209.—WALTER FROMPTON, burgess.

1423. May 5th. To be buried in the cemetery of holy Cross Temple of Bristol, to the vicar of which church, for tithes and offerings, vj^d, and each chaplain celebrating therein ij^d. To son John and his heirs, a hall in Temple-strete, situate between a tenement of Isabel Droys and that of Robert Sachefield, on condition that John Lymnour and John Godehyne, both of Bristol, receive yearly the rent of the said hall, until the sum owing by testator to William Vynour, citizen of London, be wholly paid by the same John Lymnour and John Godehyne, and that testator's wife Alice have, for her life, a shop and two chambers heretofore pertaining to the said hall; rem. to son John and his heirs and assigns for ever. To the said Alice two shops in the market, situate between a tenement of John Leyoetur and one of the abbot of Keynsham; rem. to son John. Residue of goods to be disposed of *pro anima* by the said Alice. She and my vicar Richard Janys to be executors.

Proved before John Borton, Mayor, and Thomas Halewey, Sheriff, on Wednesday next before the feast of St. Michael Archangel, 3 Henry vi. Previously proved before William Brett, clerk.

210.—JOHN HETHE, burgess and merchant.

1423. Wednesday next before the feast of the Annunciation of B.V.M. To be buried in the crypt of the parish church of St. Nicholas at Bristol, "coram ymagine se'e Crucis ib'm." Legacies to the fabric and vicar of that church, every chaplain thereof attending the funeral, and the chaplain who shall celebrate *pro anima* therein for a whole year ; to the fabric of the cathedral church of Worcester, each convent of friars at Bristol, and apprentice John Wise. To daughter Alice, £20 of good English money for her marriage, and 100 shillings for her chamber. To son John Hethe, and his heirs and assigns, all testator's lands, tenements, rents, reversions, and services in the town and suburb of Bristol, and residue of goods. The said John, dau. Alice, and Walter Carpynter, executors. To the the last named xx^s. Witnessed by Maurice Jones, clerk, Walter Carpynter, Thomas Badron, and others.

Proved before John Leycestre, Mayor, and Thomas Halleway, Sheriff, on Friday next after the feast of St. Luke Apostle and Evangelist, 3 Henry vi. Previously proved before the ecclesiastical authorities.

211.—RICHARD STEPHENES, tanner and burgess.

1421. In the feast of St. Vincent Martyr. To be buried in the church of St. James the Apostle at Bristol, to the fabric of which vj^s viij^d, and the same sum to the high altar thereof. A chaplain to celebrate *pro anima* therein, at the altar of B.V.M. for three years. To the fabric of the mother church of Worcester viij^d. To each of the orders of Friars Preachers, Carmelites, and Minors, ij^s vj^d. To son Thomas, for his life, after the death of wife Joan, the reversion of a messuage, with a curtilage adjoining, in the street called Brodemede, in the suburb, between what were formerly the tenements of John Somerwell and Thomas atte Hay, and extending from the street aforesaid to a tenement of the prior of St. James ; which tenement testator had of the gift and feoffment of Hugh Carleton, burgess of the town of Bristol, and John Richardes. The sum of xxvj^s viij^d to be bestowed among the poor on the day of burial ; and testator's anniversary to be kept yearly in the aforesaid church of St. James, first by son Thomas, and afterwards by the guardians and procurators of that church, to which the said messuage is to revert. Residue of goods to wife Joan. She, the said Thomas, and Edward Rede, executors. To the last named xiij^s iiij^d.

Proved before John Leycestre, Mayor, and Thomas Erle, Sheriff, on Wednesday next after the feast of St. Maurus Abbot, 3 Henry vi. Previously proved before John Byrymore, commissary general of the Bishop of Worcester.

212.—CECILY BUSSCHOPE. In the margin *Busshoppe*.

1422. Feb. 26th. Testatrix was relict of John Busschoppe, weaver, late a burgess of the town of Bristol, desired to be buried in the cemetery of the parish church of St. Peter in the same town, and bequeathed four pence to the mother church of Worcester. To John Shareshull of Bristol, weaver, and his heirs, a garden in the suburb, opposite the cemetery of the parish church of St. Philip, between the garden of Henry Gildeney, on the east, and the King's way as one goes towards "le Kyngesmerssch," on the west, and extending from what was lately the garden of John Beverley, on the north, to the lane called "seint Philipeslane," on the south. Residue of goods to the aforesaid John Shareshull, who was to dispose *pro anima*, and be executor.

Proved before John Byrymore, in the parish church of St. Augustine the Less of Bristol, May 7th, 1423. No record of proof before the Mayor.

213.—ISABEL SHEREWYN.

1422. March 9th. Testatrix was late wife of Thomas Sherewyn of Bristol, and desired to be buried in St. Thomas's cemetery. To daughter Joan, twelve pounds of white wool, two girdles, &c.; also part of a shop in Wynchestrete, opposite the church of the Holy Trinity. Legacies to son Matthew, son John, and Richard Shirwyn. The said Matthew and my brother Richard Shirwyn executors.

Proved before William Brett, clerk, &c., July 12th, 1430 *(sic)*; before the Mayor and Sheriff on Friday in the feast of St. Cedde Bishop, 3 Henry vi.

214.—THOMAS FYLER, mercer.

1425. Oct. 8th. To be buried in the church of All Saints of Bristol, or wherever it shall please God. To the mother church of Worcester xx^d. To the fabric of All Saints' church xl^s. To Sir Thomas Marchall, vicar there, xx^s. To each chaplain celebrating therein, and present at the mortuary offices, and mass on the day of burial, vj^d. To father John Fyler and his wife Beatrix, ten marks. To sons Thomas, John, and William, ten marks apiece. To daughters Joan, Alice, Cristina, Joan *(sic)*, and Katharine, 100 shillings apiece. Legacies also to my brother Thomas Filer, sister Margery, and kinswoman Margery Baker. Residue to wife Agnes. She and brother Thomas to arrange for the funeral, &c., and be executors.

Proved before John Berymore, commissary general of the Bishop of Worcester, in the parish church of St. Augustine the Less, at Bristol, Oct. 21st, 1425. No record of proof before the Mayor.

215.—WILLIAM MOILLE, merchant.

1422. March 12th. To be buried in the crypt of St. Nicholas's church in Bristol. Legacies to the vicar thereof, and the cathedral church of Worcester. To wife Avice, all jewels, and other necessaries in the house. Residue of goods, "tam citra mare q'm vltra," to her and kinsman William Moille, of the town of Ludlow, who are to dispose *pro anima*, and be executors. Robert Russell, merchant of Bristol, overseer.

Proved before the ecclesiastical authorities April 20th, 1423. No record of proof before the Mayor.

216.—THOMAS PAPPEWORTHE, burgess.

1424. Aug. 12th. To be buried in the church of the Holy Trinity of Bristol, in which a fit chaplain was to celebrate for two years at the altar of St. Thomas the Martyr, and have sixteen marks. To the rector of that church, for tithes and offerings forgotten, iij^s iiij^d. To Sir John Chivaler, chaplain, and Thomas Caudell, clerk, iij^s iiij^d apiece. To the fabric of the the church of Worcester iij^s iiij^d. "Jt'm lego iiij^{li} ad emendac' vestiment' eccl'ie meo p'och'." Twenty chaplains to attend the funeral rites, and have vj^s viij^d equally divided among them. To wife Julian all household utensils, jewels, &c., except armor, clothing, silver girdles, baselards, and daggers. Other effects to be equally divided into three parts; the first part *pro anima*, the second part for wife Julian, the third for children John and Joan. If the said children should die under age, or Joan before marriage, their legacies were to be divided into two portions; one for wife Julian, the other to be disposed of for the welfare of testator's soul, the souls of the said John and Joan, &c. To each order of friars at Bristol v^s. To the fraternity of St. John Baptist vj^s viij^d. To son John the best girdle, " cu' om'ibz baslardis & daggeris meis." To kinsman Robert, all the armor pertaining to testator's body. Legacies also to the fraternities of St. Katharine and the Assumption of the blessed Mary, to Thomas Filour, and his wife Joan, daughter of testator. Residue of goods " in pijs op'ibz." Wife Julian and John Milton executors ; to the latter xx^s. John Bolton, to whom xx^s, overseer. Witnessed by the said Sir John Chivaler, Simon Roger, the said Thomas Filour, and others.

Proved before the ecclesiastical authorities Dec. 18th, 1425. No record of proof before the Mayor.

217.—JAMES COKKES, burgess.

1423, May 21st. To be buried " in medio corp'is eccl'ie b'te Marie de fforo Bristoll' coram ymagine sc'e Crucis existent' in australi p'te eiusdem eccl'ie." To the fabric of that church xxvj^s viij^d. To the rector, for tithes, &c., xiij^s iiij^d. To the four orders of friars xx^s apiece, that they may attend the mortuary offices, and have testator's soul in remembrance for a month, and each find one chaplain of their own order to celebrate during that time in the said church. A thousand masses to be celebrated, with all speed after the day of his death, by divers chaplains, to whom £5. Twelve poor men to be employed about his burial for a month " ad orand' cotidie," &c., and receive from the executors meat and drink every day, two pence, and a hood and gown apiece. £10 for the fulfilling of the will, for the said twelve poor men, and for keeping the obit in the best manner. £12 to be distributed among divers poor people, each to have one penny. £20 to be bestowed upon the paralytic and sick poor within four years next after testator's death ; namely, 100 shillings yearly, the sum to be laid out in meat, drink, fuel, and candles ; in the feast of All Saints 20 shillings, in the feast of the Lord's Nativity 40 shillings, and in the feast of Easter 40 shillings. Unbequeathed jewels, as silver cups, and cups called " masers & notes hernisat'," &c., to be divided into two equal parts ; one for wife Margaret, the other for Thomas Fissche, who is to pay the executors two shillings for every oz. of the better and worse. To Sir John Coterel, chaplain, vj^s viij^d yearly, for twenty years, in the feast of Easter, if he should live so long, that he might pray for testator's soul, and the souls of his parents, benefactors, &c. To younger son John £20. To elder son John £20, to free him from his debts, according to the ordering of Thomas Fissche and John Bolton. To the said Thomas, and his wife Joan, daughter of testator, after wife Margaret's decease, the great silver cup with cover, weighing 33 oz. and 3 quarters. To Joan, testator's sister, 100 shillings. To the fraternity of St. John Baptist of Bristol xx^s sterling. Legacies to Sir Thomas Holme, chaplain, servant Joan Whitman for her marriage, servants John Batyn and Margaret, Richard Fynche, Hugh Escot, John Bolton, and the prior of the house of St. James at Bristol. To wife Margaret, a messuage in Worschipstrete, situate between shops of the abbot and convent of St. Augustine of Bristol, on the one part, and the shops held by John Spyne of the prioress of St. Mary Magdalene, on the other, and extending from the said street to a certain lane leading "ad fonte' vocat' Edde welle ;" also a messuage in the same street, situate between the messuage of the said Thomas Fissche and that of Thomas Seysell, and extending from the street to the cemetery of the aforesaid St. Mary's church ; a messuage and shop in St. Mary's street, inhabited by John Grove, situate between a messuage of the said abbot and convent, on the east, and one of Dame Joan Brook, relict of Sir Thomas Brook, on the west ; a messuage in the same street, situate between a messuage of Hugh Escot, inhabited by the said Hugh, on the one part, and one of testator's messuages, inhabited by John Bern, brewer, on the other part ; a messuage, &c., in the same street, situate between property of the said abbot and convent, and of Joan Brook, relict of Sir Thomas Brook, late of co. Somerset ; also a yearly rent due from Thomas Papworthe, burgess of Bristol, and his wife Julian, for a messuage in Wynchestrete, situate between testator's messuage inhabited by Thomas Balle, on the one part, and Towrestrete on the other ; together with the reversion of that messuage after the death of the said Thomas and Julian ; and also all that " bassam domu' vocat' le Stable," held of testator by John Osteler, and situate behind the said messuage inhabited by Thomas Papworth ; the whole of the aforesaid property to be held by the said Margaret for her life, on condition of remaining sole and chaste, taking no other man as a husband, and also providing a fit chaplain to celebrate daily *pro anima* during her life, in the parish church of the blessed Mary "de lloro." If she should fail in any point, the property to pass immediately to younger son John and his lawful issue ; in default of issue, rem. to the said Thomas Fissche and his wife Joan, and issue ; in def., rem. to elder son John Cokkes, and his lawful issue ; in def., to be sold ; one half of the money to be delivered to the Mayor and Commonalty of Bristol for their use, the other for the poor and works of charity. To wife Margaret, all the state and term in a messuage, with a shop in front, in Weste Towker strete, between the Lawdiche on the one part, and testator's shop inhabited by Thomas Taillour, on the other ; also in the rent due from Michael Rob'd and his wife Joan for the same messuage and shop, held by them in virtue of testator's grant for a term of thirty years beginning in the feast of the Annunciation of B.V.M., 9 Henry v. If the said Margaret should die before the expiration of the term, the said messuage and rent to remain to younger son John, &c. Also to wife Margaret the state and term in a shop in West Towkerstrete, situate between the shop held by the said Michael and Joan, and a tenement of the prior and convent of Witham, inhabited by the said Thomas Taillour ; also the rent due from the said Thomas for the same shop, held of testator "ad volu'tate';" rem. to younger son John, &c.; also the term in a messuage in Wynchestrete, situate between the messuage inhabited by Thomas Papworthe on the east, and a messuage of the master and brethren of the fraternity of St. John Baptist of Bristol on the west ; and the rent due from Thomas Ball and his wife Alice for the messuage held by them of testator for a term of forty years beginning Oct. 1st, 9 Henry v.; rem. as before. Also to wife Margaret, a messuage in St. Mary's street, with two shops ; rem. to elder son John and his lawful issue ; in def., rem. to Thomas Fissche, and his wife

Joan, dau. of testator, and their lawful issue; in def., rem. to younger son John and his lawful issue; in def., rem. to the Mayor and Commonalty of Bristol, and the poor, &c. Also to the said Margaret, for her life, a messuage and shop in Wynchestrete, situate between the messuage of John Clyve, inhabited by John Bolton, on the one part, and a messuage of Thomas Erle, inhabited by John Draper, on the other. To younger son John, the messuage called "le Thorowhowse," with three shops, &c., situate in St. Mary's street, between a stable held by Richard Shirwyn, and a messuage inhabited by Robert Haselwell, turner; also a shop in the High-street "in rengia cocor'," between a little lane as one goes from the same street towards the church of All Saints, on the one part, and a shop of Sir John Frampton Ch'l'r, inhabited by Thomas Dugeon, on the other; also messuages, &c., in St. Mary's street, between the messuage of Hugh Escot, on the west, and that of Bernard Brewer, on the east; and two shops on the bridge of Avon, between the shop inhabited by Philip Tornour, on the one part, and that of Henry Gildeney, inhabited by Robert Beverley, on the other; in default of issue, rem. to the said Thomas Fissche, &c. To elder son John, four shops in the suburb of Bristol, by the outer gate of Frome, as one goes to the house of the Friars Minors, lately had by testator of the gift and feoffment of Thomas Malvern; also the messuage held by Robert Prowte in "le Brodemede" between a messuage of the said Thomas Fissche, on the west, and Thomas Wellyngton's garden, on the east; a shop in the same part, between the messuage of the said Thomas Fissche, on the east, and the shop of the said Thomas Wellyngton, on the west; and the rent due from John Budde and his wife Joan for a messuage in Mersschestrete, between the said Thomas Fissche's shop, on the west, and what was lately the messuage of Adam Inhyne, on the east; the said messuage being held of testator by the said John and Joan Budde for a term of twenty years from the feast of St. Michael Archangel, 7 Henry v.; together with the reversion of the said property. If elder son John should die s.p., rem. to younger son John and his lawful posterity; in def., rem. to the said Thomas Fissche, &c. Residue of goods to wife Margaret. She, Richard Fynche, younger son John Cokkes, and Hugh Escot, executors. The said Thomas Fissche and John Bolton overseers.

Proved before John Clyve, Mayor, and Robert Colvile, Sheriff, on Monday next before the feast of St. Matthew Apostle and Evangelist, 5 Henry vi. Previously proved before the ecclesiastical authorities.

218.—JOHN AILLEWARD, burgess.

1427. March 26th. To be buried "in campanili eccl'ie sc'e Werburge" at Bristol, to the fabric of which church, for the breaking of the ground, xx^s. To the fabric of the cathedral church of Worcester iij^s iiij^d. To the fraternity of St. John Baptist of Bristol, xx^s. Legacies also to the Friars Preachers, Minors, and Carmelites at Bristol, the fabric of the church of St. Leonard there, kinsman Walter Was, and Sir Richard Fraunceys. To wife Emmot, for her life, a tenement in Oldeeorn strete, situate between what was lately the tenement of William Warmystre, inhabited by William Marcus, and John Kerdif's tenement, and extending from the said street to a garden of the lord of Burnell; remainder to Agnes daughter of testator's son William Aylleward, and her lawful issue; in def., rem. to apprentice Richard Blake and his heirs and assigns. Testator's wife to have the residue of his effects, and maintain an honest chaplain of good report to celebrate *pro anima* for three years. She and Richard Blake executors. John Grissche overseer.

Proved before Thomas Mordon, clerk, commissary general of the Bishop of Worcester, in the parish church of St. John of Bristol, Aug. 26th, 1427; afterwards before the Mayor and Sheriff.

219.—THOMAS YONGE, burgess.

1426. Friday, March 14th. To be buried in the church of St. Thomas the Martyr at Bristol, before the altar of St. Nicholas. A chaplain of good and honest conversation to celebrate therein *pro anima* for one year after testator's decease, and be paid cvj^s. viij^d. Legacies to the high altar, every chaplain, and the two clerks of that church; each order of mendicant friars in Bristol, and the poor of the almshouse in "le langrewe". To wife Joan, a messuage in Templestrete, between a tenement of Thomas Blount and what was lately the tenement of John Droys; a tenement in the suburb "in vico ffullonu'," between what was lately the tenement of John Prishton of Coventry, on the one part, and that of Nicholas Devenyssch, on the other; four messuages in Templestrete, between property of Thomas Norton and Richard Dollyng; a shop at the south end of the bridge of Avon, situate between what was lately the property of John Droys and William Colyns of co. Gloucester; the rents and services due from John Brewere and John Forde, dyer, for two messuages, situate conjointly "in vico ffullonum" between what was lately a tenement of John Droys and the tenement of Reginald Jacob of Dorchester; with the reversion of the said two messuages: remainder to son Thomas Yonge and his lawful issue; in def., rem. to son John Yonge and his lawful issue; in def., rem. to daughter Alice Yonge and her lawful issue. Also to wife Joan, a shop at Bristol "in alto vico," situate between a shop belonging to the chantry of Walter Frampton, formerly burgess of Bristol, and one belonging to the chantry of Evorard le ffrenssch, formerly burgess; a messuage in the market, situate between a tenement belonging to the parish church of St. Philip of Bristol and what was lately the tenement of William Frome; six shops in the said market, situate between property of Mark William and the shops lately held by Martin Bowcher; a garden in the same part, lying between a garden of the prior of St. James in Bristol and what was lately the garden of John Barstaple; a messuage in Baldewynstrete, situate between what was formerly the property of Richard Peawtrer and Henry Frampton; a yearly rent of three shillings of silver and one pound of pepper, due from a tenement on the Back of Avon, situate between what were formerly tenements of Thomas Coventre and Robert atte Walle, which tenement was lately held by John Clyfford; the rent due from a tenement in the same part, situate between what was lately the tenement of the said John Clyfford and the common wall of the town, which tenement Elizabeth atte Walle lately held; a yearly rent of two shillings of silver, due from a tenement "in vico sc'i Nich'i," situate between what was formerly the tenement of John Cleof and a void place near what was formerly the tenement of Richard Tylly; a yearly rent due from a tenement in the same street lately held by John

Cobyndon, and situate by the tenement of Henry Honefield; a yearly rent from the void place lying between what were formerly the tenements of Henry Honefield and Richard Tylly, in the same street; and a yearly rent from a place (placea) which was formerly Robert Holhurst's, in the same street: remainder to son John and his lawful issue; in def., rem. to son Thomas and his lawful issue; in def., rem. to daughter Alice and her lawful issue. Residue of goods to be divided into three parts: one *pro anima*, another for testator's wife, the third to be parted between his said three children. His wife and son Thomas executors.

Proved before John Nuton, Mayor, and John Sherp, Sheriff, on Friday next after the feast of St. Hilary Pope, 6 Henry vi. Previously proved before the ecclesiastical authorities.

220.—THOMAS BEWFLOUR.

1426. Sept. 18th. Testator describes himself as "compos mentis mee timens mortis p'icl'm michi imminere," and desires to be buried in the church of St. Stephen, opposite the altar of St. Katharine. To the mother church ij^s. To the high altar of my parish church "p' decimis meis negligent' decimat'" xl^s. Legacies to Sir John, parish chaplain, Sir John Herford, Sir John Cadican, and each other priest (p'sbit'o) of that church attending the mortuary offices; to Edmund the clerk, and John the suffragan of the church; to my sister; to John Crede, kinswoman Isabel, servants John Cole, Joan Rederisse, and Alice, William Pavy and his wife Joan, testator's daughter. To son John, 100 marks "sub hac condicione q'd bn' & honeste h'eat se & q'd sit sub gub'nac'oe & regimine matris sue & Will'i Pavy;" which sum is to remain to wife Agnes, if John should depart first. A fit chaplain to celebrate for the soul of testator, &c., in St. Stephen's church, and have xxiiij^{li}. To Sir Robert Londe (or Loude), Scolemaistre, vj^s. viij^d. To the fabric of the church xiij^s. iiij^d. Wife Agnes to have the third part of the effects, &c., and be co-executor with son John. William Pavy overseer.

Note of proof before the ecclesiastical authorities dated Oct. 8th, 1426. No record of proof before the Mayor.

This will is also registered at Somerset House, *Luffnam*, 7, where it is said to have been made Sept. 8th, and proved Oct. 9th, 1426.

221.—DAVID RUDDOK, burgess.

1426. Nov. 16th. To be buried in the chapel of St. Thomas the Martyr of Bristol, to the vicar of which, for tithes, xx^s. Testator's effects, wheresoever found, to be divided into three parts; one for needy people, &c., the second for wife Isabel, the third to be equally divided among his children, John, Thomas, William, and Isabel. If all these should die, the said third part to be divided equally; one portion *pro anima*, the other for wife Isabel, who is also to have all household utensils, except jewels of silver, cups, spoons, &c., which are to be divided into three equal parts, as expressed above. The said Isabel to have the keeping of all the children during their minority, finding due security before the Mayor of Bristol, according to the custom of the town. Of the third portion of goods, 100 shillings for the fabric of the chapel aforesaid. Residue " p ' ai'a mea in pios vsus." Wife Isabel and son John executors. Edmund Broun and John Yhevell overseers, to whom 20 shillings apiece.

Proved before John Bernard, bachelor in laws, commissary general of the Bishop of Bath and Wells, Jan. 14th, 1420. No record of proof before the Mayor.

222.—JOHN CLYVE, burgess.

1430. Jan. 3rd. To be buried in the chapel next the chancel of the church of the Holy Trinity in Bristol. To the mother church of Worcester vj^s. viij^d. To the said church of the Holy Trinity vj^s. viij^d, and testator's best missal. A missal also to the church of St. John. To wife Isabel, and Thomas Clyve, otherwise called Thomas Berkeley, a messuage in Bradstrete, situate between the tenement of John Berdon and that of Richard Cheddre esquire, and extending from the said street to the lane called Towrestrete ; also two tenements in Knyfsmythstrete, between the shop held of testator by Thomas Lombard and what was formerly Nicholas Wareyn's tenement, which tenements are inhabited by John Parys and Bartholomew Pytte, " vestmentmaker." Also to the same Isabel and Thomas, all the lands and tenements lately acquired by the grant and feoffment of John Stephenes, late burgess of Bristol, and formerly an executor of the will of John Castell, late burgess of the same town ; lands and tenements in the parish of the Holy Trinity, namely, in the street called Pythey, and in Wynchstrete ; a messuage in the street of the blessed Mary " de floro," inhabited by William Moret ; a messuage in the street of St. Nicholas, inhabited by the vicar of St. Leonard's of Bristol, and situate between what was lately the tenement of William Berdon and a tenement of the prior of the blessed Mary of Witham of the Carthusian order; a tenement in the town of Bristol, in Fuysterlane, inhabited by John Ryngeston " hosteler "; four shops with gardens adjoining in Brodemede, between what was lately a tenement of John Prowte and the garden of William Worcestre ; five shops with gardens in Worschupfulstrete ; a garden lying in Irysschmede, by the house of the Friars Preachers of Bristol, between what was lately Walter Wynter's land and the garden of Mark William, which garden William Moret holds ; the rents and services due from Thomas Lombard, shoemaker, for a shop, with the solar above it, in Knyfsmythstrete, between testator's tenement, lately inhabited by Walter Baker, and Frome gate ; the rents and services due from John Spaldyng and his wife Isabel for property in the same street, situate between testator's tenements inhabited by John Paryce and Bartholomew Vestmentmaker, with the reversion after the death of the tenants ; the rents and services due from John Gegge and Thomasine his wife for a tenement with adjoining shops, &c., in a lane as one goes from Merstret " versus Kayam ville," situate between what were lately the shops of Thomas Knapp and the tenement lately inhabited by John Saundres ; the rents and services due from Margery late wife of John Prowte " whyttower," and her son William, for a tenement with two shops, &c., in Brodemede, situate between tenements of William Worcestre, the elder, on either side ; the rents and services due from Joan Barette for a messuage with four shops and garden in Lewynsmede, situate between a tenement of John Frampton Ch'l'r and what was lately the tenement of John Canynges ; also a shop in

Redclyfstrete, situate between what was formerly the shop of John Bath and the shop which William Devyas formerly held, which property testator had bought of Sibil Moys, relict and executrix of Alexander Moys, late burgess of Bristol; and all interest in the tenement and adjoining lands, meadows, and pastures in Shernehampton, co. Gloucester, situate between a tenement of the Bishop of Worcester, on the one part, and a tenement of John Nuton, on the other. To Geoffrey John of Bristol, draper, and his wife Margaret, all testator's state in a tenement in Bradstrete, situate between his own dwelling house and a tenement of the fraternity of St. John Baptist. Provision to be made for a fit chaplain to celebrate for twelve years in the chapel next the chancel of the Holy Trinity of Bristol for testator's soul, and the souls of his parents, &c. To the aforesaid Isabel and Thomas Clyve, otherwise called Thomas Berkeley, all the lands, tenements, rents, &c., in the town and suburb of Bristol "apud lez Barrez," bought of Walter Wynter, formerly burgess of the town. Residue of goods, after the full payment of debts and funeral expenses, to be employed *pro anima* by Thomas Clyve, otherwise called Thomas Berkeley; but he and wife Isabel to have the use of the said goods during her life. These two, and Sir Thomas Marchall, vicar of All Saints', to be executors. In witness whereof I have put my seal to this my testament. And because my seal is unknown to most people, I have caused the seal of the dean of the deanery (decanatus) of the town of Bristol to be put to the presents. In the presence of Sir Richard Clerke, rector of the parish church of St. John, Master John Fitz waryn, rector of the parish church of the Holy Trinity of Bristol, Nicholas Excestre, Thomas Hallewey, John Twyncho, and Thomas Market.

Proved before John Leycestre, Mayor, and Hugh Withiford, Sheriff, on Friday in the morrow of the Conversion of St. Paul, 9 Henry vi. Previously proved before the ecclesiastical authorities.

223.—JOHN COKKYNG, burgess.

1430. Dec. 14th. Testator describes himself as of the parish of St. Nicholas of Bristol, in the diocese of Worcester, and desires to be buried in the parish church of St. Mary of Redcliff, "sub lapid' ib'm in qua *(sic)* nomen men' ac nomen Alicie nup' vx'is mee sunt supraseript'." To the mother church of Worcester xx^d. To every chaplain of St. Nicholas's church attending all the funeral rites ij^d. To wife Felicia, a state and term in a tenement and adjoining curtilage in Redeclevestrete, situate between a tenement of the master and brethren of the hospital of St. John Baptist, held by Richard Brokworth, on the one part, and a tenement of the abbot and convent of St. Augustine of Bristol, on the other, and extending from the King's way towards the Avon; a state in two tenements in the street called Redeclyf pitte, between a tenement of the master and brethren of the said hospital of St. John Baptist, inhabited by Richard Noreys, on the one part, and the tenement lately held by John Tylar of the said master and brethren, on the other, and extending from the street to a tenement of the said master and brethren, lately inhabited by John Swalledale; a state and term in a garden, with dovehouse built therein, by the cemetery of the blessed Mary of Redcliff, situate between the garden of the said master and brethren, on the one part, and what was lately a garden of Sir Thomas Brook knt., on the other, which garden and dovehouse Nicholas Taillour lately held ; a state and term in a croft upon Redcliff hill, by the high way leading towards "Trevell Mille," between the garden of the relict of Walter Newcombe, and what was lately Gilbert Brampton's, one ridge (capud) of the said croft extending beyond the land of the master of St. Katharine the Virgin by Bristol ; a state and term in a tenement inhabited by Thomas Webbe in Worschipstrete, situate between a tenement of the said master and brethren of the hospital of St. John Baptist and a tenement of the Commonalty of the town of Bristol, and extending from the King's way in front to the Avon behind ; a state and term in a tenement in St. Mary's street, lately inhabited by William Canon, between property held by Thomas Hallewey and the (late) shops of William Frome, and extending from the street to what was lately a messuage of John Stoke ; a state and term in three shops with a solar inhabited by John Kyppok, smith, in "seint Mariestrete," situate between the tenement lately inhabited by John Taillour and that which John Wyse lately inhabited, and extending from the King's way to the land "de Kalenders ;" and a state in the shop lately inhabited by William Worcestre in Bradstrete, situate between what was lately the tenement of William Plomer (sic), relict of Hugh Plomer, and the late dwelling house of Robert Bowyer, and extending from the street to the tenement lately inhabited by John Spyne : all this property to be held of the chief lords, &c., by the said Felicia and her assigns. Also to her, two messuages in Mersschstrete, situate between a tenement of Nicholas Excestre, on the south, and what was lately a tenement of Agnes who was wife of Henry Vyell, on the north, and extending from the street to the common wall of the town. Residue of goods to the said Felicia and son John. She to be executrix. John Eyre and John atte Wodde overseers.

Proved before John Skeffyngton, clerk, commissary general of the Bishop of Worcester, Jan. 30th, 1430 ; afterwards before the Mayor.

It is recorded in the registers which were kept by the Priors of Worcester "sede vacante," folio 259, that Master John Skeffyngton and another deputy were employed by the Prior, in the year 1433, to make a visitation at Bristol. On Sunday, Oct. 25th, they were with the Abbot of St. Augustine at dinner (in prand'). On the next day, before dinner, they visited the monastery, and, after dinner, the Master of St. Mark and his brethren. On Tuesday, Oct. 27th, before dinner, they visited the clergy and people of the deanery in the church of St. Augustine, and, after dinner, the Prior of St. James, and the Dean and chapter of Westbury.

224.—HENRY GILDENEY, burgess.

1430. Dec. 13th. To be buried in the chancel of the crypt of St. Nicholas's church at Bristol, in which church a fit chaplain is to celebrate for seven years, and pray, first for testator's soul, and the souls of Thomas and John, and afterwards especially for his soul, and the souls of his late wives Joan and Joan. Legacies to the vicar of that church, Sir John Howlegge the chaplain, and every other chaplain celebrating therein ; to the mother church of Worcester, Sir Thomas Hallewey and Sir Henry Harsfeld, chaplains, another Thomas Hallewey, Thomas Wyke of Staunton Drewe, William Pytte, John Vyell, John Gyles, Richard Morgan, clerk, the chapel of the blessed Mary on the bridge of Avon, John Assch, son of

Agnes Assch, Alexander Potckary, for his good service and painstaking, John Basset, whose legacy included a baselard with an ivory haft garnished with silver; to servants John Harry, Richard, Agnes Taillour, Margery, and Elen. To the abbot and convent of St. Augustine of Bristol, testator's pension (pensionem) yet remaining unpaid. " vt ip'i sp'ialiter orent p' ai'a mea." Two shillings sterling to be distributed every week for two years among the bedridden and other very needy people, that they also may pray. To the chaplain appointed to celebrate for seven years, £18 of the sum of £52 due to testator from Andrew Parle, burgess of Bristol; the remaining £34 to be paid to wife Margaret, and employed *pro anima*. To the said Margaret, for her life, the rents and services due from John Sherp and Joan his mother, executors of the will of John Sherp, late burgess of Bristol, for a messuage inhabited by the said John and Joan in Oldecornstrete; also the shop annexed to the said messuage in the same street, and lately inhabited by William Baret; the reversion to be sold within three years after the death of testator, and the money employed "in pios vsus." Richard Newton, "Recordator ville," to have the said reversion, if desirous, for twenty marks less than any one else might offer; if not, Thomas Wyke might have it, and give £10 less. The reversion of all lands, tenements, &c., in the town and suburb of Bristol, granted to wife Margaret for her life, to be sold within three years after testator's death, and of the money raised, 100 shillings to the fabric of the church of the blessed Mary of Redcliff, 100 shillings to the Carmelite Friars of Bristol, £3 to each of the four executors, Richard Nuton, Robert Russell, William Pytte, and Thomas Wyke, and £3 to the aforesaid Thomas Hallewey; the residue of the said money to the poor, &c. To kinswoman Agnes Roper, for her life, a tenement in the suburb in Redeclyvepytte, situate between Ralph Chaloner's tenement and testator's shop inhabited by Joan Shop, widow; the reversion to be disposed of for pious uses. Testator, having granted to Robert Russell and Thomas Hallewey, " burgens' ville," a yearly rent from property called " le Wildchows " in King's Berton by Bristol, co. Gloucester, acquired by a fine thereof levied in the court of Humphrey Duke of Gloucester, before Richard Nuton, steward of the court, and John Caffe and John Cokkes, suitors, now wills that the said Robert and Thomas shall grant to the aforesaid John Harry that rent for his life, and afterwards dispose of it " in pios vsus." Also, having granted to Richard Nuton and Thomas Hallewey, lands and tenements in Botelleres Wanstre, co. Somerset, lately acquired by the grant of John Hawkyns of Estwanstre, in the same county, now wills that the same John Harry should have this property for his life; the reversion to be religiously disposed of. To the executors before named, and wife Margaret, a tenement inhabited by Emmot Beverley, widow, on the bridge of Avon, situate between the tenement inhabited by Isabel Bolo (Bole?), widow, and the one inhabited by John Shyryngton, mercer; that they, or their assigns or executors, within half a year immediately after testator's death, should make John Eyre, John Loveney, Philip Guyen, William Lucas, John Cokkes, and Richard Bedstone, burgesses of Bristol, feoffees of the aforesaid tenement, to be held by the said six persons, their heirs and assigns, of the chief lords for ever, on condition of their finding yearly, from the feast of Easter until that of the Lord's Ascension, a certain taper, called the great Paschal, burning in the church of St. Nicholas of Bristol, according to the custom hitherto obtaining and approved in that church, without any other money payment or consideration ; the vicar of the said church, or the parish chaplain, to rehearse publicly in " le pulpite," before all the people, this present legacy, yearly in the day and feast of Easter, that they may especially pray at that time for testator's soul : his obit also, and that of his former wives Joan and Alice *(sic)*, to be kept every year on Tuesday in the week of Easter ; the vicar of the said church to be paid sixpence, each of the chaplains four pence, and the water-bearer, for bell-tolling, eight pence ; the town-crier of Bristol also to have four pence, if he will go round all the town and suburb, and proclaim the obit. To the parish church of Wanstre, co. Somerset, x^s. of the sum of thirty shillings owing to testator by Thomas Taillour, so that a cow may be bought, and with the profit thereof testator's obit kept there ; the said legacy to be publicly rehearsed every year in the pulpit of that church before the parishioners, that they may especially pray, &c. To the parson of Wanstre vj^s. viij^d, and to William Seggel, of that parish, xl^d, out of the residue of the said thirty shillings. Residue of goods to be disposed of *pro anima* by wife Margaret. She, Richard Nuton, Robert Russell, William Pytte, Thomas Wyke, and John Lucas, clerk, to be executors. Thomas Hallewey, overseer.

Proved before John Leycestre, Mayor, and Hugh Withiford, Sheriff, on Wednesday next before the feast of the Exaltation of the holy Cross, 10 Henry vi. Previously proved before the ecclesiastical authorities.

The will of Margaret, relict of Henry Gildeney, late burgess of Bristol, was made Jan. 8th, 1430. To be buried in the crypt of St. Nicholas's church at Bristol. Legacies to the vicar, and the fabric of that church, in which a chaplain was to celebrate for four years ; to her sister Elizabeth Basset, and John son of William Basset. Her brother William Basset to have the residue, and be co-executor with William Pate, merchant of Bristol. Proved Jan. 28th, 1430. Registered at Somerset House, *Luffenam*, 15.

Philip Guyen, who is named in the will of Henry Gildeney, may probably have been the Philip Geen, or Gywon, otherwise Smyth, whose will is registered in the Library at Lambeth, *Stafford*, 129. It was made Feb. 7th, 1438, and proved Oct. 20th, 1445. He desired to be buried in St. Nicholas's crypt at Bristol, and left legacies to the vicar of that church, daughter Elena, Worcester cathedral, Alice and John Stephen. Stephen ap Griffith, and his wife Emmot, executors.

225.—NICHOLAS EXCESTRE, burgess.

1434. Sept. 16th. To be buried in the crypt of the parish church of St. John Baptist of Bristol, to the fabric of which, for tithes, vj^s. viij^d, and a wine vessel of silver and gilt. Legacies also to Sir Nicholas, and Sir William, chaplains there, the parish clerk, and Sir Denis, the parish chaplain ; to the mother church of Worcester, and each order of mendicant friars at Bristol. To son Mark Excestre, and Thomas Westerley and Thomas Pavy, merchants of Bristol, a hall and five adjoining shops in the suburb, outside Frome gate, between the said gate, on the one part, and a certain common slip (slipam), on the other ; also two shops in Fysschernelane, between a shop of the abbot of Tintern and one which was formerly Robert

Gardyner's, now John Shipward's; and a yearly rent from a tenement inhabited by Alice Tyler, widow, which was lately Yvo Floyt's, now John Halle's of Redelond, situate in Brodemede, between property of the said John Halle and Thomas Griffyth; all this to be held for ten years by the said three, who are therewith to find and support a fit chaplain to celebrate *pro anima* during that time in the said church of St. John, at the altar of St. Nicholas. To William Wonder and John Frensche, procurators of the said church, a state and term in property situate in Lewynsmede, between the tenements of Richard Forster and John Whyte, barber; the said procurators and their successors to contribute therewith to the support of the chaplain. To wife Joan, household vessels, a silver cup standing on three feet, with cover, &c.; also a yearly rent issuing from a corner shop in Templestrete, situate between what was lately the tenement of Richard Jolyff and the street called Langrewe, and extending from the street to Lawdiche; also a tenement in Bradstrete called " Wryngtonstenement," situate between testator's tenement held by Thomas Westerley and a tenement of the abbot of Malmesbury; property in Cropelane, between John Sherp's tenement and what were lately the shops of John Arthur of Clopton; a hall and fourteen shops opposite St. Peter's place, situate between the shops of our lady the Queen, which Simon Olyver lately caused to be built anew, and the lane called "Stretedefence," and extending from the said place to the late shop of William Warmystre, weaver, now Richard Halle's; a shop on the Key, opposite the pipe called the Key pipe, between some shops of Lucy Stephenes and one of Walter Estcote; another shop on the Key "subtus le pentys," between and under a tenement of the aforesaid John Sharp and what were lately the shops of Mark William, and under these shops; and another in Fysschernelane, between what was lately the shop of John Harrewell and the shop of the abbot of Tintern: this property to be held by the said Joan for her life. To servant Margaret Lely, 40 shillings; also for her life, two shops in Cropelane, between property of John Twyncho and the abbot of Kingswood. To the aforesaid Thomas Westerley and his wife Margaret, testator's daughter, and their heirs and assigns, a tenement in Bradstrete, with a shop in front, situate between the tenement bequeathed to wife Joan and testator's tenement inhabited by the aforesaid William Wonder, and extending from the street to St. John's lane; also a garden and close annexed thereto in the suburb, "iux' lez Barrez," between the little lane " in qua iacet Seint Marie Well" and the common gutter by the wall of the Friars Preachers' orchard, on the one part, and the late close of William Cary, now John Bolton's, on the other, and extending from the King's way to the Frome: a barn and close adjoining in the Redelond, situate between a little lane extending to one of testator's closes and Lucy Draycote's close, on the one part, and a tenement of the prior of St. James, on the other; a small close in the same part, situate between what was formerly John Stoke's close and that of Lucy Draycote, and extending in width between what was lately John Burbache's land and the close of the prior of St. James; a close in the suburb, situate between the close of William Arch of Bedmynstre and that of the said prior; also the reversion of the aforesaid rent in Templestrete, when it shall fall after the decease of testator's wife; and the rent in Brodemede, after the term of ten years. To the aforesaid Thomas Pavy and his wife Alice, testator's daughter, and their heirs and assigns, a tenement in Bradstrete, between the tenement bequeathed to Thomas Westerley and Margaret his wife and the shop and tenement of John Twyncho; also a corner shop in Horstrete, situate between the lane leading to St. Michael's hill, on the one part, and the late shop of Robert Russell, on the other, and extending from the street to what was lately the garden of the said Robert. The tenement called "Wryngtonstenement," immediately after the death of wife Joan, and the aforesaid two shops in Fysschernelane, after the term of ten years, to remain to the said Thomas and Alice Pavy, and their heirs and assigns for ever. To son Mark Excestre, a corner tenement with shop, &c., in Gropelane, situate between the land of John Nuton, on the one part, and the shops of the lord of Burnell, held of the said lord by Joan Graunt, on the other, and extending from the King's way to the common wall of the town of Bristol; also to him and his heirs, a tenement and adjoining garden in the same street, situate between a lane where one goes towards "Loveyhate," on the one part, and the late shops of Mark William, on the other, and extending from the little lane to the common wall of the town; and the six shops in Gropelane, after the decease of testator's wife, and also those two in the same street, bequeathed above to Margaret Lely, immediately after the said Margaret's decease, and the property outside Frome gate, bequeathed, for ten years, to Thomas Westerley, Thomas Pavy, and Mark. To son Thomas Excestre, and his heirs, a corner tenement on St. Michael's hill, between the lane leading towards St. Michael's church, on the one part, and John Nuton's shops, on the other; also the rents and services due from William Hukeford, mason, for a tenement and garden in Mersschstrete, situate between what were formerly the shops of William Warmystre and the tenement of John Kenne of Wroxhale, which tenement the said William Hukeford holds of testator for a term of years; and the reversion of the same. To son William Excestre, and his heirs, a tenement in Knyfsmythstrete, situate between a tenement belonging to the chantry of St. Laurence of Bristol and the entrance of a tenement of the master of the house of St. Mark. To the aforesaid Thomas Westerley, Thomas Pavy, and Mark, the rents and services due from John Strete and Joan his wife, and Thomas their son, for a tenement held of testator by them for their life, situate on the Back of Avon, between a former tenement of Thomas Beawpyne and one of Sir Thomas Brook knt., and extending from the King's way to the entrance of what was lately Richard Spysour's tenement in Baldewynstrete; the said three persons to hold these rents and services, and the reversion, after the death of the said John, Joan, and Thomas, and dispose therewith *pro anima*; rem., after a term of ten years, to Thomas and Margaret Westerley, and their heirs. To son William Excestre, and his heirs, those two shops on the Key, after the decease of wife Joan. To son John, testator's best missal, a cup called *bolle pece*, &c. To son Thomas, a gilt spicedish, a girdle garnished with nettle leaves, &c. To son Mark, a silver cup with a star in the middle, &c. Silver cups also to Thomas and Margaret Westerley, Thomas and Alice Pavy, and testator's son William. Residue to be distributed *pro anima*. Thomas Westerley, Thomas Pavy, Mark Excestre, and Thomas Excestre, executors. Witnessed by Sir Nicholas Wousy, chaplain, Thomas Caudell, clerk, William Tyrry, John Copper, clerk, William More the writer, and others.

Proved before Thomas Hallewey, Mayor, and Thomas Fissche, Sheriff, on Wednesday next before the feast of St. Martin Bishop "in yeme," 13 Henry vi. Previously proved before the ecclesiastical authorities.

226.—JOHN FISSCHER, merchant and burgess.

1434. Friday next after the feast of St. Kalixtus Pope. To be buried in the parish church of St. Werburgh of Bristol, in which a chaplain is to celebrate for ten years for testator's soul, and the souls of his parents, and wives Joan and Alice, John Seymour, Walter Seymour, and Margaret his wife, William Folkyshull, Master Richard Bruton, and Sir John Frampton, receiving yearly the sum of eight marks. Twenty shillings for his burial in that church. Legacies to the rector, the clerk, and every priest there, and all other priests and clerks attending the funeral rites; to the mother church of Worcester, the Carmelite Friars of the blessed Mary, the Minors, Preachers, and Augustinians by Temple gate, the sisters of St. Mary Magdalene, the poor of St. Laurence outside "lafford" gate, those of the Holy Trinity "in dict' porta," and of the house of St. John "de la Redeclyne pytte," the prisoners at Monkebrigge, kinsman and servant John Diar, kinsman William Tonbrigge, kinswoman Alice, who is daughter of John Cokkes of Luttelton, servants Thomas Wytham, Margaret, and Cristina. Sixty shillings' worth of bread to the poor "in die obit' mei." To kinsman William Drivare of Luttelton xl^s. To Alice Dryvare, daughter of William Drivare vj^{li}. xiij^s. iiij^d, also a silver cup with cover, price xl^s, a maser, price xx^s, and six silver spoons, price xiij^s. iiij^d. To Joan Merbury (?), daughter of Joan Folkeshull, and her heirs, two tenements in the street of St. Nicholas at Bristol, situate between a certain "introitus" of the prior and convent of Maydenbradley, formerly inhabited by John Fuyster, on the east, and one which was formerly inhabited by John Ailmer, on the west, and extending from the street to the land of the said prior and convent. To wife Joan, for her life, testator's dwelling house and shops in Smalstrete; the reversion to be disposed of *pro anima*. To Sir Richard Luttelton, canon and prior of the monastery of St. Augustine of Bristol, x^{li}. He, wife Joan, and Thomas Passwer, executors.

Proved before the Mayor and Sheriff, on Friday next after the feast of the Conception of B.V.M., 13 Henry vi. No record of proof before the ecclesiastical authorities.

The episcopal registers at Worcester state that Richard Litulton, in company with other canons of St. Augustine's of Bristol, was ordained a religious priest in Worcester cathedral, May 27th, 1396.

227.—EDMUND BIERDEN.

1435. Aug. 18th. Testator describes himself as of Bristol, and desires to be buried in the cemetery of holy Cross Temple there, near his brother. For funeral expenses vj^{li}. xiij^s. iiij^d. To the high altar of that church, for tithes and offerings forgotten, vj^s. viij^d. Legacies also to every chaplain, and the two clerks thereof, each order of friars, the poor and leprous at St. Laurence's outside "lafford" gate by Bristol, the poor of the late shops of Elias Spelly in Berelane, the poor inmates of the hospital of St. John Baptist, of the almshouses in Langrewe and Templestrete, of Brightscowe (?), and St. Bartholomew, the prisoners at Monkebrigge, the nuns of the blessed Magdalene at Bristol, William Rook, "Hrmar' mco in Com' Herford," and his wife Katharine, each of testator's godchildren, and William Sevyer of Bristol, weaver, son of Robert Sevyer. To Agnes Bierden, late the wife of my brother William Bierden of Bristol, the tenement inhabited by her in Temple-street, situate between a messuage of Thomas Blount, on the one part, and the messuage of Isabel Droys, inhabited by William Delyn, weaver, on the other, and extending from the said street to the street of St. Thomas; also tenements, &c., in the same street, situate between what were formerly the messuages of Hugh Carleton and Henry Wyvescombe, and extending from the street to the Lawediche; a yearly rent from property in the same street, situate between shops belonging to the church of Holy Cross Temple, on the one part, and the late messuage of John Barstaple, on the other; a tenement, &c., in Redcclifstrete, situate between what were lately the messuages of John Newton and Sir Thomas Brook knt., and extending from the street to St. Thomas's cemetery; a tenement in the same street, situate between John Blekker's messuage and what was lately the messuage of Master Simon Uphulle, and extending from the street to the river Avon; the rent issuing from a messuage and land "in vico vocat' Redeclynepytte exoppo'ito Hospital' sc'i Joh'is ib'm," situate between the late messuage of Master Simon Uphull and a messuage of the said hospital, and extending from the street to a messuage of St. Katharine's by Bristol; and a tenement in Pylestrete, situate between a messuage belonging to St. Mary of Redcliff and what was lately Thomas Knap's tenement, and extending from the street "ad le Brodediche ville Bristoll';" all this property to be held by the said Agnes, for her life, of the chief lords; rem. to John Fitelton of co. Somerset, and his wife Alice, and their lawful issue; in default of such issue, to be disposed of "in pios vsus p' salute ai'e mee," &c. To the said John and Alice, silver vessels, one of them called a spicedish; also to them, and their lawful issue, a tenement in Knyfsmythstrete, situate between a messuage of the prior of the Kalendaries and one of Clement Bagot, and extending from the King's way to the said Clement's messuage; property in the same street, situate between what was lately the messuage of Sir Thomas Brook knt. and the dwelling house of William More, scrivener, and extending from the street to a messuage of the master of St. Mark of Byllcswyk; a tenement in Horstrete, otherwise called Fromebriggestrete, situate between the messuage of Mark William, inhabited by Richard Ridere "Bokebyndere," on the one part, and what was formerly the messuage of Stephen Comyn, on the other, and extending from the said street to the river Frome; a tenement situate between St. Laurence's church and St. Giles's gate, and extending from the street leading from Knyfsmythstrete "ad Keyam" to Conglane; a tenement on the Key, situate between the dwelling house of Alan Channdeler and a messuage of the prior of Bath, and extending from the street to the lane called "Bastewalles;" a tenement in St. Nicholas's street, between the dwelling house of Walter Power, merchant, and the late messuage of John Clyve; and three shops in Bradstrete, situate between a messuage of the said John Clyve, on the one part, and the late messuage of Thomas Knap, inhabited by William Chiltenham, barber, on the other, and extending from the street to what was lately the property of John Richardes: this property to be religiously disposed of, if the said John and

Alice should die s.p. "Jt'm lego noui *(sic)* op'e cancelle eec'ie b'te Marie de Redeclyne C⁸." To Sir Richard Janys, vicar "sc'e Crucis Templi," a book called *le bible*, lately bought of Thomas Boys, chaplain. The sum of x^li. xiij^s. iiij^d for celebrations in that church, for two whole years, for testator's soul, and the souls of his father John, and mother Alice, brothers William, John, and Thomas, sister Rose, &c. The aforesaid Agnes Bierdene and Sir Richard Janys to be executors. To the latter C⁸.

Proved before Nicholas Devenyssch, Mayor, and John Spicer, Sheriff, on Monday next after the feast of the Assumption of B.V.M., 14 Henry vi. Previously proved before the ecclesiastical authorities.

The will of William Bierdene, of Bristol, is registered at Somerset House, *Marche*, 48. It was made July 1st, 1420, and proved on the 16th of the following month. Testator mentions his late wife Agnes, and father John, and leaves legacies to John Deye, parson of Baggeworthe, the mendicant poor of the late shops of Elias Spelly in Berelane, and Agnes P'stwod. To his present wife Agnes, the house inhabited by him in Temple-street, between a tenement of Thomas Blount and what was lately John Sely's tenement; also property in the same street, situate between a tenement of John Droys and the late tenement of William Wermynstre of Bristol, tucker, to daughter Alice Bierdene and her issue; in def., rem. to brother Edmund Bierdene and his lawful issue; in def., rem. to John Sausemer. All other lands, rents, &c., in the town and suburb of Bristol, to the said Edmund, who is appointed co-executor with wife Agnes.

The reference to Elias Spelly suggests the addition of a note which ought to have been inserted after his will: no. 44. The will of his widow, Agnes Spelly, was made in 1393, in the feast of the Nativity of B.V.M., a "cedula" being appended Sept. 10th., in the same year. She desired to be buried in the church of the Friars Minors of Bristol, and bequeathed sums of money to Robert Spelly, his daughter Agnes, and his son, her maid-servant Isabel Ken, and the church of St. Leonard at Bristol, in which her anniversary was to be duly kept for ever. To Joan Spelly, daughter of testatrix, brazen vessels, silver cups, &c. Legacies also to John Pokelchurch, John, hermit of the chapel of St. Jordan (Gordian?), John Gamelyn, skinner, &c. Proved May 15th, 1405. Registered in *Marche*, 9.

The diocesan registers at Worcester mention a Richard Spelly of Claines, near that city, living in 1302.

228.—EDWARD REDE, parchmentmaker and burgess.

1436. Tuesday, May 1st. To be buried in the cemetery of St. James's church in Bristol, "iuxta sepultura' p'ris mei." To the fabric of that church xx^s. To the parish chaplain there xl^d. To the prior of St. James, a cow already in his keeping. To each monk living in the said priory xx^d. To the mother church of Worcester xij^d. To Thomas David "Madok de Wall'" the debt owing by William Wodynton, of Kerdyf in Wales. To Joan, daughter of the said Thomas, all the debts owing by William ap Thomas ap Prene. To my brother David Whittower, a blue gown "penulat' cu penula vulpor'." Legacies also to Sir John Ponter, chaplain, Robert David of Bristol, whittawer, William David, Edith Davy, and servants Howele and Cristina. To Joan, testator's wife, £40 of good and lawful English money; also his dwelling house in "le Brodemede," situate between what was lately the tenement of Joan Stephenes, now John Crynche's, and one of the abbot and convent of St. Augustine, and extending from the said street to the late land of Mark William; also one pepper-corn, being a yearly rent due from Joan Wocetre *(sic)*, widow, for a tenement, with garden, &c., in the same street, situate between the late tenement of John Clyve, now inhabited by Henry Hemyng, and a tenement of the Kalendaries, now inhabited by William Worcestre, whittawer, and extending from the said street to the river Frome; the reversion of this property, after the death of the said Joan Worcetre, to be held by wife Joan for her life; to be sold after the death of these two, together with the reversion of testator's dwelling house, and the money distributed *pro anima*. To servant Alice Edward, for her life, three shops in the street called Ratenrewe, in the parish of St. James the Apostle, lately bought of Richard Forster, merchant of Bristol, situate between property of Mark Somerwell and a lane leading from the said street towards the Frome; remainder to the aforesaid Robert Davy and his heirs. The executors are to sell the property in Lewynesmede, situate between Richard Forster's tenement inhabited by John y herward, tanner, and a tenement of the prior of St. James inhabited by William Bracy, tanner; also that in "le Market," situate between the tenement of William Glasier, "Belmaker," and the late shops of Margaret Martyn, and extending from the King's way in front to a lane where one goes to St. Philip's church behind; the money to be distributed *pro anima*. John Marle of Bristol, merchant, is to pay his debt of £16, in the next feast of Easter after the making of this will, or before that feast, in the church of the Holy Trinity of Bristol, and then all those lands, &c., on Redcliff hill and in Pylestrete, which testator lately acquired by the grant of the said John, shall revert to him, and his heirs and assigns, according to the tenor of certain indentures; failing to do so, the said property is to be disposed of "in pios vsus." David Thomas, "boucher" and burgess, to whom xl^s sterling, and a horse "de Baye colour," John Brandesby of Bristol, saddler, to whom xl^s and a sheaf (garba') of arrows, and Robert Davy, executors.

Testator added a codicil, bequeathing forty dozen parchments to his wife Joan, and a bullock to his servant Alice Edward; and ordering that if the parishioners of St. James's church in Bristol would buy his missal "quod de nouo fieri feci," they might pay the executors one half of its value, so that, in consideration of the other half, his name be enrolled among the other names of benefactors of that church, and be rehearsed by the parish chaplain on Sundays, in the pulpit, hereafter for ever; if not, this order to be void.

Proved before the Mayor and Sheriff on Friday next before the feast of SS. Tiburcius and Valerian, 15 Henry vi. Previously proved before the ecclesiastical authorities.

229.—ROBERT BELAMY, burgess.

1436. Saturday, March 16th. To be buried in the parish church of St. Michael of Bristol, "coram crnce ib'm," to the fabric of which church, for his burial, xl^s. To the rector, for tithes and offerings, vj^s viij^d. To the clerk of the same church, "p' classo meo pulsand'," iij^s iiij^d. To the mother church of Worcester xij^d. To the poor and needy in the parish of St. Michael aforesaid, for their prayers, 100 shillings; and the same sum for funeral expenses. Ten shillings to each order of mendicant friars at Bristol. The executors were to sell a messuage, with garden, &c., on St. Michael's hill, situate between the land belonging to the procurators of St. Werburgh's church, and held by William Bradford, on the north, and the corner messuage lately held by John Ewley and John Seynt of testator's grant and feoffment, and the late land of Walter Rodeney knt., on the south, and extending from the King's way as one goes towards the house or hospital of St. Mary Magdalene "ant'ius," on the west, as far as the garden of the master of St. Barthomew's hospital, held by John Vyell the younger, on the east; also all testator's lands, tenements, rents, &c., in the town and suburb; the money to be distributed for the benefit of his soul, and that of his late wife Agnes, the souls of her parents, John and Alice Jacob, and the souls of all the faithful dead. Residue of goods for the celebration of masses, and for the needy poor. William Tyrry of Bristol, merchant, and William More of the same place, writer, to be executors, and have xx^s apiece.

Proved before Richard Forster, Mayor, and Walter Power, Sheriff, on Friday in the morrow of St. Blaise Bishop, 15 Henry vi. Previously proved before John Harnham, commissary general of the Bishop of Worcester.

230.—JOHN LEYCESTRE, burgess and merchant.

1436. Oct. 1st. To be buried in the parish church of St. Stephen of Bristol, in the chapel of the blessed Mary, under the image of St. George. To the rector thereof, for tithes and offerings forgotten and withdrawn, xl^s. To the mother church of Worcester vj^s viij^d. To the fabric of the said church of St. Stephen £5. Legacies also to the parish clerk, and suffragan, and each chaplain thereof attending the masses of *requiem*, and other mortuary solemnities, daily for four weeks next after testator's decease; also to every other chaplain of the town who shall be present; each of the four orders of friars; the needy poor; every almshouse at Bristol; John Sergeant, and Tibot his wife, and all their children; my sisters Agnes and Margaret; my brother Ralph, and his wife and children; Laurence son of Roger Batte; the lady Emmot Payn, nun of Tarant; Janyn Reynold, and Margaret his wife, and all their children; Roger Strete, and Katharine his wife; apprentice John Rede, and servant Isabel Exale. Poor people to have £10 in money, and clothing to that amount, on the day of burial. For funeral expenses £20. To the fabric of the church of Thorleston £5. A chaplain to celebrate *pro anima* in that church for two whole years, and be paid £11. The sum of £10 for the liberation of poor prisoners at Monkebrigge; £10 for mending bad and dangerous roads near the town of Bristol; and £10 for the marriage of poor virgins. To the fraternity of St. John Baptist xl^s, and a like sum for the reparation of the chapel of St. George at Bristol. To John Streynesham, merchant of Bristol, John Bronn, and Roger Strete, tanner and burgess of the town, all testator's lands, tenements, &c., "in vico vocat' le Market;" also the property on Redcliff hill, held for a certain term of years by Henry Bisley, dyer, and his wife Joan and son Thomas; the fourteen shops in Gropelane, purchased of John Clyve, late merchant of Bristol; the shop, with solar above it, on the Key, situate between the late tenements of Roger Batte and Sir Thomas Brook knt.; and the rents and services due from the said Henry Bisley and his wife and son Thomas, for a tenement in Redclyvestrete, held by them for their life, with the reversion thereof: all this property to be held by the aforesaid three persons for twenty years, on condition of their providing a fit chaplain to celebrate *pro anima* during that time in the church of St. Stephen aforesaid; to be afterwards religiously disposed of. John Streynesham and John Broun, merchants of Bristol, being already enfeoffed in all testator's property in Fremschawe, within the manor of Hambroke, and hundred of Wynterborne, co. Gloucester, are to enfeoff therein his wife Emmot, immediately after his decease; the said property to be held by her for her life, and afterwards disposed of *pro anima*. Also to her, a tenement in the suburb of Bristol, opposite St. Stephen's church, situate between the tenement of John Blount esquire, inhabited by testator, on the one part, and what was lately the tenement of Walter Carpenter, on the other; remainder to testator's sister Margaret, widow of Roger Batte, who is to hold it for her life, and pay out of it ten shillings yearly to the executors, that they may keep up testator's anniversary in the said church of St. Stephen: the property to be afterwards religiously disposed of. The aforesaid John Streynesham, to whom £10, John Broun, to whom £10, and Roger Strete, executors. John Marler, clerk, to whom 100 shillings, overseer. To William More, the writer, xiij^s iiij^d. Witnessed by Nicholas Devenyssch, John Shipward, Hugh Withiford, John Troyt, William More, and others.

Proved before the Mayor and Sheriff on Wednesday next after the feast of the Translation of St. Thomas Martyr, 15 Henry vi. Previously proved before the ecclesiastical authorities.

231.—JOHN STEPHENES, "wolmanger" and burgess.

1440. June 20th. To be buried in the parish church of St. James of Bristol, by the altar of St. Thomas, to the fabric of which church iij^{li} vj^s viij^d. To the rector thereof, for tithes and offerings, xl^s. To Sir John Nouerton, parish chaplain there, xiij^s iiij^d. To each monk in the priory of the said St. James, for their prayers, xij^d. To the mother church of Worcester, iij^s iiij^d. To each order of mendicant friars in Bristol present at the funeral rites, ij^s vj^d. To wife Alice and her heirs, a tenement in Lewynsmede, situate between a messuage of the abbot and convent of Tewkesbury, co. Gloucester, on the one part, and the messuage of Joan lately wife of Peter Lucas, late of the said town, "Bowcher," on the other, which tenement was inhabited by Germanus Thomas, brewer; also all testator's interest in the messuage inhabited by John Chamberleyn, tailor, in Oldecornstrete. The said Alice to be executrix, and have the residue of all effects, and dispose therewith *pro anima*. Witnessed by Sir John Nouerton, John Gusshe, John Sawyer, tucker, Thomas Assche, baker, Tancred Johnson, and others.

Proved before Nicholas Freme, Mayor, and John Stanley, Sheriff, on Wednesday next before the feast of St. Matthias Apostle, 19 Henry vi. Previously proved before the ecclesiastical authorities.

232.—THOMAS BLOUNT, burgess and merchant.

1441. May 26th. To be buried in the cemetery of the parish church of holy Cross Temple, near to the wall of the chapel of the blessed Mary, on the south side of that chapel. To the said church, my book called "Antiphenall." To the vicar there, for tithes, vj^s viij^d. If the parishioners intend to build the tower of that church, they are to have forty shillings "de bonis meis cu' ip'i idem Campanile de nouo edificau'int." And if the said parishioners shall hereafter convey, or caused to be conveyed, the water of a certain conduit now being at the gate called "Temple yhate," from the said conduit in leaden pipes to the cross of the Temple aforesaid, they are to have, from testator's effects, 500 pounds of lead for that work. To the mother church of Wells xl^d. To each convent of mendicant friars at Bristol ij^s vj^d. To wife Margaret, for her life, testator's dwelling house, with the shops and gardens adjoining thereto, in Templestrete, situate between the late tenement of William Berden, inhabited by John Wawton, and Richard Forster's shops ; remainder to Richard Forster, burgess and merchant of Bristol, and his heirs and assigns. To the same Richard and his heirs, a tenement in the said street, situate between a messuage of Thomas Cheddre esquire, inhabited by Simon Yonge, tucker, and the messuage of Nicholas Caunterbury, inhabited by Henry Archer, dyer ; also a tenement in Towkerstrete, between what was lately the messuage of John Canynges, inhabited by John Berber, tucker, and the messuage of John Forde, inhabited by Patrick Devy, dyer ; also all that inclosed void place of land, and a drying-room built therein, lately held by John Lese, tucker, in "seint Thomas strete," by Houndenlane, situate between the stable and garden of testator's dwelling house and what was lately the land of John Haveryng, and extending from St. Thomas's street in front to the garden "mei p'dict' Thome Blount" and the garden of the abbot and convent of Tewkesbury behind ; the reversion of all this property to be held by the said Richard and his heirs, after the death of testator and his wife, for the £200 paid by him to testator. To wife Margaret and John Baker, bailiff of Templefee at Bristol, testator's state and term "in tota illa Turre vocat' Towrcharratz," and in a parcel of land lying behind the walls of the town, and extending in length from Temple gate to the aforesaid tower, and in breadth from the said walls to the common ditch of the town ; to hold the said tower and parcel of land, paying for the same the rents and services yearly due to the Mayor and Commonalty of the town of Bristol. The said Margaret to have during her life the use of all testator's jewels and silver vessels ; that which remains of them after her decease to be made into chalices *pro anima* for poor churches. To Thomas de la Pille testator's best gown "scarleti color' penulat' cu' penula de poleyne greye." Wife Margaret to be executrix, and have the residue of goods.

Proved before John Stevenes, bachelor in laws, and canon of the cathedral church of Wells, June 28th, 1441 ; afterwards before the Mayor and Sheriff of Bristol.

233.—ROBERT HALLE, otherwise Hegham.

1441. June 25th. To be buried in the parish church of the Holy Trinity at Bristol, to the fabric of which xl^s. Legacies also to the rector there, the cathedral church of Worcester, the poor in the Bristol almshouses, and other poor of the same town. To wife Amy, for her life, lands, tenements, rents, &c., in the town and suburb of Bristol ; remainder to sons Thomas and William ; remainder, after their decease, to John, testator's son and heir. To the said Amy, for her life, lands, tenements, &c., in Eston Gordon, Feyland, and Portbury, co. Somerset, and in Hampton and Combe, co. Gloucester ; rem. to son John. He and she to be executors. Sir John Fitz waryn, rector of the aforesaid parish church, to be overseer. Witnessed by the said Sir John, John Mede, and Robert Steynour.

Proved before William Canynges, Mayor, and John Shipward, Sheriff, on Wednesday in the feast of St. Lucy Virgin, 20 Henry vi. Previously proved before the ecclesiastical authorities.

234.—THOMAS FISSCHE, burgess and merchant.

1440. Wednesday, Nov. 2nd. To be buried in the cemetery of St. Thomas the Martyr at Bristol, outside the north porch, by the grave of late wife Joan. Legacies to the vicar, the fabric, each chaplain of that church, the two clerks there, and the mother church of Wells. To wife Agnes and her heirs, a tenement inhabited by Robert Herverd, shoemaker, in Wynchstrete, Bristol, between a tenement of the prior and brethren of the Kalendaries, inhabited by Richard Smyth, shoemaker, and that of Thomas Castelman, inhabited by John Carpenter, tailor; also the lands, tenements, &c., in the town and suburb, possessed by testator in fee simple, and lately bought of John Bathe, otherwise called Pocheon, and Robert Nemot, late burgess of Bristol, deceased ; one half of this property to be sold by the said Agnes, or by her executors, and the money distributed *pro anima*, and the other half to remain, after her decease, to William Fissche, testator's brother. Also to the said Agnes, a state and term in a messuage, garden, &c., in West Toukerstrete, situate between the lane called Westbury lane, on the one part, and a tenement of the prior and convent of the blessed Mary of Wytham, inhabited by John Sawyer, tucker, on the other part, which property testator purchased of William Fitz William, prior of the said house, for a term of ninety years ; also a state in three tenements in Towkerstrete, situate between a tenement of the said prior and convent, lately inhabited by Ralph Willond, dyer, on the one part, and the tenement lately inhabited by David Danyell, tucker, on the other ; and a state in a tenement in Templestrete, between the messuage lately inhabited by Philip Hore, tucker, on the one part, and the tenement of William Knolles, on the other ; which four tenements testator had purchased of John Cosham, late prior of the house of the blessed Mary of Wytham, and that convent, for ninety years. If Agnes should die within the said term, rem. to brother William Fissche and his assigns. To the said Agnes, a state in two messuages, with their adjoining closes, in the town of Mersschefeld "voc' Estem'sschfeld," in the south part of the said town, between the tenement inhabited by Thomas Passch, on the west, and that inhabited by Peter Gosse, on the east, which property testator bought of Thomas by divine permission late abbot of the monastery of the blessed Mary of Keynsham, and the convent there, "simul cu' Thoma ffyssche nup' p're meo defuncto," for a term of sixty years ; rem. to testator's kinsman Richard Deenys and his assigns, if the said Agnes should die within the term. Wife Agnes to be executrix, and have the residue of goods. John Burton, merchant of Bristol, overseer.

Proved before the Mayor and Sheriff on Wednesday next after the feast of the Lord's Epiphany, 20 Henry vi. Previously proved before the ecclesiastical authorities.

235.—RICHARD TRENODE, merchant.

1442. Tuesday in the week of Pentecost. To be buried in the parish church of St. Leonard of Bristol. To the mother church of Worcester vj^s viij^d. "Jt'm lego ad p'formand' nigra' sectam de'e eccl'ie sc'i leonardi de sect' capi (for *capæ* ?) p' me antea eid'm eccl'ie dat' xl^s." To wife Joan, for her life, a messuage in Baldewynstrete, with shop in front and garden behind, situate between the tenement of Thomas Cheddre, esquire, and that of William Arthur of Bedmynstre; also a yearly rent from a tenement on the back called "Avenbakke," adjoining the cemetery of the parish church of St. Nicholas at Bristol, on the south side of the cemetery: the said property to be disposed of *pro anima* immediately after her death. Wife Joan and William Pavy to be executors. John Sherpe and Nicholas Freme overseers.

Proved before John Hernham, commissary general of the Bishop of Worcester, July 23rd, 1442; also before the Mayor and Sheriff.

The will of William Pavy the elder, burgess and merchant of Bristol, was made on the day and feast of St. George Martyr, 1461. To be buried in the crypt of the parish church of St. Leonard in Bristol, in which church a chaplain was to celebrate for three years, and to which testator bequeathed his best missal, his book called *Legenda Sanctorum*, a good Psalter, and a pair of black vestments. To the vicar thereof xx^s. To the mother church of Worcester ij^s. To wife Joan, and son William Pavy, his dwelling house on the Key of Bristol, and all lands, tenements, rents, &c., in the parish of St. Stephen; two messuages in Redcliff-street, by the tenement held by Richard Kayton; four shops in the parish of St. James; two messuages on the Were at Bristol; and a messuage "sine hospiciu'" in Tewkesbury, co. Gloucester, called "le Bere." If son William should die s.p., all the said property to remain to son Robert Pavy and his issue; in default, rem. to son John Pavy; in default, rem. to son Richard Pavy; in default, rem. to daughter Margaret wife of Edmund Westcote; in default, rem. to daughter Elen Pavy; in default, rem. to daughter Elizabeth Pavy; in default, rem. to Richard Chokke the elder, of Staunton Drewe, and his lawful heirs. To wife Joan and son William, a cottage in Cornstrete, Bristol, situate between a tenement of the Mayor and Commonalty, inhabited by John Swancote, on the one part, and a tenement of the church of St. Werburgh, inhabited by Thomas Rowley, on the other. To daughter Elen, four pipes of woad, and twenty marks in silver cups, &c. To son John, for his maintenance at school for six years, twenty-four marks sterling. To son Richard, four pipes of woad, worth eighty marks. To son Robert, four pipes of woad of the same value. To William More the elder, the writer, vj^s viij^d. Residue to wife Joan and son William. They and the aforesaid Richard Chokke to be executors. Master Hugh Pavy, testator's son, overseer.

Proved in the collegiate church of Westbury, Oct. 5th, 1466, and registered at Worcester, in Bishop Carpenter's register, vol. i., folio 205.

236.—WILLIAM FISSCH, merchant.

1441. June 20th. To be buried in St. Thomas's cemetery at Bristol. Legacies to each chaplain of the church there attending the mortuary offices, and the two parish clerks, the cathedral church of St. Andrew of Wells, and the vicar of the blessed Mary of Redcliff. To wife Agnes, the best standing bowl with silver cover, &c. Jewels, goods, and merchandise within the realm of England, and in all parts beyond the sea, to be divided into three equal parts; one for wife Agnes, the second for the three children equally, the third *pro anima*. If the children should die under age, the said Agnes to have their legacies. To son William Fyssche, forty shillings of yearly rent from one half of all the lands, tenements, &c., in the town and suburb, given to testator by the will of his brother Thomas Fissche, formerly burgess of Bristol, after the death of Agnes, wife of the said Thomas. To daughter Joan, forty shillings of yearly rent from the same property, when it shall fall after the death of the said Agnes. The said lands, tenements, &c., to remain to son Thomas and his lawful issue; in default, rem. to son William; in def., rem. to daughter Joan; in def., rem. to Richard Denys "nepoti meo," son of William Denys, late of Mersschefield. If the said Richard should die s.p., the executors are to sell the said half of the property under the oversight of the Mayor of Bristol, and distribute the money in works of charity for the health of testator's soul, and the souls of wife Agnes, brother Thomas, &c. To the said Agnes for her life, after the death of the aforesaid Agnes, 100 shillings of yearly rent from the lands, tenements, &c. She, Matthew Shirwyn, and Richard Morgan executors, and Sir Nicholas Pittes, vicar of the parish church of the blessed Mary of Redcliff, overseer. To the said Matthew and Richard, 20 shillings.

Proved before John Stephenes, licenciate in laws, and canon of Wells cathedral, Sept. 12th, 1441; afterwards before Clement Bagot, Mayor, and Nicholas Hille, Sheriff.

237.—JOHN GOSSLYN, "Belyetter" and burgess.

1450. May 12th.—"compos mentis laudetur altissim' p'ponens p' dei gr'am partes Romanas causa p'egrinandi visitare condo test'm meu' in hunc modum, Jn primis lego ai'am meam deo om'ipotenti corpus q' meum sepeliend' vbicumq' deus disposuerit." To wife Margery, lands, tenements, rents, &c., in the town and suburb of Bristol, and also in New Sarum, and elsewhere in England, for her life. It shall be lawful for her to sell them *pro anima*. If she does not, the money raised by disposal of them after her decease to be distributed to chaplains, poor virgins, for their marriage, prisoners, the blind, lame, &c. To the said Margery, a state and term of years in a house in Baldewynstrete, opposite the Cross, inhabited by Robert Megges. She, John Megges, and John Strete, tanner, to be executors. William Talbot of Bristol, overseer.

Proved before John Stanley, Mayor, and Richard Hatter, Sheriff, May 22nd, 30 Henry vi. No record of proof before the ecclesiastical authorities.

We have here an ancient Bristol surname. John le Hattere, of the ward (quarterinm) of the blessed Mary of Redcliff, occurs on a Gloucestershire subsidy-roll at the Record Office, dated 6 Edward ii.

The will of Richard Hatter, burgess and merchant of Bristol, is registered at Somerset House, *Stokton*, 10. It was made September 5th, 1457. Testator desired to be buried in the church of All Saints, to the fabric of which iij^{li} vj^s viij^d. Twenty-four chaplains to be at the mortuary offices, and twelve poor men to hold torches burning thereat. To the fabric of the mother church of Worcester vj^s viij^d. To the fabric of St. Leonard's of Bristol vj^{li} xiij^s iiij^d, in which church a chaplain was to celebrate for twelve years. Legacies also to the vicar of that church, to the reparation and building of the tenements and ornaments of Thomas Hallewey's chantry, to my brother John, and brother William Hatter of London, and the children of the former, my sister Isabel Stafford, Robert Warmyngton and his wife, Master Richard Warmyngton, Thomas Devenyssh, Richard Boole, John Milleyn, apprentice Richard Marchall, and servants John Laveraunce and Maud. Wife Constance and her son John Hawke to have the residue of goods, and be executors. Given at Bristol. Witnessed by John Turnor, vicar of St. Leonard's, John Shoppe, John Prince, William Waring, chaplain, Richard Haddon, Nicholas Reede, William Moore the writer, and others.

Proved at Lambeth, Sept. 21st, 1457.

238.—JOHN CASTELMAN, burgess.

1446. Nov. 4th.—"compos mentis laudetur Altissimus eger in corp'e." To be buried in the chapel of the blessed Mary, in the parish church of holy Cross Temple at Bristol, diocese of Bath and Wells, to the vicar of which, for tithes and offerings forgotten, vj^s viij^d, and to the fabric, for grant of interment, 200 pounds of lead, wife Edith to keep the lead until there is need to repair the said church. Legacies to the fraternity of St. Katharine in that church, the mother church of Wells, and the altar of St. Citha (sc'e Cithe virginis) in the conventual church of the Augustinian friars at Bristol. To wife Edith, lands, tenements, shops, gardens, &c., in the town and suburb, for her use and *pro anima*. She and Thomas Yonge, Recorder of the said town of Bristol, executors. To the latter, for his pains, xx^s. Sir Richard Jamys (sometimes written *Janys*), vicar of the aforesaid church of holy Cross, overseer. Witnessed by the said Sir Richard Jamys, John Davy, chaplain celebrating in that church, Thomas Yonge, tucker, William Payn, Robert Core the writer, and others.

Proved before William Coder, Mayor, and Thomas Meed, Sheriff, on Wednesday next after the feast of St. Hilary Bishop, 31 Henry vi. No record of proof before the ecclesiastical authorities.

This will is also registered in the Library at Lambeth, *Stafford*, 147.

239.—JOHN BURTON, burgess.

1454. March 21st. To be buried in the parish church of St. Thomas the Martyr, diocese of Bath and Wells, by the altar of St. John Baptist. To the fabric of that church, five marks. To the cathedral church of St. Andrew of Wells, xx^d. For funeral expenses, and for the poor on the day of burial, xx^{li}. To Nicholas Pittes, Philip Mede, John Gaywode, and Richard Thyngwall, of Bristol, the reversion of the half of tenements, &c., lately purchased of Agnes, wife of John Spycer of Bristol, formerly wife of Thomas Fyssh, late burgess of that town, which property the said Agnes held of testator for her life; namely, the half of a tenement inhabited by Jen'n Deyell in St. Nicholas's street, situate between the tower (campanile) of the church of St. Nicholas, on the east, and the late cellar of Thomas Chedder esquire, held by Robert Bracy, on the west, and extending from the said street to the old wall of the town ; the half of a tenement in Wynchestrete inhabited by Thomas Griffith, smith, situate between a tenement of the Mayor and Commonalty of Bristol, inhabited by William Herbard, on the west, and a tenement of the chantry of Robert Chepe, lately founded in the aforesaid church of St. Thomas, inhabited by Richard Webbe "Corio'," on the east : the half of three shops in the said street, separately inhabited by Richard Forbour, Thomas Cotyller, and William Stappe, situate between the tenement of John Cockes, brewer, inhabited by Thomas Spenser, merchant, on the west, and the tenement of John Tydryngton and his wife Edith, inhabited by John Clerk, pointmaker, on the east ; the half of a garden in the Market "cu' vno logge in cod'm Gardino," held by John Symondes, hooper, situate between the garden of the almshouse at Laffordesyate, held by the poor of the said house, on the east, and the garden of Joan Erley, widow, held by John Newton, on the west, and extending from the King's way in front to a lane called "seint Philippeslane" behind ; the half of a garden or void place of land (placee t're) on the Were, in a way where one goes from the Were towards Erlesmede, held by Thomas Griffith, situate between a tenement of the prioress and sisters of the house of St. Mary Magdalene of Bristol, held by John Rider, tanner, on the west, and a garden of the aforesaid Philip Mede, held by John Clerk, pointmaker, on the east ; the half of a tenement held by Richard Waxmaker on the bridge of Avon, situate between a tenement of testator's inhabited by Walter Benett, hosier, on the south, and a tenement of William Taverner, gentleman, inhabited by Margaret Pyke, on the north ; the half of a tenement and two cellars on the Back of Avon, containing divers "mansiones" held by Edward William and several others, situate between a lane where one goes from the said Back towards Bastestrete, on the north, and the tenement of William Wanstre, inhabited by Thomas John, on the south ; the half of the two messuages, inhabited by Edward Mason and Nicholas Stocke in Merchestrete, situate between a tenement of the fraternity of St. John Baptist at Bristol, on the south, and the land of John Sherp the elder, on the east ; the half of a close on St. Michael's hill, held by Richard Ewyn "halyer," lying between a close of the abbot and convent of St. Augustine, held by the said Richard, on the west, and the land of the Commonalty of Bristol, on the east, and extending from the King's way where one goes towards Clifton, in front, to the garden of John Sherp the elder, behind ; the half of a tenement inhabited by John Elyott in Redeclifstrete, situate between the tenement of John Hampton of Bath, mason, on the south, and what was lately the shop of Thomas Fysshe, on the north, and extending from the street to the late tenement of Thomas Parkhous ; the half of a tenement held by Oliver Meke "chalno'" in the said street, between the tenement of Sir John Seymour knt., inhabited by Lodowic Chalnour, on the north, and a void place of land belonging to the master of St. John's hospital, and held by John Meke and others, on the south ; the half of a tenement held by William Tanner, crocker, in Redeclifstrete, situate between a tenement of Thomas Vyell, gentleman, inhabited by Thomas Taillour, on the south, and a tenement of the said John Hampton of Bath, inhabited by William Hone, weaver, on the north, and extending from the street to what was lately the tenement of the said Thomas Parkhous, inhabited by Nicholas Hyll ; and the half of a shop held by the aforesaid John Elyott in Redeclyfstrete, between the late shop of the said Thomas

Parkhous, inhabited by Thomas Tadelton, latoner, on the north, and the tenement inhabited by the said John Elyott, on the south. To the same Nicholas Pittes, Philip Mede, John Gaywode, and Richard Thyngwall, a tenement and shop in Lewenesmede, between a tenement belonging to the chantry of Thomas Halewey, late burgess of Bristol, and Joan his wife, lately founded in the parish church of All Saints, on the east, and a certain common gutter running from the said street to the river Frome, on the west; also a tenement at the north end of the bridge of Avon, between the tenement of John Thorp, inhabited by John Compton, merchant, on the south, and the late tenement of Thomas Fyssche, inhabited by Richard Wexmaker, on the north; also property in Templestrete "direct' exoppo'ito Crucis vocat' Stalegecrosse," between a tenement belonging to the chantry of Robert Chepe, lately founded in the church of St. Thomas the Martyr, on the north, and a tenement of the lady Margaret Countess of Salop, on the south; also two tenements, with garden adjoining, in St. Thomas's lane, opposite the southern entrance of St. Thomas's church, situate between a tenement of the prior and brethren of the Kalendaries, on the east, and a tenement of the procurators of the blessed Mary of Redcliff, on the west, and extending from the said lane to a path where one goes "ad latrinas situat' sup' le Lawediche;" the said Nicholas Pyttes, Philip Mede, &c., to hold this property after the death of the aforesaid Agnes, on condition that they found and duly establish a perpetual chantry, so that a chaplain may hereafter for ever celebrate divine offices at the altar of St. John Baptist in the parish church of St. Thomas of Bristol, for the good estate of our lord the King, and Margaret Queen of England, his consort, and Edward Prince of Wales, his eldest son, and for the good estate of testator and his wife Isabel, and for the souls of all these after their departure "ab hac luce," and for the performance of other works of piety: the said chantry to be called the perpetual chantry of John Burton, merchant of the town of Bristol, for ever, and the chaplain thereof for the time being to be called the chaplain of the perpetual chantry of John Burton, merchant of the town of Bristol; licence and the King's letters patent for this purpose to be procured. To wife Isabel £100, also merchandise wares, wool, &c.; also, for her life, lands, tenements, rents, &c., in the town and suburb of Bristol; rem. to daughter Isabel, wife of Thomas Yonge, and her heirs for ever. To the said wife Isabel, the fourth part of a ship called "la Marie de Bristoll," being now in "Islande," of which Robert Goteham is master, together with all its fittings, and the merchandise therein. To my brother Nicholas Burton, the true value of 200 marks in cloth, &c. To kinsman Robert Jonys, cloth, woad, coats of mail, &c. Legacies also to kinsman John Jonys, John Gaywode, kinswoman Edith Jonys, and the four orders of friars at Bristol. Thomas Yonge and Sir John Fortescu knt. to be executors, and each to have xx^{li}. Witnessed by Master Nicholas Pyttes, William Canynges, Philip Mede, John Jonys, William More, Nicholas Parker, Richard Hickes, John Edwardes, and others.

Proved at Lambeth July 28th, 1455; also "p' tres vices p'clamat' fuit in pleno hundr'o tent' apud Bristoll," in the Guildhall, before William Coder, Mayor, &c., on Friday next after the feast of the Purification of B.V.M., 36 Henry vi.

Thomas Parkhous, of Bristol, who died in 1449, bequeathed £10 to the church of Bradford in Yorkshire, " vbi oriu'dus fui," and where he then had a brother John.

240.—THOMAS JONYS, cofferer and burgess.

1464. Sept. 18th. To be buried in the crypt of St. Nicholas at Bristol. To the cathedral church of Worcester iij^s. iiij^d. To Master John Arffos, vicar of the said church of St. Nicholas, x^s. To the chapel on the bridge of Avon vj^s. viij^d. To the fraternity of St. John Baptist at Bristol vj^s. viij^d. To wife Elen, for her life, a messuage in Baldewynestrete, situate between the tenement of Richard Erle, inhabited by Elen Stourmy, and what was lately the tenement of the Lady de Lysle, inhabited by Roger Plomer, and extending from the street in front to the orchard of the said Richard ; remainder to the procurators of the aforesaid crypt, and their successors for ever ; the whole rent, after the said Elen's death, to be expended on divine offices in that crypt every year, on the vigil of St. Matthew, in the month of Sept., " cum Placebo & Dirige & die Crastino sequente Cum Missa de Requiem," at which mass the procurators are to offer a penny for the good of testator's soul and that of his wife Elen, and the souls of Robert Thomas and Edith his wife ; the vicar of the church for the time being to have twelve pence yearly for celebrating, and each chaplain four pence for taking part at the said anniversary. To the principal clerk of the church, for taking part, two pence ; " & pro pulsac'o'e maxime Campane. ad exequias anniuersarij mei Tribz Signis & ad Missam vno Signo solempniter faciendo iiij^d ;" the secondary clerk also to receive two pence from the aforesaid procurators, for taking part in the said exequies and for the preparation " de la heerce ;" and four pence yearly to the common beadle (Bedmanno Co'i) of the town for proclaiming the anniversary. The sum of eight pence out of the rent of the aforesaid messuage to be divided equally every year between the procurators for their pains ; but if they shall be found neglectful in paying and doing as ordered by testator, they are to forfeit the eight pence for that year ; the vicar of the said church of St. Nicholas to enter the said messuage and distrain. Testator's soul and his wife Elen's to be "recommended" in the pulpit every year, on Sundays ; and the vicar to be paid by the procurators on St. Matthew's day. The guardian also of the fraternity of St. John Baptist in Bristol to be paid twelve pence for ever, on condition that he and his successors provide for the due observance of the anniversary in the said church on that day. The remainder of the rent to be paid as a salary to a chaplain of the said fraternity of that crypt, who is to celebrate therein. A secular chaplain is also to celebrate *pro anima* for two years in the aforesaid church, and receive £12. Legacies also to son Thomas Jonys, and mother Isabel Jonys, Richard Ewryn, chaplain, and my brothers John and Waryn Ewryn. Wife Elen and John Skryveyn executors. To the latter, ten shillings and a gown. Witnessed by Master John Arffos, vicar of St. Nicholas's, William Weele, chaplain, John Cogan, mercer, John Stevenys, and William More.

Proved before Master John Harnham, commissary of the Archbishop of Canterbury, Sept. 24th, 1464 ; afterwards before John Shypward the elder, Mayor of Bristol, and John Hawkys, Sheriff.

Elen Sturmy was widow of Robert Sturmy, burgess and merchant of Bristol, who made his will June 27th, 1457, because he was then "passinge oner the see, vnder the mercy of God." He bequeathed forty shillings to "the Church Werk" of St. Nicholas of Bristowe, and twenty shillings to "the Crowde" therein. The sum of £30 to be expended during five years on behalf of the souls of his "ffader and moder." To the parish church of Knygton (Knighton), co. Worcester, xl^s. Legacies also to the priests of the college of "Seynt marye yeld in Ludlowe," the fraternities of the chapel on the bridge and of St. John Baptist at Bristol, the poor friars of " ye Woodehous by ye Clee in Shroppeshire," my brother John Sturmy, "Nevowe" Robert, and the other children of brother John, "Cousyn" Roger Banastre, apprentice John Penk, &c. If testator's ship and goods come home in safety, then, after his decease, a secular priest is to sing for him in St. Nicholas's church "a bone wrete" for ten years, and another in the above-written church of Knyghton, and have yearly nine marks, and forty pence "for brede wyne and light." Residue to wife "Elyne." She and brother John Sturmy to be executors. Master John Arffos, vicar of St. Nicholas's, and John Hosier, draper, of Ludlow, overseers. Proved 'at Lambeth, Dec. 12th, 1458. Registered at Somerset House, *Stokton*, 14.

The diocesan registers at Worcester give the following particulars. 1446, Apr. 2nd, Master John Arffos, master in arts, of the diocese of Worcester, was ordained a secular deacon by the Bishop of Worcester, in the parish church of Hembury in Salt Marsh, on a title conferred by Merton college in Oxford; and, at the same time, friar William Arffos, canon of St. Augustine's monastery at Bristol, was ordained a religious priest. 1446, Apr. 16th, the said John Arffos was ordained a secular priest in the church of the house of St. Mark at Bristol, on the title of his vicarage of St. Nicholas in that town. 1447, Dec. 30th, the Bishop of Worcester granted to Master John Arffos, master of arts, vicar of St. Nicholas's, Bristol, a licence to preach and expound the Word of God anywhere within the diocese. 1457, Dec. 1st, the Bishop granted to Richard Arffos esquire the office of keeper of the manor of Wythyndon, co. Gloucester, and of all the woods, &c., pertaining thereto.

241.—LODOWIC MORS, burgess and merchant. In the margin *Morse*.

1464. Feb. 7th. To be buried "in Porticu Eccl'ie b'te Marie de Redclyff Bristoll' Bathon' & Wellen' dioc' videl'it coram ymagine b'te Marie ib'm." One quarter of woad for testator's burial there. To the mother church of Worcester xx^d. To the vicar of St. Leonard's at Bristol, for tithes and offerings, vj^s. viij^d. Legacies also for the reparation of that church, and to friars John Everard and John Leyson. To wife Joan, for her life, testator's dwelling house in Oldecornstret. If son Thomas should die before the age of 22, and s.p., the said tenement to remain to son John. If John should die s.p., rem. to son Walter and his issue; in default, rem. to Lodowic John of Bristol, merchant, and his heirs. If the said Lodowic should wish to inhabit the said house, he is to pay wife Joan xl^s sterling during her life. To son John, a shop on the Key of Bristol, held of testator by John Robyn, hooper; wife Joan to receive the rent of it until the said son John shall be 22 years old. If he should die s.p., rem. to son Walter when 22; in def., rem. to son Thomas when 22; in def., rem. to Lodowic

John. To son Thomas, seven pipes of woad; seven to son Walter; and six to son John; of which pipes, six are within testator's house, and as many as fourteen in certain ships returning by the grace of God from parts beyond the sea. If any misfortune should befall the said fourteen pipes, the burden of the accident to be borne by his sons according to the discretion of his wife. If all his sons should die before coming to years "discree'o'is," the said pipes to come to the hands of his said wife; and then, eight pipes for Lodowic John; three for the reparation of the house of the Friars Minors at Bristol; two for repairing the church of the blessed Mary of Redcliff; one pipe for repairing the church of St. Leonard; two pipes to John Lewys, brother of the said Lodowic John; two to Joan and Agnes, daughters of testator's sister; one pipe to William Rede; and one to Alice sister of wife Joan. The said Joan to be executrix. Witnessed by John Streynsham and Robert Core.

Proved before William Spenser, Mayor, and John Clerke, Sheriff, on Wednesday next after the feast of the Lord's Epiphany, 5 Edward iv. Previously proved before the ecclesiastical authorities.

242.—WILLIAM CAUNTERBURY, esquire, burgess.

1459. Jan. 4th. To be buried in the parish church of St. Thomas the Martyr at Bristol, to the vicar of which, for tithes and offerings forgotten, xij^d. To the mother church of Wells xij^d. To wife Alice and her heirs, two tenements in Castelstrete, in the parish of St. Peter the Apostle, situate between the tenement of John Taverner and that of the prior of Maydenbradley, and extending from the said street in front to a tenement of William Canynges behind; also two gardens in Mershstrete, between the land of John Sherp and that of William Erleygh; and lands, tenements, &c., on the Key, which property is to be sold by her, or by her executors, and the money distributed *pro anima*. To Philip Mede, Thomas Sawyer, Robert Baron, John Jones, dyer, Richard Kayton, and Walter Fosse, all testator's lands, tenements, rents, &c., in Redeclyfstrete and Templestrete, on condition that, immediately after his decease, they make for his wife Alice a sufficient and secure estate of and in four messuages in the former street, situate between the land of Sir Walter Rodeney knt. and what was lately the land of Thomas Cheddre esquire; she to hold the said messuages for her life, paying yearly to the said Philip, Thomas, and the other feoffees, one red rose at the feast of the Nativity of St. John Baptist, if demanded, for all other services, exactions, &c. And, after her decease, the said feoffees shall find a priest, or fit chaplain, to celebrate masses and other divine offices in the aforesaid church of St. Thomas for ever, for the good of testator's soul, his wife's, &c. To his said wife, who is made executrix, and to her assigns, a state in two messuages in Bradstrete, lately occupied by Robert Hygham. To John Alwyn, tiler, "optimam meam Togam stragulatam vocat' Ray in vna p'te virid' Coloris cum furrura in eadem Toga existen'." Legacies also to wife's kinswoman Alice, and Elen Stagge, testator's servant and apprentice. Sir Maurice Berkeley knt., lord of Beverston, to be overseer.

Proved in the church of St. Thomas the Martyr at Bristol, March 3rd, 1459; afterwards before the Mayor and Sheriff.

243.—THOMAS ROGER, burgess and merchant.

1465. Jan. 16th. Testator describes himself as of the parish of St. Stephen of Bristol, in the diocese of Worcester, and desires to be buried in St. Stephen's church, before the altar of St. Katharine the Virgin. To the mother church of Worcester xl^d. To the rector of the said church of St. Stephen, for tithes and offerings forgotten, vj^s viij^d. To Master John Gomond xl^d, that he may pray for testator's soul. To Sir Geoffrey Norman, and Sir John Wodward, xx^d apiece, and to each of the other chaplains of of the said parish church, xij^d. To the procurators thereof, for testator's burial there, a quarter of woad. A fit secular chaplain to celebrate therein. To each order of friars at Bristol v^s. To the procurators of the parish church of Mersshfeld, for the work thereof, "vnn' settyng Woode." To wife Agnes, for her life, lands, rents, reversions, &c., in Bristol, and "in Com' ac Suburb' einsdem"; remainder to son William Rogers, and his lawful issue; in default, to be sold, and the money distributed *pro anima*. Residue to wife Agnes. She and son William to be executors. John Streynsham overseer. Witnessed by Sir Geoffrey Norman, John Wodward, John Emayn, li'ato (?), and others.

Proved before William Canynges, Mayor, and John Gaywod, Sheriff, March 20th, 7 Edward iv. Previously proved before the ecclesiastical authorities.

Master John Gomond, clerk, was named as an executor and legatee in the will of Thomas Norton, of the parish of St. Peter of Bristowe, brother of Walter Norton, who was father of Thomas Norton the elder, and Thomas Norton the younger; will proved Feb. 16th, 1449, and registered in the Library at Lambeth, *Stafford*, 184.

A document at the Record Office mentions that John Streynesham, John Nancothan, and some others, were employed to collect a subsidy in the town and suburb of Bristol, 24 Henry vi. And from the Worcester diocesan registers, it appears that a Thomas de Strengesham was ordained an acolyte in Worcester cathedral in 1314, and that John Strengesham was of Ashchurch, co. Gloucester, in 1369.

244.—AGNES FYLOUR, widow.

1467. Nov. 8th. Testatrix was of the parish of All Saints in Bristol, and desired to be buried in the parish church there, in the chapel of holy Cross, by the burial-place of Thomas Hallewey. To Sir Maurice Hardwyk, vicar of the said church, for tithes and offerings, vj^s. viij^d., also a chalice of silver and gilt, for his own use. Six chaplains, named by him, to take part in the mortuary offices during one month after the death of testatrix, and have forty shillings sterling equally divided among them. A fit secular chaplain to celebrate *pro anima* in that church for three years, and be paid £18 for that term. To the mother church of Worcester viij^d. To son Thomas Fylour of London, mercer, a messuage in the High-street at Bristol, inhabited by testatrix, situate between the messuage "voc' le Grene latyce" inhabited by John Compton, on the north, and land belonging to the abbot and convent of Tewkesbury, and held of them by testatrix, on the south, and extending from the said street to the land of the master of St. Laurence by

Bristol. The said Thomas to keep the anniversary of testatrix every year, expending twelve shillings on the same; that is to say, giving to eight priests four pence apiece; to the poor five shillings in bread; to the clerk "Classicu' pulsanti" twelve pence, and for his other duties two pence: to the town-crier two pence; to the vicar for the time being, for wax to burn, twelve pence, and that he may see to the fulfilment of these orders, and have her "recommended" among the other benefactors of the said church, twelve pence; and to the procurators, that they may attend to the holding of the said anniversary, twelve pence, equally divided. After the death of the said Thomas, the messuage is to be held by daughter Joan, on condition of her keeping the anniversary in the same manner; after the said Joan's decease, rem. to Sir Maurice Hardwyk, vicar of All Saints', and John Compton and William Rowley, procurators of the said church, to be held by them, and their assigns, on the same condition; which parties are to have and keep all the muniments relating to the aforesaid messuage immediately after the decease of testatrix. To daughter Joan "duas pecias de Crescloth," a kirtle, &c., and two pieces "de Rawe flemyssh." To son Thomas's wife, a gown of scarlet. A sum of money to be laid out "in Camisijs & Smokkys" for poor men and women. Clothing also for servants Isabel Abell, Dionisia, and "Theodur." Son Thomas to be executor, and dispose of the residue after payment of debts, &c. Richard Haddon to be overseer, and have "p' suo labore vnu' Nobile."

Proved before Thomas Bevyr, bachelor in decrees, commissary in the town and deanery of Bristol for the Bishop of Worcester, Nov. 30th, 1467 also before Robert Jakys, Mayor, and John Hoper, Sheriff.

245.—WILLIAM SHEPWARDE, otherwise Barstaple, of Marlborough, co. Wilts, gentleman.   In the margin *Shipward*.

1467. July 23rd. To be buried in the church of the blessed Mary of Marlborough, to the vicar of which, for tithes, and for his prayers, xx^s. For the sustentation of the light of the blessed Mary "de Pytte," in the said church, a cow. To the fabric of St. Peter's church in the same town iij^s iiij^d. To Sir John Aspsen, chaplain, vj^s viij^d. To the fabric of the cathedral church of the blessed Mary of Salisbury iij^s iiij^d. To the fabric of the church of All Saints at Burbache vj^s viij^d, and those two cows in the keeping of Robert Kember, so that the guardians of the said church keep testator's obit therein yearly for ever. To the fabric of St. Thomas's church in the city of Worcester (a mistake for *Winchester*), vj^s viij^d. To the fabric of the church of the Holy Trinity at Mottesfont vj^{li} xiij^s iiij^d sterling, that the prior and convent thereof may keep testator's obit every year, after the sale of his capital messuage or tenement, lately that of Hugh Crane, in the aforesaid city of Worcester (*Winchester*). To the fabric of the church of St. Margaret at Poughley co. Berks, five marks sterling, that the prior and convent thereof may yearly keep his obit. To John Hardy, "ad orand' p' ai'a mea," vj^s viij^d. To William Shepward otherwise Barstaple, "Nepoti meo," forty shillings, after the sale of the tenement in Cornestrete at Bristol. To Isabel Newbury, after the sale of the capital messuage or tenement in the aforesaid city of Winchester, 100 shillings sterling. To Robert Erley, brother of the said Isabel, a gown, &c., and twenty shillings in money, after the sale of the said capital messuage. To

William Manger, and his wife Emmot, testator's sister, six marks, and all the moveable goods in the said capital messuage; also a tenement in Radclyfstrete at Bristol, for their life, and a rent issuing from the messuage or tenement "in alto vico voc' le Starretau'ne in villa Bristollie;" and a rent from a messuage on the bridge of Bristol, late the property of my mother Joan Erley, lately wife of Robert Erley, who was of Wolsale, co. Wilts, esquire; remainder to John Shepward otherwise Barstable, "nepoti meo," and his lawful issue; in default, rem. to Robert Shepward otherwise Barstable, and his lawful issue; in def., rem. to the aforesaid William Shepward otherwise Barstable, and his lawful issue; in def., rem. to Thomas Shepward otherwise Barstable; in def., rem. to John Shepward the elder, merchant of Bristol. To the aforesaid John Shepward otherwise Barstable, two tenements with adjoining gardens in Marleburgh; one of them called "Caleys," and situate in Seyntmarigrene there, between the tenement of William Dolman, on the north, and the tenement of Yorke (sic), on the south; the other tenement being situate in the street as one goes towards the Castle "extra lez barres," and held by John Frenshman, weaver. But if the said John Shepward otherwise Barstable does not conduct himself well towards the executors, they are to have the said two tenements. To the said executors, the lands and tenements in the city of Winchester, in which Robert Pytte otherwise Cornyssh, citizen of Winchester, is enfeoffed; also the aforesaid tenement in Cornestrete at Bristol, inhabited by Thomas Shiplode, wherein Henry Vaughan and others "ad meam deno'icac'oem ex confidencia ffeoffat' exist';" the said property to be sold for payment of debts and legacies, and for masses and charitable purposes *pro anima*. Meadow and other lands in Groston, and Westledwyn, "ac de Fourde," in which Robert Roo "de hospic' d'ni Regis," and others, are enfeoffed for testator's use, to be held, immediately after his decease, by William Manger and his wife Emmot, testator's sister, and their heirs and assigns, on condition that they keep his obit every year in the aforesaid church of the blessed Mary of Marleburgh. The said William and Emmot, and John Wyse, vintner, citizen of New Sarum, to be executors.

No record of proof.

Walter Bardestaple occurs on the Gloucestershire subsidy-roll, 6 Edw. ii, above referred to; he, and William de Pridie, Richard de Pridie, Thomas de Pridie, Blissota Vallet, and Thomas Hemyng, weaver, possessed goods in the ward of the blessed Mary in the Market, in the town of Bristol.

246.—JOHN JAY, burgess.

1468. April 13th. To be buried in the choir of the parish church of St. Mary of Redcliff, Bristol, to which church, for his burial, xx^s, and to the vicar, for tithes, vj^s viij^d. To the mother church of Wells xij^d. To the church of St. Thomas the Martyr, at Bristol, vj^s viij^d. Testator's wife Joan to have 100 marks in ready money, in silver bowls and cups, and 100 marks in salt and other articles of merchandise. Household vessels, "hoc est in Aula in Parlario in Cameris et in Coquina," to be divided into three equal parts; wife Joan to take the first part; the two other parts to be for the five children. To elder daughter Joan, a pipe of woad, and two whole cloths; her mother's legacy also to be for her. Testator's share of the ship called "Trinite" to be for his sons John and Henry. To the said Henry, the house in Templestrete lately inhabited by John Bukke; also "vnu' vas et vnu' fforneys." To younger daughter Joan £20 in money, in merchandise wares, and in utensils. The same to daughter Julian. If all the children should die, "q'd absit," the effects bequeathed to them to be disposed of *pro anima*. Son John to be executor, and have the ordering of the residue of goods. John Dunstar, prior of the monastery of Bath, Master Nicholas Pittes, vicar of Redcliff, my brother John Jaye, and John Godard, merchant, to be overseers.

Proved before Robert Jakys, Mayor, and John Hoper, Sheriff, on Wednesday in the feast of St. Margaret Virgin, 8 Edward iv. Previously proved before the ecclesiastical authorities.

247.—TANGELA A CLONNE, widow. In the margin *Aclonne*.

1468. Feb. 10th. To be buried in the cemetery of the church of St. James of Bristol "iuxta Sepulturam Parentum & ffamuliar' meor'." To the mother church of the blessed Mary the Virgin at Worcester iiij^d. To the parish church of St. James aforesaid a brass dish. To the sustentation of St. Katharine's altar in that church "vnu' Palliu' de le Twylly." To William Payne, son of daughter Alice, £4 of lawful money of England; and the same to his brother Thomas Payne. John Houndesley, merchant, and his wife Alice, the said daughter of testatrix, to be executors, and dispose of the residue of goods *pro anima*. Sir William Nuport, prior of the priory house and church of St. James aforesaid, overseer; to whom ij^s for tithes and offerings, and for his prayers.

Proved before Philip Mede, Mayor, and Robert Strannge, Sheriff, March 13th, 9 Edward iv. Previously proved before Thomas Bevir, commissary in the town and deanery of Bristol for the Bishop of Worcester.

248.—JOHN NANCOTHAN.

1469. Oct. 14th. To be buried in the chapel of St. John Baptist within the church of St. Ewen of Bristol. Legacies to the rector that church, the fraternity of St. John Baptist there, the mother church of Worcester, the parish church of All Saints at Bristol, the fabric of the church of the Holy Trinity there, the fabric of the church of the blessed Mary of Yatton, of the parish church of Congresbury, and of the church of St. Paul "iuxta Porthynes" in Cornwall. To Sir Robert Dewy, chaplain of the aforesaid fraternity, a gown "Coloris Blacke a lire engreyned Cum quadam ffurrura voc' le Croppes of Grey." To John, son of testator, £20 sterling, also "men' Salsare Optimn' Argenteu'," six silver spoons, having a maiden's head at the end of every spoon, an entire bed, &c. To daughter Margaret £20, also "men' Optimn' Nucem," and other six spoons, having "in ffine cuiuslib't Coeliar' Caput Puelle." To daughter Edith forty shillings sterling, a cup, &c. To daughter Isabel forty shillings, a cup, &c. Twelve pence sterling to each of the children "quos a Sacro fonte leuaui." To the venerable (venerabili viro) Philip Meed, merchant, forty shilings. Wife Margaret to be executrix. The said Philip Meed overseer.

Proved before John Shipward, Mayor, and William Brydd, Sheriff, Aug. 6th, 10 Edward iv. Previously proved before the ecclesiastical authorities.

249.—WILLIAM ROKES.

1469. March 11th. To be buried in the chancel of the parish church of St. Stephen at Bristol, beside the burial-place of former wife Joan. To the cathedral church of Worcester xij^d. To the rector of the aforesaid church of St. Stephen, "Curato meo," xx^d; and to the use of that church, on account of testator's interment therein, vj^s viij^d. To daughter Elizabeth a pipe of woad, and a silver cup. To daughter Katharine one whole cloth, and a silver cup. To son John a whole cloth, &c. To Elizabeth, wife of testator, for her life, his dwelling house in Merschstrete, situate between the tenement belonging to St. Stephen's church, on the south, and one of the Lady de Seymour, on the north, and extending from the street to the tenement of the said church; remainder to son John and his lawful issue. If all testator's children should die s.p., rem. to John Rokes "Nepoti meo," and his heirs; in default of issue, the said property to be sold, and the money distributed for the good of testator's soul, and that of his uncle Thomas Rokes, &c. Wife Elizabeth to be executrix. William Spencer overseer.

Proved at Lambeth June 28th, 1470; before John Shipward, Mayor, and William Brydd, Sheriff, Aug. 11th, 10 Edward iv.

The Lady de Seymour here referred to was probably Isabel relict of Sir John Seymour knt., who is mentioned in the will of John Barton, burgess of Bristol: no. 239. Bishop Carpenter's register at Worcester, vol. i., folio 192, states that Isabel Seymour, widow, took the vow of perpetual chastity in the collegiate church of Westbury "int' missar' solempnia," in the presence of the said bishop, who gave her his benediction, and put upon her the vidual vesture, June 3rd, 1465.

250.—JOAN FORDE. In the margin *Foorde*.

1463. Feb. 8th. Testatrix had been wife of John Forde deceased, and desired to be buried "iuxta Sepultura' de'i Joh'is fforde. scil't in Cimiterio Eccl'ie P'och' Se'e Crucis Templi" at Bristol, in the diocese of Bath and Wells. To the vicar thereof, for his prayers, and for tithes and offerings forgotten, vj^s viij^d. A fit secular chaplain to celebrate in that church for two whole years for the welfare of her soul, and the soul of her husband, parents, &c. To the mother church of Wells xl^d. To John Bryd, son of my son John Bryd, the value of £30 in money and instruments pertaining to the craft of a dyer, and household goods. If he should die under the age of twenty, £10 to remain to John Strafford of London, grocer, £5 to Isabel wife of William Kemys, mercer, and £5 to the Carmelite Friars of Bristol, where the parents of testatrix were buried, provided that her name and that of the aforesaid John Fo.de, and the names of her parents are especially named among the other benefactors "in Pulpito P'dicat' temp'e cciam Missar' & di'or'." Master Walter Hunt, brother of testatrix, and her kinsman Henry Chestir to be executors, and dispose of the remaining £10, and also have the keeping of the aforesaid John Bryd. Edith Wolf, overseer, to whom a gold ring, &c.

Proved in the parish church of Redcliff, Nov. 16th, 1464. No record of proof before the Mayor.

251.—JOHN GAYWODE, burgess.

1471. May 11th. To be buried in the church of the blessed Mary of Redcliff, at Bristol, by the entrance to the chapel of the blessed Mary, "sub lapide ib'm p' me ordinat'." To the fabric of that church xx^s. To my curate, Master Nicholas Pyttes, for tithes, vj^s viij^d. To the cathedral church of Wells xx^d. Forty shillings to the fabric of the church of St. Thomas the Martyr at Bristol. Four pence to Master Bulkeley, that he may be present in the said church of St. Thomas on the day of burial, or of the obit "ad Mensem." To the scholars of the said master, that they may be present therein, and say "v. p'r. n'r. v. Ave maria Cum Credo," on either of those occasions, eight pence among them "in vino causa recreac'onis." Legacies also for the repair of the tenements belonging to the fraternity of the Assumption of B.V.M. on the bridge of Avon; to the fabric of the parish church of Worle, co. Somerset; the four orders of friars at Bristol, if present at the mortuary offices; the needy poor of the fraternity of St. John Baptist; the poor of the almshouse of "longerewe," and of Richard Forster by Redcelyfyate, of the "Lazarchous apud Brightbowe," of the almshouse of William Canynges on Redcliff hill, and of John Spicer by Temple gate; the poor of the fraternity of St. Katharine; the poor and needy at the fullers' hall; the poor of the almshouse near the church of All Saints, and of the Holy Trinity "apud Laffordesyate;" the needy prisoners of Newgate; to the prior, subprior, canons, and priests of the priory house of Wursprynge, co. Somerset, also eight pence among them for a flagon of wine; to Margaret Palmer, for her marriage; to Master Thomas Palmer, rector of Wynterborne, Nicholas Palmer, Sir William Palmer, canon of Wursprynge, John Palmer, the elder, and John Palmer, the younger; wife's daughter Joan Coklonde, and her husband Philip Coklonde; William Browne, husband of sister Agnes; Katharine Bury, Joan Poleyne, servants Alice Crosse and Agnes Burye, and apprentice Thomas Skynner. To Agnes, testator's wife, his dwelling house in Redclyf Strete, situate between a tenement of William Rogers, on the north, and a certain void place of Richard Arthour of Clopton, esquire, on the south, and extending from the street to "le Lawedyche;" also a tenement inhabited by Joan Newe, widow, in the same street, situate between the tenement of John Bagod, on the north, and that of John Merbury, esquire, on the south, and extending from the street to the river Avon behind; a tenement inhabited by Thomas Taillour in Wynchestrete, between a tenement belonging to St. Augustine's monastery, on the east, and one belonging to the Commonalty of Bristol, on the west, and extending from the street to the house of Richard Haddon; and a garden "iuxta le Were" in the suburb, as one goes towards Elebrigge, opposite the tenement inhabited by Thomas Oseney: all this property to be held by the said Agnes for her life, and to remain afterwards to son John Gaywod and his lawful issue; in default of such, rem. to daughter Katharine and her lawful issue; in def., rem. to daughter Isabel and her lawful issue; in def., rem. to testator's brother John Gaywod of Pevesey; in def., rem. to testator's sister Agnes Browne and her lawful issue; in def., rem. to William Gaywode of Stamfourde; in def., rem. to the rightful heirs "Sanguinis mei." To son John a tenement in the suburb "in Angulo Redclyf Pytte," opposite the hospital of St. John Baptist, between a tenement belonging to the said hospital, on the north, and Pylestrete, on the south; the said John to make a yearly payment to testator's daughter Katharine. To brother John Gaywode, of Pewesey, for his life, a tenement and garden on Redcliff hill, opposite the cemetery of the blessed Mary of Redcliff, situate between the tenement of Master Nicholas Pyttes, vicar of Redcliff, on the north, and property of John Whitton of Bakwell, co. Somerset, on the south, and extending from the street to the garden of Redcliff vicarage; which tenement formerly belonged to testator's uncle, Richard Stamforde of West Tekynham; rem. to son John and his lawful issue; in def., rem. to the procurators of the church of the blessed Mary of Redcliff for ever. To son John, a garden with a well therein, by Brightbowe, extending in length from the King's way to a close of the master of St. John Baptist's hospital, opposite the cross standing in the King's way, by the almshouse "de Lazares," and extending in width between a tenement of the Lady Lysle and the garden of William Rogers of Bristol; also two closes and a garden at Brightbowe, extending, on the west, from the King's way to Redeclyf Mede, and, on the south, to a close of the master of St. Katharine's hospital by Bristol, and, from the north part, to the small close of the Lady Lysle; half an acre of meadow in Redeclyf Mede, containing in length 391 feet (pedes regales) towards the south-west and north-east, and in width, to the end of the said Mede south-west, 56 feet, and in the end of the said Mede north-east, two feet and upwards; and a tenement in Worshuppstrete "alias vocat' Shamels," inhabited by John Goldesborough, boucher, situate between a tenement of the prior of St. James of Bristol, on the west, and the tenement of John Halle of Redelande, on the east, and extending from the street to a tenement of Thomas Norton, inhabited by William Isegar; the said son John and his lawful issue to hold this property, and the sum of twenty shillings from the tenement in Worschuppstrete to be paid to Agnes, sister of testator, yearly throughout her life. To the same John, a tenement in St. Mary's street, "exoppo'ito eccl'iam b'te Marie de fforo," between John Sherp's tenement, on the west, and a tenement belonging to the fraternity of the Assumption of the blessed Mary, on the east; rem. to the use of the Commonalty of Bristol, at the ordering of the Mayor and Chamberlain, if John should die s.p. To daughter Isabel, for her marriage, twenty marks sterling; if she should die before marriage, ten marks to son John, and ten for the marriage of Margaret Palmer, daughter of testator's sister; also to the said Isabel, "vnam Tabulam duplicatam de Wayneskott cu' quatuor pedibz & vnu' Beste in eadem," &c.; also two small gardens in the lane by Elebrigge, where one goes towards Laffordesyate, which gardens extend from the said lane to the King's way in "Olde Market," and are situate between the garden of John Yonge of London, on the west, and that of William Boxe, on the east; a house in the corner by the Were "apud watryngplace," extending from the King's way by the castle wall to the garden of the chantry "Eborardi le ffrenssh," and, in the eastern direction, towards the garden of the Lady Isabel Seymour; and a void place at the Barres, "pro gardino," between the tenement of Thomas Asshe, on the north, and a certain void place of the Lady Isabel Seymour, widow, on the south; which property testator had bought of Sir Nicholas Barstaple, clerk, and John Warmystre of Wynterborne, co. Gloucester: rem. to son John for his life, and afterwards to the use of the Commonalty of Bristol, if the said daughter Isabel should die s.p. To son John, a purse of cloth of gold, a pair of beads " de Calsydonyes ;" also, after the death of testator's wife Agnes, tapestry for the hall and parlor, with bankers and cushions to match ; two pairs of cuirasses complete " cu' dualz Saletes viscrat' iacent' in nouo barello vocat' hogyshed ;" a pair of brigandines covered with red worsted, with buckles and pendants of silver ; the two best pollaxes, "cu' vno longedbeef garnisat' cu' Cerico ;" a spear standing in the hall by the entrance to the kitchen ; a candlestick of latten hanging in the hall ; two great andirons for the hall, in use at the feast of Christmas (ad ff'm Cristysmas) ; a silver cup " de Paryce fact' cum Curto Pede Ac Cum vno Signo Ju Medio Colorat' cum Amell' ;" twenty marks sterling ; &c. To Richard Selar, husband of daughter Katharine, the second best gown of black "pennlat' cum Wylde-ware," a pair of cuirasses complete, with a salet and visor. Wife Agnes to be executrix. Edmund Newe overseer. Testator's seal being unknown to most people, he caused the seal of the mayoralty of Bristol to be put to his will, July 18th, 11 Edward iv., Thomas Kempson being then Mayor.

Proved before John Cogan, Mayor, and John Jay, Sheriff, Oct. 24th, 12 Edward iv. Previously proved before the ecclesiastical authorities.

252.—JOHN SEYNTE, burgess.

1471. Dec. 25th. To be buried in the parish church of the Holy Trinity at Bristol. For burial there vj^s viij^d, and the same sum to the rector for tithes. To the mother church of Worcester xij^d. To wife Alice, son John, and daughter Joan, tenements in Stipestrete, in the parish of St. Michael in Bristol. To Alice, wife of testator, and to his and her children, two other tenements in the same street, situate near the void place of the sisters of the Magdalene, for the keeping of his obit in the church aforesaid, in the vigil of the Apostles Simon and Jude, the obsequies of the dead to be had in the vigil, and mass on the morrow following, attended by six chap-lains, to be nominated by the rector, or any one else occupying his place ; remainder, after the death of the said Alice and the children, to the use of the procurators of the said church for ever, who are to have the obit kept in the aforesaid form. The said Alice is also to find a secular chaplain in the said church of the Holy Trinity for the space of one year. Testator grants full power to his son John, and makes him heir of all his lands and tene-ments within and about the town of Newport in Wales, formerly the property of John Clerke ; namely, the " hospicium " opposite the tenement of William Kemmys, situate a little way beyond the high cross, and extending from the street to the well "vocat' Payneswell ;" and another tenement in the middle of that town, formerly called " Coyte place," which tenement Morgan Jenkyn ap Philipp built on testator's land, and held for a long time, " et adhuc ininste detinet," with divers other lands and tene-ments, to our cost and detriment and the hurt of his soul. To the said John all things pertaining to the craft of brewing, " vnu' par Sereticar' de le Plate," a salet, the best pollaxe, a pair of brigandines covered with blue velvet, and adorned with embossed work (cu' pustulis), and pendants, &c. To wife's daughter Alice twelve silver spoons, and a coverlet "de Arace." Legacies also to John Mayhowe " wexmaker," William Proute, purser, and John Seynt upon the Back. Wife Alice and son John to be executors. Thomas Proute overseer. Witnessed by John Bagod, John Mayhowe, "Wexchaundeler," and others.

Proved at Lambeth, March 31st, 1473; afterwards at Bristol, before the Mayor and Sheriff.

253.—WILLIAM ROGERS, of Bristol.

1471. May 6th. To be buried in the church of St. Stephen in Bristol, by the tomb of his father. To the church of Mary at Worcester twelve pence. To the fabric of the said church of St. Stephen three measures of woad. Legacies also to the rector of that church, Master Geoffrey the curate, and William the suffragan there; to kinsman John Croke, and John Wodeward, chaplain. To eldest son William a tenement in Redcliffstrete, lately held by William Hurne, between the tenements of Thomas Yonge and John Gaywode. To son Thomas the other tenement situate in that street. Wife Maud to possess the said two tenements for her life. If she should die during the minority of the said sons, the property is to be under the management of the executors until they are of full age. If both sons should die under age, it is to be at the disposal of the said Maud and her executors and assigns. To John Skryven, merchant, "meam Tunicam Squamatatam, vulgariter nuncupat'. A pair of Brigandyrons." Residue of goods to wife Maud and her assigns. She to be executrix, and to dispose for the health of testator's soul. John Wodeward and John Skryven overseers.

Proved at Lambeth, Nov. 21st, 1471; afterwards at Bristol, before the Mayor and Sheriff.

254.—JOHN CLERKE, mercer.

1473. April 3rd. Testator was of the parish of St. Thomas the Martyr at Bristol, and desired to be buried in the church there. To the fabric of that church two quarters of woad. To the cathedral church of Wells ij^s iiij^d. To Master Nicholas Pittes, vicar of the parish churches of Bedminster and Redcliff, and testator's curate, xx^s for tithes and funeral lights. To elder son John, son William, and younger son John, two pipes of woad apiece; the said six pipes to be paid to them out of the woad then being in parts beyond the sea. To the parish church of Warmyster a pair of green vestments. Residue to wife Giles (Egidia) and son William, who are made executors. Witnessed by Philip Meede, merchant, Richard Dugmore, chaplain, William Wykam, John Reynold, John Smyth, and John White, burgesses of Bristol, and others.

Proved at Lambeth, April 13th, 1473; afterwards at Bristol, before the Mayor and Sheriff.

255.—JOHN BROWNE, baker and burgess.

1473. Jan. 20th. "Compos mentis mee laudetur altissimus." To be buried in the church of the Apostles SS. Philip and Jacob, within the chapel of St. Nicholas. For the use of that church, and for testator's burial there, x^s. To his curate, that he may pray "p' ai'a mea," iij^s iiij^d. To the cathedral church of Worcester xij^d. Twelve chaplains to take part in the mortuary offices, and have iiij^d apiece. Twelve torches to burn on the day of burial and at the month's mind. Wife Alice to find for herself meat, drink, and clothing, during her life. To the said Alice a tenement in the suburb of Bristol "in vico vocat' Olde Markett," situate between the garden of Thomas Yong, on the west, and the King's way towards Elbrigge, on the east, and extending from the street to the garden of Sir Edward Grey knt. Lord Lisle; to remain, after the death of the said Alice, to son William and his lawful issue; in default, rem. to son Humphrey and his lawful issue; in def., rem to son Henry; in def., rem. to son Thomas; in def., rem. to daughter Margery; in def., rem. to daughter Joan; in def., rem. to John Browne, son of testator's late son John, and his lawful issue; in def., rem. to the procurators of the church of the Apostles Philip and Jacob, for the use of the said church for ever. Gowns to testator's brother Thomas, and his brother in law (ffratri in lege). To his sister Agnes "vnn' Curtell' Cloth." Residue to wife Alice, who is made executrix. Thomas Keamys overseer, to whom four marks sterling. Witnessed by the said Thomas Keamys, Richard Batheryn, John Calicote, and others.--Oseney.

Proved at Knoll, April 2nd, 1474; afterwards at Bristol, before William Spenser, Mayor, and Edmund Westcote, Sheriff.

256.—WILLIAM CODER, burgess and merchant. In the margin *Codder*.

1473. March 14th.—"sanus mente laudetur altissimus." To be buried in the crypt of the parish church of St. Nicholas at Bristol, under testator's marble stone, beside the bodies of his wives there interred. To the procurators of the said crypt, for his burial there, xiij^s iiij^d. To the chaplain of the fraternity, celebrating therein, that he may pray for testator's soul, vj^s viij^d. To the said church of St. Nicholas a hundred marks for a set of vestments. To the mother church of Worcester xiij^s iiij^d. To the parish church of St. Leonard in Bristol £40 for a set of vestments. To the fabric of the campanile, and for the reparation of the parish church of St. Laurence of Ludlow twenty marks. To the friars of the blessed and glorious Virgin Mary of Mount Carmel at Ludlow aforesaid xx^s, that they may pray for testator's soul, and devoutly celebrate the mortuary offices and mass; and the same sum to the Augustinian friars there. To the Friars Preachers of Bristol xx^s, that they may be present at various mortuary offices, and on the day of the anniversary. Sums of money also to the three other orders of friars at Bristol, that they may be present; and to each curate of Bristol, each annuellere priest, and every parish clerk in the town, if present on the day of burial. Twenty poor people to hold torches about testator's body on that day, or at least on the day of his trental, and have a gown with a hood of Welsh cloth. Bread and ale to be distributed among the poor, feeble, and needy on the day of burial, and on that of the trental. Forty shillings to the parish church of Westbury, that the parishioners there may recommend testator's soul in their prayers. To Thomas Withyford, gentleman, two pipes of woad, reckoning sixteen measures in each pipe. To kinsman John Coder all those books of Latin (Latinales) already in his keeping, and all the Latin books in a chest within testator's house, together with the said chest, and ten marks in money. To William Coder of Newland £10. To his son Richard £5. To John Mason xx^s, &c. The debt of five marks is remitted to the mother of the said John Mason, on condition of her providing him with necessaries at school. To William Colwell, son of testator's daughter Agnes Coder (*sic*), a hundred marks, and five pipes of woad; the said William Colwell and his legacies to be in the keeping and governance of William Hoton, merchant of Bristol, until he be of full age, namely, 21; the said William Hoton finding sufficient security to the Mayor of the town of Bristol, as the custom is. If the said William Colwell should die under age, his effects are to go to testator's issue. To Thomas Oseney, clerk to the Mayor and Commonalty of Bristol, three yards of scarlet cloth, and forty shillings in ready money. To William Hoton, merchant of Bristol, and his heirs, a tenement in "Ooldcornestrete," situate between the cemetery of the parish church of St. Leonard and the tenement inhabited by William Water, and extending from the said street to the garden of Sir Edmund Hungreford knt. The said William Hoton to keep testator's anniversary in the said church of St. Leonard, with six chaplains, and tolling of the bells there, and distribute ten shillings yearly among the feeble and needy poor, and order the burning of four tapers, to the value of iij^s iiij^d, at the said anniversary, and lay out yearly, *pro anima*, xl^s in pious uses and works of charity. To the fraternity of the holy Cross at the church of St. John Baptist of Bristol xx^s. Legacies also to the prioress and convent of the blessed Mary Magdalene at Bristol, the poor of long Rewe and at Laffordesyate, Alice Hoton, Lodowic Jonnys, merchant of Bristol, Katharine Aphowell, Maud Coder, Margaret Lewes, each of testator's maid servants, John son of William Hoton, John son of William Wodyngton, merchant of Bristol, William Hoton, canon of St. Augustine's monastery at Bristol, and son of the aforesaid William, Philip Puton of Ludlow, Walter Puton, and Sir Richard Warens, chaplain. The aforesaid William Hoton and William Wodyngton to be executors, and have £10 apiece. Witnessed by Sir John Torner, clerk, vicar of St. Leonard's in Bristol, Sir Richard Warens, chaplain, Richard Coder of Newland, and many others.

Proved at Knoll, April 2nd, 1474; afterwards at Bristol, before the Mayor and Sheriff.

257.—WILLIAM HYNDE, burgess and whittawer.

1473. Feb. 27th. To be buried in the cemetery of the church of St. James in Bristol. To the mother church of Worcester iij^s iiij^d. To the new bell, bought of John Callicote, to serve in the church of St. James aforesaid, iiij^l. A fit chaplain to celebrate therein for three years. To the prior of St. James, and Laurence the parish chaplain there, iij^s iiij^d apiece. Ten shillings to be equally divided among the four orders of friars on the day of burial, and the same sum to be laid out in bread for the poor. To Daniel Sheldon a horse. To Thomas Proud "meam Togam de Kendall." To Roger Wotton a new gown "pellipat' cu' flechewes." To John, son of testator's son John, ten marks of silver when eighteen years of age. To Joan, sister of the said John, ten marks when she is married. If both should die under age, the twenty marks are to be distributed *pro anima*. Legacies also to Joan, late wife of son John, the chamber of the town of Bristol, John Swayn, and testator's maid Edith. Half of the residue of goods to wife Joan; the other half to be under the control of the aforesaid John Swayn and the said Joan for her life, if she remains unmarried. These two to be executors, and the aforesaid Roger Wotton overseer. Witnessed by Laurence Preston, chaplain, Thomas Skydmore, Thomas Proude, and others.

Proved before Robert Carewe, master of arts, commissary of the Bishop of Worcester, in the parish church of St. James at Bristol, Aug. 11th, 1474; afterwards before the Mayor, &c.

258.—WILLIAM CANYNGES. In the margin—"Test'm Will'i Canynges nup' decani de Westbury, antea p' quinq' vices nup' Maioris ville Bristoll'."

1474. Nov. 12th. Testator describes himself as clerk, dean of the collegiate church and college of the Holy Trinity of Westbury upon Trym, by Bristol, in the diocese of Worcester, and lately a merchant of the town of Bristol aforesaid. He commends his soul to Almighty God, the B.V.M., and all the saints, and desires to be buried in the church of the blessed Mary of Redcliff at Bristol, in the place which he had constructed and made on the south side of that church, by the altar of St. Katharine, where the body of his late wife Joan was buried. To the mother church of Wells xx^d. To Master Nicholas Pittes, vicar of the said church of Redcliff, v^{li}, on condition that the lights on the day of burial and the month's mind be borne and lighted freely, and without further payment, within that church and the limits thereof, and that the executors arrange on the day of burial twenty-four torches "nouit' empt' quolib't eor' ponderis xxj^{li} cere," with other tapers according to their discretion; the said torches, after the month's mind, to be distributed to twenty-four parish churches outside and nearest to Bristol in either direction. To every chaplain of the said church of Redcliff vj^s viij^d, on condition of their being present on the day of burial, and through the whole month immediately following testator's death, and saying daily by note, in the choir of the said church, the exequies of the dead, and mass of *Requiem*. To each of the three clerks serving in the said church iij^s iiij^d, on condition of their being present. To each of the three procurators of the church vj^s viij^d. To the keeper of the box for oblations at the north doorway of that church xx^d. To each of the fellows of the collegiate church and college of Westbury aforesaid vj^s viij^d, and to each chaplain and deacon of the same college v^s, on condition of their personal attendance at the obsequies and mass in the said church of Westbury, and afterwards conducting his body to the church of Redcliff, to the place of burial. To John Hampton iij^s iiij^d, on the same condition. To John Gardyner xx^d, on the same condition. To Thomas Norman xx^d, on the same condition. To William Whetenhall xx^d, on the same condition. To William Clerk, "aquebainlo de Westbury p'dict'," iij^s iiij^d, on the same condition. To each of the twelve chorister boys of Westbury viij^d, on the same condition. To the six priests of the new chapel, lately founded in Westbury aforesaid by the venerable father in Christ and lord John bishop of Worcester, iij^s iiij^d apiece, to pray for testator's soul. To each of the six poor almsmen of Westbury, lately founded by the said lord bishop, xij^d. To each of the six poor widows of Westbury, lately founded by the same, xij^d. To the fabric of the church of Westbury xl^s. To the fabric of the church of Compton Craynefeld, and to the tower thereof, xl^s. To testator's poor almsmen dwelling on Redclyfhull at Bristol, to each one of them living at the time of his death, xx^s. To the order of Friars Minors of Bristol xx^s, on condition of being at the mortuary offices and mass on the day of burial, and of the month's mind, in the aforesaid church of Redcliff, and on the day of the anniversary in the first year after testator's death. Legacies to each of the other orders of friars at Bristol, on the same condition; to the fraternities of the Assumption of the blessed Mary on the bridge of Avon, St. John Baptist founded in the church of St. Ewen, St. Katharine of Bristol founded in holy Cross Temple, and the fraternity of the Commemoration of Souls founded in the church of the blessed Mary of Redcliff; to Thomas Warley, William Cooke, John Wadnyng. Richard Hikkes, William Trowell, and Gregory Greemer, servants of testator; to Janen Cooke, and John Boriet, servants of the college of Westbury. The sum of xx^{li} to be distributed to the poor, lame, blind, decrepit, and needy dwelling in Bristol on the day of burial; a further sum of xx^{li} to them at the month's mind; and xx^{li} to the poor on the day of the anniversary. To the church of Redcliff aforesaid testator's two books" voc' liggers cu' integra legenda," on condition that one of the said books be in the choir of that church before one of his chaplains there, "p' me p' p'petuo fundat'," on one side of the choir, and the other book on the other side, before his other chaplain for the time being, as need may require. To his chaplain Peter Lawles, and his successors, serving or ministering at the altar of St. Katharine of Redcliff aforesaid, the best pair of vestments of velvet. To his chaplain Thomas Hawkesok, and his successors, a pair of vestments of damask "blodij Coloris" for ministration at the altar of St. George in the said church. Another pair of vestments of red damask for the use of the hospital of St. John Baptist in Redclifputte for ever. To William Canynges, nephew of testator, a tenement in the corner of Bradstrete at Bristol, by St. John's gate, inhabited by Richard Deryk, shoemaker, in which tenement Elizabeth Sherp, widow, has the half of one chamber by right of inheritance; also a tenement annexed thereto in St. Laurence's lane, where one goes from Bradstrete towards Smallestreet, opposite the church of St. Laurence the Martyr, inhabited by John Robyns, hooper; testator's whole state in a tenement inhabited by William Wykham, dyer, in Redclyfstrete, between a tenement of Philip Meede and one belonging to the monastery of St. Augustine at Bristol; a close lying between the meadow called Redclyfmede and testator's garden opposite the cemetery of the blessed Mary of Redcliff; an orchard in Pilestrete, held by John Tyler, weaver, between the King's way and a small garden of testator's; also that small garden held by the same John Tyler in Redelane; also the reversion of tenements, lands, &c., in Bristol and the suburb, in the hand of Isabel Powlett, late wife of William Canynges, testator's deceased son, by the gift of testator for her life only; namely, two tenements in Westowkerstrete, in the parish of St. Thomas the Martyr, situate between property of the prior of the Carthusian house of Witham on either side; also two messuages on the bridge of Avon, situate between a messuage of Isabel, late wife of Sir John Seymour knt., on the north, and a lane where one goes to a certain draught called "Avenprevey," on the south, and extending from the King's way to a void place of land belonging to the Mayor and Commonalty of Bristol; also the messuage inhabited by Richard Griffith, waxmaker, on the bridge of Avon, between the tenement of Thomas Yong and his wife Isabel, on the south, and that of John Taverner, on the north; a large tenement with fourteen shops opposite St. Peter's cross, between the shops of our lady the Queen, which Simon Olyver lately caused to be built anew, and a lane called "Strete of defence;" and two messuages "sup' le Weer," between land belonging to the prior and convent of Witham and the tenement of Hugh Mulle, gentleman: all this property to be held by the said William after the said Isabel's death. If he should die s.p., it is to remain to Isabel (Elizabeth) Canynges, niece of testator, and sister of the said William, and to her lawful issue. If she should die s.p., it is to be sold by the Mayor and Common Council of Bristol, and the procurators of the church of the blessed Mary of Redcliff; one half of the money to be delivered to the said procurators for the use and sustentation of his two perpetual chantries founded by him in that church, and the other half to the Chamber of Bristol for the use of the said town. To Elizabeth Canynges, late wife of testator's son John, a messuage in St. Nicholas's street, "simul cu' vno magno vaute" pertaining thereto, held by John Penke, merchant; also another messuage annexed thereto, in the same street, held by the same John; and another in "le Thoroughows," between the aforesaid street and Baldewynestrete, held by Edward Bery, baker; another messuage in Baldewynestrete, "in Occidentali p'te dict' Thoroughous," with a large cellar lying next to the said messuage of the said Edward, held by John Janyns; and another messuage in the same street, with two cellars situate in the "Thorowehous" aforesaid, held by Robert Megges; and a large cellar in the east part of the same Thorowehous: the aforesaid Elizabeth Canynges to hold this property, for her life only, of the chief lords of that fee; to remain afterwards to the aforesaid Isabel, testator's niece, and to her lawful issue; in default of such, to be sold by the Mayor and Common Council of Bristol, and the procurators of the church of the blessed Mary of Redcliff; one half of the money to be delivered to the said procurators for the use and sustentation of testator's perpetual chantries in that church, and the other half for the use of the town of Bristol. The residue of all and singular his unbequeathed goods, chattels, jewels, and debts, to William Spenser, merchant of Bristol, and servant Richard Hykkes, who are to be executors, and distribute therewith "p' ai'a mea." Witnessed by Master Philip Hyette, subdean of the collegiate church of Westbury, Thomas Hexton, merchant of Bristol, John Grene "Cirurgico eiusd'm ville," and others.—Hardyng.

Proved at Lambeth, Nov. 29th, 1474; also at Bristol, before Robert Straunge, Mayor, and John Forster, Sheriff, Jan. 12th, 14 Edward iv.—T Oseney.

"Hardyng" probably stands for Matthew Hardyng, whom the diocesan registers at Worcester mention as chaplain to the Mayor of Bristol, and from whom, as from other Bristol clergy, a subsidy was due in 1475. The will of William Canynges, as registered in the Orphan Book, is followed by a memorandum to the effect that John Holden, citizen and cloth-merchant of London, who had married Elizabeth (Latinized *Isabella* in the said will and bond), daughter of Thomas Canynges, late citizen and alderman of London, and niece of William Canynges, late dean of the church and college of the Trinity of Westbury upon Trym, was bound, Sept. 11th, 19 Edward iv., to the Mayor and Commonalty of Bristol, in the sum of £100, to make no alienation or "discontynuaunce" of and in five tenements in St. Nicholas's street, in the town of "Bristowe," and in Baldwyn-street, in the suburbs thereof; which five tenements had come to Elizabeth, then wife of the said John Holden, by the devise and will of the testament of the said William Canynges. The will of William Canynges, son of the said testator, was made June 8th, 1458, in the dwelling house of Stephen Forster, citizen and merchant of London, in the parish of St. Botulph by Billingsgate. He describes himself as son of William Canynges, merchant of the town of Bristol, and leaves funeral arrangements to his father, who is to be executor. All his lands, tenements, rents, &c., in Bristol and "Wellis," after the decease of his wife Isabel without issue by him, to John Canynges, his brother, with remainder to his father William, in case of John's death s.p. Witnessed by the aforesaid "honorabilis vir" Stephen Forster, and John Jaye of Bristol, merchant. Proved Nov. 20th, 1458. Registered at Somerset House, *Stokton*, 14. In the same year, old style, the eminent merchant is mentioned as a correspondent of Sir John Fastolf knt. : *Paston Letters*, Gairdner's edition, i. 425. The surname occurs at an early date in the Worcester diocesan registers :—1308, 12th kal. Jan., brother Thomas de Canyngges, of the order of Friars Minors, was ordained a priest by the bishop of Worcester in the parish church of "Foleham," diocese of London. The same registers contain the following particulars. 1467, Aug. 16th, in the house of Sir John Lewys otherwise Turnor, vicar of St. Leonard's in Bristol. Sir Richard Countasse, chaplain, was admitted to the vacant perpetual chantry founded by Richard Spycer, late burgess of Bristol, in the church of St. Nicholas ; to which chantry he was presented "p' Egregiu' viru' Will'm Canynges Maiore' ville Bristollie," patron by right of his mayoralty. 1467, Sept. 19th, in the chapel within the college of Westbury, the bishop of Worcester admitted William Cannynges (*sic*), rector of St. Alban's in Worcester, to the order of acolyte, on the title of his said benefice. 1467, March 12th, in the chapel within the bishop of Worcester's manor of Northwick, the said bishop admitted William Cannynges, of the diocese of Bath and Wells, upon letters dimissory, to the order of subdeacon, on the title of his patrimony. 1468, April 2nd, in the chapel within the manor of Northwick, the bishop of Worcester admitted William Cannynges, of the diocese of B. and W., upon letters dimissory, to the order of deacon,—"ad ti'm patrimonij sui de quo reputauit se contentu' in diaconu' rite & cano'ice ordinauit." 1468, April 16th, in the same chapel, the bishop of Worcester admitted William Cannynges, of the diocese of B. and W., upon letters dimissory, to the order of priest, on the title of his patrimony. On the same day, the said bishop collated Sir William Cannynges, chaplain, to a canonry in the collegiate church of Westbury, and the prebend of "Goderynghill alias dict' Wodeford aut Trekchill vel Bryan" in the same, vacant by the free resignation of Master Robert Slymbrygg, last canon and prebendary thereof. The said Robert had been collated to this preferment, which was of the yearly value of forty shillings, in 1467, Nov. 7th, and, on Dec. 27th, he took an oath of obedience to the dean, or, in his absence, the subdean. The possessor of this preferment had a right to a stall in the choir, and a place and voice in the chapter of Westbury. 1468, May 5th, the bishop collated Sir John Lewys otherwise Turnor, chaplain, to the rectory of St. Alban's in Worcester. 1469, June 3rd, Sir William Cannynges, chaplain, was collated by the bishop of Worcester to the office of dean of the collegiate church and college of Westbury, vacant by the free resignation of Master Henry Sampson ; and took an oath that he would observe all the statutes and ordinances appointed by the said bishop, the founder and patron, would be content with the sums set forth in the statutes, and would not reveal the secrets of the said church and college to the detriment thereof. He was inducted and installed on the same day, by virtue of a mandate issued to Master Philip Hyett, subdean, or president of the chapter there, in the presence of Master Thomas Hawkyns, archdeacon of Worcester, Thomas Balsall, professor of sacred theology, William Mogys, archdeacon of Stafford, "ac me Rob'to Enkbarow, et multis alijs Socijs & ministris d'ce Eccl'ie." The canonry vacated by Canynges was accepted, on the same day, by Henry Sampson, master in the faculty of arts, who had been presented to the deanery of Westbury Jan. 20th, 1458, five months after Philip Hyett had been collated by the bishop to the office of subdean. This Sampson appears to be identical with Henry Sampson, master of arts, whom the bishop collated to the rectory of Tredington, co. Worcester, Sept. 11th, 1451, and who died Nov. 17th, 1482, as stated on his monumental brass in Tredington church, which represents him as wearing the almuce of a canon. The diocesan registers mention that the bishop, being in his college of Westbury, within a certain oratory there, selected Robert Multon, one of the seven monks nominated by the chapter or convent at Worcester, for the office of prior in the cathedral church, in succession to Thomas Musard deceased ; in the presence of William Vauce, or Vauxe, the bishop's chancellor, who was, or had been, one of the canons of Westbury, William Cannynges, dean of the said college, Master Thomas Balsall, &c., Aug. 19th, 1469. Canynges, it appears, died Nov. 17th, and the bishop appointed as his successor Master Robert Slymbrygg, doctor of decrees, Dec. 5th, 1474 ; the entry of the appointment containing a note that the main portion of the fruits and profits of the vicarage of Kempsey, co. Worcester, with the annexed chapels of Stoulton and Norton, had lately (Sept. 2nd, 1473) been made over to the church and college of Westbury for the use of the dean thereof. About forty-one years afterwards, according to the registers, the name of Canynges became again connected with this place. Sept. 14th, 1515, Master William Canynges, master of arts, was instituted to the office of subdean and vicar in the collegiate church of Westbury, vacant by the death of John Wellow ; being presented by the dean and chapter there, and promising on oath to obey and reverence the dean and his successors, to reside constantly and personally, to observe the statutes of the reverend father in Christ, John lord bishop of Worcester, the illustrious founder, to be content with the appointed yearly sum of £10, and to abstain from revealing to any man the secrets of the said collegiate church and college to the detriment thereof. At the end of one year however the office was vacant by his resignation ; the institution of his successor bearing date Oct. 1st, 1516.

259.—WILLIAM HOTON, merchant. In the margin *Hotton*.

1474. Sept. 3rd. To be buried in the north porch of the church of St. Werburgh, by the burial-place of Master William Sutton, clerk, rector of that church, there interred. Legacies to the said church, and the rector, who was to have one of testator's gowns "penulat' cu' lever ;" to the mother church of Worcester ; each order of friars in Bristol, if present at the mortuary offices, &c., and offering masses and prayers *pro anima* ; the poor of the almshouses of St. Katharine and "longe Rewe," of the almshouse by the church of All Saints in Bristol, and of that at "laffordys yate ;" servants Maud Codder, Elizabeth Hunte, Katharine Whight, Joan Byrch, and Joan Bury ; apprentices John Askell, Edmund Dovandre, and John With, on condition that they kindly and diligently serve testator's wife ;

Lodowic John, merchant of Bristol; Thomas Oseney, clerk of the Mayor and Commonalty of the town; Katharine Buntyng, and William Buntyng. A chaplain to celebrate for testator's soul every day for four years in the aforesaid church of St. Werburgh, and have £24 sterling. Twelve poor men to be provided with a black gown of Welsh cloth on the day of the trental, and to hold twelve torches. To son William Hoton, canon of St. Augustine's at Bristol, five marks in ready money, a standing silver cup with cover, &c. To servant Elizabeth Cromwell £8, and two yards and a half of woollen cloth "de Sadde morrey;" also fifty shillings, if her brother George Cromwell be dead on the day of testator's burial. To son John and his heirs, a tenement in "Old Cornestrett" in Bristol, situate between the cemetery of St. Leonard's church and the tenement inhabited by William Water, and extending from the street to the garden of Sir Edmund Hungerford knt.; which property testator had by the gift and grant of William Coder, late merchant of Bristol, on condition that the said John Hoton and his heirs duly keep the said William's anniversary every year in the parish church of St. Leonard aforesaid, with six chaplains, "et pulsac' Campanar' ib'm," and distribute ten shillings in bread among the poor, feeble, and needy, also arrange for the burning of four tapers, of the value of iij^s iiij^d, at the said anniversary, and yearly dispose of forty shillings for pious purposes, for the welfare of the said William Coder's soul, by the advice and counsel of William Wodyngton, merchant of Bristol, and his heirs. Wife Alice and son John to be executors: two parts of the residue of testator's effects to the former, and the third part to the latter. William Wodyngton to be overseer, and have £10 sterling. Witnessed by Master Thomas Pyttes, rector of St. Werburgh's, John Alberton, and John Swancote of Bristol, "M'cator'," and many others.

Proved before the Mayor and Sheriff, Sept. 20th, 15 Edward iv. Previously proved at Lambeth.

260.—ROBERT JACOB, otherwise Jakes, merchant.

1475. May 24th.—"sanus mente laudet' altissimus." To be buried in the church of St. Werburgh, at the discretion of wife Elizabeth. To the said church, for burial there, xx^s. To the mother church of Worcester iij^s iiij^d. To the rector of St. Werburgh's, for tithes, "meam sengle Armulausam de Skarlette." If testator's moveable goods should not be enough to pay all his just debts, there was to be a sale of his messuage, toft, and void place in Cornestret, situate between what was formerly the messuage of Robert Shypward, lately inhabited by Philip Geynan (?), on the west, and the messuage lately held by Isabel Power, on the east, and extending from the said street to what was formerly Robert Russell's land; the surplus of the money so raised to be expended on celebrations *pro animâ* for one year in the parish church of St. Werburgh. If the said goods should suffice for the payment of all just debts, wife Elizabeth to hold the aforesaid property for her life. To son John and his lawful heirs, after the death of testator's brother Humphrey Jacob of Tamworth, lands, tenements, reversions, and services in Brantyngthorp, Great Petelyng, Little Petelyng, and Wheston, co. Leicester. To wife Elizabeth, for her life, a tenement in Tamworth, co. Warwick, situate in Chirchstret, between the prebendal land of Sirescote and what was lately the land of John Aston, and extending from the King's way to the King's fosse; also a burgage in Tamworth, situate in Chirchstret, between the land of Richard Archar of Stotfold, esquire, and his wife Alice, and the land of Henry Jeke, and extending from the King's way " vna cu' ffossa d'ni Reg's " to the land of Thomas Ferreys : another burgage in Tamworth " p'ut situat' in Alto vico vocat' Chirchstret. exopposito stansili (?) Cimit'ij," between the prebendal land of Cirescote and testator's own land ; also his state and term of years in a messuage at Bristol in Cornestret, situate between the late tenement of John Wythyford " & Mesuagiu' Abbat' se'i Augustini & Neth," lately inhabited by David Sergeaunte, and extending from the street to the messuage of the Lady Elizabeth Russell : remainder to sons John and William ; the former to possess all the aforesaid lands, tenements, &c., in co. Leicester ; and William to have the state and term of years in the aforesaid messuage in Cornestrete, also testator's dwelling house, toft, and void place in the same street, if they shall not have been sold by wife Elizabeth, and the remaining property in Tamworth. If William should die s.p., rem. to son John and his lawful issue ; in def., rem. to daughter Margaret and her heirs for ever. Residue of goods to wife Elizabeth, who is to be sole executrix, and dispose " p' salute ai'e mee," and give to sons John and William, out of the said residue, £20 apiece. Witnessed by Master Thomas Pyttes, rector of St. Werburgh's, John Forster, merchant and sheriff of Bristol, Robert Bolton, John Estoefeld, Henry Dale, Nicholas Slyke, merch : of Bristol, and others.

Proved before William Byrde, Mayor, and Thomas Rowley, Sheriff, Jan. 24th, 15 Edward iv. Previously proved at Lambeth.

261.—PHILIP MEDE, burgess.

1471. Jan. 11th. To be buried in the church of the blessed Mary of Redcliff, by the altar of St. Stephen the Martyr. To the vicar of that church, for tithes and offerings, xx^s. To the fabric of the same church a pipe of woad. To the mother church of St. Andrew of Wells xij^d. To the church of St. Thomas the Martyr at Bristol £4 sterling, " de quibz dicta Eccl'ia michi debet iij^{li} v^s." To wife Isabel, for her life, lands, tenements, &c., in the county of Somerset and in Bristol ; rem. to son Richard Mede and his lawful posterity ; in default of issue, rem. to Maurice Berkley and his wife Isabel, testator's daughter, and their lawful issue ; in def., rem. to Philip Ryngston and his lawful issue ; in def., rem. to Robert Ricarde and his heirs and assigns. A fit chaplain to celebrate and pray for testator's soul, and the souls of his parents, and be paid £40 sterling. Residue of goods to wife Isabel. She, and son Richard Mede, and Maurice Berkley to be executors. Witnessed by Master John Mede, rector of Wraxal, William Wykam, Robert Baron, John Laucrance, Ed'o Bracy, and others.

Proved before William Brid, Mayor, and Thomas Rowley, Sheriff, March 26th, 16 Edward iv. Previously proved at Lambeth.

262.—THOMAS KEMPSON, the elder, burgess.

1475. Nov. 29th. To be buried within the church of the blessed Mary of " Radeclif." To the cathedral church of Wells xx^d. Legacies to Sir Thomas Smith, vicar of holy Cross Temple, testator's curate, for tithes, Sir Roger Kempson, chaplain, his brother, Sir William Kempson, chaplain, John Hone, and Richard Radifford. To wife Joan, in money, 100 marks sterling ;

in jewels of silver, the worth of 100 marks; five pipes of woad, and all household utensils: she to find a fit secular chaplain, who is to celebrate *pro anima* for seven years in the aforesaid church of holy Cross, and receive a yearly stipend according to the usage of the town of Bristol. To kinsman Thomas Kempson the best coat of mail, &c. To Robert Bouok a barrel of oil. To twelve needy men a gown of "Russet ffrise." Wife Joan to be executrix, and have the residue of goods. John Screveyn to be overseer, and have ten marks sterling. Witnessed by Sir Thomas Smyth, vicar of holy Cross Temple, and John Screveyn, merchant.

Proved at Lambeth, Jan. 16th, 1475. No record of proof at the Guildhall.

263.—ROBERT HYNDE, goldsmith and burgess.

1476. May 17th. To be buried in the parish church of the Holy Trinity at Bristol. To the cathedral church of Worcester xij^d. To the aforesaid church of the Holy Trinity, for the use of the high altar, "vnu' l'axbrede Argenti & deaurat' ponder' quindecim vnc' ad orand' p' ai'a mea," &c. To Master Robert Carewe, rector of that church, and testator's curate, for tithes, xx^s sterling. To each of the chaplains celebrating therein, and present at the burial and month's mind, xij^d. To a fit secular chaplain, to celebrate *pro anima* therein for a whole year, vj^{li}. To the water-bearing clerk of that church, "p' classis pulsand' diem sepulture mee et indies videl't vnam pulsac'o'em apud le Curfew vsq' ad mensem," xvj^s viij^d. For the use of the chapel of St. James in the parish church of Newent "in floresta" vj^s viij^d. To the church of St. Ewen at Bristol vj^s viij^d. To each of the four orders of friars there, present at the funeral rites, v^s. To every parish church of the town of Bristol, situate within the diocese of Worcester, the churches of the Holy Trinity and St. Ewen only excepted, iij^s iiij^d. To the King's way between Chepnam and Calle, towards London, vj^s viij^d. Legacies also to the chapel of St. Katharine in the church of holy Cross Temple at Bristol, the fabric of the chapel of St. Anthony, opposite the chapel of St. Anne, John Balle at "Manyswyhope in ffloresta," and John Gylbert "Cariar." Residue of goods to testator's wife Elen and his children. Edward Kyte and John Birde, of Bristol, to be executors, and take £40 for the fulfilling of the will, &c., reserving for themselves forty shillings apiece.

Proved before John Bagott, Mayor, and William Wykeham, Sheriff, Nov. 18th, 16 Edward iv. Previously proved at Lambeth.

264.—JOHN SHIPWARD, the elder, merchant.

1473. Dec. 14th. To be buried in the chancel of St. Stephen's church at Bristol, by the high altar, "in loco quo *(sic)* de nouo construxi de petra," beside wife Katharine. To the mother church of Worcester v^s. To the rector of the said church of St. Stephen, for tithes, xl^s. The sum of x^{li} to be distributed in bed-clothes "die obitus mei" among poor householders in the parish of St. Stephen, according to the discretion of the executors, and the advice of the rector there. Five marks for the poor on the day of burial, and the same sum at the month's mind, in bread and ale. Four large and four small tapers, weighing ten pounds, to stand burning upon the hearse from the day of burial to that of the month's mind, "cu' duobus

Standarddez cu' olio ardent' die ac nocte a die p'dict' Obitus mei vsq' ad die' Mensalis mee." Twenty-four torches to burn about testator's body on those occasions, and to be held by twenty-four poor men, to each of whom a gown of black frize with a hood of white frize, and four pence in money. Two torches to burn daily at the mass of *Requiem* in the said church of St. Stephen, from the day aforesaid to the month's mind, to be held by two poor men, who are to have a daily payment of a penny apiece, and meat and drink at the charges of the executors. Of the aforesaid twenty-four torches, after the month's mind, two are to be given to the said church of St. Stephen, two to the church of All Saints in Bristol, for the use of the fraternity of Jesus there, two to the church of St. Bartholomew's hospital, for the use of the fraternity of St. Clement, one to the chapel of the blessed Mary on the bridge of Avon, and one to each of the other parish churches and chapels in Bristol, where most needed, according to the discretion of the executors. To the said church of St. Stephen two missals, and a chalice of silver and gilt; also six pairs of vestments, namely, one pair of "velwett sup' velwet Browderyd cu' vna Cruce de Redde velwett," another of black damask, embroidered with a cross of cloth of gold, another of white baudkin with a cross of red, another of green "Borde Alisonder," &c.; on condition that testator's priests, singing in the said church, shall have and use the said vestments at the high altar on every needful occasion, to the praise of God, without contradiction of the rector or procurators. Legacies to each chaplain, clerk, and singing boy at the said church of St. Stephen, and all the curates, chaplains, and parish clerks of the town, attending the mortuary offices; each order of friars in Bristol, if present; every prisoner in the King's gaol of Newgate, every man and woman in any almshouse in the town of Bristol on the day of testator's death, each inmate of the almshouse of the Holy Trinity at Lafford's gate, and the chapel of the blessed Mary on the bridge of Avon. To John, son of testator, his "hospicium" in the High-street at Bristol, called "Gillowes," inhabited by David Osteler; a tenement annexed thereto, lately inhabited by John Leynell, draper; a tenement and cellar there, held by Hugh Forster, saddler; a tenement there, inhabited by William Atkyns and his wife Maud, lately inhabited by the aforesaid John Leynell; a tenement there called "le Cokke," inhabited by Clement Wiltshire, with a stable and chamber behind the "Gillowes," held by William Peynt'; a tenement in "seynt Nicholas Strete," held by John Furnyvall, pewterer, with a cellar there held by the said Clement Wiltshire; a cellar there held by John George; also a tower in a large garden "apud Lafforddes yate," together with the garden itself; five other gardens there, held by Edmund Wescote, Thomas Daske, Richard Boteler, John Cely, and Thomas Wodward and his wife Isabel; also seven acres of meadow in Radclyff Mede, held by David Hosteler; and a garden "extra Temple yate," lately held by John Gregory, merchant; all this property to be had and held by said John Shipward and his lawful posterity, on condition that two chaplains be found for twenty-five years to celebrate daily at the high altar of the aforesaid church of St. Stephen, for testator's soul, and the souls of his parents John Shipward, late merchant of Bristol, and Guynot his wife, of William Philippys, late of Bath, draper, and Agnes his wife, &c.; and after the said twenty-five years, one fit chaplain is to celebrate for ever *pro animo* at the high altar of that church; the said chaplain, and each of the said chaplains, vested in surplices, shall on the days in future "post meridie' & ante vesp'ar' decantac'onem" say distinctly and openly the offices for the dead according to the use of Sarum before the high altar aforesaid, and on the morrow of those days the mass of *Requiem*; the aforesaid chaplains, during the said term and years, to say mass in honor of the most blessed Name of Jesus on every Friday in the week, unless other feasts occur, or any other lawful cause prevent : the said priests to be present daily in surplices in the choir of St. Stephen's church, and sing mattins, mass, and vespers with the other ministers of the said church : son John and his lawful heirs to pay yearly to the said chaplains nine marks, and for bread, wine, and wax, two shillings ; the anniversary to be kept in that church every year, the exequies on the 2nd of August, and mass of *Requiem* on the morrow, the rector attending with nineteen chaplains and the clerks of the church, he to be paid, for celebrating and singing, iiij^d, and for having a light in the church at the time of the said exequies and mass, ij^s ; each priest then present iiij^d, each clerk ij^d, each procurator xij^d, and to a hundred poor people dwelling within the said parish j^d apiece. To the Mayor of Bristol, personally attending the said rites, and making an offering at the said mass, vj^s viij^d. To the Sheriff and Recorder of the town, personally attending, iij^s iiij^d apiece. To the bailiffs of the said town, the clerk to the Mayor and Commonalty, and the Mayor's sword-bearer, personally attending, xij^d apiece. To other persons in the service of the Mayor and Sheriff, and to the itinerant bailiff, personally attending, iiij^d apiece. To the clerk of the said church of St. Stephen, for tolling the bells, xx^d. To the crier iiij^d. The said Mayor, Sheriff, and Recorder to take the oversight of the keeping of the said anniversary every year on the aforesaid day for ever. If the intention of this will should be neglected by son John and his posterity, the aforesaid property is to pass to testator's daughter Agnes, wife of Edmund Wescote, and to her daughter Isabel Norton, in equal portions, to be held by them and their lawful heirs, on condition that the said chaplains be provided, and the anniversary kept, &c. If the said Agnes and Isabel should die s.p., rem. to testator's daughter Joan, wife of Thomas Norton esquire, and her lawful issue, on the same conditions. If the said Joan should be neglectful, or die s.p., rem. to Master John Harlowe, rector of the said church of St. Stephen, and John Scryven and Henry Vaughan, procurators of that church, and their successors, and to the parishioners there, and their heirs for ever, on the same conditions. If they should fail to carry out testator's intention, rem. to William Bridde, Mayor of Bristol, and his successors, and the Commonalty of the town for ever, to be held on the same conditions. To the said son John and his lawful heirs a tenement on the Key of Bristol, inhabited by Gillam de la Founte, merchant ; a tenement in Fysshereslane, inhabited by Robert Bridde, with a void place of land adjoining it ; a tenement "apud le Pyll yende," inhabited by Benedict Crose, mason, and another there, inhabited by Richard Makwell, tailor, from which tenement a yearly rent of assize has gone to the rector, procurators, and parishioners of the aforesaid church of St. Stephen ; also a tenement in Mersshestrete, inhabited by John Colle, with two cottages opposite to the said tenement : a newly built tenement in the same street, between the tenement of Thomas Yong, the Judge, and that of John Wykys, gentleman ; two tenements in the same street, inhabited by Richard Spenser and Richard Bulloke; two newly built tenements in the same street, inhabited by Katharine Whyte and Thomas Sutton; a tenement in the same street, inhabited by Thomas Knokke; a house called "le Masthous," situate on the Key next that of John Bagod; the house called "le Scolehous," with a long cellar underneath, at the end of the said Key, near the tower there; a tenement in "Seynt Marystrete," purchased of William Joce, late merchant of Bristol; two tenements on the Were, between what was lately the tenement of John Innyng, gentleman, and a tenement of the Lady Isabel Stanshawe; and testator's state and term of years in the tenement inhabited by him. If son John should die s.p., all this property to remain to daughter Agnes, wife of Edmund Wescote, and Isabel Norton, her daughter, in equal portions. If both of these should die s.p., rem. to daughter Joan, wife of Thomas Norton esquire, and her lawful heirs. If the said Joan should die s.p., the property is to be expended on the celebration of masses, on poor bedridden people, the marriage of young virgins, defective highways, &c. To Edmund Wescote, merchant of Bristol, and his wife Agnes, and their lawful heirs, the tenement inhabited by them in "Balwynestrete." If they should die s.p., rem. to the aforesaid Isabel Norton. To the same Isabel a tenement in Cristemastrete, inhabited by John Stokys, merchant; also a tenement in Balwynestrete, by the church of St. Leonard, lately inhabited by Geoffrey Jankyn, mariner; a tenement in Gropelane, inhabited by Roger Purches "halyer;" and a tenement in Mersshestrete, inhabited by John Fowke, baker. If the said Isabel should die s.p., rem. to Edmund Wescote and his wife Agnes; in default of issue, rem. to son John Shipward; in def., rem. to Joan wife of Thomas Norton esquire. If the said Joan should die s.p., the property is to be religiously disposed of for the health of testator's soul, and that of his wife Katharine, &c. Son John and Edmund Wescote to have the residue of goods, and be executors. Witnessed by Thomas Oseney, Thomas Newton, Thomas Lane, and others.

Proved at Lambeth, Jan. 1st, 1476; afterwards before the Mayor and Sheriff.—Oseney.

265.—HENRY BROUN, brewer.

1464. Dec... To be buried in the church of the Holy Trinity in Bristol. Legacies to the high altar and fabric of that church, and the mother church of Worcester. To son Richard a silver cup. Residue of goods to wife Isabel, who is to be executrix, pay debts, and dispose *pro anima*. Master Robert Carew, rector of the aforesaid church, to be overseer.

Proved before Master Thomas Bevir, "in decreto Bacallar'," &c., in the church of St. Peter of Bristol, Jan. 15th, 1464. No record of proof before the Mayor.

266.—WILLIAM ROWLEY, burgess.

1478. Nov. 25th. To be buried in the chapel of St. George within the church of the Carmelite Friars "apud Burdeaux." To the use of the said friars "1 ffrankes monete Acquitanie" in addition to funeral expenses. To wife Elizabeth household goods, and the third part of the jewels. To Thomas Rowley, testator's father in Bristol, the sum of £10 sterling, that he may bestow it on the most needy poor, &c. The said Thomas to provide a fit chaplain to celebrate "vnu' trigentale p' ai'a mea, sicut ip'e quondam

Ordinauit p' ai'a ffratris mei Ricardi." Testator's four daughters to be provided for out of his goods, and the will fulfilled by his father, "Cuius conscienciam Jlluminet Sp'us veritatis." To father's apprentice George xl^s. To my boy Nicholas xx^s. Kinsman John Chestre to have £10 sterling, and be overseer of all the effects in those parts, both of merchandise and "de Gubernacione Nauis," and render a good and faithful account to testator's father after the arrival of the ship at the port of Bristol. His said father to have the residue of goods, and be executor. Witnessed by Janycot Barero, Richard Seynt, Roger Taillour, Richard Vaughan, Thomas ap Howell, Robert Barero, and others.

Proved before William Spencer, Mayor, and John Skryven, Sheriff, Sept. 15th, 19 Edward iv. Previously proved before the ecclesiastical authorities.

This will is followed by two notes relating to administration; from which it appears that Thomas Rowley, testator's father, died before the will was proved, and that administration was committed, first to Margaret Rouley, widow, and John Esterfield, of Bristol, and afterwards to testator's uncle William Rowley. The notes make mention of Master William Vauxe (spelling the name thus, and also Vauce), dean of the collegiate church of Westbury; who, according to the Worcester diocesan registers, was dead in 1479, and was succeeded by Master John Lyndesey, professor of sacred theology, Aug. 25th, in that year.

267.—WILLIAM ROWLEY, merchant.

1479. Nov. 6th. Testator is described as "de Bristoll' Mercator. nacion' Anglican' dei gr'a mente sanus. corporea licet egritudine detentus." His will is nuncupative, and was made in the town of "Dam in fllandria," in the dwelling house of the honorable Roger de Dam, citizen and inhabitant of that town. He desired to be buried in the parish church of the blessed Mary there,—" in ambitu elegit retro chorum," and bequeathed Flemish money to the fabric of that church "pietatis intuitu ac fauore Sepulture," and to the church itself "p' testamento;" also to each curate and chaplain, and to the guardians "seu matricularijs" thereof. To the religious ladies of St. Agnes there, of the order of St. Augustine, "p' humanitate p' easd'm p'stita in extremis," &c., eight crowns of French money to be once paid (semel leuan'). Testator's effects moveable and immoveable to be parted between his wife Joan and children, provision being made *pro anima*. Legacies to the vicar of St. Ewen's in Bristol, the hospital of the town of "la Rentarya in Hispania," and the church of the blessed Mary of "Hurenheranso" in Spain. John Estirfield of England, to whom £5 sterling of English money, and testator's beloved wife Joan to be executors. "Acta fuerunt in villa de Dam." Witnessed by Master Francis Caen', licentiate in decrees, "Alterius porc'onis ib'm vicesgeren'," Arnold Helle and Nicholas Horenbord, priests of the diocese of Tournay, and chaplains of the aforesaid parish church, brother John Bond, hospitaller, Nicholas Vaud', "veet'ens (?) Burgi," Master John ooex (?), Englishman, Peter Aernondts (?), Christopher Maereolff, Francis Reinghooolt (?), and more witnesses worthy of credit. inhabitants of the same town. "Ei Ego Marcus Cryn P'b'r oriu'dus de Ghistolla Torn'cens' Dioc' sacris Ap'lica & imperiali auct' Notarius juratus Quia," &c.

Proved at Knoll, May 3rd, 1480; afterwards at Bristol, before the Mayor and Sheriff.

268.—JOAN KEMPSON.

1479. Sept. 10th. Testatrix was widow of Thomas Kempson, burgess of Bristol, in the diocese of Bath and Wells, and desired to be buried in the parish church of holy Cross Temple there, before the altar dedicated in honor of SS. Andrew and Nicholas, to which altar she bequeathed a missal. To the vicar of that church a bowl, worth four marks, and six of her best towels. To the said church xx^s, and to the chapel of St. Katharine there vj^s. viij^d. The sum of £100 for the support of a perpetual chaplain in the church aforesaid; the sum to be laid out in tenements, but to be safely kept in a chest by Sir John Mason, vicar of the church, Robert Bonnok, and John Jay, merchant of Bristol, each of whom is to have a key, until the tenements are obtained and peaceably held. To the cathedral church of Wells xvj^d. To Alice wife of Richard Mathowe a cloth "voc' le forste cloth ;" and a similar one to the daughters of Thomas Egleston. To my chaplain Sir Richard four yards of green cloth. The best loom to Thomas Dexe, the second to Thomas Penlowe, the third, being near the Avon, to Thomas Wigan. To each of the sons of my sister vj^s viij^d. To the church of St. Peter in Bristol "ij Tortell'." Legacies also to the wife of John Hoppis, the house of the Augustinian friars at Bristol, the church of St. Augustine the Less, the church of Clifton by Bristol, the chapel of St. Anthony, and Joan daughter of Richard Rastforth. Residue of goods, lands, and tenements to the executors, namely, Robert Bonnock, and his wife Elen, daughter of testatrix. The aforesaid Sir John Mason to be overseer. Witnessed by the said Sir John, William Sodbury, and John Crykald of Bristol, weavers, and others.

Proved at Mathfeld, Oct. 8th, 1479. No record of proof before the Mayor.

This will is followed by two blank pages; after which there is a writing, dated July 1st, 1561, relating to the foundation of the Grammar School in Bristol, and addressed to "all. trewe. xp'en. people." by Nicholas Thorne of the city of Bristowe, merchant. The writing is followed by twenty-three blank leaves.

269.—PETER DREWZ, burgess and merchant.

1487. Sept. 18th. To be buried in the parish church of St. Stephen, to the fabric of which "idest le Rode lofte" xl^s. To the rector of that church, for tithes, vj^s viij^d. To the cathedral church of Worcester xij^d. To daughter Margaret £10 sterling. To Margery "filie mee Medie" £10. To daughter Katharine £10. To son Robert £10. If the said Margaret should die s.p., or before coming to years of discretion, her portion is to be divided equally between the survivors. If all except one "diem claudant extremum," that one is to take the whole sum of £40. If all should decease, "q'd absit," before their lawful age, a fit priest is to celebrate *pro anima* in the aforesaid church of St. Stephen, and receive nine marks yearly of the £40, as long as it will last. Twenty shillings' worth of bread to be distributed to the imprisoned and the poor. To brothers Richard and John Drewz fifty shillings apiece. John Balle to have testator's part of the salt in the cellar of John Burton. Legacies also to John Bray, apprentice John Quyrke, and servant Joan Cory. Residue of goods to wife Joan. She and the aforesaid John Drewz to be executors. Richard Vaughan overseer. Witnessed by Master Walter Morice, bachelor in decrees, Robert Warner, chaplain, and John Ball, merchant.

Proved at Moretelake, Oct. 1st, 1487; afterwards at Bristol, before the Mayor and Sheriff.

270.—ELIZABETH FERRE.

1487. Feb. 11th. Testatrix describes herself as "late the wyf of william fferre somtyme the wife of John Alberton nowe beyng widdowe." To be buried in the church of St. Stephen of Bristowe. "Jtem y bequeth to the Cathedrall of Worcestre xij^d." To son Andrew Alberton a signet of gold, two pairs of sheets, a covering of a bed "of luxbon worke," &c. To son John Alberton "a nother Signet of golde. ij peire of Shetes w^t a Bedde white and blewe a mete cloth and a Towell of workes And a Carpette." To daughter Joan Alberton the state and term of years now to come of the place inhabited by testatrix, and the residue of household effects after the payment of the bequests before written. If Joan should die unmarried, the said state to remain to son John and his assigns. If all the children should so die, their legacies "shall be bysette in fynding of Seculer preeste" to sing in the aforesaid church of St. Stephen as long as "the saide goodez shalle suffice." Residue to the said children, "to be departed egally emongest them." They are made executors. John Walshe and John Drewez overseers. Witnessed by Sir John Edwardez, George Hunte, and others.

Proved before John Esterfeld, Mayor, and John Chestre, Sheriff, Aug. 6th, 3 Henry vii. Previously proved before the ecclesiastical authorities.

271.—EDWARD KYTE, burgess.

1487. June 18th. To be buried in the parish church of the Holy Trinity of Bristol. To the cathedral church of Worcester vj^d. To daughter Joan Kyte xviij^{li} xiij^s iiij^d. in money; also "vnu' Noote harnisat' cu' argento & deaurat',...meu' optimu' ffethirbedde," &c. If she should die "ante annos nubiles," her legacies are to be distributed "in pijs vsibz & Caritat' p' salute ai'e mee," &c. A measure of woad for the use of the aforesaid parish church. A secular chaplain to celebrate therein for two years, at the altar of St. Katharine, and be paid £12. Sir Thomas Lyncoln to have testator's horse. Wife Agnes to have the residue of goods, and be executrix. Sir Thomas Lyncoln and John Kyte overseers: to the latter articles of clothing, including testator's best doublet. Witnessed by John Bale, Simon Passhley, John G'unte (Graunte?), and others.

Proved in the parish church of the blessed Mary "in Foro," July 13th, 1487; afterwards before the Mayor and Sheriff.

272.—AGNES KYTE.

1487. Dec. 17th. Testatrix was widow of Edward Kyte, late of Bristol, merchant, and desired to be buried in the parish church of the Holy Trinity, to which she bequeathed a measure of woad. To the cathedral church of Worcester vj^d. To son John a gown which belonged to the late husband of testatrix, also a whole cloth called a "See Cloth," six cushions, "vnu' Table cloth," and all the wares beyond the sea already in his governance. To daughter Alice a gown " coloris morrey," a pair of beads, &c. To daughter Joan " vnam Note " with the cover, and a pair of beads " de Coralle." If the said Joan should die under age, "videli't ante Annos nubiles," her legacies are to be distributed *pro anima*. Residue to the executors, Sir Thomas Lyncoln, chaplain, and Thomas Davye. Witnessed by Hugh Bruer, John Sadiller, and others.

Proved in the parish church of the Holy Trinity of Bristol, Jan. 24th, 1487; afterwards before the Mayor and Sheriff.

273.—RICHARD ERLE, esquire, burgess.

1491. June 15th. Testator commends his sinful soul to Almighty God, his Creator and Redeemer, the B.V.M. " Regine misericordie," and all the saints, and desires to be buried in the chapel of St. Michael the Archangel, on the north side of the high altar of the parish church of the Holy Trinity at Bristol; to which altar, for tithes and offerings forgotten, iij^s iiij^d. The sum of four pence to the mother church, the cathedral of the blessed Mary of Worcester. Legacies also to the high altars of the parish churches of St. Philip and St. Leonard of Bristol. Residue of goods to the executors, namely, William Joh'nes, clerk, John Wareyns, and Thomas Howell, for payment of legacies, &c. To Sir Edmund Gorges knt. and his heirs and assigns testator's dwelling house in the Old Market at Bristol. Reference is made to a deed, bearing date May 7th, 6 Henry vii., by which testator made over to William Joh'nes, clerk, George Monoux, William Gauncell, Hugh Joh'nes, Thomas Howell, John Wareyns, John Sokett, Simon Passheley, and John Davy, the younger, nineteen tenements and a garden in Bristol and the suburb; the said feoffees being required to find, out of the rents of that property, a fit and honest chaplain to celebrate daily, in the aforesaid chapel of St. Michael, for testator's soul, and that of Thomasine his late wife, and the souls of Thomas and Margery Erle, his parents, and others, in all succeeding years ; the said feoffees and their heirs and assigns to pay the chaplain ten marks yearly ; the said chaplain to sing in the aforesaid church of the Holy Trinity at all mattins, masses, and vespers, and at other canonical hours. And if the chaplain should be neglectful, he is to be removed "infra tres moniciones." The executors, or their heirs or executors, are to sell, after testator's death, all his other messuages, cottages, lands, tenements, rents, &c., in the town and suburb, and dispose of the money thus :—to Tristram Fulbroke, Robert Fulbroke, and Margaret Launde, testator's daughter, the sum of twenty shillings apiece yearly during their lives ; also to William White, dyer, and his wife Elizabeth, for her service "michi impenso," twenty shillings yearly during the said Elizabeth's life. The executors are also to keep, or cause to be kept, in the aforesaid church, testator's obit or anniversary on June 15th, or the day following, with "Placebo & dirige" at night, and mass of *Requiem* on the morrow, for eighty years next after his decease ; paying and distributing the sum of vj^s viij^d among the priests, clerks, and poor people attending the exequies, and for bell-tolling and the burning of tapers. The anniversary to be kept also in the same form on June 16th, or the day following, for eighty years, in the conventual church of the blessed

Mary of "Wyttham," in the cathedral church of St. Andrew the Apostle in Wells, and in the church of St. Augustine's monastery at Bristol; the sum of vj^s viij^d to be yearly paid in each of these three churches. Witnessed by Sir Robert Carter, parish chaplain of the aforesaid church of the Holy Trinity, George Monoux, one of the bailiffs of the Mayor and Commonalty of Bristol, John Davyson "auctoritate ap'lica Notario," Hugh Joh'nes, William Walshe, and others.

Proved at Lambeth, Aug. 5th, 1491; also before John Stephens, Mayor, and William Regent, Sheriff, and George Monoux and Richard Vaughan, Bailiffs of the town, on Friday, Aug. 12th, 6 Henry vii., in the Guildhall, "in pleno hundred' tunc ib'm tent' s'c'd'm lib'tates & consuetudi'es eiusd'm ville. per sacr'm d'ni Ric'i Hopkyns Confessoris de'i defuncti."

274.—EDMUND NEWE, burgess and dyer.

1491. Jan. 16th. To be buried in the cemetery of the parish church of St. Thomas at Bristol, to the use of which church, and chiefly for the reparation of the porch on the north side, a quarter of woad. To the vicar of Redcliff, testator's curate, for tithes, vj^s viij^d. To wife Agnes "duas Saltes Argenti cu' vno coop'culo, ... vnu' Spyce disshe," twelve silver spoons, &c. To son John a pipe of woad, a cup "voc' A horne" garnished with silver, six silver spoons, &c. To son Robert a pipe of woad, &c. To son Richard a pipe of woad, twenty ounces of silver "p' vno Cipho sibi fact'," &c.; also to the said Richard and his lawful heirs, testator's dwelling house in Redde-clifstrete, situate between the tenement of John Bagod, on the north, and the tenement inhabited by John Brooke, gentleman, on the south, with all the fittings "& instrumentis artis mee." In default of issue, rem. to son John; in def., rem. to son Robert; in def., rem. to daughter Margaret and her lawful heirs. To the said Margaret a pipe of woad, a silver salt-cellar, without cover, "vnu' hedde bonde," a maser "harnizat' cu' signo in medio videli't Rosa," a girdle, &c. To John Stalworth, the younger, a green girdle "harnizat' & stipat' velut grossos." To Alice Coker a standing maser bound with silver and gilt, with a silver cover, and three lions under the feet thereof; also a cup, &c. To Margaret Newe, daughter of John Newe, a standing silver cup with silver cover, "et illu' Ciphu' voc' A Costard." Legacies also to the cathedral church of Wells, servant John Cokkes, and Isabel Dolle. Residue to wife Agnes and son John, who are to be executors, and dispose for the health of testator's soul "vt ip'i reddant racionem in die iudicij." Thomas Flexhall overseer. Witnessed by Master Nicholas Pittes, master of arts, "Curato meo," John Hawley, notary public, and many others.

Proved at Lambeth, Feb. 21st, 1491; afterwards at Bristol, before the Mayor and Sheriff.

The surname of this testator was anciently at Cheltenham. William le Newe, of that town, occurs on a Gloucestershire subsidy-roll, 1 Edward iii., at the Record Office. And the diocesan registers at Worcester state that Henry Newe, of Cheltenham, was ordained a secular acolyte in the parish church of Hartlebury, Dec. 21st, 1370.

275.—CLEMENT WILTESHIRE, merchant.

1488. June 30th. To be buried in the parish church of All Saints at Bristol, in the chapel of the blessed Mary there, if a convenient place can be found, if not, in any place (in alico loco) according to the discretion of the executors and the parishioners. To that church, for burial there, xx^s. To the mother church of Worcester xx^d. A fit priest, chosen by the vicar of the said church of All Saints, to celebrate therein *pro anima* for three years, receiving yearly £6 of lawful English money. To Sir John Thomas, vicar of that church, for tithes, xl^s; also a gown of scarlet, formerly belonging to William Coddar, that he may pray for the soul of testator and that of Margery his wife, and the souls of their parents, brothers, sisters, &c., on every Sunday, among the other dead of the said church, according to the usage there. To sons Richard, Clement, Henry, and Daniel Wilteshire, £10 apiece. To son Clement the state and term in the tenement lately purchased of John Shipward of Bristol, merchant, for a term of sixty years, situate in the High-street, " iuxta Le Cok in the Hope," and inhabited by John Jay, tailor. To son Henry the state and term in the cellar purchased, for the same length of time, of the said John Shipward, situate in " saint Nicholas strete iuxta portam," at the hinder part of the tenement called " Gelows June," on the west side of that tenement. To son Daniel the state and term of and in the cellar purchased, for the same length of time, of the said John Shipward, situate in the same street, by the said gate, at the hinder part of the same tenement, on the east. To daughter Alice the state and term in a tenement in the High-street, lately purchased for a term of sixty years of John Newlond, abbot, and the convent of St. Augustine's monastery by Bristol ; rem. to son Richard, if the said Alice should die before marriage. To daughter Anne the state and term in the tenement in Templestrete, lately purchased for a term of ninety-nine years of Isabel Hosyer of Bristol, widow. Testator's wife Joan Batyn to have, for her life, his state and term in the tenement inhabited by him in the High-street, called " Le Cok in the Hope," purchased of the aforesaid John Shipward for a term of sixty years ; rem. to daughter Katharine. To daughter Agnes and her lawful heirs, the tenement lately purchased in fee simple of John Gaywode of Bristol, merchant, situate " in vico vocat' Wynestrete ;" rem. to her brother Richard Wilteshire, if she should die s.p. If Richard should so die, rem. to son Clement ; in def., rem. to son Henry ; in def., rem. to son Daniel ; in def., rem. to the rightful heirs of testator for ever. To each of his daughters, twenty ounces of silver ; also a girdle of silver and gilt, each of the girdles being worth xl^s " ad minus." To Henry Weston, " Seneseallo Cur' Tols' ville," a standing cup with a cover of silver and gilt, formerly belonging to Robert Bolton, merchant of Bristol. Testator wills that Richard Andrewe, his father-in-law (pat' meus in lege), receive weekly, out of his effects, xij^d sterling for his support during his life. To apprentice Robert Russell a cloth " vocat' A See clothe." Legacies also to apprentices William Forest and John Sandy, and servants John Ryppe, Isabel Wilteshire, and Margery. Residue of goods to wife Joan Bateyn and son-in-law John Parnand, who are to be executors, and dispose for the health of his soul, and the souls of his children by his late wife Margery. John Pollard of Bristol, mercer, to be overseer, and have xl^s for his pains. Witnessed by Henry Weston esquire, Sir John Thomas, testator's curate, William Sare, notary public, and many others.

Proved at Knoll, Jan. 7th, 1492; also at Bristol, before John Hawkes, Mayor, and John Dreux, Sheriff, on Friday, Feb. 1st, 8 Henry vii.

276.—THOMAS BAKER, grocer.

1492. Feb. 14th. To be buried in the parish church of All Saints, if he should happen to die in Bristol. Forty shillings to the fabric of the nave of that church, for his burial. Twenty shillings to Sir John Thomas, vicar of the said church, for tithes and offerings, and that he may on every Sunday exhort the parishioners especially to pray for testator's soul. Twelve pence to the mother church of the blessed Mary in the city of Worcester. Forty shillings to the fabric of the parish church of St. Briavels in the Forest of Dean, on condition that the guardians of the goods of that church keep testator's obit there in the week next after his decease. To the prior and convent of each house of mendicant friars at Bristol twenty shillings, that they may attend the mortuary offices on the day of burial, and also "in die Mensis." To eldest son Thomas Baker 100 marks of lawful English money, and 50 ounces "ponderis troie" in silver cups, bowls, salt-cellars, and spoons, when he is twenty-four years of age. To daughter Alice Baker 100 marks, and silver cups, spoons, &c., when sixteen years of age. Also to daughters Margaret, Joan, Elizabeth, Anne, and Maud, 100 marks, &c., when sixteen years of age. If all the children should die under age, wife Maud is to enjoy their portions during her life, if she keeps herself single and unmarried. A fit chaplain to celebrate for six years in the aforesaid church of All Saints, and receive yearly £6 sterling. Testator's obit or anniversary to be kept also in the same church year by year for ten years, with "Placebo & dirige" at night, and mass of *Requiem* on the morrow, on the day upon which he shall happen to migrate "ab hac luce." The sum of ten shillings to be expended on each anniversary, of which twelve pence to the aforesaid Sir John Thomas, and the remaining nine shillings to the priests and clerks taking part in the said offices, and for lights, and tolling of the bells. Wife Maud to provide due security before the Mayor of Bristol "p' viam recognic'o'is," according to the laudable custom of the town, in respect of the aforesaid 700 marks and 350 ounces of silver bequeathed to the children. To John and William, sons of John Hutton, late merchant of Bristol, 100 shillings apiece, when aged twenty-four. If they should both die under that age, the said legacies are to be divided equally among testator's own children. To Magdalene Baker, daughter of James Baker, late merchant of Bristol, deceased, £20 sterling when she is sixteen years of age. If she should die under that age, or be unwilling to obey the governance of testator's wife Maud and John Stevyns, his own children are to have the said legacy. To his sister Elizabeth, and Elizabeth daughter of his brother William Baker, 60 shillings apiece. To his said brother 100 shillings, on condition of being "benivolus" to wife Maud in all transactions. To David Whitecastell, chaplain, 20 shillings, that he may pray for testator's soul. To servant Katharine Trcheron, for her marriage, a pipe of woad, containing "sexdecim mensuras quarterij Bristoll." Legacies also to servant Alice Bernard, and her daughter Joan Bernard when sixteen years of age; servant John Willys; apprentices Thomas Paty, Ralph Walshe, and John Carpynter; John Bale; Agnes Furboure, servant of Maud Wodyngton, widow, for her marriage; the aforesaid John Stevyns, for his pains, &c.

Residue to wife Maud and her executors, on condition of keeping herself single and unmarried. To the same Maud, who is appointed executrix, all testator's lands, tenements, and rents in the town and suburb of Bristol, for her life; rem. to son Thomas and his lawful heirs. Also, for her life, lands, tenements, &c., in the aforesaid parish of St. Briavels, and in Hewellesfeld, within the Forest of Dean, lately bought of brother William Baker, Thomas Dull, and others. Witnessed by Sir John Thomas, dean of the deanery of Bristol, and vicar of All Saints', Sir Henry Scurlag, clerk, David Whiteeastell, chaplain, John Stevyns, merchant, Thomas Snyg, mercer, Thomas Pernaunte, grocer, William Smyth and John Colles, literates, Thomas Bale, and others.

Proved before John Hawkes, Mayor, and John Dreux, Sheriff, April 17th, 8 Henry vii. Previously proved at Lambeth.

To this will there is appended a memorandum, to the effect that on Oct. 14th, 9 Henry vii., Thomas Wodyngton came before the Mayor and Sheriff, and with the assent of the Mayor and the Aldermen of Bristol, and also of Maud, widow and executrix of Thomas Baker, late of Bristol, grocer, espoused Alice, daughter of the said Thomas, and acknowledged the receipt, from the aforesaid Mistress Maud, of the 100 marks of lawful money of England, and 50 ounces of silver, bequeathed to the said Alice by the aforesaid Thomas Baker's will, enrolled in the court there.

277.—EDWARD DAWES, merchant.

1493. July 21st. To be buried before the altar of the blessed Mary in the parish church of the blessed Werburgh of Bristol, to the high altar of which church, for tithes and offerings, twenty shillings. Eight measures of woad, of Bristol warranty and measure, towards buying a pair of new organs for that church. A fit chaplain to celebrate there for four years next after testator's decease, and be paid £24. All debts to be paid. The sum of £10 for funeral expenses, and for distribution at the month's mind. Two shillings to the mother church of St. Mary of Worcester. Forty shillings to the fabric of the nave of the parish church of St. Leonard at Bridgnorth. Six shillings' worth of bread to be divided among the poor in the gaol of Newgate at Bristol. Twenty shillings for the most needy poor. Legacies also to the prior, or guardian, and convent of each house of mendicant friars at Bristol; Thomas Dawes, chaplain, Hugh Dawes, John Dawes, and Roger Dawes, brothers of testator; his god-daughter Elen Dawes, daughter of the said Roger; Thomas Patte; servants Robert Rowlowe, Margaret Spycer, and Elizabeth Edwardes. To son Richard Dawes, " in recompensac'o'em sibi de & pro tota p'parte sua ip'm contingen' de bonis meis," sixty ounces of silver, and five pipes of woad, worth £40 sterling; also the half of all testator's implements and household utensils, jewels and wares excepted; to be delivered to the said Richard when twenty-one years of age. If he should die before that age, wife Joan to have one half of the said legacy, the executors bestowing the other *pro animu*. To wife Joan, in the name of her whole rightful portion of the moveable goods and chattels, ten pipes of woad, worth £80 sterling, and twenty woollen cloths, worth eighty marks; also £30 in money, eighty ounces of silver, and the other half of all household goods, except the before excepted articles. Testator's most beloved brother Roger Dawes and John Robertes, merchants, to be executors, and John

Esterfeld, merchant, overseer; to each of whom a pipe of woad, good and merchantable. Witnessed by John Esterfeld, Richard Hoby, Richard Hemmyng, merchants, Robert Birche, chaplain, "Confessore meo," Thomas Walmesley, chaplain, and others.

Proved at Lambeth, Aug. 6th, 1493; afterwards at Bristol, before the Mayor and Sheriff.

278.—THOMAS BEELL, burgess.

1493. July 30th. To be buried in the crypt of the parish church of St. Nicholas at Bristol, in which church a fit chaplain is to celebrate *pro anima* for one year, and be paid nine marks. Legacies to the high altar thereof, the fabric of the nave, and the reparation of the said crypt, for his burial therein; the mother church of St. Mary of Worcester; John Sherp, gentleman; each of testator's brothers; the boys of his hospice, staying in London; John Frankeleyn, and —— Forster, gentleman. To son Thomas twenty marks when 21 years of age. To sons John and Henry Beell twenty marks apiece when of that age. To daughters Alice and Elen twenty marks apiece when married. Residue to wife Katharine, who is made executrix. John Dreux to be overseer, and have three yards of scarlet cloth. Witnessed by Sir Robert Birche clerk, testator's confessor, to whom ten shillings, Janycote Barrero, Patrick Cole, John White, Thomas Calmady, and others.

Proved at Lambeth, Aug. 6th, 1493; afterwards at Bristol, before the Mayor and Sheriff.

279.—DAVID AP POLLANGHAN, burgess.

1495. May 9th. To be buried in the crypt of St. Nicholas at Bristol. To the cathedral church of Worcester xx^d. To Master John Burton, testator's curate, for tithes, vj^s viij^d. For the use and reparation of the said church of St. Nicholas vj^s viij^d. A fit secular chaplain to celebrate for two years in the crypt aforesaid, at the altar of St. Citha, and have £12. To son Sir John, the canon, a silver cup called "A flatte Pece," and six silver spoons "cum Maidenheddis." To the other John, son of testator, a pipe of woad, a standing silver cup with cover, and six silver spoons "de Maidenheddis." To son Thomas £10 in money and a pipe of woad. To daughter Joyce £30 in money. To wife Margaret, for her life, two tenements on the Back of Avon; rem. to son Thomas during the term of years not yet complete therein. Residue of goods, after deduction of debts and funeral expenses, to wife Margaret, who is made executrix. Thomas Vaughan and Patrick Cole overseers, to whom ten shillings apiece. Witnessed by John Hawley, notary public, Sir William Carpynter, chaplain, and many others.

Proved at Lambeth, July 23rd, 1495; afterwards at Bristol, before John Esterfeld, Mayor, and Matthew Jubbes, Sheriff.

280.—WILLIAM DE LA FOUNTE, merchant.

1493. Feb. 12th.—"compos mentis in bona memoria existens et corporis sanitate p'ponens visitare terram Rome." My body to ecclesiastical burial "vbicunq' deus disposuerit me obire." To the mother church of Worcester xij^d. To Sir John Vaughan, parish priest of St. Stephen's church at Bristol, and testator's curate, vj^s viij^d sterling, for tithes. To the works of that church xx^s. An honest priest to celebrate therein for seven years for testator's soul, and the soul of his late wife Alice, his parents, brothers, sisters, &c., and receive yearly £6 sterling. Forty pence to each of the four orders of friars at Bristol. To sons Edmund and John £20 apiece at the age of 21. To elder daughter Joan, daughter Anne, younger daughter Joan, and daughter Elizabeth, £20 apiece at the age of 15. If all should die under the said ages, their portions are to be distributed *pro anima*. To servants Isabel Skydmore and Margaret Sawee forty shillings apiece. To servant Margaret Mathewe twenty shillings. Wife Elizabeth to be executrix. Philip Ryngstone and John Barryero, merchants of Bristol, to be overseers, and have forty shillings apiece. Witnessed by the aforesaid Sir John Vaughan, John Barryero, William Sare, notary public, and many others.

Testator added a codicil on April 8th, 1495, bequeathing £40 in salt, after four pence the bushel, to his parish church of St. Stephen, and legacies to his children, to St. Clement's chapel, &c. Witnessed by Master Philip Ryngstone, Sir John Vaughan, Sir John Hawley, and others.

Proved before William Regent, Mayor, and Nicholas Broun, Sheriff, Sept. 11th, 12 Henry vii. Previously proved at Lambeth.

281.—JOHN PENKE the younger, merchant.

1493. Sept. 14th. To be buried in the parish church of "Alhalowyn in Bristowe." To the cathedral church of Worcester xij^d. To the use of the aforesaid parish church four measures of woad. To "my Curate vicary of the saide Churche, iiij mesures of wode." A secular priest to sing in that church "at dyuynes" by the space of two years, and have £12. To wife Alice Penke eight pipes of woad "and x ton wyne." To "my suster Annes Pynke" two pipes of woad, a coverlet "of verdour colour," a dozen of pewter vessels, &c. To "my suster Johane Penke iij ton of Gascoyn wyne the fust that shall come fro Burdeux of myn." To my brother Thomas Penke "iij ton wyne co'myng first fro Burdeux of myn And J forgeve him all suche money as J haue lent hym before this tyme." To Master Thomas Cornyssh, suffragan at Wells, and Sir John of London a pipe of wine apiece. Legacies also to John Bouwey, Thomas Baron, Simon Gerveys, and John Shipman. Wife Alice to be executrix, and have the residue of goods. Testator's "ffader" John Penke and Thomas Snygge the younger "to been as ou'seers." To the former "x mesures wode, nowe being in his owne keping redy." To Thomas Snygge iij^{li} vj^s viij^d. Witnessed by John Bowley, merchant, Simon Gerveys, merchant, Edward Gibbes, mariner, and others.

Proved before John Dreux, Mayor, and Hugh Joh'nes, Sheriff, on Friday, March 3rd, 12 Henry vii. Previously proved at Lambeth.

282.—JOHN HENLOVE, dyer.

1498. March 18th. To be buried in the cemetery of the parish church of the Holy Cross at Bristol, under a yew-tree growing there. To the procurators of the said church, for testator's burial, vj^s viij^d. To Edmund Burley, vicar of the church, for his prayers, forty shillings sterling, also a standing silver cup, &c. To the mother church of Wells xij^d. To daughter Margery a pipe of woad good and merchantable, of the real value of twenty marks sterling, containing sixteen measures, of Bristol measure, "s'cd'ng assaiam & p'bacionem cons'ilis guide in eadem villa antiquit' vsitat'; " also cups, &c., and a pair of coral beads, worth twenty shillings; to be delivered to her when married. If she should die before marriage, the said legacies to be expended *pro anima*. To the same Margery a tenement in Templestrete, situate between the tenement belonging to the abbot and convent of the blessed Mary of Keynsham, and occupied by John Yong, on the south, and the tenement of Humphrey Hervy and Anne his wife, held by Richard Snowe, weaver, on the north, and extending from the said street to a ditch " vulgarit' nu'cupat' le Lawediche " ; which tenement the aforesaid John Henlowe *(sic)* by the name of John Henlove of Bristol, dyer, purchased for himself, and his heirs, of John Forster of London, gentleman ; the said tenement to be held by daughter Margery and her heirs after the death of wife Isabel. To kinsmen Robert Henlove, Gregory Henlove, and Thomas Henlove, a whole woollen cloth apiece, price £3 sterling, or else that sum of money. To the said Gregory and Robert, after the death of wife Isabel, all the utensils and instruments pertaining to testator's craft of dyeing, divided equally between them. To John Tyler, weaver, "vna Cratera' argenti & in p'cell deaurat' ponderant' sexdeci' vnc' ponderis Troie," &c. Residue of goods to wife Isabel. She, and the aforesaid Edmund Burley, and John Tyler to be executors—" quor' conscienc' illuminet sp'us sc'ns." Witnessed by Thomas Smyth, tucker, Thomas Broke, tucker, John Piers, dyer, and many others.

Proved before Richard Vaughan, Mayor, and Hugh Elyot and John Bateyn " vic' eiusdem ville," on Friday, Feb. 5th, 16 Henry vii. Previously proved at Lambeth.

283.—JOAN JONS.

1501. Aug. 13th. Testatrix was relict of John Jons, otherwise Morgan, late of Bristol, brewer, and desired to be buried in the cemetery of the church of St. Peter at Bristol. To the high altar of that church, for tithes and offerings, iij^s iiij^d ; also a linen cloth. To the chapel of the blessed Mary in the same church iij^s iiij^d. To the mother church of Worcester xij^d. To sister Katharine Joh'nes my best cap of velvet. To Cristina Hawkyng, widow, " vnam togam vna' tunica' voc' le Sloppe Mantell & vnam tunicella' vocat' le petycote." To Joan Henewod half a dozen " de garnyssh vessell'," &c. To my curate Sir Thomas Schaftspere " vnu' collitegiu' de veluet cum laqueo cerico." Legacies also to Anne wife of Robert Howlet, cooper, Agnes wife of John Baker, Margaret Phill, widow, servant Joan Gronowe, and John Davys, baker. Residue of goods to sons John Jons otherwise Morgan, master in arts, and Thomas Jons otherwise Morgan, who are made executors. Master Hugh Joh'nes overseer. Witnessed by Sir Thomas Schaftspere, curate, John Davys, baker, Matthew Cotynton, and many others.

Proved before George Monoux, Mayor, and Thomas Parnant and Thomas Snyg, Sheriffs, on Friday, Dec. 17th, 17 Henry vii. Previously proved at Lambeth.

The name of the above mentioned " curate " occurs as Thomas Sheftspere, Shafftes]er, Shakespeir, and Shakespeire, in some Bristol wills registered at Somerset House.

284.—JOHN FUYSTER, burgess and merchant.

1501. July 2nd. Testator bequeathed his soul to Almighty God, and his body " to be buryed in the Crowde of seint Nicholas by my Moder and vnder the same stone." To the mother church of Worcester xij^d. To the vicar of St. Nicholas " for Satisfaccion of my tythes forgoten " xx^s. To " the werkes " of the said church xl^s. To Robert Fuyster, testator's son and heir, all his lands and tenements " within Herford and the ffraunchise of the same accordyng to my ffaders last will And he to haue possession of the same. And to put his moder in suertie to pay her yerely x^{li} clere. Without any other charge." To wife Elizabeth five pipes of woad, household goods, half of the plate, &c.; also the state and term of testator's dwelling house and gardens " in the Bartilmewes." If son Robert, who is to have the other half of the plate, should die before her, the said plate is to be " departed " between John Wyot and Joan Fuyster. To Robert Fuyster articles of clothing, " iij paire of Brigandynys," &c. To daughter Joan two pipes of woad, twenty marks in plate, " and xx marke of my Cabbowe, in money or dettes, or otherwise, to the value." To the works of " the mynist' of Herford " xl^s. To " the vicaires of the same Monastery to their werkes " xl^s. To " Alhalowen Church " there xl^s. To servant Joan xx^s. To the chapel on " the Brigge " vj^s viij^d. To John Wyot the best ring, &c.; also four yards of " violet in grayn' and oon of my gownes that he will chose." Testator wills that after the payment of his debts, and all the cost of burying, month's mind, and twelve months' mind, " all the Residue of my Cabbowe be departed in two wherof J bequeth to (sic) oon half to Robert my son and the other half to be disposed for my sowle And my fryndez soules in fyndyng a Preste to pray for vs in seint Nicholas churche by the orden'nce of myn' Executrix whome J make chef Elizabeth my wyf and Robert my sonne. And John Wyot to be ou'seer."

Proved before George Monoux, Mayor, and Thomas Parnaunt and Thomas Snyg, Sheriffs, on Monday, March 21st, 17 Henry vii. Previously proved at Lambeth.

285.—THOMAS EDWARDE.

1503. Sept. 17th.—" p'nu'c manens in villa Bristoll' Wellen' & Bathon' dioc'." To be buried in the parish church of the blessed Mary of Redcliff. To the mother church of St. Andrew at Wells vj^d. To the high altar of my parish church, namely, of St. Thomas the Martyr, for tithes and offerings, xij^d. To wife Joan " om'ia clenodia argentea & deaurat'," and other household utensils; also, for her life, lands and tenements in or about the town of Stanford. But if she should take another husband, all the said property is to pass to Henry Edward, testator's son and heir, except one messuage situate in the parish of St. Andrew in that town. If the said Henry should die s.p., the property is to be disposed of *pro anima*. An honest priest to celebrate daily for four years. To daughter Agnes x^{li}, on condition that she properly serves and pleases her mother. To William, Henry, and John Edwarde, x^s apiece. Legacies also to the mendicant friars of Bristol and Stanford, and testator's sister Agnes. Residue to wife Joan. She, John Wynter of Stanford, and Sir Richard Moskam, priest, of the same town, to be executors: to these two xx^s apiece. Master Richard Meryeke to be overseer, and have xx^s. Witnessed by Nicholas Broun, Richard Meryck, James Baker, Thomas Devyncher, John Barbour, Richard Skansby, John Wynter " de villa Stanfordie," and Sir William Moskam of the same town.

Proved before Roger Dawes, Mayor, and Thomas Elyot and John Harrys, Sheriffs, on Friday, Jan. 14th, 21 Henry vii. Previously proved before the ecclesiastical authorities.

286.—THOMAS ELYOT, burgess.

1505. Feb. 9th—"beyng hole of mynde & in good memory thanked be Jh'u." To be buried within "the Church hey of the p'issh church of seynt Thomas the Martir in the Town of Bristowe nygh vnto the tombe or place where the body of Alice late my wyf lieth ther buryed." To the mother church of Wells xij^d. To the high altar of the said parish church of St. Thomas, for tithes, &c., iij^s iiij^d. To Thomas Hoskyns "a Crucifix of golde." To my brother John Elyott "a hors beyng w^t John Payne of Elborowe." To Sir John Russell "a gown of Tawney which his ffader william Joly" gave to testator; also "a paire of hosen of Puke." To Isabel Tanner, over and above her wages, vj^s viiij^d, and "asmoche cloth as woll make the saide Jsabell a gowne." To wife Joan all household goods, plate, &c., which she brought unto testator at her marriage, and "the Nutte" made of her own stuff and plate; also the state and term of years in testator's dwelling house "sett in Redclifstrete in the p'issh of Seynt Thomas aforseid." But if she "do mary ageyn. and kepe her not sole or woll not dwell in the saide ten't her self," the said house or tenement is then to remain unto son Nicholas. To the same Nicholas all the "ffate ffurneys Cestren," &c. If he should die s.p., the state and term of years then to come is to remain to son Thomas Elyot. To the said Thomas all the state, title, interest, and "termes of yeres" of the house in Barton hundred, and the stuff belonging to the same, he "payeng yerely vnto thabbot of Seynt Austynes the rent therof." Also to the said Thomas Elyot all "the wynes beeng in the Celer wherof. he berith the key," and other wines and goods in the hands of cousin Robert Elyot, and all the money and debts owing by Richard Baker, merchant, and also "my stonding place in Seynt James chirch hey w^t the sayes therto belonging." To son William and his lawful heirs a tenement on the east side of Redclyfstrete, in "the parisshe of o^r Lady of Redclyf" in the suburb of the town of Bristowe. If he should die s.p., rem. to son Thomas and his lawful heirs; in def., rem. to Robert Elyot, son of testator's brother John. If Robert should die s.p., rem. to "the right heires of John Jay thelder m'chant of Bristowe." Testator's children to have the residue of his goods. His sons Thomas and William Elyot to be executors. John Jay, John Elyot, and Thomas Hoskyns, overseers. Testator wills, requires, and charges his said two sons "vpon my blissyng that they vse & ex'cise thexecucion of this my testament in eu'y thyng bi thaduyce & agrement of my foresaide overseers & none otherwise." The said executors and overseers to have free entry and issue into and from his dwelling house or tenement aforesaid, "at all tymes Lefull & convenyent by the space of one yer. & one day next ensuyng after my decesse w'oute eny impedyment or contradiccion' of my wyf or of eny other p'sone or p'sones." Witnessed by Sir John Russell, priest, William Bedford and Thomas Devonshire, "Burgeisez" of the town of Bristowe, and others.

Proved at Lambeth, March 5th, 1505.—Jo Yong. Also proved at Bristol, before John Vaghan, Mayor, and John Edwardes and Simon Gervys, Sheriffs, on Monday, Feb. 14th, 23 Henry vii.

287.—JOAN RYNGSTON, widow.

1509. April 15th. Testatrix was of the parish of St. Stephen in Bristol, in the diocese of Worcester, and desired to be buried in St. Stephen's church, "in the Sepultre where the body of my late dere husbond Philip Ryngston nowe lyeth buryed." She bequeathed to "the modre church of o^r blessid Lady of worcestr'" xx^d. To the reparation of the said church of St. Stephen a pipe of woad good and merchantable, and "a Standing cupp of silu' ou'gilt w^t a cover of the same weyeng xxiij vnces." The executors are to find "or doo to be founde" an honest priest of good name and fame "for to pray & syng for my sowle and for the Sowle of my dere husbond abouesaid and all xp'en Sowles bi the space of two yeres next aft' my decesse within the saide p'issh Church of scynt Stephens. at the aulter of Seynt John baptist there;" the same priest to say "his masse" there every day during the said two years, unless hindered by a reasonable cause, and to receive yearly for his salary £6 sterling. To daughter Joan Rowlowe (*sic*), wife of Robert Rolowe, "ij p'pez of wode good and m'chauudable;" and a like bequest to daughter Agnes Snyg, wife of John Snyg, mercer. To youngest son John Ryngston forty ounces in silver plate, and two pipes of woad good and merchantable, to be delivered to him by the executors when he shall come to his age of xxiiij years. If he should die before that age, "which god defend," the said goods to be equally divided among "others of my children aboue & w^tin named then ou'lyving." The forenamed son John Ryngston, with all his bequests contained as well in the testament of "my saide dire husbond Philip Ryngston. as in this my p'sent testament," to be committed and delivered unto Robert Thorn' of Bristowe, merchant. The executors are to "fynde vnto the same John Ryngston sufficient Lernyng in Gramer clothing and all other necessaries belonging to his body vntil the saide John co'me to his age of discrecion that is to say. xiiij yeres," or until the time of his being apprenticed with some honest man, after the advice and discretion of the said Robert Thorn and the executors; during all which space, "that is to wete fro my deth or decesse vntil the saide age of xiiij yeres," or until he be apprenticed, the same John Ryngston is to be in the custody, ward, governance, and guiding of the forenamed Robert Thorn, or of such a "sad & discrete" person as the same Robert shall depute or assign; and as soon as he shall come to his age of xxiiij years, all his whole bequests to be delivered to him. All "beddys Shettes blankettes Cou'lettes Napry hangynges pottes pannes," &c., to be equally divided among the children of testatrix. To John son of William Burley forty shillings in money, and a pipe of woad good and merchantable, to be delivered to him when aged xxj years. To Agnes Ryngston, daughter of eldest son John, twenty "vnces" of silver plate when aged xvj. To servants Water Alpe and Agnes Anthony, "Senglewoman," half a pipe of woad apiece. To the "pore prisoners of Newgate in Bristowe eu'y Wednesday in the weke oon aft' another. ymmediatly folowing during an hole yere next aft' my decesse. vj^d in brede," to be equally distributed. The executors are to fulfil the last will of "my saide late dire husbond," whereof the date is the xxth day of August, mccccvij. Residue of all "goodes catalx. Juelx," &c., not bequeathed, debts being fully contented and paid, and "my buryeng. monethes mynd and yeres mynd worshipfully kept," &c., to be equally divided between sons Thomas and William, in the presence of the overseers of this will, and William Edwardes, mercer. The "half parte or halvendele" of the said goods, &c., to be delivered to the aforesaid William Edwardes "to thuse and behoof" of son William, if apprenticed with the same William Edwardes; the latter to be bounden in a certain sum of money, "for to relyn'e (relyvere, for relevy?) or doo to be relyn'd" unto the said William Ryngston all his bequests as soon as the same William "shall co'me oute of his App'ntise-wike or assone as his app'nticewyk shalbe fynysshed, or ended." The said Thomas and William Ryngston to be executors. Robert Thorn' and Robert Rolowe overseers. To "eu'ych of my saide Ou'seers" vj^{li} xiij^s iiij^d. Witnessed by Sir William Hawkes "my Curate," Sir John Hewys, chaplain, Nicholas Box, merchant, and many others.

Proved before John Caple, Mayor, and John Williams and John Wilkyns, Sheriffs, on Monday, Aug. 26th, 2 Henry viii. Previously proved at Lambeth.

288.—STEPHEN FORSTER, merchant.

1508. Sept. 16th.—"beyng in good and stedfast mynd," and desiring that his body be "buryed in xp'en grave where please god." To the parish church "a pipe of oode of vj m're warantise conteynyng xvj mesures." Executrix to cause that a trental be said on "the day of my deeces," and on other two or three days, "w^t xxx prestes eu'y prest having for his labour iiij^d sterling," with all things belonging to the same "for the welth of my soule and all xp'en soules." The sum of iiij^s iiij^d for the prayers of thirteen poor men. A priest of good name and fame to sing and pray for the space of three years next after testator's death "w^{t}in the parisshe chirch where J dwell and inhabit at the tyme of my deth," and be paid ix marks sterling for his labor, and xx^d for light, &c., every year. A measure of woad "of vj m're warantise" to every house of "the iiij ordres of frreres in Bristowe to pray for my good fryndes & me." To the chapel of "Seynt Clement set beside the Marsshe in Bristowe" two measures of woad. To the poor prisoners of Newgate, every Friday for the space of a whole year, xij^d sterling "in ferthing bred." Towards the reparation of the Temple pipe, and the conduits of Redcliff, All Saints', and St. John's in Bristowe, "that is to sey to eu'y of them" a measure of woad. To brother John Forster "a pipe of ode (sic) of vj m're warantise." To brother Richard Forster a pipe of woad, and "oon of my gownes and an other to my brother John aforenamed." To the children by "my wyf Johane" lands and tenements "set in the town of Bristowe or elswhere w^{t}in Englond;" but she to have the rule and profit of the same lands "vnto the tyme that he or they be of the age of xxij yere olde." If the said child or children die before that age, brother John Forster and his heirs to have the said lands; and "for defaute" of heirs, rem. to the next of testator's kin. To son Richard xij pipes of woad, &c. And if another child shall be born to testator by his wife Joan, the same child is to have x pipes of woad, iij tons of iron, and x^{li} in silver plate. But if there shall be no child to live to the age of twenty-two years, "then J. will that x of the aforenamed xxij pipes oode be delyu'ed vnto the holy churche of seint Stephen in Bristowe, so that the parisshens of the saide churche doo let fynde a good prest for to Syng and pray for my soule and all my good frendes soules for the space of vj yeres." Wife Joan to have the residue of the woad, iron, &c., and of all testator's other goods, and be full and sole executrix, pay all debts, and "doo for my soule and for her fathers soule as J was bounde by conscience." My "good frynde" John Messam to be overseer of this will and testament, and to have for his labor a pipe of woad "of vj m're," testator's best gown, and best ring of gold. "J haue writen it w^t myn' oune hand."

Proved at Lambeth, May 7th, 1510. No record of proof before the Mayor.

289.—MAUD ESTERFELD.

1491. July 21st. Testatrix was wife of John Esterfeld of Bristol, merchant, and made her will by his leave. She commended her soul to Almighty God, her Creator and Redeemer, to the B.V.M. "Regine misericordie," and to all the saints, and desired to be buried by (iuxta) the chapel of the blessed Mary "de Belhous" in the parish church of St. Peter at Bristol, to the use of which chapel she bequeathed her wedding ring. Another ring of gold to the use of the chapel of the blessed Mary "situat' in portico" of the parish church of the blessed Mary of Redcliff; and another to the use of the chapel of St. Anne by Bristol, co. Somerset. Four shillings for the reparation of the cathedral church of the blessed Mary of Worcester. Twelve pence to the high altar of the parish church of St. Werburgh the Virgin at Bristol, for tithes. Ten shillings for the renovation of the tabernacle of the blessed Mary in the same church. To son John Esterfeld, the younger, two tenements held by William Malteman in Templestrete, in the parish of holy Cross, and a garden held by John Spenser in the Old Market "iuxta portam Lafford." If the said John should die s.p., rem. to son Henry Esterfeld; in def., rem. to daughter Isabel; in def., rem. to daughter Joan. To the said two daughters "ornamenta corporis mei." To son William Rogers two dozen napkins, four towels, twelve dishes, twelve amber salt-cellars, &c. Legacies also to the mendicant friars of Bristol, Lucy Nete, Alice Dee, and servant Agnes. John Esterfeld, husband of testatrix, to be executor. Sealed with her seal and his.

Proved at Lambeth, Feb. 6th, 1492. No record of proof before the Mayor.

The will of John Esterfeld of Bristol, merchant, husband of the aforesaid Maud, is registered at Somerset House, *Holgrave*, 26. It was made Feb. 5th, 1504. To be buried in "the holy Oratory of our blessed Lady of Belhowsse" within the church of St. Peter in Bristowe; to which chapel of our Lady "my best masse boke my chalice of siluer and gilt and my Cruettes of siluer." To the high altar of St. Werburgh's church in Bristowe vj^s viij^d. To the "moder chirch of Worcestre" xij^d. An honest priest to "sing before my Wif in saint Warbrois chirch in Bristowe by the space of au hoole yere," and be paid vj^{li}. To wife "Scolast" certain goods, and £100 in money; also the state possessed by testator in his dwelling place, if disposed to dwell therein, she paying the rent, £4 by the year, to Sir John Rodney knt., and finding reparations; also the garden in St. Leonard's lane, as long as she dwelleth in the said house. The executors are to restore to St. Werburgh's church the house held by testator at a yearly rent of xiij^s iiij^d. To Master John Esterfeld, son of testator, and "Chanon of saint Georges chapell within the castell of Windesore," three of the best gowns

N

furred with such as he shall choose; also articles of silver plate, and the best "coverpayne otherwise called a bredecloth." To son Henry Esterfeld a coverlet of arras work "the which J had of maister ffoster"; also a feather-bed and bolster, "ij pylowes garnesshed," a Psalter-book, a "matens boke," the best chain of gold with the cross thereunto belonging, a pair of complete harness, pots, pans, ewers, &c., and "my clothe presse to pak in clothes"; also two new houses built by testator in Smalstrete, and inhabited by John Jamsye and William Hurst. If the said Henry should die s.p., rem. to "my yong Son John Esterfeld" and his heirs; in def., rem. to daughter Jane Poppheyne. If he "doo mary in my lif dayes," he is to have in money xl^{li}, in plate xxx^{li} "after iij^s iiij^d the vnce," in iron xij tons, price the ton five marks. If he marry afterwards, "wisely and discretely by the advisement of my Son maister John Esterfeld and myn Executours," he is to receive in money, plate, and iron, "as is afore rehersed," and to have a state in the house of Richard Hobbes; also in gardens held by Genet Boole and John Wassh, laborer; and the garden in St. Leonard's lane, after the decease of testator's wife, or her departing from his dwelling house in Smalstrete. To younger son John the money in the hands of "his maist^r Dauid Philip alias Dauid Cogan;" a "cheyne of gold with a Sanguinarye;" the "best matens boke" covered with velvet; pots, pans, &c.; also all the lands that "his moder" bequeathed him by her testament, namely, a house in Templestrete, lately inhabited by William Maltman, and a garden in the Old Market-place, held by John Spenser, mercer; the rent to be kept in the hands of the aforesaid Master John Esterfeld until the younger John be of lawful age; the latter also to have the house in Templestrete next to Maltman's house. If he should die s.p., rem. to son Henry Esterfeld and his heirs; in def., rem. to testator's daughter and her lawful heirs male. If at length there should be no heir, these houses and gardens are to remain to "the Almeshowses of the iij Kinges of coleyn." To the said sons Henry and John, the younger, all "my weybernes with all my weights of lede" equally divided. Certain goods to be shared by them and daughter Jane. To the said Henry "alle my bonetts shurts and stomachers and my knif called an hanger." To Robert Poppham the money owing by him, and a ton of iron, price iiij^{li}. To William Grevell "s'iaunt at lawe Recorder of Bristowe," John Esterfeld, clerk, Henry Esterfeld, and John Esterfeld, sons of testator, John Rowland and Richard Hoby, merchants, Thomas Hardyng, common clerk of the town, and John Knottyng, the reversion of seven messuages and two parcels of land "vsid with fullers Rakkes with their appurten'nces set and being in the parisshe of the holy crosse of temple," and of a messuage in Marshstrete held by Alice Wicham for her life, and the reversion of two parts of the messuage in Cornestrete held by Agnes Weston, widow, for her life; that the said William Grevell, John Esterfeld, &c., may execute and fulfil "diuerse devises and intentions" specified in certain indentures. Testator willed that, before his decease, his executors or their assigns should have in their rule and possession all "bokes of my dettes alle my obligacions and billes obligatory and also alle my keys of alle my Cellers with alle the Salt therin," and sell his merchandise "to the moost value," and dispose of the money in good works. Eldest son John Esterfeld and John Vaughan to be executors; the latter to have £10 in ready money. Residue of goods to be employed by the executors "for the welth of my Soule and in especiall to have Remembraunce to the Almashowse." Witnessed by Sir Richard Wode, parson of St. Werburgh's, John Rowland and William Lane, merchants of Bristowe, and many others.

290.—THOMAS HARTE, merchant.

1541. March 29th. To be buried in "saint Jones Crowdes" at Bristowe. Towards the reparation of the said Crowdes "where the People doo walke to make the Grounde playne and to repaire the Pewes there" xx^s sterling. To "Mr Parson of saint Jones my Curate," for tithes, xxvj^s viij^d. To Sir John Jeffreys, priest, "synging at saint Jones Parishe," xx^s. To Mr. Henry Collyns, vicar of "saynt Austens by Bristowe," xx^s. The sum of £3 to be distributed on the day of burial among the poor people in the almshouses within the town of Bristowe and "the Suburbies of the same Towne," and the sum of xl^s "peny dole" among other poor and needy people. The same amount of money to be distributed in like manner at the month's mind and year's mind. To each of testator's "wurkemen," William Denys, William Edmonds, Richard Wynnall, Laurence Nashe, and Thomas Bense, v^s sterling. He releases and forgives Thomas Lasingbie, dyer, "almaner dettes whiche he owethe vnto me." To every godchild v^s sterling. To servant Agnes Bronne xxvj^s viij^d. To every other servant, as well men as women, "doyng their duties to my wife," xx^s apiece. To John Wyllie, Chamberlain of the town of Bristowe, "my vyolet in Grayne Gou'ne." To daughter Katharine and her lawful heirs, lands, tenements, and pastures within the said town and without. If she should die s.p., rem. to the Chamber of Bristowe, to "thentent it may helpe make free the yates of bristowe, for en'y good man and woman to resorte and co'me to the said Towne frelic w^{t}out paiyng any tollage at the same Gates." Immediately after testator's burial, all the evidences of his said lands were to be put into the Chamber of Bristowe, to be safely kept there for the use of his said daughter and her lawful issue, and there to "remayne vnto suche tyme as my said doughter Katheryn haue borne a Childe or twoo of hir owne body lawfully begoten." If she should die s.p., the said "Chambre of bristowe or Chambreleyn" to cause an obit to be kept for testator and his wife within St. John's church, to the sum of forty shillings yearly for ever; "that ys to witt," to the parson of St. John's, and for his wax, xij^d; to four priests, and one clerk, xx^d; to the sexton, and for the bells, xij^d; to the bellman iiij^d; to Mr. Mayor for the time being, if he be there, v^s; to Mr. Recorder, if he be there, iij^s; to "en'y of the Shrifs" ij^s vj^d; to the eight Serjeants ij^s viij^d; to the waiting men viij^d; and xvj^s to be yearly distributed among poor and needy people, some j^d and some ij^d, where most need is, as the Chamberlain shall think best to bestow it upon the parish. The sum of £100 to the Chamber of Bristowe, to be bestowed and set into some good use, as the chief Masters of the town for the time being "shall thinke moost p'fett for the pore Comynaltie." To daughter Katharine £150 when seventeen years of age, "orels be maried." If she should die first, £50 to remain to the son and heir of Edward Twynyhoo, and £100 to be bestowed in making and amending of highways about Bristowe, where "nede clothe requyre," by the counsel of the Masters of the said town. And if "the said Twynyho happen to deccace or he shall accomplishe thage of xvij yeres," his legacy "shalbe bestowed in highe wayes as afore is rehersed." A priest of an honest conversation to say mass in the "Crowdes" aforesaid, and pray for testator's soul and all Christian souls yearly, as long as the sum of £20 sterling shall endure. Wife Alson to be sole executrix, and have the residue of goods. Mr. Thomas White, alderman of Bristowe, overseer, to whom "twoo Portag.'" Witnessed by Mr. Thomas Whyte, John Willye, and William Nashe, of the said town, notary public.

Proved "apud London" May 27th, 1541.'

Thomas Argall.

291.— ROBERT THORNE.

1532. May 17th.—"humbly beseching almyghtie god and our Lady Saint marye and all the Sayntes of heuen to be intercessors for me." To be buried in some convenient church, and "at my buriyng to be said Masse and dirige as a cristen man' ought to haue." Testator refers to two chests "in the whiche ar 33 peces blacke app'teynyng to Georgio Catanio more ij helles of Perles m'ked w^t a Spectacles. in the which is cc peerles that ar also the said Georgio." To the children of sister Katharine Woselay £100 apiece. To sister Alice Jackman five hundred marks; also to the said Alice and her children "all that Thomas Jackman hir husbonde dothe rest owyng me at this p'sent day whiche is ffive hundreth poundes and not certen dettes that hathe p'ceded of Oyle and Sheepe whiche dettes do app'teyne to me and not hym. but oonly J bequethe the ready money that he owethe me for rest of accompte. to his wife and Childerne to the Su'me of the said ccccc poundes litle more or lesse." To Edmund Wythypoll £50 sterling; and to Elizabeth Wythipoull his sister "other ffyftye poundes." To the children of John Wythypoull of Maumsbury £50, to be "rep'ted among them after the discrecion of my Master Poule Wythipoll." To James and Thomas Thorne, children of my uncle William Thorne deceased, £50 apiece; and "asmuche more to the ij doughters of the said Willyam Thorne the oon maried in the Citie the other in Maydestone." Towards the making up of "the ffree Scole of Saint Bartholomeus in Bristowe" £300 sterling, "and more that my lorde Dalaware Onethe as by his Obligacion Apperethe." To the relief of "the pore Co'mons of Bristowe" £300, to be "rep'ted after the discrecion of ij of the best men of coneyens that may be founde in cu'y p'isshe of the said Towne." Towards the redemption of the fee-farm and prisage of the said town of Bristowe £200, if "redemed w'in this iij yeres." To Agnes Amayne, and to her sister "there maried in Bristowe," £30 apiece. To godson Robert Thorne, son of brother Nicholas Thorne, £100. To son Vincent Thorne, being in Spain, £3000 sterling, "whiche J will that Carolo Catanio that hathe the kepyng of hym at this p'sent in Spayne shall reteyne of the goods of myne that the said Carlo Catanio and his brother hathe to the vse & benefitt of my said Childe till he be of lawfull age and setting it at Seynt Georges in Jeane." If the said Vincent should die before he come to lawful age, his said legacy is to return to testator's heirs. To Anagaria (Anna Garrera), mother of the said Vincent, £50, on condition of her renouncing all pretence of inheritance of the bequest of her said son. To the five almshouses in Bristowe £100. To Thomas Lucar, William Ballarde, Francis Fowler, Thomas Cornell, John Shipman, John Messam, Thomas Tyson, Humphrey Coston, William Pyckeryng, William Harper, and John Woseley, £10 apiece. To Emanuel Lucar £10. To Thomas Moffett, master in the Grammar School in Bristowe,

£25. To Robert Moffett, his son, £10. The sum of £500 for poor householders in the twenty-five wards of the city of London, "of whiche is p'te alredy delyv'ed. by Manuel Lucar to my Maister Poule Wythypoull." The debts owing by the said Poule, and by William Dyott (?), of Bristowe, Ralph Onley, William Pepwall, and Benet Jaye, all "thise forsaid dettes J forgeue And bequethe it to en'y of them and wuld not it be axed." To sister Alice "late wife of Thomas Jackman for her. ij. Childerne. c. poundes Apece beside that bequest beforewrytten." To Manuel Lucar, testator's servant, £100 sterling in money "for to occupy for his owne behofe for the space of. v. yeres vpon his owne Obligacion w'out any Suerties." Towards the relief of prisoners in this city of London £50. Towards the "mariage of pore Maydens" in London £50. To the relief of poor prisoners in Bristowe £50. For the marriage of poor maidens there £50. To the making of a place for merchants "in the Strete where it shalbe thought by my Executors" £100, on condition that it be made within three years after testator's decease. To the reparation of the highways from Co'mer marsh to Bristowe £100; also "towardes the Rep'acyons Abowte bristowe of the highe ways. c. poundes." To Aldermary church in Watling-street £10. To St. Nicholas's church of Bristowe £20. The sum of £20 to each of the four orders of friars in Bristowe, the one half for the reparation of their churches and houses, and the other for their sustentation. To the four prisons about London, that is to say, Newgate, Ludgate, King's Bench, and Marshalsea, £100, to be delivered by the executors, a noble every quarter of a year to every house in bread, till the said £100 be consumed and paid. To the prisons of Bristowe £100, to be bestowed in like manner. The sum of £300 to be "disposed" in the Chamber of Bristowe, "to thentent that yerely may be made p'vision of Corne And wudde for the Succor of the pore Com'ons a'd to be bought as muche Corne and wudde as that amounteth to. in tyme of best Chepe. And to be delyuered vnto them at that Price in tyme of best chepe. when it is wurthe more, So that always the said ccc poundes do contynue in the said Chambre." Testator also willed that £500 be "deposed in the said Chambre of bristowe" for the succor of young men minded to clothmaking in that town; so that "he that wulde bynde hymselfe and geue best Suertie and make in dede moost Clothe shall enyoye moost money w'out payng any intresses. but that he shall retorne the Money that he receavethe into the Chambre at thende of xij monethes After suche forme as my Executors shall devise." To Collyngs wife "of this Citie," daughter to cousin William Thorne, £20. Brother Nicholas Thorne to "inherytt" all the rest of the goods, and "to rep'te it in good dedes of mercy to the relyef of the Comons of bristowe;" the poor people to have £500 above the bequests aforesaid. The sum of £1000 to be "distributed and ordred As my Executors shall seme best for my Soule." The residue of all goods "Aswel onthisside the See as beyonde the see," to brother Nicholas Thorne. William Wythypoule, "my Maister," and Emanuel Lucar to be executors, and have £20 apiece. Harry Hubberthorne overseer, to whom £20. Witnessed, May 18th, 1532, by Richard Reignolde, mercer, and Thomas Howson, William Macham, and Edward Bawne, clothworkers.

Proved at London, Oct. 10th, 1532.

A note states that William Shipman, Mayor of the town of Bristowe, and the Commonalty acknowledged the receipt of £500 at the hands of

Emanuel Lucar, executor of the will of Robert Thorne, late of London, merchant tailor, Nov. 3rd, 25 Henry viii.; and of £300 "by thendes" of Nicholas Thorne, Feb. 18th, 25 Henry viii. Then follow the "ordinances," to which reference has been made in the *Introduction*.

The families of Thorne and Lucar were connected by marriage with the Wythipools; as appears by the pedigree of Wythipool, entered at the visitation of Suffolk in 1561, and that of Lucar, entered at the visitation of Somerset in 1623.

292.—ROBERT ELLYETT, merchant.

1545. Aug. 23rd. To be buried in the crowde of St. John Baptist "nexte vnto my wifes." To the said parish church vj^s viij^d. To the parson thereof, for tithes, v^s. To daughter Barbara xxx^{li}; also four crocks, a pair of the best andirons, six candlesticks, "and ij ffeete to the Candelstykes," &c. To daughter Elizabeth xx^{li}, that is to say, in money twenty marks, and the rest in household stuff, "and my wives seconde girdell." To daughter Katharine xx^{li}, my wife's "best beades," &c. To son Robert a scarlet gown and frock, a damask jacket, "my Signe of gold," &c. To eldest son John a "vyolett in Grayne Gowne w^t his ffurr and x^{li} in money if his Condicions be honest and good." To son William v^{li}, and "other v^{li} when my Clothes be sold." To base son Richard, dwelling with William Mericke, tailor, "at his setting vp of his Crafte," iij^{li}. vj^s. viij^d, a great counting board, &c. Forty shillings "vnto his brother John," if alive, and "if his Condicions be good." To base son John a crimson satin doublet, &c. To sister Joan Mershe forty shillings in money, and "an honest Gowne of my wives." To sister-in-law, Mr. Bewsam's wife, a hoop of gold, three yards of "pewke Clothe," &c. To Sir John Kerne a velvet doublet, &c. To my kinswoman of "the Gillowes Jnn," the good wife of the house, a taster of silver "waing by estymacion vj vnces," &c. To Robert Ellyet, in Barton hundred, "my wurst Gowne of ffoynes and my beest peir of hoses." Mr. Richard Pryn, "my Gossipp" John Seibright, and neighbour William Jones, merchant, the tutors and governors of testator's daughters Barbara, Elizabeth, and Katharine, to occupy and use money and household stuff, and "find my said Children vntill they com' vnto their lawfull age and be maried." If they should die before that age, and unmarried, £40 to be divided among son Robert Ellyett's children in Salisbury, and the rest of the money to go to son William, and towards highways, poor people, &c. The said tutors and governors to find sureties "to be bounden vnto the Chambre of Bristowe;" the Mayor to have "for his paynes takyn" iij^s iiij^d, and the Chamberlain xij^d. To poor householders in the aforesaid parish, and to every "pore body" dwelling in the Bristol almshouses at the time of testator's burial, "orels at my monethes mynde," a penny; and among the poor in bread vj^{li}. Son Robert Ellyett and Mr. Richard Pryn' to be executors, and have iij^{li} vj^s viij^d apiece. Mr. William Jay overseer, to whom xl^s. Witnessed by Sir John Kerne, Thomas Harris, John Seibright, William Jones, Sir Nicholas Jones, with others.

Proved at London, Oct. 7th, 1545.

Thomas Argall.

293.—NICHOLAS WUDHOUSE, tanner.

1532. July 30th.—"at this p'sent being p'feete in mynde and witt and sick in my bodie." To be buried in the parish church of St. Peter within the town of Bristowe. To the high altar of that church v^s sterling. To the "mother churche of wurcoter" iij^s iiij^d. To daughter Agnes xx^{li} sterling, and she to be ordered at the will of the executrix. To "eu'y tw'oo Sisters" vj^s viij^d. To cousin Margery Cowper xx^s. To "the reperacions of highe waies" iij^s iiij^d. To poor people vj^s viij^d. To poor prisoners in Newgate iij^s iiij^d. To Joan Payne vj^s viij^d. To my brother Sir Thomas Wudhouse "my litle Nutt p'cell gilte." Wife Margaret to have the residue of goods, and be sole executrix. Ralph Leche and Rouland Cowper overseers, to each of whom xl^s. Witnessed by Thomas Willyams "my Curate," Mr Roger Cooke, John Clerke, with others.

Proved at London, May 2nd, 1548.

294.—MARGARET WUDHOUSE.

1548. Sept. 24th.—"of the Citie of Bristowe widowe late the wif and executrix of the testament and last will of Nicolas Wudhouse late of the same Citie tanner deceased." To be buried in the parish church of St. Peter there. To the high altar of the same, "for my teithes and oblacions negligentlie forgoten in discharge of my soule," v^s. Agnes Wudhouse, daughter of the said Nicholas, to have £20 of lawful money, according to his will, and other £20 of the money owing by Robert Butler and others, "for dyvers consideracions." But if the said Agnes and Richard Cawse "at any tyme herafter to vex (sic) or troble" the executors before the day of payment, the £20 due from Robert Butler is not to be paid to her. To the said Agnes "twoo Gownes of my owne wearing clothes wherof oon is lyned w^t saie and thother is lyned w^t chamblett;" also three partlets, four smocks, &c. To Richard Cause, and the said Agnes, his wife, and their lawful heirs, the dwelling house of testatrix, "sett and liyng vpon the were in the Suburbies of the Citie of bristowe;" and another house or messuage in the same part, lately purchased of Harry Brayne, esquire; also "a nother house or stable," set and lying in "saint Marye strete," purchased of Francis Stradling, esquire. In default of issue, rem. to William Cowper and his wife Margery and their lawful heirs. The executors to have the rents and profits of the property "vnto suche tyme that the said Richard Cawse com' and be of the full age of xix yeres," distributing the profits among the poor. To the said Richard and Agnes all the interest possessed by testatrix for a term of years in a certain garden adjoining her house; also "tenne diker of lether," &c. To the said Richard Cause "all the barke being in my house concernyng tanners crafte." When William Ballarde and others have paid their debts, the sum of £10 is to be bestowed for the reparation of highways beside Stokes Croft, co. Gloucester. To the "rep'acions and mayuteynyng of saint Peters Plompe" x^s. To Thomas son of William Cowper x^s. To Giles Cowper and Agnes Cowper, "doughters" of the same William, xx^s apiece, to be paid in money for the salt sold to the aforesaid Robert Butler. Legacies also to Elizabeth Willyams, Agnes Tomkyns, Edith Darbie, William Jones, the younger, and Eleanor, Margaret, and Joan, daughters of William Jones, John Jurden, tanner, servant Agnes Willyams, and late servant Joan Evan. The sum of £6 for expenses at the month's mind and burial. Forty shillings to be distributed at "the tyme of my dethe" to priests, clerks, and poor people. William Cowper and William Jones to be executors, and distribute the residue for the soul of testatrix and that of her husband "in wurkes of marcie pittie and charytie." To the said executors £10. Hugh Jones overseer, to whom £5. Witnessed by Rouland Cowper, Philip Frier, shoemaker, William Knyght, Griffith Jones, and Thomas Lewys.

Proved in the cathedral of the Holy and Undivided Trinity at Bristol, Oct. 31st, 2 Edward vi.

295.—NICHOLAS THORNE.

1546. Aug. 4th.—"Citizen and marchaunte of the towne or Citie of Bristowe." To be buried, "yf J dye in bristowe," in the church of St. Werburgh, where late wife Mary Thorne was buried. At the time of his burial there is to be said and sung "Dirige and masse w^t all other dyuyne s'nice as a true cristen man ought to haue;" and a sum of money, not passing £15 sterling, to be spent and given to poor people; also £15 at the month's mind, and the same amount at the twelve-months' mind. Twelve poor men, eight of them to be dwellers within the parish of St. Nicholas, and four within the parish of St. Werburgh aforesaid, "that haue byn housholders and fallen in decaye, to have a gown apiece, "of mowster or Russett of the price of euery gowne twentie shillinges sterling," and xiij^s iiij^d in ready money. Testator willed that above all things his debts be paid. To poor householders within the city of Bristowe 100 marks sterling. The sum of forty shillings to the church of St. Nicholas there "towardes the reparac'ons and maynten'nce of the clocke and of the chyme in the said churche." To William Harpar, testator's brother-in-law, "a gowne wherof the foreparte is lyned w^t damaske a Jacket of tawny damaske a gown furred w^t boge," &c., and £10 in money. To "my Sister his wif" £10, also "a ring w^t a dyamount and more a ring w^t an esmyrall and a ring w^t a ruby," &c. To Francis Woseley £10 in salt "after xx^s the tone." To Nicholas Woseley, his brother, £20 in salt. To Vincent Thorne, resident "in Jane," 200 ducats, and the residue of the debt that "the palabyzenes genewys" oweth of the bequest of testator's brother Robert Thorne, deceased; "the whiche legacie J will be paid for hym vnto leonarde Cattaynes Genewys or to his assignes And to be put in saynte Georges of Geane to and for those behofe profett and advantage" of the said Vincent. If the said Vincent Thorne should die under the age of twenty-one, his bequest is to be delivered to the use and behoof of "the house of the bartilmews" in Bristowe, and be employed in the building and reparation of the same house, or in the purchase of land for the maintenance of the free school there. To Robert Thorne, prentice with William Ostriche of London, haberdasher, £100 sterling. To Nicholas Thorne, "my bastarde sonne nowe being in Biskaye," lxvj^{li} xiij^s iiij^d sterling; he with whom the said Nicholas is "printice" to have the rule and keeping of the said money for the term of seven years, "fynding suffycient Surties to the Chambre of bristowe." The sum of £100 to the said Chamber, to be employed "in maner the hankes in the marshe in the said towne and Citie of bristowe where as (sic) it shalbe thought mooste nede." And lxxx^{li} of the said money to go towards the making of a "gro narde to kepe suche prouision of corne as shalbe prouyded for the comons of the said towne and citie." The £100 to be expended by the advice and order of "my neighbo' John Drewes thelder," to whom £40, to be discounted and deducted to him of such debts as he "dothe owe me at this p'sente day;" also to him a black gown, price xxx^s. The sum of £25 towards the making of a dam-head with stone to the dock at the Key, for the making and repairing of ships ; the same dam-head to be made by the advice and counsel of Thomas Hickes and Edward Jones, to whom xx^s apiece. To Master Harrys, "Scole m^r of the free Scole at the bartilmews," five marks sterling, and a black gown. If the lands of the said "bartelmewes" may be hereafter improved, and the rents become more, then "J will that his wages be enlarged to twentie poundes by the yere." To John Sariaunte, "yssher of the grammerschole," three tons of salt. To twenty poor maidens of good name and fame, dwelling within the city of Bristowe, intending there to inhabit and dwell, five marks apiece at the day of her marriage. The sum of £6, of the goods of Mistress Tonnell deceased, remaining in testator's hands, to be paid to her daughter Joan when married. To Robert Thorne, the younger, legitimate son of testator, 100 marks sterling, and "one hunderth vnces of siluer half gilte and half parcell gilte," also a share in household stuff. The same amount of money, and certain goods, to each of the other legitimate sons, Nicholas, Edward, and John. To Frances, Mary, and Bridget Thorne, testator's legitimate daughters, 200 marks apiece, &c. To wife Bridget £150 sterling, and 150 tons of salt "of watermesure ;" also the farm of Aller Court, held by lease of the earl of Huntington, and "nowe in the tenure of Thomas Clerke paing for the same xxix^{li} by the yere ;" to remain, after her decease, to legitimate son Robert Thorne and his assigns. To the said Bridget, for her life, testator's dwelling house in Small strete, with the garden, &c. To her three daughters, Alice, Barbara, and Katharine, "to euery of them xx tonne of Salte." To legitimate son John Thorne, the money "wch master John Myles of Hampton stande bounden by his obligacyon" to pay testator. If the four legitimate sons and three legitimate daughters should die before lawful age or marriage, one third part of their legacies to remain to Frances and Nicholas Woseley, the children of "my Sister Katheren abowen," and to Robert and Nicholas "my baste sonnes," or the longest liver of them : the second third part to be bestowed "vppon the house of the Bartilmews in bristowe aforesaid towardes The buylding and purchasing of landes for the maynten'nce of the free Scole therefore (sic) the bringing vpp of youthe in vertue and goodnes" : the other third part to the Chamber of Bristowe, towards the making and repairing of the bridge, and the highways about the said city. The rents and profits of the farm of Knowle, held by testator for a term of years of the demise and grant of James Clyforde esquire, deceased, to be for "the finding of my children during there mynoritie ;" rem. to the four legitimate sons, who are also to have all lands and tenements held by lease for a term of years, or by copyhold or otherwise, within the city and elsewhere. The executors are to recover all things appertaining to testator of right under the will of his brother Robert Thorne, or by any other means, as heir to his said brother, "on whose Soule and all xp'en soules god take mercy." Towards the maintenance of the free school aforesaid, and to make a library in such place as Sir John Barloo "late deane of the disolued house and college" of Westbury-on-Trym, John Drewes, and Francis Codrington of Bristowe, merchants, shall think best or meetest within the said Bartilmewes, £30 sterling. Testator also bequeaths all such of his books as may be meet for the said library, and his astrolabe "whiche is in the keping of John Sprynte poticary," with charts, maps, &c., belonging to the science of astronomy. The sum of xxxvj^{li} xiij^s iiij^d for the garnishing of altars, vestments, altar-cloths, glazing, &c., at the said house of "the bartilmewes." The sum of xx^{li} sterling to be paid by the advice of the said John Barlowe, John Drews, and Francis Codrington, and of John Harris "scole master of the said scole," to retain learned counsel to assure and convey the lands belonging to the said Bartilmewes to the Chamber of Bristowe, for the assurance and continuance of the said school, the said Chamber to be bound for the performance of covenants, &c. To the said "master barloo" a black gown, price xl^s, and £5 in money. To testator's parish church of St. Werburgh in Bristowe vj^{li} xilj^s iiij^d towards reparations, and maintaining of the place for assembling of merchants "late buyldyd agaynst the said Churche wall;" the money to be put in the treasure coffer of the same church. To divers debtors "suche porcons and parte of the debtes owing" as is expressed, &c., "w^t my owne hande." To my brother Cockescy a gown "furred w^t foynes," &c., and to his wife "two tonne of baye Salte and lxvj^s viij^d in money and more fyve poundes every yere for the charges and tables of my two daughters w^t all other charges as she hathe layed oute for my said ij daughters nowe in the keping of them." To the Chamber of Bristowe 250 tons of salt, and £150 in money, amounting to £400, whereof £200 is of the gift of Thomas Howell "whiche died in Civill," and was by his testament assigned to be paid to testator for the use of clothmaking and helping young men, "of the whiche Some is delivered to certen clothers w^{tin} this towne or Citie of bristowe aforesaid cc^{li};" the Mayor and his brethren, within the space of three years next after testator's decease, to employ the money, with the £800 given to the Chamber by his brother Robert Thorne, in good land, the rent of which to be for the same use and intent as "one master Thomas White of london purpose (*sic*) for the making and helping of yong men" within the city of Bristowe. If the said money bequeathed by testator's brother Robert Thorne, and that bequeathed by himself, be not employed in land for the use aforesaid, then the £200 of testator's bequest shall not be paid to the Chamberlain, but be "reparted" among the aforesaid seven legitimate children "by yeven porcions." If they, and illegitimate son Robert, should all die s.p., the dwelling house to be for the use of the Chamber. To the "reparacions of the highe waies aboute the said Citie of bristowe and for the mayntenyng of Condittes the pitty well and of saynt peters plumpe thirtie tonne of Salte." Legacies also to cousin John Thorne, and his wife, Thomas Clarke of Aller, John Sare, notary, Martin Atlilde, Thomas Warden, William Cooke, Francis Coston, cousin John Amayne, John Hunteley esquire, and his wife, cousin Agnes Saunders, father-in-law John Mylles, and his wife, Eliz. Deane, Eliz. Percie, and servant Eleanor Cornyshe. Thomas Shipman to "charge vnto myne Accompte one hunderth markes in repompee' (*sic*) and towardes the buylding of the shippe called the Savio^r, and be devided oute of my porc'on at the fynishing of the said Accompte." Testator had referred to his partnership with Thomas Shipman, and with Edward Pryn, and others, bequeathing his share of the profits to his three daughters, and four legitimate sons when twenty-one years of age. Roger Barloo and Edward Pryn', merchants, to be executors, and have £20 apiece. Francis Codrington and cousin John Thorne overseers, to each of whom £5 and a black gown. To the said John Thorne "my gowne furred w^t Jenettes." Witnessed by Francis Codrington, Thomas Shipman, Giles White, John Sare notary, and Thomas Shewarde. Two hundred ducats of the legacy of Thomas Howell remain "in thaundes of Thomas Harrys of Civill;" but testator's executors are to furnish the said ducats "in one w^t the two hundrethe poundes aforesaid So Amounte the hole legacie of the said Thomas Howell that was appoynted to be paid vnto me the said Nicholas Thorne to the vse aforesaid Two hunderthe and fiftie poundes sterling." To Christopher Capper one ton of salt "to pray for my Sole and all xp'en Soules."

It is not stated in the Orphan Book when this will was proved; but the copy at Somerset House, *Alen*, 18, supplies the date, — Oct. 15th, 1546. The diocesan registers at Worcester record the appointment of the above mentioned John Barlow, professor of arts, to the office of dean of Westbury, June 15th, 1530, vacant by the death of John Hughes.

296.—WILLIAM PYKES, mercer.

1550. Jan. 12th. Testator makes his will in the name of the Father, and of the Son, and of the Holy Ghost, and confesses Christ to be "the verye true and onlie merito^r for as many as shalbe savid, And that no good wurkes that I haue doon nor that other canne do for me can save me, But onlie the mooste holsome passion, and glorious resurrection of mye Savio^r Jh'us Criste." To be buried within "my parrishe Churche co'menly called Saint Thomas Churche in Bristowe." Ten shillings to "my Curate" there. The executors are to provide at the time of burial "some well learned man to declare the mooste pure sincere and lyvely worde of god to the Cristen congregacion." The sum of £20 for the poor people in Bristowe; the first distribution to be made on the day of "my buryinge," the second before the end of six months following, the third "by thende of twelve monithes nexte after my deceas." The twelve poor men and twelve poor women of the almshouse called St. Thomas's almshouse, in the Longe Rowe, to have twenty-four shillings of that sum "at every tyme of this distribucion." The executors are to purchase in fee simple so much good land as shall amount to the clear yearly value of £6. 13. 4; the fourth part of which to be paid by the Chamberlain of Bristowe to the poor people of the said almshouse every quarter, at the four principal feasts of the year most commonly used within the said city: "And this my p'sent gifte to haue a contynnaunce for ever while the worlde shall endure." To wife Maud Pykes 1000 marks, and all testator's plate and household stuff; also, for her life, all the higher part of his dwelling house, bought of Anthony Norton, gentleman, and the higher part of the adjoining house, held by lease of Mr. Rodney, with the garden thereto adjoining, and the other garden lying by St. Thomas's church; upon condition that she do continually dwell in the said higher parts of the houses; the shops, cellars, and warehouses underneath to be held jointly by "John Pykes my Elder sonne and John Pykes my Seconde sonne" during the space of "one whole yere nexte after my deceas." The said sons are also to hold for one year in like manner "my Shoppe of my corner tenement in the highe strete," and also "my wurkehouse in Tuckers strete" held of Mr. David Harris. After the end of the said year, the house bought of Anthony Norton "shall hollie remayne" to eldest son John, who is also to have all the shops, cellars, and warehouses belonging to the house held by lease of the said Mr. Rodney, and the garden lying by St. Thomas's church. To second son John, after the said year, the corner house and shop in the High-street, and also "my said warkehowse in Tuckers strete," and all the title, state, and term of years of and in the same. To the six children of "mye doughter" Cecily Wilson, by John Hillacre, her first husband, and by Roger Wigmore, her second husband, that is to say, Polidorus Hillacre, William Hillacre, Joan Hillacre, and Elline Hillacre, and to William and Mary Wigmore, £100, to be equally divided, and paid to them at their day of marriage, or their age of "twentie and one yeres;" the said money to be delivered by the executors to "my sonne in lawe Myles Wylson w'in one yere nexte after my deceas." To son Water Pykes £100. To sister Joan £10. To her children, Amy, Joan, and Richard, £10 apiece. To Joan Bysse "my doughters doughter" twenty marks of money at her day of marriage. To "my Cosyn Johane Precye" forty shillings. To old John Hacket "my nighte gowne and a grote in money" every week during his life. The sum of £50 to be bestowed "vppon the mendinge of the highe waies aboute Bristowe;" of which sum, £20 for the highway "betwene Bedmyster and the farther ende of the cawseye called the longe cawseye" beyond Stoke; £20 "vppon the highe waye betwene Laffordes yate, and the fote of the hill called Toghill whiche is the highe waye from Bristowe towardes London;" and £5 to be bestowed "vppon the highe waye Betwene Bristowe and Keynesham, And thother fyve poundes to be bestowed vppon the slippe in the shambles of Bristowe called the Bochers slippe." The sum of £20 towards "the charges of fetchinge whome of the water to sainte Thomas Pipe in Bristoll," if the same be done before the end of two years after testator's decease. All his unbequeathed apparel to his three sons. To his neighbour Mighell Kettill and Margaret his wife "twentie nobles of money." Residue of goods to his two sons, "John Pykes thelder and John Pykes the yonger," who are made executors. Mr. David Harris and Water Pykes overseers, to whom a gown and twenty shillings apiece. Witnessed by Richard Dakins, Edmond Rogers, and Robert Burgin.

Proved at London, Feb. 23rd, 1550.

297.—ROBERT ESTEGATE, innholder.

1552. Sept. 4th. To be buried in "the churche yearde of Saint Phelippes and Jacobe in the Citie of Bristoll." To son Oliver £30 of lawful money, also "a Stonding bedstede wth a fether bed," &c. If he should die before the age of twenty-one, testator's brothers Thomas and John to have £10 of that money, equally divided. To the said brothers twenty shillings between them. To uncle Robert Estgate "ij fusten doblettes Also more I forgeve hym all that money as he oweth me excepte the viij^s that he shall paie for the half yeres rent." To father-in-law "my golde ringe." To brother-in-law John Smyth the best gown. To my curate Thomas Beede "my lyned gowne, my tawny Jacket my best doblet and ij^s of money." To the "poremens boxe" xiij^s iiij^d. Residue to wife Agnes, who is made sole executrix. Oliver Brigg and John Evance overseers, to whom x^s apiece. Witnessed by Thomas Beede, clerk, and Agnes Estgate "cu' alijs."

Proved Nov. 15th, 6 Edward vi.

298.—WALTER LODBROKE.

1547. June 26th. To be buried in the churchyard of St. Nicholas. To "my naturall mother" Alice Burton £10. To brothers William and Thomas Lodbroke £10 apiece. To wife Agnes, during her life, "the terme of the howse that she dwellethe in." To Jeffery Michaell and Margaret

Michaell, her son and daughter, £5 apiece. To son Jonas Lodbroke £40. To the unborn child of wife Agnes £20. The said Agnes to have the use of the aforesaid bequests to William and Thomas "my Brethrene," and to Jeffery and Margaret her children, and to Jonas and "the vnborne childe," testator's children, till they be of the age of twenty-four; she, or Mr. Roger Jones, to put in sureties for the payment thereof, "Orels to put it into the Chambre of Bristowe there to remaine till en'y of them co'me to thage of xxiiij^{ti} yeres;" but Margaret and the unborn child, if it be a woman child, "shall receve their porcions at the daies of their mariages." If the said William, Thomas, or Jeffery die before the appointed age, the portions of them that die are to "return to Agnes my wief and to none other." If she should die before son Jonas is twenty-four, the house in which she dwelleth is to be "lette or sett," and the said Jonas to have the profits, and the house itself when he is of that age. Legacies to Thomas Gwynne, priest, John Fric, Thomas Williams, and the poor. Wife Agnes to be executrix. Mr. Roger Jones overseer, to whom xl^s and a satin doublet. Witnessed by the said Roger, John Fay, Thomas Gwyn' clerk, and Thomas Williams, "wth other."

Proved at London, Aug. 8th, 1547.

299.—THOMAS JONYS.

1554. July 9th. Testator described himself as a "wodseller and Citesin of the Citie of Bristowe," and desired to be buried in the churchyard of St. Nicholas; "fullie p'swaded that when J shalbe lossed from this (nowe corrupte tabernacle) to accompanie those at goddes pleasure w^{che} alredie ar revested wth the firste stole that is the glory of the soule," and expecting "to receave the seconde stole w^{che} is the glorie of the bodie at the laste daie of iudgement." To eldest daughter Jane, after wife's death, half a dozen of silver spoons "weying vj vnc' iij q'," and then also "a fetherbedd." To second daughter Jone £10 of money at the day of her marriage, and a goblet parcel-gilt, weighing ten ounces, after "her mothers daies." To daughter Elizabeth twenty nobles when married, and, after "her mothers daies," a salt of silver "wth his cover" parcel-gilt, "waying vj vnc' iij q^{rs}." To eldest son John Jones (sic), "after my wiefes daies," a house and garden "adioyning to the towne wall in Bastestreat," held of John Grene by lease. To son William "an other Te'nt wth a garden adioyning to the other foresaid Te'nt and garden w^{che} also J holde of the said John Grene by lease after my wiefes daies." To son Richard, and younger son John Jonys, five marks apiece. Wife Welthian to be sole executrix, and have the residue of goods, some portion of which "vnto the pore people" at her discretion. Witnessed by John Rastall, clerk, Edmond Jonys, and John Jonys, "wth other."

Proved in the cathedral church of "Bristoll," Aug. 23rd, 1554.

300.—JOHN BEYNTON, carpenter.

1558. June 9th. The name of this testator, who was "of the Citie of Bristowe," is written *Baynton* in one part of his will, and in the note of proof. To be buried "in cristyan buriall." All his lands to remain to his sister's son, Robert Lemyng, dwelling "in Midleton besides Lynne," and to his heirs "for eu'more." If the said Robert Lemyng should sell the lands within the city of Bristowe, a whole year's rent is to be distributed to poor people, who are also to have the residue of testator's goods immediately after his decease. Harry Gervys, otherwise called Harry Davis, and David Mathew to be executors, and have xl^s apiece. Mr. John Stone overseer, to whom xl^s "for his paines taking." Witnessed by Thomas Owen, David Tailor, and Richard Langton, notary.

Approved before Robert Adams, Mayor, and John Browne and John Pruett, Sheriffs of the City, on Friday, April 14th, 1 Eliz. No record of proof before the ecclesiastical authorities.

301.—WILLIAM TYNDALL, merchant.

1558. Sept. 13th. Testator beseeches the B.V.M., and all the saints in heaven, to pray for him, and with him, to the Saviour, "that his wrathe w^{che} J haue instely des'uid, maie be pacified & his mercy extended." To be buried at the discretion of the executors. The sum of £20 for the poor within the city and suburbs of Bristoll. To wife Jane, for her life, "my howse in Mershestreat wherein J dwell." No furniture to be removed out of the said house, but to remain, with the house itself, to son Thomas Tyndall and his heirs and assigns for ever. To the said Thomas 100 marks in money; also to him and his legitimate heirs, house property toward the Key and "toward m'shestreate," with a stable in the latter, and two houses in Christmas-street in the several tenures of William Yonge, merchant, and John Erothe, hooper, "with all my grounde in Lewens meade sometyme the graie ffriers," a house in Fisher lane in the tenure of Julian More, widow, and a lease of "a certaine grounde in m'shestreat" held of Mr. Pacie for certain years; remainder to testator's daughters, if the said Thomas should die s.p., and to my brother Robert Tyndall, if they should so die. To daughter Joan 100 marks; also the lease of a garden in St. Michael's parish "w^{che} J holde of the Bartlemewes for certaine yeres yet to co'me;" but Joan Olde, testator's kinswoman, was to have it until his said daughter should marry, or come to the age of twenty-one. To his three children, all such plate and household stuff, remaining in the house at the day of his death, "as was myne before J maried wth my wief;" the said legacies to be delivered unto them "at the daie of mariage of euery of them, or at thage of xxj^{ti} yeres." If they should all die "before the tymes before appointed," the third part of their legacies to be equally divided among the children of testator's brothers Richard and Thomas Tyndall, and his sisters Annes and Isabel, "J meane the children of them foure that remaine in Lincolne shire" with or about their parents; and the other two third parts to be bestowed upon the building of a house for twelve aged poor people to dwell in rent-free; the said house to be built at the ground in Lewen's mead, "late the churche of the graye ffryers w^{thin} the Citie of Bristoll," toward the garden held by Mrs. Jaye. If wife Jane continues unmarried, and has the children with her, she is to keep Thomas "to the scole," and Joan and Faith "to service in the howse, and to vse their nedills," finding them meat, drink, and clothes, with other things necessary, until they are of the age of sixteen: at which time, testator wills that Thomas "shalbe bounde apprentice to suche misterie or science as he shalbe moste apte, or els kepte to his lerning in Oxforde if he be apte and haue mynde therevnto;" and the daughters kept at the appointment of testator's overseers by the counsel of his wife, "if she be not mynded still to haue them wth her." If she should marry again, or will not be "so content to vse my children," giving good sureties to the Mayor of Bristol, and the executors and overseers, she is immediately to deliver up the children's portions to the said executors and overseers ; and then he or they that have the governance thereof " shall putt in sufficient suretie to the Maio^r of Bristoll for the tyme being " for the safe delivering of the said legacies. Testator's wife to have and enjoy, during her life, his stable in Marsh-street, the lease whereof he bought of William Donnynge. After his said wife's " tyme," his daughter Joan and her legitimate heirs are to have "the howse vppon the Kaye" inhabited by Robert Tailor, with the shop and little vault occupied by testator ; in default of such heirs, rem. to son Thomas and his heirs ; in def., rem. to daughter Faith and her heirs : in def., rem. to the lawful heirs of " my brother Robert Tyndall here in this realme of englonde ; " in def., rem. to my right heirs for ever. To daughter Faith and her legitimate heirs "my howse in Christmas streat, w^{che} Sampson Hamersley nowe dwelleth in;" rem. to son Thomas, if she should die s.p.; to daughter Joan, if he should so die ; to my brother Robert and his heirs, if the said Joan should so die. To Thomas Tyndall, son of brother Richard, vj^{li} xiij^s iiij^d. To James Olde and his wife the lease of the house wherein he dwelleth. To wife Jane all and singular such plate and stuff of household as she brought with her from Tewkesbury ; also " one pece of golde of xx^{ti} ducketts whiche J sent her for a token," and two hundred marks. To "the Cathedrall churche of Bristoll" v^s. To Mr. Hugh Jones "my goastly father" v^s. Residue of all goods, leases, ships, &c., to the executors, namely, brother Robert and son Thomas, except only the price wines that James Olde had " w^{che} J will that my Cosin Johan Olde shall haue during my yeres therevppon, paying as her husbonde James paid." Overseers to be John Willy of Bristol "chambrelaine," to whom v^{li}, John Sprinte, to whom " my beste gowne w^{che} J made in london," and Nicholas Crosbie, to whom " three yardes of clothe that J bought in london." Witnessed by Mr. Thomas Sylke, prebendary of the cathedral church of Bristol, Mr. Hugh Jones, parson of St. Stephen's, "my goastely father," and Robert Tailer, merchant, " my brother in lawe." Unto wife Jane three ale cups parcel-gilt, and "the foure poundes of money w^{che} sainte Stephins churche owithe me." To cousin Joan, wife of James Olde, " my lease vppon the prise wynes," paying the sums of money specified in the said lease, and no more; " wch lease is in my Cownter; " also to the said Joan "tenne poundes in money w^{che} J p'mysed her husbonde and her for to paie for the dynner and charges of their wedding." Witnessed by the aforesaid Hugh Jones, clerk, and " Johan Tyndall my wief."

No record of probate is given in the Orphan Book ; but from the copy at Somerset House, *Chayney*, 7, we learn that the will was proved April 27th, 1559.

302.—RICHARD WYECKAM, tailor.

1558. Jan. 19th. Testator was of " the p'isshe of saint Mary Porte w^{thin} the Citie of Bristowe," and desired to be buried in the church there, near to his wife Mary. To his daughter Anes (*sic*) xx^{li} of " currant money of Englonde," and a silver goblet " the w^{che} was her graundfathers." To the said Agnes two silver spoons, &c. To sons William, Edmond, and Harry, and to daughters Katharine and Alice, £20 apiece. To the child "my wief goeth nowe wth" £20. The said sons to have their money when twenty-four years of age, and the daughters at "the daie of their mariage." If they should all die before such time, one half of their legacies to go to brother John Wyckam and his children, and the other to the executrix of this will. To the said John the third best gown, "and J clerely forgive him all suche debtes as he doth owe vnto me." Legacies also to every almshouse within the city of Bristowe or the suburbs of the same, the poor people, the Tailors' hall, and Gilbert Barnsley. Wife Margery to have the residue, and be executrix. Brother John Wyckam and William Donnyng, tailor, overseers, to whom ten shillings apiece. Witnessed by Richard Overton, William Donnynge, and Gilbert Barnesley.

Proved April 24th, 1559.

303.—WILLIAM BALLARDE.

1554. April 12th. Testator, who was a "Cytisen and Marchaunte of Bristoll," describes Queen Mary as "of the Churches of Englande and Jrelande ymmediatlye vnder Christe the supreme headde;" and desires to be buried in the church of St. Stephen, or elsewhere, as "yt shall please godd to appoyntte the same." The sum of £5 for poor householders of St. Stephen's parish, and other places; and a like sum to be given "in co'mon almys" at the burial, or two days after, in bread or money. Ten shillings to every almshouse within the city and suburbs "nott havyng An'nall Rentes." To sister-in-law Syble Ballarde vj^{li} xiij^s iiij^d in money, and all the "Cattle and other furnytures" in her custody at Hardwick, on condition that "she remayne wydowe," and keep, nourish, and do honestly entreat, order, and guide testator's two sisters Jane and Joan Ballarde during their lives, "yf she do lyve so long as J trust in god she shall for theire comforts." If the said Syble should marry during the lives of the two sisters, she is to have "but iiij^{li} onely." To Anne Bolardine widow, towards her marriage, xiij^{li} vj^s viij^d; also, for her life, a tenement in "Redclyffe streate" inhabited by Humphrey Jones, shearman, of the value of forty shillings by the year; and a tenement "lying before saynt Stephyns Churche dore," inhabited by John Power, cofferer: rem. to Alice Bolardine, daughter of the said Anne, and her lawful issue; in def., rem. to kinsman Thomas Goodale of Bristol and his heirs. To the said Anne Bolardyne "one of my smalle gobletts gylte and syxe spones." The sum of £20 to be delivered unto some honest man, who is to be bound "wth suertys" to pay to John Clune, mason, during his life, xij^d weekly, and to keep the said sum, after the death of the said John Clune, until the marriage of the aforesaid Alice Bolardine. If Alice should die before her marriage, the money is to be for her mother; and if the latter be also dead, it is to be "gevyn to the mariage of pore maydens." To Anne Hem'yng three tenements on Redcliff hill, for her life; reversion to Thomas Goodale and his heirs for ever. To godson William Hemyng, and to his lawful issue, a tenement lying "in Wynestreatte," inhabited by John Outtley, goldsmith; in def., rem. to Thomas Goodale and his heirs. To servant Katharine Smythe £5 at her marriage; but if she should die unmarried, the money is to be given to the marriage of "other pore Maidens wthin the Cytie." To the forenamed John Clune "a gowne of myne of Rattes color furryd wth blake A fryse cote A marble cote two shyrtes," &c. To Robert Butler, merchant, £50, and he to pay to "my systers Jane and Johan Ballarde duryng there lyfes" £4 by the year. To wife Alice Ballarde £100 in money, and all the plate "that J hadd wth her," household stuff, &c. She is also to have and enjoy, during her life, testator's dwelling house, and all his other tenements; also £20 by the year, to be paid quarterly by Robert Butler, merchant, to whom the sum of £200 is to be delivered; the said money to be repaid at "the ende of iiij^or yeres next after the deceasse of my wyef." To the said Robert, and after his decease, to his eldest son Francis Butler, and to his heirs for ever, testator's dwelling house, with the appurtenances, "sett lying and beyng in Balland strete." To the said Robert "my Ryng wth A white camfeo;" and to Elizabeth Butler, his wife, "my Ryng wth a Rubye." To Mr. Thomas Tison "my gilte hanger wth A Christall hallte." To Mastres Tyson a gown cloth "of my fyne clothe." To George Snygg "my Sworde and A gowne clothe of my fyne clothe." To the said George's wife a gown cloth of the same. To 'servants Roger Afylde and William Tiler forty shillings apiece. To Maulbe "my woman" twenty shillings, &c. "J will that my Sister Jane or Johan' Ballarde who clothe possesse my howse and grownd therto belongyng at Hardewyke in the countie of Harforde that they or either of them at the nexte cowrte holden in that Lordeshippe do acknowlege and nomynate Thomas Goodale aforesaide o^r Kynsman' to be the nexte heire." Robert Butler, merchant, to be sole executor, and have the residue of unbequeathed goods. He is to "make ij Ryngs of the value of xl^s in golde," to be given for tokens to James Bailye and his wife. Legacies to Elizabeth and Bridget Butler, daughters of the said Robert, to the aforesaid Thomas Goodale, and Alice Bolardyne. Mr. William Carr, merchant, and Mr. Thomas Tyson to be overseers, and have a gown apiece.

Proved in the cathedral church of Bristol, April 24th, 1554.

304.—WILLIAM FLECCHAR, draper.

1552. July 10th. Testator was of the parish of St. Nicholas in Bristow, and desired to be buried in "the crowde vnder my forewritten p'ishe churche." The sum of vj^s viij^d "vnto M^r vyker my curate," and xx^s to the poor men's box of the same church. To the almshouses of the city iij^li in bread. To the five daughters of testator xxx^li apiece in money or wares. If any of them die before lawful age or marriage, her or their part to be divided equally among the longer livers. To his wife Alice the state of his house and garden during "her lief tyme, Excepte she doe marye into the countrey," in which case, son John is to have that property. If John should die before coming into possession, it is to go to the next of the children. To brother-in-law Luke "my sonday gowne." The sum of v^s to "the pore people of the Almes howse called Lawfordes yate." Legacies also to father-in-law Philip Hornar, mother-in-law Elyn, and their servants; sister Elizabeth Coke, Sysly Coke "my Sister doughter," Alice Jones, daughter to Thomas Jones, tailor, Richard Clement, tailor, Laurence Nasshe, shearman, "the Curate of Donyt," and every household of that parish, John Roberts, and servant Edith. Wife Alice and son John to have the residue of goods, and be executors. Richard Vaughan, gentleman, and Richard Davis, draper, to be overseers, and have "for their gentlenes" x^s apiece. Witnessed by "M^r doctur Austyne a phisission," William Smitheman, clerk, Thomas Jonys, tailor, and othe

Proved at London, Aug. 23, 1552.

O

Memorandum, on June 18th, 1561, was delivered to Mr William Carr, Mayor of the city of Bristowe, by Richard Standbank, draper, husband to Alice, late wife, and one of the executors of the before named William Flechar, a licence of alienation under the great Seal, with evidences, including an indenture of bargain and sale made by Sir Ralph Sadler to the said William Flechar of a 'messuage and garden in Bristoll, "w^{che} evidences were put in a white rounde box to be kepte vppon truste to the vse of the heires of the said Will'm flechar."

305.—ROBERT GRYGGE, wiredrawer.

1559. May 15th. Testator was "dwellinge in the p'ishe of o^r ladie of Redcliff" at Bristoll, and desired to be buried in the church of that parish. To his eight children, at the day of their marriage, or their lawful age, £20 apiece. If any die, his wife is to have that part of the money. To his poor workmen "a frise cote a pece, and J do forgive them and en'y of them suche debtes as they or any of them doe owe me." The sum of forty shillings to poor people. To Mr Chauncellor "my ringe wth a square dyamonde." To Mr Huys "my Ringe J were wth a cornet in him." To the goodman Mylles "my furred Jacket faced w^t foynes." Wife "Alis" to have the residue, and be sole executrix. Brother-in-law John Sprynte and John Davis, weaver, to be overseers, and have xl^s apiece. The said John Sprynte to have testator's horse and saddle.

Proved July 5th, 1559.

306.—JOHN FYSHER, skinner.

1561. Feb. 26th. Testator was "of the p'ishe of saint Warborowes in the citie of Bristowe," and desired to be buried in the church there. The sum of ten shillings to be distributed among "suche as be very pore and nedy." To son John Fisher £10 when aged twenty-one. To eldest daughter Anne £10 at the day of marriage; also, after the death of testator's wife, the years of his "howse in alhalowes p'ishe," with all implements belonging to the same. To daughter Mary £10; and a like sum to the unborn child. If any or all of the said children "chaunse to dye before the age of diskrecion," such legacies to return to wife Katharine. Forty shillings to brother-in-law William Thomas when he has served his "prentishippe wth my wyfe"; but he must "vse scalfe honestlye." The said Katharine to have the residue, and be "hole and foolle Executryx." Richard Grynwey, John Merik, and Thomas Hill to be overseers, and "to ech of them ane olde angelett a pece."

No record of proof.

307.—JAMES CHESTER, merchant.

1560. April 8th. Testator's body "vnto xp'en buryall." He desired God to give him "the power to write the truthe and nothinge but the truthe," and appointed his wife Mary executrix. To sons Edward and Thomas Chester £140 apiece: "The whiche J wolde there shulde be solde of suche merchandises as J haue at the discrecion' of my Overseers vnto three or foure honest menn, gevinge them ij yeares day of payment at an honeste price, and then at thende of their yeres to bringe their monye into the chambr' of Bristoll, according to theire bande, And it is the Maio^{rs}

dewtie so to doe for Orphanes;" the overseers to take care that the money " maye be in good sylver or golde, and that it be faste sealed in a bagge wth the Maiors seale and theirs, and to lye for the behoofe of the childern" till they come to the age "of xxij. or xxiij yeres;" but testator's brother, Thomas Chester, might take the said money at the end of the two years, he being bound, and " payinge the children xx^{li} more," and might keep the said money during the said time. If both the children should die s.p., the overseers are to purchase " fyve poundes by the yere of good rente," specified portions of which to be given " towarde the lighte of Saincte Leonardes gate," to the almshouses at Lafters gate, in the Marsh, in Lewens mead, at St. James's Back, and " in Saincte Thomas streat," and to the poor " in Tucker Halle," and at Temple gate; " the wch J wolde sholde be delivered yerelie at all Halloutyde againste xp'emas in wooll for euer;" the rest of the yearly rent to be divided " emongeste the poor of this citie," and the places before rehearsed, for ever: the rest of the money, after the purchase of the land, to remain " vnto my wife duringe her naturall lyffe," and afterwards, " thone halfe to my brothers and sisters children, and thother to her brothers children." To son Edward all the landed property given to testator by his father, which is to " goo from one to another of the Lynage from heyre to heyre to the vttermoste of the kynne called Chesters, beinge of the male kynde and beinge brothers children from ishewe to ishewe accordinge to my ffathers will and testament." The said property consisted of Radford in Westerley, with all the ground appertaining thereto, which testator had " sente foorthe" to one Symondes for ix^{li} vj^s viij^d by the year, "accordinge to a wrytinge that Mr Frize hathe made betwene him and me;" a yearly rent of ten shillings " oute of the blacke fryars" paid by my brother Dominick during my mother's life, "and after her tyme Domynick muste pay xx^s by the yeare;" and parcel of a piece of land " that my ffather bought of Sr Jhon Howse wyfe wch liethe at Michell Hill, a lodge and ij gardyns wherof J haue made the lease to my wyfe duringe her lyfe;" also " after my tyme my brother Domynick to have the bowlinge ally wth the litle orcharde and wth a little house to hit in the said orcharde," he paying to my wife and heirs a yearly rent of ten shillings, and the fruit of two trees. To son Thomas Chester, and to his issue, all lands " wch J haue purchased my sealfe." Brothers Thomas and Dominick, and brothers-in-law Edmond and Robert Smythe, to be overseers, and each of them to have " a gowne of xij^s a yarde." A gown also to each brother and brother-in-law, and to " euerye of their wyfes a Cassocke clothe of x^s a yard." To " my wyfe" 100 oz. of the best plate, and the rest unto the children in equal portions. To brother-in-law John Roberts "a blacke colte wch goethe in puckle churche pareke." To Mr Offley " my litle gim'oll of gynny gold." Legacies also to the poor " where nede is," John Wilshyre, Ralph Smythe, and servant Robert Clerk. Witnessed by James Chester, Thomas Chester, Dominick Chester, Edmond Smythe, Robert Smythe, " and other."

Proved at London, July 12th, 1560.

308.—RICHARD WATLEY, brewer.

1555. July 13th. Testator was of the parish " of Chrystchurche" in Bristowe, and desired to be buried in the church there. To Sir Thomas Pynchyn " my Curate" vj^s viij^d. To the mother church of the city of

Bristowe, called "the Trynitie," vjs viijd. To daughter Margery Wyckeham £20, to be paid "wthin one twelvemoneth after my decesse by the handes of Johane Watley my wyffe." To second daughter Elizabeth Smythes, and third daughter Goodlove Smethes (*sic*), £20 apiece, &c. To Richard Dudmester, son of the aforesaid Margery Wyckeham, when twenty-one years of age, all the stuff pertaining to the brewhouse wherein testator dwelt; rem. to wife Joan, if the said Richard should die before that age. To Richard's sister, Goodlove Dudmester, three tons of iron at the day of her marriage, or when aged sixteen. If all the said children should die before their said ages, wife Joan to have their legacies "yff she be then in playn lyff." To the said Joan, for her life, lands in "the Countie and shere of Bristowe and lib'ties of the same." To daughter Margery Wickeham and her lawful issue, after the said Joan's death, testator's dwelling house, with two shops, and tenements in the tenure of John Davis, cooper, James Braughton, tailor, and John Tawnye; also a tenement called "the iij Coppes" in the tenure of Thomas Young, grocer. To daughter Elizabeth Smythes, after the said Joan's death, a tenement in "saint Mary port strett" in the tenure of John White, shoemaker; another in "saint Mary port churche yeard" in the tenure of John Frye, saddler; and another in the tenure of Joan Hoke, widow. To daughter Goodlove Smythes, after the death of wife Joan, a tenement in the said street in the tenure of Richard Wyckeham, tailor; also a cellar adjoining to the same; a garner for grain; a tenement in the tenure of John Turner; cellars in the tenure of Thomas Whetocke and Arthur Hamons; a garner in the tenure of John Cutley; and a tenement in the tenure of Danyell, the hooper. To William Warman "my gowne faced wth coney," &c. To "the Mayor Burgeses and Coiltie of the Cytie of Bristowe," after the death of the said Joan, to the use of the Chamber for ever, a corner tenement "in a strett called Cornestrett wthin the p'ishe of all sayntes" in the tenure of David Jones, barber; the said Chamber paying ten shillings yearly to the alms-people of All Saints' almshouse towards "there Reliffe and mayntaynyng" for ever. The said Joan to have the residue of goods, and be "hole executrixe." Stephen Cole of Bristow, gentleman, and John Willy "of the same cytie Chamb'layn," to be overseers, and have xs apiece.

Proved at London, Nov. 13th, 1555. Tho' Argall.

309.—JAMES DOWLE, grocer.

1564. Feb. 27th. To be buried in "the Churche of Alhallows" in Bristoll. To eldest son John Dowle, at the age of twenty, £170 "curr'unt money of Englond;" also a house at Newland "in the forrest of Deane," co. Glouc., in the tenure of uncle Christopher Dowle, who is to enjoy the same during his life, "and the liffe of Alice his wiffe," paying yearly xijd for rent to son John, or to his heirs. To son Arthur Dowle £120. To the child, or children, which may perhaps be born, £50 apiece. If all the children should die under age, their portions to be divided equally among "all my susters children" and my brother's. To mother Alice Bell "two angeletts of golde." To uncle Christopher Dowle one of "my signetts of golde, I say the lighter colored stone." To my said uncle's wife one angelet of gold. To father-in-law James Bell "my other signett of golde." The sum of £10 for the erection of "an hospitall in the marshe for poore children;" and £10 to "the buylding and maytaignenyng of the Calsey betwixte Bristoll and Aust." Legacies also to the children of my four sisters, aunt Seyrry, Anne Seyrry "my mayde," and other maid servants, apprentices Morris, William Smothie, and "my other twoo prentices," brothers-in-law William Ricardes and Clement Cradock, brother Henry Dowle, and "good wyfe Poyner." Residue to wife Elizabeth, who is made full executrix. If "my said wief do happen to entend to mary before the said legasies of my said children be deliu'ed into the chamber of Bristowe aforesaid," she is to make delivery of them to the said Chamber before her marriage. George Higgins, merchant, Thomas Colston, linen draper, father-in-law James Bell, and uncle Christopher Dowle, overseers. Witnessed by Thomas Colston, George Higgins, Robert Halton, Christopher Dowle, William Yeman, and John Dye.

No record of probate is inserted here : but the will is also registered at Somerset House, *Morisson*, 10, where it is said to have been proved March 22nd, 1564.

310.—THOMAS HILL, skinner.

1564. March 20th.—"hole in bodye and so in mynde praysed be to god therefore." To be buried in the crowde of the parish church of St. John Baptist in Bristoll, after the discretion of the executrix and overseers, "withe out any pompe or pride there to be done." To son Bartholomew twenty marks. To sons John and Richard, and daughter Prudence, £10 apiece. To the child "wch my wife is now at this p'sente time co'seued withe all" £10. If all the children should die, wife Joan or her assigns to have the said bequests. Legacies to brother Anthony Hill, sister Elizabeth, and brother's son Anthony. Wife Joan to have the residue, and be executrix. John Merike of Bristol, skinner, and Richard Younge, merchant there, to be overseers, and have ten shillings apiece. Witnessed by John Myrike, Richard Younge, and others.

Proved Aug. 20th, 1565. "Dat' London."

Laur' Argall.

311.—JOHN SUCHE, merchant.

1565. March 21st. Testator, who was "of the citye of Bristow," bequeathed to his daughter Anne £100 ; also "my Jland paynted Cheste," &c., and a dozen of silver spoons, which had belonged to Mr. William Appowell of "the Backe hall," when she is of the age of twenty-one, or at the day of her marriage ; also all interest and term of years in a tenement in the tenure of Alice Appowell, widow, "lyinge in Balanstrete of Bristow," and all "the lynene that was my fyrste wines her mother." To son William £100 when aged twenty-one ; also "my gilte salte Seller wth his cover. one ringe of golde wth a turkes that was his mothers, a Levente shorte and my owne signete of golde gravene wth my owne m'ke." If the said Anne or William should die before the said "daie and tyme," the survivor to take the legacy of the other. If both happened to die, £20 of their money to be divided "indeferentlie" between the children of David Olfyld and his wife, testator's cousin, and the remaining amount to be divided among the children of brothers Silvester Souche and William Soche, and of sister Cristiane Batche. To son William the "house in saynte Nicolas strete called the blacke Boye," during testator's interest and term of years ; rem. to son George, if

William should die under age. The legacies to be assured to the said children according to the charter concerning orphans. To son Robert 100 marks when twenty-one years of age. If the said Robert and his heirs have and enjoy, after the decease of testator's wife, the dwelling house "in Ballanstrett," to which he is "now verye heyre," he is to hold himself well contented with the said amount. But if "my wyfe" do, or cause to be done, any act to deprive the said Robert, she is then, immediately after such act, to pay him 200 marks over and above that amount. To son George 100 marks when twenty-one years of age; also to him and his legitimate heirs a tenement in Cornestrete, in the tenure of William Gryne, tailor; rem. to son William, if George should die s.p., and to son Robert, if William should so die. To daughter Mary Souche 100 marks, and the second gilt goblet, at the age twenty-one, or day of marriage. To daughters Dorcas, Charity, and Elizabeth, 100 marks apiece at such time or day. If all the said children should die before "the tymes lymitted," the sum of £40 is to be given among the poor in Bristow, and £40 to be bestowed in the making of "highe wayes a boute brystow;" the residue to the executrix, but, if she be dead, to be equally divided among the next of "my kynne." Testator forgives all the debts of William Barret, Richard Langton, and William Sprate. To William son of Richard Appowell iiij^{li}, to be paid to him by xx^s a year towards "his exhibic'on" in Oxford. Legacies also to each of testator's brothers and sisters "naturall," and all their children, to the poor in Bristow, the maintenance of "the scole" in the Marsh, David Olfylde, and his wife, Robert Smythe, and his wife, Richard Appowell, Richard Cole, apprentice Richard Hodson, maid Agnes, and William Broune "my boye." Wife Agnes to have the residue, and be sole executrix. Brother William Suche, brothers-in-law William Stevans and Robert Smythe, and Richard Cole, overseers, to whom xl^s apiece.

No record of probate occurs in the Orphan Book: but the will was proved April 3rd, 1566, as appears by the copy at Somerset House, *Crimes*, 10.

312.—WALTER WEST, baker.

1567. April 24th. Testator's body to be "puryed (*sic*) in xp'en buryall." To the poor of St. Thomas's parish in Bristow xl^s. Wife Elizabeth to have, for her life, the tenement in Redcliff-street "whereas" Robert Hixe, clothier, dwelleth; the rents of the same to remain afterwards to the use of the poor within the parish aforesaid, and "to the relese of the pore p'soners in the gale of newgate of the sayd cytic" for ever. To daughters Alice and Joyce, at the day of their marriage, £20 apiece; also silver spoons, some marked with the Apostles' heads, and others round-headed; and each of the said daughters to have "a brasse crocke of the best in the house," &c. If either daughter should happen to decease before marriage, half of her legacy to remain to "thother lyvinge," and the other half to John and Arthur West, sons of testator's brother. To the said John and Arthur xx^s apiece when twenty-one years of age. To son-in-law John Corfield vj^{li} xiij^s iiij^d besides the twenty marks of the bequest of the said John's father; also "my second best gowne my best doublet of grograyne and my Jerkyn of spanishe Lether." Legacies also to my "naturall brother" John West, my sister in London, my other sister dwelling in Carmarthen in Wales, sister-in-law

Margaret More of Tewkesbury, and Thomas More "my boye." Wife Elizabeth to be sole executrix, and have the residue of goods, and lands, tenements, &c., in the city and suburbs; rem. to daughters Alice and Joyce, and to their heirs for ever; in def., rem. to the sons of testator's brother. Mr. John Wade, Thomas Horner, John Palmer, and Thomas Bellingam to be overseers, and have vj^s viij^d apiece. Witnessed by William Hancock, Anthony Phillipps, Richard Langton, notary, and "the foresayd ou'seers."

Proved June 6th, 1567.

313.—THOMAS APRICE, tucker.

No date. Testator was of the parish of Temple. "my body to the E'rthe from whense it came." To eldest son Thomas xxvj^{li} xiij^s iiij^d, when twenty-one years of age; also a "rynge of golde wth the picture of deathes heade therevppon." To eldest daughter "allies," and daughter Elizabeth, £20 apiece on the day of their marriage. To sons William and John £20 apiece when twenty-one. To the child "my wyfe goeth wth all" £10, to be delivered at the age of twenty-one. If all the children should die, one half of their goods and legacies to go to "the poore people," and the other to the maintenance of the Tuckers' hall. The sum of £6 for "the pore." To Roger Dere "a doblet of mokkadoe," &c. To William Ryce "my workinday gowne of sheppes collower." Two shillings to my maid servants. To Robert Dawkins "that I lent him owt of my purse wch is ij^{li}." Legacies also to brother Thomas Leweas, John Barons, the younger, Alice Flowen', and apprentices Robert and Thomas. Wife Joan is to surrender £50, the Chamber's money, unto Mr. Roberts, he being one of testator's sureties; unless she will keep it in her power "any longer then twoo monethes after god hath called me to his m'sye," in which case she is to put in two sufficient sureties for the payment thereof. Thomas Symons and Richard Yonge, merchants, are to pay to her the money due from them, namely, xlij^{li} x^s; also Mr. Thomas Aldeworth and John Carr, merchants, Nicholas Blake, Mr. Saxey, and Philip Jenkins are to pay her what they owe. The said Joan to be full executrix. Brother Thomas Leweas and John Barons overseers. Witnessed by Roger Dere, Thomas Leweas, Elizabeth, wife of the said Thomas, and Katharine Deare.

Proved Aug. 8th, 1567.

314.—RICHARD ALKYNE, soapmaker.

1567. Sept. 11th. Testator was of the parish of St. Thomas "wthin the cytie of Bristowe." His body "to thearthe whereof it came." The sum of twenty shillings for the poor of the said parish. To John Thew, curate there, ij^s vj^d. To son John Alkyne, after the decease of wife Joan, all the drapery, &c., in the dwelling house, with the glass in the windows; also a gown "lyned withe crograyne." To sons Robert, Michael, Richard, and William, £20 apiece at the age of twenty-one. To daughters Joan, Frances, Elizabeth, Susan, Margaret, and Sara, £20 apiece at the day of marriage. The sum of £100 for "the bringinge vp of my aforesaid children in erudic'on and Learninge." To Mr. William Coxe "my cassocke of damaske gardid withe velvet." Legacies also to kinswoman Margaret Alkyne, wife's kinswoman Agnes Launsdon, Richard Swetnam, and sister Elizabeth Wheitley. Wife

Joan to have the residue, and be executrix. Robert Alflat and Richard Swetnam supervisors. Witnessed by John Thewe, curate, Mr. William Coxe, Robert Alflate, and Richard Swetnam.

Proved at London, Oct. 20th, 1567.

Law' Argall.

315.—EDMOND ROGERS, innholder.

1566. Jan. 21st. Testator was of "the p'ishe of Saint Thomas wthin the citie of Bristowe." His body "vnto the earthe." To the curate of the said parish vj^s viij^d. "Jtem J will that there shalbe but one bell ronge at my dep'tinc or buriall and my wief to cause a sermond to be made at my buriall." To the parish of Bristoltonn, for the mending of the highway between the houses of Smithe and John Newman, xx^s. To eldest son Thomas Rogers £6 at the day of his marriage; also, after the decease of wife Elyn, all the lands in Nympsfield, and within the city of Bristowe, "excepte the howse in Redcliffe streate;" rem. to son Ralph, if the said Thomas should die before his mother, or s.p. To the said Ralph £6 at the day of his marriage; also, after his mother's decease, the house in "Redcliffe streate" in the tenure of Barnes, the baker; rem. to eldest daughter, if then alive, and to her lawful heirs, in case of Ralph's death before his mother, or s.p. The said house to descend and remain to "the next of my bloud," if all the children should die s.p. To eldest daughter Elizabeth, second daughter Elizabeth, and daughters Alice, Jane, and Charity, £10 apiece at the day of marriage. Legacies also to every man and woman servant "in my howse," and kinswoman Marion. Wife Ellyn to have the residue, and be executrix. Thomas Coningham and John Palmer overseers, to each of whom vj^s viij^d. Witnessed by Thomas Horner, Walter West, John Cradocke, James Abolton, and others.

Proved Sept. 11th, 1567.

316.—MICHAEL COLSTONNE, draper.

1565. Aug. 26th. Testator's name is written thus, and also *Colston*, in the will. He desired to be buried in the parish church of All Saints in Bristowe. To sons Robert and Thomas, and daughters Margaret and Alice, vj^{li} xiij^s iiij^d apiece. The said Alice was "dowghter by my first wief." To son Robert the leases of the "two howses wch J doe nowe dwell in," and also "my garden grownd." Wife Edith to enjoy and occupy the said property "duryng her naturall lief," have the residue of goods, and be executrix. To kinsman John Addyson "my best cote," &c. My "welbeloved in christ" Thomas Colston, William Yemanns, and Walter Davys, overseers.

Proved Jan. 8th, 1565.

317.—ROBERT SMYTHE, merchant.

1569. June 29th. Testator describes himself as "of the Citie of Bristowe m'chant, and one of the shiriffes of the same Citie." To be buried in the parish church of St. Stephen the Martyr there. To wife Katharine, for her life, the house, garden, &c., "wherin I nowe dwell," bought of brother-in-law William Spratt, and situate "in Ballan strete," within the parish of St. Stephen aforesaid; rem. to son Peter Smythe and his lawful issue; in def., rem. to daughters Mary and Agnes Smythe. To the said Peter a house in Marsh-street " within Bristowe," bought of John Gryne (Grene) ; testator's wife to hold the said house until the said Peter is aged twenty-one, and to pay daughter Agnes xl^s a year during the said term. The said Peter to have £100 at the age of twenty-four. To daughters Mary and Agnes £150 apiece when aged eighteen, or married. If all the children should die before " the tyme lymitted," £100 of the said amount to be paid to the " mayor and co'i'altie of Bristowe," and disposed of in wood and coal yearly, to be bought in the summer, and sold out in the winter at cost price, for the benefit of the poor. The remaining £300 to be divided equally among " my brethren " Ralph and Edmund Smythe, and their children, and the children of sister Mary Higgines. To daughter Mary all interest and term of years in the great messuage or tenement held of William Barrett, situate " in Ballan strete," and in the tenure of John Sachfelde; also "my Cipres cheste therin." To daughter Agnes " my seconde beste Jlande cheste with his locke and key." Legacies also to brother-in-law William Spratt, brother Ralph Smythe, the said Ralph's son Edmund, apprentice to Thomas Colstone, mercer, the said Ralph's children Samuel and Letice Smythe, " my iiij mayde s'vantes," apprentice Roger Johnsonne, Robert Davies and David Lewis, tuckers, Edmund Olfilde, and his son David, brother Edmund Smythe, brother Richard Cole, cousin Anne White, and the poor in Bristowe. Wife Katharine to have the residue, and be sole executrix. Mr. John Cutt, John Carr, brother Edmund Smythe, and cousin Thomas Smythe, overseers. To the said Mr. Cutt " my baye nagge." To the said John Carr " iiij yeardes of fine puke clothe to make him a gowne." To cousin Thomas Smythe all interest in "that backehouse or Tenement" adjoining the tenement that "the saide Thomas dwelleth in in Ballan strete ;" also "my fowerthe gowne." To cousin Edward Chester " the ringe that his mother gaue me, remayninge in maister Higgins handes." Witnessed by Thomas and Edmund Smythe, John Carr, and John Die.

Testator added a codicil, July 6th, 1569 :—"out of suche p'te and porc'on of myne Adventure that is to saie of my goodes and m'chaundizes beinge to the value of iijCxlvj^{li} imbarged or stayed in Luxborne and the ylandes of Surry that happen to be loste or not to be recou'ed, the thirde p'te of the same shalbe deducted and defawked out of my legacies of money geven to my Children."

No record of probate occurs in the Orphan Book : but the will was proved Aug. 5th, 1569, as appears by the copy at Somerset House, *Sheffeld*, 19.

The next entry in the Orphan Book is an "acquitaunce conc'nyng money receyved and geven by John Mathows (sic) m'cer vnto his children." Toby Mathewe, son and heir of John Mathewe " late of the cytie of Bristowe m'cer deceassed," Andrew Cotterell of the same city, merchant, who espoused and took to wife Judith Mathewe, one of the daughters of the said John, and Hugh James of the same city, merchant, who espoused and took to wife Elizabeth Mathewe, the other daughter of the said John, " have remysed, relaxed quite discharged and exon'ated, to Robert Pressey of the cytie of Bristowe m'chaunt," and his heirs, &c., all obligations by which the said Robert Pressey was bound or charged for the legacy of the said John

Mathewe, by his last will and testament, or the gift and bequest of Ellynor Higgyns, now wife of George Higgyns, merchant, and late the wife of the said John Mathewe deceased, " in her widdowhodd to the Chambre of the said cytie for the Mayor and Aldermen of the same by waye of Recognizau'nce or otherwise to the vse of the foresaid children " of the said John; and for all actions, suits, &c. Bill made Oct. 3rd, 14 Eliz., and signed by the said Toby, Hugh, and Andrew, on the same day : " cognitu' coram Joh'e Browne Maiore et Ric'o Willymott See^{lo} ib'm," Oct. 31st, 14 Eliz.

318.—EDMUND WOODD. In the margin *Wood*.

1571. Oct. 23rd. Testator was a "m'chaunt of the cytie of Bristowe," and desired to be buried in the crowde of St. Nicholas. To eldest son William Woodd " my howse att Borton," with all the cattle there, namely, " ffyftene Kyne, ffyve yowng cattle named yerlinges alitle more or lesse one hundreth and twentie shepe ;" also £80 at the day of marriage, or age of twenty-one. To son John Woodd £80 in like manner. Wife Ellyn to have, during her natural life, the profits of the house, appurtenances, and cattle " before mencioned." To daughters Alice and Joan £50 apiece at the day of marriage. To daughter Elizabeth £10. To "the poore Almes howses " of the city £5. To son John the fee simple of the little tenement " in Ballance strete ;" also the lease of my dwelling house, and the lease of the house " app'tey'ing to the companey of the Taylors," inhabited by John Rowland. Wife Ellyn to have and enjoy, during her life, " the forenamed howse in ffee symple," and also the two leases, and the profits of the same. To servants Roger Freeman and Joan Bradforde forty shillings apiece. Testator's goods being " directted in trades of the sea and otherwayes in venter," he willed that if any part of them should miscarry or be lost, the legacies of his said children should bear their portion of the losses. His wife to be executrix, and have the residue of goods. Within three months next after his decease, she is to discharge Mr. John Browne and John Bysse, merchants, " my suerties for the so'me of fliftie powndes to the Chambre of Bristowe." Mr. John Browne, Thomas Powell, and Robert Kytchin, merchants, to be overseers. Signed, Edmond Wood. Witnessed by John Browne, Robert Kytchin, Thomas Powell, and Nicholas Hickes.

No record of probate occurs in the Orphan Book ; but the will was proved Nov. 22nd, 1571, as appears by the copy at Somerset House, *Holney*, 41.

319.—JOHN WHYTE, merchant.

1569. Nov. 26th. Testator was of " the cittie of Bristowe," and willed that his body be buried " in suche place as it shall please god to call me," and that " maister laurence shall make A s'mone at my buriall to whome J doe gyve for his paynes takinge in that behalf sixe shilinges and eighte pence." To wife Edith White £400, some part of which to be received of Edward Cullymore, her brother ; also a " Tenement with the howses therevnto belonginge wherein she nowe dwellethe," and one garden belonging to the same, called " Michaell Hill garden ;" rem. to son George and his heirs. Also to the said Edith, for her life, the garden " at Marke Lanes end ;" rem. to daughter Edith White and her assigns during all the years contained " in

A lease thereof made vnto me." To the said daughter Edith 100 marks when twenty-one years of age, or married; also a goblet parcel-gilt, and "one cuppe of silu' called the rocke." To son Thomas £100 when twenty-one; also a dozen of silver spoons parcel-gilt, called "the Twleve Apostelles," three gilt goblets, &c., after the death of wife Edith; also to him, and his heirs, a tenement "sitting and beinge in the highe streate," in the farm and occupation of one Ralph Hurte. To son George 100 marks of lawful English money when twenty-one; also "my beste awndyorns," &c., and "my goulde rynge wth deathes hedd in it." To daughter Susan £60, and a goblet parcel-gilt; also testator's lease and term of years in three tenements "wth A Orcharde at Lawfordes gate," which he had by the demise of his father-in-law Walter Philippes. To daughter Elizabeth £50 when twenty-one, or married; also £10, to be paid to her by one John Whitte of London, merchant, at the end of her "apprentishoode," or at the day of her marriage; and a goblet parcel-gilt. To daughters Maud and Grace £50 apiece at the age of twenty-one, or day of marriage: to the former "my oulde goblett p'cell gylte;" and to the latter "my taster of silu' and eighte silu' spones." To the prisoners in Newgate in Bristowe £5 "in brede chese and bere and other victualls." The sum of £20 "vnto the moste porest howsholders dwelling in Bristowe beyonde the haven in temple streate St Thomas streate and Raclill streate." Legacies also to the poorest householders "in marshestreate in the p'ishe of St Stevens," the poorest people dwelling in St. Werburgh's parish, servant Ellyn Harrys, alms-people in Bristowe, brother Richard Willymotte, brother-in-law Edward Cullymore, sister Cullymore, cousin Joan Williams, Ralph Hooper, and Joan Skynner. Residue to wife Edith for her life; to be afterwards divided equally among all the children. Dominick Chestar, and Thomas Williams "my nevewe," merchants of Bristowe, to be executors, and each to have £5. Witnessed by John Gislingham, Robert Coulye, and William Norton.

Proved at London, May 1st, 1570.   Law. Argall.

320.—WILLIAM CHESTER, whittawer.

1572. Dec. 1st. Testator was of "the cytie of Bristowe," and desired to be buried near vnto his father and brothers. To eldest son William £20; also the land consisting of three tenements "which J nowe dwell in," and which "my father gave me;" also two tenements at "the corners" of St. James's Back, inhabited by the good wife Mathewe and a brewer; three tenements by "the bars;" and three tenements before St. Stephen's church door "that the good wief Moore made one of." Wife Joan to occupy the first mentioned three tenements during "her widowe estate," paying to son William twenty shillings a year. But when she is married "then J doe geve him the three howsen that J dwell in," with all the implements, "that is ye back parlor wth waynescote and a faire folding table," and the fore parlor "hanged wth saies and borders, and the chambers aboue wth stayned clothes," and the standing bed that testator lay in, "wth certayne Coffers that was (sic) my fathers, and other tryfling implementes wch J doe not remembre." To son Harry £10; also to him, and wife Joan, all the houses in Barton hundred "wch J bowght for lieves" of Sir Morrys Dennys, and those bought of brother Thomas. If son Harry should "dye wthowt issue," rem. to Walter Chester; in def., rem. to James Chester; in def., rem. to

Thomas Chester; in def., rem. to eldest son William; in def., rem. to daughter Elizabeth Chester; in def., rem. to daughter Mary Chester; in def., rem. to my brother Thomas and to "his Successors for ever." To son James £20, and two of the tenements "at Brode meade ende;" the other two tenements to son Thomas; the garden to be shared equally by them and their heirs. To daughter Elizabeth £8. 3. 4, and "the litle crewes covered wth silver." To daughter Mary £30, and the second salt with the cover. Articles of plate also to sons William, Harry, Walter, James, and Thomas. To my sister Roberts "one olde Angellett." To son Walter £10; also to him, and to his heirs, two tenements in the tenure of William Yate and Elizabeth Cradock, widow; wife Joan to receive out of this property forty shillings yearly, and a like sum yearly out of son William's lands. To the servants of the house "one ffryse amongest them." Legacies also to brothers Thomas and Dominick, and the poor. Wife Joan to have the residue, and be sole executrix. Witnessed by Thomas Chester "ar," Robert Smythes, William Pyll, John Horte, John Jacob, Christopher Burkhed, and others.

Proved at London, March 7th, 1572.

321.—WILLIAM CLEMOND, innholder.

1569. Nov. 29th. To be buried in the parish church of St. Philip at Bristowe, "in such place as yt shall seme beste to my wief to laie me." The sum of xx^s to the poor of that parish; and iij^s iiij^d toward "aboord cloth for the co'mu'yon table." To son Thomas, after the death of wife Elizabeth, the house "lying wthout Laffordes gate," inhabited by the goodwife Lambe, and lately bought of Mr William Bede. Also to son Thomas twelve pieces of brass, &c., and £10 in money; of which goods and money "my wief shall haue the custody" till he come to the age of twenty-one, "and thus the Almightie god blesse him." To son William two houses in the same part, the one bought of the said Mr. Bede, and inhabited by Edward Baker, "arrowhedd maker," and the other bought of Edmond Grove, pointmaker, and inhabited by one Fissher and Margaret Sknowe; also three silver spoons, &c., and " in currant money x^{li}." The goods and money of the said William to be kept in like manner as those of his brother till he "com' to thage of xxj^{ti} yeres." If these sons should both die before that age, rem. to son John. If all the children should die s.p., rem. to wife Elizabeth, who is made sole executrix. My neighbours John Warren and Thomas Colman to be overseers, and have x^s apiece. Witnessed by Roger Chaloner, curate of the said St. Philip's, John Warren, David Harris, Joan Harris, and Robert Graie.

Nov. 25th, 1569, is here given as the date of proof. But according to the copy at Somerset House, *Daper*, 27, the will was made Oct. 29th, 1569, and proved Aug. 2nd, 1572.

322.—WILLIAM YEMAN, glover.

1573. Dec. 21st. Testator was of "the cytie of Bristoll," and desired to be buried "in Christian buriall." To son William three houses, two of them being within the parish of St. Peter, and the other in St. James's parish "in Brodemeade;" also £20 of money, with "my best goblett," to him and his heirs for ever. William Yeman the younger, grocer, to have the custody of this son William, and of his goods and lands. To daughters Alice, Margery, Katharine, and Joan £20 apiece, and to "base dowghter" Katharine £5; to be paid to them at the age of twenty. If any die before that age, the portion of such "to be equallie devided among the rest vivent." To my father John Yeman one silver spoon. Wife Joan to have the residue, and be executrix. William Yeman the younger, grocer, to be overseer.

Proved April 5th, 1574.
This will is also in the Bristol probate office.

323.—JOHN KETTINGALL, mercer.

1569. March 14th. Testator was of "the Citie of Bristowe," and willed that his body be buried "in the earth from whense yt came." To eldest son John Kyttingall £20 when twenty-one years of age. To sons Tobit and George £20 apiece when twenty-one. To daughter Elizabeth Kyttyngall £20 at the day of her marriage. To "my Childe that my wief nowe goeth wthall," £20 at the age of twenty-one, "if that it be a boye," but at the day of marriage, if "a wench." If all the children should die before receiving their legacies, one half to remain to wife Elizabeth, and the other to brother-in-law John Hylhowse, or Agnes his wife; and for any such lack, to my sister Alice Kittingall, or to the children of the said John and Agnes Hilhowse. To brother John Cother "my wedding gowne lyned wth Taffata." To "the poore of this citie" xx^s in wood and bread. Legacies also to brother John Hilhowse, servant John Foliett, and cousin James. Wife Elizabeth to have the residue, and be full and sole executrix. Brother John Cother, and cousin Hugh James, overseers. Unto "my brother Cawfylde my ringe of golde wth the Onyxe stone whose frindshippe towardes my poore Children and wief J trust J nede not to crave." Witnessed by Mr. Roger Jones, Mr. George Higgyns, John Huntington, and John Cother.

Proved at London, April 26th, 157. *(sic)*. The year was 1570, as appears by a copy of the will at Somerset House, *Lyon*, 10.

324.—RICHARD MERICK, tailor.

No year given. July 17th. Testator was of "the p'ishe of St Tuens in the citie of Bristowe," and desired to be buried "in Christen buryall." To each of his three sons, Robert, John, and William, iij^{li} vj^s viij^d. If they should all die "before they be able to make any will," rem. to the daughters of sister Maud and of brother Walter "by equall porc'ons." To son Robert the lease of testator's house, if he shall live "to thage of xxiiijth yeres," if not, to "the rest Successivelie one after the other." To brother John Mirick, the elder, "a yarde and half of puke kersey of iij^s the yarde." To William Merick, of Redyker, "my bowe and my arowes and a dosen of bowe stringes that are in my Cownter." To each brother and sister "a paire of hose of xij^d apaire." Legacies also to Elenor Jurdon, daughter of sister Maud, every almshouse in Bristowe, and godfather William Merick. Wife Anne to have the residue, and be executrix. Brother John Mirick, the younger, and Philip Browne, overseers, to each of whom four yards of "the best kersey in my shoppe orelles vj^s viij^d apece."

Testator added a codicil, Sept. 10th, 1573, in order to give twenty nobles to each of his three sons; also the best gown and a ring to son Robert;

"my other Puke gowne" to son John; and "my shepes Color gowne" to son William. Witnessed by John Mirick of Bristowe, Thomas Ryder, Laurence Wally, and Mr Dove of London.

Proved at London, Oct. 26th, 1573.

325.—RALPH PILKINGTON.

1570 (?). June 12th. Testator was of "the p'ishe of all Saintes within the Citie of Bristowe," and desired to be buried in the church there. The sum of xx^s to "the poore people of the Cytie of Bristoll" at the time of burial; and v^s to the curate of All Saints'. Forty shillings to Alice wife of Robert Mellye of Bristowe, goldsmith. To Jane Serche, daughter of John Serche, after the deecase of wife Joan, all the money that shall be then unpaid of one obligation of £90, bearing date Jan. 28th, 10 Eliz., due from one Richard Proctor, of the city of London, merchant tailor, or from his heirs or assigns. To wife Joan "my part of all the rest of the yeres of Pile Hills and Ware meades the Conye close and brode meade," with three acres adjoining to Temple mead; the lease of "my dwelling howse called gillardes June," with seven acres of mead "lying in Redclief meade"; also eight kine "going vppon the said grounde," and two oxen. All other "my free purchased landes wthin the Cytie of Bristowe J doe freelie geve vnto the foresaid Jane Sarche." Wife Joan to have the residue of goods, and be sole executrix. Robert Saxcey, alderman, and Thomas Wysshe, gentleman, overseers, to each of whom xx^s. Witnessed by Robert Saxcey, William Hastling, and Robert Cole, writer.

Note of probate dated the last day of Feb., 1574.

326.—GEORGE GRAYE, innholder.

1567. Nov. 26th. Testator was a "Citezen of the Citie of Bristowe in the p'ishe of Saint Marye Port," and desired to be buried in the church or churchyard of the said parish. To the poor men's box there ij^s vj^d. To the poor prisoners of Newgate ij^s vj^d. To eldest son William Graye "two gownes furred one wth bugge and the other with black branched damaske;" also "my marbell riding cote laied with laces," &c. To youngest son George Graie the lease of a house inhabited by one John Filian, grinder, "in St Marie port Strete;" also twenty marks at theage of twenty-one; rem. to wife Alice Graie, if he should die before that age. The said Alice to be sole executrix, and have the dwelling house, and all unbequeathed goods, lands, and tenements; she to be bound "with suertie" to the overseers in the sum of £40 for the performance of the will, &c. John Cowper alias Rowland, "Citezen and drap' of the Citie of Bristowe," and William Yate, citizen and soapmaker of the same city, to be overseers. Witnessed by John Cowper, William Yate, and David Roberts.

Proved Aug. 17th, 1573.

327.—ROGER JONES, grocer.

1574. Sept. 23rd. Testator was of "the Citie of Bristowe," and desired to be buried " in the ground as nere my sonne Edward Jones as maye be;" also that before all things his debts be "paied to all men." To a preacher that will preach "at my buryall" vj^s viij^d. To sister Higgyns "ablack gonne & hoode." Gowns to "my cosen doctor Mathewe," and cousins Buckford, Cother, and Elizabeth Benett. Two gowns to "my sonne and dowghter," and £20 to their daughter "litle Besse" at her marriage. To cousin Synell a gown, or forty shillings in money. Testator having a bond of "my lord Staffords" of £40, bequeaths one half of that sum to cousin Synoff, "yf J doe receyve and be paied the same." Legacies also to my six servants, cousin Richard White, and the poor. Wife Elizabeth to have the residue, and be sole executrix. Son-in-law Richard Moore to be overseer, and have xl^s. Witnessed by John Bosswell, Henry Millard, and Nicholas Hill.

Proved at London, Oct. 20th, 1574.

328.—WILLIAM CARR, merchant.

1574. Jan. 10th. To be buried in the parish church of St. Werburgh, by my late wife, "yff J dy in Bristoll." The executors are solemnly charged to see that all debts be justly and truly paid. The sum of £10 a year to the poor within the said city, out of lands and tenements; the Mayor and Commonalty to attend to the yearly bestowal of the money. If the good order used within the city should be dissolved and discontinued, then "the maior & comynalltie of the said citee for the time being shall yeerly forever" pay and distribute the same amount, out of the rents of such lands and tenements, to the poor in the almshouses on St. James's Back and in Lewens mead, and in those of "the three kinges of Culleine" and St. John's; £4 of the amount to be for "the poore prisoners of Newgate wch live vppon the bagge." If the Mayor and Commonalty at any time hereafter "make defalte," then all persons "and boddies politique" standing and being seized of such lands and tenements, shall then and from thenceforth stand and be seized thereof, and of every part thereof, "to thonly vse and behooff" of testator's right heirs for ever. To wife Anne all goods, plate, jewels, household stuff, &c., and £200; also, for her life, a yearly rent of £20 out of lands and tenements in Woodspring, in the name of "her Joincture;" also testator's dwelling house, garden, and orchard "in Balldwinstreete within the said city of Bristoll, during her widdowhed," and half of all the stuff in the said house; also 100 oz. of "plate percell guilte," and 50 oz. of "guylte plate." To son John, and to his heirs for ever, the said dwelling house, garden, and orchard; also a messuage in the same street, in the tenure of Walter Standfast, and a messuage called "Beards land" in Congresbury, co. Somerset; also half the stuff in the dwelling house, and 100 oz. of "plate guilte." Testator being bound with Thomas Alldwoorth, merchant, unto the Queen's Majesty, for and with the said John Carr, in one obligation of £800, bearing date Aug. 20th, 15 Eliz., for and concerning "certeine Portingall goods" delivered to the said John Carr, in respect of certain goods of the said John "staied in Portingall;" if the said John, and his executors and administrators, will at all times acquit and discharge testator's heirs, executors, administrators, and assigns, as the said Thomas Alldwoorthe, his heirs, &c., for and concerning the said obligation, and the penalty therein contained; the said John Carr, and his heirs, &c., at all times permitting testator's executors to execute their office; then testator releases unto his said son John all debts and duties "wch he oweth vnto me either for moneys or wares lente or sould vnto him : " in case of refusal, " this my releasse shall be voied and of none effecte." Testator having already executed an estate in tail to his son Edward Carr, of and in "the Scite and demeansues" of Woodspringe, co. Somerset, and assigned to him a lease in reversion for the term of twenty-one years of and in the parsonages of Worle and Kewstoke, and all right, title, and interest in one close of pasture called "Collam," in the said county; now moreover bequeaths to the said Edward all the stock and store of oxen, kine, &c., going or pasturing "in or vpon the demesnes" of Woodspringe, or in Worle, or Kewstoke, geldings and mares excepted; also implements and furniture of husbandry in Woodspringe, and some of the stuff in the house there; growing corn, 100 oz. of plate parcel-gilt, and a counting-chest standing on a frame in "my bedd Chamber aforestreete." To son-in-law William Younge and his wife Anne, testator's daughter, and the heirs of the latter, a tenement, with garden and orchard ground, in the occupation of Henry Wyate. To Mary Ashe, daughter of John Ashe, and of testator's daughter Margaret, a tenement "in Balldwinstreete," in the occupation of Nicholas Hickes, merchant, with all the wainscot, glass, &c., therein; in default of issue, rem. to Anne Ashe, another daughter of the said John. Testator having, by indenture, Aug. 8th, 13 Eliz., conveyed to his friends in trust William Young, Richard Cole, and John Ashe, his lease and term of years in the lands and tenements called "the twelve ffarmeis of Weeke Sainct Lawrence," co. Somerset, "to thonlie vse" of his last will and testament, does now dispose of the whole profits thus :—the executors to receive the yearly rent of £60 for two years, for the benefit of son John Carr; and, for ten years afterwards, the said rent to be received and paid towards the agreement, satisfaction, or payment of £2000, payable hereafter to Richard Owen for the manors of Congresbury and Lawrence Weeke : and when the person who shall have immediate inheritance of the said manors, at the decease of "ladie Mary Allen," or hereafter, shall make agreement with the said Richard Owen, his executors and assigns, in the discharge of the said £2000, then testator's executors shall forthwith upon request render up, satisfy, and pay to such person, having inheritance, as shall make such agreement and satisfaction of the said sum, all such yearly rent as before that time, since the expiration of the said two years, they have received, &c. To the children of William Young, by my daughter Anne, £20 yearly, equally divided among them out of the said rent of £60, for and during twelve years after the expiration of the aforesaid time. To Mary and Anne, daughters of John and Margaret Ashe, £12 out of the said rent, equally divided, for the space of twelve years. To "my sonne" Richard Colle, and Alice his wife, £18 yearly for the space of twelve years. The residue of the said rent, and all rents and profits during the remainder of the time after the expiration of the twelve years, to be paid to the person having inheritance of the said manors, and making satisfaction or agreement of or for the £2000. To son-in-law Richard Cole and his wife Alice, testator's daughter, 300 oz. of parcel-gilt plate. A considerable amount of plate also to son-in-law William Younge, and his wife Anne, and daughters Alice and Anne; to son-in-law John Ashe, and his daughters Mary and Anne. The sum of £25 for the making or repairing of "highewaies" within fifteen miles of Bristoll. To the marriage of poor maidens in that city xxvj^{li} xiij^s iiij^d; no one maid to have to her marriage above xl^s. For the clothing of the poor "where neede ys in Bristoll" lx^{li}. To servant Edward Barrowe the lease in reversion for twenty-one years in a tenement in Porteshedd, co. Somerset, in the occupation of Thomas Chappell. To servant William Oliver the lease in reversion of twenty-one years in one close of pasture called "Carrells hamme," containing eight acres within "the seawall," and three acres "withoute the seawall" in Porteshedd aforesaid, in the occupation of John Stevens, or John Cottrell. To the poor prisoners of Newgate "wch live by the bagg," £20 weekly in bread. To every poor man and woman in every almshouse within Bristoll xij^d "to the some of tenn poundes." To servant Edmund Cooke the lease in reversion for twenty-one years in a messuage and tenement, with lands thereunto belonging, in Carswell, in the parish of Portbury, co. Somerset, in the occupation of William Parker *alias* Locker, or his assigns. To each of "my frinds" Thomas Kelke, Thomas Alldwoorth, Thomas Rowlannde, and Thomas Symons, merchants, xx^s for a ring. To "my frinde" Robert Dowe xx marks "for his chilldren." To "my cosen" William Bithesea v^{li}, and a good gown. To the marriage of the daughter of Thomas Haines of Bristoll, dwelling "wth William James wyfe widowe in Sainct James p'ishe," £10. Legacies also to every maid servant, "my freind" John Jacob, John Blande, and Elizabeth Blande. All "myne apparell" unto my children and friends. Richard Colle and John Ashe to be executors, and have £20 apiece. Residue of goods to go towards the payment of the said sum of £2000 to that person, or persons, which shall make agreement or satisfaction of the same to the said Richard Owen, or to his assigns. William Younge, Thomas Alldwoorth, Thomas Rowlannde, and Thomas Simons, overseers. Witnessed by Thomas Alldwoorth and Thomas Rowlannde.

"Probatum fuit in cur' prerogativa Anno d'ni 1575": no mention of day or month. There is however a copy of the wil at Somerset House, *Pyckering*, 21, from which we learn that it was proved on May 16th, in that year.

329.—JOHN CUTT.

1571. Jan. 10th. Testator, who was "of Bristow marchaunte and late Maior there," desired to be buried in the parish church of St. Werburgh. To his wife Joan the manor and lordship of Burnett, co. Somerset, with all houses, lands, &c., appertaining thereto, and all other lands, tenements, &c., in Wells, Burnett, and elsewhere in that county, for the term of sixty years, "if she so longe lyve:" rem. to son William Cutt and his lawful heirs male; in def., rem. to son Nicholas Cutt and his heirs male; in def., rem. to son Matthew Cutt. To the said Joan, for sixty years, the parsonage of Chewton Keinsham in Somerset, with the tithes and profits belonging to the same, and the yearly profits and commodities in Broadmead lying in the same parish; rem. to son Matthew for eighty years, he paying £4 yearly to William Cutt and his heirs male, who are afterwards to inherit this property; in def., rem. to the said Nicholas Cutt and his heirs male; in def., rem. to the said Matthew. To the said Joan, for sixty years, testator's dwelling house in Bristowe, in Cornestreet, and all his other lands, tenements, &c., in the city, except the property already given to son Nicholas; rem. to the said Nicholas. To son William £100, on condition of his being bound to his mother in the sum of £500, that she and her assigns shall or may

P

quietly have and enjoy the aforesaid manor of Burnett, &c. To son Matthew £100 at the age of twenty-one. To daughter Bridget £33 6s. 8d. over and above the £100 delivered to brother-in-law John Ritche; the said sums to be paid at the day of her marriage. To the said John Ritche a ring of gold of the value of forty shillings. A scarlet gown to son Nicholas. A gown "furred with gennyttes" to son-in-law John Bisse; and a cassock of damask and satin coat to the children of the said John. A gown lined with satin, &c., to son-in-law Robert Sanforde. A velvet coat to brother-in-law Thomas Kelke. Son William to have the rest of the apparel. The sum of £4 to the poor people of the almshouse " in the marshe in Bristowe." To "my poore woorckmen," the tuckers, and others, £6. Wife Joan to have the residue, and be sole executrix. The aforesaid Thomas Kelke, John Bisse, Robert Sanford, and Nicholas Cutt, overseers. Testator forgives and remits to his said son William "all suche debtes as he doethe owe vnto me," on condition of his entering into the abovesaid bond of £500 to his said mother. Witnessed by Thomas Kelke, Robert Sanford, John Dye, and Nicholas Cutt.

Proved "in cur' prerogatiua" before Thomas Godwin, dean of the cathedral church, 1575: no mention of day or month. The will was proved on June 10th, in that year, as appears by the copy at Somerset House, *Pyckering*, 24.

330.—JOHN ROCKWELL, brewer.

1572. July 18th. Testator was of "the p'yshe of St Mariporte within the citee of Bristoll," and desired to be buried in the church of that parish, "by Mr Edwardes tombe." Mr. Huntington, the preacher, was to "make a Sermon in the daye of my buriall " in the said parish church, and have for his pains vj^s viij^d sterling. To William Gibbes twenty quarters of malt. To William Greene twenty quarters of malt, and iij^{li} x^s sterling; also ij^{li}, due to testator from William Mays of Laffords Yate, and ij^{li} viij^s, due from Mr Lacy of the same part. To John Rockwell £14, due from Stephen Spurlock "of the redlion in redclyff Streete," and two dozen of "Standes." To son William Rockwell both the furnaces, with "all the vates Trendills and kives," the mill, the well, and all other implements "that belongethe vnto my brewhowse;" but wife Katharine to have and occupy all these things during her life. The dwelling house, after her decease, to son Gilbert. To Joan Tailor xl^s; also, for her life, the tenement inhabited by John Fillian; rem. to her brother Richard Tailor for his life, and afterwards to testator's son William and his heirs. To son-in-law William Gibbes "two Crewses of Silver," &c., but wife Katharine to have the use of them while a pure widow. To sons Gilbert and William twenty quarters of malt apiece, and wood to " brew it withall." To William Rockwell of Barton hundred ij^{li} sterling; also " his bed wch he lieth vpon," &c. Legacies also to Nicholas Greene, and his brother Anthony Greene, Richard Tailor, and servants Ellin and Hugh. Wife Katharine to have the residue, and be sole executrix. Mr John Horte and William Gybbes overseers: and "J geve to the said Master John Horte for his pains to be taken in this behaulf xiij^s iiij^d." Witnessed by John Gregory, clerk, Nicholas Robins, John Kemsham, Anthony Phillips, William Greene, and others.

Proved " in cur' prerogatiua," Oct. 9th, 1572.

The register of burials in the parish of St. Mary-le-port, Bristol, contains these entries:—John Rockewell, brewer, July 22nd, 1572 ; Gilbert Rockewell, householder, Aug. 9th, 1573 ; John Gregorie "the minister," April 10th, 1579 ; Katharine Rockewell, widow, April 8th, 1583.

331.—ROGER CLASBOCK.

1575. June 10th. Testator was of the parish of Temple, in the city of Bristow, and desired to be buried in the churchyard there. To William, Maud, Alice, and Elizabeth Clasbock, the children of his son John late deceased, £20 13s. 4d. equally divided, that sum being in the hands of his son-in-law Jenkine Apphowell ; to be paid within twenty days after testator's death to the Mayor of this city, who is to dispose of the same to such person or persons as seem most meet and convenient according to his discretion with the advice of the overseers ; the same person or persons putting in sufficient sureties to bring up the said children at his or their own proper costs and charges, and pay the portions bequeathed to them at the age of twenty, or when married, according to "the custome for orphantes vsed wthin *(sic)* this Citie." All household stuff to Jane Powell, daughter of testator's daughter, except one platter and one pottinger, which his kinswoman Elizabeth Clasbock is to have. The aforesaid Jenkine Aphowell to be sole executor, and have all the rest of the goods and money. Mr. John Barnes, Mr. Randall Hassald, William Nicholls, and Milles Evans, overseers, to whom vj^s viij^d "to be bestowed vppon a breakefast at suche time as they shall thincke goode." Witnessed by Mr. Edward Porter.

No record of proof.

The Temple parish register records the burial of Maud Clasbock, a child, Aug. 1st., and of Roger Clasbock, Aug. 8th, 1575 ; the letter "p," evidently standing for "plague," being inserted opposite to both, and indeed nearly all the entries of burials (a very considerable number) which took place in that year.

332.—JOHN NORTHALL, pewterer.

1572. Feb. 16th. Testator was of "the cytee of Bristoll," and desired to be "honestlie and decently buried" within his parish church called Christ Church ; and that an "honest preacher" should preach a sermon at his burial, and be paid vj^s viij^d. He willed that those feoffees whom he had chosen and put in special trust, named and specified in a deed of feoffment bearing date "the said xxvjth daie *(sic)* of February," 15 Eliz., and their heirs, should stand and be seized of his dwelling house and appurtenances in "Wine streete," in the aforesaid parish, to his use for life and that of his wife Elizabeth during her life, in full recompense of her jointure, and dower of all his lands, tenements, &c., within Bristoll or elsewhere ; rem. to the use of son Rowland Northall and his wife Elizabeth during their lives ; rem. John to Northall, eldest son of the said Rowland, and his legitimate heirs ; in def., rem. to the heir male of the said Rowland ; in def., rem. to the said Rowland's daughters ; in def., rem. to "theirs" of John Ades of Bristoll, pewterer, by his late wife Elizabeth, testator's daughter ; in def., rem. to brother Thomas Northall and his legitimate heirs. The said feoffees, after testator's decease, are to stand seized of the messuage in the High-street, held by the said John Ades at a rent of "vij^{li} by theere," to the use of the said Rowland, and of Elizabeth his wife, during their lives ; rem. to the said John Northall, son of Rowland, and his legitimate male issue ; rem. to the heirs of the said John and Elizabeth Ades, if the said Rowland should leave no male or female heirs ; rem. to brother Thomas Northall, if the said John and Elizabeth should be s.p. The feoffees are also to stand and be seized of a tenement in Baldwin-street inhabited by William Mills "the Searcher," and also of a tenement in the said parish of Christ Church, in the tenure of Humphrey Androwes, and a tenement in the tenure of George Roselie, fletcher, to the use of the said Rowland and his wife Elizabeth during their lives ; rem. to John, son of Rowland, and his heirs. To the said Rowland a messuage or tenement in Wolverhampton, co. Stafford ; rem. to the use of the said John Northall, son of Rowland, and his legitimate heirs. Any doubt or question that may arise as to the disposition of the inheritance of these lands, tenements, &c., to be explained by testator's friend Mr. Reade, to whom "J have imparted my mynde at lardge before the making of the same will." Wife Elizabeth to have the use of all furnaces, brewing utensils, horse-mills, mill-horses, drays, &c., and be bonnd with two good and sufficient sureties to Thomas Younge of Bristol, grocer, William Reade of Bristoll, esquire, and John Athall, the overseers of this will, to yield up these things to son Rowland, his executors and assigns "ymeadiatlie after my decease ;" Rowland to occupy for his life ; rem. to his said son John. To wife Elizabeth all the money she has "to bie and sell withall ;" also all the malt and wood in the mansion-house, and certain household stuff. To each of the three daughters of the said Rowland, at the age of eighteen, or the time of marriage, £20, out of the £200 due from John Ades. To the children of my said son-in-law John Ades, by daughter Elizabeth, £20 "by even porcions" at the age of eighteen, or the time of marriage. To the poor of the city of Bristoll £10. To Ellen Northall, daughter of son Rowland, a "nutt enclosed wth Silver and gilte of accorne woorcke and a cover gilte for the same." Legacies also to Joan and Elizabeth Northall, the other daughters of the said Rowland, and Elizabeth his wife, Leonard Pope, and John Hall "my wyves kynsman," and the overseers of the will. The said John Northall, son of the said Rowland, to have the residue, and be sole executor. William Reade and Thomas Younge, or the survivor of them, to assign and appoint what fee the said John Athall shall yearly have for the gathering and paying of the rent of "my said landes." Witnessed by Edward Dowting, Hugh Barrett, and Leonard Pope.

Testator added a "Codicill nuncupatyve" in his dwelling house in Wine-street, in the presence of his daughter-in-law Elizabeth, wife of Rowland Northall, July 29th, 1574, in order to bequeath certain sums of money to Elizabeth "his owne wief," his three maid-servants, and the three daughters of his son Rowland. Witnessed by John Hunte, Agnes Collman, Elizabeth Risby, John Greene, Alice Reade, Joan Cox, and others.

Proved "in cur' p'rogat'," June 5th, 1575.

333.—GEORGE ROWSLEY.

...... Sept. 26th. Testator was of "the cytee of Bristowe and of the parishe of Christchurch," and desired to be buried within the church of that parish. To brother Anthony "my rugg gowne my fryse ierkin and my mouldes of breeches and the breeches." To servant Robert Priest £10, to be "paied of the rent of my shoppe r'c'd at St James tide from yere to yere at my wyves discretion." To Edith Priest, and cousin Agnes Priest, £10 apiece. Wife Alice to have the residue, and be sole executrix. Witnessed by Richard Howseman, Margaret Thurston, and others.

Proved Oct. 22nd, 1575.

334.—THOMAS BETTES, "yeman."

1575. Oct. 13th. Testator, who was of the parish of St. Nicholas "within the cytee of Bristoll," desired to be buried in "St Nicholas crowde." To every one of "my wives childrens children" forty shillings apiece. To son-in-law John Bonner all the debts owing to testator. Loving wife Welthian to have the residue, and be sole executrix. Witnessed by Thomas Addams, ropemaker, Thomas Grove, "sayler," Joan wife of Lewes Philippes, baker, with divers others.

Proved "in cur' p'rogativa," Nov. 29th, 1575. Administration to the aforesaid Welthian.

335.—HUGH MATHOW.

1575. July 24th. To be buried at the discretion of "my executrice." To my three children, Thomas, Margaret, and Amy, xx^{li}, to be equally divided, and paid at the age of eighteen, "and not before." If all should die before that age, wife Agnes to have the said money. To brother Nicholas Mathew (sic) forty shillings, and all wearing garments "saving only my best gowne." Wife Agnes to have the residue, and be sole executrix. Brother-in-law John Adies, overseer. Witnessed by John Burrowes, Edward Davis, James Farley, and Roger Rice "person of St Johnes in Bristowe."

Proved Aug. 18th, 1575.

336.—WILLIAM RIDGES, tailor.

1575. Sept. 26th. Testator was of "the cytie of Bristow," and bequeathed his body "to the earth from whence yt came." To son William a standing bed, with "a tester of drapry and hedd of ye same;" also a great chest, a table board, "wth all thimplem^{tes} in the Parlo^r and a bible." To daughter Elizabeth Ridges a new standing bed, &c., and "a spruse chest of xl^s." Wife Mary to have the residue, and be executrix. Witnessed by John Grigg, clerk, Hugh Jones, and Davy Philippes.

Proved before William Jones, doctor of laws, official of the whole diocese of Bristoll, Oct. 7th, 1575. Adm'on to Mary Ridges, executrix named in the will.

The register of the parish of St. Nicholas, Bristol, records the burial of William Ridges, Sept. 27th, 1575.

337.—JOHN PAINE alias FLETCHER, draper.

1575. July 22nd. Testator, who was of the parish of St. Nicholas "wthin the cytee of Bristow," willed that his body be "buryed in xp'ien buriall wthin the parish church of Abergainy," and bequeathed to John James, vicar of that town, ten shillings for a mortuary. To eldest son Toby, sons William and John, eldest daughter Alice, and daughters Agnes, Mary, and Elizabeth, £5 apiece. Unto Hughes xx^s. To wife Alice Paine the lease of the dwelling house, all household stuff, &c.; also, during her "wydowhedd," after the decease of testator's mother, the house inhabited by his said mother; rem. to eldest son Toby. My "welbeloved wyfe Alice Paine" to be sole executrix. Mr. Robert Saxey and Mr. John Browne, aldermen of "the cytee of Bristoll," overseers. Witnessed by Frances Jones, "Elynor Jones al's viz' Rees, Joane viz' Thomas," and James Blan.

Proved "in cur' p'rogativa," Nov. 2nd, 1575.

338.—JOHN BOYDELL.

1575. Aug. 15th. Testator was "of the cytee of Bristoll vyntener," and desired to be buried "wthin the parish church of the holy Trynitee of Bristoll comonly called Christchurche;" also that at his burial there be made a sermon by Mr. Northbroke, or by some other "learned and discreete person," and "for the same sermon so to be made J geve xl^s." To son Benjamin Boydell £20. To son Giles Boydell £20 at the age of twenty-three. To son Robert Boidle £20 at the age of twenty-one. To sons Nicholas, Richard, William, and John Boydell £20 apiece at the age of twenty-one. To son Ralph Boidell £20 at the same age. To daughter Alice Boydell £40 at the same age, or when married. To daughter Elizabeth, wife to Christopher Wodward, one of testator's "stone Cuppes or cruses wth a cover of Sylver." To daughter Anne, wife to Richard Honye, "one other of my stone Cruses," &c. To son-in-law Richard Honie £20. To Mary Woodwarde, daughter of the said Christopher, £5 at the age of twenty-one; and £5 to her brother Richard Woodwarde at the same age. Wife Elizabeth to occupy testator's dwelling house "beinge now a Taverne and called by the name of the Horshedd scituate in Wynestreete in Bristowwe (sic) aforesaid;" also to have "the occupac'on" and profits of that tenement in "the Highe streete of Bristowe" in the occupation of William Newton, and lately in the tenure of Arthur Hamonde, for the term of sixty years, if she "doe so longe lyve;" and of the tenement in the occupation of William Yeman, the elder, in the same street; the said three messuages or tenements being held by two several leases, the one made to testator by David Harries, grocer, for forty-nine years, and ratified and confirmed by "the Deane and Chapter of the Cathedrall churche of the holly Trynitie of Bristowe lordes of the premisses;" the other, by the said dean and chapter for sixty years: son Benjamin to have the use, occupation, and profits of all three tenements after the death of wife Elizabeth. If the said Benjamin should decease before "the determinac'on" of the said terms of years, son Giles to succeed him. If all the sons should decease, then daughter Alice, &c. The said Benjamin, while holding the three tenements, to provide for his sister Alice, and, after her marriage, to pay her a yearly sum of twenty shillings: the holder of the said three tenements to be bound to the Mayor and Commonalty in the sum of £1000, to observe the leases, &c. Wife Elizabeth to have the residue, and be sole executrix. Mr. Richard Cole, Christopher Woodwarde, Edward Lewes, and John Dye, overseers, to whom five shillings apiece. Witnessed by Richard Honie, Giles Boydle, and John Dye.

No record of probate: but the will was proved Oct. 29th, 1575, as appears by the copy at Somerset House, *Pyckering*, 37.

Then follows a schedule of the wainscot, "sealinge worke," &c., in the tavern called the "Horsse hedd in Wynestreete." There was "a presse wth iiij^{or} romes to sett Tavern pottes vppon;" also "a seate of Drapery wth iij^e Cupbordes and lockes and keis to the same" for him or her that receiveth the money for the "wyne;" also "a glassewindlowe all glased," &c. The tenement in the High-street, "wherein Will'm Yeman' thelder nowe dwellethe," contained hall, parlor, kitchen; also the "Aller" in which there was "an oulde Cheste."

339.—JOHN STONE.

1575. June 24th. Testator was of the parish of Temple in "the citie of Bristowe," and desired to be buried in the church of that parish "in the north syde of the chancell by the northe wynde." To Mr. Northbrocke "to preache my ffuneraull Sermon x^s, yf he be at whome at that time," otherwise some other preacher "shall have yt to preache at my funeraull tenne shillinges." The sum of forty shillings unto the vicar of Temple, Sir Richard Barwycke. To "the Catheadraull churche of Saynete Augustines" iij^s iiij^d. To the poor people of the parish of Temple £3. To those of the city £5. To those of the city almshouses £5. Forty shillings unto "the poore prysoners" of Newgate. To John Freeman "my wyves dawghtors sonne" £20, after the said wife's decease. Sums of money also, after her decease, to the three children of Henry Stone, to Anthony son of William Stone, Thomas Appowell, William Oldbearye, Robert Wolforde's two children, and William "my boy." To John son of William Stone, after her decease, the fee simple of testator's dwelling house, and the drapery about the house, "withe the Brewhowse," &c.; also the mill, three horses, &c. If the said John should die under the age of twenty-one, or without lawful issue, rem. to Anthony Stone. If the said Anthony should so die, rem. to "the nexte of my kynne," namely, William Oldbearie, otherwise called Lamberd. To the same William Oldbearye, after wife Joan's decease, the house inhabited by Edward Buscon, "payeing therfore to the chamber of Bristow by theere xv^d." Legacies also to my mother-in-law M^{ris} Standbancke, men-servants, maid-servants, and Elizabeth Stone, widow. Wife Joan to have the residue, and be whole executrix. Mr. Anthony Standbancke and Edmund Robartes, overseers, to each of whom forty shillings. Witnessed by Richard Barrwyck, vicar of Temple, and Mr. Anthony Standbancke, with others.

Proved "in cur' p'rogativa," Aug. 1st, 1575.

340.—JOHN COTTRELL.

1575. Oct. 28th. Testator was "of the City of Bristoll march'unte," and desired that his body be buried "wheare it shall pleas my lorde god & Savioure Jhesus christe for the vppon the departure to Sea." To son James the sum of £200 "starling in monie" of the goods "wch J lefte in England;" also the lease of testator's dwelling house "in Chrestmas street in Bristoll," with all implements and furniture; but wife Alice to have the same house "vntill my sayed Sonne come to the ffull age, yff she do so longe lyve;" also to him "my Chayne of golde whiche J leafte at whom." To daughter Alice £200; also "my best dyamounte Gold rynge," &c. If God should "send the myniken and the domynycke of Bristoll well whome in

Saffetye then J do geve more vnto my Sonne James £300, my leas Chayne," &c. To daughter Katharine £50, &c.; also, after "the Save aryvaull of the said Shippes won hundreth pounde;" and £100 to daughter Alice. To every godchild "a noble A pese of Corraunte monney wch is vj^s viij^d." Legacies also to sisters Ydde Silvester and Joan Frye, brother Silvester, and the poor people of the almshouses in the Marsh and at Michael's hill. Wife Alice to have the residue of goods, lands, &c., and be executrix. Mr. Thomas Chester "of Bristoll Allderman," overseer, to whom "J do geve for a Token a gould rynge withe a torkes stone." Witnessed by Richard Barrett, Edward Morris, and Thomas Barnes.

No record of probate ; but the will was proved April 5th, 1576, as appears by the copy at Somerset House, *Carew*, 7.

341.—THOMAS ROBARTES, clothier.

1574. Sept. 7th. Testator was "of the parrishe of the Temple in the cytie of Bristoll," and desired to be buried in the church of that parish. The sum of £5 to the poor there ; and £5 to the poor of the city. Unto "the Tenne Almeshousses" ten shillings apiece. Unto "the mendinge of highe waies aboute Bristoll" £10. Forty shillings unto the prisoners of Newgate. To my mother Margaret Robertes £10. To "my suster Margaret Cee" £10; and £10 to each of her three children. Unto "myne Aunte Langeforde" and cousin Browne forty shillings apiece. Unto my servants, besides their wages, xiij^s iiij^d "a peece." To brother William Robartes "all suche debte as he owethe me." To brother Harry all that he oweth, as well for John Large as himself. Testator's apparel to be equally divided between his brother Edmund Robertes, Peter See, and Arthur See "his sonne." Wife Alsey to have the residue, and be sole executrix. Thomas Kyrklande, testator's "Brother Lawe," and Edmund Robartes, his brother, to be overseers, and have forty shillings apiece. Witnessed by Richard Barwick, "vickar of Temple," and John Barrons.

On Sept. 10th, 1574, additions were made to the will and testament : Sister See to have "one Chaine of goulde beinge in valew woorth iiij^{li};" and her two daughters xx^s apiece. To brother John Robartes "my golde rynge wth the seale of Armes." To Mary Robartes, brother Edmund's daughter, "one Portigewe of goulde." To William Cooke "one peece of goulde of xx^s." To the wife of brother John Robertes, and the wife of brother Edmund Robartes, xx^s apiece. Witnessed by Sir Richard Barrwick, vicar of Temple, and John Barons.

No record of probate ; but the will was proved Aug. 5th, 1575, as appears by the copy at Somerset House, *Pyckering*, 32.

342.—JOHN WHITE.

No date. Testator describes himself as "of the citie of Bristowe and of the p'yshe of the blessed Trynitie in the same Citie Showmaker and Inholder." To be buried within the church of the said parish. To Richard Howseman "oure Curate" iij^s iiij^d. To son Thomas the lease of a house ; testator's wife to enjoy it till he is twenty-one, giving him vj^s viiij^d "everee yeere" for the rent. If Thomas should die before that age, she is to "dispose" it to one or more of the children. The sum of £10 "to ffinde him at Scoole." To daughter Margaret £20 at the day of her marriage. To daughters Joyce, Joan, and Agnes, £10 apiece when married. If "my wief do mary agayne," she is to pay to "everie of them xx^{li} apece." John Rothell to have the best gown, and Thomas Nelmes the second gown. Wife Joan to have the residue, and be sole executrix. John Rothell and Thomas Nelmes overseers, to whom ten shillings apiece. Witnessed by the said John and Thomas, and Richard Howseman, " withe other more."

Proved before William Jones, doctor of laws, Nov. 11th, 1575.

343.—EDMOND JONES.

1573. Nov. 15th. Testator was of the city of Bristol, clothier, and willed that his body be "buryed as the Tabernacle of a Christian mans Soule in the parrishe churche yeard of Saincte Nich'as w^{thin} the said citie wheare my father and mother do lye." To "the vicarye" there, for tithes forgotten, vj^s. Wife Agnes to have, for her life, all the lands and tenements possessed by testator in fee simple " in the parrysshe of Saincte Mighill within the coun'tye of the citie of Bristowe ;" rem. to Edmond Jones, son of brother John Jones of the said city, draper, and to his legitimate heirs; the property to be enjoyed by the said Agnes without any suit or trouble on the part of the said John, and of Edmond and John, his sons; in default of issue, rem. to the said John Johnes *(sic)*, brother of the said Edmond, and his heirs, "vppon like condic'on above wrytten"; in def., rem. to William Jones, son of brother Thomas; in def, rem. to " my righte heires foren'more." Wife Agnes to have the use of the dwelling house upon the Back of the said city, during testator's term of years; if she should decease before the end of the term, rem. to the aforesaid " Edmond Jones the Sonne " during the rest of the said term. She is also to have the use and occupation of a "wonrek house," four tenements, and six gardens, and of all the houses held by lease "for terme of yeeres" of the demise of Henry Weston, esquire, situate in Bristow, " in a Streete theare called Rackly " within the parish of St. Nicholas ; also of two furnaces, &c., in that street ; rem. to the said John Jones, brother to the said Edmond, if she should decease before the end of the term or lease. To brother John Jones a great spruce table board, standing " in my Haull above " in the dwelling house ; also a standing cup with a cover of silver and double-gilt "wch was my fathers," on condition that wife Agnes is allowed peaceable occupation of all this legacy during " her naturall lief." To Roger Jones, son of brother John, a silver goblet parcel-gilt, weighing by estimation xvj oz., and two dozen silver spoons weighing eight oz. To my brother Thomas Cooke "a Cloke cloth" of the value of vj^s viij^d the yard. To Elizabeth and ——, daughters of the same Thomas, " and to everye of them v yardes of ffyne ffryse," of the price of xx pence the yard. To Nicholas Gaynsforde and Walter Dowle " a goulde ryng " apiece. To Jane Dixon, Joan Bonner, and Elizabeth Ingeman, daughters to brother Thomas Jones, " a Cassocke clothe " apiece. To John Jones, son of the said Thomas, " a gowne clothe of Sheepes colloure." Legacies also to Roger, Richard, and William, sons of the said Thomas Jones, John son of Thomas Cooke, Letice Dall, and " Luce " Gainsford. Wife Agnes to have the residue, and be sole executrix. Philip

Langley and George Badram overseers, to each of whom a gown cloth of the the value of xl^s, " or elles xl^s a peece in money at theyre ellection." Witnessed by Leonard Pope, George Badram, and Philip Langleye.

Proved " in cur' p'rogatina," April 7th, 1576.

344.—WILLIAM BODMAN, shipwright.

1575. Sept. 4th. Testator was of the parish of St. Stephen, in the city of Bristowe, and desired to be buried in the "churchiarde" of that parish. To the relief of the poor, sick, and needy there, vj^s viij^d. To "my fower Chilldren" £10 apiece. Unto "eu'ie of my p'ntices one pece of eu'y kinde of my Tooles." To John Warfourde "my best Jerkin and breeches Saving one." One suit of apparel to be bought for son John "that is in the marget." Twenty shillings to "Mathew my maide." The sum of £10, "that was the bequeaste of my ffather," to be paid to "my Systre Wellthiane or to her Assign'." Testator leaves " the purchase of Weste Weston" to his son Thomas, "to enioie it as his owne for it is his purchase." But wife Margaret to have the goods, household stuff, &c., there; also the rest of the goods in Bristowe, and be sole executrix. William Evance, of Weare, and Randall Wilbram overseers, to each of whom x^s. Witnessed by John Knighte, "ghostly counselor," John Fletcher, John Gryffith, mariner, John Whyte, and others.

Proved " in cur' p'rogativa," Dec. 5th, 1575.

345.—THOMAS FITTZ JEFFREIS, ironmonger. In the margin *Fitzieffrey*.

1575. Oct. 3rd. Testator was of the parish of St. Nicholas. His body "to thearthe." The sum of £5 to the poor of Bristoll, at the discretion of Mr. Northebroock, preacher, and Mr. Thomas Simondes, merchant. To William Willson, son of wife's first husband, one standing bed, &c. To Alice Mefflin, sister of the said William, a " bedsteede," &c., and xx^s in money. To wife's son Lewes Coston xx^s. To Alice Coston, her daughter, x^s : the legacies of the said Lewes and Alice to remain in the keeping of their mother Anne while they are under age. If they should both die, rem. to brother John Fittz Jeffrey, to whom also £10. To testator's sister, Robert Abbott's wife, dwelling " in Tesbury p'ish," £10. To Thomas Fittz Jeffrey, son of brother Edward, and Matthew Fytts' Jeffrey, " my Sister Elyzabethes Sonne," £10 apiece. Wife Anne Fittz Jeffreie to have the residue, and be executrix. Master John Northbroock, preacher, Thomas Symons, and Christopher Flower, supervisors. Witnessed by Mr. John Northebrock, William Thomas, Hugh Watkyns, Agnes Hailes, Jane Jones, and Lewes Coston. " By me Thoms' flittz Jeffreye."

Proved before William Jones, doctor of laws, Dec. 5th, 1575.

The register of the parish of St. Nicholas records the burial of Thomas *fcetsyefferis*, Oct. 6th, 1575.

346.—AMBROSE DAVIES.

1575. Aug. 28th. Testator was of " the Mydle Temple of the citie of London," and desired to be buried in the parish church of Temple (at Bristol). The sum of £5 unto the poor folks of that parish. To Richard Davies the fee simple of all testator's lands. If the said Richard should decease before the age of twenty-one, or otherwise without lawful issue, rem. to Katharine Davies. To the same Katharine the house inhabited by John Barro. To Richard Horner £10. To Davye Owldfielde £8. Alice Horner to have the best "ffetherbedd." Legacies also to Hugh Carroo, John James, and his wife, and Dorothy Bene. Richard and Katharine Davies to be executors, and enjoy the residue of the goods when twenty-one years of age. Sir Richard Barwick and Richard Horner to be overseers, and "see me honestly brought in yearthe." To the former xl[s]. Witnessed by David Ouldfielde, John James, Hugh Carowe, Sir Richard Barwick "vicker of Temple," and others.

Proved before Thomas Goodwyn, "sacre Theolog' professore," Sept. 6th, 1575.

The Temple parish register records the burial of Ambrose Davis, Sept. 1st, 1575; the letter "p" being opposite to the entry.

347.—JOHN ROWLAND.

No date. Testator's wife Elizabeth to have all his household stuff; also, on the safe arrival of all his adventures, amounting to £300 and upwards, "as by my boke of remembraunce appereth," she is to enjoy the one half, "howsoever yt fall out wth Losse or gaines;" and son Thomas the other half; on condition of their giving to testator's sisters, "Luce" and Agnes, twenty marks apiece, and to his father, Richard Rowland, £20. If wife Elizabeth should bear another child, and it "do come to age," it is to have £50 out of "his mothers & brothers porcion." If the said Elizabeth should marry again, uncle Mark Wardford is to take unto him the aforesaid Thomas, with his portion of goods, until he is twenty-one years of age, putting in "suffycient suerties." If "the child happen to dye" before that age, testator's father and mother to have the use of his goods, which are afterwards to remain equally to sisters "Luce" and Agnes. The best gown to brother Nicholas Langford; and to my sister Joan, his wife, "my ring wth the Turkey stone w[ch] J weare." To father-in-law John Langley "my ring of Jemolles"; and unto my mother-in-law "my bachelers salt being silver and guilt." To brother-in-law Thomas, their son, "my whistle w[ch] hath a Toothe Piker in him" both of silver and gilt. Legacies also to brother Richard Langley, sister-in-law Elianor Young, and William and Mark, children of uncle Mark Wardford. Testator leaves for overseers of this last will, to be accomplished according to his true meaning, Mr. George —, John Webb, father-in-law John Langley, and aforesaid uncle Mark, to whom xx[s] apiece. Witnessed by Marks Warford and Lewes Dawkin.

Proved "in cur' p'rogativa," May 18th, 1576.

348.—JOHN CURTIES.

1576. May 16th. Testator was "of the citie of Bristoll Cooke," and desired to be buried in the church of "all saintes otherwise called Alhallowes w[th]in the citie of Bristoll aforesaid, where my mother was buryed." The sum of twenty shillings for the poor on the day of burial. To son Thomas £24 when twenty-one years of age; wife Elizabeth to have the bringing up of him; also, to the said Thomas and his heirs, testator's dwelling house with all "drapery wayneskott glasse wyndowes," &c., after the said Elizabeth's death. If Thomas should decease s.p., rem. to daughter Margery and her heirs. The said Margery to have £24 "in the daye of her mariage"; also a whole "garnishe" of pewter vessels of the best sort, a "brasse crock," &c., and "one table bourde wth a frame standing over the Walters Jnne dore." Testator gives and bequeaths vj^s viij^d to "the M^r and Company of taylors w^thin the city of Bristoll for a token of remembraunce." To Joan Burchall "my maide" vj^s viij^d. To son Thomas "my golde ringe wth a seale in yt." Wife Elizabeth to be sole executrix, have the residue of goods, and possess and enjoy the messuage or tenement "for terme of her naturall liffe." Walter Davies, glover, and David Jones, innholder, to be overseers, and have xij^d apiece. Witnessed by Richard Langton, notary public, Julian Betham, Joan Burchall, William Hobbes, and others.

Proved before Felix Lewes "legu' doctore," June 8th, 1576.

349.—EDWARD PORTER, draper.

1577. April 12th. Testator was of "the cytee of Bristoll," and desired to be buried "in the crowde of St Nicholas at the staires foote there," bequeathing the sum of twenty shillings for repairing and mending "the staires there," to be paid to "the Proctors" of the parish "ymediatly after the same ys amended." The sum of £20 to "poore people" in the said city. To brother Simon Porter £10, to be paid yearly in sums of forty shillings at the feast of St. James the Apostle, until the said money be "truely contented & paied"; the said yearly payment to cease, if the said Simon should decease before any or all of the days of payment. To brother John Porter £10, to be paid in like manner. To Joan, Rose, William, and Margaret Porter, children of the said brother John, now and long before in testator's keeping, £400, equally divided; the said William to have his money at the age of twenty-six, and the others to have theirs at their marriage, or at the age of twenty, if not then married. Wife Elizabeth to have the occupation of £200 of that sum in the mean time, putting in good and sufficient sureties to "the father of Orphantes w^thin the said cytee"; the other £200 to be in the keeping of testator's overseers. The said Elizabeth to have the residue of goods, and be sole executrix. Brother-in-law Thomas Kelke "of the cytee of Bristow Alderman," Walter Pikes, Richard Cole, and Thomas Pytt, overseers. Witnessed by Thomas Kelke, Walter Pikes, Thomas Pytt, and George Baldwin.

Proved "in cur' p'rogativa," April 19th, 1577.

350.—JOHN HOLLAND, glover.

1575. Aug. 14th. Testator was of "the citye of Bristoll," and willed that his body be "buryed at the discretion of my Executrix." To son Harry, after the decease of wife Dorcas, and to his heirs for ever, the garden "att Stony Hyll"; the forepart of the house which was one Murcock's tenement, "viz all the yeres vnexpyred in the same"; "my Bedd that J Lye on," &c.; and also, after "my mothers deathe," the house in Conway; and all the goods bequeathed to testator by his father. In default of issue, the said house in Conway to remain to Hugh Thomas, "my sustors sonne," and his heirs; in def., rem. to "my syster" and her heirs for ever. To daughter Alice the second bed in the forechamber, five silver spoons, "my greate crock," &c. ; also all the years unexpired in the whole house inhabited by Kerry. To brother Sir Harry Holland " my best gowne faced wth boudge." To Hugh Browne " my Chamlett bretches & the mouldes & also a cassock silke grograine," being in the house of Nicholas Rice, tailor. Legacies also to Justinian Elston, James Thomas, Robert Sadler, and Roger Rice " p'son." Wife Dorcas to have the residue, and be sole executrix "yf so be that she shall recover of this her Sicknes." If she should die, testator's two children to be executors : and if they also " do decease of this Sicknes," then Hugh Thomas, Katharine Taylor, and testator's two "systrein in Law," Margaret and Charity Greneway, to be executors. Sir Humphrey Brickdall, Justinian Elston, and Hugh Browne, smith, to be overseers, and each to have xij^d. Witnessed by John Yeroth the younger, Justinian Elston, Robert Sadler, James Thomas, and the aforesaid Roger Rice.

Proved " in Cur' prerogativa," Oct. 24th, 1575.

The register of the parish of St. John records the burial of John Holland, Aug. 15th, 1575 ; also the baptism of his son Henry, Oct. 11th, 1572, and of his daughter Alice, April 7th, 1574.

351.—JOHN HOLLYSTER. In the margin *Hollaster*.

1575. July 29th. Testator was " of the citie of Bristoll Marchaunt." His body " to the yearth wherehence yt came." To the Chamber of Bristoll £10, to be " ymployed in woode att the key at every springe of the yere," to serve the poor of the city in winter, they paying no more for it than what it cost, " whereby my Tenne poundes may remayne wholy contynually to that vse." To Edith Hollyster, testator's daughter, his lands in Congresbury, after her mother's death, "contayninge by Estimac'on lxj acres & halfe," the gift of his father-in-law John Iryshe ; also £20, given her by the will of her grandfather, the said John ; and a further sum of £20, which " J do geve her in reddy money." To daughter Annis Hollister £40 ; also, after her mother's death, the fee simple of two tenements, bought of Mr. Henry Doddington, one being in Cornestreete, and occupied by testator, the other inhabited by Samuel Gough, skinner. To daughter Mary Hollister, the lease of the half of Thomas Hollister's windmill ; also the lease of a house in Cornestreete inhabited by William Cutt, merchant ; and the adventure " wch J have wth me in the Prymrose for the Matheras (?) wth that wch J have lyeing there allreaddy wch is litle more or lesse of a Hundred and Twenty poundes as by my booke shall appere." Wife Joyce to have the residue, and be executrix. If daughter Annis should die s.p., daughter Mary to have the two tenements ; and the £40 to be parted between the other daughters. If all should die before marriage, wife Joyce to take their portions, and the " heire of my Bodye " to have the lands. To daughter Annis " all my Boordes " at brother Richard Hollester's at Westerley, with all those " in my house," to help her " to Buylde in Bristoll." Thomas Symons " thelder m'chaunt," William Seman, Willliam Avery, Thomas Hollester, and brother Richard Hollester be to overseers, and have xx^s apiece.

Proved " in Cur' prerogativa," July 29th, 1577.

352.—EDWARD FRENCHE, grocer.

1577. July 27th. Testator was "of the citye of Bristoll," and desired to be buried in the parish church of St. Thomas there. The sum of twenty shillings to the poor of the said parish. Forty shillings yearly unto "my mother." To sons Toby and Richard £60 apiece at the age of twenty-four. To daughter Katharine £60 at the day of her marriage. Testator forgives all the debts of his brother-in-law Humphrey Griste; and bequeaths twenty shillings to each of the three children of the said Humphrey "by my suster," to be paid when they are twenty-one years of age. He also forgives his brother Thomas Frenche £5 of the debt of £17; and gives ten shillings to each of the said Thomas's three children. Wife Anne to have the residue, and be executrix. Richard Fuller of Exbridge, co. Somerset, and Thomas Tagg, overseers. Witnessed by George Baldwyn, John Alkyn, and Buckforde (sic).

Proved "in Cur' p'rogat'," Aug. 22nd, 1577.

353.—ROGER ADDAMS.

1562 (?). March 15th. Testator was a soapmaker "of the citye of Bristoll," and desired to be buried in "the churche of St Tewens." To son Nicholas, when twenty-one years old, the house "wth all the implementes as J bought yt in Broadestrete whereiin dwelleth nowe Grace Borry widowe"; also £10, the furnace, &c. Wife Joan to have the use of the said furnace, on allowing the said Nicholas £7. To daughters Mary, Elizabeth, and Agnes Addams £10 apiece; also to "the childe wch my wife goeth wth all" £10; to be "d'd vnto them" at the day of their marriage. If the expected one should be a "manchilde," he is to have his portion at the age of twenty-one. If any should happen to die before marriage, sister Elizabeth Addams to have £5 out of that portion; the rest of the money to be divided equally among the remaining daughters. If they should all die before marriage, and a "manchilde" should survive, he is to enjoy one half of the premises with his brother Nicholas. If all the legitimate sons and daughters should die before their lawful age, wife Joan to have the house, and one half of their bequests; and Richard Mydleton, son of brother-in-law James Mydleton, to have the other half. Legacies to the said James, and sister Elizabeth Addams. Wife Joan to have the residue, and be sole executrix. My "lovinge gossipp James Dowle" and James Mydleton to be overseers. To James Dowle "my Bow wth my Quyver and all my shaftes."

No record of probate. A note states—"Concordat cum Reg'ro Walter Gliston." The register of the parish St. Ewen records the baptism of Nicholas son of Roger Adams, March 14th, 1554, and the burial of Roger Adimse (or Admise?), June 12th, 1564.

354.—GILES HOBBES, vintner.

1575. Nov. 26th. Testator's body to the "yearthe" from whence it came. To his sister Anne Pepwall £40 in money, and his best gold ring. To brother Thomas £40, which he oweth testator upon an obligation; also "one golde Ringe wth a dyamond stone wch he hathe allreddy of mine." To Jane Hobbes, daughter of the said Thomas, "one payre of Virgynalles." To Mrs. Maud Moore, testator's mother, £10. To Mr. Moore, his father-in-law, all right, title, term, and interest yet to come in "the Bargaine wch J have in East Brynte," with £11 rent due from John Bysse for that bargain; also £5 due from Wall for rent. Unto "myne vnckle and Auntc," Peter See and his wife, £20, &c. The sum of forty shillings towards "the maynten'nce and rep'ac'ons of my parrishe churche called St Mary Porte;" twenty shillings to Mr. Wade "to make merry amongest the parrishners" there; and twenty shillings to the poor of the said parish. The sum of £5 to "the poore of the citye of Bristoll," to be distributed by the hands of Mr. Northbroke. Frise gowns and cassocks, and "eight kerchers" unto eight poor men, and eight poor women, who are to accompany testator's corpse to the grave. To "my brother Michell Pepwall," and his wife, a mourning gown and a mourning cassock. To Mr. Michael Pepwall "sheryff" the best gold ring "sauinge one." To "the mendinge of Bryntm'sshes Cawsey" xl^s. To "the Taylors haull" vj^s viij^d. Legacies also to Arthur, Anne, and Mary See, George Higgins the younger, son of Mr. George Higgins, John Cecill, Michael Gadburye "my Boye," maid-servent Emlyn Borrage, and servants Joan Cecyll, Alice Borrage, Thomas Hydden, and Agnes. Brother Nicholas Hobbes to have the residue, and be sole executor. Mr. Michael Pepwall and Mr. John Wade overseers. Witnessed by Mr. John Northebrock, preacher, and John Harris, with divers others.

Proved "in Cur' prerogat'," Nov. 24th, 1576.

The register of the parish of St. Mary-le-Port records the burial of this testator; also of Mr. Nicholas Hobbes "of ye Raven," Oct. 17th, 1594, and of Giles Hobbes, "slayne in fight," Aug. 3rd, 1611.

355.—THOMAS WARDEN.

1579. Aug. 10th. Testator was "of the City of Bristoll marchaunte," and desired to be buried in St. Werburgh's church. To sons Thomas and Nicholas £300, "lying in Maister Carrs hands." To daughters Mary and Elizabeth £100 apiece. To wife Joan £100, and all the household stuff. Thomas Aldworth and son-in-law Erasmus Write to be executors. Witnessed by Thomas Aldwourth and Robert Pressye.

Proved "in Curia p'rogativa," Sept. 11th, 1579.

356.—JOHN CHAMBERS, tailor.

1580. Sept. 20th. Testator was "of the Cyty of Bristow," and desired to be buried in "the Crowde of Sainct Nich'as Parrishe church." Three shillings and four pence to "the poore." To eldest son Dominick "a dossen of postle spoones at the price of five poundes wch yf they way more, the ou'plus J will to remaine to the vse of my wief Alice." To second son Thomas £4. To third son John the bill of £5 due from Master John Bradstone of Winterbourne. To fourth son William £5. To daughter Alice £5, if she come to age to enjoy the same; if not, two of "her bretheren," William and Thomas, to share that sum equally, if they survive her. The sum of £5 to "the childe vnborne, wherwth my wief now goith be yt boy or maide." Wife Alice to have the residue, and be sole executrix. Mr. William Hopkins and brother William Chambers overseers. Witnessed by George Harris, clerk, William Hopkins, and William Chambers.

Proved Oct. 13th, " mill'mo quingentesimo septuagesimo octogesimo."
The register of the parish of St. Nicholas records the marriage of John
Chameres and Alice Morgan, Nov. 23rd, 1561 ; the burial of Morgan Harris,
Aug. 2nd, 1580 ; and the burial of John Chambers, Sept. 23rd, 1580.

357.—MORGAN HARRIS.

1580. July 29th. Testator was of the parish St. Nicholas "the
confesser," within " the dioc' of the cyty of Bristoll," and desired to be
buried in the crowde of St. Nicholas. To wife Elizabeth thirteen horses
"wth chaines bedstalls dreyes," &c.; also, for her life, the dwelling house
on the Back, with " the forehowse " inhabited by John Eaton, and the shop
under the same ; and all testator's lands in Bristoll ; rem. to his brother
William Harris ; and all his lands in Wales, the rent thereof being " her
ioincture." To the eldest son of brother William one standing bedstead, &c.
To Katharine, testator's mother, one chamber within his said dwelling
house, already occupied by her ; also xx^s, and "meate and drinck during
her lief." Ten shillings to "the Master and fellowshipp of the bakers of
the city of Bristoll." Wife Elizabeth to be executrix. John Henry and
William Vawer overseers.

Proved " in Cur' prerogatiua," Sept. 12th, 1579 *(sic)*.

358.—JOHN DRAPER, the elder.

1578. Jan. 27th. Testator was "of the cyty of Bristoll marchaunt,"
and desired to be buried in St. John's church. To "a precher to exhorte
the people in gods word at my buriall " vj^s viij^d. To son John Draper, and
his legitimate heirs, the "howse in Brodstreete " inhabited by Thomas
Wall ; also a garden in Grope lane ; and three gardens " on Michaell hill,"
two of them, with a lodge in one, being held by John Caro, and the third
by Philip Browne ; wife Anne to have the property for her life. To cousin
Richard Weaver, of Worcester, iij^s iiij^d. To William Browne £4, besides
the twenty shillings due to him when eighteen years of age. Forty shillings
to " poore people." Legacies also to " my maide" Alice Browne, my two
maid-servants, and the parson of St. John's. Wife Anne and son John to
have the residue, and be executors. Richard Langford and John Henry
overseers, to whom x^s apiece. Sealed July 6th, 1579. Witnessed by Thomas
Price, notary public, John Henry, notary public, and Roger Rice, rector of
the church of St. John Baptist.

Proved " in Cur' prerogatiua," Sept. 23rd, 1579.

359.—NICHOLAS CUTT, of the city of Bristol, merchant.

This will is dated " in the three and twentith yeere of the raigne of
oure Soueraigne Ladie Elizabeth," Feb. 21st. My body "to the earth
from whence yt came." All lands, tenements, &c., to wife Bridget and to
her heirs and assigns for ever. The sum of £5 to the poor people within
the city. Wife Bridget to have the residue, and be sole executrix. Father-
in-law Mr. Robert Saxey and Edward Morris, merchant, to be overseers.
Witnessed by Robert Saxey, William Saxey, William Hickes, John Robertes,
John Willett, and Edward Morris.

Proved " in Curia p'rogatiua," May 2nd, 1580 *(sic)*.

The register of the parish of St. Nicholas records the burial of Nicholas
Cutte, March 31st, 1581.

360.—NICHOLAS WILLIAMS.

1565. Sept. 1st. Testator describes himself as "of the citie of Bristowe Tailor and late Maio^r of the same citie," and desires to be buried "in the p'ishe (sic) of Saint Marie port of Bristoll." To Mr. Eiton, preacher, "for his good & godlie adu'tisement & counsell x^s praying him to make my funerall sermon." To wife Joan, for her life, the house called "the Crowne," inhabited by Katharine Wight, widow, "in St Marie port strete;" rem. to son Rowland and his legitimate heirs; in def., rem. to son Edward and his legitimate heirs; in def., rem. to "my cosen John White sonne of my brother Thomas White" and his legitimate heirs. To son Rowland £10 at the age of twenty-four. Wife Joan to enjoy the lenses during her life; rem. to son Edward: but the leases and interest of and in a tenement in the street aforesaid, in the tenure of William Grigg, tailor, and held by testator of the Chamber of Bristowe, and also of and in the tenement called "the Swanne" in the tenure of George Graye, in the same street, to remain to "the M^r & company of the occupac'on of Tailors wthin the same Cytie." If son Edward should die before the expiration of the leases and interest to him bequeathed, rem. to son Rowland; if Rowland should die, rem. to all the children of brother Thomas White, saving the lease of "my howse called the bore hedd being in the highstrete wch lease J geve & bequeath to my Cosen Richard Newman bocho^r after the decesse of my wief And my sonne Rowland and Edward if then the same lease or any p't thereof be vndet'myned & vnexpired." To the said Edward "my Nest of gobletts' wth their cover wch cost me xxxv^{li}," half a dozen of silver spoons, and £10 at the age of twenty-four. Testator forgives and releases to Richard Langton, notary, twelve shillings "p'cell of iiij^{li} xij^s wch he oweth me." To the said Richard Newman "my worken day gowne that J ware the last som'." To George Graye the gown worn by testator "in the wynter vppon workin daies." To David Martyn "my cloke dressed wth lace about the coller." To sister Joan White six yards and a half "of Welsh frise." To Agnes Marten six yards of frise; and testator wills that vj^s viij^d be abated yearly to her, during her life, of the rent paid by her for his house wherein she dwelleth. Twenty shillings to "the poore people in Bristoll." Legacies also to late servant Nicholas Robins, cousin John White, Thomas Jones, tailor, John Rockwell, Jenkyn Dye, and Joan Haynes. My "welbeloved wief" Joan to have the residue, and be executrix. Mr. John Woode, "vpholster," and Hugh Draper, vintner, to be overseers, and have xx^s apiece.

Proved before John Cottrell, doctor of laws, Sept. 12th, 1565.

361.—WILLIAM YEMAN.

1580. Nov. 14th. Testator was "of the cityc of Bristowe," and desired to be buried in the church of All Saints. To Mr. Haslyn, the vicar there, iij^s iiij^d; and to a preacher "at my buryall" vj^s viij^d. Six poor men to have "vj gownes of black frise" at the burial. To son William Yeman two goblets of silver parcel-gilt, &c.; also six silver spoons "wth postle heddes," weighing xj oz. iij qrs.; the best ring of gold "wth a seale in him"; twelve "voyders"; a "Custerd coffyn," a pair of dogs, &c. To Susan Yeman, at the day of her marriage, £3. 6. 8; also the best coverlet, &c. The same amount to her sister Mary Yeman, at her day of marriage; also "the frame bedd" in the fore chamber, &c. To Joan Hunt, testator's daughter, £6. 13. 4 ; also six silver spoons "wth flatt heddes"; the hanging of the parlor "of fine red saie & grene the borders of the storie of Elias "; the " Jland coffer and the busse chest in the Alarie .... a large loking glasse .... a fier slice a paire of pott hookes a rack to hange crooks' .... a blanckett of wedmole," &c. To Joan, daughter of Edward Evenet, £3. 6. 8, to be paid at her day of marriage; also "a Crock a litle skillett," &c. The same amount to Florence Evenet, her sister, at the day of marriage ; also " a payneted panne," &c. The same amount to Alice Evenet, their sister, when married ; also three platters, two pottengers, &c. Twenty shillings to Joan, daughter of John Yeman, shoemaker, at her marriage ; also a crock, a pan, &c., and " the paynted clothes in my baft chamber The hanging of the p'lor of all saye red & grene and the borders of the storie of grisell." The same amount to her sister Annis Yeman at her marriage ; also a crock, &c. The same amount to Grace Yeman, their sister in Cardiff, at her marriage. If the said Grace should die before " the daye of her Mariage," her legacy of xx^s is to be bestowed upon the town walls. Twenty shillings to cousin Joan, daughter of Stephen Tanner, "at her daie of Mariage" : if she should die before that day, the said money is to be bestowed " vppon the rep'ac'ons of the Towne walls' in Cardiffe." Legacies also to Agnes, daughter of Arthur Yeman in Cardiff, at her marriage ; and each of her sisters, Mary and Joan Yeman, in like manner. Son William to have the residue, and be executor. Testator adds the names of his well beloved in Christ, Mr. Thomas Colston and Thomas Fawkett, who are apparently to act as overseers.

Proved before Felix Lewis, doctor of laws, Jan. 7th, 1580.

362.—RICHARD LANGFORD, merchant.

1580. Nov. 18th. Testator was of the parish of St. Stephen, and desired to be buried in the church there, "as nere my doughter as it conveniently maye be." The sum of twenty shillings towards the marriage of " poore maides " in that parish ; and twenty shillings to poor people in Bristowe. To Elizabeth, wife of testator, £500. To his five children £1000, to be equally divided, and paid to them at the age of twenty-one, or when married. To brother Ellis Langford £10. To sister Elizabeth Langford £20, of which she is to enjoy the profit and increase during her life ; rem. to the executors. To brother Edmond Langford £8 : to his child, testator's goddaughter, forty shillings. To brother Richard Bailieff's children £10, whereof " my godson " shall have forty shillings. To brother Thomas Langford's children £10. To Henry Robertes "my gimmoll ringe." Legacies also to brothers Walter and William Langford, and the poor in Ludlow. Testator forgives his sister Partridge all that may be due at his death. Residue of goods, leases, money, plate, &c., to the executors, namely, wife Elizabeth, and son Richard Langford. "Mr Thomas Slocumbe nowe Maio^r of Bristowe my father in Lawe Mr John Robertes," Mr Robert Kitchin, and brother Charles Langford to be overseers, and have forty shillings apiece. Witnessed by Thomas Pryn, notary public, Henry Robertes, and Thomas Langford.

Proved before William Drury, doctor of laws, Dec. 2nd, 1580.

363.—THOMAS COXE, citizen and merchant of Bristol.

1580. Feb. 8th. To be buried "at the discreac'on of my executor." Thomas Callohill, citizen and apothecary of Bristowe, and John Bollton, citizen and goldsmith there, to be overseers, and have £4 apiece. Brother William Coxe to be executor, and have £60, and all testator's books, weapons, and apparel. To Thomas Coxe, son of the said William, £6 towards "his schoole" and maintenance in Christian religion, "as J a bonnde beinge his godfather:" the said Thomas to be placed with a teacher who is free from "papiste or Annabaptiste" notions, and believes in the sufficiency of the "workes and merites" of Christ "wthout Trentalls or any other Sacrelege." If this son of the said William should die, rem. to "the nexte childe of his bodye." To brother-in-law's second daughter, Elizabeth Callowhill, twenty marks at her day of marriage; the money to be put meanwhile in "the chambers handes," or other assured person, who is to pay towards the young maid's expenses after the rate of "Seven in the hundred for the yere." To Christopher and Philip Callowhill, "my brother lawes seconnde and thirde boyes," twenty nobles apiece "towardes their meynten'nce to schoole:" if either of them should die, his children Thomas and Constance Callowhill to have the money. To Matthew Coxe, "remayninge in my brother lawes house," £5 to maintain him in some good service, "for that he is an Jnnocente." To sister Elizabeth, wife of Thomas Callowhill, "A broken whistle wch wayeth three ownces," &c. Residue "vnto the godly poore people of the worlde, as also some parte thereof to be distributed vnto poore marryners for their meynten'nce and reliefe of suche that hathe by me hurte or meyned *(sic)* in the defense of the merchaunte and his gooddes."

Proved "in Curia prerogatiua," Sept. 25th, 1581.

364.—JOHN PREWETT, the elder.

1579. Aug. 14th. Testator was of the parish of St. James "wthin the subburb of the Citie of Bristowe," and desired to be buried in the churchyard there, hard by his wife. To "Sr Jones," minister of that parish, xx^s. To the mother church of the city of Bristowe ij^s vj^d. Twelve poor men and twelve poor women of the aforesaid parish to have gowns of frise, and £5 in money or bread. To wife Ellyn £50; also all the plate that she brought "vnto me," full and whole, &c. To son John Prewett, the lease of the dwelling house; rem. to his son Arthur, if he should decease before the end of the lease; also the lease of "my lesowe wth the ragg" held of the hospital at Lafford gate; rem. to Anthony, son of the said John; also the interest and term of years in a stable held "wthin the black friers," and in a lane called "Erlesmeade lane," with both the leases concerning the same. To the same John "my Synett & gold ring wch J were," testator's name being graven thereupon; also two presses, &c., and "fower diker of Rawe leather." To son William Prewett, the use of the best new coverlet, as long as he liveth; rem. to my said son John and Antffony his son; three of the best gowns, and my ring that hath the white stone in it; also the lease of two tenements, with all the woods belonging to them "at Hannam," held of "my lord Barkley." To daughter Margaret Tilor the lease held of Cornish Laighton "the bocher;" rem. to her son Ralph Scalter, if she should decease before the expiration of the lease, and to William Scalter, if Ralph should decease. To William Scalter and Joan Tilor, children of the said Margaret, twenty nobles apiece. To daughter Charity Cory, for her life, the two tenements bought of William Cooper; rem. to her daughter Margaret Cory and her heirs: the said Margaret to have twenty nobles at the age of sixteen. To William Cory, son of the said Charity, twenty nobles at the age of eighteen. Son William to be sole executor, and have all the plate, and the rest of the leather of "my Tanne howse." Mr John Browne, alderman, and "my loving kynsman" John Sayer of Banwell to be overseers, and have xx^s apiece. Witnessed by Richard Clark, John Clark, and Thomas Prin, notary public.

"Probatum fuit hoc testamentu' Coram Phillippo Langley Maiore in Guyhald Bristoll'," Oct. 28th, 1581.

365.—ROGER DEER. In the margin "Jhon Deere."

No date. To be buried in the churchyard of Temple, "by my neighbour John Clark." Wife Katharine to be sole executrix. To sons Henry, John, and William, twenty shillings apiece at their day of marriage or age of twenty-four. To son William, after his mother's decease, "my howse and lease"; rem. to son John Deer, if William should die s p. To son-in-law William Dane and daughter Maud Dere (sic) a broad loom, standing in the south side of "my shoppe next to Thomas Tippers howse;" also "one osset loome," two flowerpots, &c. To wife Katharine "my howse called the beer howse," with the lease thereof, at Temple gate; to go, after her decease, to "that childe wch she shall think best of."

Proved before Felix Lewes, doctor of laws, Dec. 5th, 1578.

366.—ANTHONY ROBYNS, merchant.

1581. Aug. 13th. Testator was of "the Cytie of Bristowe," and desired to be buried in St. Ewen's church. To daughter Anne £300; of which sum £100 to be delivered to Mr Michael Pepwall, with the said Anne, for her use; he to keep her, and have her "broughte vppe in Lerninge wth the said hundreth poundes till her age of one and twentye yeres or daye of Marriadge:" the other £200 to remain with the overseers, and be paid to her at the said appointed time. If she should die first, £100 to remain to "my nexte of Kynne," and £200 to wife Grace, if then living. To Alice Wadley £10; also the lease of a garden in St. Mark's lane, held of "the Chamber of Bristoll;" but the said Grace to hold it "all the yeres yf she Lyve soe longe." To each of the four children of Thomas Ryder £4. To brother and sister Mericke forty shillings apiece. To godson Anthony Crewe £5. To the use of "the poore people in the Almeshouse in ye Mershe" £5, the profits to be delivered to them yearly. Legacies also to wife's goddaughter Anne Crewe, Margaret Ryder, Mr Michael Pepwell and his wife, the writer of this will and testament, "my Maide," and three other "poore maydes," Joan Syllyvaunt, and sister's son Richard Lea. Wife Grace to be sole executrix, and have the residue of goods, and also "houlde and enioye the house J nowe dwell in duringe her liefe." Father-in-law Thomas Eddye and Thomas Ryder overseers, to whom forty shillings apiece. Witnessed by John Mericke, Thomas Eddye, Thomas Ryder, and Edward Lane.

Proved "in Cur' prerogatiua," Nov. 8th, 1581.

367.—THOMAS LAWRENCE.

1581. Jan. 11th. His body "to the yearthe." To daughter Elizabeth £20 when married. To brother Richard Lawrence twenty shillings. Wife Jane to have the residue, and be sole executrix. William Lawrence and Richard Stones overseers. Witnessed by Dyricke Dyrrickeson, George Langton, John Johns, Rice (Richard ?) Arther, with others. "M^d J geve vnto my daughter Elizabeth one standinge bedsteade and a spruce Cheaste"—Aug. 1st, 1582.

Proved before John Sprinte, S.T.P., and Felix Lewys, doctor of laws, "in Cur' Consistor' Bristoll."

The register of the parish of St. Mary-le-Port records the burial of Thomas *Lavrence*, tailor, Jan. 6th, 1582.

368.—DAVID HARRIS, grocer.

1582. Oct. 4th. Testator was "of the Citie of Bristowe Alderman," and desired to be buried in the crowde of St. Nicholas, where his father and first wife lay, "yf J dep'te in Bristoll or wthin one and Twenty myles of Bristowe." To wife Margaret a yearly rent of £26. 13. 4. out of all my lands and tenements, during "her widowhed." If she should marry, the profit of the said annuity to remain to son David Harris and his children, and my daughter Alice and her children, "ioyntly and equally." To the said Margaret and David the dwelling house "indifferently to vse betwixt them ;" but daughter Alice and her husband may, if they please, have and dwell in "a third p'te of the howse :" the fee simple to remain at length to son David and his heirs. To the said Margaret and David the profit of all the leases "for terme of yeres," equally between them ; the residue to remain to son David and his heirs. He is also to have "my Shoppe of my said howse" with the implements, paying the said Margaret during "her widowhed" £5 quarterly ; also the lower great ground in Froglane "during my terme of yeres yet to come ;" my ring "wth the Turcas," and all "my bookes of Phisick." To the said Margaret "the greate downe bedde in the greate Chamber," &c. To daughter Alice and her legitimate heirs a house "in Tuckar streate," in the tenure of the goodwife Apprice ; also seven other tenements in the tenure of Richard Shoile, Richard Jenkins, William Ricartes, Edward Hoskins, the goodwife Sutton, Mr Blake, and the goodwife Apparry ; also a stable in the tenure of Mistress Higgins, and a pavement or yard in the tenure of Morris Aprotherowe. To son John Harris tenement in Lewens mead. To son George the higher orchard in Froglane "during my yeres." To daughter Alice 100 oz. of such plate as hath not "the grocers armes ;" also my ring "wth the fflower of diamondes." If she and her heirs should decease s.p., the abovesaid property to remain to son David and his legitimate heirs. If David should die s.p., the lands held in fee simple, and given to him, to remain to daughter Alice and her legitimate heirs. The said David and son-in-law Ralph Bennett to be full executors. The former to have the residue of lands and tenements ; also "the Salt wth the Christall and the nest of gobletts' wth the ffecte of Griffins and their Cover." To servant Robert Reckcliffe £4 ; "my Riding cloke," &c. Residue of goods to be divided equally between wife Margaret, son David, and daughter Alice. Mr Standback and Mr Walter Pikes overseers: to the latter a gown; to the former a mourning gown. Witnessed by David Harris, Ralph Bennett, Alice Bennet *alias* Harris, Robert Reckcliffe, Anthony Standback, and Margaret Harris.

Proved " in Cur' p'rogativa," Nov. 20th, 1582.

369.—THOMAS KELKE, merchant and alderman.

1583. June 10th. To be buried in the church of the parish where God shall call him out of this world. To Thomas Kelke, son to testator's son Richard, £400. If he should die under the age of twenty-one, rem. to his father Richard. The said Richard to have and enjoy £200 "in his keepinge," and to disburse to the poor "at the daie of my buriall," or very shortly afterwards, the sum of £10, and the same sum yearly "for the space of xx^{tie} yeres next co'minge." To sister Kelke of London, late wife to " my brother Joⁿ Kelke deceased," and to her children, £20. To the poor in the city of Bristowe £10. To the poor prisoners of Newgate £13. To each of twenty-four poor people, twelve of whom to be women, "a fryse Gowne esteemed at xij^{li}." Fifty-two poor maidens to have vj^s viij^d each, to their marriage. To Richard Kelke's other three children, viz., John, Anne, and ———, vj^{li} xiij^s iiij^d apiece. To each servant dwelling with testator at his death xx^s. To his sister, Clement's wife, sister Cutt, and sister Garrett, each a ring of gold, worth xl^s. The sum of £10 for " the rep'ac'ons of the Cunditts' in Bristowe;" and the same amount towards repairing the highways about the city. Son Richard Kelke to be sole executor, and have the use and profits of all testator's lands, &c.; rem. to Thomas, son of the said Richard, and to his legitimate heirs; in def., rem. to the heirs of "Joⁿ Kelke my brother deceased in London;" in def., rem. to "the next of bloode." Brother Clement Kelke, "my frinde John Henry," and Mr. Thomas Aldworth, overseers, to each of whom xl^s. Testator bequeaths £20 for a stock of money, to remain for ever "in the howse of correction within the Citie of Bristoll," for the maintenance and "settinge of work of such people as shalbe therevnto co'mitted for their mysdemeanors." Read and published Sept. 2nd, 1583.

> Oh Lord into thy handes I do comitt
> my sowle wch is thye dewe
> ffor why thowe hast redeemed it
> my Lord & god most trewe.

By me Thomas Kelke. Witnessed by John Henry, Robert Temple, and Thomas Aldworth, Mayor.

Proved Sept. 24th, 1583.

370.—WILLIAM PILL, grocer.

1582. April 7th. Testator was of "the Citie of Bristowe," and desired to be buried in the church of All Hallows, "as neere my Pewe as may be." The sum of vj^s viij^d for "a Sermond at my buriall." Twelve "gownes of ffrize" to be ready against that time for twelve poor people; and twenty shillings "in bred" to the poor. To son Anthony and his lawful "heires males" my dwelling house in "the High streate of the same Citie;" in def., rem. to son Nicholas and his lawful heirs male; in def., rem. to William Pill, my brother's eldest son, and his lawful heirs male; in def., rem. to Humphrey Pill, "my brothers sonne," and his lawful heirs male ; in def., rem. to William Pill, my brother's youngest son. To the aforesaid Anthony and his heirs all other lands, and all goods, jewels, plate, &c. Wife Jane to have, during her life, the back chamber "w^{th}in my dwellinge howse," and bedding, &c., for herself and a maid-servant : the said Anthony to suffer her to have also the use of half the garden in "the Pythey," and to pay her ten shillings yearly for the rent of "my howse at Bewdley ;" also twenty shillings every quarter of a year ; and to find her and her servant meat and drink convenient, and make her a black gown "agaynst my buriall." Son Anthony to pay son Nicholas £50, and make him a black gown ; also to give and deliver unto son-in-law John Warde "my Signett," and to daughter Margery "one Silver standinge Cuppe gilt wth a Cover," and to either of them a black gown. To brother Richard a pair of breeches, and "drawers vppon them," a "felt hatte," &c. To William Pill "my brothers youngest Sonne" £10 at the age of twenty-six. Twenty shillings to Richard Cap', servant of son Anthony, "at thende of his App'ntishoode." Legacies also to William Pill, my brother's eldest son, Humphrey Pill, my brother's son, my two maid-servants, and "the company of poyntemakers." Son Anthony to be sole executor. Witnessed by Bartholomew Chappell, Richard Edwardes, and Edward Hollester.

Proved Sept. 6th, 1582.

371.—ROBERT PRESTON.

1583 (sic). Jan. 8th. Testator describes himself as "of the City of Bristoll taylor," and desires to be buried "in the p'ishe Churche of Christe churche." All his plate to be sold, and the proceeds divided equally between his wife and son Robert : the latter to have certain furniture, and also, after her decease, the lease of the dwelling house. Wife "Roes" to have the residue, and be sole executrix. Mr. Ralph Dole and Thomas Aldworth overseers. Witnessed by Ralph Dole, Thomas Aldworth, and John Grygge.

Proved before Thomas Knowles, master of arts, exercising spiritual and ecclesiastical jurisdiction throughout the whole city and deanery of Bristoll, March 6th, 1582.

The register of the parish of Christ Church records the burial of Robert *Presson*, tailor, Jan. 12th, 1582.

372.—JOHN AWSTE, baker.

1583. July 15th. Testator was of "the p'ishe of St Peters w^{th}in the Cityc of Bristoll," and desired to be buried in the churchyard there. To wife Mary the lease of three houses ; rem. equally to my three children Robert, William, and Elizabeth Awste, now under the age of twenty-one. To eldest son Robert £5. The sum of £10 to daughter Elizabeth, when married. To the poor people of this city "xx dozen of breade." Twenty shillings to brother William Awste "twoe yeres after my funerall." To sisters Agnes, Dorothy, and Alice, twenty shillings apiece. Ten shillings towards the maintenance of the bakers' hall. Wife Mary to have the residue, and be sole executrix. Thomas Poole and William Wyett overseers, to each of whom xx^s. Witnessed by Humphrey Mosely, parson of St. Peter's, Thomas Barnell, Thomas Dorrell, and James Sargente, writer hereof.

Proved Sept. 27th, 1583.

373.—KATHARINE ROCKWELL, widow.

1582. Feb. 19th. Testatrix was of the parish of St. Peter, and desired to be buried in the church of "St Marie Porte," between her husband and son Gilbert. Five shillings to the poor of those two parishes; and ten shillings in bread to be given away "at my buriall." To Ma... Rockwell, daughter of Gilbert Rockwell, one pot of silver, &c. To Thomas, son of the said Gilbert, "one greate Crock wthout legges;" also the "brue howse" held by John Lewes, "wth the drap'ie about the p'lo^r next the Streate of the same howse." To John, brother of the said Thomas Rockwell, three silver spoons. Legacies also to Agnes, wife of John Lewes, and late servant Welthian Thomas. Son William Rockwell to be sole executor, and have the residue of goods; also to hold and enjoy the lease of the dwelling house for a year; rem. to daughter Joan Greene. Nicholas Robbins and John Lewes overseers, to each of whom ij^s vj^d. Witnessed by Richard Arther, clerk, Nicholas Robbins, John Lewes, David Richartes, and Anne Robins. The following persons were owing sums of money to testatrix "at the daie of my death:"—Jo^n Barrat, Jo^n Lewes, Jo^n Robinson, Richard Harrison, John Swyfte, and daughter Joan Greene.

Proved May 6th, 158..

This will is also registered at Somerset House, *Rowe*, 25, where May 6th, 1583, is given as the date of probate.

374.—WILLIAM COXE, merchant.

1581. July 8th. Testator was of the parish of St. Stephen in Bristowe, and desired to be buried in the church there, as nigh to the place "whereas my Sonne Henric was buried as yt Conveniently may be." To daughter Margaret and her lawful heirs "my Sixe . . . and gardeyne groundes vnto them ap'teyninge"; also a stable and orchard "in Marsh streate wthin the said Citie of Bristoll"; a garden ground and stable; a "well howse;" a well in the aforesaid "streeate" bought of William Jones of Bristowe, merchant; a house "in Redcliffe streate wthin the said Citie" bought of Edward Veale of Over, and inhabited by Daniel Goughe; and a house upon the Back inhabited by William Colstone : but wife Margaret, during her life, to enjoy the profits of the said house on the Back, and of the garden, stable, well, and wellhouse bought of William Jones. To wife Margaret the lease of testator's dwelling house. To daughter Margaret a dozen of silver spoons "wth maydens heddes gilted," &c., also "a garnishe of vessel." To servant Joyce ij^s vj^d. "Jt'm Jn London Mr Pitte and J haue paide for W^m my Sonnes Rannsome one Hundreth Powndes" unto Mr. Colthurste and Simon Lawrence of London; testator paying 100 marks, and Mr. Pitte the rest; "the wch Mr Pitte hath in Suyte vppon their bande," and what he shall recover thereof "the after p'te of the Note of that as shall Co'me to my p'te" to be for daughter Margaret; and wife Margaret to have "thother iij q'ters," and also the residue of goods, and be sole executrix. Mr. Thomas Warren, merchant, and Richard Langton of the city of Bristowe, notary public, to be overseers, and have ten shillings apiece.

Proved June 20th, 1583.

The register of the parish of St. Stephen records the burial of William Cox, July 5th, 1582.

This will is followed by an inventory of the goods and chattels of Edward Pitte, late of the city of Bristowe, merchant, deceased, taken by Edward Norrice, Thomas White, and Christopher Pitte of the same city, merchants, Oct. 4th, 1583. Deceased had two Luxborne chairs, valued at xvj^s viij^d; "one little bible booke," v^s; "the worne Jrishe Cad," xxiiij^s; "ij Calyvers," xx^s; "the xxiiijth p'te of a Shippe Called the vnicorne," xvj^{li}; "an adventure in the Pellican," vij^{li} xiij^s iiij^d. Thomas White owed money to deceased; and the latter was in debt to Mr. William Birde, Mr. Richard Cole, Thomas Pitcher, Richard Rice, Griffith Berebrewer, and Edward Lewes. The order or decree for, and concerning the distribution of the goods, &c., of deceased, was made by Mr. William Drurie, doctor of laws, and commissary of the prerogative court of Canterbury: William, John, and Anne Pitte, children of the said deceased, were each to receive £25 at the age of twenty-one, or when married.

375.—JOHN PALMER, baker.

1583. June 7th. Testator was of the parish of St. Thomas in "the Citye of Bristoll." His body "to the yearthe from whence yt came." To eldest son Thomas the dwelling house "wth Pavem^t where the well ys," &c., and the little house "at Redclife gate," with the orchard there; also a "greate Spruce Cheaste," and a "greate hoope Ringe of golde," after the decease of wife Elizabeth. To son John the house "in Temple Streate" that David Barnes dwelleth in; also the new house "that ys a buildinge;" the house inhabited by David Lloyd; a "garden place called Glovyers Greene in Temple p'ishe"; three tenements "above the Pipe in St Thomas Streate wth the gardeyns belonginge to them"; the house "before St Thomas Churche" in the holding of Richard Hall of "the La'me"; the said John and his lawful heirs to possess this property, "payenge the Annual Rente": he and son Thomas to enter and enjoy their lands at the age of twenty-one. To the said John "a Silver goblette double gilte" after the decease of wife Elizabeth; also "my Lease wch J haue of Mr Sachefylde" in reversion of my daughter Dorothy Younge. If John should die under the age of twenty-one, rem. to son Thomas; and if Thomas should so die, daughters Elizabeth and Agnes to share this lease equally. To the said Thomas and John the "beste Salte" after wife Elizabeth's decease, "devyded bytwene them." To daughter Alice "the thirde best Crocke," &c.; also, when married, xiiij^{li}, which is in the hand of Thomas Tomlyne. To daughter Agnes a "fether bedd," &c., and x^{li} when married. If the aforesaid sons should die s.p., daughters Elizabeth and Agnes to have their lands, equally divided. If these daughters should die before marriage, rem. to wife Elizabeth and daughter Alice. To Thomas and John, sons of my daughter Tomlyne, and Elizabeth, her daughter, v^s each at the day of their marriage. To daughter Tomlyne "a Stone Cruse covered wth Sylver," &c. To Margaret and Elizabeth Younge, daughters of Dorothy Younge, v^s each when married. To "the Poore" xx^s. Wife Elizabeth to have the use of all the lands for twelve years, to build the houses "in Temple Streate," paying "the Lordes Rente," to "the keepinge vpp of my Children," &c.; and after the expiration of those years, to have "the thirde foote or penye of all my Landes during her naturall lyfe." She is also, during those years, to pay the supervisors of the will, to the use of testator's sons Thomas and John, v^s apiece, "as A Knowledge penney" that he has made them "heires and Lordes" of the said lands. Wife Elizabeth to have the residue of goods, and be sole executrix; and also, "wthin or at the twoe yeres ende," to make a tomb "over me and my wife." William Sayer, Richard Kitchinge, and Thomas Masone, supervisors, to each of whom x^s. Witnessed by John Thewe, curate there, Henry Slye, and Robert Rogers.

Proved Oct. 12th, 1583.

376.—RICHARD CAUSE.

1583. Sept. 8th. Testator was a "Citizen and Tann' of the Citie of Bristowe," and committed his body "to ye earth." To his wife Agnes the sum of £10 yearly out of his lands and leases; also £10 in money, and "the ij Chambers before streate the wch J lie in my selfe rent free during her life"; together with all the furniture in them. To cousin Barber of London, and cousin Elizabeth his wife, and their lawful issue, "my howse the wch J nowe dwell in wth vates & trowes" belonging thereto. To cousin Robert Leversage of London, and cousin Katharine his wife, and their lawful issue, a tenement "vppon the weare" inhabited by Joan White, widow, with a void ground "lyenge in St Marie Porte streate," held by lease of testator by Robert Risbie, furrier. Cousins Barber and Leversage to pay, each of them, xx^s yearly to wife Agnes, which shall be "towardes her x^{li} yeerly before bequeathed." All the rest of the free lands, and the leases, to Philip son of kinsman William Cause of the parish of Wollasson, within "the shere" of Gloucester, and to the heirs of the said Philip; but wife Agnes to have, during her life, £8 by the year out of this property. Legacies to the poor of that parish, and of St. Peter's, and the two sons of cousin William Cause. Margery Bushe "the mydwife" must have xiij^{li} vj^s viij^d "of the meere debt that J owe her whereof she hath c'teine Naperie of myne in Pawne for the same." I Richard Cause have written this "all wth my owne hand." Witnessed by Thomas Colman, vicar of St. Philip's "wthin the deanerie of Bristoll."

No executor having been appointed, adm'on was granted to testator's relict, Agnes *Causse*, by the archbishop of Canterbury, Sept. 28th, 1584.

Rich'us Argall.

377.—RICHARD SWETNAM, merchant.

1584. Sept. 20th. Testator was of the parish of St. Stephen, and made his will nuncupatively. To his four daughters, Frances, Anne, Judith, and Elizabeth, £10 apiece. Twenty shillings to "the poore." Wife Frances to be executrix. Witnessed by William Ellys, Richard Shore, William Swetnam, Simon Aldworthe, William Chewe, and others.

Proved "in Curia prerogativa," Oct. 9th, 1584.

378.—RICHARD SALTREN, merchant.

1584. Aug. 2nd. Testator was of "the p'ishe of St John Baptiste in the Citie of Bristowe." His body to be "laied in Cristian buriall." To his sons, John, Richard, William, and Edmond, £40 apiece. To his daughter Mary Saltren £50. The said sons to have their legacies at the age of twenty-one; the daughter to have her portion at the same age, or when married.

Wife Joan to keep their portions, putting in "sufficient suerties to the court of Orphans in the Citie of Bristowe." Forty shillings unto the poor people "whereas it is most neede" in the city. Wife Joan to have the residue, and be sole executrix. Mr. William Saltren, testator's brother, and Mr. William Ellis, "nowe Sheriffe," to be overseers. Witnessed by William Saltren, William Ellis, William Smyth, Thomas Prin, and Thomas Saltren.

No record of probate.

The register of the parish of St. John records the burial of Richard *Salteron*, Aug. 6th, 1584.

379.—JOHN WELSHE, merchant.

1584. Jan. 20th. To be buried in the church of St. Stephen, "so nighe to my Pewe as Convenyently may be." Wife Margery to have all goods, debts, lands, &c., and be executrix. John Caroe and servant Philip Hill overseers. Witnessed by the said John and Philip, and Patrick Mathewe, with others. Sums of money were due from Mr. Walcott "that married my Ladie Arnold," John Bull "the Smyeth," and Thomas Lewes: and testator owed money to his cousin Parmynter and Bodman's daughter.

Proved "in Cur' p'rogativa," Feb. 13th, 1584.

380.—WILLIAM SHUTLEWOORTH.

1584. March 17th. Testator was "of the p'ishe of temple Bearebrewer," and desired to be buried in the church there "before the Pewe wherein my wief Elizabeth lyeth." Twenty shillings to the poor people of that parish. To sister Joan Selman £10; also the money which testator had of her to keep. To wife Elizabeth, for her life, the new house inhabited by son-in-law Griffeth Perkin, and a close "att Reddclyf hill" containing two acres; also to her, and her heirs and assigns for ever, the ground called "the Leare ground" wherein testator used to lay his wood; and the tenement held "of ffee ffarme," inhabited by William Lawrence "Clarke of Temple." The said Elizabeth to be sole executrix, and to bring up "my boy William Shutlewoorth the Sonne of Edward Shutlewoorth," except it be his mother's pleasure to bestow the charges on him, and see him brought up herself. If the said William should die s.p., all testator's lands to be divided between the children of Griffeth Perkin and of John Shutlewoorth, plumber. Sums of money to the children of the said Griffeth, and to John, William, and Bridget, children of the said John. Mr. Thomas Slocombe, alderman, Mr. William Bird, and Mr. John Harte, drapers, to be overseers, and have xx[s] apiece. Witnessed by Richard Martyn, vicar, John Younge, John Shutlewoorth, Mary his "wief," and John Selman.

No record of probate.

The register of the parish of Temple gives the marriage of William Shuttleworth and Elizabeth Sellman, Nov. 30th, 1574, and the burial of the former, March 19th, 1584.

381.—WILLIAM HUKINES.

1583. June 14th. Testator was of the parish of St. Stephen "w[th]in the Cytie of Bristoll," and desired to be buried in the church there. To his mother, Agnes Hukines, twenty nobles in money, to be given to her by "my Gossipp" John Caro "att sundrye Tymes a weeke." If she should die before spending that sum, rem. to brother's daughter Elizabeth. To wife Amy the dwelling house, during "her naturall lyfe"; rem. to brother Thomas Hukines and his lawful heirs; in def., rem. to the next of kin. Legacies to the almshouses in the Marsh and "att Laffardes gate," Mr. Tyson, parson of St. Stephen's, and the clerk. Wife Amy to have the residue, and be executrix. Mr. George Badram and John Caro overseers. Witnessed by John Caro, Richard Walsh, Katharine Caro, Thomas Tyson, rector, and Matthew Need. Sums of money were due from John Griffeth, John Jones, and William Smith. At the request of testator's wife, all the debts of his brother-in-law Robert Abevan are forgiven, "Saving A Couerlett y^t J haue of his in l'awne of money the wch Couerlett J doe geve and bequeath vnto my Seru'nte Joane Darby."

No record of probate: but the will was proved Aug. 28th, 1583, as appears by the copy at Somerset House, *Rowe*, 41; in which copy the surname Badram is incorrectly written *Badna'me*.

382.—WILLIAM HAMMONDES, blacksmith.

1584. Aug. 25th. Testator dwelt in the parish of St. Peter, in "the Cytie of Bristoll," and desired to be buried in the church there. To daughter Joan £5, to be in the hands of wife Katharine "against her daie of Mariadge." To servant Ansell Slaughter forty shillings "att thend of his yeres" which he hath to serve me or my wife; also "A litle Anvill wch is nowe in my shopp." Wife Katharine to have the residue, and be sole executrix. Thomas Moone, smith, and Richard Page, barber, to be overseers. Witnessed by Humphrey Mosely, parson of St. Peter's, Walter Baynam, tailor, "and me James Sargente wryghter hereof," with others.

Proved "in curia prerogatiua," Oct. 5th, 1584.

383.—ELIZABETH SLOCOMBE, widow.

1583. Oct. 21st. Testatrix was "of the Cytie of Bristoll," and willed that her body be "layed in St Nycolas Crowd," near her first husband Thomas Goodawle. To daughter Elizabeth Goodawle *alias* Elliott, and to her heirs for ever, a yearly rent of xx^s from a messuage or tenement "vppon the weer in the Suburbes of the Cytie of Bristoll," within the parish of St. Peter, in the tenure of John Wallys, slaymaker and weaver, and situate and lying there between "a howse late builte sometyme in the occupac'on of Thomas Dye deceassed and nowe in the occupac'on of Edward Bateman," on the west side, and a tenement inhabited by Thomas Poole, tanner, on the east. To daughter's children, William, Thomas, Henry, and John Elliott, £10 apiece at the age of twenty-one; rem. to their mother, if they should die under that age. Testatrix wills that "the saied foner boyes or Chilldren shalbe putt foorth to honest and Credible p'sons and to learne some honest Craft or trade of lyving." My said daughter Elizabeth to have the residue of goods, and be sole executrix. Mr. William Prewett and Mr. Thomas Pytt overseers, to each of whom an "Angell of golld." Witnessed by William Prewett, Richard Rise, Thomas Picher, Bartholomew Hill, and Patrick Younge.

Proved June 30th, 1584.

384.—JOHN AUSTE, baker.

1583. July 25th. Testator was of the parish of St. Peter "wthin the Cytie of Bristoll," and desired to be buried in the churchyard there. Wife Mary to be sole executrix, and have the lease of the three houses enjoyed by testator; the said lease to be equally divided, after her decease, between his three children, Robert, William, and Elizabeth Auste. To eldest son Robert, and son William, £5 apiece. To daughter Elizabeth £10 at the day of her marriage. Unto the "poore people of this Cytie towardes their Releef xx^{tie} dossen of bredd." To brother William Auste, and sisters Agnes, Joan, and Alice, xx^s apiece. Ten shillings towards the maintenance of the bakers' hall. Residue to wife Mary. Thomas Poole and William Wyett overseers, to each of whom x^s. Witnessed by Humphrey Mosely, parson, Thomas Barnell, Thomas Dorrell, and James Sergent.

Proved Sept. 27th, 1583.

385.—JOHN POPLEY *alias* Deane.

1583. Feb. 27th. Testator was of the parish of St. John Baptist, in "the Cyty and dioces of Bristoll," and willed that his body be "laied in Christian Buriall." To his wife Margery, for her life, all his tenements, &c., in the city and suburbs, and all rents, fines, and profits; also the goods which she brought with her when married. To son Edmond Popley and his legitimate heirs, after the decease of wife Margery, the reversion and rents of the "messuage or tenement called the White Harte lying in Brood street wthin the Cytie of Bristoll," in the tenure of Thomas Thomas. To John Popley the younger, son of "my late owne Sonne John Popley th^e elder deacessed," those two tenements or houses "in St Nycolas Street in Bristow," now or lately held by ———Davys, cobbler; and a house "in Ballwinstreet," inhabited by John Millerd, hooper. To daughter Elizabeth Eaton a small goblet, &c., and "the greate thick panne wch was her grand-mothers"; also to her, and her legitimate heirs, "all that my vtter Corner Tenement or howse scituate vppon the key of Bristoll att the easte end there," in the occupation of William Smith, merchant, and the reversion and rents of the same, after the decease of wife Margery. To Edmond Eyton, one of the sons of the said Elizabeth Eiton (*sic*), "a stone Cruse wth Cover brim and foote of Siluer doble guilt." To daughter Prudence Longe £5, six silver spoons, &c.; also to her, and her legitimate heirs, "my inner Corner Tenement or howse also Scituate vppon the East end of the Key," inhabited by Thomas Cutt "Seriaunte," and the reversion and rents, after the decease of my said wife. To Margery Jones, daughter of John Jones, blacksmith, £10, to be levied and paid out of the tenement called "the White Harte," in the day of her marriage; also to her, and her legitimate heirs, all that void ground behind the aforesaid corner tenements upon the Key, "wherevppon was some tyme a howse & late by Casualty of flier wasted." The sum of £4 to "the poore people in the Cytie of Bristoll," and five shillings to "the p'son of St John the Baptiste." To William Starling "my Prentice," the years remaining, after my wife's decease, of the lease "in the withie Bedd or twigg bedd" in Pile street, provided he continues his service, and behaves himself "trewe and gentell towardes my wief." If any of the children, or other "legatory" shall molest, sue, or trouble "my saied wief," the legacies of such are to be distributed "amongest the poore people in the Cytie of Bristoll by the good discrec'on of the Maior and Alldermen." Wife Margery to have the residue of goods, and be sole executrix. Robert Tyndall "my Sonne in Lawe" and Thomas Prin' of Bristoll, overseers.

Proved April 15th, 1584.

386.—ELIZABETH BRAMPTON, widow.

1583. Dec. 28th. Testatrix, who was of the parish of St. Thomas, describes herself as "the vnprofitable Seru'nte of God weake in boddy not wthstanding stronge in mind." Her body to the earth "whereof yt Came." To Mr. Tewe, curate of the said parish, vj^s viij^d. To the poor of Bristoll £10, divided as followeth: twenty shillings to St. Thomas's almshouse, and vj^s viij^d to every almshouse within the city; the residue of the money to be given to poor householders of the parishes of St. Thomas, "Raclifie," and Temple. To Anne Jenson £5; also "my gowne furred wth shankes," a "Chamlett kirtle," &c. To Frances Smith, during her life, a "gillt Salt wth A Cover"; rem. to her daughter Elizabeth Smith. To cousin John Smith "his wief," and children, two obligations of £30 due from one John Harrwood. To Joan Burchall and her five children £12. To John Fursell's daughter vj^s viij^d a year; if she should die s.p., rem. to Joan Ruddock and her heirs for ever. To cousin Martha Snowe, daughter of Anne Saunders, £20 at her marriage; also "half A garnishe of pewter vessell," &c.; rem. to the children of cousin John Snowe, if she should die before marriage. To Joan May "the golde Ringe wch J were vppon my finger." To my neighbour Richard May the lease of my garden and stable, and forty shillings in money. If John Fursell should sell away the house, the drapery, glass, &c., to be for the use of the executors. Legacies to Robert Gillmam, Joan Coxe, Alice wife of James Owfford, cousin John Snowe, William Stibbes, and his wife. Of the residue of goods, one half to the said John Snowe, the other to William Stibbes: the said John and William to be executors. Richard Maye overseer. Witnessed by Richard May, John Snowe, William Stibbes, Richard Burcott, James Newton, and John Tewe.

Proved Dec. 18th, 1584.

387.—JOHN BOSSINGTON *alias* George.

1575. Aug. 26th. Testator was of the parish of Temple "in the Cytie of Bristoll." To be buried "in the p'ishe and Churchard of Temple." To daughter Alice a flockbed, a broad loom with "the harnys belonginge to the same," &c. Wife Eleanor to have the residue, and be sole executrix. Witnessed by Sir Richard Barwicke, "vicear of temple,'" and Maister Randall Hassall, with others.

Proved Sept. 17th, "Anno d'ni millesimo quingentesimo octuagesimo quinto."

The Orphan Book contains another copy of this will, in which testator desires to be buried "in the p'ishe Churche of Temple," and which gives 1575 as the year when the will was proved. The Temple parish register records the burial of John Bossington, Aug. 28th, 1575, and of Mr Richard Barwick, vicar, Jan. 7th, 1575; the letter "p" being opposite to both the entries.

388.—CHRISTOPHER FRYNDE, hooper. In the margin *Frend*.

1575. Sept. 19th. Testator was of "the Cytie of Bristoll." His body to the earth. To his children John, Joan, and Edward, £5 apiece at the age of fifteen. If all should die under that age, the whole of the money to remain to wife Margery and her assigns. To son John " my bibell." Wife Margery to have the residue, and be sole executrix.

Proved Jan. 30th, " Anno D'ni Millesimo quingentesimo quinto."

This will is registered twice; the second copy giving 1575 as the year in which it was proved.

389.—THOMAS ADDAMS, tanner.

1585. May 27th. Testator was of the parish of St. Peter in Bristoll, and desired to be buried in the church there, " in the North ille," where his father had erected a " tome " and lay buried with both his wives, and two of testator's children, namely, Thomas and Annis. To the parson there vj^s viij^d. To Robert Addams, " my Sonne and heire," £200 when aged twenty-one; also " the beste peece of Arras or tapstry wch J bought my self." To daughter Joan £200 at the age of " twentie yeres," if she will be ruled and counselled in marriage by her mother and by my overseers. If both the children should die under age or before marriage, their money to remain to the Mayor and Commonalty, for the purchase of land; the yearly rent of one moiety thereof to be lent unto " the poore Craftes men of the Citie of Bristoll " on good sureties " freely wthowt payinge anie thinge therefore " by the space of seven years; to be delivered afterwards to other such persons upon like sureties; " and so allwaies to continewe in such sorte as Sr Thomas White knighte gave his Legasey to the saied Citie of Bristoll ": the company of tanners to have " more benefytt of this my gnifte from time to time then anie other one Company wthin the saied Citie of Bristoll shall and haue." The yearly rent of the other moiety of the said lands is to be given by the advice and counsel of the Mayor and aldermen, and of the overseers of this will, to good and charitable uses, as relieving the poor, especially in St. Peter's parish, and to the " increase of relief in some Almes howses and to the increase of A stocke in the howse of correction or such like." To brother Robert Addams twenty marks; and testator does not know that he owes him anything " butt for A trusse of taffata," to the value of x^s or thereabouts. To brother Francis Addams twenty nobles, upon condition that " he wilbe thankfull and not vse such vngratefull and threateninge Speeches as at his laste being heere " to testator's wife. The same amount to the daughter of the said Francis by his first wife. To Thomas Baynam " my Nevewe " £20. To John and David Jones, children of testator's wife, £5 apiece " when they come to their severall ages," order to be taken " by the Courte of Orphanes " for the payment thereof. To Thomas Cory £20 on condition of his being " faithfull and trustie vnto my wife," and that " he doe mary my kynsewoman Jane Addams." Testator forgives the debts of John Prewet, John Christopher's wife, and " the poore Coblers wthin this Citie." Six poor men and six poor women to have a " frise gowne," &c., and " sixe pence A pece." Forty dozen of bread to the poor people of the city. Legacies also to William son of Richard Baynam, Agnes wife of Thomas Belling'am, the daughter of John Gervys and of my sister Alice,

Christopher Walker "my Vnckles Sonne," Margaret daughter of Robert Lathbury at her marriage, Joan Tyler, daughter of cousin Margaret Tyler, when married, John Leech, "my man" William Hoell, and "my Nurse wch nursed my two daughters." Wife Joan to have the residue, and be executrix. Mr. Philip Langley, alderman, Mr. Robert Smithes, and William Edmondes to be overseers. All goods and plate given to testator's children by Robert Arden deceased, their grandfather, to be "co'mitted to the Courte of Orphanes."

No record of probate: but the will was proved June 26th, 1585, as appears by the copy at Somerset House, *Brudenell*, 32; which copy gives May 17th as the day on which the will was made.

390.—ELIZABETH JONES, widow.

1575. Sept. 4th. To be buried "in the Crowde in the parishe of St Nycholas wthin the grate," by late husband Roger Jones. Debts to be paid with as convenient speed as may be. To sister Elynor Higgines £30. To "my welbeloued cossen Maister Doctor Mathewe my golld ringe sett wth an emerod." To Elizabeth daughter of Richard Moore and of Elizabeth his wife "my only daughter" a hundred marks at her marriage, "J meane wth the xx^{li} that my late husband gave her by his Will the whole to be a hundred markes"; also "my beste neste" of double-gilt goblets, &c., "my litle golld ringe sett wth arubye," and the fourth part of all the householde stuff. The sum of £100 towards the provision of the poor, who are to have "xxx^{ty} blake gownes of frise" out of this money. To cousin John Cother a black gown, and to "my Cossen his wief" a cassock "of Grograu' wth mynkes." To servant Nicholas Hill £20. To servant Anthony Hill £5. To Jane Cother "my shippes Collo^r Cassock furred wth otter and a peticote of frisadowe." To goddaughter Elizabeth Cother "one ffrocke of Chamlett garded wth velvett." To servant Elizabeth Bosewell a gown, &c., on condition that she "sarve the Residewe of her yeres wth my daughter Elizabeth Moore." To Mrs. Buckford of London "that litle Bes moore dweled wth" a gold ring set with a stone "called a Saffyer." Legacies also to cousin Katharine Buckford, John Faye, servant John Bosewell, and late servants Harry Millard and Thomas Tayler. Son-in-law Richard Moore, and his wife Elizabeth to have the residue, and be executors. Edward Porter overseer, to whom "A golld ringe."

No record of probate: but the will was proved March 10th, 1575, as appears by the copy at Somerset House, *Carew*, 4; which gives Sept. 3rd as the day on which the will was made.

391.—JULIAN ROBERTS, widow.

1584. April 22nd. Testatrix was of the parish of St. Nicholas "in the Citie of Bristoll," and commended her body "to the earth from whence yt came." Six poor men to have gowns, and six poor women to have cassocks "of blake frise." To "my Sister and Dorothie" £20. The same amount to be equally divided between the children of my brother. To "my Cosen Margarett that is my Serva'nte" £20 when married; also "two hoopes of gold to make her a weddinge ringe." To goddaughter Anne Sawll "my weddinge ringe," &c.; but Edward Longe "my ffreind" to have the keeping of the same until the day of her marriage. If the said Anne should die unmarried, her said bequests are to be divided equally among the children of my brother Richard. To Joyce Havyland " my seconde beste sallte Seller and v^{li} in monie." Unto " my ffreind " Mrs Anne Colstone a gold ring " wth A pearle sett in yt." To goddaughter Mary Powell, when married, " x^{li} in monies and her Goblett that I haue in pawne." Legacies also to John Howell, shearman, and his daughter Mary Howell, Matthew Haviland, goddaughter Mary Smithes, John Grigge, clerk, and the poor. My "trustie frindes" Edward Longe and Margery his wife to be executors, and have the residue of goods, and also " my howse in the Citie of Bristoll neere the Crowde dore." Witnessed by John Grigg, John Howell, and Thomas Williams, " Chirurgion."

No record of proof.

The register of the parish of St. Nicholas records the burial of " Jellian Roberts widdow," June 1st, 1584.

392.—PHILIP KYTE.

1585. Dec. 5th. Testator was of the parish of St. Mary Port " wthin the Cytie of Bristoll," and desired to be buried " in the South Ile " of the church there, near unto the place where his " last wyfe " Joan Kyte lieth buried. To eldest son Philip twenty marks, on condition of his permitting Katharine Kyte, " my wyfe that nowe ys," to occupy the dwelling house " in St Marie Porte streate " for eight years; in case of refusal, son John to have that money, in addition to £20, at the age of twenty-one; and also to have it, if the said Philip should die under that age. Also to the said John, after the decease of Agnes Kyte, widow, " my naturall Mother," the lease of one parcel of pasture ground in the tenure of brother William Kyte, situate in the parish of Chippenham, co. Wilts, " nere vnto the Causey or highwaie " of that parish. To the said Agnes " one olde Angell of Golde beinge of the value of Tenne Shillinges in money." To sister Alice Kyte " an olde Angell of Golde" of the same value. If both the said sons should die under the given age, £10 out of their legacies to remain to the said Alice, and other £10 to sister Katharine Kyte; and the twenty marks to wife Katharine, who is also to have the residue of goods, and be sole executrix, and stand bound " in good and sufficient Bandes to the ffathers of the Orphantes in this Case p'vided " to bring up the said Philip and John " in learninge wth meate drinck Clothinge," &c., until they are twenty-one. My brother William Kyte, to whom vj^s viij^d, and Anthony Phillippes, to whom iij^s iiij^d, overseers. William Pynder, writer, " the ffirme " of Anthony Phillippes, " the ffirme " of Philip Gwynne, shoemaker.

Proved in the prerogative court of Canterbury, Jan. 10th, 1585.

393.—ROGER SHIPMAN, mercer.

1586. July 11th. Testator was " of the Cytie of Bristoll." To sons Thomas, John, William, and Edward, £50 apiece. To daughter Margery Shipman £50 when married, or aged twenty-one. If any of the said children should die under that age, the portion, or portions, to be equally divided among those that survive. The sum of £10 unto poor householders within " this Cytie." Wife Bridget to have the residue, and be sole executrix. To the

R

child she is about to bring forth, if it shall live, "all such p'fitt and gaine as shall rise and increase vppon my parte of the Twenty Tonnes of Oile wch is betweene my Gossippe Will'm Carie and me." My "vncle" Mr. Thomas Aldworth and the said William Carie to be overseers. Witnessed by — Aldworth and the said William. Inventory stated to amount to vij^c xxiij^li vj^s x^d.

Proved in the prerogative court of Canterbury, Aug. 26th, 1586.

394.—THOMAS ROWLAND, merchant.

1584. April 20th. To be buried "in my p'ishe Churche." Twenty shillings "towardes the rep'ac'ons of the sayde Churche vnto the newe worke." To the Mayor and Commonalty of Bristoll "towardes the rep'ac'ons of the sayde Cytie" £5. To eldest daughter, Joyce Rowland, two hundred marks, with one of the best goblets, &c., and "a pann that was her graundmothers, and one garnishe of pewter vessell." To second daughter, Margery, one hundred marks; also a lease held of Merburyes, which "J boughte of John Sandiforde of Lo'. J haue as yet an eighte & twentye yeare to come or thereabouts"; also "one greate Jland chest," &c. To third daughter, Mary, £80; also a table cloth "of Hollande," &c. To fourth daughter, Anne, £20, &c., and she, for her life, "to be the flirste in a lease that J boughte of the Chamber of Bristoll in reversion of old mother Stokes." Legacies also to fifth daughter, Katharine, sixth daughter, Alice, and seventh daughter, Elizabeth. Unto Gelyan Rowland, my youngest daughter, £40, and my best dozen "of Siluer Spones of the guilte Apostells." Unto the child that my wife "goeth withall" £30, and one of "my best guilt Tanckardes." All the legacies to be paid to them "at the daye of theire lawfull Marriadge," or when aged twenty-four. Sums of money to the almshouses, each of "my apprintices," maid-servant Ellen, godson Thomas Rowland, and godson and son-in-law Richard Langford. All "my firste wines landes in Wales shall goe amongest my Seven daughters and hers" as their inheritance, to be divided equally by the rent, or as may best be devised by "learned Councell," that they have no strife, but agree "like lovinge Sisters." All the lands "in towne" to remain to wife Elizabeth during her life, and afterwards to "oure heires betwene vs begotton." She to be executrix, and have five hundred marks, "J say 333^li 6^s 8^d," and to recover all debts and goods "due vnto me aswell beyonde the seas as here within the lande." She is to trouble no person "for anie dett due vnto me that is not able nor of power to paye the same but suche J freely forgive as J hope and beleue freely to be forgiven thorowe the tender mercy of o^r Sauio^r Jesus Christ vnto whose tuic'on and mercy J Comytt my soule for ever."

Proved in the prerogative court of Canterbury, April 21st, 1586.

The register of marriages at St. Stephen's has the entry—Thomas Rowland and Elizabeth Langford, Nov. 30th, 1581.

395.—WILLIAM PEPWALL, alderman.

1571. Feb. 1st. Testator was of "the Cyttie of Bristoll," and desired to be buried in the parish church of St. Nicholas there, in decent order according to his calling. To son Michael and his heirs the manors, lands, tenements, &c., at Coldashton, Hamestwell, and Tatwicke, purchased of Sir Walter Dennis knt., deceased, and Richard Dennis esq.; but wife Elizabeth to have this property for her life, as being "ioynte purchasar thereof withe me." She is also to enjoy the parsonage there, with the mansion house, lodge, &c., "whether she marrie or not marrie"; and the dwelling house in Bristol "somtyme called the Starr," if she live sole and unmarried, with all wares, stock, and store in the shop, warehouses, &c., within the said mansion house, she paying debts and duties owing for the said wares as well in London as elsewhere; also all the plate, jewels, &c. To the said Michael and his heirs the property at Tatwicke purchased of Edward Teinte(?), in the tenure of Gnninge (?) or of his assigns: and other property there purchased of ——Goore, gent., in the tenure of John Smithe; and the grove there "nowe in myne owne possession;" also all the lands, tenements, &c., in Bristol, and those in the parish of Almesbury Hill, co. Glouc., lately purchased of Giles Ive, gent. To daughter Langley the best nest of goblets, &c., and "one Castinge bottell of silver guilt wth a litle cheine belonginge to the same." To daughter Susan Yonge "a pepper Boxe of Siluer guilte," &c., and a cross of gold. To son Timothy the advowson of the benefice of Coldashton, after the decease of the parson there; also 100 marks, &c., and two goblets of silver parcel-gilt, as soon as he (Timothy) shall be "charged to be residensarie" upon his spiritual promotion of Harford Este. To son John £100, and "a Goblett of siluer p'cell guilt." To servant Mary Roche, towards "the p'ferment of her Marriage," £20; but "yf she never Marye then this guifte to be voyde." To the mother of the said Mary £5. To the children of Rodeman of Mershfyld, being "my Kynn," £5. Twenty poor men to have a gown apiece "at my buryall." The sum of £10 to "the poore mens Boxe equallie to be devided amongest them." To son Richard a cassock of velvet, &c. Black gowns to such as shall be appointed mourners at the burial, by "thadvise" of the overseers, "that is to wyte" to sons Langley and Younge, John Pepwall, Timothy Pepwall, William Reade, and such others, besides "weomens gownes." To each of "my apprintices" and servants £5. To "my freud" Mr Rede vj^{li} xiij^s iiij^d. Legacies also to daughter Langley's son Toby, daughter Elizabeth Jones, John Pepwall, son Langley, Besse Higgens, and servant Joan Hawkins. Son Michael to have the residue, and be sole executor. Son Mr Philip Langley and friend Mr William Rede overseers.

On Feb. 11th, 1573, testator wrote an explanation of his meaning, and ordered that his son Michael should be bound to his said wife in a reasonable sum, so that she might be made the more secure in the possession of her legacies. Son John to have £50, instead of the aforesaid £100. To servant Richard Treherne "one Tnne of ledd." Witnessed by William Rede, Philip Langley, William Gittens, John Pepwall, Elizabeth Pepwall, Michael Pepwall, William Sprinte, and Richard Treherne.

Proved "—— die Junij," 1574.

The Pepwall pedigree in the Harleian MS., 1543, begins with this testator, and mentions his sons, Michael, John, and Timothy, and daughters, Mary, wife of Philip Langley, Elizabeth, wife of Richard Jones, and Susan, wife of Richard Yonge; also the children which the said Michael had by his wife Anne, daughter of Davy Hobbes.

396.—JOHN BRAMPTON, merchant.

1563. July 23rd. Testator was of the parish of St. Thomas " wthin the Cyttie of Bristoll," and desired to be buried in the churchyard there. To "the Curat" of that church xij^d. To "the Cathedrall Churche of Bristoll" xx^d. To the poor on the day of burial iij^{li}, either in money or in bread. To daughter Joan, late the wife of Thomas Fussell, xx^{li}, and "in my apparell as shalbe valued at iiij^{li}." To wife Elizabeth, for her life, the dwelling house, in "a Streate called Redcliffe Streate next thowse of Thomas Horner called the Beares Inde"; rem. to daughter Joan and her legitimate heirs, who are to pay out of the said tenement the yearly sum of vj^s viij^d towards the relief of the poor of the aforesaid parish of St. Thomas, to be received and paid by the churchwardens. And "yf yt fortune that godlie vse be broken, of the gathering for the poore," the said money to be given yearly to the poor people of the almshouse "called Burtones Almeshouse," and so to continue for ever. To wife Elizabeth and her assigns for ever a tenement or house "lyinge in Chipna' in the Countie of Wiltshere," between the tenements of Philip Smythe and Bartholomew Fustewe (?), with all the lands, leases, &c. To daughter Joan a house in Redcliff-street in the tenure of Joan Pincley, widow, next testator's dwelling house. Wife Elizabeth to have the residue of goods, and be sole executrix. Witnessed by John Tewe, curate, Richard Alkin, Thomas Horner, and William Sutton. To James Bodie of Bristoll, towards his losses that he sustained "by suertiship for Tison," xl^s. To Thomas Fussell, son of daughter Joan, xl^s, to be "paide vnto him at his Cominge out of his Apprentishippe." Robert Banner of Bristoll is released from his debt of iij^{li} iij^s iiij^d.

Proved before John Cottrell, doctor of laws, archdeacon of Dorset, Dec. 10th, 1566.

397.—THOMAS OLIVER, baker.

1557. June 19th. Testator was of "the p'ishe of St Thomas thappostell within the Cittie of Bristoll," and desired to be buried in the churchyard there. To the poor alms-people within that parish vj^s viij^d in bread. To daughter Elizabeth Oliver and her heirs a messuage "in Reckcliffe streate" inhabited by Richard Rose, shoemaker, to be enjoyed by her at the age of eighteen. To wife Margaret a messuage "vppon the Backe of thafforesaid Cyttie of Bristoll," inhabited by John Thomas. To son John, at the age of twenty-one, and to his heirs for ever, all the rest of the lands, tenements, rents, &c., in the said city and "subburbes." Wife Margaret to have the keeping of the said son and daughter "duringe theire nonage," and have the profits of the said property; and the property itself, for herself and legitimate heirs, if the said children should die under age, or s.p.; for lack of such heirs, rem. to brother-in-law Richard Alkin and his legitimate heirs; in def., rem. to sister-in-law Elizabeth Craddocke. To son John a goblet of silver parcel-gilt, and "haulf a dozen of Silver spones with Maydens heddes." To daughter Elizabeth "a standinge Cuppe of Siluer p'cell guilt," &c. Wife Margaret to have the residue, and be sole executrix. My "verie lovinge frendes" Richard Alkin and Thomas Craddocke, "my brotherlawes," to be overseers, and have x^s apiece. To William Edmondes "Surgion," for his "paines takinge wth me," vj^s viij^d. Witnessed by Richard Woodcocke, saddler, William Dawemer, tailor, Randall Hassall, shearman, Richard Alkyn, and others.

Proved July 12th, 1557.

398.—RICHARD CARY "thelder," merchant.

1570. June 11th. Testator was of "the Cyttie of Bristoll," and desired to be buried "in Saint Nicholas Crowde." To eldest son Richard Cary £10. To son William, and daughters Frances, Ann, Elizabeth, and Mary Carye, £10 each. The sum of £400 to my father William Carry (sic), "wch is a dett that J owe vnto him." To daughter Letice Mellin £5. Wife Joan to redeem all the lands, tenements, &c., "that be in mortgage." After her life, and the expiration of nineteen years, all the property to remain "in ffee Simple" to son Christopher and his legitimate heirs; in def., rem. to eldest son Richard and his legitimate heirs. Wife Joan to be executrix, and to have one part of the residue of goods; "thother twoe p'tes" to be for the said six last children. Brother William Carye and brother Robert Halton to be overseers, and have xx^s "a pece." Witnessed by Robert Halton and Christopher Pacye "Prebendarie in the Cathedrall Churche of Bristoll."

Proved Nov. 3rd, 1570.

399.—THOMAS INMAN, shearman.

1585. March 16th. Testator was of "the p'ishe of Temple within the Cittie of Bristoll," and desired to be buried in the churchyard there "at theaste end of the Chauncell of the said Churche where somtyme an old yewe tree stode." To the poor of that parish ten shillings in bread on the day of burial. Unto our vicar vj^s viij^d; and a like sum to Mr Greene, preacher and vicar of Henbury, who is to "preache a Sermon at my buryal." To wife Joan a silver-gilt ring, in token of charity, and for the remembrance of "the vowe and promise in matrimonie wch he (sic) hathe voluntarilie renounced in her wilfull sep'atinge of her self from me." To sister Alice Henshawe £15; also, for her life, a chamber "in my howse," the said chamber being over "the p'lo^r" of the house bought of William Rise. To son Thomas £12, part in money, and part in "howschould stuffe"; also the house with the lease bought of William Rise. To daughter Agnes Inman as much "blacke ffrise" as will make her a cassock, and "twoe shirtes of myne to make her smockes." Legacies also to William Rise and John Sextene. Son John to have the residue, and be sole executor. John Yonge and Henry Beale overseers, to each of whom vj^s viij^d. Witnessed by Richard Martin, Richard Mero, Dame Oldfild, John Yonge, Henry Beale, and others.

Testator added a postscript, stating that his son Thomas was to have the £12 at the age of twenty-two, or when married, and the lease of the house immediately after "my decease." Witnessed by Richard Smithe, Thomas Hamor, Robert Byde, and Richard Martyne. To brother Sir Thomas of Puxon the best gown, for the use of "my sister" or himself. Testator owed sums of money to Thomas Teige, Thomas Toningham (?), and John Griffen. "Henry Salisburye oweth me vppon a band of ffive poundes," for payment whereof Philip Jones gave his word before Robert Morris "who brought me his goldringe in token of paym^t."

Proved March 24th, 1585.

400.—WILLIAM TUCKER.

1583. July 14th. Testator describes himself as one of "the Aldermen of the Cittie of Bristoll," and desires to be buried "in Christian Buryall." Twelve poor men to accompany his corpse to the "funerall," and each to have a gown of black frise. To wife Isabel, for her life, the dwelling house upon the bridge of Avon, and a messuage in St. Nicholas street; her son Thomas Clement to succeed to the said dwelling house, and to hold it for twenty-one years, paying yearly £6, at the four principal terms in the year, to such person and persons, their heirs and assigns, as testator " shall deuise the Reu'c'on in ffe thereof." If the said Thomas Clement be not living at the death of the said Isabel, apprentice and kinsman Matthew Warren is to hold and enjoy the said messuage during the appointed time for the like rent of £6; and to possess it, if the said Thomas should die before the expiration of the twenty-one years. Four of " the Auncyent p'sons wthin the p'ishe of St Nichollas wch haue beyn Mayors or Sherives of the said Cittie," and their heirs and assigns for ever, to have the reversion " in ffee " of all and singular the aforesaid property, on condition that the said four persons, within one month next after testator's decease, grant over the same in trust to twelve, or sixteen other persons of the same parish, and to their heirs and assigns: of the issues and profits, forty shillings to be bestowed yearly for ever on the poor people in the said parish, and vj^s viij^d to a learned preacher, to preach one sermon in the parish church aforesaid yearly for ever upon the first Sunday after Trinity Sunday; all the residue to be " for and towardes the rep'ac'on." To kinswoman Sible Warren £20, one half to be paid at the day of her marriage, and the other twelve months afterwards. To apprentice and kinsman Matthew Warren £20. Wife Isabel to have the residue of goods, and be executrix. John Roberts, alderman, and Hierome Ham gent., " Towne clarcke of the said Cittie," to be overseers, and each to have four broad yards of cloth " of xv^s a yeard."

Proved Nov. 15th, 1583.

This will is followed by a memorandum that adm'on of the effects of Richard Boidell of the city of Bristol, who had died intestate, was granted to his brother William, March 5th, 1584. The will of the latter, which was made Nov. 29th, and proved Dec. 16th, 1597, is in the Bristol probate office. He therein calls himself " William Boydell of the cittie of Bristoll m'chaunt," and desires to be " buryed as neare as may be to my mothers graue in Christ churche p'ishe." Sums of money are bequeathed to every one of his sister's children, and to a preacher to preach at the burial. His brother-in-law Christopher Woodwarde to have the residue, and be executor. The register of the parish of Christ Church records the baptism of Richard son of John Boydle, April 3rd, 1562, and of William, son of the same, July 23rd, 1563; also the marriage of Christopher Woodwarde and Elizabeth Boydell, June 12th, 1570.

401.—THOMAS PITTS.

1585. Jan. 8th. Testator was of the parish of Temple in " the Cittie of Bristoll," and desired to be buried " in Temple Churche before my pewe, that is to saye, betwene the Table for Collecc'on for the poore & my pewe aforesaid." Ten shillings to " the vicare," and £5 to the poor of the said parish. To son William and his heirs and assigns, after the death of wife Joan, the dwelling house for the specified term of years. The rent of the house wherein William Howe dwelleth " shall aunswere the Churche of Temple " for the rent of the house inhabited by son Richard " in the longe Rowe," the yearly rent to be paid to the churchwardens of that church in " the behaulffe " of the said Richard. If the said Richard should depart this life before the expiration of the said lease, the rent of that house is to be equally divided among his children. The said Richard shall have "egresse and regresse into the Racke" in the backside of the house wherein John Higgens now dwelleth; but he is not to "sett nor lett the said Racke to anie other;" the said house and lease to remain, after the death of wife Joan, in the power and occupation of son William. To Margaret, daughter of the said William, the second silver salt. To William, son of the same, a silver goblet. To Elizabeth, daughter of the same, "one silver drinckinge Cuppe." The said children to have their legacies at their day of marriage, and also £10 in equal portions. To Robert Kytchin, son of Richard Kytchen (sic), £3 at the age of twenty-one. Wife Joan to be sole executrix. William Nicholls and son William Pitts overseers, to each of whom twenty shillings. Witnessed by Richard Martin, vicar.

"Probatu' fuit hoc p'sens Testamentu' in Curia p'rogativa." No date is given: but the will was proved May 6th, 1586, according to the copy at Somerset House, *Windsor*, 25. The Temple parish register records this testator's burial, April 2nd, 1586.

402.—RICHARD GOORE, shoemaker.

1586. Jan. 6th. Testator was of "the p'ishe of St Thomas the Apostle in the Cytty of Bristowe." His body "to the earth." Wife Margaret to have the dwelling house for her life; rem. to son James and his legitimate heirs; in def., rem. to second son John and his legitimate heirs; in def., rem. to the expected offspring, if a man child. If neither son should have issue, rem. to daughter Alice and her legitimate heirs; in def., rem. to the expected one, if "a maide Childe." To son John the lease of a house in Redcliff-street, held of the feoffees of St. John's parish in Bristowe. Wife Margaret to bring up the said John until his age of twenty-one, and have the profit of the said house. To sons James and John, and daughter Alice, £40 apiece; the sons to have the money when twenty-one, and the daughter when married. To the said Alice the lease of five tenements and gardens in St. Thomas street: the aforesaid Margaret to bring her up, and enjoy the profit of the lease until the said Alice is eighteen years of age. To kinsman Edward Goore £5. Wife Margaret to have the residue, and be sole executrix. Thomas Sawnders "of Coventree" and James Hurtnall of Bristowe overseers. Witnessed by James Hurtnall, Richard Davis, William Cadle of Bedminster, Edward Goore, Richard Edwards, and Thomas Prin.

"Probatu' fuit hoc p'sens Testamentu' in Curia p'rogativa s'c'do die post festu' Assenc'o'is An° snp'adict'"
Ric'us Argall."

The register of the parish of St. Thomas records the burial of Richard Gower, Jan. 9th, 1586.

403.—HUGH GYBBES. In the margin *Gibbes*.

1585. Nov. 7th. Testator was of the parish of "St Mary porte in the dioces of Bristoll," and desired to be buried in the church there. To eldest daughter Margaret Gybbes, at the day of her marriage, £10, and "one Standinge Bedd." Wife Joan, daughter Margaret's "motherinlawe," to have the residue, and be sole executrix. Witnessed by Thomas Nelmes, John Hurtnoll, Richard Arther, clerk, with others.

"Probatu' fuit hoc p'sens Testamentu' cora' Episcopo Glouc' et Bristoll'" Jan. 12th, 1585.

404.—ROBERT PRISYE, merchant. In the margin *Prisie*.

1586. Sept. 27th. Testator was of "the Cytty of Bristoll," and desired to be buried in the church "of St Warboroughes," bequeathing ten shillings towards "the rep'acions" thereof. The sum of x^{li} to Mary daughter of Richard Wryte of Wantage, when married. The same amount to "the poore Jnhabitantes of the Cytty of Bristoll." To Alice Rowland vj^{li} xiij^s iiij^d. To servant Margery xx^s. Wife Joan to have the residue, and be executrix. Thomas Aldworth "my welbeloved Brother" to be overseer.

Proved before William Blackleeche, doctor of laws, Oct. 17th, 1586.

405.—THOMAS SLOCOMBE, alderman.

1586. June 22nd. Testator was of "the Cytty of Bristoll," and desired to be buried " in St Nicholas Crowd." To daughter Elizabeth Rowland £60 ; and to each of her daughters, Julian and Sarah Rowland, £20. To daughter Bridget Chester £60 ; and to her children, James, Mary, Elizabeth, and Bridget Chester, £10 apiece. To daughter Joan Dydmyster £40 ; and to her "fyve sonnes," Thomas, Richard, Edward, Henry, and Thomas, £10 apiece ; and to her daughter, Bridget Dydmister, £10. To "my sonne" John Slocombe £100 ; also to him and his legitimate heirs male, after the death of wife Elizabeth, three tenements " in Broademead in St James p'ishe in Bristoll," and a house " in St Nicholas streat " in the occupation of Mr John Robertes. If son John should die s.p., rem. to Gilbert, son of my son Henry Slocombe, and "his yssue males"; in def., rem. to "my heyer male generall." To Thomas, John, and Elizabeth Slocombe, the three children of son John, £10 apiece at the age of twenty-one, or their marriage. To Gilbert Slocombe aforenamed £10 ; "allso J Confesse J owe him" £20. To Mary Langford a "gylt Salt" bought of John Yevans, a gilt goblet, "one beere Cruse," &c., and six silver spoons "wth Lyons heades." Legacies also to John son of my brother John Slocombe "deceassed," sister Yowen, and her three daughters, William Yowen, George Yowen, my brother John Slocombe, the parish of Willscombe, and the poor of "the p'ishe of Huyshe chamflows." To each of twelve poor men in Bristoll a gown, a cap, and four pence in money. To each of twelve poor women there a "fryse gowne," also a "kerchewe and fower pence." Wife Elizabeth to have the residue, and be executrix. Mr. John Browne, alderman, to be overseer, and have "towards A gowne" £3, also "an Angelett." Witnessed by William Chaple and Elizabeth Rowland.

No record of probate : but the will was proved Dec. 2nd, 1586, as appears by the copy at Somerset House, *Windsor*, 69.

406.—JOHN GRYFFYN.

1587. April 20th. Testator describes himself as "of the p'ishe of Temple wythin the Cytty of Bristoll Beerebrewer," and desires to be buried " wthin the interclose, in the place where the deske stoode, before it was sett att the Pulpytt." To the poor of that parish on the day of the funeral, as much bread as shall cost £5. To Sir Richard Marten "the vicker of Temple" £4. To the preacher for a funeral sermon " to bee preached at my buryall" vj^s viij. To the com.mon use of "the poore and Co'mons of the Cytty of Bristoll" £100, to be delivered unto the Mayor, &c., for the yearly purchase of corn, to be sold to the poor at a reasonable price. To Christian, wife of Thomas Vethered, £10; in case of her death, the said money to "discend" to her legitimate children. If the said Thomas Vethered shall bring in two sufficient sureties "vnto the father of the Orphanntes" within the city, he may enjoy the said "Tenne powndes" during the "minorytie of the said Childe or Children." If the children should die under the age of twenty-one, the said money is to be distributed to the almshouse of St. Thomas "in the Longe Rowe," the almshouses of the Tuckers' hall and Weavers' hall, and the almshouse "wthout Temple gate," by even portions. To Elizabeth daughter of Thomas Hilling £5 at her marriage, or age of twenty-one. If she should die before, the said money is to be parted among the Newgate prisoners, the almshouse "at the Whirkgige at Michaell Hill," the "spytle howse" and almshouse of St. Katharine at Redcliff hill, the almshouse at Tower lane, and Sir Richard Marten, the vicar of Temple, or his children in his absence. To John Hooke, and Edith his wife, ten shillings apiece. The sum of £5 towards "the Repayringe of Pedminster Calsey," half of which money to be bestowed in stuff and workmanship on "the one ende of the Calsey from Redclyffe hill vnto bright bowe," and the rest "on the other ende or p'te of the Calsey from bright bowe to Bedminsters townes ende." To Richard Kytchinge, of the parish of Temple, "a goulde ringe by estimac'on in pryce or value xx^s havinge therin a Read stone wth a mayden heade." To Robert Deane, hooper, "dwellinge in Ballandstreat," my third gown, "by the name of silke Russett soe Called wch gowne I have Co'monly woren on Sundaies." To John Barrowe of Temple parish, shearman, my gown "comonly called a Shepe Russett gowne." If wife Maud should depart this life before the lease of the dwelling house be expired, the said house, with the horse-mill, three horses, and brewhouse, shall "discend" to the relief of the poor inhabitants of the parish of Temple, and also "to the yerely Repayringe of the Condyte of the said p'ishe of Temple": the said house and lease, with the horse-mill, &c., to be ordered, set, and let by the discretion and "good Advyce" of the fraternity and brotherhood of the vestry of the parish of Temple, together with "myne overseers," to the uses aforesaid. Unto the parish of Temple "my newe howse in Tuckerstreat," between the house of Mr. Richard Kelke, on the south-east side, and a house of Thomas Lucas, dyer, "Comonly Called the Doggeshead in the Pott," on the north-west; the rent to be distributed yearly to the poor people of the said parish. Wife Maud to hold this house during her life, and to be sole executrix. William Nicholls of the parish of Temple, clothier, and Matthew Havelande of St. Leonard's parish, merchant, to be overseers, and each to have £6. 13. 4. Witnessed by Richard Martin, vicar of Temple, Matthew Havelande, and William Nicholles.

Proved "in Cur' prerogatiua," June 6th, 1587.

407.—WILLIAM GYTTINS.

1582. Jan. 1st. Testator was "of the Cytty of Bristoll marchaunte," and desired to be buried "in St Warborough Churche." To the reparation thereof xx^s; and to St Stephen's church xx^s. To son John Gyttens £100 at "the ende of one yere," and £100 at the age of twenty-one; also, after the decease of wife Mary, "my estate in feefarme of my house in Smallstreate," paying xl^s a year to "the vse of the iiij^{er} kinges vppon Michaell Hill," with all drapery, glass, &c., and twelve spoons " wth a wylde man gylt on the endes of Every of them." To son Champion Gyttons £200 at the age of twenty-one. To son Thomas Gyttyns £200, and the fee simple of a house "vppon the Keye." To son Jeffery Gyttyns £200 at the same age, and a lease for nine hundred years of a house on the Key inhabited by Michael Knott. To George and William Colston, sons of daughter Elizabeth, wife to William Colston, £25 apiece at the age of twenty-one. To daughter Margaret £50 towards her maintenance, and " all the Stocke belonginge to the grownd of my howse in Publowe," the money to be delivered to her at the discretion of " my wyffe," as she "shall see neede wth her estate" in that house, "and Afterward to Champyon." To daughter Agnes Gyttins £100 at her marriage, and £100 after her mother's decease ; also " my castinge bottell of Silver " double-gilt. To daughter Mary Gyttins £100 at her marriage, and £100 after her mother's decease ; also " one of my iij goblettes of xvj onnces double gylte," &c. To brother Robert Gyttyns £20, " wth all other debtes to him due." To " my Lovinge sister Lady Jane Pip A Portygue to make her a Jewell, acknowledginge my self to be A Thowsand tymes more in her debte." To " my good M^{rs} mystris Pepwell " a Portigue of gold, or the just value. The sum of £3. 6. 8. to " the helpe and furnyture of bedinge in mambridge nowe the howse of Correce'on." The same amount to " the Co'mon box of the poore in this Cytty." Testator forgives William Cole all the money paid " for his Redemption from Argell, Jn Considerac'on he shall doe my wyffe true and dilygent service duringe his Apprentishipp." Forty shillings to William Swetnam over and above "his dewe at the Co'minge owt of his yeeres." Legacies also to daughter Elizabeth Colston, brother Edward Gyttins, sisters Elizabeth, Cicely, Dorothy, and Katharine, and " the mayde in the howse." Wife Mary to be executrix, and have the residue of goods, debts, merchandise, &c. Michael Pepwell, Mr John Browne, Mr William Hickes, and William Ellice overseers, " to whome J doe geve xx^s J say to en'y of them." Provided always, " and yt is my determynate will that if any p'te of my Adventure, wch this daie J have at the Sea to ffraunce Spayne Portingall and Turkey which J doe esteme in 2013^{li} doe myssecarry, wch god forbid," each of my children to " beare the losse alyke," and wife Mary to have " the gaynes."

No record of probate : but the will was proved March 20th, 1586, as appears by the copy at Somerset House, *Spencer*, 13.

408.—JOHN BOSWELL.

1586. March 20th. To be buried " in the Crowde of S^t nicholas p'ishe." To the poor of that parish xx^s. The same amount to " the poore of the p'ishe of Shiffnall whereas J was borne," to be distributed at the discretion of brother George Boswell. To sons William and John xxx^{li} each at the age of twenty-one. To daughter Elizabeth xl^{li} at the same age, or when married. Also " if my wief be wth Child whether it bee a Boye or a wenche J doe geve and bequeath vnto yt xx^{li}" at the age of twenty-one, or day of marriage " yt it bee a wenche." To sister Joan Boswell forty shillings, half of which brother William Boswell gave her. To servant James Atwood forty shillings, " yf that he dothe serve owte his yeeres wth my wief." The same amount to Edward Dowle, serving out his years with " my wief," to make up " the so'me of iiij^{li} specyfied in his Jndentures." Ten shillings to

Michael Tillett " my boye." Twenty shillings to John Stinchcome, " yf he be bownde and serve his yeres." Legacies also to sister Elizabeth Benion, sister Anne Boswell, sister Elianor's daughter Margery, brother Richard Boswell, Elizabeth Watkins, Richard Yweme, John Grigge clerk, and servants Alice and Joan. If all the children should die, their legacies shall remain to brother Richard's children. Wife Elizabeth to have the residue, and be executrix. Mr John Webbe and brother Richard Boswell overseers: to the former xl^s. Witnessed by John Cothery, Adam Bynion, and George Watkins.

Proved May 13th, 1587.

409.—THOMAS GRYFFYTHE. In the margin *Griffith*.

1586. Sept. 13th. Testator was " of the Cytty of Bristoll marchaunte." His body " to the Earth from whence yt Came;" trusting by Christ's "deathe and Resurrection to obteyne forgevenes of my sinnes." The sum of iij^{li} in bread to " the poore people of Bristoll at my buryinge." To son John the lease of " my howse vppon the backe wherin J dwell," with the glass, wainscot, " the frame bourde in the Parlor of Wallnutt tree," &c.: but wife Elizabeth to enjoy it " tenn yeres after my death if she soe longe Lyve," and remains unmarried. To daughters Elizabeth and Mary two stone cruses covered double-gilt, and six silver spoons. To daughter Maud " my Turkey goldringe." To son Thomas " a Stone Cupp Covered wth silver." Of the residue of goods, money, plate, &c., one third part to wife Elizabeth, and the other parts to the children, John, Thomas, Elizabeth, Maud, and Mary, in equal portions. Wife Elizabeth and son John to be executors. Mr William Hopkins and brother Hugh Griffythe overseers. Witnessed by Hugh Griffyth and William Griffyth. The " so'me of the Jnventory is iiijC ij^{li} x^s."

Proved Oct. 11th, 1586.

410.—ROGER HAYNES, shoemaker.

1587. June 21st. Testator was of " the Cytty of Bristoll and of the p'ishe of the Holly Trinitie," and desired to be buried in St. Peter's churchyard, " neere vnto the place where my ffather and mother doe Lye buryed." Ten shillings unto " the poores box of Christ Church;" and the same amount to that of St. Peter's. To servant Mary Smyth, and to her legitimate heirs, two houses " in Defens streate " in the parish of St. Peter, in the occupation of Mary Mosly, widow, and John A Price; in default of issue, rem. to my servant and kinswoman Elizabeth Whyte and her heirs. To the said Elizabeth £5, and two houses " on Michael Hill." To Walter Pykes, alderman, and to his heirs, a house " in Wyne streate," in the occupation of John Bantinge " mynister." To Mr John Browne, alderman, and to his heirs, a house in the same street, in the occupation of Richard Coollim^r (?), saddler. To William son of Thomas Pytt of Bristoll, merchant, and to his heirs, the lease and interest in testator's dwelling house, with the wainscot, glass, and " portall," the doors, &c. To the said Thomas " my bloode stone." Unto the company of " the Shomakers of Bristoll " my great pan " and brandire and Pykes thervnto belonginge," to be kept " in the hall vntyll there be cawse to vse the same," and to be lent to every householder of that company " one daye in the yeere and noe more to boyle their pees' and not for any other vse payinge iiij'd to the vse of the poore of the said Crafte." To John Gryffyn, innholder, "my best Ringe." To Richard Stone and William Cradocke, shoemakers, twenty shillings apiece. Legacies also to servant Agnes Coorant, godsons Roger Oliley and Roger Baker, Joan Dye, daughter to Robert Dye, and goddaughter Alice Gryffyth. Roger Cooke, tanner, to have the residue, and be executor. "Mr Alderman Browne and Mr Alderman l'ykes" to be overseers. "Wytnes herevnto my fyrme and Seale, donne in the p'sence of these p'sons vnder wrytten R H Red fyrmed and Sealed in the p'sence of vs" George Baldwyn, Thomas Pyte, and Maud Pytt.

No record of proof.

411.—WILLIAM STERNOLDE, cooper.

1587. Dec. 10th. Testator was of "the Cytye of Bristoll." His body "to the Earthe." Twenty shilling to the poor of the parish of St. Nicholas. To brother Robert Sternolde my best wearing apparel; also £10, "to be paid w'thin one halfe yeere after my decease. yf yt please god that xlviij barrells of Hearinge nowe laden abourde the Tobye of Newnam, and xxviij barrells of heringe nowe Laden and A kynterkin of heringes nowe Laden abourd the Peeter of Milford be safely dischardged att the Porte of Bristoll or any other Porte of Right dischardge to the vse of me the said Willia' Sternolde or my Executors." To wife Agnes the rents of lands in "the Forest of Deane," co. Glouc., until daughter Margaret shall attain to the age of twenty-one. If the said Agnes should bear another child, it is to have £30 at that age. The said Agnes and daughter Margaret to have the residue, and be executors. "Jtem J doe hereby Release vnto my Cosen Robert A Deane all Acc'ons and demands' from the beginninge of the worlde vntill this daye." Brother-in-law John Whytson and "my Cosen xp'ofer Aileway" overseers, to each of whom ten shillings. Witnessed by Robert A deane, Matthew Cable, William Sternolde, and John Whytson.

Proved before William Drury, doctor of laws, Feb. 8th, 1587.

412.—DAVID OLDEFEILDE, shearman.

1587. June 13th. Testator was of "the Cytty of Bristoll," and desired to be buried "by my firste Wief in Temple Churche yarde." To son Edmund £10; also the lease of the house which he dwelleth in "in Tucker streate;" and also "my grindinge Stone furnished." To daughters Mary and Agnes Oldefeilde £20 apiece. To son William "the Tenne powndes w'ch was Lefte w'th John Spencer of London for the placinge of my said Sonne." To son John £C, "that ys Three powndes in menye, and more Three powndes sobers, and owinge me by Michaell Thirkell." To sister Agnes Dyer "three yardes of Weded Russett Cloth" to make her a gown. Six shillings to sister Judith; also "a Ifrize Cassoke and a Smocke." To son Thomas "my Ringe that I had of Parrye Gould smyth of London." Legacies also to Alice Oldefeilde, daughter to son Edmund, and Davye son of Thomas Tyther. Wife Cicely to have the residue, and be executrix. Thomas Pytte and William Nicholls overseers, to whom ten shillings apiece. Witnessed by the said Thomas and William.

Proved before William Drury, doctor of laws, Feb. 6th, 1587.

413.—PETER MATHEWE, draper.

1587. Oct. 1st. Testator was of "the Cytie of Bristoll," and desired to be buried in the churchyard of St. Nicholas, by the appointment of " my good frinde William Vawer shyryfe nowe of Bristoll." To wife Anne £300. To sons Bartholomew and John £200 apiece at the age of twenty-one. To daughter Penelope £200 when married. The sum of £100 unto " my onely faythfullyst frinde vnder god in the worlde William Vawer nowe one of the Sheryfes of the said Cytie of Bristoll." Unto " my by ffather Thomas Mathewe " 100 marks, and " the Graye geldinge wch he had of me at his laste beinge here." To brother James Mathewe £50. The sum of £20 to each of my sisters Joan and Susan, who are both married, " but J doe not knowe their husbandes names." To the children of Henry Elliott " who was executed at Glouc'" £20, to be equally divided. To Mistress Garrett " whoe was sometymes my Mystris " £20. To John Weste " of Andyver " the money that he " doth reste owinge me vppon accompte wch ys abowte Ten powndes or twentye Markes," but the executor is not to make him " any Acquyttaunce," by reason of " an Estatute wch J have passed to one Roberte Godfrye wth his condiscente And J have taken the same Roberte Godfrye dettor for Cxviij^{li} wch was the princypall that remayned vnpaid of the Statute " To father-in-law Peter Shee £20. Unto the poor generally of the city of Bristoll £100, for provision of corn, and other things necessary. Twenty nobles unto " my good frinde Mr Doctor Dunn ;" and the same amount to Thomas Thomas, saddler, dwelling in Bristoll " at the Signe of the Harte :" and to Shingleton, a draper " of Sowthe Hampton." To Lewys Phillippes, late baker " of the Backe of Bristoll", £10. Unto the poor of Stratford and Honnington, co. Wilts, " where J was brought vppe in my Childhode," £20 " to eyther of them." A further sum of £150 to my three children, equally divided. My " good frinde Mr Vawer " to be executor, and to bring up the said children " in Vertue and Learninge." To " my frindes " Mr Hierom Ham and Edward Lane £5 " the peece." Witnessed by William Vawer, Peter Shee, and Richard Moore.

On the day after the date of the will, testator added a " schedule :" having given unto the poor generally of the city of Bristoll £100, " for the provysion of Corne," &c., the said sum is now willed and bequeathed to remain for ever with " the Mayor and Co'mynaltye " of the city, to be from time to time converted and employed for " a Stocke in the howse of Correction to sett poore people in Worke w^{thin} the said Cytye." Witnessed by William Vawer, Hierom Ham, Thomas Saull, William Dawl....

Proved Oct. 9th, 1587.

414.—JOHN CAROE, vintner.

1588. Sept. 13th. Testator was of the parish of St Stephen in Bristoll, and willed that his body be " buried in good order in the churche of St Stephens aforesaide." To the parson and the clerk there ten shillings apiece. To the poor of the city £13. 6. 8., immediately after the burial. To wife Katharine, for her life, a messuage upon the Key, commonly called " the tower," and three other messuages there, now or late in the occupation of William Atkins, joiner, Edward Nayler, and Richard Adames ; a messuage in Small-street, now or late in the occupation of John Younge; a messuage "in Redcliffe streate," now or late in the occupation of Luke Harris, and commonly called "the Red Lion," and other messuages in the same street, now or late in the occupation of Humphrey Massis, William Jones, Elizabeth Pickerill, and Michael Vynson *(sic)*; also the messuage "towardes Marshestreate," held of Mr Standfaste, and the messuages "scituate by Froome gate," now or late in the occupation of Anthony Goodier: the said Katharine to receive the rents of all the other messuages, lands, &c., to the use of testator's five sons; and, after her decease, "the Red Lyon," and the messuage on the Key in the possession of the aforesaid William Atkyns, to remain to eldest son John Caroe and his legitimate heirs; in default of such issue, rem. to Henry Caroe and his legitimate heirs; in def., rem. to William Caroe and his legitimate heirs; in def., rem. to Richard Caroe and his legitimate heirs; in def., rem. to "Elexaunder Caroe" and his legitimate heirs. To the said Henry Caroe "my sonne," and his legitimate heirs, eight messuages "in Redcliffe streate" now or late in "the severall occupac'ons" of Michael Wynson, M^{ris} Crickland, Edward Nightingale, John Melloes, Humphrey Masics, and Philip Jones: also three messuages in Temple-street, whereof two are, or late were in the tenure of Nicholas Lyon, and one was lately purchased of William Kirke and his son, or of one of them; in def., rem. to William Caroe and his legitimate heirs; in def., rem. to the said Richard Caroe and his legitimate heirs; in def., rem. to the said Alexander Caroe and his legitimate heirs; in def., rem. to the said John Caroe and his legitimate heirs; in def., rem. to testator's right heirs. To son William and his legitimate heirs the aforesaid messuage upon the Key "Comonlye called the tower;" in def., rem. to the said Richard Caroe: also to the said William all the terms, estates, &c., in messuages on the Key "nere vnto the said howse called the tower." To son Richard and his legitimate heirs a messuage "in Temple Streate," in the possession of Thomas Davis, tucker; and those messuages now or late in the occupation of Elizabeth Pyckerell, Edward Naylor, John Young, and Anthony Goodier; in def., rem. to Alexander Caroe and his legitimate heirs; in def., rem. to the said John Caroe and his legitimate heirs: also to the said Richard all the "estates termes and interestes" in the messuage in Fisher lane, now or late in the possession of Thomas Davis, hooper; in the messuage "in Marshestreate," now or late in the possession of Robert Baynham: in two tenements in Silver-street, now or late in the possession of John Wilbram; in a messuage and garden "in Horse streate," held by lease; and in two gardens "at Michaell Hill," in the several possessions of Henry Griffyn and John Bull. To Alexander Caroe and his legitimate heirs a messuage in Fisher lane, now or late in the tenure of Richard Lambard; also two houses and gardens, and "one woorckhouse" in Horse-street, with outhouses, &c., now or late in the possession of William Atkins and others; a garden now or late in the possession of Henry Gibson, and a messuage in Horse-street, now or late in the occupation of Thomas Gamlyn; another messuage "in Horsestreate," now or late in the occupation of William Phillippes; three tenements upon Michael hill, now or late in the tenure of Philip Phylon, Roger Oliver, and Elizabeth Mason, widow; a messuage and garden "in tholde M'kett," now or late in the possession of Richard Young; and one shop "in Lewins Meade," now or late in the possession of John Bull "smythe;" in def., rem. to son John Caroe and his legitimate heirs; in def., rem. to son Henry. To the said Alexander the messuage or tenement in Temple-street, held of the Mayor, Burgesses, and Commonalty of the city. None of testator's sons, or their heirs, are to alienate or lease any of the aforesaid property before they shall come to the age of twenty-eight. Wife Katharine, after a reasonable "prysment" thereof made to the value of £100, to take "at her election" goods, plate, and "husholde stuffe" to furnish the said house called "the tower," and to enjoy and possess such goods "during her naturall liffe;" remainder to son William. She is also to have 100 marks, and all testator's timber within the city of Bristoll, for the building and repairing of the said house. To cousin Julian More £5 in money, and as much black cloth as will make her "a Gowne." To cousin Thomas Kynch, of Waterford, forty shillings to buy him three yards of satin to make him a doublet. Twenty shillings unto Joan which was my servant, and "nowe dwellethe wth Mr Kelke." Ten shillings to servant Joan, who lately dwelt with master Bisse. Ten shillings to every servant in testator's house at the time of his decease, "bothe men kinde and wemen kinde." Legacies also to Matthew Hitchinges, Katharine Kett, daughter of Philip Ket *(sic)* of Waterford, and William Scott, and his daughter Julian. Wife Katharine to be executrix, and to provide, within forty days after testator's decease "at the fartheste," gold rings of six or seven shillings apiece, and give the same unto those "my frindes" as followeth, viz., goodwife Merricke, Henry Griffythe, and his wife, goodwife Clodd, Edward Naylor, and his wife and daughter, Mrs Harte, Mrs Androes, Mrs Perrie, the wife of Henry Lucas, Elizabeth Tytherton, the wife of Richard Adames, and master Androes. The residue of testator's goods, &c., to be sold, and the money divided among his five sons. John Androwes "Customer," Robert Perrey, gent., Henry Griffithe, tailor, and Richard Adames, ropemaker, to be overseers, and each to have four marks. Witnessed by Robert Perrey, John Lardge, and Henry Griffin.

Proved Sept. 30th, 1588.

415.—CHRISTOPHER CECYLL. In the margin *Cecill*.

1587. May 30th. Testator was of "the p'ishe of St Michaell in the Subvrbes of the Cytie of Bristoll." His body "to the Earthe to Christyan Buriall." To his "very frinde" Richard Mascall of the said city, butcher, and his heirs, the messuage wherein the said Richard doth now dwell, "in the Shambles Called Worshipfull Streate, extendinge from the said Streate vnto the Churchyarde of St Mary Porte," and all testator's other lands, tenements, &c., within the same city, and elsewhere in England, paying to wife Elizabeth, during her life, four nobles a year, the payment to be made quarterly "as he dothe vse to doe." The said Elizabeth to have all the moveable goods, and be executrix. Witnessed by Richard Yorke, tanner, Richard George, brewer, Anthony Goodyer, tailor, Walter Fryer, tailor, Walter Tovye, smith, Richard Byllinge, tailor, and Thomas Pryn', notary public.

No record of proof.

416.—PATRICK WISE.

1588. Sept. 10th.—" of the Cyty of Bristoll Muzition entendinge (yf god p'mit to goe for Jrelaude doe make my last will and Testament .... my body to the earth to be enterred where yt shall please god." All my worldly goods, &c., to daughters Letice Wyse and Joan Wise. Patrick Younge, dyer, and Michael Winson to be overseers, and have " the vse of my said Children' and their porc'ons." Inventory=£161. 0. 7.

Proved Jan. 16th, 1590.

417.—WILLIAM NICHOLLS, clothier.

1589. Aug. 4th. Testator was of the parish of Temple within the city of Bristoll, and willed that his body be " buryed in o^r Lady Chappell in the p'ishe Churche of Temple neare vnto the Corpes of Johane my wyffe." Five marks to the poor of that parish at the funeral. Forty shillings to Richard Marten, vicar of Temple; and vj^s viij^d to a preacher for preaching a sermon " att my funerall." Twelve poor men to have " ffrize gownes and Cappes," and be present. To daughter Alice, wife of Walter Williams, £100; also " twoe gylte boules of sylver," &c., and " thre goulde ringes wch was my wyfes." To son-in-law Walter Williams " my blacke geldinge." To Walter, son of the said Walter, £10 at the age of twenty-one. To Alice, Mary, and Anne, daughters of the said Walter, £10 each when married. To servant Ellis Nordon xx^s, to be delivered to him shortly after " my deceasse." Legacies also to Richard Jackson, David Henton, John Gybbens, David Williams, John Browninge, and Margery wife of Owen Rogers. Son-in-law Walter Williams and Matthew Havelande to be overseers, and each to have xl^s. Son George Nicholls to be executor, and have the residue of goods, lands, &c. Son-in-law Walter to have " the tutele and goverment " of the said George with all his legacies during " the tyme of his Mynorytie," putting in " suffycient suerties to the father of the orphans," and paying v^{li} yearly for the use of every £100. If the said George should die under the age of twenty-one, daughter Alice Williams and her children to have all the goods, lands, &c. Witnessed by Richard Marten " mynister" (the writer of the will), Walter Williams, and Ellis Northerne.

Proved Nov. 18th, 1589.

418.—ANTHONY STANDBACKE.

1587. May 31st. Testator describes himself as " of the Cytye of Bristoll Late Mayor there," and wills that his body " be Layed in xpi'en buryall " in the crowde of St Nicholas. To his wife Katharine Standbacke, for her life, all his lands, tenements, rents, &c., " wthin the Cytye of Bristoll, in the County of Bristoll and in Templestreate, and in St Nicholas Streate there and els where in the Realme of Englande ;" to remain fo ever, after her decease, to all intents and purposes to that good and godly use of orphans and fatherless children " or otherwyse howsoever" as of late it was devised by Mr John Carre, deceased, " for an Hospitall to be erected wthin this Cytye of Bristoll," as by the will and testament of the said John Carre " yt maye appeere." In default of such erection of the said hospital " and soe that yt doth not take effect," all the said property to go to " my said Wyffe yf she be lyvinge," and to " my very lovinge and Trusty frinde Mr William Byrde," woollen draper, to be used to their good and godly discretion, or the discretion of one of them "survyvinge," for the best profit and commodity of the poor. Wife Katharine to have the residue of goods, and be sole executrix. The said Mr William Byrde to be overseer. Witnessed by the said William, Thomas Brooke, and Thomas Pryn, notary public.

No record of proof.

The register of the parish of St Nicholas records the burial of "Jonne the wiffe of Antonye Stanbacke," Feb. 23rd, 1575, and of "Antonye Stanbanke," June 8th, 1587; and the marriage of Thomas Callowhill and Katharine Stanbanke, widow, Sept. 25th, 1587.

419.—GEORGE MARTYN, soapmaker and chandler.

1589, Dec. 31st. Testator was of "the parrishe of St Thomas the Appostle wthin the Cyty of Bristoll," and declared his last will "nuncupatyvelye." To his son Richard the dwelling house in Redcliff-street, with the furnace and all implements and utensils for soapmaking and "for Chaundlinge;" also the land "in Jvye Lane" and in St Thomas-street. To his son George a house next adjoining unto the said dwelling house, and the house "in Redclyffe Streate" wherein Thomas Browne "the Hatter" dwelleth. All his apparel to his said two sons: and "all his wyffes apparrell" to his daughters, Anne, Elizabeth, Cecily, and Edith. Legacies to his brother Richard Martyn "of Dorsley," kinsman Harry Martin of Bristoll, Philip Juke, late servant Edith Symons, William Kearne, Richard Woodsonne, and Dorothy Hawkins. To Alice Martyn "his Pownde garnet ringe." To Harry Martyn aforesaid "his beste Lardge Byble." To the poor of Bristoll £10, "wch ys in the handes of the Chamberlen of Bristoll." To the poor of Blaisdon parish £10. Residue of goods to be equally divided among his six children. If any of the said children should die before his or their lawful age, the portion to remain among the children of his brother William Marten, late of Bleisdon, deceased. His brother Richard Marten and kinsman Henry Martyn to be overseers. Witnessed by Richard Woodson, Henry Martyn, and William Carne.

"Administracio Concessa fuit in Curia p'rogativa Thome Grayle dat' London xiiij^{to} die mens' Januarij Anno d'ni 1589."

420.—RICHARD ROGERS the elder, soapmaker.

1588, May 28th. Testator was of "the p'ishe of St Thomas Thappostle in the Cyty of Bristoll," and desired to be buried in the churchyard there "as nere the grave of my ffather and in such semely sorte as shall seme good to my executors and overseers." To the said parish church xx^s. To the poor people of St. Thomas's almshouse xx^s. For "my funerrall Sermon" vj^s viij^d. Twelve poor men and women to have gowns "of Blacke ffrize," and "to eu'y of the women a kerchewe clothe of dowles." Forty shillings to be bestowed in apparel upon kinsman William James of Bedminster, and his wife. To daughter Rachel £100 at the age of twenty, also "my frier Cuppe covered wth silver my lytle Sylver Cuppe wch J vse to warme drinke in," &c. To daughter Joan Rogers £200, and the lease of an orchard at Temple gate; also "my silver salte wch J bought of David Warren of Worle," a walnut chest, &c., and "my Crocke J bought of goodwyffe Baker."

s

Twenty marks to each of the children of son Richard Rogers. To Agnes Rogers, "the nowe wyffe of my said sonne Richard," £60. To son Nicholas Rogers £50. To son Robert Rogers three silver spoons, a silver pot marked with testator's name, and a maser; also "my right and interest of the howse att Porte Walles wch J houlde of the p'ishe Churche of the blessed lady of Redclyffe in the subvrbes of the Cyty of Bristoll." To son Richard the biggest silver salt, "my great aqua vitæ Crocke my yron Crocke," &c., and "a brasen Chaffingedishe wch was his grandmothers;" also £30 towards "the buyldinge of the lytle olde howse wherein J nowe dwell lyinge betwene the lande of John Alkin of the south side and my howse J bought of Mr Harry Braine of the north side"; the lease of the garden in Redcliff, and all the timber and trees in the orchard at Temple gate before bequeathed to daughter Joan, who is to allow the said Richard free egress and regress for the purpose of cutting, squaring, sawing, &c., the said timber during the space of five years next after testator's decease. To daughter Rachel and her legitimate heirs, the messuage or tenement in the tenure of Richard Edwardes, pewterer, in Redcliff-street, between son Richard's dwelling house, on the south side, and the tenement in the tenure of William Slany, girdler, on the north, and extending from the said street forwards "vnto the Halle" of the said messuage "nowe in the manuraunce" of the said Richard Rogers backwards; which property testator purchased of Robert Henshawe. If the said Rachel should die s.p., rem. to son Nicholas and his legitimate heirs. To sons Richard and Robert, and their heirs, a messuage or tenement "in Redclyffe streate," between the messuage in the manuraunce of George Marten, soapmaker, on the north, and the messuage in the manuraunce of William Jones, soapmaker, on the south, and extending in length from the said street forwards "vnto the Ryver of havon" backwards; which said tenement testator purchased of David Harris the younger, and used for his "worke howse." To his said son Robert Rogers and his heirs, the corner house "at the bridge ende in Bristoll," turning into Redcliff-street, in the occupation of James Inshall, goldsmith; which tenement testator bought of Mr Maurice Rodny esq.; also another messuage, adjoining the said tenement, between the aforesaid "litle oulde howse" on the south, and the said corner messuage on the north; which property was purchased of Mr Harry Brayne. Sums of money to "my prentyces" Benjamin Jen'n, John Cullymore, and Thomas Puxstone, and to servants Margaret Hentton and Elianor Dewell. Sons Richard and Robert to have the residue, and be executors. Peter Bysse and Richard Davies overseers, to each of whom xx^s. Witnessed by Peter Bysse, Richard Davys, Thomas Puxstone, and Margaret Henton.

Proved June 19th, 1588.

421.—THOMAS WALL, soapmaker.

1589. Aug. 16th. Testator was of "the p'ishe of Christchurche wythin the Cyty of Bristoll," and committed his body "to xp'ien buriall." To son John Wall the "biggeste Jlande Chayer," &c., also £20, and "my greate Sope furnes wth all vates," &c., at the age of twenty-one; but wife Margery during "her wydowehed" is to hold and use the said furnace, &c., paying yearly twenty shillings to the said John. To daughter Anne Wall the best bedstead in the higher parlor, &c., and a spruce chest "wch ys in the Cocklofte," also a little "portingall Chayer," and £50 in ready money at the age of seventeen. Wife Margery to be sole executrix, and to hold and enjoy, for her life, the house in Lewens mead, and see the yearly payments made to "the Goodwyffe Pullen." William Browne, skinner, and William Jones, baker, to be overseers. "The Totall some of the Jnventory Amountethe to the some of Cxliij^{li} xv^s viij^d."

Proved before William Drury, doctor of laws, Nov. 19th, 1589.

422.—WILLIAM SLANYE, girdler.

1589. May 27th. Testator was of "the Cyty of Bristoll," and desired to be buried in the parish churchyard of St. Thomas. Wife Katharine to enjoy, during her life, the dwelling house "att the Bridge ende"; rem. to sons John and Henry Slanye and their heirs for ever. To the said Henry a stone cruse covered with silver, and six silver spoons. All "workinge Tooles" to son John, if he will follow "my occupac'on"; if not, to his brother Henry, if he will use them; if not, to wife Katharine. Violet breeches &c., to John Robertes "my Surgion." A black doublet, &c., to "my vncle" George Slanye of Bewdley. A "Crane Colored fustian dublet" to cousin Thomas Morgan of Bewdley. A platter to "Gregorie Baylyves sonne my godson." One flockbed to Thomas Trowbridge of Hutton; and "my best hatte" to the uncle of the said Thomas. Legacies also to the poor of St. Thomas's almshouse, Thomas Lawrence, goddaughter Joyce Cother, Edmund Trowbridge, Simon Barrett of Hannam, and the goodwife Jorden. Wife Katharine to have the residue, and be executrix. Dated in Bristoll. John Cother and John Richman overseers, to each of whom v^s. Witnessed by the said overseers. Inventory = £76. 10. 3.

Proved Aug. 2nd, 1589.

423.—JAMES TURVER, glover.

1588. June 3rd. Testator was of "the p'ishe of St Thomas Thappostle wthin the Cyty of Bristoll." The sum of £5 to be paid to "every of my Children," viz., Margery, John, Nicholas, and Mary, when of lawful years and discretion; wife "Eme" to have the use of the money in the mean time, putting in sufficient assurance for the payment thereof to the overseers, "yf she shall chaunce to marry." She is also to have the residue of goods, and be sole executrix. William Higgins and George Martyn overseers. Witnessed by Thomas Thackham, preacher, Nicholas Rece, and Peter Bysse.

Proved before Gilbert Browne, doctor of laws, Feb. 5th, 1588.

424.—JOHN BRINSDON.

1588. April 3rd.—"my bodye to be buryed in the earth att the discretion of my ffrindes." To son John £100; also to him and his heirs, two houses in Wootton; in default of heirs, rem. to son William and his heirs. Brother George oweth £62, of which the sum of £32 is forgiven; so that son John shall hold an estate in reversion of a tenement "wch he hath boughte vnto him." To son William £50. To sister Margaret twenty nobles. Wife Dorothy to pay for brother Giles £10, for which testator is bound to his sister Anne. "Jtem my vncle nicholas Webbe oweth me Tenne powndes for Roberte osborne besides accompte of wheate wch J bought of my Cosen poore," and other money " wch ys noe p'te of Roger Bowmans p'te," and also £20 " wch he p'mised me wth my first wyffe in mariadge." Roger Webbe oweth £10 at his day of marriage, or death. Brother William Brinsdon to pay Mr. Langley £20, due upon Roger Bowman and testator ; on payment of which amount, the said Roger is to pay "my wyffe" £10. Mr Leea oweth £30, "whereof there ys Paulne for ten powndes." John Sachfeild is also in debt. Roger Bowman had put into stock £500, and testator £400 ; but the said Roger having taken out almost £300, " my accompte muste nedes be better then his," yet testator is content to part with him " yf he soe will." Wife Dorothy to have the residue, and be sole executrix. Witnessed by Mr William Wally, Mr William Sherston, and others.

Proved before William Drury, doctor of laws, June 18th, 1588.

425.—EDWARD ROE.

1588. Jan. 13th. To be buried "over against my pewe dore." All goods to "my wyffe," who is to pay "my debtes," and be executrix. Witnessed by Thomas Tayler, Thomas Printer, Agnes Goodyere, Alice Hamlett, Christopher Coffe, and Thomas Mors.

Proved " in Curia prerogativa " Jan. 25th, 1588.

426.—ELIZABETH ROE, widow.

1589. April 14th. Testatrix was of " the Cytie of Bristoll," and desired to be "buryed in the Churche of the p'ishe of St Thomas nere vnto my husbande." To my two children, Joan and Elizabeth Roe, £100, of which the sum of £40 has been lent to John Kidwellyter *alias* Kainshutte (?) ; also all the household stuff, plate, &c., to be equally divided, and paid at their marriage. To the said Joan " my Grogran gowne my best petycoate and my silke grograyne aprone." To the said Elizabeth " my blacke Laced gowne," &c. All the linen and twelve " goulderinges " to be equally divided between the said children. Twenty shillings to Alice Clarke. Thomas Printer, father of testatrix, to be executor, and Thomas Taylor, overseer. Witnessed by John Hinge, Alice Clarke, Anne Goodyere, Thomas Mors, and Christopher Cufe.

No record of proof.

The register of the parish of St Thomas records the burial of Edward Rooe, Jan. 24th, 1588, and that of Elizabeth Rooe, April 29th, 1589.

427.—THOMAS POLLINGTON, merchant.

1587. Jan. 20th. To be buried " in Bristoll in Christ Churche in the Channcell as nere the grave of my late wyffe Elizabethe as conveniently maye bee." To Thomas Pollington " my sonne and heyer " and his legitimate heirs, after the decease of my mother, lands, tenements, &c., " in the Towne and p'ishe of Thame in Oxforde shere late my father Will'm Pollingtons deceassed and ys two howses wth gardens ortchards and thapp'ten'nces and halfe an Acre of meade grownde app'teyninge to the greater howse." If Thomas should die s.p., rem. to son Richard and his legitimate heirs. To the said Thomas £300 at the age of twenty-two ; also " my beste gylte silver salte " ; also to him and his heirs " my howse in Bristoll that J dwell in in

Wynestreate"; in def., rem. to daughter Elizabeth Pollington and her heirs for ever. To son Richard Pollington a lease of sixty years of the parsonage of Kingston "nere to Tanton in Som's'tshere houlden of s^t Augustines in Bristoll"; also £300 at the age of twenty-two, and three silver pots parcel-gilt. To eldest daughter Elizabeth Pollington £300 at the age of twenty-one, or when married; also "her owne mothers weddinge ringe of goulde and a Gymoll of goulde and her beste gowne of Shepne Clothe and her beste Lynnen." To daughter Margery Pollington £300 at the age of twenty-one, or when married; also "one gylte ale potte," &c. If both sons should die s.p., daughters Elizabeth and Margery, and their heirs, to have the property in Thame, and also the aforesaid lease of the parsonage of Kingston. The sum of £20 to "the poore people p'itioners and Almeshowses of Bristoll." Testator forgives his brother William Pollington all his debts, and gives him "to begyn to trade wth xl^{li}." He also forgives "Johane Yevans of London my naturall sister" all her debts, and gives her xx^s. To "myne owne Mother" xl^s. Legacies also to sister Alice Cobbet, John Savadge the elder and his wife, and Thomas Savadge "my Servaunte." Wife Susan to be sole executrix, and have the residue of goods, debts, adventures, &c., and the custody and "govermente" of the children during their minority, and have and enjoy "the vse of the stockes" and legacies, to bring them up, and also the dwelling house until son Thomas come to the age of twenty-one. William Yemans, grocer, and William Ellis, merchant of Bristol, to be overseers. Witnessed by Matthew Hickman and Thomas Savadge.

Proved "in Curia prerogatiua Caut'," before William Lewen, doctor of laws, May 29th, 1590.

428.—JOAN STONE, widow.

1590. April 30th. Testatrix was of "the Cytye of Bristoll in the p'ishe of Temple there," and desired to be buried in the chancel "wthin the p'ishe Churche of Temple in Bristoll afforesaid," as near as might be to her late husband Mr John Stone. Forty shillings unto Mr Richard Marten, vicar of Temple. To son-in-law Sampson Edwardes two goblets "all gylte p oz xlix ounces," one stone pot, with a foot, lip, and cover "all gylte," six silver spoons "wth Thappostells vppon thendes," &c. To daughter Edith the second best diaper table-cloth, &c. To Edmond son of Sampson Edwardes, at the age of twenty-one, 100 marks; also "one very fayer gylt salt wth a Cover," &c., "my best Carpett for a table, wth a lesser Carpett for a syde table," &c. If the said Edmond should die under the given age, the said money to remain to daughter Edith; and the plate and other legacies to be equally divided between Thomas Brooke, the younger, and Joan, Margery, and Elizabeth Alye, the children of "my Cosen" Edward Alie of Tewkesbury. The sum of £4 unto "my syster" Elizabeth Barebone, and forty shillings to her daughter Elizabeth. To John, William, Thomas, and Walter Stone, "the flower sonnes of my Nephewe" John Stone, xx^s apiece. To son-in-law John Gostlett one pot of silver, &c. To Joan Hedges, one of the daughters of the said John, forty shillings. To Agnes and Elizabeth, two of his other daughters, £10 apiece, &c., at the day of their marriage. To the children of William Bullocke and Fortune "his wyffe" £20. To the poor people of Temple parish £5; and to the poor of other parishes of this city "other fyve powndes" on the day of "my funerall." The sum of £65 to be distributed among the poor of the parishes of Temple, St. Thomas, and Redcliff, within the term of thirteen years; that is to say, £5 yearly, first to one parish, and then another, at "than'neyacon' of o' Lady S⁺ Mary the virgin," until the said sum be "fully distributed and geven." The sum of £100 to be bestowed in cloth and other necessaries requisite and needful for the charges of "my funerall"; whereof unto twelve poor men, twelve gownes and "Cappes," and to twelve poor women "xij ffrize gownes and xij ells of dowles for kerchers." Legacies also to Thomas Brooke, the younger, at the age of twenty-one, Elianor Heriottes, John Conie and his wife Agnes, and children Robert and Mary Conie, and each of the children of Thomas Saule of Clifton. Thomas Brooke to have the residue, and be sole executor. Kinsman Edward Alie and William Sayer overseers, to each of whom "a mourninge gowne." Witnessed by Edward Alye and William Sayer.

Proved July 3rd., 1590.

429.—WALTER DAVYES, glover. In the margin *Davis*.

1589. May 24th. Testator was of "the Cytye of Bristoll," and parish of All Saints, and willed that his body be buried "in the earth whereof yt was made." To cousin Walter Davys £10 at the age of twenty-one, and one thousand of white leather. To John, Edward, and Thomas, three of the sons of brother John Davis, deceased, £5 apiece at the age of twenty-one. To sister Joan £3. 6. 8. To Roger son of Richard Davys £3 at the age of twenty-one; and to his sister Elianor £3: if these two should die before the "tymes afforesaid," the children of brother John Davys are to have their legacies in "equall porc'ons." To cousin Alice Bellamye xx^s; and to her children x^s apiece at their several days of marriage, or their "seu'all ages of xxj yeres." To James Davys of Upton xx^s; and to each of his children x^s at the age of twenty-one, or their marriage. To Elizabeth and Anne Hamlen, the children of Robert Hamlyn, late of "the Cyty of Bristoll m'chaunte deccassed," x^s apiece, to be paid to them "as ye before expressed." To Walter son of Thomas Rockwell "sayler" xl^s at the age of twenty-one: if he should die under that age, rem. to Edith the child of Thomas Rockwell. To "my wyffe" a yearly rent of £10 over and besides her other legacies; the said rent to be received out of testator's dwelling house, and the tenement in High-street in the tenure of Edward Evenet, goldsmith, the tenement in Broad-street in the tenure of John Henry, and the messuage and tenement in the tenure of Thomas Holbeck, haberdasher, "vppon the bridge of Havon, wthin the said Cyty." James Banghe to be allowed quiet possession of "my shoppe," and the chamber wherein "he nowe lyeth," and such other rooms as have been demised and granted to him by indenture of lease; and to have and use all the implements in the rooms. Testator's heirs to have and enjoy all his drapery, and "waynscott Glasse wyndowes," &c., in his dwelling house, and also in the tenement in the tenure of the said Edward Evenett, goldsmith, and in the tenement in the tenure of James Cadle, pewterer. Wife Edith to have and enjoy "the Chamber aforestreate," with "the gallery adioyninge vnto the same," during her life, without paying any rent. Twenty shillings to Walter son of Richard Yorke. Twenty shillings to the company of "white Tawers" within the city "att my Buriall." The lands and tenements before mentioned, and the tenements held by Edward

Evenett and John Henry to go to that child "my wyffe nowe goeth wth all," if the same be a man child, and to its heirs; in default of issue, rem. to daughter Joan for her life; and, after her decease, and that of the said child, to Walter Davys, son of brother John, and his legitimate heirs; in def., rem. to John, Edward, and Thomas, sons of the said John Davies, and to their heirs jointly for ever. To daughter Joan and her heirs for ever, a tenement in Temple-street, in the tenure of Richard Horner, dyer. If wife Edith should bear a "woman Childe," it is to have £60. To cousin Mabel Morgan, widow, and her daughters Margery and Alice Morgan, a yearly rent of forty shillings out of lands and tenements "somtymes the Lorde Lysles Lande," purchased by lease for certain years of the Chamber of the city of Bristoll, and held by Walter Pykes alderman, Richard May gent., and William Colston merchant. A yearly rent of fifteen shillings, during testator's term and interest of and in the messuage called "Brewe howse," situate in "the Subvrbes of the Cytye of Bristoll afforesaid," without the gate called "the Pythye gate," and held by Christopher Dyllet, brewer, to be divided equally between the poor of the almshouses of Lewens mead and St James's Back, and the prisoners in the gaol of Newgate. To cousin Walter Davys, and his heirs, executors, and assigns, all right, title, interest, and demand in a messuage upon the bridge of Bristoll, now or late in the tenure of Thomas Holbecke; paying to wife Edith the said yearly rent during her life, and also "one Suger lofle weyenge ten powndes and a box of m'malade weyenge iij^li yerely," at the feast of the Circumcision of our Lord "Comonly called newe yeres day"; and, after her decease, paying to the other executor, if then living, during her natural life, the said sugar-loaf, &c., at the feast aforesaid: also paying to the said Edith, during the space of six years, the sum of xlv^s iiij^d at the four principal feasts of the year. To Michael Bowden "my apprentyce" £3. 6. 8, to be paid to him "att thexpyrac'on of his apprentishippe." Wife Edith and daughter Joan to have the residue, and be executors. Richard Maye and John Henry gent. to be overseers, and have twenty shillings apiece. Read, published, sealed, and subscribed, Jan. 7th, 1589, in the presence of the said Richard and John.

Proved May 20th, 1590.

430.—PHILIP SCAPULIS, stationer. In the margin *Scapelis*.

1589. Aug. 9th. Testator describes himself as born in Germany "in the Auncient Citie of Tryer and dwellinge in Bristoll in England in Winstreate in the p'ishe of the holye Trinitie," and desires to be "buryed after the manner of A Christian man" in the church of that parish "before the Pewe wherein J was wonte to kneale." Ten shillings unto "the poore man John Ball the Crippell." Ten shillings unto old John Tannye, bowyer, and his wife. Ten shillings unto the poor man —— Heughes, lame man, being one of the almsmen of "the Almes howse w^thin Lattordes gate," and to Anne his wife, "the longeste liver of any of them bothe." Ten shillings unto "the poore woman the Goodwife Gere wch some tyme did dwell wth me in London and did there Nurse me A Childe in my howse dwellinge nowe in Bristoll." Five shillings in bread to the poor prisoners in Newgate "the wch haue noe thinge but that is geven them by godlie disposed people." To fifty poor men or women that be known to be "trewe p'testantes" sixpence each. Five shillings to the wife of the goodman Ryse deceased, that "some tymes" was a shearman dwelling in Temple-street, and his wife is "nowe" in one of the almshouses "wthin loffordes yate." To godson Philip, son of Thomas the gardener, and to godson Philip, son of Lewes Tayler, ten shillings each. To cousin Margaret, Thomas Tyler's kinswoman, twenty shillings besides her wages. Unto my godson (the son of Anthony Simons tailor, deceased,) called "by my name Phillippe," ten shillings. "J doe yeve vnto the poore widdowe (of) Ankerett Knighte pointmaker deceased dwellinge in Lewens meade tenne shillinges." To Richard Foorde, stationer, "wch was some tyme my prentice," the great press standing in the garden, and the three moulds made of "latten wyer," to make "paste bourdes wth all," &c. To neighbour Nicholas Woulfe, cutler, "my longeste Ridinge swoorde." To cousin Henry Nayler "my other longe Ridinge swoord." Legacies also to Robert Goodyer, smith, and Margaret his wife, dwelling in St. Peter's parish, old Richard Rudge, shoemaker, old John Faye, grocer, dwelling upon the bridge, George Brymhaye, testator's gardener, and his wife, Alice and Elizabeth Yeomans, testator's "maydes," the poor old woman "the Goodwife Ellyn one of the Almes howse of Michaell Hill," and Master Jones "our p'son." Wife Elizabeth to have the residue, and be sole executrix. Cousin Thomas Tyler, hooper, "dwellinge in Ballante streate," and friend Hugh Harvye, schoolmaster and scrivener, "dwellinge by St Peters Ploumpe," to be overseers. To the said Thomas Tyler "my beste blacke gowne "furred with white lamb, and "faced wth bodge." To the said Hugh Harvye the other best black gown "lyned wth double frysado and faced alsoe wth bodge"; also to each of them fifty shillings in money "wch they shall receave of Richard Foord stacioner of Bristoll" of that money "wch he dothe owe me," and all bows, shafts, and quivers, parted justly between them. Witnessed, on Jan. 20th, 1589, by Henry Nayler and Richard Foorde.

Proved "in Curia Prerogatiua," May 21st, 1590.

The register of the parish of Christ Church records the burial of Mary Scapulis, Aug. 19th, 1574; the baptism of Margaret daughter of Philip Scapulis, June 28th, 1581, and her burial, June 3rd, 1585; and the burial of Philip Scapulis "stacioner," May 7th, 1590. The register of Bristol apprentices states that David son of John Trewell of Chard, co. Somerset, "posuit se app'ntic' Ph'o Scapulis Stac'on' et Marie vx' eius", Aug. 25th, 1561.

431.—ANTHONY PILL, grocer.

1591. April 10th. Testator, who was of the parish of All Saints "in the Cytye of Bristoll," made his will nuncupatively, appointing his wife Elianor and only son John executors, and bequeathing all his goods to them. Witnessed by William Dyvis (Davis), Amy Brooke, Margery Butlin, Elizabeth Williams, and others.

"Probatum fuit hoc p'ns Testamentu' in Curia prerogativa se'do die post festu' sc'i Joh'is Bap'te : 1591." The Orphan Book contains another copy of this will, the probate clause stating that it was proved April 23rd, 1591; which agrees with the copy at Somerset House, *Sainherbe*, 28.

Anthony Pyll was admitted to the freedom of the city of Bristol, Sept. 19th, 12th Eliz., "quia fuit filius Will'mi Pyll groc' Burgens'."

432.—JOAN WHYTE, widow. In the margin *White*.

1592. Aug. 21st. Testatrix was of "the Cytie of Bristoll," and desired to be buried in the churchyard of Christ Church. Five shillings to the poor of St. John's almshouse; and two shillings to every other almshouse in "the Cytie of Bristoll." Forty shillings in bread unto the poor of the said city "in gen'all." To son Thomas Whyte the lease of the house commonly called "the Whyte Lyon Lyenge in Brodestreate," which lease was also given to him by his father deceased. To son-in-law John Rothell, and his wife, xx^{li}. To Elizabeth Heryforde x^{li} "at the daye of her Marryadge"; rem. to John Rothell and his wife, if she should die before marriage. To Thomas Farmer, and his wife, the three bowls, and "twoe whyte ones wch he hathe of myne." To William Waynewrighte, and his wife, xxx^{li}. To daughter Anne Waynewrighte the spruce chest in the great chamber, and a "lytle Cheste wth the Lynnen that ys yn him beinge yn the Lynnen Chamber." To the said Anne, and Joan Farmer, the best coverlet and curtains, "wth the ffrenge," each of them to have the use thereof as often as they, or either of them, lie in childbed, and "the Longeste Lyver of them twoe" to possess the said goods. To Mr. Morgan Jones "o^r p'son" x^s. To the aforesaid John Rothell xx^s. Legacies also to John Woodwarde, and Thomas, Joyce, and Anne Woodwarde, children of John, every one of Thomas Nelme's children, John and Richard, sons of Edward Herryforde, and Mr. Aberte. Son Thomas to have the residue, and be executor. John Rothell and John Woodwarde overseers. Witnessed by Morgan Jones "the wryter hereof," John Rothell, John Woodwarde, Thomas Farmer, and William Waynrighte.

Proved before Francis James, vicar general in spirituals of the bishop of Bristoll, Sept. 22nd, 1592.

The name of this testatrix suggests a reference to the will of Thomas White, of the city of Bristoll, merchant, proved in P.C.C., March 24th, 1601, *Montague*, 8, containing the words, - to son Thomas "my Ringe which I allwaies weare that S^r ffraunces Drake gave"; to daughter-in-law Alice Grice "my diamond Ring which was her mothers, and the double hoope ringe that her Mother allwaies wore which sir ffraunces' Drake gave."

433.—PHILIP LANGLEY, alderman.

1587. June 5th. Testator was of "the Cytye of Bristoll," and desired to be buried in the parish church "of Alhallowes." To wife Mary, for her life, the dwelling house in "the highe streate" of that city, and a messuage in the same street called "the George," in the occupation of John Webbe, draper, and Elizabeth Boswell, widow; also two tenements in St. Nicholas street, in the occupation of Robert Prince, John Harris, and James Bushe; two tenements "in St Mary porte streate," in the occupation of Philip Gwynne and Richard Browne, shoemakers; four tenements "in Wynestreate," in the occupation of John Thurstone, John Morgan "seriannte," Joan Lenny, widow, and William Butler: the same lands and tenements to remain to son Toby Langley and his legitimate heirs male, on condition that he does not grant or demise any part of the said property to any person for more than twenty-one years, or less, or three lives, or less, reserving thereupon the old accustomed rent, or more, "as Tente in Tayle May Lawfully doe"; if he should do so, the property shall remain to Philip Langley, son of the said Toby, and his heirs male; in def., rem. to the female heirs of the said Toby. All other lands, tenements, &c., and all lands "houlden for terme of yeeres," and leases, &c., in the city of Bristol, and in the counties of Somerset, Gloucester, and Monmouth, and elsewhere in the realm of England, except one garden, held for a term of years of the parishioners of All Saints' within the said city of Bristol, lying "neere a streate Called the Pythie," to go to son Toby, and his legitimate heirs male, on the aforesaid condition; in def., rem. to the heirs male of brother William Langley, deceased. To the said Toby 200 oz. of plate, he to make "his Choyse," save only of such plate as Mr. Pepwall "my wyves ffather" gave her; also £2000, to be paid to him in separate sums within four years; £1000 of this sum to be in the keeping of the Mayor, Burgesses, and Commonalty, until the said Toby or his heirs, by the advice of the executrix and overseers, shall conclude, and "thinke yt good and Convenyent" to purchase lands therewith; the said Mayor, &c., to pay him and his heirs, &c., "vij^{li} yeerely for eu'y hundred" for the use and possession thereof; the said Toby or his heirs to give the Mayor and Chamberlain one year's notice before he or they take out the money for the purchase of lands. If "any honest burges" shall borrow any of the said money, the said Mayor, &c., "shall not take above the rate of viij^{li} for the forbearaunce or Loane of every hundred pounde" for one year. To Philip Langley, son of the said Toby, 200 oz. of the best plate at his age of twenty-one; his father to have the use of it in the meantime, "puttinge in suffycyent securytye vppon receyte thereof vnto the Mayor Burgesses & Comynalty of the foresaid Cytye of Bristoll for the delyvery thereof vnto the said Phillippe at his full age of xxj yeeres." To Mary Langley, eldest daughter of the said Toby, £250 in money at the age of seventeen; and the same amount to Anne Langley, "my sonnes youngest daughter," at eighteen: if both should die, their brother Philip is to have their said money. To the said Philip £200 at the age of twenty-one; the said money to be divided between his two sisters, Mary and Anne, if he should die. To his said sisters 200 oz. of plate, equally divided at their age of eighteen. To son Toby all goods and chattels, plate, &c., at "or in Catchecoulde," co. Glouc., where he "nowe dwelleth"; also one garnish of pewter vessels, &c., "my Byble my booke of Statutes," a pair of "Corslettes ffurnished," and a musket furnished. Wife Mary to have, during her life, "the vse of my Andyrons," which cost £8; also the use of furniture "in my nowe dwellinge howse in the high streate in Bristoll;" rem. to son Toby for his life. To the said Mary the use and occupation of the garden in "or neere the Pyttye Hill in the Cyty of Bristoll," held for a term of years of the parishioners of All Saints', she paying the yearly rent for the same; rem. to son Toby. To Ellynor Langley, daughter of brother William, x^{li} in money. To cousin William Langley, "nowe dwellinge in Luxborne in Portingale," son to brother William Langley deceased, xl^{li} in money, to be "ymployed and bestowed to his vse in the most vendyble m'chaundyzes for Spayne and Portingale." To cousin Robert Langley, brother to the foresaid William, xx^{li}. To servant Annis Williams x^{li} when married. To cousin Sarah Pepwall xx^{li} when married. To the poor people of the parishes of St. Philip, St. James, St. Michael, Temple, and Redcliff, x^{li}, viz., xl^{s} to each parish; and xx^{s} to the poor of each of the parishes of St. Peter, Christ Church, St. Stephen, and St. Nicholas. Unto "my old s'vantes and now my good frindes," Mr. Ralph Hurte, John Hewghes, Edmond Maddock, John Wallie, and John Robertes, xxx[s] each, " to be paied them in Angells of gold. wherw[th] J pray them to make cu'y of them a signett wth my coate Armor to be graven therein, And to weare the same as a token of remembrance of me sometymes their master." Unto " my lovinge Cosens " William Williams, and Roger Williams, of Newport, xl[s] apiece, to make them " seu'all signettes of gould wth my coate armor therein " ; also to the said William Williams, and Roger Williams, £3. 6. 8., to employ and bestow the same upon the amendment of the highways, &c., "from Hysweryd to Traslon' in the p'ishe of Christchurch," co. Monmouth, and other £3. 6. 8. towards amending " the highe waies betwixt Cates ashe and Christchurch," in the said county. Wife Mary to pay fifty shillings yearly to William and Anne Langley, the two poor children of John Langley, tucker, towards the maintenance of the said William to be brought up at school until he is thirteen or fourteen years of age, and to provide apparel, &c., for the said Anne till she be "of the adge of x or xj yeeres," and both to be bound apprentice : to the said William Langley v[li] at the age of twenty-one ; and to the said Anne, his sister, v[li] when eighteen. To eighteen poor men " a fryse gowne and a new capp" and sixpence apiece ; and to eighteen poor women "a fryse gowne and a Carchife of dowlesse or Lockrome " and sixpence apiece : the men to be taken out of the almshouses " of the trynitie of Laffordes gate and of the three kinges of Collen att S[t] Michaells " ; the keeper of "the hospitall of Laffordes gate," Christopher, testator's water-bearer, Abbington, his horse-keeper, and John Langley, tucker, to be of that company ; the women to be of the same houses, and of the almshouse of " All hallon'," the goodwife Perrin to be one. To the poor inhabitants within the parish of Christ Church, co. Monmouth, xl[s], to be distributed by cousin William Williams and Ryce Langley. Legacies also to servants John Fowins, Morgan Watkins, Davie Goughe, Sander Robertes, and Anne Howell, if serving testator at the time of his death, and towards repairing the bridges of Newport, Carlyon, and Chepstow. Wife Mary to have the residue, and be sole executrix. Owen Guin esq., cousin William Williams of Newport gent., and brother Michael Pepwall esq. to be overseers, and each to have iiij[li] towards " their morninge Clotheis to be worne after my decease." If wife Mary should refuse to enter into bonds to the Mayor, Burgesses, and Commonalty of Bristoll, for the performance of all the legacies, son Toby is to have £500 besides his other legacies. Witnessed by Michael Pepwall, Owen Gyn *(sic)*, and William Williams.

On Aug. 14th, 34th Eliz., testator made the following codicil. To his wife Mary his dwelling house for her life, and for the term of thirty-one years in reversion next atter the expiration of her life ; also, for her life, " my house in broadmeade," late in the occupation of Richard Dole. She is to pay but vj[d] for "my best paire of Andiorns," and to have, for her life, all the lands "w[ch] J bought in fee farme." To servant John Fowens, and "my kinswooman" Anne, his wife, " for terme of xxj yeeres," the tenement and lands which John James and his sister Joan, or some one of them holdeth " in my mannor of Birwick," co. Glouc. My nephew William Langley being now deceased, the two daughters of "my Cosen M[r] Woodsonnes wief," sister to the said William, are to have his legacy. To John Langley, son of "my sonne"

Toby, an estate "in reuere'on for the terme of his leif" of a tenement and lands held by John Pryor and his wife, for their lives, "in my Manno^r of Berwicke aforesaied"; also the sum of £50. Twenty shillings to each of "my three maide s'vantes," Joan Hibbott, Elizabeth Smyth, and Jane Bennett. The xl^{li} bequeathed to the two daughters of son Toby, and given them by their deceased "graundmother M^{ris} Pipwall" by her will, and remaining in testator's hand, to be accepted and taken as part of the vc^{li} which he has bequeathed to them. To the Mayor and Commonalty of Bristoll xx^{li} towards redeeming the manor of Congresbury, out of the interest money "wch they Doe owe me for money lent them."

No record of proof.

The register of the parish of St. Nicholas records the marriage of Philip Langley and Mary Pepwall, Sept. 11th, 1557.

434.—MARGARET TYNDALL.

1605. March 30th. Testatrix was "of the p'ish of S^{tt} John the Baptist within the Cittie and Countie of Bristoll daughter and heire of John Sebright late of the same p'ish and Cittie Gent. deceased," and desired to be buried in the churchyard of that parish, "as neere where my father and mother lyeth as conveniently it may be. And J will that there be a tombstone there sett with my name engraved, and the day and yeere of my buriall for a memoriall." The sum of four pence yearly to the parson and his successors "for the roome of the stone there to stand." Twenty shillings unto the parson "for my duties omitted." The same amount to the poor of the almshouse of St John's aforesaid. Ten shillings to a preacher "for a sermon to be made at my buriall." As touching "my land called Esthams hay lyinge in the p'ish of Overly (Wolverley) in the Countie of Worcester," in the occupation of Thomas Best or his assigns, cousin Edward Sebright and his heirs are to have the said property, on condition of his giving "for a fine thereof" the sum of £20, to be divided among the children of cousin Thomas Such, and among Roger Goodier and his two sisters, and also on condition that he and his heirs pay out of the issues and profits of the said property a yearly rent of twenty shillings for ever for the poor in "the Citty of Bristoll." If the said Edward should refuse, cousins Thomas Goodier and Thomas Warren are to hold the property on the same condition: and if they refuse, then the said property, and the rents and reversions of the same, are to pass to Sir George Snigge knt., one of the barons of "his Ma^{tes} Court" of the Exchequer, William Ellis merchant, one of the aldermen of "the said Cittie of Bristoll," John Andros gent., Walter Gleson, Thomas Prin, and James Farly, citizens and burgesses of the same city, being cofeoffees of the lands and tenements "belonginge to the said p'ish Church of S^{tt} John the Baptist in Bristoll," and to their heirs and assigns, on condition of their performance of the said fine and "yeerly An'nitie forever." To the same cofeoffees the messuage and tenement "wherein J now dwell in Bristoll in Brodestreete." Whereas the father of testatrix did bequeath his house in Overley, wherein one Wallis dwelled at the yearly rent of twenty shillings, to remain, after the death of testatrix, and of Edith Coleman, now deceased, to William Winter of Bristoll, hooper, and to his lawful heirs; and that house being since sold; the heirs of the said William

Winter are to have twenty shillings yearly out of the issues and profits of the said dwelling house in Broad-street; and the rest of the rents and profits to be yearly distributed among the poor of Bristoll: the "seller Roome" with a little pavement adjoining to the dwelling house, and held of the Chamber of Bristoll by lease, to remain and continue "vnto my said dwellinge house." To Margery Floide the little tenement with the little shop under the Guildhall, parcel of the said Chamber's lease; she to dwell there "duringe all the yeeres to come in the said Chamberlins lease," and to pay yearly the ten shillings due to "the Chamberlin." The sum of £10 to "the poore at my buriall." To Mary Longe, "now dwellinge with me," £10, a feather-bed, &c., and "the bigger Crocke that goeth about the house." To Margery Floide "the lesser brasse Crocke wch goeth about the house," &c. To "the Com'union Table att S^{tt} Johns one Table cloth of diaper with blew at the end, and one quart present pott to be vsed to fetch wine for the Com'union Table." To Susan Walter "my best Curtins and vallence." To Edmond Popley "the Jland Chest in the great Chamber wherein his linnen was." To goodwife Haines (?), of Hambrocke, "the ringe vpon my finger." Legacies also to Margery Lucas, William Longe, Edith Sperckes, daughter of Alice Sperckes, godson Thomas Warren of Overley, old Mrs Foyns, widow, Elizabeth Cooleman, John Greeves, little Elizabeth Floid, goddaughter Mary Foyns, and servant Jane Samborne. The rest of the goods, &c., to be sold, and the money given to the poor. Testatrix desires her "verie good friendes" Mr John Foyns and Mr Hugh Murcott to "be aydinge and assistinge heerein," and to each of them, "for their gentlenes and paines," forty shillings: likewise Mr William Lewes "searcher" to be helping herein, "to whom J giue my husbandes best ringe": and also to "my Cozen" Thomas Prin, for his help, "my owne best ringe." Witnessed by John Fownes, Hugh Murcott, William Davells, Thomas Prin, and John Northall jun^r.

Administration was granted to the feoffees named in the said last will, before Morgan Jones, surrogate, and Nathaniel Pownoll, notary public and registrar, April 9th, and to Walter Gleson, before John Gooder, &c., April 12th, 1605.

This will is also in the Bristol probate office; which office contains only two of the wills registered in the Orphan Book. The register of the parish of St John records the burial of Margaret Tyndall "widowe," April 10th, 1605. It is not quite evident from the register, whether her father was buried in 1565, or in the following year. The burial of Thomas Pryn "notarie public" occurs under the date April 1st, 1607.

435.—ABRAHAM COLLMAN, mercer.

1592. March 28th. Testator was of "the Cyty of Bristoll," and desired to be buried in St Philip's churchyard "neere the place where my Grandfather was buryed." To sons Abraham and John, and daughter Margaret, £20 apiece; and the same amount to "my childe wherewth my wyef nowe goeth w^{thall}"; to be paid at their day of marriage, or age of twenty-one. If all of them should die before that time, rem. to my two sisters Katharine and Anne. Wife Margaret to have the residue, and be sole executrix. Also "J doe pray and desyer Mr Mayor of this Cyty and those to whome the cause of Orphans doth or shall app'teyne to cause good suertyes to be put in for the assuraunce of the Childrens Legacyes accordinge to the lawdable Custome of this Cytye." John Fox and Thomas Wilcockes to be overseers. Witnessed by the said John and Thomas, and by Thomas Whyte.

Proved June 8th, 1592.

436.—ELIZABETH PEPWELL, widow.

1591. June 10th. Testatrix was of " the Cyty of Bristoll," and desired to be " buryed after this my transytory lyef fynishid by the side of my husbande Will'm Pepwall at Coulde Aishton in the County of Glouc'." To son Timothy Pepwell £400, " for the payment whereof J doe appoynte " the £200 in the hands of Mr Reade, £50 in the hands of Mr Thomas Ivye, and £50 in the hands of William Osborne of Maxfield, and the other £100 " nowe Remayninge in my sonne Langlies handes," the "encrease and proffytte" whereof to be paid yearly to the said Timothy " for the maynten'nce of him his wyef and Children, vntill the the said Tymothye Pepwell and my sonne Langley shall fynde or procure some good lande to be bought wth the said mony for the better and more Certeynetye of the Lyvinge of the said Tymothie & Elizabeth his wyef." The said Timothy and Elizabeth to hold the lands "for terme of their Lyves, wth remaynder to his eldest sonne " : but if the said eldest son should die s.p., rem. to " his seconde sonne " ; and so to every one of his children, one after another. To the children of the said Timothy £40, equally divided, and " ymployed " by son Langley to the use of the said children, till the sons " be of thage of xxj yeeres," and the marriage of the daughters, or their age of twenty-one, "yf they be not marryed." To the said Timothy all the linen " wch nowe ys in the Cheste at the beddes hedde in the fore Chamber next the streate." To daughter Mary Langley £100 ; also " my best bedde in Bristoll wth the bedsteede and Curteynes of silke," the linen which she " hath alredye, and was delyvered vnto her by my mayde Elizabeth Mur when her husbande was Mayor," and also " a presente potle potte." To daughter Elizabeth Jones the use of £100, delivered to " my sonne Langley " ; rem. to her husband Ryce Jones, if then living ; if not, to such as the said Elizabeth " shall lymytte and appoynte by her discretion " ; and if she do not dispose the same accordingly, the said money to " remayne amongeste the female Children of my daughter Andros, and the females of the daughters of the said Tymothie then Lyvinge towardes their p'ferment to be equally devided amongest them": the said Ryce Jones to have the use of the said £100, if he " canne geve good and suffycyent suertyes to my said soninlawe Mr Langley " for the repayment of the said £100 " laste mene'oned," and for the use of the same during the life of the said Elizabeth, and " yf he the said Ryce Jones shall have geven over the partnershippe betweene him and Roberte Sanford." To goddaughter Anna Younge three " Bell Candlestickes," &c., at her marriage, or age of twenty-one. To Mary and Anne, daughters of Toby Langley, £20 apiece at the age of seventeen. To the three daughters of daughter Androwes £20 apiece at their marriage, or age of twenty-one. To son Timothy " a paier of Childbed sheetes and a Coople of pillowe beeres of hollande half a garnishe of vessell, Two paier of flaunders Candlestickes, ... a Turkey Carpet, ... seaven silver spoones flatte headed at the endes a Stone potte Covered wth sylver dowble gylte Wexte and footed," and " a Chayer that Came from beyonde sea." To John Pepwall " nowe p.isoner in ffraunce " £100. To Sarah

Pepwell "half a dossen of spoones Lyon headed," and £100 in money at the age of eighteene, or when married. To the two children of son John Pepwall deceased, viz., to Elizabeth £50, and to Samuel £10; to be put out to their use till "the same Samuell doe accomplishe the Age of xxj yeeres," and the said Elizabeth be of the same age, or married. To Agnes Pepwall £50 when married. The sum of £10 for "the repayringe of the highe wayes betweene Bristoll, and Colde Aisheton." The same amount unto the poor of "the p'ishe of St Nicholas in Bristoll." Forty shillings to the repairing of the church "of Colde Aishton." Six poor men and six poor women of Bristoll, and the same number "of Colde Aishton" to have "ffrize gownes" and four pence apiece, "to be delyvered at the solempnisinge of my ffunerall." Twenty shillings to "eu'y of the Almeshowses in Bristoll." Legacies also to daughter Jones, daughter Andros, wife of John Androwes, Arthur Pepwall, godson Edward Pepwall, Toby, Matthias, and Samuel Pepwall, Toby Langley, sister Botche, cousin Besse Smythe my brother's daughter, every maid and man servant, "the p'son of Colde Aishton John Tayler," and Thomas Gunninge "Baylye of Coulde Aishton." Son Michael Pepwall to have the residue, and be executor. Mr Thomas Ivye and Mr William Reade "Esquyers," and Mr Philip Langley to be overseers, "to whome J geve three of my best oxen to each of them one, And to eache of them a gowne and xl^s in mony a peece." My sons and their wives, and daughters and their husbands and all their children, and Toby Langley and his wife and children, to have "gownes at my funerall." If son Michael shall not permit son Langley to take and receive "the monyes" owing by Mr Reade, Mr Ivye, and William Osborne, to the use of son Timothy, or shall do any act to prejudice or hinder "the receyte thereof," or shall not willingly suffer John Gunninge "nowe my servaunte and apprentyce," who is to tarry and abide in the "howse and shoppe" of testatrix by the space of two years next after her decease, "to thintent" to gather her debts, and make sale of her wares: or if he do wilfully "wthstaunde to p'fourme the execution" of the will, according to the true and plain meaning of the same, "then J doe appoynte and make Marye Langley my daughter my sole executrix." To servant John Gunninge, "for his paynes," five marks in money "at the Cominge fourth of his apprentishippe." By me Elizabeth Pepwall. "Wrytten by me George Baldwyn by her appoyntment." Witnessed by Philip Langley, Michael Pepwall, John Androwes, George Baldwyn, and John Gunninge.

Proved "in Curia prerogativa" before John Hone, doctor of laws, July 24th, 1591.

437.—HUMPHREY ANDROWES, merchant tailor.

1588. May 31st. Testator describes himself as "of the Cyty of Bristoll marchant Tayler and of the p'ishe of the holy Trynytye Called Christ Church there." His body unto the earth "to be Laide in xp'ien buriall in decente manner." His wife Agnes to be "sole and only Executrix." To son Humphrey and his heirs two messuages "scytuate & lyinge vppon the Key of Bristoll wthin the p'ishe of St Stephens," in the occupation of Thomas Grove, mariner, "tenant to the same;" also all interest, right, title, "and residewe of the terme of yeeres to come" of and in all that long shop under one of the foresaid messuages, and a shop in the occupation of John Jorden, joiner, belonging to one of the same; but wife Agnes and her assigns are to hold and occupy the said tenements, shops, goods, &c., "for the terme of her naturall lyef." To the said Humphrey £100 at the age of twenty-one. To son John £100 at the same age; also all interest and term of years in a messuage "scytuate in Wynestreate in Bristoll, w^{th}in the p'ishe of Christe-churche wherein Phillippe Scapulis stac'oner doth nowe dwell for Certeyne yeeres determynable vppon his lyef, except one yeere more after his deccasse graunted for his wyef that nowe ys To houlde yt;" but wife Agnes to possess and occupy the same messuage for her life: the said John to take it with all the leases and writings belonging thereto. To daughters Abigail and Agnes Androwes £100 apiece at the age of eighteen, or when married. If all my four children should die under age, or before marriage, £100 to Thomas, Richard, and Mary Griffythe, three of the children of Edward Griffythe deceased, "my wyves Late brother," equally divided at their age of eighteen. If they should all die, rem. to the children of sister Alice Chamley equally; and one other £100 to be divided among the children of the said Alice "by even porc'ons": one other £100 to remain to wife Agnes: and of the other £100, one half to "remayne to the vse of the Chamberlen of Bristoll and his Successors for the tyme beinge for ever" to buy "certeyne Landes in ffeesimple," the rent of which to go to the repairing of "the Pyttye plumpe" for ever; and the other £50 to remain "to the Company and fellowshippe of Taylers in Bristoll," and to be "sette owte vnto fyve p'sons of the same Company to every one Ten powndes a peece for and duringe the terme of ffyve yeeres to occupye the same vppo' Condic'on that every one of them wch shall have the mony shalbe bounde wth two suffycient suertyes, bothe to the Chamberlen of Bristoll and to the Master and Company of Taylers for the tyme beinge in a reasonable some aswell to repay the Princy-pall some Receyved at the ende of the said terme of ffyve yeeres, As alsoe to pay every yere, every one of the fyve p'sons six shillinges eight pence a peece, wch amountethe to xxxiij^{s} iiij^{d} a yere And the same mony of vj^{s} viij^{d} a peece shalbe yeerely distributed amongest the poore of the Company of Taylers where moste neede shalbe by the good discrescyon and advisement of the Master and assistantes or the moste p'te of them from tyme to tyme and soe yt to Contynewe for ever." To daughter Abigail and her heirs the tenement "over against the Key Pype in Bristoll," being the tenement of Thomas Latymer; also "a voyde peece of grownde Lyinge vppon the Key," and adjoining unto the back part of "the Taverne Called the Starre," between a tenement in the occupation of Richard Addams, ropemaker, and a tene-ment in the occupation of ———, "wch said voyde grownde Thomas Good-man Joyner dothe nowe occupye and possesse;" which property "my late ffatherin lawe John Griffyth deceassed in his lyef tyme did geve and graunte vnto me the said Humfrey Androwes and Agnes my wyef his daughter for the terme of our lyves and the Longest Lyver of vs." If all the said four children should die s.p., the said two tenements and shops upon the Key are to remain unto the legitimate heirs of the aforesaid Edward Griffythe "my wyves brother;" and for lack of such issue, to testator's right heirs. To sister's daughter Agnes Chamley, "nowe dwellinge wth me in service," twenty marks at the age of twenty-one, or when married; also "one honest and Comley seate of Apparrell for hollydayes and an other suyte for working-dayes." To her brother Thomas Chamley twenty marks at the age of twenty-one. Forty shillings in money to "the goodwyef Robins nowe beinge my servaunte;" and twenty shillings to every one of testator's servants and apprentices at the time of his death. Witnessed by Thomas Prinne, notary public.

Proved April 22nd, 1592.

438.—WILLIAM PYTTES, clothier. In the margin *Pittes*.

1592. Oct. 30th. Testator was of the parish of Temple within the city of Bristoll, and his will was "wrytten by me Rychard Martin mynister of the said p'ishe." To be buried "in the Churche of Temple." Forty shillings to the poor of the said parish. To eldest son William "my howse wherein J nowe dwell wth all furnyture therevnto belonginge," which included "a standinge bedde wth a Truckle bedde vnder yt," and the best coverlet "wch J bought of Lynzye the wayte player;" wife Agnes to have and hold the said house and furniture till the said William come to the age of twenty-one; also to him £60 at that age; and the lease of the house "wherein my mother nowe Jnhabyteth," to hold after her decease; and also the house, rack, and garden in the tenure of John Higgins. If son William should die before the given age, all his legacies to pass to "the nexte of his bretheren in age wch then shall lyve," at the age of twenty-one. To sons Robert, Thomas, and John, £20 apiece at that age. To daughter Elizabeth £30, and "one brasse Crock," &c., at that age; if she should die before the said age, the two daughters of brother Richard Pyttes are to have her said money. To George "my prentyce" ten shillings. To servant Agnes, and Sir Richard Martin, vicar of Temple, ten shillings apiece. Wife Agnes to have the residue, and be sole executrix. Mr John Pykes and Thomas Hayward overseers. Witnessed by William Barnes.

No record of proof.

The Temple parish register records the burial of William Pittes, Nov. 29th, 1592.

439.—MARY NOBLE, widow.

1588. Feb. 12th. Testatrix was of "the p'ishe of St Phillipps wthin the Cytye of Bristoll," and desired to be buried at the discretion of her executors. Twenty shillings to the poor of the said parish. To eldest son Jessie £5, also "my Bedsteede in the Parlor," &c., at his age of twenty-one, or when married. To son Thomas £5, and "a fetherbed wth his app'ten'nces and my best panne and my best Crock," at that age, or when married. Money and goods also to daughter Elizabeth and son John, at that age, or their marriage. To servant Alice Burriett "a flocke bed that ys behinde the lytle Chamber Dore." Uncle John Bushe, and brother-in-law John James, "my trustie frindes," to have the residue, and be executors. Witnessed by William Edmondes, John Bushe, Nicholas Blake, and Robert Jefferis.

Proved "in Curia prerogatiua," April 30th, 1589.

440.—JOHN JONES "al's Smythe."

1592. Feb. 26th. Testator describes himself as "of the p'ishe of St Thomas wthin the Cytie of Bristoll Smythe." His body "to the earth from whence yt came." To son John Jones and his heirs "one Tyled howse wth

T

one ortcharde lyenge and beinge w^{th}in the p'ishe of St Georges in the County of Som's't nowe in myne owne handes and fforteene Acres of grownde therevnto belonginge nowe in the tenure of Richard Churchehowse." Also to the said John "my best Anvill and my third Anvill," &c., and "my Satten dublett and my signet ringe And the one halfe of my workinge Tooles ;" also £30 "at thende of his yeeres of Apprentishippe." To daughter Elizabeth Jones, and her legitimate heirs, one house and orchard " wth one stytch of lande belonginge therevnto," in the tenure of Thomas Whytinge of St Georges ; also " ten Acres of grownde " in that parish, in the tenure of John Hillseley of Leigh. To daughter Jane Jones, and her legitimate heirs, one house, and seven acres of ground thereunto belonging, in that parish, in the occupation of Elizabeth Mollgrove. To daughters Elizabeth and Jane, and their legitimate heirs, nine acres of ground, in the tenure and occupation of James Whytinge, of that parish, and Thomas Perrington, of Leigh aforesaid, to be equally divided between them ; also £20 apiece at their marriage, or age of twenty-one. To daughter Margery Jones £10 at that age, or when married. To son Thomas Jones, and his legitimate heirs, " the George Close lyinge and beinge w^{th}in the p'ishe of Redclyffe w^{th}in the Cytie of Bristoll and a styche of grownde lyinge in Redclyffe Meade," all beinge in the tenure and occupation of Thomas Thomlinson, of the parish of St Thomas ; also " the howse J nowe dwell in," after the decease of wife Margaret, and £20 at the age of twenty-one. If all the children should die before that age, or their marriage, and Michael Partridge, brother of wife Margaret, should die s.p., one half of the said houses and lands to go to the poor of the parish of St Thomas in Bristoll, and the other half to the poor of the parishes of Redcliff and Temple in the same city. To "the Company of the Smythes in Bristoll to drincke six shillinges eight pence." Legacies also to servant Thomas Jeine, William Beast " o^r mynister of St Thomas," and the twenty-four alms-people of that parish. Wife Margaret to have the residue, and be executrix. William Pryddy, William Sayer, and Laurence Reade, overseers, to each of whom xiij^s iiij^d. Witnessed by the said Laurence, and by William Pryddy, William Harris, and William Beast.

Proved " in Curia p'rogativa," May 10th, 1593.

441.—WILLIAM BITFEILDE, soapmaker.

1591. July 21st. Testator was of " the Cytie of Bristoll," and desired to be buried in St John's churchyard " next to my wief there buried." Son-in-law William Yate and daughter Margaret, his wife, to take into their charge and custody son Martin Bytfield, " beinge a simple and innocent Creature w^{th}owt discretion or goverment," and provide him with " sufficient and Convenyent meate and drincke lodginge and app'ell Duringe his naturall lyffe :" if they will do so, they are to have " my best nest of silver goblettes wth one Cover double Guilt of the value of xxxiij^{li} viij^s or thereabowtes and a nest of Silver Alecuppes Double guilt of the value of xvij^{li} or thereabowtes," &c., also " one doosen of Apostle Spoones of silver of the value of viij^{li} or thereabowtes." To wife Joan, for her life, the messuage and tenement in the occupation of Thomas Langley " scytuate and beinge in xp'omas streate w^{th}in the said Cyty of Bristoll," and the messuage " in Cornestreate," which was " sometyme p'cell of the possessions of the late dissolved monastery of Michaells Kinton," co. Wilts, in the occupation of John Staple "fturber;" also "one chief rent or yeerely rente" of twelve pence, issuing out of a tenement "in Baffestreate wthin the said Cytie," sold to John Bulbeck, deceased; and a yearly rent of four shillings, "issuinge owt of one Tenement in Redcliclfe streate wthin the said Cyty and yeerely paid by the proctors of the p'ishe of Redcliffe afforesaid"; rem. to daughter Joan, and her legitimate heirs; in def., rem. to "my Right heyres for ever." The executors are to hold the dwelling house and shop "for the terme of nynescore dayes next after my Deccasse;" rem. to son Giles Bytfield and his heirs, together with "all the glasse in the howse and the drapery and borders in the Parlo^r accordinge to a fformer bargayne betweene vs before this tyme concluded, Jn Consideracʼon of Threescore and odd powndes by him to me paid." After the ninescore days, the said Giles to have all the residue of the lease and term of years of and in the said shop, together with the original lease thereof, on condition that he "shall make scale and delyver to myne executors a generall releas of all demaundes (the Legacyes afforesaid excepted) wthin forty daies next after my deccasse." To Henry, son of the said William and Margaret Yate, "my greate signet of goulde wth a Red stone therein." To "my Lovinge ffrend Thomas Fawkett my Geneva bible and Twenty shillinges for a token of olde good will." Wife and daughter Joan to have the residue, and be executors. Son-in-law William Yate and the said Thomas Fawkett overseers. Witnessed by the said Thomas, and by William Saxey, Edmond Erond, and George Caulie.

Proved "apud Bristoll" before Morgan Jones, deputy to Francis James, doctor of laws, Oct. 21st, 1591.

442.—HENRY GOUGHE, merchant.

1592. Jan. 20th. Testator was of "the Cyty of Bristoll." No direction as to burial. To wife Mary, during her life, the dwelling house "in Baldwynstreate;" also all lands and tenements in "the forrest of Deane," co. Glouc., until son George Goughe shall accomplish the age of twenty-one, "yf she shall soe longe lyve;" if the said George should die, she is to hold the property during the minority of son Matthew, and also the orchard and garden "at Michaell Hill." To daughter Anne Goughe the lease of the house inhabited by goodwife Lecke in the parish of St Nicholas in Bristoll; the said lease and house to remain to daughter Elizabeth Goughe, if the said Anne should die before marriage; and to Matthew Goughe, if the said Elizabeth should so die; and to son John Goughe, if the said Matthew should so die. To daughter Anne £100 at the age of eighteen, or when married. To daughter Elizabeth £100, to be paid to her in like manner. To sons Matthew and John £100 apiece at the age of eighteen, except it shall seem better to "my wyef and their frindes" to be paid rather for their preferment as apprentices, or to detain the same "tyll they come to xxiij^{ty} yeeres of Age, yf they be not apprentises." And whereas "some p'te of my estate lyeth on the sea, and beyonde the sea in adventures my will ys that if any shall myscarry and be lost of my goodes," the losses shall be cast upon all the goods, plate, and chattels, and be "borne equally by my wyef and the fower children above named to whome J have geven the cccc^{li} sol' p' libro." Eldest son George, and his legitimate heirs, to have all lands and tenements "in the forrest of Deane;" also the dwelling house in St Stephen's parish, with the reversion thereof, and the garden and orchard at Michael hill, and all implements "aswell at Breme in my howse there, as in Bristoll in my dwellinge howse there," except the estate herein mentioned " to my wyef ;" in default of issue, rem. to Matthew, my second son ; in def., rem. to John, my third son. The plate to be divided among the said children. Wife Mary to be sole executrix. Brother George Gough, brother-in-law Thomas James, and "Tho: Whyt my kynsman" to be supervisors. Witnessed by Thomas James and Thomas Whyte.

Proved " in Curia prerogativa" Nov. 13th, 1593.

443.—BENEDICT WYNTER, gentleman. In the margin *Winter*.

1592. Feb. 14th.—"of the Citye of Bristoll gent' . . . at this present J ame bounde on A voyadge to the Seas and knowe not whether ever J shall returne home againe or not yet reposinge my selfe into the handes of the Almightye bothe abroade and at home and alwayes appealinge vnto Christe Jesus the sonne of god for m'eye." To brother William Wynter £200. To Anne Huntlye, daughter of Ansell Huntlye "of Hull al's Hill of the p'ishe of Barckley," co. Glouc., gentleman, " whoe marryed wth my sister marye," £100. To sister Anne, wife of George Pryce, £50, to be delivered by the executors to the Mayor and Commonalty of Bristoll to the use of the said Anne, and by them to be put forth upon good assurance for her better maintenance from time to time "soe longe as shee shalbe covert baron wth the said George Price," and no part thereof to be delivered unto him, " in considerac'on of the speciall care wch J desier the mayor to take thereof for the tyme beinge." The sum of £10 unto " the Newe erected Hospitall called the Queenes Hospitall in the Colledge Greene of Bristoll." The same amount to servant Robert More (?), if he " returne from Sea." To Thomas Knowell of Sherborne " the some of Tenne poundes to imploye in A pece of silver plate and thereon to grave my armes and name in Remembraunce of me." Brother-in-law Aunsell Huntlye to have the residue, and be executor. Witnessed by Anselme Huntlye, George Baldwyn, and Thomas Stevens.

No record of probate.

444.—ELEANOR PILL, widow.

1594. June 9th. Testatrix was of " the p'ishe of all hollandes wthin the Citty of Bristowe," and willed that her body be laid " as neere vnto my late husbande as yt convenientlie maie be." All her apparel to be equally divided between her two sisters, Agnes " the wiefe of William Nicholas of Pilston (Pilton) in devonsheere," and Grace " the wiefe of Jesper Castelman " of Bridgwater, co. Somerset. To kinsman Hugh Pearde the dwelling house, with "the vse and p'ffite of my garden grounde in St Jones p'ishe in Bristoll," adjoining to the back part of the almshouse there, until son John Pill is twenty-one years of age. If the said John should die before that age, the said Hugh to enjoy the lease, and all the whole years to come. The said John to pay and allow towards the building of a lodge in the said garden, which the said Hugh " dothe purpose to cause to be newlie builte " there, one third part of all such charges and expenses as by a just " accompte " shall appear to be laid out by the said Hugh, or his assigns, in the building of the lodge. To the said Hugh Pearde " the leas and terme of yeres of A stable Roome wch liethe in Ducklane neere the Pittie gate in Bristoll ;" also two other leases "of certeine romes p'cell of the Gillardes Inne in the Highe Streate," the one granted by Ralph Piltingetonn (Pilkington), and the other by William Davis. Gold rings to brothers George and John Pearde, and brothers-in-law John Wade of London, and Nicholas Pill. Forty shillings to the poor in "the Cittie of Bristowe." Residue of goods, leases, &c., to son John Pill at his full age of twenty-four. The said Hugh Pearde to have the tuition, custody, education, and bringing up of the said John until he shall be of the age "of xxj^{tie} yeres," and also the use and keeping of his goods, leases, plate, &c. If the said John should die before the age of twenty-four, the said Hugh to have the third part of his goods; and the children of the aforesaid sisters, Agnes and Grace, to have the other "to thurde p'tes" equally divided. The said Hugh to hold, possess, and enjoy the house and cellars "wherein J nowe dwell in the Highe streate," paying to the use and account of the said John Pill a yearly rent of £10. The said John to be sole executor. Thomas Salterne, grocer, and James Cadell, pewterer, to be overseers, and have x^s apiece. Witnessed by the said James, and by William Davis, innholder, and Thomas Prinne. Sealed, &c., June 10th, 1594.

No record of probate. Commission to administer was granted to Hugh Perde, Dec. 3rd, 1594, as appears by the copy at Somerset House, *Dixey*, 88.

445.—THOMAS DAVIS, hooper.

1593. Dec. 25th. Testator was of "the p'ishe of St Stephens w^{thin} the Cyty of Bristoll," and desired to be buried in the churchyard of that parish, "as nighe vnto my sonnes grave as may be." If wife Agnes should marry, she is to pay £10 to son Henry, and also give to him "the great Cheast at the Stayer head," &c. She is to have the use of the goods "vntill she shall marry," when brother John Davis shall have the keeping of "my said sonne," and the goods, until he come "of Lawfull yeres." A black cloth doublet to the husband of sister Joan. The best breeches to brother John. To "my brother John his daughters" x^s apiece. Wife Agnes to have the residue, and be executrix. Witnessed by John Davis, hooper, and Thomas Tyzon, parson of St Stephen's.

Proved at Bristoll, Feb. 15th, 1595.

This will is followed by a considerable number of the writings referred to in the *Introduction*.

446.—WILLIAM PREWETT, draper.

1594. April 2nd. Testator was of "the Citye of Bristoll," and desired to be buried in the churchyard of St James's parish, "in the Tombe where my father was layed." Eighteen poor men, and eighteen poor women to have "blacke frize gownes," and the men caps, and the women "Kercheiffes" at the burial. To the two almshouses in the parish of St James twenty shillings apiece. To the almshouse without Temple gate, and that "in the Tuckers Hall," twenty shillings apiece. To "the Spittell house" without Redcliff gate ten shillings yearly out of "my landes" for ever, "soe as they doe not p'cure any lisence vnto them or vnto any other for them to begge but if they shall have or procure any suche lisence then this leagasye to be voide." The sum of £5 to the repairing of "the Highe waye betwene Redcliffe Churche and the Brighte Bowe;" and the same amount to the repairing of "the Highe waye betwene Laffordes and Dungeons Crosse." To wife Joan the lease of the house at Hanam, and of the mills, grounds, &c., if she continue "sole and vnmarryed;" Thomas Pitcher to assure unto her the benefit of the grant which testator procured Richard Danvers to "make vnto him vpon truste to my vse:" after her decease, or marriage with any other, the said lease of Hanam house, mills, and grounds, had of William Lacye, as also the said interest conveyed by Richard Danvers unto Thomas Pytcher, to go to the executors: the said Thomas to assign the interest that "remanethe in him" of the premises to the uses aforesaid. To wife Joan, for her life, the dwelling house upon the Back in Bristoll, with the shop, &c., stretching unto St Nicholas-street, and all the rooms thereof, in the occupation of "my selfe," or of Thomas Pitcher; rem. to the said Thomas and his wife Prudence during their lives; rem., after their decease, to nephew Anthony Prewett and his heirs. To the said Joan the rent of the dwelling house of Richard Ryce, tailor, in Bristoll; the reversion of the house and rent, after her decease or marriage, to remain to the said Anthony, and to his heirs. Also to the said Joan £100, fourscore oz. of plate, &c., and all the household stuff in the said houses at Hanam and Bristoll, for her life. Testator having in his house two rings, "thone wth a dyamonde of John Westons in paune of fower poundes thother A Turkeys of Henrye Westons in paune of fortye seven shillinges," the said John and Henry are to have their rings again upon payment of the money; but if they shall not be redeemed, daughter-in-law Prudence Pitcher to have the ring with the diamond, and also "the beste ringe wth a turkeys" bought by testator of Richard Bennett. To son-in-law Thomas Pitcher the ring "wch my mother gave me when J was a batcheler." To brother John Prewett 100 marks; also £10 yearly, to be paid quarterly by even portions, out of all "my landes and rentes" in Bristoll, my said dwelling and Richard Rice's house excepted. To sister's son William Corye so much as shall make up the legacy bequeathed unto him by John Prewett "my father" remaining in "my handes" £40, to be paid at his age of twenty-one. To Alice Weekes, Thomas Wykes, and Charity Weekes, the children of Edward Weekes "bye my sister," £30 apiece at their marriage, or age of twenty-one; rem. to the executors, if the said children should all die. To the children of "my Neece" Joan Yorcke £10 apiece at their marriage, or age of twenty-one. The sum of £5 yearly to late servant Patrick White. To kinsman William, son of Patrick Younge, £5 when he shall "come fourthe of his app'ntishode." To Alice and Anne, the children of Thomas Pytcher, £40 apiece at their marriage, or age of twenty-one. To Bartholomew Hill, and to his heirs and assigns, the garden bought of William Lacye in the parish of St Philip in Bristoll. Edward Weekes is forgiven "all that he dothe owe vnto me." These to have black cloth gowns at "my buriall,"—wife Joan, Thomas Pitcher and his wife Prudence, brother John Prewett and his wife, William Yorcke and his wife Joan, Richard Hill, Edward Bosdon, Thomas Pytt, William Vawer, Richard Smythe sheriff of Bristoll, Christopher Walker, Patrick White, and William Younge "a Clocke." John Harris, the keeper of Newgate in Bristoll, also to have "a gowne of blacke Clothe at my buriall." To nephew Anthony Prewett all lands, tenements, reversions, &c., and the residue of goods. Wife Joan to leave the executors £50 after her decease. Legacies to the parishioners of the church of St Nicholas in Bristoll "to the vse of theire said church thadvowson of the same wch J boughte of William Jones," to sister Charity's daughter Margaret Burnell, wife of John Burnell of Exeter, son-in-law Richard Hill, Joan wife of William Wyott, servant John Cosson, Edward Bosdon, and Thomas Pytt. Edward Bosdon, Thomas Pytt "chamberlayne" of Bristoll, and late servant Patrick White to be executors "of truste to thuse of my said Nephewe Anthonye Prewett" until he is twenty-five years of age, when he is to be full and whole executor. Master William Vawer, and the aforesaid master Richard Smythe, overseers. Thomas Pitcher to "instructe and bringe vpp my said Nephewe in the trade of drap'ye" until he is twenty-five. Witnessed by William Carey, draper, and Roger Longe.

Proved at London, June 14th, 1594.

447.—ROBERT TAYLOR, merchant. In the margin *Tayler*.

1594. Aug. 24th. Testator was of "the Citty of Bristoll," and desired to be buried where his executrix should think it convenient. Forty shillings to be distributed among the poor of Bristoll "at the tyme of my buriall." To son Robert £20, whereof the sum of £10 is paid; also "my signett of golde," &c. To daughter Katharine Childe £20, whereof the sum of £10 was paid in June 1587; also some plate. To daughter Jane Taylor £80, &c. To daughter Anne Tayler £70, &c. Twenty shillings "in golde" to sister Margaret Robins. The legacies of my two young daughters, Jane and Anne, to be delivered in ready money unto "Credible men in the Citty of Bristoll" for a reasonable annuity for the maintenance of the said children; which men are to give good assurance with sureties to the executrix and overseers; and "neither the ffather of the orphantes nor the Chamber of the citty of Bristoll" is to be troubled in the matter. Wife Katharine to be sole executrix, and to have the residue of goods, and the debts owing by son Robert and others. Brother-in-law John James of Wollaston, Thomas Durlinge, and son Robert, overseers, to each of whom x^s. Witnessed by Thomas Watkins "Ser'" and Robert Taylor.

No record of probate: but the will was proved Oct. 23rd, 1595, having been made Aug. 16th, 1594, according to the copy at Somerset House, *Scott*, 57.

448.—RICHARD COOKE.

1593. Feb. 4th. Testator, who was of "the p'ishe of Littell St Austins by Brist'," was then "meaninge by the sufferance of god to make my voyadge on' the Seas." His body to the earth. Ten shillings to "the poore of the same p'ishe." To son John £10; also "my Whistell and Chaine and my Jnstrumentes belonginge to the Sea." To daughter Anne £10, &c, and a "Table Boorde in the Cockloftе." To son William £10, and "A Salte of Silver." To son Thomas £10; also a stone cup covered and bound with silver and gilt, and a counter "beinge of spruce." To son Philip £10, &c., and half a dozen "of Silv^{er} spoones doble gilte." To (daughter?) Agnes Cooke the lease and years to come "of the howse that Nicholas Barnes dwellethe in." To son Thomas and his legitimate heirs, after the decease of his mother, "the howse that J doe dwell in;" in def., rem. to son Philip; in def., rem. to son William; in def., rem. to son John; in def., rem. to daughter Agnes and her heirs for ever. The pewter and brass given to the children by their grandmother, to be equally divided among them. The daughters to have their legacies at the age of sixteen, and the men children at twenty-one. Wife Joan to have the residue, and be excentiix. Witnessed by Thomas Batten, Clement Goddell, William Merrike, "wth other more."

No record of proof.

449.—THOMAS NEATHWAY, mariner.

1595. Feb. 7th. Testator describes himself as " of Bristoll in the County of Som's't Marryner." His body to the earth " whereof yt was flirste made." To youngest son Thomas Neathway £100 at the age of twenty-one: " my good frinde " John Younge of Bristoll to have " the puttinge fourth of the said hundred powndes to the beste vse," and to put in sufficient surety for the repayment of the said money, with the profits thereof. If the said Thomas die before the given age, the said money to come to eldest son George Neathway. And whereas "J was p'te victualler at the tyme of my hurte in the good shippe called the Swan of Bristoll in the some of ffortye fyve powndes tenne shillinges J also will and bequeathe, that if yt shall chaunce the said Shippe to take any purchase in this her voyadge that the quarter thereof shall come and be to the vse of my youngest sonne Thomas Neathway, and alsoe to be putt fourth to the beste p'ffytte, by the foresaid John Younge, vntill he shalbe of age, And if he chaunce to dye before, then to co'me vnto my other sonne George Neathway." To apprentice Robert Trippett " my sea Chiste," sea apparel, and all sea instruments. Wife Elizabeth Neathway and son George to be executors. The said John Younge, overseer. Witnessed by John Hoggett, Thomas Greves, John Chesses, and John Armerer.

This will is also registered in the third volume of wills at the Council House; but neither that volume nor the Orphan Book gives the date of probate. There is however a copy at Somerset House, *Drake*, 15, from which we learn that the will was proved Feb. 26th, 1595.

CORRECTIONS AND ADDITIONS.

For "Porteshened," in the note of probate after the will of John Stoke, p. 7, read *Portesheued.*

For "p'ochus," in the first line of Bernard Obeleye's will, p. 26, read *p'och'us.*

The clause in the will of Thomas Tanner, p. 63, relating to the tapers, may seem to require some explanation. Testator desired that eight poor people should carry eight tapers to the cathedral church of St. Andrew, and hold them "in exequijs meis circa corpus meum ib'm de nocte & in Crastino ad missam;" and also—"lego alijs viij paup'ibz deferent' alios viij Cereos ab eccl'ia se'i Andree p'dict' ad eccl'iam se'i Cuthb'ti Well' circa corpus meum in exequijs meis de nocte & in missa in Crastino."

A legal document, 10 Richard ii., preserved at Bristol, was witnessed by William *de* Ele, as the name is also written in the Orphan Book, pp. 12, 52; not *le* Ele, as on p. 75.

The names of Laurence Wermystre and his wife Maud, by whom certain rents and services were paid, were accidentally omitted from the sixth line of the will of Margaret Stephenus, p. 97. The will of Laurence Warmestre, burgess of Bristol, was made April 11th, 1421, and proved May 6th, in the same year, in P.C.C., *Marche*, 51. He bequeathed sums of money to the mother church of Worcester, St. Stephen's church in Bristol, where he desired to be buried, the cathedral church of Waterford in Ireland, the church of St. Mary of "Roos," &c., and left all his lands and other possessions in the town and fields of Weymouth to Agnes Gros, relict of Henry Gros. The sum of £7 for a chalice and pair of vestments for the use of the chapel or parish church of Weymouth. Forty shillings to Thomas Knapp's daughter when married. John Troyt and Robert Panys executors.

For "Halleway," in the note of probate after the will of John Hethe, p. 110, read *Hallewey.*

The original of the clause relating to the solemn remembrance of the soul of Thomas Jonys, and his wife Elen's, p. 137, may suggest a more desirable rendering:—"volo insuper q'd p' ffelici Reco'mendac'o'e A'i'e mee ac A'i'e p'd'ee Elene vx'is mee in D'm'icis in Pulpito faciend' quilibet vicar' d'ee Eccl'ie se'i Nich'i qui p' tempore erit sing'lis Annis imp'petuu' p'cipiat p' manus procurator' eiusdem Cripte Die se'i Mathei de redditu Mesuagij p'd'ci."

In the second note on p. 138, fifth line, omit "friar."

Insert *of* before "that church," in the second line of the will of John Nancothan, p. 143. It may be mentioned that a John Nancothan, grocer, was admitted to the freedom of the city of Bristol, on Feb. 24th, in the 5th year of the reign of Elizabeth.

In the heading of the will of William Canynges, p. 151, omit the comma, and insert *&* before "antea." It appears that Thomas Hawkesok, whose name occurs in the will, was ordained a secular priest in the church of St. Nicholas at Worcester, obtaining his title from Great Malvern, March 14th, 1466. The copy of this will at Somerset House, *Wattys*, 17, has Isabel *Powett* instead of "Powlett."

For "Estoefeld," at the end of Robert Jacob's will, p. 157, read *Estrefeld*.

For "Ei," in the last sentence of William Rowley's will, p. 162, read *Et*.

The word "Cabbowe," in John Fuyster's will, p. 173, is explained in the will of John Rowley, merchant and burgess of Bristowe, dated Sept. 2nd, 1489, and proved Nov. 10th, in the same year, in P.C.C., *Milles*, 29. That testator speaks of "alle my Cabowe or stuf in March'undise."

For "especiall," in the last line of p. 178, read *especciall*.

The will of Robert Thorne, p. 180, differs in several places from the copy at Somerset House, *Thower*, 18. The latter has *Gregorio* Catanio, *Anthony* Cornell, *Robert Ondeley*, &c. The will of Robert Thorne, father of this testator, which was proved July 6th, 1519, may be seen there, in *Ayloffe*, 19 ; and that of his mother, Joan Thorne, proved May 16th, 1523, in *Bodfelde*, 8.

The will of John Awste, or Auste, is entered twice, with different dates, in the Orphan Book, and was inadvertently copied a second time into this work ; pp. 231, 237.

INDEX.

Abbington,—, 267.
Abbott, Robert, 218
Abell, Isabel, 141
  ,, Richard, 83
Aberte, Master, 265
Abevan, Robert, 236
Abolton, James, 200
Abraham, Adam, 65
  ,, Joan, 16, 18, 19
Aclonne, Tangela, 143
Adames, Richard, 253, 255, 272
Adams, Nicholas, 58, 67
  ,, Robert, 190, 239
Addams, Agnes, 222
  ,, Elizabeth, 222
  ,, Francis, 239
  ,, Jane, 239
  ,, Roger, 222
  ,, Thomas, 213, 239
Addyson, John, 200
A Deane, Robert, 252
Ades, Elizabeth, 212
  ,, John, 211, 212
Adekyn, Richard, 21
Adies, John, 213
Aeruondts, Peter, 162
Affilde, Martin, 186
Afylde, Roger, 193
Alleway, Christopher, 252
Allleward, John, 114
Ailly, John, 16
Allmer, John, 124
Alberton, Andrew, 164
  ,, Joan, 164
  ,, John, 156, 164
Aldeworth, Thomas, 199, 207, 209, 223, 230, 231, 242, 248
Aldworthe, Simon, 234
Aleyn, Isabel, 9
Alflat, Robert, 200
Algode, Simon, 59, 76
Alkin, Richard, 244
Alkyne, John, 199, 222, 258
  ,, Margaret, 199
  ,, Richard, 199
Allen, Lady Mary, 208
Alpe, Water, 175
Alwey, Nicholas, 70
Alwyn, John, 139
Alye, Edward, 261, 262
  ,, Elizabeth, 261
  ,, Joan, 261
  ,, Margery, 261
Amayne, Agnes, 180
  ,, John, 186
Amyet Robert, 8
Andreas, John, 96
Andrewe, Richard, 167
Androwes, Abigail, 272
  ,, Agnes, 272
  ,, Humphrey, 212, 271, 272
  ,, John, 255, 268, 271
Anketill, Andrew, 19, 43, 57
Anthony, Agnes, 175
ap Griffith, Stephen, 121
ap Howell, Thomas, 162
ap Philipp, Morgan Jenkyn, 147

Aphowell, Katharine, 150
Apparry, goodwife, 229
Apphowell, Jenkine, 211
Appowell, Alice, 197
  ,, Richard, 198
  ,, Thomas, 215
  ,, William, 197, 198
ap Pollangha', David, 170
  ,, John, 170
A Price, John, 251
Aprice Thomas, 199
Apprice, goodwife, 229
Appulby, Richard, 73
Aprotherowe, Morris, 220
ap Thomas ap Prene, William, 126
Arch, William, 122
Archar, Richard, 157
Archer, Henry, 130
Archor, John, 27
Arden, Robert, 240
Ardern, John, 93
Arffos, John, 137, 138
  ,, Richard, 138
  ,, William, 138
Argall, Laurence, 197, 200, 203
  ,, Richard, 234, 247
  ,, Thomas, 180, 182, 196
Armerer, John, 280
Armys, Richard, 55
Arnold, Lady, 235
Arondell, John, 97
Arther, Richard, 232, 247
Arthour, Richard, 145
Arthur, Adam, 64
  ,, Isabel, 6, 28, 41
  ,, John, 37, 106, 122
  ,, Thomas, knt., 6, 41
  ,, William, 132
Arvas, Richard, 108
Asby, Robert, 63
Asch, Richard, 43
  ,, William, 26
Ashcote, William, 49
Ashe, Anne, 208
  ,, John, 208, 209
  ,, Margaret, 208
  ,, Mary, 208
Askell, John, 155
Aspsen, John, 141
Assch, Agnes, 120
  ,, John, 119
  ,, Rose, 53
Assche, Thomas, 129, 146
Assheworthy, Joan, 20
Asshton, Denis, 70, 83
  ,, Joan, 16
  ,, Robert, 70, 71
Aston, John, 156
at Berkyng, Agnes, 76
Athall, John, 212
Atkins, William, 253, 254
Atkyns, Maud, 159
  ,, William, 159
atte Barugh, Peter, 26, 47
atte Celer, John, 64, 108
  ,, Thomas, 69
atte Corner, Adam, 11
atte Feiradon, Richard, 23

atte Hay, Thomas, 18, 23, 32, 55, 110
atte Hulle, Thomas, 44
atte Lane, William, 29, 33
atte Mede, Thomas, 42
atte Rode, Alice, 105
,, Walter, 105
atte Walle, Elizabeth, 115
,, Robert, 115
atte Water, William, 63
Attewelle, John, 89
atte Welle, William, 102
atte Wode, Peter, 22, 86
Atwood, James, 250
Aumiger, William, 8
Auncell, Elen, 94
Aungell, Isabel, 84
Auste, or Awste, John, 231, 237
,, Elizabeth, 231, 237
,, Mary, 231, 337
,, Robert, 231, 237
,, William, 231, 237
Austyn, John, 25, 73, 85
,, Richard, 39
Austyne, Doctor, 193
Avery, William, 221
Avynce, Hugh, 106
Aylleward, William, 115

Baath, John, 42
Babbeeary, Henry, 36
Babestoke, John, 37
Backe, Thomas, 41, 81
Backwell, Joan, 93
Badecok, Gilbert, 94
,, John, 36
Badram, George, 218, 236
Badron, Thomas, 110
Bagenham, Alexander, 96, 97
Baggewell, John, 45
Bagod, John, 145, 147, 161, 166
Bagot, Clement, 125, 133
Bagott, John, 158
Bagpath, Henry, 102
,, John, 53, 70
Bailieff, Richard, 226
Baillebien, Thomas, 33
Bailly, John, 24, 85
Bailye, James, 193
Baker, Alice, 88, 168
,, Anne, 168
,, Edward, 204
,, Elizabeth, 168
,, goodwife, 257
,, James, 168, 173
,, Joan, 168
,, John, 130, 172
,, Magdalene, 168
,, Margaret, 130, 168
,, Margery, 111
,, Maud, 168
,, Ralph, 52
,, Richard, 174
,, Roger, 252
,, Thomas, 168, 169
,, Walter, 88, 117
,, William, 77, 106, 168, 169
Bakkester, Robert, 65
Baldwin, George, 220, 222, 252 271, 276
Bale, John, 164, 168, 169
Ball, Alice, 113
,, John, 158, 163, 164
,, Thomas, 113
Ballarde, Alice, 193
,, Jane, 192, 193
,, Joan, 192, 193
,, Syble, 192

Ballarde, William, 150, 183, 192
Balsall, Thomas, 155
Bannebury, John, 33, 52, 70
Banner, Robert, 244
Bantinge, John, 251
Barber, 234
Barbor, Richard, 6, 41
Barbour, Geoffrey, 43
,, Joan, 19
,, John, 51, 173
,, William, 89
Barebone, Elizabeth, 261
Barell, John, 18, 21, 25, 38
,, Robert, 18
Barero, Janycot, 162, 170
,, Robert, 162
Baret, Margery, 95
,, William, 95, 120
Barette, Joan, 117
Barloo, Roger, 186
Barlow, John, 185, 186, 187
Baruell, Thomas, 231, 237
Barnes, 200
,, David, 233
,, John, 211
,, Nicholas, 279
,, Thomas, 216
,, William, 273
Barnesley, Gilbert, 192
Baron, Robert, 139, 157
,, Thomas, 171
Barons, John, 199, 216
Barough, Thomas, 77
Barrat, John, 232
Barret, William, 198, 201
Barrett, Hugh, 212
,, Richard, 216
Barri, Thomas, 38
Barro, John, 219
Barrowe, Edward, 209
,, John, 249
Barry, Elena, 47
,, Stephen, 47
Barryero, John, 171
Barstaple, Isabel, 5, 86
,, John, 5, 16, 59, 63, 65, 68, 74, 86, 115, 125
,, Maud, 35
,, Nicholas, 146
,, Robert, 80, 81
,, Walter, 142
Barstaple, alias Shepward, John, 142
,, ,, Robert, 142
,, ,, Thomas, 142
,, ,, William, 141
Bartelote, Thomas, 69
Barton, Thomas, 67, 76
Barwicke, Richard, 215, 216, 219, 238
Baskervile, John, 107
Basset, Elizabeth, 121
,, John, 29, 85, 120, 121
,, William, 121
Batche, Cristian, 197
Bateman, Edward, 236
Bath, alias Pochyn, John, 74, 131
Bathe, John, 46, 66, 71, 73, 118
Batte, Laurence, 128
,, Margaret, 129
,, Roger, 86, 87, 128, 129
Batten, Thomas, 280
Batter, John, 93
Batyn, Joan, 167
,, John, 112
Baughe, James, 262
Bawdon, Alice, 42
Bawne, Edward, 181
Baylyve, Gregory, 259

Baynam, Richard, 239
,, Thomas, 239
,, Walter, 236
,, William, 239
Baynham, Robert, 254
Bayon, John, 108
,, Robert, 108
Beale, Henry, 245
Beast, William, 274
Beauflour, Agnes, 46, 116
,, Edmund, 20, 42
,, Geoffrey, 6, 48
,, Thomas, 116
,, Walter, 16
Beaupyne, Margaret, 78
,, Thomas, 28, 77, 78, 127
Beche, de le, Richard, 43
Bede, William, 204
Bedford, William, 174
Bedhampton, Richard, 61
Bedstone, Richard, 120
Beede, Thomas, 188
Beell, Henry, 170
,, John, 170
,, Katharine, 170
,, Thomas, 170
Bekeford, Maud, 50
Bekeswell, Walter, 34
,, William, 34
Beket, John, 36, 37
,, Maud, 37
Belamy, Robert, 127
Bell, Alice, 196
,, James, 196, 197
Bellamye, Alice, 262
Bellingam, Thomas, 199, 239
Bene, Dorothy, 219
Benet, Robert, 82, 99
,, Thomas, 52, 53, 54, 57, 58, 74
,, Walter, 135
,, William, 74
Benham, John, 16
Benion, Elizabeth, 251
Benley, Alice, 81
,, Joan, 97
,, John, 97
,, Robert, 98
,, Thomas, 97
,, William, 81, 90, 103
Bennet, alias Harris, Alice, 230
Bennett, Jane, 268
,, Ralph, 229, 230
,, Richard, 278
Bense, Thomas, 179
Beoff, John, 73, 74
Berber, John, 130
Berdon, John, 117
,, William, 65, 117
Berebrewer, Griffith, 233
Berelay, John, 59
Berford, William, 35
Berkeley, Alice, 16, 48
,, Maurice, knt., 139
,, alias Clyve, Thomas, 117
Berkley, Isabel, 157
,, Maurice, 157
Bern, John, 113
Bernard, Alice, 168
,, Joan, 168
,, John, 117
Bernelee, John, 41
Bertlot, Thomas, 83
Bertram, John, 92
Bery, Edward, 153
,, John, 59
Best, Thomas, 268

Betham, Julian, 220
Bettes, Thomas, 213
,, Welthian, 213
Beverley, Emmot, 120
,, John, 110
,, Robert, 114
Bevyr, or Bevir, Thomas, 141, 143, 161
Bewsam, Master, 182
Beynton, John, 189
Bierden, Agnes, 125, 126
,, Alice, 126
,, Edmund, 48, 124, 126
,, William, 10, 40, 48, 94, 125, 126
,, 130
Birche, Robert, 170
Birde, John, 158
,, William, 233, 235
Bisley, Henry, 128, 129
,, Thomas, 129
Bissy, John, 19
Bitfield, Giles, 275
,, Martin, 274
,, William, 274
Bithesea, William, 209
Blake, John, 20, 87
,, Master, 229
,, Nicholas, 199, 273
,, Richard, 115
Blakeford, Walter, 89
Blakemore, Richard, 101, 107
Blakeney, William, 60
Blan, James, 214
Blancombe, Stephen, 102
Blande, Elizabeth, 209
,, John, 209
Blanket, John, 16, 52
,, Ralph, 19
Blecker, John, 61, 68, 125
Bleys, John, 82
Blith, John, 63
Bloundel, Richard, 39
Blount, Alice, 82
,, John, 120
,, Thomas, 24, 25, 31, 48, 80, 81, 82, 92, 96, 100, 115 125, 126, 129
Bloys, John, 101
Bluet, Agnes, 60
Bocher, Thomas, 48
Bodie, James, 244
Bodman, John, 218
,, Thomas, 218
,, William, 218
Body, John, 85
Boilon, Richard, 39
Bokebynder, James, 38
Bokelond, Alice, 102
,, Joan, 101
,, Margery, 102
,, Richard, 101
,, Thomas, 74
Bokerell, Henry, 46, 106
,, John, 106
Bolardine, Alice, 192, 193
,, Anne, 192
Bole, Isabel, 120
,, Joan, 31
,, John, 97, 108
,, Richard, 50, 134
Bollton, John, 227
Bolton, John, 100, 112, 114, 122
,, Robert, 157, 167
Bonce, Robert, 105
Bonde, John, 80, 162
Bonnor, John, 213
Bonok, Robert, 158, 163
Bonwey, John, 171
Boole, Genet, 178

Bord, John, 14
Bore, Roger, 39
Borgeys, Thomas, 17
Boriet, John, 152
Borne, John, 5, 13
,, William, 50
Borrage, Alice, 223
,, Emlyn, 223
Borry, Grace, 222
Borton, John, 66, 109
,, Richard, 66, 93, 90
Bosdon, Edward, 278, 279
Bosewell, Elizabeth, 240
,, John, 240, 250
Bossington, John, 238
,, *alias* George, John, 238
Bosswell, John, 207
Boswell, Anne, 251
,, Elizabeth, 265
,, George, 250
,, Joan, 250
,, Richard, 251
,, William, 250
Botch, ——, 271
Boteler, Henry, 56
,, Richard, 159
Boteman, Philip, 62
Botener, Thomas, 57
Botiller, John, 84
,, Maud, 84
Botoner, William, 90
Boucher, Martin, 77, 87, 115
Bougham, Nicholas, 31
Boughan, William, 66, 67, 100
Bount, John, 14, 73
,, Roger, 74
Boure, John, 99
Bourne, 79
Bowde, Joan, 106
,, William, 106
Bovy, or Bony, Richard, 50
Bowden, Michael, 263
Bowley, John, 171
Bowman, Roger, 260
Bownes, John, 5
Bowyer, Joan, 48
,, Robert, 49, 119
Box, Nicholas, 176
Boxwell, Joan, 104
,, John, 104
,, Robert, 104
Boydell, Alice, 214
,, Benjamin, 214
,, Elizabeth, 214, 246
,, Giles, 214
,, John, 214, 246
,, Nicholas, 214
,, Ralph, 214
,, Richard, 214, 246
,, William, 214, 246
Boys, Thomas, 126
Braci, William, 40
Bracy, Ed., 157
,, Robert, 134
,, William, 127
Bradford, Joan, 202
,, John, 63
,, William, 128
Bradstone, John, 223
Braillys, Richard, 27
Brampton, Elizabeth, 238
,, Gilbert, 119
,, John, 80, 244
Brandesby, John, 127
Branktre, Henry, 32
Brathelyn, Dayowe, 30
Bray, John, 164

Brayle, Richard, 73
Brayn, Henry, 96
,, Robert, 71
Brayne, Harry, 183, 258
,, Joan, 23
Bremcote, Andrew, 6
Brent, Henry, 78, 99
,, William, 33, 70
Brett, or Britt, William, 108, 109
Brewer, Agnes, 22
,, Bernard, 114
,, Joan, 47
,, John, 37
,, Richard, 67
,, William, 63, 95
Brickdall, Humphrey, 221
Brid, William, 23
Bridle, Robert, 160
Bridport, John, 65, 66
Brigg, Oliver, 188
Briggewatir, John, 65
Brinsdon, John, 259
,, William, 259, 260
Bris, Richard, 39
Bristelton, Julian, 31
,, Thomas, 31
Broforde, Robert, 28
Broke, John, 44, 80, 166
,, Julian, 35
,, Lady, 48, 113
,, Thomas, knt., 27, 30, 37, 48, 52, 55, 57, 77, 78, 82, 94, 100, 103, 106, 113, 118, 123, 129, 130
,, William, 33, 44, 70, 71, 83
Brokeworth, Agnes, 56
,, John, 56
,, Richard, 56, 73, 118
Brokke, Laurence, 91
Bromdon, Richard, 65
Brompton, Joan, 27
,, John, 47
Brond, Richard, 87
Brooke, Amy, 264
,, Thomas, 44, 172, 257, 261, 262
Broun, Beatrix, 105
,, Edmund, 67, 100, 108, 117
,, Elen, 100
,, Henry, 161
,, John, 63, 77, 102, 105, 128, 129
,, Nicholas, 171, 173
,, Philip, 9
,, Richard, 161
,, Walter, 23, 79
,, William, 29, 92, 100
Brounenesyng, David, 52
Browne, Agnes, 145, 179
,, Alice, 224
,, Gilbert, 250
,, Hugh, 221
,, Humphrey, 149
,, John, 148, 149, 190, 202, 214, 228, 248, 250, 251, 252
,, Philip, 205, 224
,, Richard, 265
,, Robert, 105
,, Thomas, 257
,, William, 145, 149, 198, 224, 259
Browninge, John, 256
Brownwyn, Richard, 87
Bruer, Hugh, 165
,, John, 52
Brues, John, 101
Bruton, John, 85
,, Richard, 63
Brwton, John, 77
Bryd, John, 144
Brydd, John, 97

Brydd, William, 143, 144
Bryghtlampton, William, 10, 55
Brymlaye, George, 264
Brynt, Marion, 43
,, Robert, 43
Brynyng, Walter, 38
Bryt, John, 33, 52
Buckford, ——, 222
,, Katharine, 240
,, Mrs., 240
Budde, Joan, 114
,, John, 114
Buffin, Margery, 264
Bulbeck, John, 275
Bulkeley, Master, 145
Bull, John, 235, 254, 255
Bullocke, William, 261
Bulloke, Richard, 161
Bunt, John, 18
Buntyng, Katharine, 156
,, William, 156
Burbache, John, 81, 90, 105 122
Burchall, Joan, 220, 238
Burcott, Richard, 238
Burdon, William, 103
Burford, John, 62, 95
Burgeys, Joan, 31
,, John, 58
Burgin, Robert, 188
Burkhed, Christopher, 204
Burlas, Robert, 86
Burley, Edmund, 171, 172
,, John, 175
,, William, 175
Burnell, John, 279
,, Margaret, 279
Burriett, Alice, 279
Burrowes, John, 213
Burton, Alice, 188
,, Joan, 6
,, John, 44, 45, 131, 134, 136, 144, 164, 170
,, Nicholas, 136
,, William, 31, 35
Bury, Agnes, 145
,, Joan, 155
,, John, 25
,, Katharine, 145
,, Robert, 40
Buscon, Edward, 215
Bushe, James, 265
,, John, 273
,, Margery, 234
Busshoppe, Cecily, 110
,, John, 110
Butler, Bridget, 193
,, Elizabeth, 193
,, Francis, 193
,, Robert, 183, 192, 193
,, William, 205
Buttiller, Katharine, 85
Byddeston, Richard, 35
Byde, Robert, 245
Bydow, Thomas, 97
Bydowe, 24
Byllinge, Richard, 255
Bynion, Adam, 251
Byrch, Joan, 155
Byrde, William, 157, 160, 256, 257
Byrymore, John, 108, 109, 110, 111
Bysse, Joan, 188
,, John, 202, 210, 223
,, Peter, 258, 259

Cable, John, 49, 101
,, Matthew, 252
Cabull, Richard, 106

Cabull, William, 66
Cadbury, John, 58
,, Robert, 44
Cadell, James, 277
Cadican, John, 116
Cadle, James, 262
,, William, 247
Caen, Francis, 162
Cake, John, 80
Calf, Henry, 22, 23, 39, 83
,, Katharine, 22, 83
,, Roger, 58, 60
Calicote, John, 149, 150
Callowhill, Christopher, 227
,, Constance, 227
,, Elizabeth, 227
,, Philip, 227
,, Thomas, 227, 257
Calmady, Thomas, 170
Camel, Robert, 11
,, Thomas, 82
Cameleigh, John, 24
Cammell, *alias* Arnald, Robert, 45
Camvyle, John, 85
Camylle, John, 103
Candevere, John, 16, 28, 39
Candover, John, 58
Canon, Ralph, 19, 30, 44, 46, 52
,, William, 89, 119
Cantwell, Adam, 73
Canyng, Maud, 73
Canynges, Agnes, 41, 48, 58
,, Elizabeth, 152, 153
,, Joan, 25
,, John, 25, 40, 48, 54, 55, 56, 77, 117, 130, 153, 154
,, Margaret, 90
,, Simon, 48, 90
,, Thomas, 90, 153, 154
,, William, 5, 6, 7, 14, 29, 41, 48, 58, 131, 136, 139, 140, 145, 151, 152, 154, 155 282
Capella, de, William, 69
Caple, John, 176
Capper, Christopher, 187
Carew, Robert, 150, 158, 161
Carey, William, 279
Carie, William, 242, 245
Carleton, Hugh, 77, 85, 110, 125
Carne, or Carue, John, 70
,, William, 257
Caroe, Alexander, 254
,, Henry, 254
,, John, 224, 235, 236, 253, 254, 255
,, Katharine, 236
,, Richard, 254
,, William, 254
Carowe, Hugh, 219
Carpenter, Bishop, 132, 144, 151
,, Henry, 13
,, John, 131, 163
,, Richard, 25
,, Th., 38
,, Thomas, 58
,, Walter, 110, 129
,, William, 38, 170
Carr, Anne, 207
,, Edward, 208
,, John, 199, 201, 207, 208, 256
,, William, 193, 194, 207
Carse, Hugh, 70
,, Thomas, 70
,, William, 70
Carsewell, John, 11, 12
Carter, Alice, 22, 39
,, Robert, 166
Cary, Anne, 245

Cary, Elizabeth, 245
,, Frances, 245
,, Gervase, 46
,, Joan, 245
,, John, 46
,, Mary, 245
,, Richard, 245
,, William, 46, 122
Castell, Alice, 60, 87
,, John, 16, 42, 44, 60, 117
,, William, 59, 64
Castelman, Edith, 134
,, Jasper, 276
,, John, 134
,, Thomas, 131
Catanio, Carolo, 180
,, Georgio, 180
Cattaynes, Leonard, 184
Caudell, Thomas, 111, 123
Caulie, George, 275
Cauntelbury, John, 8
Caunterbury, Alice, 139
,, John, 30, 73, 82, 84, 89
,, Nicholas, 80, 130
,, William, 139
Cause, Agnes, 234
,, Richard, 234
,, William, 234
Causy, Hugh, 8
Cave, or Cane, Philip, 50
Cawfylde, —— 205
Cawse, Richard, 183
Cecill, Christopher, 255
,, Elizabeth, 255
,, Joan, 223
,, John, 223
Cely, John, 159
Chalnour, Lodowic, 135
Chaloner, Peter, 99
,, Ralph, 120
,, Richard, 38
Chamberleyn, John, 129
Chambers, Alice, 223
,, Dominick, 223
,, John, 223, 224
,, Thomas, 223
,, William, 223
Chamley, Agnes, 272
,, Thomas, 272
Champenes, Alice, 25
,, John, 25
Champency, John, 21
Champeneys, Richard, 36
Champion, William, 35
Chapeleyn, John, 12, 22, 109
,, Maud, 22
,, Richard, 22
,, Thomas, 21
Chaple, William, 248
Chappell, Bartholomew, 231
,, Thomas, 209
Chauncellor, Master, 194
Chaundeler, Alan, 125
,, Roger, 12, 20
Chaunger, Letice, 16
Cheddre, Richard, 117
,, Robert, 6, 9, 17, 20
,, Thomas, 130, 132, 134, 139
,, William, 9
Cheltenham, or Chiltenham, John, 24, 25
29, 33, 34, 51, 92
,, Walter, 12, 15
,, William, 125
Chepe, Robert, 70, 135, 136
,, William, 80
Chepman, John, 89, 105
,, Nicholas, 8, 81

Chepstowe, Joan, or John, 33
,, John, 21, 63
,, Nigel, 21
,, Robert, 21
Chesewell, Cristina, 80
,, John, 80
Chesses, John, 280
Chester, Bridget, 248
,, Dominick, 195, 203, 204
,, Edward, 194, 201
,, Elizabeth, 204, 248
,, Henry, 144, 203, 204
,, James, 194, 203, 204, 248
,, Joan, 203
,, John, 162, 164
,, Mary, 248
,, Thomas, 194, 195, 204, 216
,, Walter, 203
,, William, 203, 204
Chewe, John, 28, 29, 30, 32, 40, 42, 59, 60
,, William, 234
Chichelew, Edith, 12
,, John, 12
Childe, Katharine, 279
Chippenham, Richard, 20
Chivaler, John, 111, 112
Chokke, Richard, 132
Christopher, John, 239
Churchehowse, Richard, 274
Churchey, Nicholas, 42
Chynham, Richard, 93
Clarke, Alice, 260
,, John, 228
,, Richard, 228
,, Thomas, 186
Clasbeck, Alice, 211
,, Elizabeth, 211
,, John, 211
,, Maud, 211
,, Roger, 211
,, William, 211
Clement, Richard, 73, 193
,, Robert, 68
,, Thomas, 246
Clemond, Thomas, 204
,, William, 204
Cleof, John, 115
Clerk, Joan, 87
,, John, 71, 98, 135, 139, 147, 148, 183
,, Nicholas, 28
,, Richard, 37, 118
,, Robert, 195
,, Thomas, 17, 32, 59, 76, 185
,, Walter, 99
,, William, 47, 148, 151
Cleyvile, Robert, 28
Clifford, Agnes, 10, 84
,, John, 10, 84, 115
Clodd, goodwife, 255
Clune, John, 192
Clyforde, James, 185
Clyve, Isabel, 117
,, John, 64, 74, 83, 89, 114, 117, 125,
127, 128
,, William, 96
Clyve, alias Berkeley, Thomas, 117
Clyvedon, Alexandre, 96, 97
,, Alice, 77
,, Joan, 96
Cobbe, Joan, 62
Cobbet, Alice, 261
Cobyndon, Henry, 39, 83
,, John, 25, 116
,, Richard, 20, 39
Cockes, John, 135
Cockesey, ——, 186
Cocus, Thomas, 17
Codde, David, 33, 42, 43

Coder, Agnes, 149
 ,, John, 149
 ,, Maud, 150, 155
 ,, Richard, 150
 ,, William, 134, 136, 149, 156, 167
Codrington, Francis, 185, 186
Codyngton, Cristina, 48
 ,, John, 48
Coferer, Richard, 99
Coffe, or Cufe, Christopher, 260
Cogan, John, 137, 147
 ,, Walter, 16, 28, 38
Cogan, alias Philip, David, 178
Coke, Elizabeth, 193
 ,, John, 35
 ,, Richard, 48
 ,, Sysley, 193
 ,, Thomas, 13
 ,, William, 6
Coker, Alice, 166
Cokkes, James, 32, 34, 77, 79, 81, 83, 84, 102, 104, 105, 112
 ,, John, 102, 112, 113, 114, 120, 124, 169
 ,, Margaret, 112
Cokking, John, 82, 118, 119
 ,, Felicia, 118
Coklonde, Joan, 145
 ,, Philip, 145
Cole, John, 104, 116
 ,, Patrick, 170
 ,, Richard, 198, 201, 208, 209, 214, 220, 233
 ,, Robert, 12, 205
 ,, Stephen, 196
 ,, William, 250
Coleman, Edith, 208
 ,, Elizabeth, 209
Colet, Edith, 25
Colle, John, 160
Colles, John, 169
Colhnan, Abraham, 269
 ,, Agnes, 212
 ,, John, 269
 ,, Margaret, 269
Collyngs, ——, 181
Collyns, Henry, 179
Colman, John, 87
 ,, Thomas, 204, 234
Colmere, Henry, 5
Colne, or Collys, Ralph, 29
Colston, Anne, 241
 ,, Elizabeth, 250
 ,, George, 250
 ,, Michael, 200
 ,, Thomas, 5, 6, 17, 28, 35, 78, 197, 200, 201, 226
 ,, William, 92, 99, 232, 250, 263
Colthurste, Master, 232
Colvyle, Robert, 76, 90, 104, 114
Colwell, William, 149, 150
Colyns, Thomas, 104, 107
 ,, William, 115
Combe, Elias, 66
 ,, John, 88
 ,, William, 17, 27, 94
Comber, John, 51, 66, 67
Comer, John, 48
Compton, John, 136, 140, 141
Compaignon, Katharine, 78
 ,, Nicholas, 78
Comyn, Stephen, 125
Conic, Agnes, 262
 ,, John, 262
 ,, Mary, 262
 ,, Robert, 262
Coningham, Thomas, 200

Cooke, Edmund, 209
 ,, Janen, 152
 ,, John, 21
 ,, Philip,
 ,, Richard, 21
 ,, Roger, 183, 252
 ,, Thomas, 32, 38, 217
 ,, William, 33, 152, 186, 216
Coollimor, Richard, 251
Cooper, William, 228
Coorant, Agnes, 252
Copper, John, 123
Corby, John, 16
Cordy, Robert, 16
Core, Robert, 134, 139
Corfield John, 198
Cornell, Thomas, 180
Cornewale, Richard, 52
Cornysh, Eleanor, 186
 ,, Joan, 25
 ,, Thomas, 171
 ,, alias Pytte, Robert, 142
Cory, Charity, 228
 ,, Henry, 58
 ,, Joan, 164
 ,, Margaret, 228
 ,, Thomas, 239
 ,, William, 228
Coryour, Hugh, 98
Cosham, John, 131
Cosson, John, 279
Coston, Alice, 218
 ,, Francis, 186
 ,, Humphrey, 180
 ,, Lewes, 218
Coterel, John, 112
Cother, —— 207
 ,, Elizabeth, 240
 ,, Jane, 240
 ,, John, 205, 240, 259
 ,, Joyce, 259
Cothery, John, 251
Coton, Agnes, 105
 ,, John, 25, 46, 82, 105
Cotterell, Andrew, 201
 ,, James, 215
 ,, John, 209, 215, 225, 244
Cotyller, Thomas, 135
Coueley, Maud, 13, 24
Couley, Robert, 203
 ,, William, 20, 21
Countasse, Richard, 154
Courtenay, William, 97
Covyntre, or Coventre, John, 104
 ,, Thomas, 115
Cowper, Agnes, 183
 ,, Giles, 183
 ,, John, 206
 ,, Margaret, 232
 ,, Margery, 183
 ,, Rouland, 183, 184
 ,, William, 183
Coxe, Joan, 212, 238
 ,, Matthew, 227
 ,, Thomas, 227
 ,, William, 199, 200, 227, 232
Cradock, Clement, 197
 ,, Elizabeth, 204, 244
 ,, John, 200
 ,, Thomas, 244
 ,, William, 252
Cragge, William, 101
Crane, Alice, 69
 ,, Hugh, 141
Crede, John, 116
 ,, Thomas, 10
Crewe, Anne, 228

2 c

Crewe, Anthony, 228
Cristishaun, Nicholas, 64
Croke, John, 148
Crokker, Richard, 42
Crompe, John, 15
Cromwell, Elizabeth, 156
,, George, 156
Cropenel, William, 98
Cros, Robert, 13
Crosbie, Nicholas, 191
Crose, Benedict, 160
Crosman, Agnes, 75
,, Robert, 75
Croter, John, 63
Croume, John, 67
Croute, Nicholas, 29
Crull, Thomas, 88
,, Robert, 88
Crykald, John, 163
Cryn, Marcus, 162
Crynche, John, 127
Cuffe, John, 120
Cullymore, Edward, 202, 203
,, John, 258
Curteys, Edward, 63
Curties, Elizabeth, 219
,, John, 219
,, Thomas, 219
Cutley, John, 196
Cutt, Bridget, 224
,, John, 201, 209
,, Matthew, 209
,, Nicholas, 209, 210, 224
,, Thomas, 237
,, William, 209, 210, 221

Dagyn, Thomas, 103
Dakins, Richard, 188
Dale, Henry, 157
Dam, de, Roger, 162
Dane, William, 228
Danvers, Richard, 278
Danyell, David, 131
,, Thomas, 55
Darbie, Edith, 183
Darby, Joan, 236
Darleston, Henry, 5, 78, 8
Daske, Thomas, 159
Daton, John, 94
Dauburne, John, 89, 96
Daunteseye, Hugh, 82
Davells, William, 209
David, Janyn, 19
,, Robert, 126
,, Thomas, 126
,, William, 10, 126
Davies, Ambrose, 218, 219
,, Katharine, 219
,, Richard, 218
,, Robert, 201
,, Walter, 220
Davis, or Davys, Agnes, 277
,, Edward, 213
,, Henry, 190, 277
,, James, 262
,, John, 172, 194, 196, 262, 263, 277
,, Richard, 193, 247, 258, 262
,, Roger, 262
,, Thomas, 254, 262, 277
,, Walter, 200, 262, 263
,, William, 261, 277
,, ——, 237
Davy, Edith, 126
,, John, 59, 131, 165
,, Robert, 127
,, Thomas, 165

Davyson, John, 166
Dawemer, William, 244
Dawes, Elen, 169
,, Hugh, 169
,, Joan, 169
,, John, 169
,, Richard, 169
,, Roger, 169, 174
,, Thomas, 169
Dawkin, Lewes, 219
Dawkins, Robert, 199
Deane, Elizabeth, 186
,, Robert, 249
Deane, *alias* Popley, John, 237
Deare, Katharine, 199
Dedbroke, Joan, 24
,, Robert, 24
Dee, Alice, 177
Deenys, Richard, 131
Deer, or Dere, Henry, 228
,, John, 33, 228
,, Katharine, 228
,, Roger, 199, 228
,, William, 228
Delaware, Lord, 180
Delyn, John, 31
,, William, 125
Dene, John, 16
,, William, 75
Denebawde, Thomas, 5
Dennis, or Dennys, Morrys, 203
,, Richard, 133, 242
,, Walter, knt., 242
,, William, 133, 179
Derby, Margaret, 49
,, Nicholas, 49
,, Walter, 5, 6, 7, 15, 28, 108
Deriton, de, John, 58
Derlyng, Nicholas, 91
Derneford, John, 25, 43, 61, 73
,, Richard, 22
Deryk, Richard, 152
Devenysch, Ismaeta, 43
,, John, 37, 53, 64
,, Nicholas, 80, 85, 115, 126, 129
,, Thomas, 134
Devonshire, Thomas, 174
Devy, Patrick, 130
Devyas, William, 118
Devyncher, Thomas, 173
Dewell, Elianor, 258
Dewy, Robert, 143
Dexe, Thomas, 163
Deye, John, 17, 65, 126
Deyell, Jen'n, 134
Didbrok, Alice, 91
,, Robert, 91
Dier, or Dyar, Agnes, 252
,, John, 5, 87, 124
,, Philip, 17
,, Richard, 66
,, Roger, 20
,, Stephen, 55
,, Thomas, 66, 90, 91, 94, 95, 98, 99, 126
Dixon, Jane, 217
Doddesley, John, 54, 55
Dodlyng, John, 13
Dole, Ralph, 231
,, Richard, 267
Dolle, Isabel, 166
Dollyng, Cristina, 101
,, Richard, 101, 102, 115
Dolman, William, 142
Don, John, 43, 45
Donhede, Edith, 45
,, John, 45

Donne, John, 71
,, Thomas, 71
Donnynge, William, 191, 192
Donster, Isabel, 45
,, John, 31, 50, 75, 143
Dorrell, Thomas, 231, 237
Dorset, Matthew, 35
Dovandre, Edmund, 155
Dove, Master, 206
Dowe, Robert, 209
Dowle, Arthur, 196
,, Christopher, 196, 197
,, Edward, 250
,, Henry, 197
,, James, 196, 222
,, John, 196
,, Walter, 217
Downe, Thomas, 51
,, William, 51
Dowting, Edward, 212
Drake, Francis, knt., 265
Draper, Anne, 224
,, Hugh, 225
,, John, 82, 97, 99, 100, 114, 224
,, William, 9, 10
Draycote, John, 49, 88
,, Lucy, 49, 122
,, Thomas, 49
,, William, 49
Dreux, John, 169, 170, 171
Drewes, John, 184, 185, 186
Drewz, John, 163, 164
,, Peter, 163
,, Richard, 163
,, Robert, 163
Dreyse, John, 68, 69
Drivare, Alice, 124
,, William, 124
Droys, Isabel, 99, 109, 115, 125
,, John, 67, 79, 80, 84, 90, 91, 94, 95, 98, 99, 126
Drury, William, 226, 233, 252, 259, 260
Drynkewater, Thomas, 43, 69
Dudbroke, David, 79, 84, 94, 96, 99, 100
,, Robert, 21, 28, 57, 69
Duddellesbury, William, 107
Dudmester, Goodlove, 196
,, Richard, 196
Dugeon, Thomas, 114
Dugmore, Richard, 148
Dull, Letice, 217
,, Thomas, 160
Dunclent, de, John, 7, 9, 14, 15
Dunn, Doctor, 253
Durlinge, Thomas, 279
Dybon, Walter, 94
Dydmister, Bridget, 248
,, Edward, 248
,, Henry, 248
,, Joan, 248
,, Richard, 248
,, Thomas, 248
Dye, Jenkyn, 225
,, Joan, 252
,, John, 197, 201, 210, 214
,, Robert, 252
,, Thomas, 236
Dyhuee, John, 61
Dyllet, Christopher, 263
Dyme, Adam, 46
,, William, 46, 60
Dyrrickeson, Dyricke, 229

Eaton, or Eiton, Edmond, 237
,, Elizabeth, 237
,, John, 224

Eddye, Thomas, 228
Edmonds, William, 179, 240, 244, 273
Edward, Agnes, 67, 173
,, Alice, 127
,, Henry, 173
,, Joan, 173
,, John, 173
,, Thomas, 173
,, William, 173
Edwardes, Edmond, 261
,, Elizabeth, 169
,, John, 136, 164, 174
,, Master, 210
,, Richard, 231, 247, 258
,, Sampson, 261
,, William, 176
Egger, Richard, 22, 42
Eglesale, William, 88
Egleston, Thomas, 163
Eiton, Master, 225
Elcok, Joan, 46
Ele, de, and le, William, 12, 52, 75
Elliott, or Ellyett, Barbara, 182
,, Elizabeth, 182
,, Henry, 236, 253
,, Hugh, 172
,, Joan, 174
,, John, 135, 136, 174, 182, 236
,, Katharine, 182
,, Nicholas, 174
,, Robert, 174, 182
,, Thomas, 174, 236
,, William, 174, 182, 236
Ellis, William, 235, 261
Elston, Justinian, 221
Emayn, John, 140
Engelond, Julian, 72
,, Thomas, 72
England, Margaret, Queen of, 136
Englissh, John, 33
,, Maud, 33
Enkbarrow, Robert, 155
Erle, Margery, 165
,, Richard, 137, 165
,, Thomas, 57, 108, 114, 165
,, Thomasine, 165
Erley, Joan, 135, 142
,, Robert, 141, 142
Erleygh, William, 189
Erlyngham, de, Sibil, 5
Erneawey, Agnes, 7
,, John, 7
Erond, Edmond, 275
Erothe, John, 190
Escote, Elizabeth, 52
,, Hugh, 112, 113, 114
,, Walter, 52
,, William, 52, 53
Estcote, Walter, 122
Estcourt, John, 96, 98, 101
Estegate, Agnes, 188
,, Robert, 188
Esterfeld, Henry, 177, 178
,, John, 157, 162, 164, 170, 177, 178
,, Maud, 177
Eston, Thomas, 68, 101
Evan, Joan, 183
Evance, John, 188
,, William, 218
Evans, Milles, 211
Evenet, Alice, 226
,, Edward, 226, 262, 263
,, Florence, 226
,, Joan, 226
Everard, John, 138

Eweyn Richard, 48
Ewley, John, 128
Ewryn, John, 137
" Richard, 137
" Waryn, 137
Ewyas, David, 33
Ewyn, Richard, 135
Exale, Isabel, 128
Excestre, Elias, 27
" Joan, 122, 123
" John, 123
" Margaret, 27
" Mark, 121, 123
" Nicholas, 86, 94, 118, 119, 121
" Philip, 5, 16, 23, 27, 28, 29, 45
" Thomas, 123
" William, 123
Eyre, John, 119, 120

Fader, William, 75
Fagan, John, 5
" Tibot, 5
Falaunce, John, 66
Famer, John, 52
Farley, James, 213, 268
Farmer, Joan, 265
" Thomas, 265
Fastolf, John, knt., 154
Faunt, John, 43
" Philip, 72, 109
Fawkener, William, 13
Fawkett, Thomas, 226, 275
Fay, John, 189, 240, 264
Fayreford, Henry, 31
Fembrigg, Richard, 74
Ferant, Ralph, 64
Ferour, Felicia, 64
" Richard, 64
Ferre, Elizabeth, 164
" William, 164
Ferreys, Thomas, 157
Ferrour, John, 24
" Stephen, 24
Ferthyng, Isabel, 48
" John, 51
" Walter, 48
Filberd, Alice, 28
" John, 28
" William, 5, 28
Fillian, John, 206, 210
Filter, Alice, 74
" Thomas, 74
Fissche, Agnes, 131, 133
" Thomas, 112, 113, 114, 124, 131
133, 134, 135, 136
" William, 131, 132, 133
Fisscher, Joan, 124
" Nigil, 20
Fissher, or Fysher, Anne, 154
" John, 83, 84, 85,
124, 194
" Katharine, 194
" Simon, 76
" ———, 204
Fitzjeffrey, Anne, 218
" Edward, 218
" John, 218
" Matthew, 218
" Thomas, 218
Fitzwaryn, John, 118, 131
Fitz William, William, 131
Flecchar, or Fleccher, Alice, 193, 194
" John, 6, 193
" William, 193, 194
Fletcher, John, 218
Fletcher, *alias* Paine, John, 213
Flexhall, Thomas, 166

Floide, Elizabeth, 269
" Margery, 269
Florys, John, 17
Flowen', Alice, 199
Flower, Christopher, 218
Floyt, or Fluyt, Agnes, 62
" John, 7, 62
" Nicholas, 62
" William, 62
" Yvo, 20, 122
Fodygndon, Henry, 45
Folkyshull, John, 72, 124
" William, 72, 124
Folyot, or Follett, John, 51, 77, 205
Foorde, Richard, 264
Forbour, Richard, 135
Forde, Joan, 144
" John, 115, 144
Forest, William, 167
Forster, Adam, 71
" Alice, 71
" Edward, 103
" Hugh, 159
" Joan, 176
" John, 49, 71, 80, 153, 157, 172, 176
" Richard, 122, 127, 128, 130, 145, 176
" Stephen, 153, 176
" William, 66, 69, 70, 72, 73, 74
Fort, William, 45
Fortescu, John, knt., 136
Fosse, Walter, 139
Founte, de la, Alice, 171
" Anne, 171
" Edmund, 171
" Elizabeth, 171
" Gillam, 160
" John, 171
" William, 170
Fourbour, Agnes, 168
" William, 93
Fowens, John, 267
Fowke, John, 161
Fowler, Francis, 180
Fownes, John, 269
Fox, John, 270
Foxhull, William, 44
Foyns, John, 269
" Mary, 269
" Mistress, 269
Frampton, Henry, 115
" John, knt., 114, 117, 124
Frank, John, 82
Frankeleyn, John, 170
Frauncys, John, 36
" Richard, 114
Freeman, John, 215
" Roger, 202
Freman, Alice, 54
" Joan, 56
" John, 54
" Thomas, 54
Freme, Nicholas, 129, 132
Frenche, Edward, 222
" Katharine, 222
" Richard, 222
" Thomas, 222
" Toby, 222
Frensch, Adam, 49
" Alice, 49
" Maud, 11, 16, 49
Frensch, le, Eborard, 32, 115, 146
Frenshman, John, 142
Frenssh, Joan, 56, 57
" John, 56, 122
Frenssh, Julian, 56

,, Thomas, 36, 54
Frere, Agnes, 103
,, Henry, 103
,, Isabel, 103
,, Joan, 103
,, John, 28, 35, 78, 103
,, Richard, 27, 74, 103
,, Roger, 103
,, Thomas, 103
,, Walter, 103
,, William, 94
Freweyn, Joan, 33
,, John, 32
Frie, or Frye, Joan, 216
,, John, 189, 196
Frier, or Fryer, Philip, 184
,, Walter, 255
Frize, Master, 195
Frome, William, 13, 14, 28, 42, 57, 115, 119
Frompton, Agnes, 60
,, Alice, 109
,, Isabel, 19
,, Joan, 41
,, John, 109
,, Richard, 13, 20
,, Roger, 20, 21, 60
,, Walter, 13, 19, 20, 21, 41, 97, 109, 115
Frost, Margaret, 42
,, William, 42
Frox, Julian, 71
Frynde, or Frend, Christopher, 239
,, Edward, 239
,, Joan, 239
,, Margery, 239
Fulbroke, Robert, 165
,, Tristram, 165
Fuller, Richard, 222
Furnyvall, John, 159
Fursell, John, 238
Fussell, Joan, 244
,, Thomas, 244
Fustewe, Bartholomew, 214
Fuyster, Elizabeth, 173
,, Joan, 173
,, John, 124, 172
,, Robert, 173
Fyl, Thomas, 54
Fyler, Agnes, 111
,, Beatrix, 111
,, John, 111
,, Thomas, 111
Fylle, Thomas, 101, 106
,, William, 82
Fylour, Agnes, 140
,, Thomas, 105, 112, 140
Fynche, Joan, 58
,, Katharine, 58, 107
,, Richard, 34, 58, 107, 112, 114
Fysshprest, Walter, 59
Fytelton, Alice, 125
,, Elizabeth, 56
,, John, 56, 125

Gadburye, Michael, 225
Gainsford, Luce, 217
,, Nicholas, 217
Galon, John, 37
Gamelyn, John, 126
Gandyn, Thomas, 254
Gardener, Robert, 33
,, William, 33
Gardyner, John, 70, 151
,, Robert, 13, 70, 122
Garewey, Matthew, 94
Garnet, John, 106

Garrett, Mistress, 253
,, ———, 230
Gasquyn, Peter, 66
Gate, William, 36
Gauncell, William, 165
Gaveler, Gilbert, 81
Gaywode, Agnes, 145, 147
,, Isabel, 146
,, John, 134, 136, 110, 115, 116, 147, 148, 167
,, William, 145
Gegge, John, 117
,, Thomasine, 117
Gele, John, 103
George, John, 159
,, Richard, 255
,, *alias* Bossington, John, 238
Gere, goodwife, 263
Gerveys, John, 239
,, Simon, 171, 174
,, *alias* Davis, Harry, 190
Geyl, Nicholas, 6
Gibbes, or Gybbes, Edward, 171
,, Hugh, 247
,, Joan, 247
,, John, 50
,, Margaret, 247
,, Walter, 15
,, William, 210
Gildeney, Henry, 110, 111, 119, 121
,, Joan, 119
Gillman, Robert, 238
Gislingham, John, 203
Glaseare, William, 74
Glasier, Henry, 100
,, William, 127
Gleson, Walter, 268, 269
Glise, John, 22
Gliston, Walter, 222
Gloucester, Humphrey, Duke of, 120
Gloucestre, Isabel, 81
,, Margaret, 105
,, Robert, 33
,, Thomas, 11, 77, 81, 105
Glover, John, 102
,, Julian, 9
,, Thomas, 9
,, Walter, 9
Godard, John, 143
Goddell, Clement, 280
Godefelawe, Thomas, 105
Godehyne, John, 109
Godereste, or Goterest, John, 39
Godesone, Denis, 80
Godewyn, William, 16
Godeyer, ———, 13
Godfrye, Robert, 253
Godwin, Thomas, 210, 219
Golde, Agnes, 41
,, John, 89
Goldesborough, John, 116
Goldsmyth, William, 93
Golsmyth, Frederick, 59
Gomond, John, 140
Gonette, John, 99
Goodale, Thomas, 192, 193
Goodawle, Elizabeth, 236
,, Thomas, 236
Goode, Thomas, 32, 35
Goodechild, Richard, 99
Gooder, John, 269
Goodman, Thomas, 272
Goodson, John, 104
,, Margaret, 104
Goodyere, or Goodier, Agnes, 260
,, Alice, 260
,, Anthony, 254, 255

Goodyer:, or Goodier, Margaret, 264
"	Robert, 264
"	Roger, 268
"	Thomas, 268
Googh, Edward, 103
Goore, Alice, 247
"	Edward, 247
"	James, 247
"	John, 247
"	Margaret, 247
"	Richard, 247
"	———, 243
Goos, John, 26
"	Walter, 10, 13, 85
Gorges, Edmund, Knt., 165
Gosham, John, 107
Gosse, Peter, 131
Gosslyn, John, 133
"	Margaret, 133
Gostlett, John, 261
Goteham, Robert, 136
Gough, Anne, 275
"	Daniel, 232
"	Davie, 267
"	Elizabeth, 275
"	George, 275, 276
"	Henry, 275
"	Jeun', 62
"	John, 275, 276
"	Mary, 276
"	Matthew, 275, 276
"	Samuel, 221
Gradeley, Cristina, 10, 11
"	Robert, 10
Graic, Robert, 204
Graunt, Elena, 56
"	Joan, 123
"	John, 56, 164
"	Thomas, 20, 56, 62
Grawnte, *alias* Wyoote, Robert, 58
Graye, Alice, 206
"	George, 206, 225
"	William, 206
Grayle, Thomas, 257
Greemer, Gregory, 152
Greene, Anthony, 210
"	Joan, 232
"	Master, 245
"	Nicholas, 210
Greeves, John, 269
Gregory, John, 159, 210, 211
Grene, John, 189, 201, 212
"	William, 44, 210
Greneway, Charity, 221
"	Margaret, 221
Grevell, Margaret, 43
"	William, 178
Greves, Thomas, 280
Grey, Edward, Lord Lisle, 149
Greynton, John, 64
Greynyle, Robert, 26
Grice, Alice, 265
Griffen, or Griffyn, Henry, 251, 255
"	John, 245, 252
"	Thomas, 49
Griffethe, or Griffith, Alice, 252
"	Edward, 272
"	Elizabeth, 251
"	Geoffrey, 108
"	Henry, 255
"	Hugh, 251
"	Joan, 108
"	John, 218, 236, 251, 272
"	Mary, 272
"	Richard, 152, 272
"	Thomas, 108, 122, 135, 251, 272

Grigg, John, 213, 231, 241, 251
"	William, 225
Grissche, John, 115
Griste, Humphrey, 222
Gronowe, Joan, 172
Gros, Agnes, 281
"	Henry, 281
Grove, Cristina, 33
"	Edmond, 204
"	John, 113
"	Margaret, 105
"	Margery, 55
"	Richard, 55
"	Thomas, 213, 271
Gryffyn, John, 248
"	Maud, 249
Grygge, Alice, 194
"	Robert, 194
Grynder, John, 102
Gryne, William, 198
Grynwey, Richard, 194
Guin, Owen, 267
Gunnett, Dionisia, 80
Gunninge, John, 271
"	Thomas, 271
Gusshe, John, 85, 120
Guyen, Philip, 120, 121, 156
Gwynne, Philip, 241, 265
"	Thomas, 189
Gy, Alice, 109
"	John, 109
Gyhbens, John, 256
Gylbert, John, 158
Gylemyn, or Gilmyn, Thomas, 11, 14, 34, 67
Gyles, John, 119
Gyna, John, 27
Gyttins, or Gittens, Agnes, 250
"	Champion, 250
"	Edward, 250
"	Jeffery, 250
"	John, 249
"	Mary, 249, 250
"	Robert, 250
"	Thomas, 250
"	William, 243, 249
Gywon, or Geen, Philip, 121

Hachet, John, 23
Hacket, John, 188
Haddon, Richard, 134, 141, 145
"	Robert, 6
Hadecombe, John, 33
Hailes, Agnes, 218
Haines, Thomas, 209
Halewey, Alice, 71, 72
"	Joan, 71, 72
"	John, 23, 54, 71
"	Margery, 23
"	Richard, 23
"	Simon, 6, 23
"	Thomas, 23, 54, 71, 72, 109, 110, 118, 119, 120, 121, 124, 134, 136, 140
Hall, or Halle, Cristina, 43, 88
"	John, 60, 122, 146, 212
"	Richard, 43, 76, 88, 89, 122, 233
"	Thomas, 43
Halle, *alias* Hegham, Amy, 130, 131
"	John, 130
"	Robert, 130
"	Thomas, 130
"	William, 130
Halperton, John, 91
Haltchy, William, 48
Halton, Robert, 197, 245

Ham, Hierome, 246, 253
Hame, Agnes, 6
  ,,   John, 44
Hamersley, Sampson, 191
Hamlen, or Hamlyn, Anne, 262
  ,,   Elizabeth, 262
  ,,   Robert, 262
Hamlett, Alice, 260
Hamme, John, 24, 63
  ,,   Walter, 63, 64
Hammondes, Joan, 236
  ,,   Katharine, 236
  ,,   William, 236
Hamond, Arthur, 214
  ,,   Richard, 57
Hamons, Arthur, 196
Hamor, Thomas, 245
Hampton, John, 135, 151
Hanam, John, 19
Hancock, William, 190
Hanham, Richard, 48
Hansford, Margaret, 92
Harderley, Richard, 11
Hardwyk, Maurice, 140, 141
Hardy, John, 141
Hardyng, Matthew, 153
  ,,   Thomas, 178
Harethorn, Thomas, 97
Harewell, de, John, 53
Harlowe, John, 160
Harnham, or Hernham, John, 128, 132, 137
Harper, John, 95
  ,,   Nicholas, 61
  ,,   Thomas, 95
  ,,   William, 95, 180, 184
Harrewell, John, 78, 122
Harries, David, 214
Harris, David, 187, 188, 204, 229, 230, 258
  ,,   Elizabeth, 224
  ,,   George, 223, 229
  ,,   Joan, 204
  ,,   John, 223, 229, 265, 278
  ,,   Luke, 254
  ,,   Margaret, 229, 230
  ,,   Morgan, 224
  ,,   Thomas, 182
  ,,   William, 224, 274
Harrison, Richard, 232
Harrwood, John, 238
Harry, John, 108, 120
Harrys, Ellyn, 203,
  ,,   John, 48, 77, 87, 174, 186
  ,,   Master, 185
  ,,   Robert, 99
  ,,   Thomas, 187
Harsfeld, Henry, 119
Harte, Alson, 180
  ,,   John, 235
  ,,   Katharine, 179
  ,,   Mistress, 255
  ,,   Thomas, 179
Harvye, Hugh, 264
Haselwell, Robert, 114
Haslyn, Master, 225
Hasplond, John, 76
Hassald, or Hassall, Randall, 211, 235, 244
Hassefeld, Henry, 69
Hassok, Philip, 93, 98, 106
Hastling, William, 206
Hastyne, Julian, 56
Hastyng, John, 90
  ,,   Margery, 53
  ,,   Nicholas, 53, 72
Hathewey, John, 12
  ,,   William, 12

Hatter, Constance, 134
  ,,   Richard, 133
  ,,   William, 134
Hauker, William, 8, 14
Haukeslow, Joan, 91
  ,,   Richard, 91
Hau'sam, William, 73
Haveryng, Joan, 98
  ,,   John, 78, 98, 130
  ,,   Philip, 98
  ,,   Thomas, 98
Haviland, Joyce, 241
  ,,   Matthew, 241, 249, 256
Hawke, John, 134
Hawkes, John, 168, 169
  ,,   William, 176
Hawkesok, Thomas, 152, 282
Hawkins, or Hawkyns, Dorothy, 257
  ,,   Joan, 243
  ,,   John, 120
  ,,   Thomas, 155
Hawkyng, Cristina, 172
Hawley, John, 106, 166, 170, 171
Hawvyle, William, 86
Hay, Thomas, 29
Hayles, William, 84, 86
Haynes, Joan, 225
  ,,   Roger, 261
Hayward, Roger, 6
  ,,   Thomas, 273
Hede, Cristina, 103
  ,,   John, 103
Hedges, Joan, 261
Hegg, Richard, 14
Helle, Arnold, 162
Hellewyse, John, 102
Hemyng, Anne, 192
  ,,   Henry, 62, 94, 127
  ,,   Richard, 170
  ,,   Thomas, 142
  ,,   William, 192
Hendy, Thomas, 29, 34, 68, 81
  ,,   William, 36
Henewod, Joan, 172
Henlove, Gregory, 172
  ,,   Isabel, 172
  ,,   John, 171, 172
  ,,   Margery, 172
  ,,   Robert, 172
  ,,   Thomas, 172
Henry, John, 224, 230, 262, 263
Henshawe, Alice, 245
  ,,   Robert, 258
Henton, David, 256
  ,,   Margaret, 258
Henx. ——, 20
Herbard, William, 135
Herford, John, 97, 116
Heriottes, Elianor, 262
Herverd, Robert, 131
Hervy, Alice, 9
  ,,   Anne, 172
  ,,   Cecily, 43
  ,,   Humphrey, 172
  ,,   Joan, 36
  ,,   John, 9, 43
  ,,   William, 36, 73
Herward, y. John, 127
Heryforde, Edward, 265
  ,,   Elizabeth, 265
Heryng, John, 370
  ,,   William, 63
Heth, Alice, 110
  ,,   John, 31, 109, 110
Heughes, ——, 263
Hewghes, John, 267

Hewyhs, Cecily, 19
" William, 18, 19
Hewys, John, 176
Hewyssche, William, 16
Hexton, Thomas, 153
Heynes, William, 54, 55
Heytesbury, Joan, 108
" John, 108
Hibbott, Joan, 268
Hickes, Nicholas, 202, 208
" Richard, 136, 152, 153
" Thomas, 185
" William, 224, 250
Hickman, Matthew, 261
Higgens, John, 247, 273
Higgins, Besse, 243
" Elynor, 202, 240
" George, 197, 202, 205, 223
" Mary, 201
" Master, 201
" Mistress, 229
" William, 259
Hilde, Geoffrey, 7
Hilhowse, Agnes, 205
" John, 205
Hill, Anthony, 197, 240
" Bartholomew, 197, 236
" Joan, 197
" John, 197
" Nicholas, 240
" Philip, 235
" Richard, 197, 278, 279
" Thomas, 194, 197
Hillacre, Elline, 188
" Joan, 188
" John, 188
" Polidorus, 188
" William, 188
Hillard, John, 66
Hilling, Elizabeth, 249
" Thomas, 249
Hillseley, John, 274
Hitchinges, Matthew, 255
Hobbes, Davy, 243
" Giles, 222, 223
" Jane, 222
" Nicholas, 223
" Richard, 178
" Thomas, 222
" William, 45, 220
Hoby, Richard, 170, 178
Hodson, Richard, 198
Hoell, William, 240
Hogekyn, William, 27
Hoggett, John, 280
Hoke, Joan, 196
" Philip, 22
" William, 81
Hoker, Edith, 94
" Nicholas, 40, 94
Holbeck, Thomas, 262
Holden, Elizabeth, 153
" John, 153
Hole, Geoffrey, 36
Holchrond, William, 88
Holewey, Felicia, 103
" Joan, 54
Holhurst, Robert, 116
Holland, Alice, 220, 221
" Dorcas, 220, 221
" Harry, 220, 221
" John, 220, 221
Hollyster, Annis, 221
" Edith, 221
" Edward, 231
" John, 221
" Joyce, 221

Hollyster, Mary, 221
" Richard, 221
" Thomas, 221
Holme, Thomas, 90, 112
Hone, John, 157, 271
" William, 135
Honefield, Henry, 116
Honie, Richard, 214
Honsome (?), Henry, 72
" Maud, 72
Hooke, Edith, 249
" John, 249
Hooper, Ralph, 203
Hope, John, 52
Hoper, Hugh, 77
" John, 143
" Reginald, 33
" Richard, 44
" Robert, 19
" William, 79
Hopkins, or Hopkyns, David, 90, 105
" Richard, 166
" William, 223, 251
Hoppis, John, 163
Hore, John, 17
" Philip, 131
" Thomas, 63
Horenbord, Nicholas, 162
Horlok, Richard, 65
Hornar, Elyn, 193
" Philip, 193
Hornecastell, John, 6
Horner, Alice, 219
" Richard, 219, 263
" Thomas, 199, 200, 244
Horte, John, 204, 210
Horugge, Walter, 54, 72
Hosier, Isabel, 167
" John, 138
Hoskins, or Hoskyns, Edward, 229
" Thomas, 174
Hosschekyns, John, 109
Hosteler, David, 159
Hoton, Alice, 150, 156
" John, 156
" William, 149, 150, 155, 156
Houghlot, John, 64
Houndesley, Alice, 143
" John, 143
Howe, William, 264
Howell, Anne, 267
" John, 241
" Mary, 241
" Thomas, 165, 186, 187
" William, 70
Howlegge, John, 119
Howlet, Anne, 172
" Robert, 172
Howse, John, 195
Howseman, Richard, 213, 216, 217
Howson, Thomas, 181
Howys, William, 76
Hubberthorne, Harry, 181
Huchons, Agnes, 33
Hughes, John, 187
Hukeford, William, 123
Hukines, Agnes, 235
" Amy, 236
" Thomas, 236
" William, 235
Hull, or Hulle, John, 17, 66
" Nicholas, 66
Hungerford, Edmund, Bart., 150, 156
Hunt, Elizabeth, 155
" George, 164
" Hugh, 28, 39, 50, 84

Hunt, Joan, 86, 226
 ,, John, 24, 38, 212
 ,, Katharine, 23, 24
 ,, Walter, 144
 ,, William, 86
Hunte, *alias* Calf, John, 86
Hunteley, John, 20
Huntington, Earl of, 185
 ,, John, 205
 ,, Master, 210
Huntlye, Anne, 276
 ,, Anselm, 276
Hurdeman, Joan, 100
 ,, William, 53, 67, 71, 100
Hurell, John, 77
Hurne, William, 148
Hurst, William, 178
Hurte, Ralph, 203, 267
Hurtnall, James, 247
 ,, John, 247
Huth, Julian, 63
Hutton, John, 168
 ,, William, 168
Huys, Master, 194
Hydden, Thomas, 223
Hyett, Philip, 153, 154, 155
Hygham, Robert, 139
Hykedon, ——, 24
Hyll, Nicholas, 135, 207
Hynde, Elen, 158
 ,, Joan, 150
 ,, John, 150
 ,, Robert, 158
 ,, William, 150
Hyndebest, or Hynebest, John, 20, 82
Hywes, Robert, 91

Ilinge, John, 260
Inet, Henry, 36, 76, 88
Ingeman, Elizabeth, 217
Inhyne, Adam, 26, 81, 102, 114
 ,, John, 26
 ,, Katharine, 102
 ,, Margery, 26
 ,, Richard, 24, 25, 31, 36, 16
 ,, Thomas, 17
 ,, William, 102
Inman, Agnes, 245
 ,, Joan, 245
 ,, John, 245
 ,, Thomas, 245
Innyng, John, 161
 ,, Richard, 78
Inshall, James, 258
Iryshe, John, 221
Isegar, William, 146
Ive, Giles, 243
Ivye, Thomas, 270, 271

Jacelyn, Paul, 96
Jackman, Thomas, 180, 181
Jackson, Richard, 256
Jacob, Alice, 128
 ,, Elizabeth, 156, 157
 ,, Humphrey, 156
 ,, Joan, 22
 ,, John, 128, 156, 157, 204, 209
 ,, Reginald, 115
 ,, William, 157
 ,, *alias* Jakes, Robert, 156
Jakys, Robert, 141, 143
James, Francis, 265, 275
 ,, Hugh, 201, 205
 ,, John, 213, 219, 267, 273, 279
 ,, Thomas, 276
 ,, William, 209, 257

Jamsye, John, 178
Jankyn, Geoffrey, 161
Janyns, John, 153
 ,, Thomas, 95
Janys, or Jamys, Richard, 109, 126, 134
Jaye, Benet, 181
 ,, Henry, 143
 ,, Joan, 142
 ,, John, 106, 142, 143, 147, 163, 167, 174
 ,, Mistress, 190
 ,, William, 182
Jefferis, Robert, 273
Jeffreys, John, 179
Jeine, Thomas, 274
Jeke, Henry, 157
Jenkins, Philip, 199
 ,, Richard, 220
Jenson, Anne, 238
Jeu'n, Benjamin, 258
John, Geoffrey, 118
 ,, Lodowic, 138, 139, 156
 ,, Margaret, 118
 ,, Thomas, 135
Joh'nes, Hugh, 165, 166, 171, 172
 ,, Katharine, 172
 ,, William, 165
Johnson, Tancred, 129
Johnsonne, Roger, 201
Joly, William, 174
Jolyff, Richard, 122
Jones, Agnes, 217
 ,, Alice, 193
 ,, David, 196, 220, 239
 ,, Edmond, 217
 ,, Edward, 185, 206
 ,, Eleanor, 183, 214
 ,, Elias, 63
 ,, Elizabeth, 240, 243, 270, 274
 ,, Frances, 214
 ,, Griffith, 184
 ,, Hugh, 184, 191, 213
 ,, Humphrey, 192
 ,, Jane, 218, 274
 ,, Joan, 183
 ,, John, 139, 217, 236, 237, 239, 273, 274
 ,, Margaret, 183
 ,, Margery, 237, 274
 ,, Maurice, 110
 ,, Morgan, 264, 265, 269, 275
 ,, Nicholas, 182
 ,, Philip, 245, 254
 ,, Richard, 217, 243
 ,, Roger, 189, 205, 206, 217, 240
 ,, Ryce, 270
 ,, Thomas, 193, 217, 225, 274
 ,, William, 182, 183, 213, 217, 218, 232, 254, 258, 259, 270
Jons, *alias* Morgan, Joan, 172
 ,, John, 172, 229
 ,, Thomas, 172
Jonys, Edith, 136
 ,, Edmond, 189
 ,, Elen, 137
 ,, Elizabeth, 189
 ,, Isabel, 137
 ,, Jane, 189
 ,, Joan, 189
 ,, John, 136, 189
 ,, Lodowic, 150
 ,, Richard, 189
 ,, Robert, 136
 ,, Thomas, 137, 189
 ,, Welthian, 189
 ,, William, 189

Joos, or Joce, Agnes, 58, 60
,, Alice, 58
,, Anthony, 58
,, Gilbert, 34, 35, 50, 58, 59, 60, 94
,, Robert, 59
,, William, 161
Jorden, goodwife, 259
,, John, 271
Jubbes, Matthew, 170
Juke, Philip, 257
Jurdon, Elenor, 205
,, John, 183

Kaynell, Richard, 82
,, William, 82
Kayton, Richard, 132, 139
Keamys, Thomas, 149
Kearne, William, 257
Kebbe, Thomas, 36
,, Walter, 35, 36
Kedwelly, William, 53
Kelke, Clement, 230
,, John, 230
,, Richard, 230, 249
,, Thomas, 209, 210, 220, 230
Kember, Robert, 141
Kempe, Maud, 53
Kempson, Joan, 157, 158, 163
,, Roger, 157
,, Thomas, 147, 157, 158, 163
,, William, 157
Kemsham, John, 210
Kemys, Isabel, 144
,, William, 144, 147
Kendall, William, 72
Kene, William, 17, 44, 45, 66
Kenfeke, Henry, 70
,, John, 70
,, Katharine, 70
,, William, 70
Kenne, John, 123
,, lord of, John, 41
Kerdif, John, 114
,, William, 33
Kerne, John, 182
Kerry, ——, 221
Kett, Katharine, 255
,, Philip, 255
Kettill, Mighell, 188
Kettingall, or Kyttingall, Alice, 205
,, Elizabeth, 205
,, George, 205
,, John, 205
,, Tobit, 205
Keynesham, John, 62
Kidwellyter, John, 260
Kilderton, William, 100
Kirke, William, 254
Kitchin, Richard, 234, 247, 249
,, Robert, 202, 226, 247
Knap, or Knappe, Avice, 68
,, Reginald, 91
,, Thomas, 5, 28, 29, 68, 117, 125, 281
,, William, 68
Knighte, Ankerett, 264
,, John, 218
Knokke, Thomas, 161
Knolles, William, 131
Knott, Michael, 250
Knottyng, John, 178
Knowell, Thomas, 276
Knowles, Thomas, 231

Knyght, Nicholas, 35
,, Richard, 77
,, William, 26, 35, 154
Knyghton, John, 14, 20, 21, 41, 43, 65
Kynch, Thomas, 255
Kynge, Cristina, 93
Kyngton, Philip, 27
Kyppok, John, 119
Kyte, Agnes, 164, 241
,, Alice, 241
,, Edward, 158, 164
,, Joan, 164, 165, 241
,, John, 164, 241
,, Katharine, 241
,, Philip, 241
,, William, 241

Lacy, Master, 210
,, William, 278
Laighton, Cornish, 227
Lambard, Richard, 254
Lambe, goodwife, 204
Lambert, *alias* Oldbeary, William, 215
Lancastre, John, 19
Lane, Alice, 78
,, Edward, 228, 253
,, John, 78
,, Thomas, 161
,, William, 179
Lang, John, 98
Langford, Charles, 226
,, Edmond, 226
,, Elizabeth, 226, 242
,, Ellis, 226
,, Joan, 219
,, Mary, 248
,, Nicholas, 219
,, Richard, 224, 226, 242
,, Thomas, 226
,, Walter, 226
,, William, 226
,, ——, 216
Langley, Anne, 266, 267, 270
,, Ellynor, 266
,, John, 107, 219, 267, 270
,, Mary, 243, 265, 266, 267, 270, 271
,, Master, 260
,, Philip, 218, 228, 240, 243, 265, 266, 268, 271
,, Richard, 219
,, Robert, 266
,, Ryce, 267
,, Thomas, 219, 274
,, Toby, 243, 265, 266, 267, 268, 270, 271
,, William, 266, 267
Langton, George, 229
,, Richard, 190, 198, 199, 220, 225, 232
Large, John, 216, 255
Lasingbie, Thomas, 179
Lathbury, Margaret, 240
,, Robert, 240
Latymer, Thomas, 272
Launde, Margaret, 165
Launsdon, Agnes, 199
Laurence, William, 98
Laveraunce, John, 134, 157
Lavynton, John, 79, 80
Lawles, Peter, 152
Lawrence, Elizabeth, 229
,, Jane, 229
,, Richard, 229
,, Simon, 232
,, Thomas, 229, 259
,, William, 229, 235

INDEX. 399

Lea, Master, 260
,, Richard, 228
Leche, Ralph, 183
Ledbury, Agnes, 90
,, Richard, 42, 67
,, Robert, 90, 91
Leech, John, 240
Leicestre, John, 83, 98, 100, 110, 118, 121, 128
Lekas, Henry, 58
Lely, Margaret, 122, 123
Lemenstour, Robert, 44
Lemman, Agnes, 72
,, John, 73, 83
,, Thomas, 72, 73
Lemyng, Robert, 189
Lenam, John, 44
Lench, William, 15
Lenny, Joan, 265
Leonus, Richard, 28, 29
Lese, John, 99, 130
Leveden, John, 57
Leversage, Katharine, 234
,, Robert, 234
Leweas, Elizabeth, 199
,, Thomas, 199
Lewen, William, 261
Lewes, Edward, 214, 233
,, Felix, 220, 226, 228, 229
,, John, 232
,, Margaret, 150
,, Thomas, 235
,, William, 269
Lewys, David, 201
,, John, 139
,, Thomas, 184
,, *alias* Turnor, John, 154
Ley, John, 43
Leyeetur, John, 109
Leye, John, 29
Leyg'ue, Hugh, 25
Leynell, John, 159
Leyson, John, 138
Libbe, Roger, 64, 86
Littilton, John, 85
Lloyd, David, 233
Locker, *alias* Parker, William, 209
Lodbroke, Agnes, 188, 189
,, Jonas, 189
,, Thomas, 188, 189
,, Walter, 188
,, William, 188, 189
Lodelow, Agnes, 101
,, Robert, 100
,, Roger, 101
,, William, 101
Lokier, Henry, 95
,, Margery, 44
Lombard, Ralph, 99
,, Thomas, 117
Londe, or Loude, Robert, 116
London, Agnes, 34
,, Alice, 34
,, Henry, 33
,, John, 171
,, Maud, 34
,, Thomas, 48
Long, Edward, 240, 241
,, John, 62, 97
,, Margery, 241
,, Mary, 269
,, Prudence, 237
,, Roger, 279
,, William, 269
Loryng, Walter, 34
Loterell, Hugh, knt., 97
Loue, Agnes, 34

Loveney, John, 120
Lucar, Emanuel, 180, 181, 182
,, Thomas, 180
Lucas, Henry, 254
,, Joan, 129
,, John, 104, 121
,, Margery, 169
,, Peter, 120
,, Stephen, 52, 53
,, Thomas, 249
,, William, 120
Luk, John, 27
Lumbard, Thomas, 60
Luttelton, Richard, 124
Lydeford, Martin, 12
Lye, Joan, 52
,, Thomas, 52, 53, 71, 78, 82, 87, 91, 104
Lygh, Agnes, 61
,, Joan, 61
,, John, 61
,, Margaret, 61
,, Maud, 61
,, Nicholas, 61
,, Robert, 61
,, Thomas, 61
,, William, 105
Lyme, Adam, 68
,, John, 79
,, Walter, 68
Lymnour, John, 94, 109
Lyncoln, Thomas, 164, 165
Lyndesey, John, 162
Lyndraper, William, 31
Lynton, John, 32
Lynzye, ——, 273
Lyon, Nicholas, 254
Lyonns, Thomas, 23
Lysle, de, Lady, 137, 146
,, Lord, 149, 263
Lytell, John, 33
Lyveden, Roger, 106, 107

Mablie, Alice, 11
Macham, William, 181
Maddock, Edmond, 267
Macreolff, Christopher, 162
Maistre, Thomas, 62
Makentose, Robert, 22
Makwell, Richard, 160
Maltman, William, 177, 178
Malverne, Thomas, 10, 99, 114
Malyns, John, 99
Mamfras, John, 27
Manger, Emmot, 142
,, William, 142
Marchall, John, 55
,, Richard, 134
,, Thomas, 71, 78, 87, 107, 111, 118
Marcus, William, 114
Mareschall, William, 58
Markes, William, 60, 79
Market, Thomas, 118
Marle, John, 127
Marler, John, 120
,, Nicholas, 29, 30
Martell, John, 33
Martyn, or Marten, Agnes, 225
,, Alice, 257
,, Anne, 257
,, Cecily, 257
,, David, 225
,, Edith, 257
,, Elizabeth, 257
,, George, 257, 258, 259
,, Harry, 257
,, Margaret, 127

Martyn, or Marten, Richard, 235, 245, 247, 248, 249, 256, 257, 261, 273
,, Walter, 16, 19, 28
,, William, 257
Maryon, Joan, 15, 57
Mascall, Richard, 255
Mason, Edward, 135
,, Elizabeth, 254
,, John, 149, 163
,, Nicholas, 10
,, Richard, 106
,, Thomas, 234
,, William, 36
Massis, or Masies, Humphrey, 254
Mathew, or Mathowe, Agnes, 213
,, Amy, 213
,, Anne, 253
,, Bartholomew, 253
,, David, 190
,, Doctor, 207, 240
,, Elizabeth, 201
,, goodwife, 203
,, Hugh, 213
,, James, 253
,, John, 201, 202, 253
,, Judith, 201
,, Margaret, 171, 213
,, Nicholas, 58, 213
,, Patrick, 235
,, Penelope, 253
,, Peter, 253
,, Richard, 163
,, Thomas, 213, 253
,, Toby, 201, 202
Maulhe, ——, 193
Mavyle, John, 88, 92, 93
May, Agnes, 42
,, Joan, 238
,, Richard, 42, 238, 263
,, Robert, 42
,, Walter, 42
Mayes, Thomas, 93
,, William, 210
Mayhowe, John, 147
Meddon, Reginald, 8
Mede, or Meed, Isabel, 157
,, John, 131, 157
,, Philip, 134, 135, 136, 139, 143, 148, 152, 157
,, Richard, 157
,, Thomas, 134
Mefflin, Alice, 218
Megges, John, 133
,, Robert, 133, 153
Meke, John, 135
,, Oliver, 135
Mellin, Letice, 245
Melloes, John, 254
Mellye, Alice, 206
,, Robert, 206
Menyber, Walter, 63
Merbury, Joan, 124
,, John, 145
Merick, or Merycke, Anne, 205
,, goodwife, 255
,, John, 194, 197, 205, 206, 228
,, Richard, 173, 205
,, Robert, 205
,, Walter, 205
,, William, 182, 205, 206, 280
,, ——, 228
Merk, atte, Clement, 14
Mero, Richard, 245

Mershe, James, 88
,, Joan, 182
Merston, John, 99
,, Thomas, 98
Mertok, Richard, 59
Messam, John, 177, 180
Mey, John, 45
Michaell, Jeffery, 188, 189
,, Margaret, 188, 189
Michell, Isabel, 22
,, John, 22, 94
,, Richard, 22
,, Robert, 22, 81
,, Thomas, 22, 75, 92
,, Walter, 20, 22
Middelton, de, John, 36
Millard, or Millerd, Henry, 207, 240
,, John, 237
Milleyn, John, 134
Mills, William, 212
Millyng, John, 14
Milman, Stephen, 48
Milton, John, 112
,, Robert, 15
,, Walter, 15
,, William, 15
Modeford, John, 42
Moffett, Robert, 181
,, Thomas, 180
Mogys, William, 155
Moille, Avice, 111
,, William, 111
Mollgrove, Elizabeth, 274
Momfort, John, 18
Monoux, George, 166, 172, 173
Monyngton, Walter, 6
Moone, Thomas, 236
Moore, Elizabeth, 240
,, goodwife, 203
,, Master, 222
,, Maud, 222
,, Richard, 207, 240, 253
Mordon, Thomas, 115
More, Cristina, 17, 44
,, John, 81
,, Julian, 190, 255
,, Margaret, 190
,, Nicholas, 63, 64
,, Robert, 276
,, Thomas, 199
,, William, 17, 76, 88, 123, 125, 128, 129, 132, 134, 136, 137
Morell, Thomas, 73
Moret, William, 117
Morewey, Richard, 16
Morgan, Alice, 224, 263
,, John, 265
,, Mabel, 263
,, Margery, 263
,, Richard, 119, 133
,, Thomas, 159
,, alias Jons, John, 172
,, ,, Thomas, 172
Morice, Walter, 164
Morris, Edward, 216, 221
,, Robert, 245
,, ——, 197
Mors, Joan, 138
,, John, 138, 139
,, Lodowic, 138
,, Thomas, 138, 139, 260
,, Walter, 138, 139
Morys, Agnes, 90
Mosely, Humphrey, 231, 236, 237
,, Mary, 251
Moskam, Richard, 173
,, William, 173

Mounford, John, 19
Mourton, Henry, 78
Moygne, or Moigne, Anketill, 25, 43
,, Thomas, 52
Moys, Alexander, 36, 45, 118
,, Sibil, 46, 118
Muleward, Bernard, 16, 18, 19, 84
,, Edith, 16, 18
,, Joan, 53
,, John, 16, 18, 19, 53
,, Richard, 16, 18, 19
,, Walter, 18
Mulle, Hugh, 152
Multon, Robert, 155
Mur, Elizabeth, 270
Murcock, ——, 220
Murcott, Hugh, 209
Muryweder, John, 5
Musard, Thomas, 155
Myagh, James, 33
Mydleton, James, 222
,, Richard, 222
Myles, John, 185
Mylles, goodman, 194
,, John, 186
Mynde, Roger, 69, 84
Mynty, Thomas, 23

Naillesey, John, 59
,, Thomas, 59
Nancothan, John, 140, 143, 281
,, Margaret, 143
Nansmoen, Avice, 96
,, Belinus, 96, 97
,, Isabel, 96
Nashe, Laurence, 179, 193
,, William, 180
Nawdyn, John, 21
,, ——, 21, 24
Nayler, Edward, 253, 254, 255
,, Henry, 264
Neathway, Elizabeth, 280
,, George, 280
,, Thomas, 280
Need, Matthew, 236
Neel, or Nele, Agnes, 51
,, Alice, 100
,, John, 75
,, William, 69, 100
Nelmes, Thomas, 217, 247, 265
Nemot, Margaret, 80
,, Robert, 80, 131
Nete, Lucy, 177
Netherhaven, Henry, 19, 28, 45, 48, 49, 50, 52, 53, 56, 61
Newbury, Isabel, 141
Newcombe, Alice, 68, 101
,, Walter, 44, 68, 101, 119
Newe, Agnes, 166
,, Edmund, 147, 166
,, Henry, 166
,, Joan, 145
,, John, 166
,, Margaret, 166
,, Richard, 166
,, Robert, 166
,, William, 166
Newlond, John, 167
Newman, John, 200
,, Richard, 225
Newmaystre, Robert, 23, 39
Newnton, David, 21
Newton, David, 11
,, James, 238
,, John, 16, 18, 19, 66, 74, 90, 100, 101, 102, 116, 118, 123, 125, 135,

Newton, Richard, 120, 121
,, Thomas, 161
,, William, 214
Nicholas, Agnes, 276
,, William, 276
Nicholls, George, 256
,, Joan, 256
,, William, 211, 247, 249, 252, 256
Nightingale, Edward, 254
Noble, Elizabeth, 273
,, Jessie, 273
,, John, 273
,, Mary, 273
,, Thomas, 273
Nordon, or Northerne, Ellis, 256
Noreys, Richard, 118
Norman, Geoffrey, 140
,, Thomas, 151
Normore, William, 99
Norrice, Edward, 233
North, Richard, 81
Northall, Elizabeth, 211, 212
,, Ellen, 212
,, Joan, 212
,, John, 211, 212, 269
,, Rowland, 211, 212
,, Thomas, 211, 212
Northbroke, John, 214, 215, 218, 223
Northton, Thomas, 51
Norton, Anthony, 187
,, Isabel, 160, 161
,, Joan, 160, 161
,, John, 18, 30
,, Robert, 82
,, Thomas, 18, 19, 27, 28, 59, 87, 90, 92, 93, 115, 140, 146, 160, 161
,, Walter, 140
,, William, 25, 30, 35, 36, 52, 54, 55, 82, 203
Nouerton, John, 129
Nuport, William, 143
Nuton, see *Newton*.
Nywbury, William, 14

Obeleye, Agnes, 26
,, Bernard, 26, 55
Offley, Master, 195
,, Roger, 252
Okeley, Richard, 37
Okerforde, John, 14
Oldbeary, *alias* Lamberd, William, 215
Olde, James, 191
,, Joan, 190, 191
Oldefeilde, or Oldfild, Agnes, 252
,, Alice, 252
,, Cecily, 252
,, Dame, 245
,, David, 252
,, Edmund, 252
,, John, 252
,, Mary, 252
,, Thomas, 252
,, William, 252
Olfylde, David, 197, 198, 201
,, Edmund, 201
Oliver, or Olyver, Agnes, 104
,, Elizabeth, 244
,, John, 28, 35, 104, 244
,, Margaret, 244
,, Roger, 254
,, Simon, 20, 23, 24, 28, 29, 34, 52, 85, 104, 122, 152
,, Thomas, 244
,, William, 209
Ombersey, John, 27
Onley, Ralph, 181

402 INDEX.

Ooex (?), John, 162
Orchard, Robert, 78
Oseborne, Elen, 32
" Robert, 260
" William, 270, 271
Oseney, Thomas, 145, 149, 150, 153, 156, 161
Osteler, David, 159
" John, 113
Ostriche, William, 184
Ouldfielde, Davy, 219
Outtley, John, 192
Overton, Richard, 192
Owen, John, 8
" Richard, 208, 209
Owfford, Alice, 238
" James, 238
Oysell, *alias* Spert, Simon, 52

Paans, Alice, 79, 80
" Richard, 79
" William, 79, 80
Pacy, Christopher, 245
" Master, 190
Padirstowe, Geoffrey, 19
Paine, *alias* Fletcher, Alice, 213, 214
" John, 213
" Toby, 213, 214
" William, 213
Page, Richard, 236
Pakker, John, 20
Palmer, Agnes, 67, 233
" Alice, 233
" Edith, 67
" Edward, 67
" Elizabeth, 233, 234
" John, 8, 32, 50, 67, 84, 145, 199, 200, 233, 234
" Margaret, 145, 146
" Nicholas, 145
" Robert, 67
" Thomas, 145, 233, 234
" William, 35, 145
Paltysmore, William, 93
Panys, Alice, 31, 32
" John, 32, 63
" Richard, 31, 32, 43, 49, 59
" Robert, 281
" William, 32
Pappeworthe, Joan, 111, 112
" John, 111, 112
" Julian, 111, 112, 113
" Thomas, 111, 113
Parice, or Parys, John, 81, 117
" ———, 107
Parker, *alias* Locker, William, 209
Parkhous, John, 137
" Thomas, 135, 136, 137
Parle, Andrew, 97, 120
Parlebien, Thomas, 10
Parmynter, ———, 235
Parmyter, John, 85
Parnand, John, 167
Partridge, Michael, 274
" ———, 226
Pascowe, William, 97
Passeh, Thomas, 131
Passemer, Thomas, 24
Passhley, Simon, 164, 165
Passwer, Thomas, 121
Patte, Thomas, 169
Paty, Thomas, 168
Pavy, Alice, 123
" Elen, 132
" Elizabeth, 132
" Hugh, 132
" Joan, 116, 132

Pavy, John, 75, 80, 132
" Margaret, 132
" Richard, 132
" Robert, 132
" Thomas, 121, 122, 123
" William, 116, 132
Pay, John, 32
Payne, Alice, 143
" Emmot, 128
" Joan, 183
" John, 174
" Thomas, 143
" William, 134, 143
" ———, 60
Pays, Agnes, 106, 107
" Alice, 48, 107
" John, 106, 107
" Thomas, 106, 107
" William, 48, 77, 106
Pearde, or Perde, George, 277
" Hugh, 276, 277
" John, 277
Peautrer, Agnes, 87
" Isabel, 11, 12
" Richard, 11, 20, 59, 69, 90, 115
Pecche, Hugh, 6
Pedewell, Emmot, 58
" John, 12, 20, 58
" Julian, 12
" Margaret, 14
" Peter, 84
" Richard, 56, 101
" Robert, 93
" Thomas, 14
" Walter, 12
" William, 58
Pedmore, Thomas, 43
Peggo, Agnes, 104
Pembroke, Isabel, 81
" John, 81
Penard, John, 66
Penke, or Pynke, Alice, 171
" Annes, 171
" Joan, 171
" John, 76, 138, 153, 171
" Thomas, 171
Penlowe, Thomas, 163
Penrice, John, 68
Penseford, Richard, 74
" William, 68, 69, 74
Peny, Roger, 68
Pepwall, Agnes, 271
" Anne, 222
" Edward, 271
" Elizabeth, 242, 243, 270, 271
" John, 243, 270, 271
" Mary, 268, 270
" Matthias, 271
" Michael, 223, 228, 242, 243, 250, 267, 271
" Mistress, 250, 268
" Richard, 243
" Samuel, 271
" Sarah, 266, 270
" Timothy, 243, 270
" Toby, 271
" William, 181, 242, 266, 270
Percie, Eliz., 186
Perell, Katharine, 22
Percnt, John, 10
Peris, or Perys, John, 104
" Thomas, 104
Perkin, Griffeth, 235
Perle, Emmot, 13
Perlour, William, 50
Pernaunte, Thomas, 169, 172, 173

INDEX.   403

Perrey, Mistress, 255
,,   Robert, 255
Perrin, goodwife, 267
Perrington, Thomas, 274
Persevale, Ralph, 65
Person, Isabel, 97
,,   John, 32
,,   Thomas, 17, 48
Pert, Simon, 25
Peseley, Thomas, 95
Peu'ell, Thomas, 17
Peyntour, Alia, 102
,,   John, 63
,,   William, 159
Peytevyn, Reginald, 87
Peto, William, 16
Phelpys, Joan, 69
Philip, *alias* Cogan, David, 178
Philippes, Agnes, 159
,,   Anthony, 199, 210, 241
,,   Davy, 213
,,   Joan, 213
,,   Lewes, 213, 253
,,   Walter, 203
,,   William, 159, 254
Phill, Margaret, 172
Phylon, Philip, 254
Pickerell, Elizabeth, 254
Piers, Alice, 43
,,   John, 104, 108, 172
,,   Thomas, 37
Pikes, Walter, 229
Pilkington, Joan, 206
,,   Ralph, 206, 277
Pill, or Pyll, Anthony, 230, 231, 264
,,   Elianor, 264, 276
,,   Humphrey, 231
,,   Jane, 231
,,   John, 264, 276, 277
,,   Nicholas, 230, 277
,,   Richard, 231
,,   William, 204, 230, 231, 264
Pille, de la, Thomas, 130
Pincley, Joan, 244
Pip, Lady, 250
Pitcher, Alice, 278
,,   Anne, 278
,,   Prudence, 278
,,   Thomas, 233, 236, 278, 279
Pitte, or Pyt, Anne, 233
,,   Bartholomew, 117
,,   Christopher, 233
,,   Edward, 233
,,   John, 233
,,   Master, 232
,,   Maud, 252
,,   Thomas, 220, 236, 251, 252, 278, 279
,,   William, 119, 120, 121, 233, 251
Pittes, or Pyttes, Agnes, 273
,,   Elizabeth, 247, 273
,,   Joan, 246, 247
,,   John, 273
,,   Margaret, 247
,,   Nicholas, 133, 134, 136, 143, 145, 146, 148, 151, 166
,,   Richard, 246, 247, 273
,,   Robert, 273
,,   Thomas, 156, 157, 246, 273
,,   William, 246, 247, 273
Plastrer, Stephen, 22
Plomer, or Plommer, Agnes, 56
,,   Edith, 59, 64, 65
,,   Hugh, 20, 59, 64, 119
,,   John, 53, 59, 64

Plomer, or Plommer, Laurence, 59
,,   Richard, 59
,,   Roger, 137
,,   William, 59, 119
Pochen, John, 73, 77
Pochyn, *alias* Bath, John, 74, 131
Poculchurch, or Pokelchurch, Amy, 27
,,   ,,   John, 27, 28, 126
Poleyne, Isabel, 15
,,   Joan, 145
,,   John, 62, 63
Pollard, John, 167
Pollesworth, Stephen, 6
Pollington, Elizabeth, 260, 261
,,   Margery, 261
,,   Richard, 260, 261
,,   Susan, 261
,,   Thomas, 260, 261
,,   William, 260, 261
Polton, Thomas, 31, 35, 36, 37, 38, 51
Ponter, John, 126
Poole, Thomas, 231, 236, 237
Pope, Leonard, 212, 218
Popley, Edmond, 237, 260
,,   *alias* Deane, John, 237
,,   ,,   Margery, 237, 238
Poppham, Robert, 178
Poppheyne, Jane, 178
Popylton, William, 79
Portbury, Agnes, 54
,,   Henry, 54
,,   Joan, 54
,,   Julian, 52
,,   Nicholas, 52
,,   Richard, 11
Porter, Edward, 211, 220, 240
,,   Elizabeth, 220
,,   Joan, 220
,,   John, 69, 220
,,   Margaret, 220
,,   Rose, 220
,,   Simon, 220
,,   Richard, 61
,,   William, 220
Portingale, or Portyngale, Richard, 16, 23, 25
Portlond, Walter, 54
Possebury, John, 64
Possh, Joan, 71
Potekary, Alexander, 120
Poul, John, 42
Poulet, William, 43
Pounde, Agnes, 62
,,   Alexandra, 61
,,   Alice, 61
,,   Margaret, 61
,,   William, 61
Pounsot, Amy, 94
,,   Edward, 94
Pountfreyt, Adam, 11
,,   Eve, 11
,,   William, 11
Powell, Jane, 211
,,   Mary, 241
,,   Thomas, 202
Power, Alice, 69
,,   Isabel, 156
,,   John, 87
,,   Walter, 69, 125, 128
Powke, Agnes, 72
,,   Thomas, 72
Powlett, Isabel, 152
Powlysham, John, 100
Pownam, William, 99, 102
Pownoll, Nathaniel, 269
Poyner, goodwife, 197

Poynez, Elizabeth, 55, 56
", William, 55
Prat, Robert, 71
Preeye, Joan, 188
Predy, Isabel, 72
", William, 72
Pressey, or Prisye, Joan, 248
", ", Robert, 201, 223, 248
Prestbury, Thomas, 35
Preston, Laurence, 150
", Robert, 231
", Rose, 231
P'stwod, Agnes, 126
Prewett, Anthony, 227, 278, 279
", Arthur, 227
", Ellyn, 227
", Joan, 278
", John, 227, 230, 278
", William, 227, 228, 236, 277
Price, or Pryce, Anne, 276
", ", George, 276
", ", Thomas, 224
Pridie, de, Richard, 142
", Thomas, 142
", William, 142
Priest, Agnes, 213
", Edith, 213
", Robert, 212
Primlok, John, 10
Prin, or Prynne, Edward, 186
", Richard, 182
", Thomas, 226, 228, 235, 238, 247, 255, 257, 268, 269, 273, 277
Prince, or Prynce, John, 134
", ", Margaret, 85
", ", Robert, 265
Printer, Thomas, 260
Priour, Cristina, 16, 18, 19
", Richard, 95
Prisshton, or Pryschton, John, 36, 40, 42, 60, 115
Proctor, Richard, 206
Proude, Thomas, 150
Prowte, John, 108, 117
", Margery, 117
", Robert, 114
", Thomas, 147
", William, 117, 147
Pruett, John, 190
Pryddy, William, 274
Pryor, John, 268
Pullen, goodwife, 259
Purches, Roger, 161
Pute, William, 121
Puton, Philip, 150
", Walter, 150
Puxstone, Thomas, 258
Pycheford, John, 106
Pyckering, William, 180
Pygas, John, 12
Pyke, Margaret, 135
", Thomas, 19
Pykenham, Adam, 34
Pykes, Alderman, 252
", John, 187, 188, 273
", Maud, 187
", Walter, 188, 220, 251, 263
", William, 187
Pynchyn, Thomas, 195
Pynder, William, 241
Pytte, alias Cornyssh, Robert, 142

Quyrke, John, 164

Radifford, Richard, 157
Ralegh, Thomas, 8

Randolf, John, 62
Rastall, John, 189
Rastforth, Richard, 163
Rawe, Nicholas, 30
Rawlyn, or Raulyn, John, 13, 20, 21, 24
Reade, Alice, 212
", Laurence, 274
", William, 212, 270, 271
Rece, Nicholas, 259
Reckeliffe, Robert, 229, 230
Rede, Alice, 39
", Edward, 110, 126
", Joan, 127
", John, 39, 40, 86, 128
", Nicholas, 134
", William, 39, 139, 243
Redeberd, Thomas, 5
Rederisse, Joan, 116
Rees, Elynor, 214
Regent, William, 166, 171
Reignolde, Richard, 181
Reinghoodt, Francis, 162
Reve, Richard, 43
", Stephen, 37, 62
Reynald, John, 52, 53
Reynesbury, Thomas, 81
Reynold, Janyn, 128
", Joan, 16
", John, 148
", Margaret, 128
Ricarde, or Ricardes, Robert, 157
", ", William, 197
Ricartes, William, 229
Rice, or Ryce, Nicholas, 221
", Richard, 233, 278
", Roger, 213, 221, 224
", William, 190
Richard, or Richardes, John, 24, 86, 88, 92, 110, 125
", ", Julian, 88, 92
Richartes, David, 232
Riche, Julian, 35
Richman, John, 259
Ridges, Elizabeth, 213
", Mary, 213
", William, 213
Rigelyn, Philip, 62
Riggewey, Robert, 94
Rijs, (Rys?), William, 86
Ripe, Roger, 62
Riper, Adam, 24
", John, 24
", Maud, 24
", Robert, 24
Rirran, Henry, 21
Risbie, or Risby, Elizabeth, 212
", ", Robert, 234
Rise, Richard, 236
", William, 245
", ———, 263
Ritche, John, 210
Robartes, Alsey, 216
", Edmund, 215, 216
", Margaret, 216
", Mary, 216
", Thomas, 216
", William, 216
Rob'd, Joan, 113
", Michael, 113
Roberts, David, 206
", Henry, 226
", John, 169, 193, 195, 216, 224, 226, 246, 248, 259, 267
", Julian, 240, 241
", Master, 199
", Sander, 267
", ———, 204

Robins, or Robyns, Alice, 107
,, Anne, 228, 232
,, Anthony, 228
,, goodwife, 273
,, Grace, 228
,, Joan, 107
,, John, 107, 152
,, Margaret, 279
,, Nicholas, 210, 225, 232
,, Richard, 107
Robinson, John, 232
Robrok, William, 74
Robyn, John, 138
Roche, Mary, 243
Rockwell, Edith, 262
,, Gilbert, 210, 211, 232
,, John, 210, 211, 225, 232
,, Katharine, 210, 211, 232
,, Thomas, 232, 262
,, Walter, 262
,, William, 210, 232
Roddeney, John, 94
Rodeman, ———, 243
Rodney, John, knt., 177
,, Master, 187
,, Maurice, 258
,, Walter, knt., 128, 139
Roe, Edward, 260
,, Elizabeth, 260
,, Joan, 260
Roger, and Rogers, Agnes, 140, 258
,, Alice, 200
,, Charity, 200
,, Edmond, 188, 200
,, Elizabeth, 200
,, Elyn, 200
,, Jane, 200
,, Joan, 257
,, Margery, 256
,, Maud, 148
,, Nicholas, 258
,, Owen, 256
,, Rachel, 257, 258
,, Ralph, 200
,, Richard, 257, 258
,, Robert, 234, 258
,, Simon, 112
,, Thomas, 140, 148, 200
,, William, 54, 140, 145, 146, 148, 177
Roke, or Rook, Walter, 41, 43, 45
,, William, 125
Rokell, John, 81, 82, 85
Rokes, Elizabeth, 144
,, Joan, 144
,, John, 144
,, Thomas, 144
,, William, 144
Romesay, John, 54
Roo, Robert, 142
Roper, Agnes, 120
,, Cristina, 50
,, Henry, 46, 50
,, Joan, 50
,, John, 20, 31, 32, 50, 80
,, Julian, 31, 32
,, Peter, 50
,, Richard, 50
,, Thomas, 50
,, William, 31, 32
Rose, Richard, 244
Roselie, George, 212
Rothell, John, 217, 265
Rowberwe, John, 44
,, Margaret, 44
Rowe, Joan, 73
,, Robert, 73

Rowland, Alice, 248
,, Elizabeth, 219, 242, 248
,, Gelyan, 242
,, John, 178, 179, 202, 219
,, Joyce, 242
,, Julian, 248
,, Richard, 219
,, Sarah, 248
,, Thomas, 209, 219, 242
,, *alias* Cowper, John, 206
Rowley, Elizabeth, 161
,, Joan, 162
,, John, 282
,, Margaret, 162
,, Richard, 162
,, Thomas, 132, 157, 161, 162
,, William, 141, 161, 162
Rowlowe, Joan, 175
,, Robert, 169, 175, 176
Rowsley, Alice, 213
,, Anthony, 212
,, George, 212
Ruddock, David, 104, 116
,, Isabel, 116, 117
,, Joan, 238
,, John, 35, 116, 117
,, Thomas, 116
,, William, 116
Rudge, Richard, 264
Ruspyn, John, 8
Russell, Agnes, 51
,, Edmund, 51
,, Lady Elizabeth, 157
,, Emma, 58
,, Joan, 97
,, John, 51, 56, 174
,, Peter, 97
,, Robert, 32, 76, 95, 98, 99, 100, 111, 120, 121, 123, 156, 167
,, Roger, 39, 58
,, Thomas, 97
Ryder, or Rider, John, 135
,, Margaret, 228
,, Richard, 125
,, Thomas, 206, 228
Rye, John, 59
Ryngston, Agnes, 175
,, Joan, 175
,, John, 117, 175
,, Philip, 157, 171, 175
,, Thomas, 176
,, William, 176
Ryppe, John, 167
Ryner, Nicholas, 15

Sachefield, John, 201, 206
,, Master, 233
,, Robert, 109
Sadler, John, 165
,, Ralph, 194
,, Richard, 30
,, Robert, 86, 221
Salisburye, or Salesbury, Henry, 245
,, William, 27
Salop, Countess of, 136
Salterne, Thomas, 277
Saltren, Edmond, 234
,, Joan, 235
,, John, 234
,, Mary, 234
,, Richard, 234, 235
,, Thomas, 235
,, William, 234, 235
Samborne, Jane, 260
Sampson, Henry, 154, 155
,, Joan, 16, 17
,, Thomas, 17, 44
,, William, 16, 17, 44

Sandiforde, John, 242
Sandy, John, 167
Sanford, Robert, 210, 270
Sare, John, 186
„ William, 167, 171
Sariaunte, John, 185
Saull, and Sawll, Anne, 240, 241
„ Thomas, 253, 262
Saundres, or Saunders, Agnes, 186
„ Alice, 30
„ Anne, 238
„ Joan, 22
„ John, 40, 117
„ Robert, 30, 51
„ Thomas, 247
„ William, 30, 51
Sausemer, John, 126
Savage, John, 38, 261
„ Thomas, 261
Saverey, John, 38
Sawee, Margaret, 171
Sawyer, John, 129, 131
„ Thomas, 139
„ Walter, 84
Saxey, Master, 199
„ Robert, 206, 214, 224
„ William, 224, 275
Sayer, John, 228
„ William, 234, 262, 274
Scalter, Ralph, 227
„ William, 228
Scapulis, Elizabeth, 264
„ Margaret, 264
„ Mary, 264
„ Philip, 263, 264, 272
Schaftspere, or Shakespeire, Thomas, 172
Scherhay, Alice, 76
„ Robert, 76
Scherman, Thomas, 40
Scosy, Edmund, 83
Scot, John, 32
„ William, 86, 87, 225
Screven, or Scriven, Alice, 45
„ Hugh, 45
„ John, 137, 148, 158, 160, 162
„ Richard, 49
„ Thomas, 20
Scurlag, Henry, 169
Scyrry, Anne, 197
„ ———, 197
Sebright, Edward, 268
„ John, 182, 268
See, Anne, 223
„ Arthur, 216, 223
„ Margaret, 216
„ Mary, 223
„ Peter, 216
Seggel, William, 121
Selar, Katharine, 147
„ Richard, 147
Selcok, Joan, 80
„ William, 57, 80, 89
Selke, John, 61
Selman, Elizabeth, 235
„ John, 235
Selsy, John, 9
„ Lucy, 10
„ Margaret, 10
„ Thomas, 9
Selwode, John, 28, 66
Sely, Isabel, 92
„ John, 27, 57, 86, 91, 126
Seman, William, 221
Sendel, Robert, 92
Serche, Jane, 206
„ John, 206

Sergeant, and Sargente, David, 157
„ James, 231, 236, 237
„ John, 128
„ Tibot, 128
Seriaunt, William, 84
Sevyer, Robert, 125
„ William, 125
Seward, Roger, 9
Sextene, John, 245
Seydon, Beatrix, 59
„ Henry, 59
Seymour, Isabel, 144, 152
„ John, 25, 26, 84, 85, 124, 135, 144, 152
„ Lady, 144, 146
„ Margaret, 58, 84, 85, 124
„ Walter, 26, 51, 58, 72, 77, 84, 124
Seynt, Alice, 147
„ Joan, 147
„ John, 128, 147
„ Richard, 162
Seynt Mariechurche, Isabel, 69
Seys, David, 20
„ Joan, 42
„ John, 42
Seysdon, Margaret, 67
Seysell, Thomas, 103, 113
Shareshull, John, 110
Sharp, or Sherp, Elizabeth, 152
„ Joan, 95, 120
„ John, 18, 40, 63, 83, 89, 95, 104, 116, 120, 122, 132, 135, 139, 146, 170
Shee, Peter, 253
Sheldon, Daniel, 150
Shephurd, John, 45
„ William, 43
Shepisby, Elen, 83
Sherborne, John, 34, 36
Sherman, John, 93
Sherrer, Philip, 17
Sherston, William, 260
Shewarde, Thomas, 186
Shingleton, ———, 253
Shiplode, Thomas, 142
Shipman, Bridget, 241
„ Edward, 241
„ John, 171, 180, 241
„ Margaret, 241
„ Roger, 241
„ Thomas, 186, 211
„ William, 181, 241
Shippester, Cristina, 19
Shipward, or Shepward, Guynot, 159
„ Joan, 87
„ John, 122, 129, 131, 137, 142, 143, 144, 158, 159, 160, 161, 167
„ Katharine, 158, 161
„ Robert, 79, 84, 86, 87
„ alias Barstaple, John, 142
„ Robert, 142, 156
„ Thomas, 142
„ William, 141
Shirwyn, or Sherewyn, Isabel, 108, 111
„ John, 108, 111
„ Matthew, 108, 111, 133
„ Richard, 94, 111, 114
„ Thomas, 108, 111

Shiryngton, John, 81, 120
Shoile, Richard, 229
Shop, Joan, 120
" John, 95, 134
Shore, Richard, 234
Shutleworth, Bridget, 235
" Edward, 235
" Elizabeth, 235
" John, 235
" Mary, 235
" William, 235
Silvester, Ydde, 216
Skansby, Richard, 173
Skeffyngton, John, 119
Sknowe, Margaret, 204
Skragge, William, 107
Skydmore, Isabel, 171
" Thomas, 150
Skynner, Joan, 203
" Sara, 43
" Thomas, 145
Slanye, George, 259
" Henry, 259
" John, 259
" Katharine, 259
" William, 258, 259
Slape, John, 36
Slaughter, Ansell, 236
Slocombe, Elizabeth, 236, 248
" Gilbert, 248
" Henry, 248
" John, 248
" Thomas, 226, 235, 248
Sloo, John, 13, 19, 28, 41, 69
" Margaret, 69
" Richard, 13, 69
Slye, Henry, 234
Slyke, Nicholas, 157
Slymbrygg, Robert, 154, 155
Smert, John, 81
Smith, or Smythe, Agnes, 201
" Besse, 271
" Edmond, 195, 201
" Elizabeth, 238, 268
" Frances, 238
" John, 148, 188, 238, 243
" Katharine, 192, 200, 201
" Letice, 201
" Mary, 201, 251
" Peter, 200, 201
" Philip, 63, 121, 244
" Ralph, 195, 201
" Richard, 131, 245, 278, 279
" Robert, 195, 198, 200
" Roger, 90
" Samuel, 201
" Thomas, 69, 71, 73, 101, 158, 172, 201
" William, 60, 169, 235, 236, 237
" ———, 200
Smitheman, William, 193
Smothie, William, 197
Smythes, or Smithes, Elizabeth, 196
" Goodlove, 196
" Margery, 48,
" Mary, 241
" Robert, 204, 240
Snigge, or Snygg, Agnes, 175
" George, 193, 268
" John, 175
" Thomas, 169, 171, 172, 173
Snowe, John, 238
" Martha, 238
" Richard, 172

Sodbury, John, 76, 78
" William, 163
Sokett, John, 165
Solas, Alice, 93
" William, 93
Solers, Agnes, 25
" William, 25
Sollers, Agnes, 65
" Elen, 65
" Margaret, 65
" Thomas, 65
" William, 65
Somervyle, or Somerville, Agnes, 82
" Elizabeth, 81, 82
" John, 28, 81
Somerwell, Alice, 59
" Cassandra, 34
" John, 14, 34, 59, 110
" Mark, 127
" William, 10, 24, 34, 59
Sopemaker, Adam, 79
Southfolke, John, 78
Southwode, Julian, 28, 65
Sowey, Edith, 11
Spaldyng, Isabel, 117
" John, 117
" Margaret, 90
" Richard, 89
Sparewe, Joan, 22
Spaynell, John, 16
" Mark, 30, 103
" Richard, 30
" Soneta, 30
" William, 30
Specheley, Henry, 28
" Roger, 28
Spelly, Agnes, 27, 126
" Elen, 27
" Elias, 26, 28, 57, 124, 126
" Henry, 27
" Joan, 126
" Richard, 126
" Robert, 126
" William, 28
Spenser, or Spencer, John, 177, 178, 252
" Richard, 160
" Thomas, 135
" William, 139, 144, 149, 153, 162
Sperekes, Alice, 269
" Edith, 269
Spert, Margery, 52
" Roger, 27
" Simon, 19, 52
" Thomas, 16, 52, 53
Spicer, Agnes, 134
" Henry, 41
" John, 23, 41, 49, 134, 115
" Margaret, 169
" Richard, 11, 34, 154
" Stephen, 6, 41
" Thomas, 90
" William, 86
Spisour, and Spyser, Alice, 69
" Avice, 69
" Cecily, 89
" John, 69, 89
" Richard, 89, 123
" Robert, 69
" Roger, 69
" Thomas, 69
Sprate, William, 198
Spratt, William, 200, 201
Spray, John, 33
Sprinte, or Sprynte, John, 185, 191, 194, 229
" William, 243

Spryngot, John, 48
Spurlock, Stephen, 210
Spynaw, de, Arnald, 78
Spyne, John, 24, 59, 80, 87, 108, 113, 119
Squihere, Alice, 87
Squyer, Matthew, 87, 92
Stafford, Isabel, 134
　,,　Lord, 207
Stagge, Elen, 139
Stalworth, John, 166
Stamforde, Richard, 146
Standbank, or Standback, Anthony, 215, 230, 256, 257
　,,　Joan, 257
　,,　Katharine, 256, 257
　,　Master, 229
　,　Mistress, 215
　,　Richard, 194
Standfast, Master, 254
　,,　Walter, 207
Stanes, Joan, 14
　,,　John, 14
　,,　Margaret, 14
Stanley, Henry, 108
　,,　John, 129, 133
Stanshawe, John, 33
　,,　Lady Elizabeth, 161
Stanys, John, 9
Staple, John, 274
Stappe, William, 135
Stapulton, ——, 43
Starling, William, 237
Staunford, John, 28, 93
Stede, William, 26
Steph', John, 42
Stephanys, John, 93
Stephen, Alice, 121
　,,　John, 121
Stephens, Alice, 129
　,,　Joan, 110, 127
　,,　John, 17, 28, 60, 81, 86, 117, 129, 166
　,,　Lucy, 83, 122
　,,　Richard, 110
　,,　Thomas, 110
　,,　William, 79, 80
Stephenus, John, 91, 97
　,,　Margaret, 91, 97
Stephenys, John, 16, 25, 26, 37, 42, 67
　,,　Richard, 27
Stephyn, John, 73
Sternolde, Agnes, 252
　,,　Margaret, 252
　,,　Robert, 252
　,,　William, 252
Stevans, William, 198
Stevens, and Stephenes, John, 130, 133, 137, 168, 169, 209
　,,　Maud, 21
　,,　Thomas, 276
　,,　William, 88
Steyl, Alice, 50
　,,　John, 50
　,,　Sarah, 50
　,,　Thomas, 50
　,,　William, 50
Steynour, Robert, 131
Stibbes, William, 238
Stiel, John, 67
　,,　Maud, 67
　,,　William, 9, 44
Stincheome, John, 251
Stocke, Nicholas, 135
Stodeley, Elen, 25, 26
　,,　Joan, 26

Stodeley, John, 25
　,,　Richard, 26
　,,　Walter, 25
Stoke, Agnes, 6
　,,　Alice, 6
　,,　Isold, 6
　,,　Joan, 5, 6, 41
　,,　John, 5, 41, 119, 122
　,,　Margaret, 43
　,,　Robert, 6
　,,　Roger, 6
　,,　William, 31
Stokes, or Stokys, John, 48, 161
Stokmer, Henry, 27
Stone, Anthony, 215
　,,　Edith, 95
　,,　Elizabeth, 215
　,,　Henry, 215
　,,　Joan, 215, 261
　,,　John, 37, 95, 190, 215, 261
　,,　Richard, 252
　,,　Thomas, 261
　,,　Walter, 261
　,,　William, 215, 261
Stones, Richard, 229
Storthwait, John, 93, 98, 101, 102, 105, 106, 107
Stourton, William, 73
Stoventon (?), Hugh, 77
Stowell, Dame Joan, 96
　,,　Thomas, knt., 97
Stradling, Francis, 183
Strafford, John, 144
Stratton, John, 88
Straunge, Robert, 143, 153
Strech, Thomas, 94
Strengesham, de, Thomas, 140
Strete, Joan, 23, 123
　,,　John, 123, 133
　,,　Katharine, 128
　,,　Roger, 128, 129
　,,　Thomas, 123
Streynesham, John, 128, 129, 139, 140
Strode, John, 52, 53
Sturmy, Elen, 137, 138
　,,　John, 138
　,,　Robert, 138
Suche, or Souche, Anne, 197
　,,　Charity, 198
　,,　Dorcas, 198
　,,　Elizabeth, 198
　,,　George, 197, 198
　,,　John, 197
　,,　Mary, 198
　,,　Robert, 198
　,,　Silvester, 197
　,,　Thomas, 268
　,,　William, 197, 198
Suelle, John, 101
Sutton, goodwife, 229
　,,　Joan, 58, 95, 96
　,,　John, 29, 40, 60, 72, 84, 95, 98, 102
　,,　Mabilla, 96
　,,　Richard, 37
　,,　Thomas, 20, 29, 40, 55, 58, 94, 161
　,,　William, 155, 244
Swalledale, John, 118
Swalwe, John, 50
Swancote, John, 132, 156
Swayn, John, 150
Swell, Alice, 24, 25
　,,　John, 14, 24
　,,　Margaret, 24, 25
Swetnam, Frances, 234
　,,　Richard, 199, 200, 234
　,,　William, 234, 250
Swyfte, John, 232

Swyfte, Thomas, 60
Sydbury, William, 35
Sydenham, Henry, 36
,, Joan, 35, 36
,, Richard, 36
,, Simon, 35, 36
Sylke, Thomas, 191
Sylly, Roger, 95
Syllyvaunt, Joan, 228
Sylney, Agnes, 97
Symondes, or Symons, Anthony, 264
,, Edith, 257
,, John, 135
,, Philip, 264
,, Thomas, 199, 200, 218, 221
,, ———, 195
Syneff, ———, 207

Taber, John, 6
Tadelton, Thomas, 136
Tagg, Thomas, 222
Taillour, or Tailor, Adam, 22, 39
,, Agnes, 120
,, David, 190
,, Elen, 39
,, Joan, 55, 210
,, John, 35, 119
,, Nicholas, 38, 93, 118
,, Reginald, 54
,, Richard, 210
,, Robert, 191
,, Roger, 19, 162
,, Thomas, 113, 121, 135, 145
,, William, 73
Talbot, John, 98, 104
,, William, 133
Tamworth, William, 81
Tankard, Thomas, 5
Tanner, Edward, 70
,, Isabel, 63, 174
,, Joan, 70, 102, 226
,, John, 30, 36, 77
,, Stephen, 226
,, Thomas, 63
,, William, 32, 135
Tannye, John, 263
Taunton, Alice, 7
,, Joan, 7
,, Roger, 7
,, Walter, 108
Taverner, John, 139, 152
,, Perot, 34
,, Walter, 26
,, William, 135
Tawnye, John, 196
Taylor, or Tayler, Anne, 279
,, Jane, 279
,, John, 271
,, Katharine, 221, 279
,, Lewes, 264
,, Philip, 264
,, Robert, 279
,, Thomas, 240, 260
Tedistille, Agnes, 13
,, Joan, 13
,, Margaret, 13
,, Walter, 13, 60
Teffent, John, 91
,, Margaret, 91
Teige, Thomas, 245
Teinte (?), Edward, 243
Temple, Robert, 230
,, William, 38, 95
Templecombe, de, Master, 46

Tewe, John, 238, 244
,, Master, 238
Thackham, Thomas, 259
Thewe, John, 199, 200, 234
Thirkell, Michael, 252
Thlau (?), Joan, 81
Thluyt, John, 7
Thomas, David, 127
,, Edith, 137
,, Germanus, 129
,, Hugh, 220, 221
,, Isabel, 100
,, James, 221
,, Joan, 214
,, John, 43, 70, 107, 108, 244
,, Robert, 137
,, Thomas, 237, 253
,, Welthian, 232
,, William, 194, 218
Thomlinson, Thomas, 274
Thomme, John, 18
Thommys, John, 19
Thorne, Bridget, 185
,, Edward, 185
,, Frances, 185
,, James, 180
,, Joan, 282
,, John, 185, 186
,, Mary, 184, 185
,, Nicholas, 163, 180, 181, 182, 184, 185, 186
,, Robert, 175, 176, 180, 182, 184, 185, 186, 282
,, Thomas, 180
,, Vincent, 180, 184
,, William, 180, 181
Thornebury, Elen, 81
Thorp, John, 5, 48, 74, 136
,, Thomas, 86
Thurston, John, 265
,, Margaret, 213
Thyngwall, Richard, 134, 136
Tibbys, alias Bailly, John, 21
Tiler, see Tyler.
Tillett, Michael, 251
Tilly, Alice, 8
,, Elianor, 8
,, Joan, 8
,, John, 8, 95
,, Margaret, 8
,, Richard, 115, 116
,, Robert, 7
Tiperton, Nicholas, 31
Tipet, John, 43
Tipper, Thomas, 228
Toftrang, John, 25
Toker, William, 80
Tomkyns, Agnes, 183
Tomlyne, Elizabeth, 233
,, John, 233
,, Thomas, 233
Tommas, John, 57
Tommes, John, 79
Tonbrigge, William, 124
Toningham (?), Thomas, 245
Tonnell, Mistress, 185
Torner, or Tornour, John, 150
,, Philip, 114
Torre, John, 87
Torrynton, or Torynton, Isabel, 94
,, John, 39
Tostrong, Agnes, 45
,, John, 45
Tought, William, 62
Touker, or Tucker, Isabel, 245, 246
,, Peter, 46
,, Walter, 85

Tonker, or Tucker William, 245
Tovy, John, 65
„ Walter, 255
Treherne, Richard, 243
Treheron, Katharine, 168
Trenode, Joan, 132
„ Richard, 132
Trewell, John, 264
Trippett, Robert, 280
Tristy, Agnes, 94
„ John, 94
Trowbridge, Edmund, 259
„ Thomas, 259
Trowell, William, 152
Troyt, John, 129, 281
Tryne, Joan, 48
Turke, Walter, 38
Turnour, or Turner, John, 134, 196
„ Thomas, 99, 100
Turtle, Roger, 65
Turver, Eme, 259
„ James, 259
„ John, 259
„ Margery, 259
„ Mary, 259
„ Nicholas, 259
Twyneho, or Twynyho, Edward, 173
„ John, 118, 122, 123
Tyderley, Matthew, 85
Tydryngton, Edith, 135
„ John, 135
Tye, William, 99
Tyler, or Tylor, Alice, 122
„ Elias, 55
„ Joan, 228, 240
„ John, 75, 108, 118, 152, 172
„ Margaret, 227, 240, 264
„ Thomas, 264
„ William, 98, 193
Tymtenhull, Margery, 19
„ Nicholas, 19
Tyndall, Faith, 190, 191
„ Jane, 190, 191
„ Joan, 190
„ Margaret, 268, 269
„ Richard, 190, 191
„ Robert, 190, 191, 238
„ Thomas, 190, 191
„ William, 190
Tyrry, William, 123, 128
Tyson, Mistress, 193
„ Thomas, 180, 193, 236, 277
„ ——, 244
Tyther, Thomas, 252
Tytherton, Elizabeth, 255

Ulage, John, 34
Umfray, John, 95
Uphull, John, 90
„ Simon, 19, 30, 49, 50, 57, 94, 125

Vaghan, John, 109, 174
Vallet, Blissota, 142
Vand', Nicholas, 162
Vauce, or Vauve, William, 155, 162
Vaughan, Henry, 142, 160
„ John, 170, 171, 178
„ Richard, 162, 164, 166, 172, 193
„ Thomas, 170
Vawer, William, 224, 233, 278, 279
Veale, Edward, 232
Veel, John, 84
Venour, or Vener, Cristina, 48, 72
„ Richard, 72, 90

Vestmentmaker, Bartholomew, 117
Vethered, Christian, 249
„ Thomas, 249
Viel, see *Vyell*.
Virly, ——, 43
Voghan, William, 88
Vyell, Agnes, 119
„ Alice, 57
„ Elizabeth, 57, 81
„ Henry, 57, 119
„ John, 10, 20, 22, 57, 67, 84, 91, 119, 128
„ Thomas, 135
Vyne, Thomas, 9
Vynour, John, 91
„ Walter, 62
„ William, 109

Wade, John, 199, 223
Wadham, John, knt., 56
Wadley, Alice, 228
Wadnyng, John, 152
Waky, Thomas, 93
Walcott, Master, 235
Wale, John, 74
„ Margaret, 74
„ Walter, 74
Wales, Edward, Prince of, 136
„ Margery, 38
„ Nicholas, 38
Waleys, Agnes, 31
„ Alice, 31
„ Joan, 24, 31
„ Margery, 65
„ Nicholas, 65
„ Richard, 31
„ Walter, 31
„ William, 25, 31
Walker, Christopher, 240, 278
Wall, Anne, 258
„ John, 258
„ Margery, 258, 259
„ Thomas, 224, 258
Wallis, ——, 268
Wallop, William, 6
Wally, John, 260
„ Laurence, 260
„ William, 260
Wallyce, Richard, 58
Wallys, John, 236
Walmesley, Thomas, 170
Walsh, David, 32
„ John, 107
„ Katharine, 107
„ Ralph, 168
„ Richard, 236
„ Simon, 107
„ Thomas, 99
„ William, 166
Walter, John, 21
„ Susan, 269
Wanstre, Alice, 94
„ Roger, 94
„ William, 135
Warde, John, 231
Warden, Joan, 223
„ Nicholas, 223
„ Thomas, 186, 223
Wardford, Marks, 219
„ William, 219
Warens, John, 165
„ Richard, 150
Wareyn, see *Warren*.
Warfourde, John, 218
Waring, William, 134
Warley, Thomas, 152

INDEX. 311

Warman, William, 196
Warmyngton, Richard, 134
  ,, Robert, 134
Warmynstre, or Wermystre, Alice, 5, 45, 73, 74, 94, 99
  ,, Cristina, 18
  ,, John, 18, 55,94, 146
  ,, Laurence, 281
  ,, Maud, 281
  ,, Thomas, 45
  ,, William, 5, 16, 17, 45, 52, 74, 94, 114, 122, 123, 126
Warner, Robert, 164
Warren, or Wareyn, David, 257
  ,, John, 204
  ,, Matthew, 246
  ,, Nicholas, 5, 24, 40, 41, 117
  ,, Sible, 246
  ,, Thomas, 232, 268, 269
Warwyk, John, 16, 23, 40, 50, 57, 59
Was, Walter, 114
Wassh, John, 178
Water, William, 150, 156
Waterfall, Alice, 102
Waterman, Walter, 93
Watkins, Elizabeth, 251
  ,, George, 251
  ,, Hugh, 218
  ,, Morgan, 264
  ,, Thomas, 279
Watley, Joan, 196
  ,, Richard, 195
Wattis, Joan, 40
  ,, John, 40
Wawton, John, 130
Waxmaker, or Wexmaker, John, 89
  ,, Richard, 135, 136
Wayn, Richard, 92
Waynewrighte, Anne, 264
  ,, William, 264
Weaver, Richard, 224
Webbe, Cristina, 89
  ,, John, 219, 251, 265
  ,, Joyce, 19
  ,, Nicholas, 259
  ,, Peter, 66
  ,, Richard, 135
  ,, Roger, 260
  ,, Thomas, 119
  ,, William, 88
Weekes, or Wykes, Alice, 278
  ,, Charity, 278
  ,, Edward, 278
  ,, Thomas, 278
Weele, William, 137
Well', de, Felix, 26
  ,, John, 26
Wellew, John, 155
Wellischotte, Roger, 106
Wellyngton, or Whelyngton, John, 7
  ,, Thomas, 109, 114
Wellys, John, 40
Welshe, John, 235
  ,, Margery, 235
West, Alice, 198, 199
  ,, Arthur, 198
  ,, Elizabeth, 198, 199
  ,, John, 198, 253
  ,, Joyce, 198, 199
  ,, Walter, 198, 200
Westcote, Agnes, 160, 161

Westcote, Edmund, 132, 149, 159, 160, 161
  ,, Margaret, 132
Westerley, Margaret, 122, 123
  ,, Thomas, 121, 122, 123
  ,, William, 98
Westley, William, 39
Weston, Agnes, 178
  ,, Amy, 31
  ,, Henry, 167, 217, 278
  ,, John, 31, 89, 90, 91, 93, 95, 278
Wetham, John, 101
Wether, Robert, 55
Wever, John, 85
Wheitley, Elizabeth, 199
Whete, Thomas, 70
Whetenhall, William, 151
Whetocke, Thomas, 196
Whight, Katharine, 155
Whitawyer, or Whittower, David, 126
  ,, Elias, 7, 10
  ,, Milcensia, 7
White, or Whyte, Agnes, 217
  ,, Alice, 71
  ,, Anne, 201
  ,, Edith, 73, 202, 203
  ,, Elizabeth, 165, 203, 251
  ,, George, 202, 203
  ,, Giles, 186
  ,, Grace, 203
  ,, Joan, 217, 225, 234, 265
  ,, John, 64, 65, 95, 122, 148, 170, 196, 202, 203, 216, 218, 225
  ,, Joyce, 217
  ,, Katharine, 161
  ,, Margaret, 217
  ,, Maud, 203
  ,, Patrick, 278, 279
  ,, Richard, 38, 207
  ,, Roger, 31
  ,, Thomas, 6, 71, 180, 186, 203, 216, 225, 233, 265, 270, 276
  ,, Thomas, knt., 239
  ,, Warine, 76
  ,, William, 8, 19, 29, 35, 56, 73, 84, 165
Whitecastell, David, 168, 169
Whitman, Joan, 112
Whitton, John, 146
Whityng, or Whytinge, Beatrix, 5
  ,, James, 274
  ,, John, 56
  ,, Thomas, 274
Whych, Maurice, knt., 6
Whytson, John, 252
Wicham, Alice, 178
Wiche, William, 16
Wigan, Nicholas, 30
  ,, Thomas, 163
Wight, Katharine, 225
Wigmore, Mary, 188
  ,, Roger, 188
  ,, William, 188
Wilbram, John, 254
  ,, Randall, 218
Wilcockes, Thomas, 270
Wilkyns, John, 39, 176
Willett, John, 224
William, Edward, 135
  ,, Mark, 57, 74, 84, 108, 115, 117, 122, 123, 125
Williams, Alice, 16, 25, 33, 256
  ,, Anne, 256
  ,, Annis, 266
  ,, David, 256
  ,, Edward, 225

Williams, Elizabeth, 183, 264
„ Joan, 203, 225
„ John, 5, 176
„ Mary, 256
„ Nicholas, 225
„ Roger, 267
„ Rowland, 225
„ Thomas, 74, 183, 189, 203, 241
„ Walter, 256
„ William, 267
Willy, or Wyllie, John, 59, 179, 180, 191, 196
„ Richard, 53
Willymott, Richard, 202, 203
Willys, John, 168
Wilshyre, John, 195
Wilson, Cecily, 188
„ Myles, 188
„ William, 218
Wilteshire, Alice, 167
„ Clement, 159, 167
„ Daniel, 167
„ Henry, 167
„ Isabel, 167
„ Margery, 167
„ Richard, 167
„ Robert, 90
„ William, 24
Winchecombe, Richard, 33, 34, 37, 40, 73
Winson, or Wynson, Michael, 254, 256
Winterborne, William, 36
With, John, 155
Withyford, Hugh, 118, 121, 129
„ John, 157
„ Thomas, 149
Wode, Richard, 179
Wodeford, Alice, 83
„ William, 77, 84
Wodeley, Alice, 76
„ John, 46, 57, 76
„ Thomas, 76
„ Walter, 76
Wodelond, William, 12
Woderoue, Agnes, 5
„ Avice, 5
„ Cristina, 5, 8
„ John, 5, 6, 7, 8, 36
„ Richard, 31
Wodevile, John, 106
Wodeward, see Woodwarde.
Wodynton, Maud, 168
„ Thomas, 169
„ William, 126, 150, 156
Wolf, Edith, 144
„ John, 25
„ Thomas, 18
„ William, 82
Wolforde, Robert, 215
Wolleye, de, William, 7
Wonder, William, 122
Wonsy, Nicholas, 123
Wood, Alice, 202
„ Edmund, 202
„ Ellyn, 202
„ Joan, 202
„ John, 202, 225
„ William, 202
Woodcorke, Richard, 241
Woodson, Richard, 257
„ ———, 267
Woodwarde, or Wodeward, Anne, 265
„ Christopher, 214, 216
„ Elizabeth, 214
„ Isabel, 159
„ John, 140, 143, 265

Woodwarde, or Woodward, Joyce, 265
„ Mary, 214
„ Richard, 214
„ Thomas, 159, 265
Worcestre, or Wircestre, Joan, 107, 108, 127
„ Richard, 39, 63
„ William, 12, 95, 107, 117, 119, 127
Woseley, Frances, 185
„ Francis, 184
„ John, 180
„ Katharine, 180
„ Nicholas, 184, 185
Wotton, Robert, 59
„ Roger, 150
„ Walter, 38, 73
Woulfe, Nicholas, 264
Write, Erasmus, 223
Wroxale, W., 38
Wroxhale, William, 61
Wryngton, or Wrington, Alan, 28, 29, 43, 51, 77, 86
„ Robert, 28
Wryte, Mary, 248
„ Richard, 248
Wudhouse, Agnes, 183
„ Margaret, 183
„ Nicholas, 182, 183
„ Thomas, 183
Wyate, William, 208
Wybbe, Thomas, 42, 44, 45, 46, 47, 50, 51, 53, 56, 58
Wycombe, Agnes, 52
„ John, 36, 52, 53, 64
Wydeboruwe, William, 75
Wyeekam, Agnes, 191
„ Alice, 191
„ Edmond, 191
„ Harry, 191
„ John, 192
„ Katharine, 191
„ Margery, 192, 196
„ Mary, 191
„ Richard, 191, 196
„ William, 191
Wyett, William, 231, 237
Wygan, ———, 43
Wyke, John, 26, 36, 37, 39, 42, 43, 58, 79, 90
„ Thomas, 119, 120, 121
Wykeham, Bishop, 74
Wykham, William, 148, 152, 157, 158
Wykyng, John, 63
„ Julian, 105
„ Richard, 105
Wykys, John, 160
Wylde, Robert, 55
Wylmott, Thomas, 194
Wynchestre, Isabel, 37
„ John, 37
Wyncley, and Wyngtley, Thomas, 33, 39
Wynkeley, John, 59
Wynnall, Richard, 179
Wynne, John, 30
Wynter, or Winter, Benedict, 276
„ Constance, 82
„ John, 82, 173
„ Philip, 82
„ Thomas, 82
„ Walter, 117, 118
„ William, 268, 276
Wycote, alias Grawnte, Elizabeth, 58
„ Robert, 58
Wyot, Joan, 279
„ John, 173

,, Robert, 39
,, William, 279
Wyppay, Maud, 106
Wyse, or Wise, Joan, 256
,, John, 110, 119, 142
,, Letice, 256
,, Patrick, 256
Wysebeche, Martin, 97
Wyseman, John, 21
Wysshe, Thomas, 206
Wyte, John, 70
Wytham, Thomas, 124
Wythipoll, Edmund, 180
,, Elizabeth, 180
,, John, 180
,, Paul, 180, 181
,, William, 181
Wythsyd, John, 51
Wyveliscombe, Clarice, 35, 36
,, Gunnilda, 35
,, Henry, 5, 29, 35, 55
,, John, 35
Wyvescombe, Henry, 125

Yalton, John, 94
Yate, Henry, 275
,, Margaret, 274, 275
,, William, 204, 206, 274, 275
Yeman, Agnes, 226
,, Alice, 205
,, Annis, 226
,, Arthur, 226
,, Grace, 226
,, Joan, 205, 226
,, John, 205, 226
,, Katharine, 205
,, Margery, 205
,, Mary, 225, 226
,, Susan, 225
,, William, 197, 204, 205, 214, 215
   225, 226
Yemanns, William, 200, 261
Yeomans, Alice, 264
,, Elizabeth, 264
Yerdesleigh, Maud, 37
Yeroth, John, 221

Yeuele, Amy, 93
,, Cristina, 93
,, Ralph, 93
Yeuelton, Beatrix, 84
,, John, 84
Yevans, Joan, 261
,, John, 243
Yevyll John, 103
Yewen, John, 62
Yhevell, John, 117
Yonge, Isabel, 136, 152
,, Joan, 115
,, John, 27, 31, 115, 146, 172, 174
   235, 245, 254, 280
,, Simon, 89, 130
,, Thomas, 80, 87, 106, 107, 115, 116
   134, 136, 148 152, 160, 196, 212
,, William, 91, 190, 208, 209, 278
Yorke, Joan, 278
,, Richard, 255, 262
,, Walter, 262
,, William, 278
,, ———, 142
Young, Alice, 208
,, Anna, 270
,, Anne, 208
,, Dorothy, 233
,, Elianor, 219
,, Elizabeth, 233
,, Margaret, 233
,, Patrick, 236, 256, 278
,, Richard, 101, 197, 199, 243, 254
,, Susan, 243
Yowen, George 248
,, William, 248
,, ———, 248
Yweme, Richard, 251

Omitted :—
Axston, John, 11
Barth, John, 41
Bonner, Joan, 217
Boswell, John, 250
Braughton, James, 195
Cooke, Richard, 279
Dawes, Edward, 169

www.ingramcontent.com/pod-product-compliance
Lightning Source LLC
Chambersburg PA
CBHW030810230426
43667CB00008B/1147